SOMETHING ABOUT THE AUTHOR®

Something about the Author *was named an "Outstanding Reference Source,"* *the highest honor given by the American Library Association Reference and Adult Services Division.*

ISSN 0276-816X

SOMETHING ABOUT THE AUTHOR®

**Facts and Pictures about Authors
and Illustrators of Books for Young People**

volume 180

THOMSON

GALE

Detroit • New York • San Francisco • New Haven, Conn. • Waterville, Maine • London

THOMSON

GALE

Something about the Author, Volume 180

Project Editor
Lisa Kumar

Editorial
Dana Ferguson, Amy Elisabeth Fuller, Michelle Kazensky, Kathy Meek, Jennifer Mossman, Joseph Palmisano, Mary Ruby, Robert James Russell, Amanda D. Sams, Marie Toft

Permissions
Margaret Chamberlain-Gaston, Jacqueline Key, Kelly Quin

Imaging and Multimedia
Leitha Etheridge-Sims, Lezlie Light

Composition and Electronic Capture
Tracey L. Matthews

Manufacturing
Drew Kalasky

Product Manager
Peg Knight

LIBRARY OF CONGRESS CATALOG CARD NUMBER 62-52046

ISBN-13: 978-0-7876-8804-2
ISBN-10: 0-7876-8804-5
ISSN 0276-816X

This title is also available as an e-book.
ISBN-13: 978-1-4144-2944-1, ISBN-10: 1-4144-2944-4
Contact your Gale Group sales representative for ordering information.

Printed in the United States of America
10 9 8 7 6 5 4 3 2 1

Contents

Authors in Forthcoming Volumes ix

Introduction xi

SATA Product Advisory Board xiii

A

Alchemy, Jack
    See Gershator, David 61

B

Barrows, Annie 1962- 1

Benedetto, William R. 1928- 2

Bernstein, Nina 1949- 3

Blume, Lesley M.M. 1975- 4

Briant, Ed 4

C

Chin-Lee, Cynthia 1958- 7

Chin-Lee, Cynthia D.
    See Chin-Lee, Cynthia 7

Cohen, Deborah Bodin 1968- 9

Collins, Suzanne 10

Copeland, Mark 1956- 12

D

Delaney, M.C.
    See Delaney, Michael 14

Delaney, Michael 1955- 14

Delaney, Michael Clark
    See Delaney, Michael 14

DeMatteis, J.M. 1953- 16

DeMatteis, John Marc
    See DeMatteis, J.M. 16

De Wire, Elinor 1953- 20

Donaldson, Julia 1948- 21

Dorfman, Joaquín 1979- 26

Dorfman, Joaquin Emiliano
    See Dorfman, Joaquín 26

Dowden, Anne Ophelia Todd 1907-2007
    Obituary Notice 27

Downes, Belinda 1962- 28

E

Ensor, Barbara 30

Evans, Lezlie 31

F

Ferguson, Sarah 1959- 32

Ferguson, Sarah Margaret
    See Ferguson, Sarah 32

Flanagan, John 1944- 35

Flanagan, John Anthony
    See Flanagan, John 35

Fountas, Angela Jane 36

Friedman, D. Dina 1957- 37

G

Geras, Adèle 1944- 39
    Autobiography Feature 45

Geras, Adèle Daphne Weston
    See Geras, Adèle 39

Gershator, David 1937- 61

Gilliland, Judith Heide 63

Gordon, David 1965- 65

H

Hart, Philip S. 1944- 68

Hausman, Gerald 1945- 70

Hausman, Gerry
    See Hausman, Gerald 70

Hawes, Louise 1943- 75

Haycak, Cara 1961- 78

Hopkinson, Deborah 1952- 80
    Autobiography Feature 85

Horne, Richard 1960-2007
Obituary Notice 97

Horne, Richard George Anthony
See Horne, Richard 97

Horse, Harry
See Horne, Richard 97

Huntington, Amy . . . .

Hurwin, Davida Wills 1950- 98

J

Johnston, Tony 1942- 102

K

Kadohata, Cynthia 1956- 109

Kann, Elizabeth 113

Kann, Victoria 113

Kimmelman, Burt 1947- 114

Klise, M. Sarah 1961- 115

L

Ljungkvist, Laura 119

Look, Lenore 121

Love, D. Anne 1949- 123

Lutz, John 1939- 127

Lutz, John Thomas
See Lutz, John 127

M

Mack, L.V.
See Kimmelman, Burt 114

Mattheson, Jenny 131

Matthews, Aline
See De Wire, Elinor 20

Menotti, Gian Carlo 1911-2007
Obituary Notice 132

Mlynowski, Sarah 1977(?)- 133

Morales, Yuyi 1968- 136

Morgan, Michaela 139

Murphy, Rita 141

N

Naidoo, Beverley 1943- 144

Nelson, Marilyn 1946- 149
Autobiography Feature 152

Nicholson, William 1948- 176

Nikola-Lisa, W. 1951- 179

P

Pfeffer, Susan Beth 1948- 183

Polacco, Patricia 1944- 188

Prince, April Jones 1975- 195

R

Reiser, Lynn 1944- 197

Reiser, Lynn Whisnant
See Reiser, Lynn 197

Reynolds, Jan 1956- 201

Rodríguez, Rachel 205

Rodríguez, Rachel Victoria
See Rodríguez, Rachel 205

Roth, Julie Jersild 205

S

Sarah, Duchess of York
See Ferguson, Sarah 32

Scamell, Ragnhild 1940- 208

Scheffler, Axel 1957- 210

Scott, Jessica
See De Wire, Elinor 20

Shaw, Mary 1965- 212

Stein, David Ezra 213

Stiegemeyer, Julie 214

Stolz, Mary 1920-2006
Obituary Notice 215

Stolz, Mary Slattery
See Stolz, Mary 215

Sturtevant, Katherine 1950- 215

Suzanne, Jamie
See Hawes, Louise 75

Swiatkowska, Gabi 1971(?)- 217

T

Taylor, Kim 220

Todd, Anne Ophelia
See Dowden, Anne Ophelia Todd 27

Tulloch, Richard 1949- 221

Tulloch, Richard George
See Tulloch, Richard 221

V

Valério, Geraldo 1970- 225

Varela, Barry 1963(?)- 226

Vitale, Stefano 1958- 227

Voake, Charlotte 1957- 230

W

Waniek, Marilyn Nelson
See Nelson, Marilyn 149

Wilkins, Rose 234

Willems, Mo 235

Williams, Laura E. 240

Williams, Laura Ellen
   See Williams, Laura E. 240

Williams, L.E.
   See Williams, Laura E. 240

Winstead, Rosie 243

Wood, Douglas 1951- 244

Wood, Douglas Eric
   See Wood, Douglas 244

Z

Zappa, Ahmet 1974- 249

Zappa, Ahmet Emuukha Rodan
   See Zappa, Ahmet 249

Authors in Forthcoming Volumes

Below are some of the authors and illustrators that will be featured in upcoming volumes of *SATA*. These include new entries on the swiftly rising stars of the field, as well as completely revised and updated entries (indicated with *) on some of the most notable and best-loved creators of books for children.

*Alma Flor Ada ▌ Cuban-born writer Ada is a noted storyteller whose works reflect her advocacy of bilingual education. Her Spanish/English picture books, such as *The Malachite Palace, Where the Flame Trees Bloom,* and the Christopher Award-winning *The Gold Coin,* promote literacy among children in both languages, while her retelling of traditional folk tales in *Medipollito/Half Chicken* and other works promote cross-cultural understanding. Her books in the "Puertas al Sol/Gateways to the Sun" series, with frequent co-author F. Isabel Campoy, collect verse, plays, art, and nonfiction biographies, providing children a chance to understand the depth and history of Hispanic culture.

Marge Bruchac ▌ Sister of noted Native-American writer Joseph Bruchac, Bruchac shares her brother's love of the traditional stories of the tribes of the Northeastern United States. A historian, musician, and storyteller as well as a writer, Bruchac lectures and performs all over the world. Her books include *Malian's Song,* an account of the British attack on the Abenaki people of New England in 1759 that attempts to right the historical record while also captivating young readers.

Henry Cole ▌ Cole was a science teacher before becoming an illustrator of children's picture books. In addition to *Boston Tea Party, Warthogs Paint: A Messy Color Book,* and his many other collaborations with friend, the writer Pamela Duncan Edwards, Cole has illustrated humorous picture books by popular writer Margie Palatini, among others. In his work with actor Harvey Fierstein for *The Sissy Duckling,* a reactionary yellow duck named Elmer comes alive for readers courtesy of Cole's whimsical art.

Polly Dunbar ▌ The daughter of well-known children's book author Joyce Dunbar, Dunbar has been writing and illustrating books professionally since age sixteen. Beginning her career with *Help! I'm out with the In Crowd, and Other Saturday Nightmares* and *Help! I've Forgotten My Brain, and Other Exam Nightmares,* Dunbar's original books were inspired by her own childhood memories. In addition to creating art for her own stories, Dunbar's cartoon illustrations also bring to life Margaret Mahy's *Down the Back of the Chair,* her mother's picture book *Shoe Baby,* and Jeanette Baker's, *A Survivor's Guide to Families,* among many others.

Emmanuel Guibert ▌ Paris-based cartoonist Guibert created story boards for videos and films before publishing his first comic, the politically themed *Brune,* in 1992. His more recent work with writer Joann Sfar include the saga of *Sardine in Outer Space* and the stand-alone graphic novel, *The Professor's Daughter,* both of which are available in English translation as well as in the original French.

Marlee Matlin ▌ Matlin is best known for her career as an award-winning actress, a field in which she has been successful despite her hearing impairment. She is also a writer, and her novels for children focus on what it is like to be deaf. Her first novel, *Deaf Child Crossing,* narrates the story of two nine year old girls—one terribly shy and one deaf—who become best friends. The girls are reunited in *Nobody's Perfect* and *Leading Ladies,* as their relationship changes and they each deal with the challenges of their personal handicaps.

*Kadir Nelson ▌ Nelson, an African-American artist who works primarily in oils, has exhibited his detailed paintings in art galleries and museums throughout the United States and abroad, as well as in many major periodicals. The lead conceptual artist for the motion pictures *Spirit: Stallion of the Cimarron* and *Amistad,* Nelson is also a respected children's book illustrator. His award-winning collaborations with a variety of authors include *Just the Two of Us, Thunder Rose,* and an illustrated version of the well-known spiritual *He's Got the Whole World in His Hands.*

*Michael Rosen ▌ Rosen's love of words, his talent for combining them in fresh and exciting ways, and his delightful ability to speak the words of a child in the way a child would speak them has made him one of the United Kingdom's most popular children's poets. In his work, which has been collected in books such as *Action Replay, That'd Be Telling,* and *Freckly Feet and Itchy Knees,* is a patchwork of anecdotes, jokes, songs, folktales, fairytales, vignettes, and nonsense verse. As a prose writer, his novels *You're Thinking about Doughnuts* and *The Deadman Tapes* weave short stories into a larger plot, while picture books such as *Bear's Day Out* feature his characteristic levity. In addition to his collections of original verses, Rosen has also edited several illustrated poetry anthologies for children, among them *The Kingfisher Book of Children's Poetry,* which contains 250 poems, and the *Classic Poetry,* which pairs short biographies of noted English-language poets from William Shakespeare to Langston Hughes with selections from their works.

*Carole Boston Weatherford ▌ African-American culture and history is celebrated in the many books by author Weatherford. The picture book *Juneteenth Jamboree* celebrates the day in 1865 when Texas slaves learned of their emancipation, while her verse collection *Sidewalk Chalk: Poems of the City* celebrates urban life in twenty short poems that focus on a child's experiences in a supportive black neighborhood: jumping rope on the sidewalk, getting a haircut, and going to church. Weatherford captures the inspiring lives of many figures in black history in *Remember the Bridge: Poems of a People,* while in the picture book *Dear Mr. Rosenwald* she tells the true story of a young African-American girl who is able to attend a new black school because of the support of several caring benefactors during the 1920s.

Leo Yerxa ▌ Native American artist Yerxa is also a picture book author and illustrator who pairs simple poetry with his vibrantly colored, detailed paintings to depict the beauty of nature. In his book *Ancient Thunder* Yerxa captures the interrelationship between wild horses and the tribes of the North American plains, while *Last Leaf First Snowflake to Fall* highlights the changes in the natural world as a young boy is taught by his father how to tell when autumn ends and winter begins. Based in Canada, Yerxa exhibits his work at numerous galleries featuring Indian art.

Introduction

Something about the Author (*SATA*) is an ongoing reference series that examines the lives and works of authors and illustrators of books for children. *SATA* includes not only well-known writers and artists but also less prominent individuals whose works are just coming to be recognized. This series is often the only readily available information source on emerging authors and illustrators. You'll find *SATA* informative and entertaining, whether you are a student, a librarian, an English teacher, a parent, or simply an adult who enjoys children's literature.

What's Inside *SATA*

SATA provides detailed information about authors and illustrators who span the full time range of children's literature, from early figures like John Newbery and L. Frank Baum to contemporary figures like Judy Blume and Richard Peck. Authors in the series represent primarily English-speaking countries, particularly the United States, Canada, and the United Kingdom. Also included, however, are authors from around the world whose works are available in English translation. The writings represented in *SATA* include those created intentionally for children and young adults as well as those written for a general audience and known to interest younger readers. These writings cover the entire spectrum of children's literature, including picture books, humor, folk and fairy tales, animal stories, mystery and adventure, science fiction and fantasy, historical fiction, poetry and nonsense verse, drama, biography, and nonfiction. Obituaries are also included in *SATA* and are intended not only as death notices but also as concise overviews of people's lives and work. Additionally, each edition features newly revised and updated entries for a selection of *SATA* listees who remain of interest to today's readers and who have been active enough to require extensive revisions of their earlier biographies.

Autobiography Feature

Beginning with Volume 103, many volumes of *SATA* feature one or more specially commissioned autobiographical essays. These unique essays, averaging about ten thousand words in length and illustrated with an abundance of personal photos, present an entertaining and informative first-person perspective on the lives and careers of prominent authors and illustrators profiled in *SATA*.

Two Convenient Indexes

In response to suggestions from librarians, *SATA* indexes no longer appear in every volume but are included in alternate (odd-numbered) volumes of the series, beginning with Volume 57.

SATA continues to include two indexes that cumulate with each alternate volume: the Illustrations Index, arranged by the name of the illustrator, gives the number of the volume and page where the illustrator's work appears in the current volume as well as all preceding volumes in the series; the Author Index gives the number of the volume in which a person's biographical sketch, autobiographical essay, or obituary appears in the current volume as well as all preceding volumes in the series.

These indexes also include references to authors and illustrators who appear in *Gale's Yesterday's Authors of Books for Children, Children's Literature Review,* and *Something about the Author Autobiography Series.*

Easy-to-Use Entry Format

Whether you're already familiar with the *SATA* series or just getting acquainted, you will want to be aware of the kind of information that an entry provides. In every *SATA* entry the editors attempt to give as complete a picture of the person's life and work as possible. A typical entry in *SATA* includes the following clearly labeled information sections:

PERSONAL: date and place of birth and death, parents' names and occupations, name of spouse, date of marriage, names of children, educational institutions attended, degrees received, religious and political affiliations, hobbies and other interests.

ADDRESSES: complete home, office, electronic mail, and agent addresses, whenever available.

CAREER: name of employer, position, and dates for each career post; art exhibitions; military service; memberships and offices held in professional and civic organizations.

MEMBER: professional, civic, and other association memberships and any official posts held.

AWARDS, HONORS: literary and professional awards received.

WRITINGS: title-by-title chronological bibliography of books written and/or illustrated, listed by genre when known; lists of other notable publications, such as plays, screenplays, and periodical contributions.

ADAPTATIONS: a list of films, television programs, plays, CD-ROMs, recordings, and other media presentations that have been adapted from the author's work.

WORK IN PROGRESS: description of projects in progress.

SIDELIGHTS: a biographical portrait of the author or illustrator's development, either directly from the biographee—and often written specifically for the *SATA* entry—or gathered from diaries, letters, interviews, or other published sources.

BIOGRAPHICAL AND CRITICAL SOURCES: cites sources quoted in "Sidelights" along with references for further reading.

EXTENSIVE ILLUSTRATIONS: photographs, movie stills, book illustrations, and other interesting visual materials supplement the text.

How a *SATA* Entry Is Compiled

SATA editors examine a wide variety of published sources to gather information for an entry. Biographical and bibliographic sources are consulted, as are book reviews, feature articles, published interviews, and material sometimes obtained from the biographee's family, publishers, agent, or other associates. Whenever possible, the author or illustrator is sent a copy of the entry to check for accuracy and completeness.

Entries that have not been verified by the biographees or their representatives are marked with an asterisk (*).

Contact the Editor

We encourage our readers to examine the entire *SATA* series. Please write and tell us if we can make *SATA* even more helpful to you. Give your comments and suggestions to the editor:

Editor
Something about the Author
The Gale Group
27500 Drake Rd.
Farmington Hills MI 48331-3535

Toll-free: 800-877-GALE
Fax: 248-699-8070

Something about the Author Product Advisory Board

The editors of *Something about the Author* are dedicated to maintaining a high standard of excellence by publishing comprehensive, accurate, and highly readable entries on a wide array of writers for children and young adults. In addition to the quality of the content, the editors take pride in the graphic design of the series, which is intended to be orderly yet inviting, allowing readers to utilize the pages of *SATA* easily and with efficiency. Despite the longevity of the *SATA* print series, and the success of its format, we are mindful that the vitality of a literary reference product is dependent on its ability to serve its users over time. As literature, and attitudes about literature, constantly evolve, so do the reference needs of students, teachers, scholars, journalists, researchers, and book club members. To be certain that we continue to keep pace with the expectations of our customers, the editors of *SATA* listen carefully to their comments regarding the value, utility, and quality of the series. Librarians, who have firsthand knowledge of the needs of library users, are a valuable resource for us. The *Something about the Author* Product Advisory Board, made up of school, public, and academic librarians, is a forum to promote focused feedback about *SATA* on a regular basis. The nine-member advisory board includes the following individuals, whom the editors wish to thank for sharing their expertise:

Eva M. Davis
Youth Department Manager,
Ann Arbor District Library,
Ann Arbor, Michigan

Joan B. Eisenberg
Lower School Librarian,
Milton Academy,
Milton, Massachusetts

Francisca Goldsmith
Teen Services Librarian,
Berkeley Public Library,
Berkeley, California

Susan Dove Lempke
Children's Services Supervisor,
Niles Public Library District,
Niles, Illinois

Robyn Lupa
Head of Children's Services,
Jefferson County Public Library,
Lakewood, Colorado

Victor L. Schill
Assistant Branch Librarian/Children's Librarian,
Harris County Public Library/Fairbanks Branch,
Houston, Texas

Caryn Sipos
Community Librarian,
Three Creeks Community Library,
Vancouver, Washington

Steven Weiner
Director,
Maynard Public Library,
Maynard, Massachusetts

SOMETHING ABOUT THE AUTHOR

ALCHEMY, Jack
    See GERSHATOR, David

*   *   *

BARROWS, Annie 1962-

Personal

Born 1962, in San Diego, CA; married; children: Clio, Esme. *Education:* University of California, Berkeley, graduate (medieval history); Mills College, M.F.A. (creative writing).

Addresses

E-mail—annie@anniebarrows.com.

Career

Author and editor.

Awards, Honors

100 Titles for Reading and Sharing inclusion, New York Public Library, and Best New Books for the Classroom designation, *Booklinks,* both 2006, and American Library Association Notable Book designation and *Booklist* Editor's Choice and Best Books designations, both 2007, all for *Ivy and Bean.*

Annie Barrows (Photograph by Barbara Lipson. Courtesy of Annie Barrows.)

Writings

Ivy and Bean, illustrated by Sophie Blackall, Chronicle Books (San Francisco, CA), 2006.

Ivy and Bean and the Ghost That Had to Go, illustrated by Sophie Blackall, Chronicle Books (San Francisco, CA), 2006.

Ivy and Bean Break the Fossil Record, illustrated by Sophie Blackall, Chronicle Books (San Francisco, CA), 2007.

The Magic Half, Bloomsbury USA (New York, NY), 2008.

Biographical and Critical Sources

PERIODICALS

Booklist, April 1, 2006, Ilene Cooper, review of *Ivy and Bean*, p. 42; October 15, 2006, Ilene Cooper, review of *Ivy and Bean and the Ghost That Had to Go*, p. 44.

Bulletin of the Center for Children's Books, June, 2006, Deborah Stevenson, review of *Ivy and Bean*, p. 440.

Kirkus Reviews, May 1, 2006, review of *Ivy and Bean*, p. 454; September 15, 2006, review of *Ivy and Bean and the Ghost That Had to Go*, p. 946.

Publishers Weekly, May 15, 2006, review of *Ivy and Bean*, p. 72.

School Library Journal, July, 2006, Even Ottenberg Stone, review of *Ivy and Bean*, p. 68; February, 2007, Adrienne Furness, review of *Ivy and Bean and the Ghost That Had to Go*, p. 84.

Tribune Books (Chicago, IL), January 7, 2007, Mary Harris Russell, review of *Ivy and Bean and the Ghost That Had to Go*, p. 7.

ONLINE

Annie Barrows Home Page, http://www.anniebarrows.com (April 28, 2007).

*   *   *

BENEDETTO, William R. 1928-

Personal

Born May 11, 1928, in Chisholm, ME; son of Fiorindo (a laborer) and Erminia (a homemaker) Benedetto; married Barbara A. Sherlock, (a legal assistant), September 4, 1948; children: Cheryl Ann Pataki, Liana M. Martin, Valerie Koepnick, William, Jr. *Ethnicity:* "Italian." *Education:* Portland State University (Portland, ME), P.S., 1977; University of Oregon Law School, J.D., 1980. *Hobbies and other interests:* Golf, reading, chess.

Addresses

Home—Wilsonville, OR. *Agent*—Agnes Birnbaum, Bleecker Street Associates, 532 LaGuardia Place, No. 617, New York, NY 10012. *E-mail*—AtyBill@aol.com.

Career

Attorney and author. U.S. Coast Guard, 1946-70, attained rank of chief warrant officer-4 (CWO-4); called to Oregon state bar, 1981; trial lawyer until 2001. Member of Washington County Civil Service Commission; member of Volunteer Lawyers Project.

Member

American Bar Association.

Awards, Honors

U.S. Coast Guard Letter of Appreciation, 1974, for life-saving work during Hurricane Betsy; U.S. Maritime Literature Award, 2006, for *Sailing into the Abyss*.

William R. Benedetto (Photograph by Barbara A. Benedetto. Courtesy of William R. Benedetto.)

Writings

Sailing into the Abyss: A True Story of Extreme Heroism on the High Seas (military history), foreword by Howard V. Thorsen, Citadel Press (New York, NY), 2005.

Contributor to periodicals, including *Harper's* and *USCG Magazine*.

Sidelights

William R. Benedetto told *SATA:* "I always had a hankering to put words to paper, to string along syllables in a rhythmic fashion, and, ultimately, to convey information to others in an interesting fashion. But life intervened.

"I was a latecomer. My first career consisted of surviving childhood—hard work in a crowded family left emotionally and financially adrift by the untimely death of Dad during the Great Depression. The Coast Guard provided a challenging welcome mat for a second career spanning twenty-eight years. Then came the mind blower: college. Thirteen years of part-and full-time studies resulted in a law degree, and a third chapter in life as a lawyer. With my wife, Barbara, as my legal assistant—she had joined me in attending college—we opened a 'Grandma and Grandpa' law office in the Portland area.

"Twenty years of considerable excitement and great challenges elapsed before I decided to exorcise that itch to write. The subject: the unique true story of a merchant ship carrying bombs to Vietnam in 1969—the bombs broke out of their containers and eventually roamed free inside the vessel—one I had heard about during my sailing days.

"Digging into government documents and newspaper clippings, tracking down survivors, and doing general research about everything connected with ships and sailing, with emphasis on the SS *Badger State* and the U.S. Merchant Marine generally, consumed a year or two. Finally, the writing and the countless revisions occupying my time seven days a week on occasion; obtaining an agent; and then her success in obtaining a national publisher, all resulting in the magic moment of national publication.

"And so the journey continues with research about another sea story looming ahead. A final phase to this challenging life? I don't foreclose any options. The sky is truly the limit in this incredible country, and there may yet be new dragons to slay out there!"

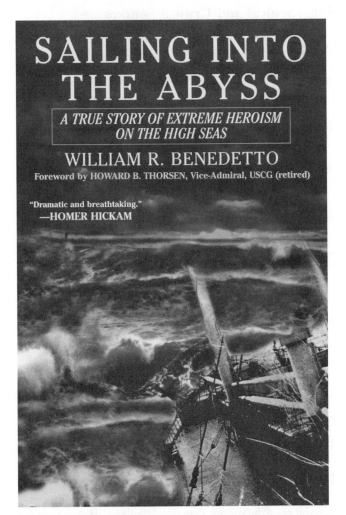

Cover of Benedetto's Sailing into the Abyss, *a nonfiction account of the travails of the* SS Badger State *during the Vietnam War.* (Citadel Press, 2005. Reproduced by permission of the author.)

Biographical and Critical Sources

PERIODICALS

Booklist, March 15, 2005, Frieda Murray, review of *Sailing into the Abyss: A True Story of Extreme Heroism on the High Seas,* p. 1260.
Publishers Weekly, December 20, 2004, review of *Sailing into the Abyss,* p. 43.
Sea Power, September, 2005, David W. Munns, review of *Sailing into the Abyss,* p. 57.

ONLINE

William R. Benedetto Home Page, http://www.williambenedetto.com (June 1, 2007).

*   *   *

BERNSTEIN, Nina 1949-

Personal
Born October 7, 1949, in New York, NY; daughter of Lester (a journalist) and Mimi Bernstein; married Andreas Huyssen (a professor of literature), June 22, 1975; children: Daniel, David. *Education:* Radcliffe College, Harvard, B.A. (history and literature), 1970.

Addresses
Home—New York, NY. *Office*—Gloria Loomis, Watkins/Loomis Agency, 133 E. 35th St., New York, NY 10016.

Career
Journalist and author. Formerly worked as a reporter in Des Moines, IA; *Milwaukee Journal,* Milwaukee, WI, reporter, 1972-86; *New York Newsday,* New York, NY, foreign correspondent, 1990-91, then reporter, 1991-95; *New York Times,* New York, NY, reporter, 1995—.

Awards, Honors
Nieman Foundation fellowship, Harvard University, 1983-84; Mike Berger Award, Columbia University School of Journalism, 1994, for *New York Newsday* series on Shirley Wilder; Alicia Patterson Foundation fellowship; George Polk Award for distinguished media coverage, 1995; National Book Award finalist, National Book Critics Circle Award finalist, Helen Bernstein Award for Excellence in Journalism, New York Public Library, PEN/ Martha Albrand Award for First Nonfiction, and Holtzbrinck fellowship, American Academy, all 2002, all for *The Lost Children of Wilder.*

Writings
The Lost Children of Wilder: The Epic Struggle to Change Foster Care (nonfiction), Pantheon Books (New York, NY), 2001.

Magic by the Book (children's novel), illustrated by Boris Kulikov, Farrar, Straus & Giroux (New York, NY), 2005.

Author's work has been translated into German, Turkish, Portuguese, and Slovenian.

Adaptations

Magic by the Book was adapted as an audiobook, read by Katie Firth, Recorded Books, 2005.

Biographical and Critical Sources

PERIODICALS

Advocate, January, 2002, Tom Gove, review of *The Lost Children of Wilder: The Epic Struggle to Change Foster Care,* p. 125.
America, October 1, 2001, Michael S. Kugelman, review of *The Lost Children of Wilder,* p. 26.
Booklist, February 15, 2001, Mary Carroll, review of *The Lost Children of Wilder,* p. 1089; April 15, 2005, Jennifer Mattson, review of *Magic by the Book* p. 1464.
Bulletin of the Center for Children's Books, February, 2005, Timnah Card, review of *Magic by the Book,* p. 244.
Choice, April, 2002, B.A. Pine, review of *The Lost Children of Wilder,* p. 1459.
Denver Post, April 8, 2001, Steve Weinberg, "Wicked Child-Care System Unveiled."
Kirkus Reviews, February 15, 2005, review of *Magic by the Book,* p. 225.
Nation, May 28, 2001, Daphne Eviatar, review of *The Lost Children of Wilder,* p. 244.
New Yorker, April 23, 2001, review of *The Lost Children of Wilder,* p. 194.
New York Times Book Review, March 25, 2001, Tanya Luhrmann, "A Perfect Test Case," p. 8.
New York Times Review of Books, May 17, 2001, James Traub, review of *The Lost Children of Wilder,* p. 24.
Publishers Weekly, December 18, 2000, review of *The Lost Children of Wilder,* p. 64; April 25, 2005, review of *Magic by the Book,* p. 57.
School Library Journal, March, 2005, Caitlin Augusta, review of *Magic by the Book,* p. 206.

ONLINE

New York Public Library Web site, http://www.nypl.org/ (May 9, 2002), "Nina Bernstein Wins the 2002 New York Public Library Helen Bernstein Book Award for Excellence in Journalism."*

*　　*　　*

BLUME, Lesley M.M. 1975-

Personal

Born 1975, in New York, NY; mother a concert pianist. *Education:* Attended Williams College and Oxford Uni-

versity; Cambridge University, M.A. (history). *Hobbies and other interests:* Travel.

Addresses

Home and office—New York, NY. *Agent*—Christine Earle, International Creative Management, 825 8th Ave., New York, NY 10019.

Career

Journalist and novelist. ABC News, New York, NY, researcher and reporter for *Nightline* based in Washington, DC.

Writings

Cornelia and the Audacious Escapades of the Somerset Sisters, Knopf (New York, NY), 2006.
The Rising Star of Rusty Nail, Knopf (New York, NY), 2007.

Biographical and Critical Sources

PERIODICALS

Booklist, July 1, 2006, Francisca Goldsmith, review of *Cornelia and the Audacious Escapades of the Somerset Sisters,* p. 55.
Bulletin of the Center for Children's Books, October, 2006, Karen Coats, review of *Cornelia and the Audacious Escapades of the Somerset Sisters,* p. 58.
Kirkus Reviews, June 15, 2006, review of *Cornelia and the Audacious Escapades of the Somerset Sisters,* p. 631.
Publishers Weekly, September 4, 2006, review of *Cornelia and the Audacious Escapades of the Somerset Sisters,* p. 68.
School Library Journal, September, 2006, Tracy Karbel, review of *Cornelia and the Audacious Escapades of the Somerset Sisters,* p. 200.

ONLINE

Lesley Blume Home Page, http www.lesleymmblume.com (April 28, 2007).*

*　　*　　*

BRIANT, Ed

Personal

Born in Brighton, England; married; children: two daughters. *Education:* Bowdoin College, B.A.; Southern Illinois University, M.A.; University of New Hampshire, Ph.D.

Addresses

Home and office—Maplewood, NJ. *E-mail*—ed_briant@ mindspring.com.

Career

Artist and children's book writer. Maine College of Art, Portland, associate professor of liberal arts and editor of Writing across the Curriculum Awards annual publication.

Writings

SELF-ILLUSTRATED

Seven Stories, Roaring Brook Press (New Milford, CT), 2005.
A Day at the Beach, Greenwillow (New York, NY), 2006.

ILLUSTRATOR

Sarah Weeks, *Paper Parade,* Atheneum (New York, NY), 2004.
Barry Varela, *Gizmo,* Roaring Brook Press (New Milford, CT), 2007.

Contributor of illustrations to *Gentleman's Quarterly, Newsweek, New York Times, Atlantic Monthly, New Yorker, Los Angeles Times, Washington Post,* and *Sports Illustrated.* Contributor to *French Connections: Hemingway and Fitzgerald Abroad,* St. Martin's Press (New York, NY), 1998. Creator of Web comic "Tales of the Slush Pile," beginning 2005.

Sidelights

Before Ed Briant wrote and illustrated children's books, he was an illustrator and caricature artist for such periodicals as *Newsweek,* the *New York Times,* and *Sports Illustrated. Paper Parade,* his first picture-book project, was a collaboration with author Sarah Weeks.

Paper Parade is the story of a young artist who, when she cannot see the parade down the street from her house, creates her own parade of paper-crafted performers. "Constructed out of paper, the artwork consists of colorful figures and backgrounds that parallel the girl's activities," explained Roxanne Burg in her *School Library Journal* review. "The pictures—striking paper constructions on clean flat backgrounds—tell most of the story," wrote *Horn Book* reviewer Lolly Robinson. A *Kirkus Reviews* contributor considered Briant's first picture book a "high-stepping debut," while a *Publishers Weekly* critic wrote that *Paper Parade* "spotlights the imaginative puppet-like constructions."

Briant's next picture-book project features an original story. Titled *Seven Stories,* the work "began as a picture book, expanded to a five-thousand-word chapter book,

a wordless graphic novel, and finally became once again a picture book," as the author/illustrator explained on his home page. Although he finished the artwork quickly, the writing took Briant three years to complete. The story focuses on a young girl living in a downtown apartment building in which the other tenants are all characters playing out various fairy tales. Jack, of Beanstalk fame, lives in Apartment Five, while Hansel and Gretel's witch makes her home in Apartment Three. The young narrator has to unravel her own tale in order to finally fall asleep. "Most of the spreads bubble with a loopy, almost animated spontaneity," wrote a *Publishers Weekly* contributor, and a *Kirkus Reviews* writer praised Briant's "simply drawn setting and . . . multiethnic (not to mention multi-species) cast." Joanna Rudge Long, writing in *Horn Book,* noted Briant's combination of "freely limned art, offbeat characterizations, retro urban setting, and perky snatches of dialogue."

Briant moves from an urban landscape to the seaside in his self-illustrated *A Day at the Beach.* A panda family plans to spend the day at the seashore, but just as the group arrives at its destination, family members realize they have forgotten something. Back to the house the pandas go, again and again remembering something else they would like to have upon arriving back at the beach. *A Day at the Beach* "is a warm family story that youngsters will enjoy," wrote Wanda Meyers-Hines in *School Library Journal.* As a *Kirkus Reviews* critic explained, the illustrator's use of "computer compos[ed] . . . digital photos of wire and clay figures and cardboard sets," gives his art a three-dimensional feel. "Briant keeps the writing low-key . . . and lets his clay-and-wire figures take center stage," wrote a contributor to *Publishers Weekly* in a review of *A Day at the Beach.*

Biographical and Critical Sources

PERIODICALS

Booklist, January 1, 2006, Karin Snelson, review of *Seven Stories,* p. 108.
Horn Book, July-August, 2004, Lolly Robinson, review of *Paper Parade,* p. 443; November-December, 2005, Joanna Rudge Long, review of *Seven Stories,* p. 702.
Kirkus Reviews, April 15, 2004, review of *Paper Parade,* p. 402; October 1, 2005, review of *Seven Stories,* p. 1077; May 15, 2006, review of *A Day at the Beach,* p. 514.
Publishers Weekly, May 3, 2004, review of *Paper Parade,* p. 190; August 8, 2005, review of *Seven Stories,* p. 232; April 24, 2006, review of *A Day at the Beach,* p. 59.
School Library Journal, June, 2004, Roxanne Burg, review of *Paper Parade,* p. 121; January, 2006, Holly T. Sneeringer, review of *Seven Stories,* p. 92; June, 2006, Wanda Meyers-Hines, review of *A Day at the Beach,* p. 107.

ONLINE

Adams Literary Agency Web site, http://www.adamsliterary.com/ (August 28, 2007).

Ed Briant Home Page, http://www.edwardbriant.com (April 28, 2007).

Maine College of Art Web site, http://www.meca.edu/ (April 28, 2007), "Ed Briant."*

C

CHIN-LEE, Cynthia 1958-
(Cynthia D. Chin-Lee)

Personal

Born October 14, 1958, in Washington, DC; daughter of William (a doctor) and Nancy (an artist) Chin-Lee; married Andrew J. Pan, April 3, 1983 (divorced, 1998); married Peter Ching, June 26, 1999; children: (first marriage) Vanessa; (second marriage) Joshua. *Education:* Harvard University, B.A. (East-Asian studies; magna cum laude), 1980; East-West Center, graduate study, 1980-81. *Religion:* Christian. *Hobbies and other interests:* Reading, walking, swimming.

Addresses

Home—Palo Alto, CA. *E-mail*—cynthia_chin-lee@post.harvard.edu.

Career

Freelance writer and consultant in technical writing, 1983—. De Anza College, instructor, 1984-89; Santa Clara University, adjunct lecturer, 1988-92; professional speaker, 1991—. Sun Microsystems, documentation manager, 2003—.

Member

Society of Children's Book Writers and Illustrators, Organization of Chinese American Women.

Awards, Honors

National Council on Social Studies/Children's Book Council Notable Children's Book in Social Studies designation, 2000, for *A Is for the Americas,* 2005, for *Amelia to Zora,* 2006, for *Akira to Zoltán;* National Parenting Publications Gold Award, Amelia Bloomer Project Award, International Reading Association/Children's Book Council Children's Choice designation, New England Book Show Juvenile Book Award, and Texas Association for the Gifted and Talented Legacy Award, all for *Amelia to Zora.*

Cynthia Chin-Lee (Photograph © by Pat Willard. Reproduced by permission.)

Writings

FOR CHILDREN

Almond Cookies and Dragon Well Tea, illustrated by You Shan Tang, Polychrome Publishing (Chicago, IL), 1993.

A Is for Asia, illustrated by Yumi Heo, Orchard Books (New York, NY), 1997.

(With Terri de la Peña) *A Is for the Americas,* illustrated by Enrique O. Sanchez, Orchard Books (New York, NY), 1999.

Amelia to Zora: Twenty-six Women Who Changed the World, illustrated by Megan Halsey and Sean Addy, Charlesbridge (Watertown, MA), 2005.

Akira to Zoltán: Twenty-six Men Who Changed the World, illustrated by Megan Halsey and Sean Addy, Charlesbridge (Watertown, MA), 2006.

Author's work has been translated into Spanish.

FOR ADULTS

It's Who You Know: Career Strategies for Making Effective Personal Contacts, Avant Books (San Marcos, CA), 1991, revised as *It's Who You Know: The Magic of Networking, in Person and on the Internet,* Book-Partners, 1998.

It's Who You Know has been translated into Chinese.

Sidelights

Cynthia Chin-Lee is the author of children's picture books that allow young armchair travelers to tour the world. Her first work, *Almond Cookies and Dragon Well Tea,* draws on Chin-Lee's own childhood and takes place in the Chinese laundry owned by her grandparents. In *A Is for Asia* she leads readers on a tour of Asia, where places as diverse as Indonesia and Mongolia are brought to life in illustrator Yumi Heo's collage art. Reviewing *A Is for Asia* for *Booklist,* Hazel Rochman wrote that the book's "alphabet arrangement" provides "a panoramic introduction to the geography, culture, holidays, traditions, and animals" of Asia, while a *Kirkus*

Reviews contributor noted that Chin-Lee "combines facts . . . with the ABC format in a book admirable for its ambitions." Calling the work a "fact-filled, fun alphabet book," a *Publishers Weekly* critic concluded that the author's focus on "different religious observances gives [*A Is for Asia*] . . . added value."

Similar in format to *A Is for Asia, A Is for the Americas* finds Chin-Lee joining coauthor Terri de la Peña and illustrator Enrique O. Sanchez on a trip through North, Central, and South America, from Niagara Falls to the land of the Zuni native people. According to Rochman, the coauthors effectively showcase "the diversity of landscape, culture, and language across borders," while the book's large, colorful paintings "evoke the stretch of history" encompassed by ancient cultures such as the Aztec, Maya, and New Mexican Zuñi.

In both *Akira to Zoltán: Twenty-six Men Who Changed the World* and *Amelia to Zora: Twenty-six Women Who Changed the World* Chin-Lee characteristically crosses cultural borders as well as vocation, profiling artists, athletes, politicians, scientists, and others who have made a positive impact on human society. Indian paci-

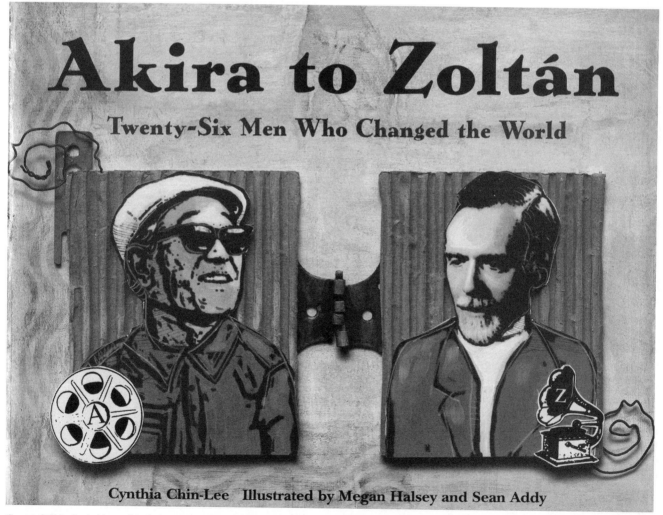

Cover of Chin-Lee's biographical picture book Akiro to Zoltán, *featuring illustrations by Megan Halsey and Sean Addy.* (Charlesbridge, 2006. Illustrations

fist Mohandas Ghandi, Japanese filmmaker Akira Kuro-sawa, and anti-apartheid activist Nelson Mandela are among those profiled in *Akira to Zoltán,* while athlete Babe Didrikson Zaharias, Mexican painter Frida Kahlo, and Egyptian physician Nawal el Sadaawi are included in *Amelia to Zora.* In her *Booklist* review of the first volume, Rochman wrote that Chin-Lee's "profiles are clearly, even eloquently written, and include just the right amount of detail" for elementary-grade readers," while *School Library Journal* contributor Ann Welton cited the author's "succinct, readable prose." The "striking mixed media" illustrations by Sean Addy and Megan Halsey also attracted comment, *School Library Journal* contributor Peg Glisson noting in her review of *Amelia to Zora* that the book's images "illustrate . . . the essence of the person" depicted. In the opinion of *Booklist* contributor Ilene Cooper, *Amelia to Zora* is "very smart—in design, art, and choice of subject" and Chin-Lee's short prose entries are "enticing." Praising the author's use of anecdote and "spirited language," a *Kirkus Reviews* writer dubbed *Amelia to Zora* "an inspiration and a delight."

Chin-Lee once told *SATA:* "I began writing poetry when I was in sixth grade, and I kept on writing through my school and college days. I wrote for publication and for self-understanding, finding joy and comfort in the act of committing words to paper.

"Both sets of my grandparents came to the United States from China in the early 1900s, so many of my stories have an Asian theme. I majored in East Asian studies at Harvard and spent part of my junior year in Taiwan. I eventually worked in China and have led tour groups through China a few times.

"Most of my professional career has been writing for business, especially computer companies. My first book, *It's Who You Know: Career Strategies for Making Effective Personal Contacts,* is a career book for adults, on networking and on the Internet. When my daughter was born in 1989, I became interested in writing for children. Writing for children seemed to bring together the best of many worlds: collaboration with an artist, poetry, and my own sense that children see the world more truthfully than adults do."

Biographical and Critical Sources

PERIODICALS

Booklist, March 1, 1997, Hazel Rochman, review of *A Is for Asia,* p. 1165; September 1, 1999, Hazel Rochman, review of *A Is for the Americas,* p. 135; April 1, 2005, Ilene Cooper review of *Amelia to Zora: Twenty-six Women Who Changed the World,* p. 1358; June 1, 2006, Hazel Rochman, review of *Akira to Zoltán: Twenty-six Men Who Changed the World,* p. 97.
Bulletin of the Center for Children's Books, May, 1997, review of *A Is for Asia,* p. 16.

Kirkus Reviews, March 15, 1997, review of *A Is for Asia,* p. 459; March 15, 2005, review of *Amelia to Zora,* p. 349; June 15, 2006, review of *Akira to Zoltán,* p. 632.
Publishers Weekly, February 3, 1997, review of *A Is for Asia,* p. 106; October 4, 1999, review of *A Is for the Americas,* p. 77.
School Library Journal, October, 1999, Kit Vaughan, review of *A Is for the Americas,* p. 135; April, 2005, Peg Glisson, review of *Amelia to Zora,* p. 147; March, 2006, John Peters, review of *Amelia to Zora,* p. 89; July, 2006, Ann Welton, review of *Akira to Zoltán,* p. 118.

ONLINE

Cynthia Chin-Lee Home Page, http://www.geocities/com/Cynthia_Chin_Lee/ (June 1, 2007).

*   *   *

CHIN-LEE, Cynthia D.
See CHIN-LEE, Cynthia

*   *   *

COHEN, Deborah Bodin 1968-

Personal

Born 1968, in Columbia, MD; married Dave Cohen (a newspaper editor); children: Arianna. *Education:* University of Michigan, B.A. (English); Hebrew Union College, ordained, 1997.

Addresses

Office—Temple Emanuel, 1101 Springdale Rd., Cherry Hill, NJ 08003. *E-mail*—dcohen@templeemanuel.org.

Career

Rabbi and writer. Religious Action Center of Reform Judaism, Washington, DC, legislative assistant; Advocacy Institute, Washington, DC, former program associate; Beth Shalom, Cary, NC, rabbi and education director, 1997-2000; Temple Emanuel, Cherry Hill, NJ, rabbi, 2000—.

Writings

The Seventh Day, illustrated by Melanie Hall, Kar-Ben (Minneapolis, MN), 2005.
Lilith's Ark: Teenage Tales of Biblical Women, Jewish Publication Society (Philadelphia, PA), 2006.
Papa Jethro: A Story of Moses' Interfaith Family, illustrated by Jane Dippold, Kar-Ben (Minneapolis, MN), 2007.

Biographical and Critical Sources

PERIODICALS

Publishers Weekly, February 14, 2005, review of *The Seventh Day,* p. 78.

School Library Journal, August, 2005, Amy Lilien-Harper, review of *The Seventh Day,* p. 86.

ONLINE

Temple Emanuel Web site, http://www.templeemanuel.org/ (April 28, 2007), "Deborah Bodin Cohen."*

*   *   *

COLLINS, Suzanne

Personal

Born in NJ; daughter of a soldier in the Air Force; married; husband's name, Cap; children:.

Addresses

Home and office—CT.

Career

Novelist and television scriptwriter. Television writer, beginning 1991. Worked previously as a clinical director of services for adults with learning disabilities, Cambridge Health Authority.

Member

Authors Guild.

Awards, Honors

New York Public Library 100 Books for Reading and Sharing selection, 2003, for *Gregor the Overlander.*

Writings

"UNDERLAND CHRONICLES"; MIDDLE-GRADE NOVELS

Gregor the Overlander, Scholastic (New York, NY), 2003.

Gregor and the Prophecy of Bane, Scholastic (New York, NY), 2004.

Gregor and the Curse of the Warmbloods, Scholastic (New York, NY), 2005.

Gregor and the Marks of Secret, Scholastic (New York, NY), 2006.

Gregor and the Code of Claw, Scholastic (New York, NY), 2007.

OTHER

When Charlie McButton Lost Power (picture book), illustrated by Mike Lester, Putnam (New York, NY), 2005.

Also author of numerous television scripts, including for programs *Clarissa Explains It All, The Mystery Files of Shelby Woo, Little Bear, Oswald, Santa, Baby!, Clifford's Puppy Days,* and *Generation O!*

Adaptations

Dan Yaccarino's picture book, *Oswald's Camping Trip,* was based on Collins' script for the *Oswald* television program. The "Underland Chronicles" were adapted as audiobooks.

Sidelights

Suzanne Collins, who has worked as a writer on such television programs as *Clarissa Explains It All, Little Bear,* and *Oswald,* did not plan to write a novel for children. After a conversation with children book's author and illustrator Joe Proimos, however, she was convinced to give it a try. The resulting middle-grade novel, *Gregor the Overlander,* became the first installment in Collins' "Underland Chronicles," a series of *Alice in Wonderland*-esque tales that find Gregor traversing an urban environment. Collins, who lived in New York City for sixteen years, wanted to gear her fantasy toward cosmopolitan young readers who are more familiar with city streets that sunlit meadows. As a contributor to the Scholastic Web site noted of Collins' inspiration, "in New York City, you're much more likely to fall down a manhole than a rabbit hole and, if you do, you're not going to find a tea party."

Gregor's adventures begin in *Gregor the Overlander* when he pursues his two-year-old sister, Boots, through an air duct and into the world below. What he finds in the Underland is not only a hidden human society, but also a world in which giant-sized rats, cockroaches, and spiders that are able to communicate in human language. When Gregor arrives, the Underland is on the brink of war—a war that threatens to spread into the Overland, first to Manhattan and then throughout the world. Gregor's first thought is to get home—until he overhears that his father, who has gone missing, may now be in the Underland and need his son's help. Gregor makes new friends in the giant rat Ripred, Temp the cockroach, and Luxa, a mysterious human girl. Together they search for the missing man and put Gregor on track to his destiny.

As Collins told Jen Rees in an interview posted on Collins's home page, she selected the Underland setting because "I liked the fact that this world was teeming under New York City and nobody was aware of it. That you could be going along preoccupied with your own problems and then whoosh! You take a wrong turn in your laundry room and suddenly a giant cockroach is right in your face. No magic, no space or time travel, there's just a ticket to another world behind your clothes dryer." She "creates a fascinating, vivid, highly original world and a superb story to go along with it," wrote Ed Sullivan in a *Booklist* review of *Gregor the Overlander,*

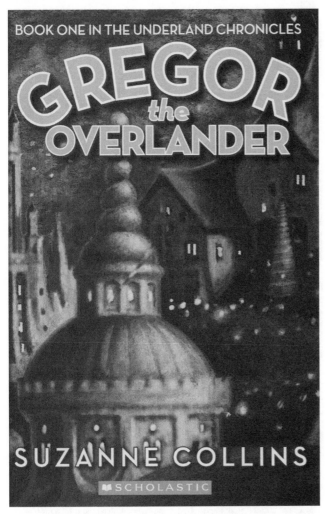

Cover of Suzanne Collins' middle-grade fantasy novel Gregor the Overlander, *featuring artwork by Daniel Craig.* (Scholastic Inc., 2003. Reproduced by permission of Scholastic, Inc.)

while a *Kirkus Reviews* contributor described Collins' storyline as a "luminous, supremely absorbing quest." Steven Engelfried, writing in *School Library Journal,* wrote that the novel's "plot threads unwind smoothly, and the pace of the book is just right."

As the "Underland Chronicles" series continues, Gregor fulfils a prophecy and becomes a leader in the Underland. Joined again by companions Ripred, Temp, and Luxa, *Gregor and the Prophecy of Bane* continues Gregor's adventures, undertaking to rescue Boots, who has been kidnapped. In her sequel Collins once again showcases her "careful attention to detail, pacing, and character development," in the opinion of *Horn Book* reviewer Kitty Flynn, while Sullivan dubbed Collins' protagonist "courageous, selfless, and ultimately triumphant."

In the third book in the series, *Gregor and the Curse of the Warmbloods,* Gregor's enemy is not an army, but a plague, one that his mother contracts. "Collins maintains the momentum, charm, and vivid settings of the original title," wrote Tasha Saecker her *School Library Journal* review of this title. *Gregor and the Curse of*

the Warmbloods "delivers the breakneck adventure and strong characters readers have come to expect," wrote a contributor to *Kirkus Reviews,* and Flynn concluded that, with this third series installment, the author's "character development, plotting, pacing, and description all shine."

Gregor returns again in *Gregor and the Marks of Secret,* which finds some of the humans' allies in trouble. Together with Gregor, Luxa and Temp attempt to save the day, and "the breathless pace, intense drama, and extraordinary challenges" of their quest "will leave fans clamoring" for more, according to *School Library Journal* reviewer Mara Alpert. In *Horn Book* Flynn commented that "vivid description, expert pacing, and subtle character development all enhance" Collins' fourth "gripping fantasy adventure."

Along with her "Underland Chronicles," Collins has produced a picture-book text featuring illustrations by Mike Lester. In the rhyming text of *When Charlie McButton Lost Power* Charlie spends most of his time playing video games, but must find a new way to entertain himself when his home's power goes out. A contributor to *Children's Bookwatch* called Collins' tale "refreshingly original and moving."

Biographical and Critical Sources

PERIODICALS

Booklist, November 15, 2003, Ed Sullivan, review of *Gregor the Overlander,* p. 608; September 1, 2004, Ed Sullivan, review of *Gregor and the Prophecy of Bane,* p. 120; July, 2005, Ed Sullivan, review of *Gregor and the Curse of the Warmbloods,* p. 1924.

Bulletin of the Center for Children's Books, January, 2004, Janice Del Negro, review of *Gregor the Overlander,* p. 185; October, 2004, Timnah Card, review of *Gregor and the Prophecy of Bane,* p. 65; September, 2005, Timnah Card, review of *Gregor and the Curse of the Warmbloods,* p. 11.

Children's Bookwatch, June, 2005, review of *When Charlie McButton Lost Power.*

Horn Book, September-October, 2003, Kitty Flynn, review of *Gregor the Overlander,* p. 609; September-October, 2004, Kitty Flynn, review of *Gregor and the Prophecy of Bane,* p. 578; July-August, 2005, Kitty Flynn, review of *Gregor and the Curse of the Warmbloods,* p. 467; July-August, 2006, Kitty Flynn, review of *Gregor and the Marks of Secret,* p. 437.

Kirkus Reviews, August 1, 2003, review of *Gregor the Overlander,* p. 1014; August 1, 2004, review of *Gregor and the Prophecy of Bane,* p. 739; May 1, 2005, review of *When Charlie McButton Lost Power,* p. 536; June 15, 2005, review of *Gregor and the Curse of the Warmbloods,* p. 680; May 15, 2006, review of *Gregor and the Marks of Secret,* p. 515.

Publishers Weekly, September 8, 2003, review of *Gregor the Overlander,* p. 77.

School Library Journal, November, 2003, Steven Engelfried, review of *Gregor the Overlander,* p. 134; October, 2004, Beth Meister, review of *Gregor and the*

Prophecy of Bane, p. 160; July, 2005, Tasha Saecker, review of *Gregor and the Curse of the Warmbloods,* p. 100; July, 2005, Barbara Auerbach, review of *When Charlie McButton Lost Power,* p. 71; September, 2006, Mara Alpert, review of *Gregor and the Marks of Secret,* p. 202.

Voice of Youth Advocates, April, 2004, review of *Gregor and the Prophecy of Bane,* p. 21; December, 2004, review of *Gregor and the Prophecy of Bane,* p. 402.

ONLINE

Scholastic Web site, http://www.scholastic.com/ (April 28, 2007), "Suzanne Collins."

Suzanne Collins Home Page, http://suzannecollinsbooks.com (April 28, 2007).*

* * *

COPELAND, Mark 1956-

Personal

Born 1956, in England; married Sarah Munro. *Education:* Attended Cambridge School of Art, 1973-74; Canterbury College of Art, degree (graphic design), 1977.

Addresses

Home and office—Insect Circus Society, 25 Church Rd., Great Livermere, Bury St. Edmunds, Suffolk IP31 1JS, England.

Career

Performance artist, model maker, illustrator, and author. Worked as model maker and prop designer for television and film, including on productions of *Hard Times, Cold Lazarus, The Borrowers,* and *Gormenghast. Exhibitions:* Paintings exhibited at Portal Gallery, London, England, 1979 and solo shows 1991, 1993, 1997, 1999; Wally Findlay Galleries, New York, NY, 1983; Halesworth Gallery, Suffolk, England, 1986, 1988; and Heffer Gallery, Cambridge, England. Copeland's Insect Circus Museum toured England, c. 2005-06.

Writings

The Bundle at Blackthorpe Heath, Houghton Mifflin (Boston, MA), 2006.

Sidelights

For British artist and model maker Mark Copeland, writing is a sideline to his main career. In fact, his children's book *The Bundle at Blackthorpe Heath* was inspired by its author/illustrator's work as the creator, proprietor, and—under the stage name Ronald McPeak—ringmaster of the touring Insect Circus Museum.

Copeland's Insect Circus Museum is a touring work of performance art in which an antique truck is transformed into a miniature, magical world. Purporting to

Mark Copeland's quirky self-illustrated novel The Bundle at Blackthorpe Heath *was inspired by his interest in the caravan shows that toured England during the Victorian era.*

commemorate the 300-year history of a traveling circus operated by the Piper family, the museum features posters, stage costumes, props, and other creations, all focusing on the work of generations of human-sized insect performers. Whether viewed through dioramas, accessed through push-button peep shows, or revealed in an accompanying stage spectacular, patrons are introduced to Ephemera the Evanescent Mayfly, the Mighty Mites, Dungo the dung beetle, high-wire butterflies, and dancing snails, as well as to the human wasp tamers and worm charmers that share the center ring.

Copeland draws on the history of his fanciful Insect Circus Museum in *The Bundle at Blackthorpe Heath,* a novel that introduces the Piper family's young scion, Art Piper. On his twelfth birthday, Art is given a brass spyglass by Sir Henry Piper, reigning ringmaster of the insect circus. Although warned not to spy by Sir Henry, Art peers through the glass and discovers a threat to his family's long-standing livelihood when he witnesses a furtive meeting between Sir Henry's ant advisor and a member of a rival circus. Together with Rufus the pet ladybug, an Australian stick bug, and a young bareback beetle rider named Daisy, Art must uncover the plot and save the family business. Noting the book's late-nineteenth-century setting, *School Library Journal* reviewer Caitlin Augusta praised Copeland's detailed pen-and-ink art and called *The Bundle at Blackthorpe Heath* "a charming balance of mystery, drama, and the allure of insect-circus life." The author/illustrator's "old-fashioned storytelling and somewhat quaint prose" pairs with his nostalgic illustrations to "create a book with a distinctly retro feel," Norah Piehl noted in a review for *Kidsread.com,* while *Booklist* critic GraceAnne A. De-Candido described the work as "cheerfully tongue-in-cheek, resolutely old-timey, and intensely imaginative." The novel's "expertly tightened suspense builds to a magnificently funny climax with an entirely satisfying closing twist," concluded a *Kirkus Reviews* writer, while Piehl dubbed *The Bundle at Blackthorpe Heath* a "rollickingly clever, old-fashioned adventure."

Biographical and Critical Sources

PERIODICALS

Booklist, June 1, 2006, GraceAnne A. DeCandido, review of *The Bundle at Blackthorpe Heath,* p. 67.

Kirkus Reviews, May 15, 2006, review of *The Bundle at Blackthorpe Heath,* p. 515.

Peterborough Evening Telegraph (Peterborough, England), June 1, 2005, "Circus: Wasp Tamer Is Some-sting Good."

Publishers Weekly, July 10, 2006, review of *The Bundle at Blackthorpe Heath,* p. 83.

School Library Journal, July, 2006, Caitlin Augusta, review of *The Bundle at Blackthorpe Heath,* p. 100.

ONLINE

Insect Circus Web site, http://www.insectcircus.co.uk/ (May 1, 2007).

Kidsread.com, http://www.kidsread.com/reviews/ (May 1, 2007), Norah Piehl, review of *The Bundle at Blackthorpe Heath.*

Portal Gallery Web site, http://www.portal-gallery.com/ (May 1, 2007), "Mark Copeland."

SideshowWorld.com, http://www.kidsread.com/reviews/ (May 1, 2007), "The Insect Circus."*

D

DELANEY, M.C.
See DeLANEY, Michael

* * *

DELANEY, Michael 1955-
(M.C. Delaney, Michael Clark Delaney)

Personal

Born April 7, 1955; son of Thomas (a stockbroker) and Antoinette (an author and illustrator of children's books) Delaney; married Christine Hauck (a graphic artist), September 24, 1988; children: Emma. *Education:* New York University, B.A. (English), 1977.

Addresses

Agent—Wendy Schmalz, Harold Ober Associates, 425 Madison Ave., New York, NY 10017.

Career

Writer and illustrator. *Gourmet* magazine, freelance illustrator, 1981-96; J. Walter Thompson, advertising copywriter, 1985-90.

Writings

FOR CHILDREN

(Under name M.C. Delaney) *The Marigold Monster,* illustrated by brother, Ned Delaney, Dutton (New York, NY), 1983.

(Under name M.C. Delaney) *Henry's Special Delivery,* illustrated by Lisa McCue, Dutton (New York, NY), 1984.

(Under name M.C. Delaney) *Not Your Average Joe,* illustrated by Chris Burke, Dutton (New York, NY), 1990.

Michael Delaney (Photograph by Molly Delaney. Reproduced by permission of Michael Delaney.)

FOR CHILDREN; SELF-ILLUSTRATED

(Under name M.C. Delaney) *Deep Doo Doo,* Dutton (New York, NY), 1996.

Deep Doo Doo and the Mysterious E-Mail, Dutton (New York, NY), 2001.

Birdbrain Amos, Philomel (New York, NY), 2002.

The Great Sockathon, Dutton (New York, NY), 2004.

Birdbrain Amos, Mister Fun, Philomel (New York, NY), 2006.

OTHER

Cartoons and illustrations published in the *New York Times, National Lampoon,* and *Saturday Review.*

Sidelights

Michael Delaney began his career masquerading as M.C. Delaney, and under this alias he authored the first three of his entertaining stories for children. With his

Cover of Delaney's middle-grade novel **The Great Sockathon,** *featuring artwork by Deborah DeSaix.* (Dutton Children's Books, 2004. Jacket illustration © 2004 by Deborah DeSaix. Reproduced by permission of Dutton Children's Books, a division of Penguin Putnam.)

1996 chapter book *Deep Doo Doo* and its sequel, Delaney took on illustration duties as well. He has continued to create art for each of the lighthearted children's stories he has written since, such as *Birdbrain Amos, Birdbrain Amos, Mister Fun,* and *The Great Sockathon.* Noting the "appealing cast of characters" that figures in the last-named story, *School Library Journal* contributor Beth L. Meister praised Delaney for concocting a "popular summer read" that mixes a small-town ghost story and the fast-moving adventures of four middle-grade friends with a dollop of "action and suspense."

In *Deep Doo Doo* Delaney introduces inventive twelve year olds Bennet and Pete, who create an electronic apparatus able to interrupt the televised speech of a gubernatorial candidate. When they replace the incumbent's image with film footage of Pete's dog and add a voice-over script revealing the hypocrisy of the candidate, their media hijinks result in the demise of the governor. When Bennet and Pete return in *Deep Doo Doo and the Mysterious E-Mail,* they are busy running the Deep Doo Doo Web site when a series of e-mails from a self-

styled Mad Poet hints at a deep secret. Soon helped by sixth-grade classmate Elizabeth, the boys find themselves embroiled in local politics and the quest to discover who hoisted a pumpkin up the town-hall's flagpole. Linda Perkins, reviewing *Deep Doo Doo* for *Booklist,* declared that, although Delaney's grown-up characters "are caricatures" and his "premise far-fetched," the story's young protagonists are "believable and very funny." A critic for *Publishers Weekly* predicted that elementary-grade readers will enjoy the tale's "swift action and political puns," while a *Bulletin of the Center for Children's Books* contributor cited *Deep Doo Doo* for serving up a "generous helping of political satire." Noting the series' roots in 1970s culture, Catherine Andronik wrote in a *Booklist* review of *Deep Doo Doo and the Mysterious E-Mail* that the novel will appeal to "technologically savvy middle-graders who happen to like mysteries." "Delaney's breezy colloquial style brings a couple of potentially nerdy boys to life," wrote *School Library Journal* contributor Ann Cook in a review of the same book, dubbing *Deep Doo Doo and the Mysterious E-Mail* a good choice for reluctant middle-grade readers.

Birdbrain Amos, a book for younger readers, follows a soft-hearted hippo as he searches for a way to escape from a swarm of pesky biting insects. Advertising for help, Amos is contacted by several birds, the third of which is Kumba the tick bird. While the hippo's bug problem is solved, he now has a new problem: Kumba has taken Amos at his word to "make yourself at home" and built a nest right between Amos's ears! When Kumba's three eggs hatch, the hippo is too caring to force the bird family to find a new home, even when a flock of assorted bird relatives arrives. Determined to show how good a friend he can be, Amos takes his tick-bird friends on a vacation to Africa's Serengeti in *Birdbrain Amos, Mister Fun.*

In a *Horn Book* review of *Birdbrain Amos,* Susan P. Bloom wrote that Delaney "gets the humor just right," while a *Publishers Weekly* critic dubbed the story a "humorous romp for readers just graduating to full-length fiction." According to *Booklist* contributor Susan Dove Lempke, the author/illustrator's "droll, cartoon drawings" "embellish the very funny story," while Bloom added that Delaney's "delicately caricatured line drawings capture the befuddled" quality of his endearing hippopotamus hero. In *Birdbrain Amos, Mr. Fun* the author/illustrator wins new fans, according to Bloom, the *Horn Book* critic citing Delaney's use of "snappy repetition, some very funny repartee, and comic cartoon pen-and-ink drawings."

Delaney once told *SATA:* "I began writing because I'm really not a very articulate person and I tend to say things that, later, I wish I'd said better and in a funnier way. Writing allows me to show that I am not quite the dunderhead I often think I sound.

"I strive to create books that readers, both young and old, enjoy reading. My hope, my dream, is to write a

Fans of Delaney's popular picture book **Birdbrain Amos** *were pleased when the engaging hippo hero returned in* **Birdbrain Amos, Mister Fun.**

Biographical and Critical Sources

PERIODICALS

Booklist, January 1, 1997, Linda Perkins, review of *Deep Doo Doo,* pp. 858-859; March 1, 2001, Catherine Andronik, review of *Deep Doo Doo and the Mysterious E-Mail,* p. 1275; April 1, 2002, Susan Dove Lempke, review of *Birdbrain Amos,* p. 1323; August, 2004, Kay Weisman, review of *The Great Sockathon,* p. 1933.

Bulletin of the Center for Children's Books, July, 1984, review of *Henry's Special Delivery,* p. 202; February, 1997, review of *Deep Doo Doo,* p. 202; April, 2002, review of *Birdbrain Amos,* p. 278.

Horn Book, March-April, 2002, Susan P. Bloom, review of *Birdbrain Amos,* p. 211; July-August, 2006, Susan P. Bloom, review of *Birdbrain Amos, Mister Fun,* p. 439.

Kirkus Reviews, February 1, 2003, review of *Birdbrain Amos,* p. 179; July 15, 2004, review of *The Great Sockathon,* p. 683; May 15, 2006, review of *Birdbrain Amos, Mister Fun,* p. 516.

Publishers Weekly, April 15, 1983, review of *The Marigold Monster,* p. 51; June 1, 1984, review of *Henry's Special Delivery,* p. 65; November 18, 1996, review of *Deep Doo Doo,* pp. 75-76; February 25, 2002, review of *Birdbrain Amos,* p. 67.

School Library Journal, May, 1983, review of *The Marigold Monster,* p. 58; October, 1984, review of *Henry's Special Delivery,* p. 156; December, 1989, Susan L. Rogers, review of *Not Your Average Joe,* p. 98; December, 1996, John Sigwald, review of *Deep Doo Doo,* p. 120; March, 2001, Ann Cook, review of *Deep Doo Doo and the Mysterious E-Mail,* p. 246; April, 2002, Linda L. Plevak, review of *Birdbrain Amos,* p. 103; August, 2004, Beth L. Meister, review of *The Great Sockathon,* p. 120; July, 2006, Quinby Frank, review of *Birdbrain Amos, Mister Fun,* p. 71.

Voice of Youth Advocates, February, 1990, review of *Not Your Average Joe,* p. 342.

Washington Post Book World, June 25, 2006, Elizabeth Ward, review of *Birdbrain Amos, Mister Fun,* p. 11.*

book that one day finds its way into the 'Classics' section of the children's books section of the bookstore. (Ideally, I'd like it to be put there by an employee of the bookstore, rather than by some customer who happened to misplace it.)

"While writing *Deep Doo Doo,* I wanted to create a world in which the adults have made a real mess of things (in this case, politics) and children save the day. My other goal was to write a book that was fun to read. My writing has been influenced by, among others, F. Scott Fitzgerald and E.B. White.

"In addition to these outside influences, I come from a family of children's book authors and illustrators, all of whom, I am happy to say, are still very much on the scene. My mother has written and illustrated several picture books as well as illustrated for *Sesame Street.* My older brother, Ned, has written and illustrated dozens of picture books. And my sister, Molly, has written and illustrated a picture book. If only I had a sibling who was a children's book reviewer for the *New York Times,* I'd be all set."

*   *   *

DELANEY, Michael Clark
See DELANEY, Michael

*   *   *

DeMATTEIS, J.M. 1953-
(John Marc DeMatteis)

Personal

Born December 15, 1953, in Brooklyn, NY; married; children: one son, one daughter. *Religion:* Hindu. *Hobbies and other interests:* Travel, playing guitar and piano, spending time with family.

Addresses

Home—Upstate New York.

Career

Comic-book writer and musician. Formerly worked as a music critic; DC Comics, New York, NY, writer, c. 1970s, late 1980s-91; Marvel Comics, New York, NY, writer for *The Defenders* and *Captain America* series, 1980s, c. 1991—. Musician, performing on *How Many Lifetimes?,* produced 1997.

Awards, Honors

American Library Association Ten Best Graphic Novels designation, for *Brooklyn Dreams;* Eisner Award for Best Humor Publication (with others), 2004, for *Formerly Known as the Justice League.*

Writings

GRAPHIC NOVELS

Greenberg the Vampire, illustrated by Mark Badger, Marvel Comics (New York, NY), 1986.

Stan Lee Presents Spider Man: Fearful Symmetry—Kraven's Last Hunt (originally published in comic-book format), illustrated by Mike Zeck and others, Marvel Comics (New York, NY), 1989.

Moonshadow (originally published in comic-book format), illustrated by Jon J. Muth and others, Marvel/Epic Comics (New York, NY), 1989, published as *The Compleat Moonshadow,* DC Comics (New York, NY), 1998.

Blood (originally published in comic-book format), illustrated by Kent Williams, Marvel/Epic Comics (New York, NY), 1989, reprinted, 2004.

(With Keith Giffen) *Justice League International: The Secret Gospel of Maxwell Lord,* illustrated by Bill Willingham and others, DC Comics (New York, NY), 1992.

Mercy, illustrated by Paul Johnson, DC Comics (New York, NY), 1993.

Brooklyn Dreams (originally published in comic-book format by Paradox, 1994–95), illustrated by Glenn Barr, Vertigo/DC Comics (New York, NY), 2003.

(With Sherilyn Van Valkenburgh) *Wings,* DC Comics (New York, NY), 2001.

Green Lantern: Willworld, illustrated by Seth Fisher, DC Comics (New York, NY), 2001.

Batman: Absolution, illustrated by Brian Ashmore, DC Comics (New York, NY), 2002.

(With Phil Jimenez and Joe Kelly) *Wonder Woman: Paradise Lost* (originally published in comic-book format), illustrated by Jimenez and others, DC Comics (New York, NY), 2002.

(With others) *Superman: President Lex,* DC Comics (New York, NY), 2003.

(With Keith Giffen) *Formerly Known as the Justice League* (originally published in comic-book format), DC Comics (New York, NY), 2004.

(With Keith Giffen) *I Can't Believe It's Not the Justice League* (originally published in comic-book format), DC Comics (New York, NY), 2005.

"ABADAZAD" GRAPHIC-NOVEL SERIES; FOR CHILDREN

The Road to Inconceivable (originally published in comic-book form by CrossGen), illustrated by Mike Ploog, Hyperion Books for Children (New York, NY), 2006.

The Dream Thief (originally published in comic-book form by CrossGen), illustrated by Mike Ploog, Hyperion Books for Children (New York, NY), 2006.

The Puppet, the Professor, and the Prophet (originally published in comic-book form by CrossGen), illustrated by Mike Ploog, Hyperion Books for Children (New York, NY), 2007.

OTHER

Author of original comic-book series "Abadazad" (also see below), illustrated by Mike Ploog, CrossGen, 2004; and *Stardust Kid,* illustrated by Mike Ploog, Boom! Studios, 2005. Author, with Keith Giffen, of comic-book series *Hero Squared,* for Atomeka Press, and *Planetary Brigade* for Boom! Studios, 2006. Author of graphic miniseries *Into Shambhala,* 1986; *Farewell, The Last One,* and *Seekers into the Mystery.* Writer for ongoing comic-book series, including *The Amazing Spider-Man, The Defenders, Superman, Captain America, Justice League, Doctor Strange, Daredevil, Man-Thing, The Silver Surfer, Wonder Woman, Doctor Fate, Spectre,* and *Batman.*

Also author of episodes for television series, including *The Twilight Zone, The Adventures of Superboy, Earth: Final Conflict, The Real Ghostbusters, Justice League Unlimited,* and *Legion of Super-Heroes.* Also author of unproduced screenplays and of installments in *Justice League* (animated television program), for Cartoon Network. Contributor of reviews to periodicals, including *Rolling Stone.*

Sidelights

Considered among the most versatile writers working in contemporary comics, J.M. DeMatteis is noted for creating compelling characters and plots involving complex themes. Starting as a music critic, the Brooklyn-born DeMatteis moved into writing for comic books in the late 1970s. In the years since, he has contributed to numerous well-known comic-book series as well as creating acclaimed original stories that have been published in graphic-novel format. In his work for well-known publishers DC Comics and Marvel Comics, he has made his creative mark on such series as *The Defenders, Spider-Man, Superman, Batman,* and the superhero spoof *Justice League International,* while in *Brooklyn Dreams, Moonshadow,* and *Abadazad* he presents original stories that appeal to both teens and adult fans of the graphic-novel medium. He has also worked for

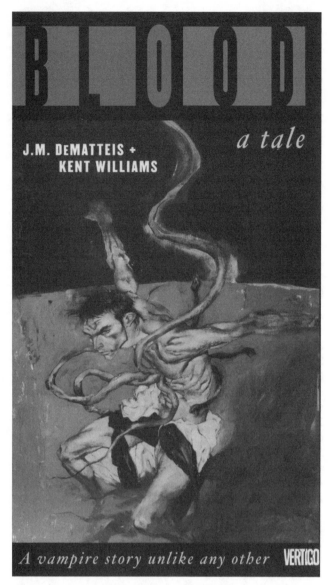

J.M. DeMatteis' comic-book series **Blood,** *featuring artwork by Kent Williams, was eventually published in book form by DC Comics.* (Vertigo, 1996, 1997. Cover illustration by Kent Williams. Reproduced by permission of DC Comics, Inc.)

indie comics publishers such as Boom! Studios, which began publishing DeMatteis' children's comic *Stardust Kid* in 2005.

DeMatteis played a significant role in founding DC's Vertigo imprint, which began publishing horror comics during the 1970s. He then went on to collaborate with artist Mike Zeck on Marvel's *Captain America* series, as well as on "Kraven's Last Hunt," a story arc that ran in the *Spider-Man* series before appearing in graphic-novel format as 1989's *Stan Lee Presents Spider Man: Fearful Symmetry—Kraven's Last Hunt.* DeMatteis also worked with artist Jon J. Muth to produce *Moonshadow,* a work published in book form by Marvel that was noted for being the first fully painted comic series.

Remaining with Marvel throughout much of the 1980s, DeMatteis followed *Moonshadow* with *Blood: A Tale,* a

vampire story with mythic undertones that features art by Kent Williams. Returning to DC by the time *Blood* hit bookstores, he took over the reins of the long-running *Justice League of America* superhero saga. When characters from that series, such as G'nort, Mr. Nebula, and Mister Miracle, were recast in the more-humorous *Justice League International,* he worked with coauthor Keith Giffen on developing both the series and its various spin-offs. In 2003 DeMatteis joined with Giffen to receive an Eisner award recognizing the story arc published in book form as *Formerly Known as the Justice League.* After five years, he returned to Marvel and shepherded the *Spider-Man* series down a darker path in story arcs such as "The Child Within," working with artist Sal Buscema.

In DeMatteis' autobiographical miniseries *Brooklyn Dreams,* a collaboration with artist Glenn Bart that was issued by DC Comics in 1994, forty-something narrator Carl Santini looks back on his high-school years in the late 1960s. Issues in the teen's tumultuous multicultural family, his questions of faith, his friendships, experimental drug use, and romantic entanglements highlight his memoir, bubbling to the story's surface in the form of what *Booklist* contributor Ray Olson described as "richly detailed" and humorous "digressions." Against Santini's teen reality is the narrator's memory of meeting with his guardian angel, a scruffy, stray hound, and this memory also resonates throughout DeMatteis's story. Praising *Brooklyn Dreams* as "a classic of the [comic-book] form," Olson deemed the work "as graphically distinguished and creatively novelistic a graphic novel as has ever been." In *Publishers Weekly* a critic called DeMatteis' tale "hypnotic," adding that Barr's illustrations follow "the plot's twists, . . . captur[ing] . . . the wild enthusiasms and fears of Carl's world." First published by DC Comics' Paradox Press imprint, *Brooklyn Dreams* was reissued in one volume by Vertigo in 2003.

In 2004 DeMatteis teamed with veteran British artist Mike Ploog to create "Abadazad," a fantasy comic published by Florida-based publisher CrossGen. Two installments appeared in soft-cover editions before Cross-Gen went bankrupt, leaving both author and illustrator in a quandary. Fortunately, the series was acquired by Walt Disney Corporation, and the media giant allowed DeMatteis and Ploog to return to the proverbial drawing table and reconfigure their story as a hybrid melding picture book and comic book. The "Abadazad" series resurfaced in 2006 as the illustrated novels *The Road to Inconceivable, The Dream Thief,* and *The Puppet, the Professor, and the Prophet.* The saga is an amalgam of *The Wizard of Oz, Alice in Wonderland,* and the Arabian Nights, with nine-year-old Katie Jameson its Shaharazad. In the story, Katie is a fan of the book series "Martha in Abadazad," and she shares these books with her younger brother Matt. The two have a close relationship until Matt mysteriously vanishes while on a ride at a local carnival. Guilt over Matt's fate transforms Katie's nature, and by her early teens she has become glum and taciturn. A meeting with a quirky neighbor who claims that Martha's Abadazadian adventures were, in fact, real rekindles Katie's fascination with the fantasy world. When the woman provides the teen with the means by which she can enter Abadazad, fourteen-year-old Katie willingly takes a chance, propelled by the belief that there she will discover Matt's fate. Discussing the initial comic-book version of the saga in a *Magazine of Fantasy and Science Fiction* review, Charles De Lint noted that "Abadazad" is engaging due to DeMatteis' "inventiveness" and "attention to real world detail and problems [which] . . . slightly subvert everything in the magical land." Calling the series "kid-friendly," De Lint also noted that DeMatteis' story contains "enough meat and sly asides and bits of humor that adults will enjoy it as well."

The "Abadazad" saga's first book-length installment, *The Road to Inconceivable,* follows Katie into the fantasy world, where the Brooklyn teen confirms that Matt is being held hostage there. DeMatteis' text is multi-level; it alternates between Katie's diary entries and the overarching story line and is cemented by Ploog's animé-style art. Although her search proves fruitless, by the end of the book Katie has started down the path she will follow in *The Dream Thief.* Helped by the benevolent Little Martha in the saga's second installment, the teen learns that her little brother is being held captive by the sinister Lanky Man. While Sharon R. Pearce wrote in *School Library Journal* that the format of the "Abadazad" books might be "too confusing" for some readers, a *Publishers Weekly* reviewer maintained that the series "expertly blends art and text" and "Katie's emotionally messy but honest diary" is enhanced by Ploog's "deft brushwork." Writing that the book's "black-and-white art is an appealing mix of realism and exaggeration," Jesse Karp added in *Booklist* that DeMatteis' heroine "makes the story shine," resulting in a "thoughtful read with surprising psychological nuance."

Discussing his "Abadazad" series with Mike Jozic in an online interview for Silver Bullet Comics, DeMatteis noted: "When I look at fantasy books I've enjoyed—from *Alice in Wonderland* to *Oz,* from [J.M.M.] Tolkien to Ray Bradbury—I think it comes down to one essential ingredient: the sense of wonder. Whether you're seven years old or a jaded adult, if your sense of wonder is blown open, if you're drawn into a world that intrigues and excites you and if you believe in that world, then the story is going to appeal. Which is why the best fantasy seems to work on so many levels, for so many age groups." Noting the growing popularity of the fantasy genre in the wake of J.K. Rowling's "Harry Potter" books, DeMatteis told *Comicon.com* interviewer Jennifer M. Contino that when an idea for a story comes to mind, "I have to trust it . . . let it lead me on a journey . . . and reveal the events, and the characters, to me as we go along." According to DeMatteis, "writing is ultimately an act of channeling: it's as if you're opening yourself up to—and transcribing the events in—a world that ALREADY EXISTS. A writer's job . . . is to honor that world and represent it as faithfully as possible. I think if you can do that, your story . . . and your characters . . . will have uniqueness and life."

Biographical and Critical Sources

PERIODICALS

Booklist, July, 2003, Ray Olson, review of *Brooklyn Dreams,* p. 1855; July 1, 2006, Jesse Karp, review of *The Road to Inconceivable,* p. 55.

Kirkus Reviews, May 15, 2006, review of *The Road to Inconceivable,* p. 516.

Magazine of Fantasy and Science Fiction, September, 2004, Charles De Lint, review of *Abadazad,* p. 32.

Publishers Weekly, September 29, 2003, review of *Superman: President Lex,* p. 45; August 11, 2003, review of *Brooklyn Dreams,* p. 259; June 12, 2005, review of *The Road to Inconceivable,* p. 53.

DeMatteis and illustrator Mike Ploog adapted a popular comic-book series into the graphic novel **Abazad: The Road to Inconceivable.** (Hyperion Books for Children, 2006. All rights reserved. Reprinted by permission of Hyperion Books for Children.)

School Library Journal, November, 2006, Sharon R. Pearce, review of *The Road to Inconceivable* and *The Dream Thief,* p. 166.

Wilson Library Bulletin, October, 1993, review of *Moonshadow,* p. 136.

ONLINE

ComicFanatic.com, http://www.comicfanatic.com/ (December 9, 2004), interview with DeMatteis.

Comicon.com, http://www.comicon.com/ (May 5, 2005), Jennifer M. Contino, interview with DeMatteis.

Silver Bullet Comics Web site, http://www.silverbulletcomicbooks.com/ (January 14, 2004), Mike Jozic, interview with DeMatteis.*

* * *

DeMATTEIS, John Marc
See DeMATTEIS, J.M.

* * *

De WIRE, Elinor 1953-
(Aline Matthews, Jessica Scott)

Personal

Born August 3, 1953, in Frederick, MD; married Jonathan De Wire (a retired Navy officer), December 30, 1972; children: Jessica, Scott. *Education:* University of Connecticut, B.G.S. (general studies), M.A. (education).

Addresses

Home—Seabeck, WA. *E-mail*—lighthousekitty@msn.com.

Career

Educator, historian, author, and editor, beginning 1980. Workshop presenter and speaker; has appeared on television documentary programs. Historical preservationist and consultant.

Member

U.S. Lighthouse Society, American Lighthouse Foundation, Washington Lightkeepers Association (founder and president, 2005—).

Awards, Honors

National League of American Pen Women award for short fiction, 1992; Coast Guard Book Award, 2003, for *Lighthouses of the Mid-Atlantic Coast,* and 2004, for *Lighthouses of the Southern Coast*; Ben Franklin Book Award, 2005, for *Lighthouses of the Southern Coast.*

Eleanor DeWire (Photograph courtesy of Elinor DeWire.)

Writings

The Guide to Florida Lighthouses, Pineapple Press (Englewood, FL), 1987, 2nd edition, 2001.

Journey through the Universe, Mystic Seaport Museum (Mystic, CT), 1987.

Activities for Young Astronomers, Mystic Seaport Museum (Mystic, CT), 1990.

Reach for the Sky, Mystic Seaport Museum (Mystic, CT), 1994.

Guardians of the Lights: The Men and Women of the U.S. Lighthouse Service, Pineapple Press (Englewood, FL), 1995, 2nd edition, 2007.

The Lighthouse Activity Book, Sentinel Publications, 1995.

Lighthouse Victuals and Verse, Sentinel Publications, 1996.

Sentries along the Shore, Sentinel Publications, 1997.

The Lighthouse Almanac, Sentinel Publications, 2000.

The Florida Night Sky: A Guide to Observing from Dusk till Dawn, Pineapple Press (Sarasota, FL), 2002.

Lighthouses of the Mid-Atlantic Coast: Your Guide to the Lighthouses of New York, New Jersey, Maryland, Delaware, and Virginia, Voyageur Press (Stillwater, MN), 2002.

Lighthouses: Sentinels of the American Coast, photographs by Laurence Parent, Graphic Arts Center Publishing (Portland, OR), 2003.

Lighthouses of the Southern Coast: Your Guide to the Lighthouses of Virginia, North Carolina, South Carolina, Georgia, and Florida, photographs by Daniel E. Dempster, Voyageur Press (Stillwater, MN), 2004.

Florida Lighthouses for Kids, Pineapple Press (Sarasota, FL), 2004.

The Field Guide to Lighthouses of the Pacific Coast: California, Oregon, Washington, Alaska, and Hawai'i, Voyageur Press (Stillwater, MN), 2006.

The Field Guide to Lighthouses of New England, MBI Publishing (St. Paul, MN), 2007.

The Lightkeeper's Menagerie: Stories of Animals at Lighthouses, Pineapple Press (Sarasota, FL), 2007.

Contributor of articles and columns to periodicals, sometimes under pseudonyms Jessica Scott and Aline Matthews, including *Aloha, American History Illus-*

trated, Beachcomber, Birder's World, Cat Fancy, Compass, Cricket, Dog Fancy, Florida Keys, Heading Out, Horseman, Lighthouse Digest, Mariners Weather Log, Navy Times, Offshore, Sacramento, Sea Frontiers, Soundings, Trailer Boats, Ventura County Coast Reporter, Weatherwise, Western Boatman, and *Yachtsman.* Editor of *Focal Point* (quarterly newsletter of Washington Lightkeepers Association), 2005—.

Sidelights

Elinor De Wire has been researching, photographing, and writing about lighthouses since 1972, and she shares her interest in books such as *Sentries along the Shore, Field Guide to Pacific Coast Lighthouses,* and *Florida Lighthouses for Kids.* Through her lectures, workshops, articles, and books, De Wire has been an instrumental force in turning public attention toward the importance of preserving the many lighthouses that dot both U.S. coastlines: the "sentinels along the shore," to quote from the title of one of De Wire's many books.

While many of her books are written for a general readership, De Wire has also focused on a younger audience with *The Lighthouse Activity Book, The Lightkeepers' Menagerie: Stories of Animals at Lighthouses,* and *Florida Lighthouses for Kids,* as well as with her kid-oriented column in the periodical *Lighthouse Digest.* In a review for *Children's Bookwatch,* a reviewer praised De Wire's "informed and informative text" in *Florida Lighthouses for Kids* and added that the "form and format" of the book is "ideal for young readers."

Biographical and Critical Sources

PERIODICALS

Children's Bookwatch, August, 2005, review of *Florida Lighthouses for Kids.*

Tampa Tribune, June 14, 2004, Steve Kornacki, "Anclote Lighthouse Has Special Place in Author's Heart," p. 2.

Yachting, October, 1995, Tyler Lifton, review of *Guardians of the Lights: Stories of U.S. Lighthouse Keepers,* p. 36.

*   *   *

DONALDSON, Julia 1948-

Personal

Born September 16, 1948, in London, England; daughter of James (a geneticist) and Elizabeth (a secretary) Shields; married Malcolm Donaldson (a pediatrician), September 30, 1972; children: Hamish, Alastair, Jesse. *Education:* Bristol University, degree (drama and French), 1970. *Politics:* Tory. *Religion:* "Agnostic." *Hobbies and other interests:* Piano, singing, walking, flowers, fungi.

Addresses

Home—Glasgow, Scotland.

Career

Children's book author and playwright. Former songwriter for children's television.

Awards, Honors

Smarties Gold Medal Award for picture books, and Kate Greenaway Medal nominee, both 1999, and Blue Peter Award for Best Book to Read Aloud, and Experian Big Three Book Prize, both 2000, all for *The Gruffalo;* Blue Peter Award for Best Book to Read Aloud, Children's Book Award shortlist, Sheffield Children's Book Award shortlist, and Scottish Children's Book Award, all 2002, all for *Room on the Broom;* W.H. Smith Children's Book of the Year honor, 2005, for *The Gruffalo's Child;* Blue Peter Award for Best Book to Read Aloud, 2005, for *The Snail and the Whale.*

Writings

FOR CHILDREN

A Squash and a Squeeze, illustrated by Axel Scheffler, Margaret K. McElderry (New York, NY), 1993.

Birthday Surprise (play), Ginn (Aylesbury, England), 1994.

Names and Games (play), Ginn (Aylesbury, England), 1995.

(Reteller) *Turtle Tug* (play), Ginn (Aylesbury, England), 1995.

(Reteller) *The Three Billy Goats Gruff* (play), Ginn (Aylesbury, England), 1995.

(Reteller) *The Boy Who Cried Wolf* (play), Ginn (Aylesbury, England), 1995.

(Reteller) *The Magic Twig* (play), Ginn (Aylesbury, England), 1995.

Space Girl Sue, illustrated by Clive Scruton, Ginn (Aylesbury, England), 1996.

(Reteller) *Town and Country Mouse,* illustrated by Nick Schon, Ginn (Aylesbury, England), 1996.

Mr. Snow, illustrated by Celia Canning, Ginn (Aylesbury, England), 1996.

(Reteller) *Counting Chickens,* illustrated by Jeffrey Reid, Ginn (Aylesbury, England), 1996.

The King's Porridge, Ginn (Aylesbury, England), 1996.

The Wonderful Smells (play), illustrated by Jan Nesbitt, Ginn (Aylesbury, England), 1997.

Top of the Mops (play), Ginn (Aylesbury, England), 1997.

The Brownie King, illustrated by John Eastwood, Heinemann (Oxford, England), 1998.

Books and Crooks (plays), Stanley Thornes (Cheltenham, England), 1998.

The False Tooth Fairy (plays), Ginn (Aylesbury, England), 1998.

Waiter! Waiter!, illustrated by Jim Kavanagh, Heinemann (Oxford, England), 1998.

All Gone!, illustrated by Alexa Rutherford, Ginn (Aylesbury, England), 1998.

The Gruffalo, illustrated by Axel Scheffler, Dial Books for Young Readers (New York, NY), 1999.

Steve's Sandwiches, Ginn (Aylesbury, England), 1999.

Clever Katya, Ginn (Aylesbury, England), 1999.

The Noises Next Door, Ginn (Aylesbury, England), 1999.

Monkey Puzzle, illustrated by Axel Scheffler, Macmillan (London, England), 2000.

(Reteller) *The Strange Dream,* illustrated by Thomas Sperling, Oxford University Press (Oxford, England), 2000.

Problem Page (play), illustrated by David Mostyn, Heinemann (Oxford, England), 2000.

The Boy Who Talked to Birds, illustrated by Suzanne Watts, Oxford University Press (Oxford, England), 2000.

One Piece Missing, Rigby Heinemann (Oxford, England), 2000.

Jumping Jack, Rigby Heinemann (Oxford, England), 2000.

The Giant Jumperee, Rigby Heinemann (Oxford, England), 2000.

Follow the Swallow, illustrated by Martin Ursell, Mammoth (London, England), 2000, Crabtree (New York, NY), 2002.

(Reteller) *The King's Ears,* illustrated by Lisa Berkshire, Oxford University Press (London, England), 2000.

The Monsters in the Cave, Ginn (Aylesbury, England), 2001.

Stop, Thief!, Ginn (Aylesbury, England), 2001.

Room on the Broom, illustrated by Axel Scheffler, Dial Books for Young Readers (New York, NY), 2001.

The Dinosaur's Diary, illustrated by Debbie Boon, Puffin (London, England), 2002.

Night Monkey, Day Monkey, illustrated by Lucy Richards, Egmont (London, England), 2002.

The Smartest Giant in Town, Macmillan Children's (London, England), 2002, published as *The Spiffiest Giant in Town,* illustrated by Axel Scheffler, Dial Books for Young Readers (New York, NY), 2003.

The Trial of Wilf Wolf, illustrated by Martin Ursell, Longman (Harlow, England), 2003.

Princess Mirror-Belle, illustrated by Lydia Monks, Macmillan (London, England), 2003.

The Head in the Sand: A Roman Play, illustrated by Ross Collins, Hodder Wayland (London, England), 2003.

The Magic Paintbrush, illustrated by Joel Stewart, Macmillan (London, England), 2003.

Conjure Cow, illustrated by Nick Sharratt, Puffin (London, England), 2003.

Brick-a-breck, illustrated by Philippe Dupasquier, A. & C. Black (London, England), 2003.

Bombs and Blackberries: A World War II Play, illustrated by Philippe Dupasquier, Hodder Wayland (London, England), 2003.

The Snail and the Whale, illustrated by Axel Scheffler, Macmillan Children's Books (London, England), 2003.

One Ted Falls out of Bed, illustrated by Anna Currey, Macmillan (London, England), 2004, Holt (New York, NY), 2006.

The Wrong Kind of Bark, illustrated by Garry Parson, Egmont (London, England), 2004.

Wriggle and Roar!: Rhymes to Join in With, illustrated by Nick Sharratt, Macmillan (London, England), 2004.

Crazy Mayonnaisy Mum: Poems, illustrated by Nick Sharratt, Macmillan (London, England), 2004.

Sharing a Shell, illustrated by Lydia Monks, Macmillan (London, England), 2004.

The Gruffalo's Child, illustrated by Axel Scheffler, Macmillan (London, England), 2004, Dial Books for Young Readers (New York, NY), 2005.

Rosie's Hat, illustrated by Anna Currey, Macmillan (London, England), 2005.

Chocolate Moose for Greedy Goose, illustrated by Nick Sharratt, Macmillan (London, England), 2005.

The Gruffalo's Song, and Other Songs (includes compact disk), illustrated by Axel Scheffler, Macmillan (London, England), 2005.

Princess Mirror-Belle and the Magic Shoes, illustrated by Lydia Monks, Macmillan (London, England), 2005.

The Giants and the Joneses, illustrated by Greg Swearingen, Holt (New York, NY), 2005.

Charlie Cook's Favorite Book, illustrated by Axel Scheffler, Macmillan (London, England), 2005, Dial Books for Young Readers (New York, NY), 2006.

(With John Henderson) *Fly, Pigeon, Fly!,* illustrated by Thomas Docherty, LIttle Tiger (London, England), 2006.

Hippo Has a Hat, illustrated by Nick Sharratt, Macmillan (London, England), 2006.

Princess Mirror-Belle and the Flying Horse, illustrated by Lydia Monks, Macmillan (London, England), 2006.

Tiddler, illustrated by Axel Scheffler, Arthur A. Levine (New York, NY), 2007.

Also author of educational materials for Oxford University Press and Walker Books.

The Gruffalo has been published in over twenty languages.

"TALES FROM ACORN WOOD" SERIES

Postman Bear, illustrated by Axel Scheffler, Campbell (London, England), 2000.

Fox's Socks, illustrated by Axel Scheffler, Campbell (London, England), 2000.

Hide and Seek Pig, illustrated by Axel Scheffler, Campbell (London, England), 2000.

Rabbit's Nap, illustrated by Axel Scheffler, Campbell (London, England), 2000.

OTHER

Also author of songs, scripts, and stories for BBC television and radio (mainly children's programs). Author of *Cat Whispers,* Rigby. Author of unpublished musicals *King Grunt's Cake* and *Pirate on the Pier.* Contributor of poetry and plays to anthologies.

Adaptations

The Gruffalo was adapted into a board book, an oversized-format book, and an audiobook, and was adapted as a musical stage production produced in London, England, 2005. *The Giant and the Joneses* was adapted as an audiobook, read by Patricia Conolly, Recorded Books, 2006, and was optioned for film by Warner Bros., 2004.

Sidelights

A storyteller and songwriter who performs her own material accompanied by her guitar-playing husband, Julia Donaldson did her first prose writing for television and radio in her native Great Britain. These creative activities, with their focus on young children, led the Scots-born writer to move into picture-book writing in the early 1990s. "My book *A Squash and a Squeeze* started life as a song on a television programme," she once explained to *SATA.* In the years since, Donaldson has become one of the most beloved writers for young chil-

dren, and her book *The Gruffalo* has become a modern-day picture-book classic. Another of her many popular works, *Charlie Cook's Favorite Book* captures the magic of reading in eleven linking stories that were praised by a *Kirkus Reviews* writer as "masterfully rhymed" and "clever" in their approach.

Donaldson retells the well-known story about an elderly woman who wishes for a larger house in *A Squash and a Squeeze.* Dubbed a "jolly version" of the traditional folk tale by *Books for Keeps* reviewer Liz Waterland, Donaldson's retelling finds an elderly woman frustrated over the lack of room in her tiny home. Taking the advice of a wise man, she invites all her farm animals into the house. After subsequently ousting the cumbersome creatures, the woman realizes that her home is large enough after all.

Julia Donaldson's humorous picture book **Room on the Broom** *is one of many collaborations with German-born illustrator Axel Scheffler.* (Dial Books for Young Readers, 2001. Illustration © 2001 by Axel Scheffler. Reproduced by permission of Dial Books for Young Readers, a division of Penguin Putnam Books for Young Readers.)

The Gruffalo, *one of Donaldson and Scheffler's most popular picture books, inspired several sequels and even a television series.*

Donaldson continues in the same humorous vein in many of her other picture books, including *The Gruffalo, Room on the Broom, The Snail and the Whale, The Giants and the Joneses,* and *One Ted Falls out of Bed.* Told in rhyming verse, *The Gruffalo* introduces an imaginary creature invented by a frightened mouse as a means of scaring off potential predators. After the mouse escapes becoming the tasty snack of, in turn, a hungry fox, owl, and snake, it comes upon the very Gruffalo it has created in its imagination, complete with fangs, claws, and a healthy appetite. Donaldson continues her story in a sequel, *The Gruffalo's Child,* which finds the daughter of the Gruffalo determined to search out the fearsome but tiny creature her father warned her about. In a *Publishers Weekly* review of *The Gruffalo,* a contributor wrote that Donaldson "manipulates the repetitive language and rhymes to good advantage," and London *Observer* reviewer Sam Taylor dubbed the book "a modern classic." In *Booklist,* Stephanie Zvirin praised Donaldson's text, noting that its "bouncy, humorous text flows smoothly," while *Books for Keeps* reviewer Clive Barnes called *The Gruffalo* "cleverly constructed." Praising Alex Scheffler's "humorous, cartoonlike illustrations" for *The Gruffalo's Child, Horn Book* contributor Jennifer M. Brabander noted of the sequel that the images "work well with Donaldson's pleasingly repetitive" rhyming text, resulting in "a story that . . . is clever rather than truly scary."

With *Room on the Broom* Donaldson uses a folktale format to tell the story of how helpful animals hitch a ride on the broomstick of a generous witch. A striped cat, spotted dog, green parrot, and frog each help the witch out of a jam, and in return they are given a ride on what ends up being a very comfortable conveyance. Noting that Donaldson's "rhythm and rhyme are lively and quick," *Booklist* reviewer GraceAnne A. DeCandido added that Scheffler's illustrations "partake equally of silly and spooky." While the storyline's "metrical rhyme and goofy suspense aren't groundbreaking," according to a *Publishers Weekly* contributor, young readers will "find it refreshing" to see a witch cast in a new role in Donaldson's entertaining story. Pamela K. Bomboy, writing in *School Library Journal,* predicted that because *Room on a Broom* is "full of fun, and not at all scary," it will be a "surefire read-aloud hit."

The Snail and the Whale follows the journey of a tiny snail and the fast-swimming whale that helps the tiny creature along. Noting the story's environmental subtext, a *Publishers Weekly* reviewer added that *The Snail and the Whale* "lightly demonstrates that friendships come in all shapes and sizes." A stuffed animal stars in *One Ted Falls out of Bed,* a counting picture book featuring art by Anna Currey. In Donaldson's tale, after a teddy bear is nudged out of his child's bed and onto the floor in the middle of the night, he enlists the help of three mice in waking the sleeping child and returning to his place under the covers. Noting that Currey's illustrations "capture the giddy, magical fun" of Donaldson's story, a *Publishers Weekly* reviewer added that *One Ted Falls out of Bed* gives pre-readers ample opportunities to elaborate on the story's rhyming text. In *Kirkus Reviews,* a critic dubbed the book "a sweet addition to any bedtime routine."

Giants figure in several of Donaldson's books. *The Spiffiest Giant in Town,* which follows George the giant as he attempts a clothing make-over, features a rhyming text contains about which a *Publishers Weekly* reviewer wrote: "joie de vivre and the characters' droll camaraderie will almost certainly prove infectious." *The Giant and the Joneses* moves readers into a fairy-tale realm, as Donaldsen puts a new spin on the story about Jack and the beanstalk. In this tale, a giant's child named Jumbeelia lives up above the clouds. Fascinated with human children, she grows a beanstalk down to earth and kidnaps the three young Jones siblings—Colette, Poppy, and Stephen. Trapped in Jumbeelia's playhouse in the sky, where they are the victim of the giant's brother's teasing, the children must find a way to escape the misguided young giantess and return to earth. In her novel story, Donaldsen even includes a glossary of Groilish terms, Groil being the language spoken by giants. Praising Donaldson's ability to create a dual narrative mixing human English and giant Groilish, *School Library Journal* reviewer Elaine E. Knight called *The Giants and the Joneses* "an exciting story with a subtle message about respect and cooperation."

Biographical and Critical Sources

PERIODICALS

Booklist, April 26, 1993, review of *A Squash and a Squeeze,* p. 78; July, 1999, Stephanie Zvirin, review of *The Gruffalo,* p. 1950; September 1, 2001, GraceAnne A. DeCandido, review of *Room on the Broom,* p. 120; March 1, 2003, Carolyn Phelan, review of *The Spiffiest Giant in Town,* p. 1201; May 1, 2006, Carolyn Phelan, review of *Charlie Cook's Favorite Book,* p. 88; June 1, 2006, Kathy Broderick, review of *One Ted Falls out of Bed,* p. 80.

Books for Keeps, May, 1995, Liz Waterland, review of *A Squash and a Squeeze,* p. 8; May, 1999, Clive Barnes, review of *The Gruffalo,* p. 21.

Childhood Education, fall, 1999, Kelly Krawczyk, review of *The Gruffalo,* p. 44.

Children's Book Review Service, August, 1993, review of *A Squash and a Squeeze,* p. 158.

Horn Book, January-February, 2005, Jennifer M. Brabander, review of *The Gruffalo's Child,* p. 75; July-August, 2006, Kitty Flynn, review of *One Ted Falls out of Bed,* p. 424.

Kirkus Reviews, June 1, 1999, review of *The Gruffalo,* p. 882; August 1, 2001, review of *Room on the Broom,* p. 1121; January 1, 2003, review of *The Spiffiest Giant in Town,* p. 60; February 15, 2004, review of *The Snail and the Whale,* p. 176; August 15, 2005, review of *The Giant and the Joneses,* p. 912; May 1, 2006, review of *Charlie Cook's Favorite Book,* p. 455; May 15, 2006, review of *One Ted Falls out of Bed,* p. 516.

Los Angeles Times Book Review, May 2, 1993, review of *A Squash and a Squeeze,* p. 7.

Observer (London, England), April 4, 1999, Sam Taylor, "When You've Been Traumatized by a Teddy, There's Only One Way Out. . . ."

Publishers Weekly, April 26, 1993, review of *A Squash and a Squeeze,* p. 78; June 21, 1999, review of *The Gruffalo,* p. 67; September 10, 2001, review of *Room on the Broom,* p. 92; January 6, 2003, review of *The Spiffiest Giant in Town,* p. 59; February 23, 2004, review of *The Snail and the Whale,* p. 75; December 13, 2004, review of *The Gruffalo's Child,* p. 68; May 15, 2006, review of *Charlie Cook's Favorite Book,* p. 71; May 22, 2006, review of *One Ted Falls out of Bed,* p. 50.

School Library Journal, April, 1993, Nancy Seiner, review of *A Squash and a Squeeze,* pp. 95-96; August, 1999, Marianne Saccardi, review of *The Gruffalo,* pp. 132-

133; September, 2001, Pamela K. Bomboy, review of
Room on the Broom, p. 187; March, 2003, Bina Will-
iams, review of *The Spiffiest Giant in Town,* p. 191;
February, 2004, Kathleen Kelly MacMillan, review of
The Snail and the Whale, p. 111; March, 2005, Marge
Loch-Wouters, review of *The Gruffalo's Child,* p. 170;
October, 2005, Elaine E. Knight, review of *The Gi-
ants and the Joneses,* p. 112; June, 2006, Marge Loch-
Wouters, review of *One Ted Falls out of Bed,* p. 110;
July, 2006, Jill Heritage Maza, review of *Charlie
Cook's Favorite Book,* p. 71.
Times (London, England), November, 1993, review of *A
Squash and a Squeeze,* p. 45.

ONLINE

Gruffalo Gang Web site, http://www.gruffalo.com/ (June 1,
2007).
Julia Donaldson Home Page, http://www.juliadonaldson.
co.uk (June 1, 2007).
Northern Children's Book Festival Web site, http://www.
ncbf.org.uk/ (June 1, 2007), "Julia Donaldson.'*

*   *   *

DORFMAN, Joaquín 1979-
(Joaquin Emiliano Dorfman)

Personal

Born February, 1979, in Amsterdam, Netherlands; immigrated to United States, 1980; son of Ariel Dorfman
(a playwright). *Education:* Attended New York
University.

Addresses

Home and office—NC.

Career

Novelist, playwright, and script writer.

Writings

(With father, Ariel Dorfman) *Burning City,* Random House
(New York, NY), 2003.
Playing It Cool, Random House (New York, NY), 2006.

Also author of plays and screenplays, some with Ariel
Dorfman.

Sidelights

Joaquín Dorfman and his father, playwright and activist
Ariel Dorfman, have shared many experiences, ranging
from being arrested and deported during a visit to Chile
when Dorfman was age six to writing the collaborative

Cover of Burning City, *a collaborative novel by Joaquín Dorfman and
father, Ariel Dorfman.* (Random House, 2003. Cover photo: fire image copyright ©
Lester Lefkowitz/Corbis. Biker image courtesy of csaimages.com. All rights reserved. Reproduced by permission of Random House Children's Books, a division of Random
House, Inc.)

novel *Burning City.* "Ariel is a lot busier than I am, so I
did most of the work," the younger Dorfman quipped to
Nadine O'Reagan in an interview for Ireland's *Sunday
Business Post* regarding the joint work of fiction. "I
took care of the consonants, he took care of the vow-
els." Even before cowriting his first novel, Dorfman
was no stranger to the world of literature. His first play
opened at the Edinburgh Festival when he was nineteen
years old, and he also coauthored two screenplays with
his father.

Burning City recounts the events of a single summer in
the life of teenage bicycle messenger Heller. While
dreaming of becoming the youngest winner of the Tour
de France, Heller rides through New York City on various assignments, often delivering bad news to his company's customers. Heller's ability to empathize with his
clients allows him to familiarize himself with a wide
variety of people, thereby gaining a different sense of
his city environment. "Taut writing matches the fast,
sweaty pace of Heller's extreme cycling through a siz-
zling New York summer," wrote Lauren Adams in her
Horn Book review, and *School Library Journal* con-

tributor Sarah Couri commented that the coauthors' "descriptions of summer in Manhattan are flawless; the city seethes as Heller surges through its streets like an electron, connecting people and lives in complicated ways."

"The pattern was togetherness and separateness," Dorfman told O'Reagan in describing the father-son writing process. "I would go to my apartment in New York at around midnight . . . and sit down and write until morning. Then I would walk to my father's house and show him what I had written. He would say, 'Change this, change that.' Usually I wouldn't listen because I'm very strong-willed." Holly Koelling, reviewing the resulting novel in *Booklist* praised the Dorfmans as "deft writers, smoothly intertwining characters and events in a highly imaginative, intriguing, and almost dreamlike story."

Dorfman moves to solo fiction in *Playing It Cool,* where readers meet master problem solver Sebastian. Sebastian can fix things, locate people, and help make tough decision. Despite the fact that so many people confide in him, however, no one really knows Sebastian. However, when he takes on the task of tracking down Jeremy's father, the over-competent sleuth must face some of his own personal struggles—including his need for a father that he never knew. Dorfman "writes with a compassion and an energy that will propel readers along," Krista Hutley concluded in her *Booklist* review of *Playing It Cool,* while *School Library Journal* reviewer Susan Oliver considered the book "a sophisticated, mystery/romance/coming-of-age story full of red herrings and elaborate schemes." While some critics, including Hutley and a writer for *Kirkus Reviews,* found the author's reliance on fragmentary sentences and the text's lack of pronouns somewhat daunting, Claire E. Gross wrote in *Horn Book* that "Dorfman's restless, pointed prose perfectly defines his narrator's fragmented perspective."

Biographical and Critical Sources

PERIODICALS

Booklist, April 15, 2005, Holly Koelling, review of *Burning City,* p. 1448; May 1, 2006, Krista Hutley, review of *Playing It Cool,* p. 80.
Bulletin of the Center for Children's Books, September, 2005, Karen Coats, review of *Burning City,* p. 14; September, 2006, Karen Coats, review of *Playing It Cool,* p. 11.
Horn Book, May-June, 2005, Lauren Adams, review of *Burning City,* p. 323; May-June, 2006, Claire E. Gross, review of *Playing It Cool,* p. 312.
Kirkus Reviews, May 1, 2005, review of *Burning City,* p. 537; May 15, 2006, review of *Playing It Cool,* p. 517.
Kliatt, May, 2005, Paula Rohrlick, review of *Burning City,* p. 10; May, 2006, Claire Rosser, review of *Playing It Cool,* p. 8.

Publishers Weekly, June 6, 2005, review of *Burning City,* p. 66; June 19, 2006, review of *Playing It Cool,* p. 64.
School Library Journal, January, 2006, review of *Burning City,* p. 130; June, 2006, Susan Oliver, review of *Playing It Cool,* p. 152.
Voice of Youth Advocates, June, 2005, Liza M. David, review of *Burning City,* p. 128.

ONLINE

Joaquín Dorfman Home Page, http://www.joaquindorfman. com (April 28, 2007).
Random House Web site, http://www.randomhouse.com/ (April 28, 2007), "Joaquín Dorfman."
Sunday Business Post Online (Ireland), http://archives.tcm. ie/businesspost/ (May 11, 2003), Nadine O'Reagan, "Escaping Pinochet's Shadow."*

*   *   *

DORFMAN, Joaquin Emiliano
See DORFMAN, Joaquín

*   *   *

DOWDEN, Anne Ophelia Todd 1907-2007
(Anne Ophelia Todd)

OBITUARY NOTICE— See index for *SATA* sketch: Born September 17, 1907, in Denver, CO; died January 11, 2007, in Boulder, CO. Artist, educator, and author. Dowden was a renowned botanical artist and nature illustrator. Born near the Rocky Mountains, she gained an early love of nature and began drawing as a child. By the time she was a teenager, her skills were such that her father, a pathologist at the University of Colorado, enlisted her skills to create medical illustrations. For her formal education, Dowd attended what is now Carnegie-Mellon University, earning a B.A. in 1930. She also studied at the Art Students League of New York City and the Beaux Arts Institute of Design. In 1930, she tried to launch a career in book illustration but, meeting with no luck in this area, she instead found work as a drawing instructor at New York's Pratt Institute. Dowd next taught at Manhattanville College in Purchase, New York, where she was art department chair from 1932 until 1953. After retirement, her initial desire to be a book illustrator was realized. She earned commissions from various magazines and in 1961 released her first self-illustrated title, *The Little Hill: A Chronicle of Flora on a Half Acre at the Green Camp.* She went on to write and illustrate a dozen books, as well as illustrating books by other authors. Specializing in publications for children and young adults, Dowd's books earned awards from library and teaching associations. *The Blossom on the Bough: A Book of Trees* (1975), her most honored work, was named a National Science Teachers Association outstanding science book for children, a notable book by the American Library Association, and a Children's Book Council showcase selection. Known for the realistic accuracy of her drawings of flowers, birds, insects, and other plants and creatures, Dowd also had her work exhibited around the country, including at the Smithsonian Institution, the Denver Art Museum, and the New York City Public Library.

OBITUARIES AND OTHER SOURCES:

PERIODICALS

New York Times, January 16, 2007, p. A29.

* * *

DOWNES, Belinda 1962-

Personal

Born 1962, in England. *Education:* Attended Loughborough College of Art.

Addresses

Office—Paper and Cotton, Ltd., P.O. Box 2723, Bristol B56 9DQ, England.

Career

Author, illustrator, and embroiderer. Worked in antique textile repair and as a costume designer; Paper and Cotton, Bristol, England, card designer. Artist-in-residence at Hampton Court Palace. *Exhibitions:* Work exhibited throughout the United Kingdom, United States, Germany, and Japan.

Awards, Honors

British Council grant, 1995.

Writings

SELF-ILLUSTRATED

A Stitch in Rhyme: A Nursery Rhyme Sampler with Embroidered Illustrations, Knopf (New York, NY), 1996.
Every Little Angel's Handbook, Dial (New York, NY), 1997.
Baby Days: A Quilt of Rhymes and Pictures, Candlewick Press (Cambridge, MA), 2006.

Contributor of illustrations and articles to magazines, including *Embroidery, Textilforum* (Germany), *Pins and Needles,* London *Sunday Telegraph, Needlecraft, World of Embroidery, Country Craft* (Japan), *Homes and Antiques,* and *Bien Fait* (Japan).

ILLUSTRATOR

Thomasina Beck, *The Embroiderers' Garden,* David & Charles (London, England), 1988.
Thomasina Beck, *The Embroiderers' Flower,* David & Charles (London, England), 1992.
Thomasina Beck, *The Embroidery Story,* David & Charles (London, England), 1995.
Silent Night: A Christmas Carol Sampler (printed music), Knopf (New York, NY), 1995.
Juliet Bawden, *Appliqué,* Mitchell Beazley (England), 1998.
Annie Dalton, *The Starlight Princess, and Other Princess Stories,* Dorling Kindersley (New York, NY), 1999.
Joan Aiken, *Snow White and the Seven Dwarves,* Dorling Kindersley (New York, NY), 2002.

Sidelights

A talented embroiderer, Belinda Downes channeled her skill with a needle into antique textile repair and costume design before turning to a task she loves: illustration. Combining textiles and embroidery fibers rather than paper and pen and paint to form her illustrations, Downes' unique style has earned her attention in her native United Kingdom as well as in the United States, Germany, and Japan, where she has featured her art in various exhibitions. As noted on the *Images of Delight* Web site, Downes at first worried that her ambition to create embroidered illustrations might be unattainable because of the lengthy time required. "Producing pictures isn't just a job, but a passion!," the illustrator explained.

As an illustrator, Downes has created embroidered images for well-known writers such as Annie Dalton and Joan Aiken, and her artwork has been paired with a beloved musical score in *Silent Night: A Christmas Carol Sampler.* "Collections of Christmas carols are readily available, but not with glorious pictures like these," wrote Ilene Cooper in a *Booklist* review of the holiday-themed offering. Of her illustrations for Aiken's *Snow White and the Seven Dwarves,* Gillian Engberg wrote in *Booklist* that "Downes coaxes extraordinary atmosphere and expression from her fabric and thread."

Along with her illustrations for others, Downes also creates unique self-illustrated books, combining traditional verses with embroidered art in *A Stitch in Rhyme: A Nursery Rhyme Sampler with Embroidered Illustrations* and *Baby Days: A Quilt of Rhymes and Pictures.* Of *A Stitch in Rhyme,* Cooper noted that familiar nursery rhyme characters "are executed in snippets of material highlighted with tiny stitches." In *Baby Days* Downes similarly combines traditional rhymes and games with questions for young readers, encouraging children to interact with the text. "Combining the looks of a sampler and a quilt, Downes's remarkably detailed artwork is a mixture of embroidery, appliqué and watercolor," explained a *Kirkus Reviews* contributor of the volume.

The intricate embroidered art of Belinda Downes appears in picture books such as **Snow White and the Seven Dwarves,** *an adaptation of the traditional tale by Joan Aiken.* (DK Publishing, Inc., 2002. Illustrations copyright © 2002 by Belinda Downes. All rights reserved. Reproduced by permission of DK Publishing, Inc.)

In *Every Little Angel's Handbook* Downes presents a host of embroidered angels, each accompanied by a short introduction. The angels watch over a group of younger angels while performing wintertime activities that range from cutting out snowflakes to baking angel food cake. "It's hard not to be charmed by the engaging, embroidered cutouts that bring individuality to each angel," concluded Cooper in her *Booklist* review of the work.

Each of Downes' book-length illustration projects takes up to two years to complete, and each one incorporates a unique history of its own. "I have drawers and cupboards full of fabrics, threads, wools, paint, paper and everything I need to help me design and make embroidered collages," the illustrator explained on the *Images of Delight* Web site. "Friends give me fabrics and beautiful clothes they no longer want and I save them until I see an opportunity to use them in my work."

Biographical and Critical Sources

PERIODICALS

Booklist, September 15, 1995, Ilene Cooper, review of *Silent Night: A Christmas Carol Sampler,* p. 169; November 1, 1996, Ilene Cooper, review of *A Stitch in Rhyme: A Nursery Rhyme Sampler with Embroidered Illustrations,* p. 503; December 1, 1997, Ilene Cooper, review of *Every Little Angel's Handbook,* p. 640; February 1, 2000, GraceAnne A. DeCandido, review of *The Starlight Princess, and Other Princess Stories,* p. 1019; January 1, 2003, Gillian Engberg, review of *Snow White and the Seven Dwarves,* p. 894; February 1, 2006, Ilene Cooper, review of *Baby Days: A Quilt of Rhymes and Pictures,* p. 54.

Bulletin of the Center for Children's Books, January, 2003, review of *Snow White and the Seven Dwarves,* p. 186.

Kirkus Reviews, March 1, 2006, review of *Baby Days,* p. 228.

Publishers Weekly, September 18, 1995, review of *Silent Night,* p. 96; October 20, 1997, review of *Every Little Angel's Handbook,* p. 78; October 25, 1999, review of *The Starlight Princess, and Other Stories,* p. 82; November 4, 2002, review of *Snow White and the Seven Dwarves,* p. 86.

School Library Journal, October, 1995, Jane Marino, review of *Silent Night,* p. 41; December, 1996, Dawn Ibey, review of *A Stitch in Rhyme,* p. 112; December, 1997, Dawn Ibey, review of *Every Little Angel's Handbook,* p. 88; January, 2000, Margaret A. Chang, review of *The Starlight Princess, and Other Princess Stories,* p. 118.

Times Educational Supplement (London, England), December 24, 1999, review of *The Starlight Princess, and Other Princess Stories,* p. 26.

ONLINE

Embroiderer's Guild Web site, http://embroidery. embroiderersguild.com/ (April 28, 2007), "Belinda Downes."

Images of Delight Web site, http://www.imagesofdelight. com/ (April 28, 2007), "Belinda Downes."

Paper and Cotton Web site, http://www.paperandcotton. com/ (July 10, 2007), "Belinda Downes."

Walker Books Web site, http://www.walkerbooks.co.uk/ (April 28, 2007), "Belinda Downes."

E-F

ENSOR, Barbara

Personal
Children: two. *Education:* Attended Brown University.

Addresses
Home and office—Brooklyn, NY. *E-mail*—info@ barbaraensor.com.

Career
Illustrator and writer. Worked previously as a puppeteer.

Writings

Paul Trapido, *Don't Even Think of Parking Here!: The New York City Guide to Parking and Driving,* Simon & Schuster (New York, NY), 1986.
Cinderella (As If You Did'nt Already Know the Story), Schwartz & Wade Books (New York, NY), 2006.

Sidelights
Barbara Ensor was raised in London, England, is a graduate of Brown University, and also has a distinctive background as a former puppeteer. As an author and illustrator, she has established a unique career as a writer by penning children's titles that reweave traditional fairy tales into a story with a contemporary spin. *Cinderella (As If You Didn't Already Know the Story),* for instance, frames the classic fairy tale from a third-person point of view by telling it via Cinderella's diary letters to her deceased mother. Cinderella's letters detail her daily struggles and express the distress the young woman experiences with her new stepmother and stepsisters. Not surprisingly, Ensor's version of *Cinder-*

Barbara Ensor brings a new twist to an old tale in her self-illustrated novel Cinderella (As If You Didn't Already Know the Story). *(Schwartz & Wade Books, 2006. Used by permission of Schwartz & Wade Books, an imprint of Random House Children's Books, a division of Random House, Inc.)*

ella does not end in the traditional happy-ever-after fashion; she adds to the story by describing the young woman's life after marriage to the prince. By story's end, Cinderella is happily wedded and has grown from a helpless damsel in distress to a powerful politician working to reshape her kingdom.

Ensor's text for *Cinderella (As If You Didn't Already Know the Story)* is accompanied by her original cut-paper silhouettes, which Amy Krouse Rosenthal described in the *New York Times Book Review* as "the perfect visual solution." The black-and-white silhouettes separate Ensor's text "into manageable chunks, making this tale suitable for reluctant readers" noted a *Kirkus Reviews* critic. Susan Riley, reviewing the book for *School Library Journal,* described Ensor's version of the well-known fable as a tale that will "please girls who like undemanding and familiar stories with a twist," while Rosenthal dubbed it "light and playful yet fairy-tale-ish."

Biographical and Critical Sources

PERIODICALS

Bulletin of the Center for Children's Books, July-August, 2006, Deborah Stevenson, review of *Cinderella (As If You Didn't Already Know the Story),* p. 495.
Kirkus Reviews, May 1, 2006, review of *Cinderella (As If You Didn't Already Know the Story),* p. 456.
New York Times Book Review, September 10, 2006, Amy Krouse Rosenthal, review of *Cinderella (As If You Didn't Already Know the Story),* p. L18.
School Library Journal, July, 2006, Susan Riley, review of *Cinderella (As If You Didn't Already Know the Story),* p. 100.

ONLINE

Barbara Ensor Home Page, http://www.barbaraensor.com (April 28, 2007).*

*   *   *

EVANS, Lezlie

Personal
Married; children: six.

Addresses
Home and office—VA.

Career
Children's book author.

Member
Utah Children's Writers and Illustrators.

Writings

Rain Song, illustrated by Cynthia Jabar, Houghton Mifflin (Boston, MA), 1995.
If I Were the Wind, illustrated by Victoria Lisi, Ideals Children's Books (Nashville, TN), 1997.
Snow Dance, illustrated by Cynthia Jabar, Houghton Mifflin (Boston, MA), 1997.
Can You Count Ten Toes?: Count to 10 in 10 Different Languages, Houghton Mifflin (Boston, MA), 1999.
Sometimes I Feel like a Storm Cloud, illustrated by Marsha Gray Carrington, Mondo (Greenvale, NY), 1999.
Can You Greet the Whole Wide World?: 12 Common Phrases in 12 Different Languages, illustrated by Denis Roche, Houghton Mifflin (Boston, MA), 2006.
The Bunnies' Picnic, illustrated by Kay Chorao, Hyperion (New York, NY), 2007.
The Bunnies' Trip, illustrated by Kay Chorao, Hyperion (New York, NY), 2008.

Sidelights

Lezlie Evans creates children's books that cover a range of themes while helping children explore and enjoy the world around them. Evans uses poetry in her children's titles, which include *Rain Song, Sometimes I Feel like a Storm Cloud,* and *The Bunnies' Picnic,* creating rhyming and lilting verses that capture and engage young readers. A few of Evans' picture-book titles feature bilingual texts, introducing young children to the many different languages that are spoken around the world. Reviewing *The Bunnies' Picnic* in *Booklist,* Carolyn Phelan drew attention to Evans' "bouncy, rhyming text" and Kay Chorao's sun-filled illustrations, dubbing the picture book "a cheerful romp for young children."

In *Can You Count Ten Toes?: Count to 10 in 10 Different Languages* the narrator teaches young readers how to count in languages that include Japanese, Russian, Zulu, French, Tagalog, and Spanish. Children are also presented with an array of unique items to count, from toes and lightning bugs to angelfish and planets. Hazel Rochman, reviewing the work for *Booklist,* noted that Evans' educational and rhyming text will allow "children to see the fun of words in translation." A similar work, *Can You Greet the Whole Wide World?: 12 Common Phrases in 12 Different Languages* teaches children how to greet others in a dozen unique ways. In her book, Evans also includes a pronunciation guide as well as a world map that indicates where each language is spoken. *School Library Journal* critic Margaret R. Tassia regarded Evans' globally focused title as a "great way to introduce the many similarities and interests of children around the world," while Carolyn Phelan wrote in *Booklist* that *Can You Greet the Whole World?* "encourages courtesy as well as multilingual expression."

Lezlie Evans' entertaining concept book Can You Count Ten Toes? *is energized by Denis Roche's brightly colored cartoon art.* (Houghton Mifflin Company, 1999. Illustration © 1999 by Denis Roche. All rights reserved. Reproduced by permission of Houghton Mifflin Company.)

Biographical and Critical Sources

PERIODICALS

Booklist, March 15, 1995, Hazel Rochman, review of *Rain Song,* p. 1331; August, 1997, Ilene Cooper, review of *If I Were the Wind,* p. 1905; October 1, 1997, Lauren Peterson, review of *Snow Dance,* p. 336; March 15, 1999, Hazel Rochman, review of *Can You Count Ten Toes?: Count to 10 in 10 Different Languages,* p. 1331; December 15, 1999, Hazel Rochman, review of *Sometimes I Feel like a Storm Cloud,* p. 789; May 1, 2006, Carolyn Phelan, review of *Can You Greet the Whole Wide World?: 12 Common Phrases in 12 Different Languages,* p. 85; December 1, 2006, Carolyn Phelan, *The Bunnies' Picnic,* p. 51.

Bulletin of the Center for Children's Books, March, 1995, review of *Rain Song,* p. 234; December, 1997, review of *Snow Dance,* p. 123.

Kirkus Reviews, May 1, 2006, review of *Can You Greet the Whole Wide World?,* p. 457; December 1, 2006, review of *The Bunnies' Picnic,* p. 1219.

Library Media Connection, January, 2007, review of *Can You Greet the Whole Wide World?,* p. 68.

Publishers Weekly, March 13, 1995, review of *Rain Song,* p. 69; March 22, 1999, "Increase Your Foreign Word Power," p. 94.

School Library Journal, July, 1995, Karen K. Radtke, review of *Rain Song,* p. 61; June, 1997, Sally R. Dow, review of *If I Were the Wind,* p. 86; December, 1997, Karen James, review of *Snow Dance,* p. 88; June, 1999, JoAnn Jonas, review of *Can You Count Ten Toes?,* p. 114; June, 2006, Margaret R. Tassia, review of *Can You Greet the Whole Wide World?,* p. 135; January, 2007, Julie Roach, review of *The Bunnies' Picnic,* p. 92.

*   *   *

FERGUSON, Sarah 1959-
(Sarah Margaret Ferguson, Sarah, Duchess of York)

Personal

Born October 15, 1959, in London, England; daughter of Ronald Ivor Ferguson (in the military) and Susan Barrantes; married Andrew Mountbatten-Windsor (a naval officer), July 23, 1986 (divorced 1996); children: Beatrice, Eugenie. *Education:* Queen's Secretarial College, graduated.

Addresses

Home—Sunninghill Park, England.

Career

Worked for various public relations and publishing firms in London, England; writer, beginning 1973. Children in Crisis (humanitarian group), founder, 1993. Spokesperson for Weight Watchers, beginning 1997, and SOS Children's Villages—USA, beginning 2004; correspondent for *Today* show; talk-show host of *Sarah, Surviving Life* for British television, and *Fergie!* for U.S. television, 2003. Featured in television programs, including *Adventures with the Duchess,* p. 1997, and *Larry King Live.*

Writings

FOR CHILDREN

Budgie the Little Helicopter, illustrated by John Richardson, Simon & Schuster (London, England), 1989.

Budgie at Bendick's Point, illustrated by John Richardson, Simon & Schuster (London, England), 1989.

Budgie and the Blizzard, illustrated by John Richardson, Simon & Schuster (London, England), 1991.

Budgie Goes to Sea, illustrated by John Richardson, Simon & Schuster (London, England), 1991.

The Adventures of Budgie, illustrated by John Richardson, Simon & Schuster (London, England), 1992.

The Royal Switch, illustrated by Jacqueline Rogers, Delacorte (New York, NY), 1996.

Bright Lights, illustrated by Jacqueline Rogers, Bantam Doubleday Dell (New York, NY), 1997.

The Haunted Spaceship, Pocket Books (New York, NY), 1997.

Little Red, illustrated by Sam Williams, Simon & Schuster (New York, NY), 2003.

Little Red's Christmas Story, illustrated by Sam Williams, Simon & Schuster (New York, NY), 2004.

Little Red's Summer Adventure, illustrated by Sam Williams, Simon & Schuster (New York, NY), 2006.

OTHER

To the Place of Shells, Chatto & Windus (London, England), 1975.

Skiing from the Inside: The Self-Help Guide to Mastering the Slopes, Simon & Schuster (London, England), 1989.

(With Benita Stoney) *Victoria and Albert: Life at Osborne House,* Weidenfeld & Nicolson (London, England), 1991.

(With Benita Stoney) *Travels with Queen Victoria,* Weidenfeld & Nicolson (London, England), 1993.

(With Jeff Coplon) *My Story,* Simon & Schuster (New York, NY), 1996.

(With Weight Watchers) *Dining with the Duchess: How to Make Everyday Meals a Special Occasion,* Simon & Schuster (New York, NY), 1998.

(With Stephanie Seymour) *Beauty Secrets for Dummies,* IDG Publishing, 1998.

(With Weight Watchers) *Dieting with the Duchess: Secrets and Sensible Advice for a Great Body,* Simon & Schuster (New York, NY), 1998.

(With Weight Watchers) *Win the Weight Game: Successful Strategies for Living Well,* Simon & Schuster (New York, NY), 2000.

(With Weight Watchers) *Dishing with the Duchess: Sarah the Duchess of York and Weight Watchers International,* Simon & Schuster (London, England), 2000.

Dining Royally, Simon & Schuster (London, England), 2000.

Reinventing Yourself with the Duchess of York: Inspiring Stories and Strategies for Changing Your Weight and Your Life, Simon & Schuster (New York, NY), 2001.

(With Jeff Coplon) *What I Know Now: Simple Lessons Learned the Hard Way,* Simon & Schuster (New York, NY), 2003.

Adaptations

Ferguson's "Budgie" character was adapted as an animated television series, 1995-96, and c. 2000.

Sidelights

A celebrity figure as much for her work as a longtime spokesperson for the Weight Watchers chain of weighloss centers as for her status as the former daughter-in-law to England's Queen Elizabeth II, Sarah Ferguson also has a following among young children as the author of picture books such as *Budgie the Little Helicopter, Little Red,* and *Little Red's Summer Adventure.*

Growing up in the village of Sunninghill, England, Ferguson never dreamed that she would one day live in Buckingham Palace as a member of royalty. However, when she wed Prince Andrew in 1986, in a ceremony televised around the globe, she became the duchess of York, and her two daughters, Beatrice and Eugenie, are real-life princesses. Although she did not grow up in the limelight like Prince Andrew, Ferguson assumed her role as a royal bride with gusto, emerging as one of the most colorful—and sometimes controversial—members of England's royal family.

An average student who excelled at sports, especially swimming, riding, and tennis, Ferguson was popular with her peers at school, and she was voted head girl during her senior year at Hurst Lodge secondary school. After graduating at age sixteen, she enrolled at Queen's Secretarial College in Kensington. There she studied typing, shorthand, bookkeeping, and cooking, but graduated at the bottom of her class due to her strong interest in skiing, tennis, and parties. After graduation, she traveled and also worked in London at public relations firms and art galleries. As part of an upwardly mobile social set, she became good friends with Diana Spencer, who, as the wife of Prince Charles, was the Princess of Wales. As a friend of Princess Diana, Ferguson became a frequent guest at Buckingham Palace; in 1985, Diana asked her to be Prince Andrew's date during Royal Ascot Week, and the rest is history.

During her marriage (Ferguson and Prince Andrew divorced in 1996) the duchess kept busy, continuing at her job while also taking on charitable work and fulfilling her obligations as a member of the royal family. In 1988, she gave birth to Beatrice, all the while maintaining a busy schedule that included writing the children's books *Budgie the Little Helicopter* and *Budgie at Bendick's Point.* Amanda Smith, writing in *Publishers Weekly,* revealed that the duchess was inspired to write because of "her own experiences as a pilot"; Ferguson holds both helicopter and fixed-wing piloting licenses. As the duchess told Smith, the "Budgie books came very easily from learning to fly a helicopter."

Over the years, Ferguson has remained highly visible in the press, for her divorce, her high-profile social life, and her weight problem. Her work as spokesperson for Weight Watchers has also kept her in the news and has let to diet guides and self-help books that bear her byline. Working with writer Jeff Coplon, Ferguson has also produced several memoirs for an interested public: *My Story* was published in 1996 and *What I Know Now: Simple Lessons Learned the Hard Way* reached bookstore shelves in 2003.

In addition to raising her two daughters and writing diet and lifestyle books, Ferguson has continued to write for children. In *The Royal Switch,* a novel loosely based on Mark Twain's classic *The Prince and the Pauper,* she introduces Princess Amanda, a feisty eleven-year-old redhead. In *The Royal Switch* Amanda changes places with look-alike American tourist Emily Chornak, and a sequel, *Bright Lights,* finds the two preteens continuing their adventures in New York City.

Like the "Budgie" books, Ferguson's "Little Red" picture books are geared for very young readers. Featuring engaging watercolor and pencil illustrations by Sam Williams, *Little Red* introduces a red-haired, gingham-clad doll who lives in idyllic Buttercup Cottage, surrounded by toy animal friends Gino the spotted puppy dog, Roany the pink pony, and Squirrel, as well as a boy doll named Little Blue. During a picnic lunch of sherbet and cake in Bluebell Wood, Red and her friends hear a frightening sound that ultimately leads them to rescue a small, frightened bunny that is stranded on a lily pad. In *Little Red's Summer Adventure* the friends find their efforts to build a watercraft for a local boat-building contest threatened by a mischievous magpie, while *Little Red's Christmas Adventure* finds them

The adventures of a little girl and her animal friends is brought to life by illustrator Sam Williams in Ferguson's large-format picture book **Little Red.** (Aladdin Paperbacks, 2003. Illustration © 2003 by Sam Williams. Reproduced by permission of Simon & Schuster Books for Young Readers, an imprint of Simon & Schuster Children's Publishing Division.)

hitching a ride on Santa's sleigh. Williams' "detailed watercolor illustrations add considerable, genuine charm to the effort," wrote a *Kirkus Reviews* writer of *Little Red,* while *School Library Journal* critic Kirsten Cutler maintained that Williams' pencil drawings "do a nice job of conveying" Ferguson's simple storyline. As another *Kirkus Reviews* writer noted of *Little Red's Summer Adventure,* Ferguson's "sweetly innocent tale, filled with whimsy, is . . . just the thing to share with little ones."

Biographical and Critical Sources

BOOKS

Seward, Ingrid, *Sarah: HRH the Duchess of York: A Biography,* HarperCollins (London, England), 1991.

Hutchins, Chris, and Peter Thomson, *Sarah's Story: The Duchess Who Defied the Royal House of Windsor,* Smith Gryphon (London, England), 1992.

Starkie, Allan, *Fergie: The Very Private Life of the Duchess of York,* Pinnacle (New York, NY), 1996.

PERIODICALS

Booklist, January 1, 1989, Barbara Jacobs, review of *Dieting with the Duchess: Secrets and Sensible Advice for a Great Body,* p. 813.

Entertainment Weekly, December 13, 1996, Dana Kennedy, review of *The Duchess of York: My Story,* p. 72.

Good Housekeeping, April, 1998, Joanna Powell, "A Royal Survivor" (interview), pp. 94-99.

Kirkus Reviews, November 15, 1996; September 1, 2003, review of *Little Red,* p. 1122; June 15, 2006, review of *Little Red's Summer Adventure,* p. 632.

Ladies' Home Journal, April, 1999, p. 136; June, 2004, Jeanne Marie Laskas, "Sarah's New Day" (interview), p. 118; July, 2006, Merle Ginsberg, "The Duchess Diaries," p. 92.

People, January 15, 2007, Allison Adato, "Catching up with Sarah Ferguson," p. 108.

Publishers Weekly, September 29, 1989, Amanda Smith, profile of Ferguson, p. 34; July 21, 2003, review of *Little Red,* p. 193.

School Library Journal, April, 2003, Karen Sokol, review of *What I Know Now: Simple Lessons Learned the Hard Way,* p. 195; September, 2003, Nancy A. Gifford, review of *Little Red,* p. 177.*

* * *

FERGUSON, Sarah Margaret
See FERGUSON, Sarah

* * *

FLANAGAN, John 1944-
(John Anthony Flanagan)

Personal

Born 1944, in Sydney, New South Wales, Australia; married; wife's name Leonie; children: Michael.

Addresses

Home and office—Sydney, New South Wales, Australia.

Career

Writer. Formerly worked in advertising in Sydney, New South Wales, Australia, London, England, and Singapore; Seven Network, Sydney, head writer for television series *Hey Dad!* 1987-94; freelance writer, beginning 1970s.

Writings

(With Gary Reilly) *The Betty Wilson Secretarial Companion* (based on the television series *Hey Dad!*), Penguin (Ringwood, Victoria, Australia), 1990.

"RANGER'S APPRENTICE" FANTASY NOVELS

The Ruins of Gorlan (also see below), Random House Australia (Milsons Point, New South Wales, Australia), 2004, Philomel (New York, NY), 2005.

The Burning Bridge (also see below), Random House Australia (Milsons Point, New South Wales, Australia), 2005, Philomel (New York, NY), 2006.

The Icebound Land, Random House Australia (Milsons Point, New South Wales, Australia), 2005, Philomel (New York, NY), 2007.

Oakleaf Bearers, Random House Australia (Milsons Point, New South Wales, Australia), 2006.

Ranger's Apprentice: One & Two (contains *The Ruins of Gorland* and *The Burning Bridge*), Random House Australia (Milsons Point, New South Wales, Australia), 2006.

The Sorcerer in the North, Random House Australia (Milsons Point, New South Wales, Australia), 2006.

The Siege of Macindaw, Random House Australia (Milsons Point, New South Wales, Australia), 2007.

Author's books have been translated into over a dozen languages.

Adaptations

The "Ranger's Apprentice" novels have been adapted as audiobooks.

Sidelights

Beginning his career in advertising, Australian novelist John Flanagan eventually moved into writing for television, spending eight years as head writer for the popular Australian sitcom *Hey Dad!* In his spare time, Flanagan also wrote for fun, developing short stories for his growing son, Mike. "He didn't like reading, and so I based the character on him and [he] did the kinds of things Mike did," Flanagan explained to Ron Charles in an interviewer for the *Washington Post Book World.* Several years later, Flanagan decided that it might be fun to rework these stories into book form; he showed them to his agent, and the "Ranger's Apprentice" series was born. "The book grew and grew and I decided it had better be two books," Flanagan later recalled on the Christ Church, New Zealand Libraries Web site. "It kept growing and growing and ended up being four."

The first volume of the "Ranger's Apprentice" is *The Ruins of Gorlan;* first published in Australia in 2004, it has since been released in fourteen countries. The novel introduces Will, a teen who anxiously desires to be accepted into Battleschool as an apprentice, but is denied because of his short stature. Instead, he is apprenticed to a mysterious Ranger and taught skills of speed and stealth. In the larger world, the evil Lord Morgarath sends assassins to murder leaders from Will's society. Now Will and his sometime rival/sometime friend

Cover of John Flanagan's "Ranger's Apprentice" series installment **The Burning Bridge,** *featuring artwork by John Blackford.* (Philomel Books, 2005. Illustration © 2006 by John Blackford. All rights reserved. Reproduced by permission of Philomel Books, a division of Penguin Putnam Books for Young Readers.)

Horace must hone their skills quickly, because their country is becoming a more dangerous place. Reviewing *The Ruins of Gorlan* for *Booklist,* Carolyn Phelan wrote that the novel's appeal comes from Flanagan's skill at building a convincing fantasy world. "It's the details of everyday living and the true-to-life emotions of the people that are memorable," Phelan noted. Steven Engelfried, writing in *School Library Journal,* commented that the author's "descriptions of Ranger craft are fascinating."

As *The Burning Bridge* opens, Lord Morgorath's army of monstrous wargals gathers. Meanwhile, Will and Horace discover a nearly completed bridge, built by Morgorath's forces as a way to sneak into their kingdom. Aided by disguised noblewoman Evanlyn, the two apprentices must now journey into enemy territory to discover the true extent of Morgoroth's plans. "Will's vivid world will entice fantasy readers who are drawn by the lure of high adventure," wrote Phelan, while a *Kirkus Reviews* contributor concluded of *The Burning Bridge* that "it all adds up to a winning formula that should prove out to a long, steady run." wrote

On the Christ Church, New Zealand Libraries Web site Flanagan talked about the satisfaction he gains from writing fantasy fiction. The best part of his job? "Planning the story, watching the meat grow on the bones of the framework, realising that your characters are taking on a life of their own and beginning to determine their own actions and how the story develops. Letting it mull round in your head for days or weeks. Putting it aside for a week and them coming back to find it's grown more detail in your subconscious while you weren't thinking about it. Great stuff. Great fun."

Biographical and Critical Sources

PERIODICALS

Booklist, June 1, 2005, Carolyn Phelan, review of *The Ruins of Gorlan,* p. 1796; May 15, 2006, Carolyn Phelan, review of *The Burning Bridge,* p. 58.

Kirkus Reviews, May 15, 2005, review of *The Ruins of Gorlan,* p. 588; May 1, 2006, review of *The Burning Bridge,* p. 458.

School Library Journal, June, 2005, Steven Engelfried, review of *The Ruins of Gorlan,* p. 158; August, 2006, Beth L. Meister, review of *The Burning Bridge,* p. 120.

Washington Post Book World, July 23, 2006, Ron Charles, interview with Flanagan, p. 9.

ONLINE

Christ Church, New Zealand Libraries Web site, http://library.christchurch.org.nz/ (April 28, 2007), interview with Flanagan.*

*   *   *

FLANAGAN, John Anthony
See FLANAGAN, John

*   *   *

FOUNTAS, Angela Jane

Personal

Female. *Education:* University of Pittsburgh, B.A. (liberal studies), 1993; University of Alabama, M.F.A. (creative writing), 2001.

Addresses

Home—Seattle, WA. *E-mail*—afountas@writehabit.org.

Career

Author and editor. Committee for Children, assistant editor, 2001-04. Writing instructor at schools, including University of Washington Women's Center, Phinney Neighborhood Center, and Hugo House. Judge for writing contests; visiting writer at schools and workshops.

Member

Editorial Freelancers Association, Northwest Independent Editors Guild, Richard Hugo House, Seattle Writergrrls, Teachers & Writers Collaborative, Women in Digital Journalism, 826 Seattle, Artist Trust, Digital Eve.

Awards, Honors

4Culture grant, 2006; Office of Arts & Cultural Affairs in Seattle grant, 2006; Jack Straw Writer, 2006.

Writings

(Editor and contributor) *Waking Up American: Coming of Age Biculturally: First-Generation Women Reflect on Identity,* Seal Press (Emeryville, CA), 2005.

Contributor to periodicals, including *Sentence, Uncaped, Northwest Asian Weekly, Writer, Rewrite, Red Mountain Review, Redivider, elimae, Bitter Oleander, Monkeybicycle, Diagram,* and *Syntax.*

Biographical and Critical Sources

PERIODICALS

Booklist, September 15, 2005, Hazel Rochman, review of *Waking Up American: Coming of Age Biculturally: First-Generation Women Reflect on Identity,* p. 12.
Kliatt, March, 2006, Patricia Moore, review of *Waking Up American,* p. 35.

ONLINE

Angela Fountas Home Page, http://www.writehabit.org/ (April 28, 2007).
Writergrrls Web site, http://www.seattlewritergrrls.org/ (April 28, 2007), "Angela Jane Fountas."*

*　　*　　*

FRIEDMAN, D. Dina 1957-

Personal

Born June 13, 1957, in Takoma Park, MD; daughter of Stanley (a writer and television producer) and Susan (a professor of mathematics) Friedman; married Shel

D. Dina Friedman (Photograph © 2005 by Andrew Morris Friedman. Courtesy of D. Dina Friedman.)

Horowitz (a writer and marketing consultant), October 9, 1983; children: Alana, Rafael. *Education:* Cornell University, A.B. (English), 1978; University of Connecticut, M.S.W., 1985. *Religion:* Jewish. *Hobbies and other interests:* Reading, political activism, hiking, gardening, cross-country skiing, music, performing arts events.

Addresses

Home and office—P.O. Box 1164, Northampton, MA 01061. *Office*—Isenberg School of Management, University of Massachusetts, Amherst, MA 01003. *E-mail*—dina@ddinafriedman.com.

Career

Educator and author. Accurate Writing and More, Hadley, MA, writing coach and marketing consultant. Mount Holyoke College, South Hadley, MA, workshop coordinator in speaking, arguing, and writing program, 1997-2002; University of Massachusetts—Amherst, lecturer in School of Management, 2000—.

Awards, Honors

Voice of Youth Advocates Top-Shelf Fiction selection, 2006, and New York Public Library Best Books for the Teen Age selection, Association of Jewish Libraries Notable Book for Older Readers citation, American Library Association Best Books for Young Adults nominee, and Children's Book Council/National Council for the Social Studies Best Trade Book designation, all 2007, all for *Escaping into the Night*; Best Children's Book of the Year designation, Bank Street College of Education, 2007, for *Playing Dad's Song*.

Writings

Escaping into the Night (young-adult novel), Simon & Schuster (New York, NY), 2006.
Playing Dad's Song (middle-grade novel), Farrar, Straus (New York, NY), 2006.

Sidelights

D. Dina Friedman always knew that writing was her calling. "I've wanted to be a writer since I was eight, and before writing my novels, I wrote many poems and short stories," she noted on her home page. Her novels for young readers—*Escaping into the Night* is a work of historical fiction for young adults while *Playing Dad's Song* is geared for middle-grade readers—feature teens discovering their own identity, and learning what their Jewish heritage means to them.

Escaping into the Night is based on the actual historical events around a little-known Holocaust story. Fleeing the Warsaw ghetto, Halina travels to hidden *ziemlankas*—underground caves where a community of Jews are hiding. "Friedman realistically captures the terror of the situation, but, refreshingly, also depicts Halina experiencing her first kiss," noted a *Publishers Weekly* contributor. According to Hazel Rochman in *Booklist*, "Friedman never idealizes the refugees or their rescuers," instead presenting the moral dilemmas Halina and her friends go through in order to survive. "In Halina, Friedman has created a reluctant heroine who is also a believable adolescent," wrote Renee Steinberg in her *School Library Journal* review of *Escaping into the Night*, while a *Kirkus Reviews* contributor concluded that "Halina's experience demonstrates maturity and a resignation that life is worth living at any price."

Friedman grew up in New York City, the setting of *Playing Dad's Song*. Gus Moskowitz wishes he could change the past: make September 11th never happen, which means that his dad would still be alive. Mourn-ing his father's death and jealous of his talented older sister, Gus struggles emotionally until he begins taking oboe lessons from a Holocaust survivor. Their relationship inspires Gus with the means by which he can honor his father in his own way. As a *Kirkus Reviews* contributor noted of the conclusion, "as Gus looks at the empty skyline, it's no longer a hole but a new beginning." "The honest personal drama brings the grief and loss of the terrorist attack home to the reader," wrote Rochman in a review of *Playing Dad's Song*.

Along with her writing, Friedman is involved in anti-poverty work, land-protection issues, and anti-war campaigns. "While writing is one of the central things in my life, equally important is working for a better world," she wrote on her home page. She also offered the following advice to young writers: "In my experience, the hardest thing about writing is to keep going and believe in yourself."

Biographical and Critical Sources

PERIODICALS

Booklist, January 1, 2006, Hazel Rochman, review of *Escaping into the Night*, p. 83; November 15, 2006, Hazel Rochman, review of *Playing Dad's Song*, p. 47.
Bulletin of the Center for Children's Books, February, 2006, Loretta Gaffney, review of *Escaping into the Night*, p. 263.
Kirkus Reviews, January 15, 2006, review of *Escaping into the Night*, p. 84; August 15, 2006, review of *Playing Dad's Song*, p. 840.
Publishers Weekly, February 13, 2006, review of *Escaping into the Night*, p. 90.
School Library Journal, March, 2006, Renee Steinberg, review of *Escaping into the Night*, p. 222; September, 2006, Miriam Lang Budin, review of *Playing Dad's Song*, p. 204.
Voice of Youth Advocates, April, 2006, Eileen Kuhl, review of *Escaping into the Night*, p. 42.

ONLINE

Children's Literature Network Web site, http://www.childrensliteraturenetwork.org/ (April 28, 2007), "D. Dina Friedman."
D. Dina Friedman Home Page, http://www.ddinafriedman.com (April 28, 2007).

G

GERAS, Adèle 1944-
(Adèle Daphne Weston Geras)

Personal

Surname pronounced with a hard "G" and rhymes with "terrace"; born March 15, 1944, in Jerusalem, Palestine (now Israel); immigrated to England, 1955; daughter of Laurence David (a lawyer) and Leah Weston; married Norman Geras (a retired professor and writer), August 7, 1967; children: Sophie, Jenny. *Education:* St. Hilda's College, Oxford, B.A., 1966. *Religion:* Jewish. *Hobbies and other interests:* Films, detective fiction.

Addresses

Office—10 Danesmoor Rd., Manchester M20 3JS, England. *Agent*—Laura Cecil, 17 Alwyne Villas, London N1 2HG, England. *E-mail*—adele@adelegeras.com.

Career

Children's book author. Fairfield High School, Droylsden, Lancashire, England, French teacher, 1968-71; writer, 1976—. Actress in *Four Degrees Over* (play), 1966.

Awards, Honors

Taylor Award, 1991, for *My Grandmother's Stories: A Collection of Jewish Folktales;* National Jewish Book Council Award, 1994, for *Golden Windows, and Other Stories of Jerusalem;* Houseman Society prize, 2000, for *The Sampler Alphabet;* British Arts Council award, 2000; shortlisted for Whitbread Children's Book Award, 2000, Carnegie Medal highly commended designation, and *Boston Globe/Horn Book* Award Honor Book designation for fiction/poetry, both 2001, all for *Troy;* HH Wingate Jewish Quarterly Poetry Award and Smith Doorstop Poetry Pamphlet Award, both for adult poetry.

Adèle Geras, 2002 (Photograph © Jerry Bauer. Reproduced by permission.)

Writings

CHILDREN'S FICTION

Tea at Mrs. Manderby's, illustrated by Doreen Caldwell, Hamish Hamilton (London, England), 1976.

Apricots at Midnight, and Other Stories from a Patchwork Quilt, illustrated by Doreen Caldwell, Hamish Hamilton (London, England), 1977, Atheneum (New York, NY), 1982.

Beyond the Cross-Stitch Mountains, illustrated by Mary Wilson, Hamish Hamilton (London, England), 1977.

The Painted Garden, illustrated by Doreen Caldwell, Hamish Hamilton (London, England), 1979.

A Thousand Yards of Sea, illustrated by Joanna Troughton, Hodder & Stoughton (London, England), 1980.

The Rug That Grew, illustrated by Priscilla Lamont, Hamish Hamilton (London, England), 1981.

The Christmas Cat, illustrated by Doreen Caldwell, Hamish Hamilton (London, England), 1983.

Little Elephant's Moon, illustrated by Linda Birch, Hamish Hamilton (London, England), 1986.

Ritchie's Rabbit, illustrated by Vanessa Julian-Ottie, Hamish Hamilton (London, England), 1986, Random House (New York, NY), 1987.

Finding Annabel, illustrated by Alan Marks, Hamish Hamilton (London, England), 1987.

Fishpie for Flamingoes, illustrated by Linda Birch, Hamish Hamilton (London, England), 1987.

The Fantora Family Files, illustrated by Tony Ross, Hamish Hamilton (London, England), 1988.

The Strange Bird, illustrated by Linda Birch, Hamish Hamilton (London, England), 1988.

The Coronation Picnic, illustrated by Frances Wilson, Hamish Hamilton (London, England), 1989.

Bunk Bed Night, Dent (London, England), 1990.

My Grandmother's Stories: A Collection of Jewish Folktales, illustrated by Jael Jordan, Knopf (New York, NY), 1990, published as *My Grandmother's Stories: A Collection of Jewish Folk Tales,* illustrated by Anita Lobel, Knopf (New York, NY), 2003.

Nina's Magic, Hamish Hamilton (London, England), 1990.

Pink Medicine, Dent (London, England), 1990.

A Magic Birthday, Simon & Schuster (London, England), 1992.

The Fantora Family Photographs, illustrated by Tony Ross, Hamish Hamilton (London, England), 1993.

Golden Windows, and Other Stories of Jerusalem, HarperCollins (New York, NY), 1993.

Baby's Bedclothes, illustrated by Prue Greener, Longman (Essex, England), 1994.

The Dolls' House, illustrated by Prue Greener, Longman (Essex, England), 1994.

Keith's Croak, illustrated by Prue Greener, Longman (Essex, England), 1994.

Mary's Meadow, illustrated by Prue Greener, Longman (Essex, England), 1994.

Mimi; and Apricot Max, illustrated by Teresa O'Brien, Longman (Essex, England), 1994.

Josephine, illustrated by Teresa O'Brien, Longman (Essex, England), 1994.

The Return of Archibald Gribbet, illustrated by Sumiko, Longman (Essex, England), 1994.

Toey, illustrated by Duncan Smith, Heinemann (London, England), 1994.

Gilly the Kid, illustrated by Sue Heap, Simon & Schuster (New York, NY), 1995.

Stories for Bedtime (with cassette), illustrated by Amanda Benjamin, HarperCollins (New York, NY), 1995.

A Candle in the Dark ("Flashbacks" historical fiction series), A. & C. Black (London, England), 1995.

(Compiler) *Kingfisher Book of Jewish Stories,* illustrated by Jane Cope, Kingfisher (London, England), 1995, published as *A Treasury of Jewish Stories,* Kingfisher (New York, NY), 1996.

(Adapter) *Beauty and the Beast, and Other Stories,* illustrated by Louise Brierley, Viking (New York, NY), 1996.

The Magical Storyhouse, illustrated by Joanna Walsh, Macdonald (Brighton, England), 1996.

Chalk and Cheese, illustrated by Adriano Gon, Transworld (London, England), 1996.

Cinderella, illustrated by Gwen Tourret, Macdonald (Brighton, England), 1996.

From Lullaby to Lullaby, illustrated by Kathryn Brown, Simon & Schuster Books for Young Readers (New York, NY), 1997.

Picasso Perkins, illustrated by Tony Ross, Transworld (London, England), 1997.

Blossom's Revenge, illustrated by Tony Ross, Transworld (London, England), 1997.

Silent Snow, Secret Snow, Hamish Hamilton (London, England), 1998.

The Fantora Family Files, illustrated by Tony Ross, Avon (New York, NY), 1998, published as *The Fabulous Fantoras, Book One: Family Files,* illustrated by Eric Brace, Avon (New York, NY), 1998.

Callie's Kitten, illustrated by Tony Ross, Transworld (London, England), 1998, published as *The Cats of Cuckoo Square: Callie's Kitten,* Dell Yearling (New York, NY), 2003.

Geejay the Hero, illustrated by Tony Ross, Transworld (London, England), 1998, published as *The Cats of Cuckoo Square: Geejay the Hero,* Dell Yearling (New York, NY), 2003.

The Gingerbread House, Barrington Stoke (Edinburgh, Scotland), 1998.

The Six Swan Brothers, illustrated by Patrick Benson, Scholastic (New York, NY), 1998.

Lolly, Orchard (London, England), 1998.

The Fabulous Fantoras, Book Two: Family Photographs, illustrated by Eric Brace, Avon (New York, NY), 1999.

Sleep Tight, Ginger Kitten, Dutton (New York, NY), 2001.

The Cats of Cuckoo Square: Two Stories, illustrated by Tony Ross, Delacorte (New York, NY), 2001.

My Wishes for You, illustrated by Cliff Wright, Simon & Schuster (New York, NY), 2002.

The Ballet Class, illustrated by Shelagh McNichols, Orchard (London, England), 2003, published as *Time for Ballet,* Dial (New York, NY), 2004.

Rebecca's Passover, illustrated by Sheila Moxley, Frances Lincoln (London, England), 2003.

(Reteller) *Sleeping Beauty,* illustrated by Christian Birmingham, Orchard (New York, NY), 2004.

Lizzie's Wish ("Historical House" series), Usborne, 2004.

Lily: A Ghost Story ("Quick Reads" series), Orion (London, England), 2007.

Cecily's Portrait ("Historical House" series), Usborne, 2007.

Cleopatra, Kingfisher (New York, NY), 2007.

Little Ballet Star, Orchard House (London, England), 2008, published as *Like a Real Ballerina,* Dial (New York, NY), 2008.

Also author of *Josephine and Pobble* and *Sun Slices, Moon Slices.*

"LITTLE SWAN" SERIES

Little Swan, illustrated by Johanna Westerman, Random House (New York, NY), 1995.

Louisa's Secret, illustrated by Karen Popham, Red Fox (London, England), 1997.

Louisa in the Wings, illustrated by Karen Popham, Red Fox (London, England), 1997.

Louisa and Phoebe, illustrated by Karen Popham, Random House (London, England), 1997.

A Rival for Louisa, illustrated by Karen Popham, Red Fox (London, England), 1997.

Louisa on Screen, illustrated by Karen Popham, Red Fox (London, England), 2001.

Good Luck, Louisa!, illustrated by Karen Popham, Red Fox (London, England), 2002.

"MAGIC OF BALLET" SERIES

Giselle, illustrated by Emma Chichester Clark, David & Charles (New York, NY), 2001.

Sleeping Beauty, illustrated by Emma Chichester Clark, David & Charles (New York, NY), 2001.

Swan Lake, illustrated by Emma Chichester Clark, David & Charles (New York, NY), 2001.

The Nutcracker, illustrated by Emma Chichester Clark, David & Charles (New York, NY), 2001.

The Firebird, illustrated by Emma Chichester Clark, Gullane (London, England) 2001.

Coppélia, illustrated by Emma Chichester Clark, Gullane (London, England), 2002.

My First Ballet Stories (collection; contains *Giselle, Coppélia, Swan Lake, Sleeping Beauty, The Nutcracker,* and *Firebird*), illustrated by Emma Chichester Clark, Gullane (London, England), 2004.

YOUNG-ADULT FICTION

The Girls in the Velvet Frame, Hamish Hamilton (London, England), 1978, Atheneum (New York, NY), 1979.

The Green behind the Glass, Hamish Hamilton (London, England), 1982, published as *Snapshots of Paradise: Love Stories,* Atheneum (New York, NY), 1984.

Other Echoes, Atheneum (New York, NY), 1983, reprinted, David Fickling, 2004.

Voyage, Atheneum (New York, NY), 1983, reprinted, Harcourt (Orlando, FL), 2007.

Letters of Fire, and Other Unsettling Stories, Hamish Hamilton (London, England), 1984.

Happy Endings, Hamish Hamilton (London, England), 1986, Harcourt (San Diego, CA), 1991, reprinted, 2006.

Daydreams on Video, Hodder & Stoughton (London, England), 1989.

The Tower Room, Hamish Hamilton (London, England), 1990, Harcourt (San Diego, CA), 1992.

Watching the Roses, Hamish Hamilton (London, England), 1991, Harcourt (San Diego, CA), 1992.

Pictures of the Night, Harcourt (San Diego, CA), 1993.

A Lane to the Land of the Dead, Hamish Hamilton (London, England), 1994.

Troy, Harcourt (San Diego, CA), 2001.

Ithaka, Harcourt (Orlando, FL), 2006.

OTHER

(With Pauline Stainer) *Up on the Roof* (adult poetry), Smith Doorstep (Huddersfield, England), 1987.

Yesterday (memoirs), Walker (London, England), 1992.

Voices from the Dolls' House (adult poetry), Rockingham Press (Ware, England), 1994.

The Orchard Book of Opera Stories, Orchard (London, England), 1997, published as *The Random House Book of Opera Stories,* Random House (New York, NY), 1998.

Facing the Light (adult novel), Thomas Dunne (New York, NY), 2004.

Hester's Story (adult novel), Orion (London, England), 2005.

Made in Heaven (adult novel), Orion (New York, NY), 2006.

A Hidden Life (adult novel), Orion (London, England), 2007.

Contributor to of reviews and articles to periodicals, including London *Guardian, Times Educational Supplement, Armadillo Online,* and *Cricket.* Geras's work has been translated into several languages, including Dutch and German.

Adaptations

Troy was adapted as an audiobook by Listening Library, 2002. *Hester's Story* was adapted as an audiobook by Clipper Audio, 2006.

Sidelights

A childhood spent following her father on his wide-ranging assignments for the British colonial service had a great influence on the work of novelist and short-story writer Adèle Geras. Using her experiences in historic Jerusalem, where she was born, as well as exotic Africa and Great Britain, where she attended boarding school and now lives, Geras weaves a strong sense of place and time into her fiction. Trained as both a performing artist and a teacher, Geras did not intend to be a writer, although it had been a hobby for her as a child. As she explained to an interviewer at *Wordpool Online,* "I've written for fun since I could write. I started with poetry, and when I was at school, the main thing I did was write plays for my friends and me to perform." "I came to writing by accident," she ezplained to an interviewer at BlogCritics Online. "I went in for a story competition in 1973 and enjoyed writing my piece so much that I decided to try and write some more." The story, "Rose," was joined by several other short tales and published by Geras in 1977 as *Apricots at Midnight, and Other Short Stories from a Patchwork Quilt.* This collection of story "patches" is narrated by a dressmaker named Aunt Piney as she works on a quilt with her young niece. A *Publishers Weekly* reviewer called the book "unusual and entrancing," while *Horn Book* contributor Kate M. Flanagan praised the tales as "rich in detail and delightfully recounted."

Geras's enthusiasm for her newfound craft also found an outlet in writing picture books for young children; the first, *Tea at Mrs. Manderby's,* is a story about a young girl who resigns herself to taking afternoon tea with an elderly neighbor at her parents' urging. Several more books for young readers followed, including *A Thousand Yards of Sea,* about a fisherman who releases a mermaid from his net and is rewarded with beautiful sea-colored cloth that the women of his village make into skirts; and *Toey,* about two children who hope for a new pet and end up with a pair of playful kittens. Geras has also published many short stories in magazines such as *Cricket,* and several of these short tales are collected as *Stories for Bedtime.*

In addition to short stories and picture books for young children, Geras is the author of several collections of short fiction written with older readers in mind. In 1983 she wrote *The Green behind the Glass,* a set of eight tales about young love that was released in the United States as *Snapshots of Paradise: Love Stories.* Called "an intriguing departure from the sunny sentimentality of so many romance collections for young adults" by *Booklist* reviewer Stephanie Zvirin, *The Green behind the Glass* includes "Don't Sing Love Songs," narrated by a young woman who is on her own with a friend in Paris until their shared attraction for handsome Jim threatens their friendship; the title story, in which a woman's older sister knows herself to be the real object of the sister's now-dead fiancée's true affections; and "Tea in the Wendy House," in which a young, pregnant woman laments for her soon-to-be-lost youth as she faces a shotgun wedding and a future as wife and mother in a tiny house. *Horn Book* writer Mary M. Burns hailed the variety of styles and settings of Geras's love stories, calling them "distinguished by perceptive insight into human nature, dexterity in plot construction, and a sense of style remarkable for its readability and its imagery and constraint."

In *A Lane to the Land of the Dead,* Geras uses suspense and elements of the supernatural to add spice and a touch of melancholy to the lives of her young protagonists. The author "shows her usual lightness of touch," Elspeth S. Scott observed in the *School Librarian,* predicting the collection would have wide appeal. In contrast, the five tales in *Golden Windows, and Other Stories of Jerusalem* show readers what life was like in early twentieth-century Jerusalem. In "Beyond the Cross-Stitch Mountains," one story from this collection, eleven-year-old Daskeh conspires with friend Danny to escape the care of her aunt Phina and visit Danny's

family, despite the danger in leaving the bomb shelter where they routinely spend each nights during Israel's 1948 War for Independence. "Dreams of Fire" shows the after-effects of this wartime experience on young Danny as memories of death and violence return to haunt him in the form of a memorial built to honor the war. Reviewer Ellen Mandel praised *Golden Windows* in *Booklist* as "well-written, laced with subtleties of history, and rich in personal emotion."

Beyond the Cross-Stitch Mountains, which was published as a separate book in the United Kingdom, draws on the author's Jewish heritage. Similarly, Geras's novel *The Girls in the Velvet Frame* takes as its setting the city of Jerusalem circa 1913 and focuses on five sisters whose brother Isaac left for the United States and has been out of contact for months. "The appeal of this charming book comes . . . from the accurate, penetrating and quite unsentimental portraits of the five children and of their elders," Marcus Crouch noted in a review of *The Girls in the Velvet Frame* for the *Times Literary Supplement.* Cyrisse Jaffee praised the story's fictional characters, and added in *School Library Journal* that "marvelous descriptions of time and place add contours" to the novella.

The full-length novel *Voyage* also focuses on the history of the Jewish people, this time by following a group of characters who flee from the poverty of Eastern Europe by enduring a fifteen-day crossing of the Atlantic Ocean aboard a tightly packed ship. The sight of the Statue of Liberty in New York Harbor at journey's end is the beginning of a new life for the characters. The book's vignettes "cleverly [reveal] not only the happenings on board but the thoughts, hopes, fears, and memories of the little community," Ethel L. Heins wrote in *Horn Book.*

Among Geras's most notable novels for young adults are the books comprising the "Egerton Hall" series. Set in Egerton Hall boarding school in 1963, the stories revolve around three friends: Alice, Bella, and Megan. In *The Tower Room* modern-day Rapunzel Megan is freed from the boarding school's lackluster tower room after falling in love with a handsome young laboratory assistant at Egerton Hall. In *Watching the Roses* Geras draws from the Sleeping Beauty legend in telling Alice's story. On the night of her eighteenth birthday party, Alice is attacked and raped by the son of her family's gardener. Her story is told in the diary entries she writes as she tries to recover from the shock of the event. Time seems to stop while Alice deals with her concerns over how the rape will affect her relationship with Jean-Luc, her own handsome prince. Florence H. Munat praised *Watching the Roses* in the *Voice of Youth Advocates,* noting that Geras "has deftly added just the right modern twists and details to allure older readers back to the story that enchanted them as children." The author's fairy-tale trilogy is completed with a modern-day retelling of Snow White's story, casting eighteen-year-old Bella in the lead. *Pictures of the Night* finds evil stepmother Marjorie so jealous of her stepdaughter's budding singing career that she tries to kill the young woman. In a *Kirkus Reviews* assessment of the novel, one critic called Geras "a writer distinguished for her imaginative power and fresh, vivid writing."

With *Troy,* Geras brings the tumultuous Trojan War to life through the eyes of four teenagers living in ancient Greece, each of whom is connected to a major figure in the epic conflict. Xanthe is nursemaid to Andromache and Hector's infant son; her sister, Marpessa, is maidservant to Helen and Paris. Polyxena, identified as the granddaughter of the "singer"—Homer—is her grandfather's caretaker. Stable hand Iason, who adores Xanthe, is too shy to express his feelings; he is more comfortable talking to Hector's war horses. "It's a domestic and youthful view of Troy," the author told Julia Eccleshare in a London *Guardian* interview, "rather than the heroic and traditional one." The teens in *Troy,* while learning about the realities of love and war, also encounter the gods, as when Eros shoots his arrow at Xanthe.

Ruminator Review contributor Christine Alfano notes that Geras integrates myth and reality by presenting the gods and goddesses in *Troy* "as living characters. They are strongly present throughout the novel and keep their fingers on the strings of fate." Patricia Lothrop-Green, reviewing the book for *School Library Journal,* found some of the key characters "thin, one-dimensional figures." A *Publishers Weekly* contributor stated that the novel accomplishes two goals: "Mythology buffs will savor the author's ability to embellish stories of old without diminishing their original flavor; the uninitiated will find this a captivating introduction to one of the pivotal events of classic Greek literature." *New York Times Book Review* critic Elizabeth Deveraux, citing Geras's "contemporary" attitude, noted that *Troy* performs "a valuable service: it paves a road into the realm of Homer, then lures young readers along its course."

Drawing on the events figuring in both the epic *The Odyssey* and *Illiad, Ithaka* focuses on the events occurring on Odysseus's home front while the hero strives to return to his kingdom. The novel is told through the eyes of Klymene, a girl in the service of Odysseus's wife Queen Penelope. Assumed to be a widow because her husband has not returned, the wealthy Penelope is plagued by suitors hoping to convince her to remarry. While the actual epic depicts Penelope as the essense of faithfulness, here Geras portrays her as a real woman with real emotions, as plagued by loneliness and human desire as is the starry-eyed and idealistic young Klymene. Klymene is in love with Prince Telemachus, but the prince has already been smitten by another: the young maid Melantho, who has also stolen Klymene's brother's heart. When one of Penelope's suitors falls in love with Klymene, the teen must navigate the tricky world of court intrigue and avoid upsetting the fickle Greek gods as she pursues the attention of her beloved. "Lovers of Greek mythology will appreciate the authen-

tic flavor of this book, but readers need not be familiar with *The Odyssey,*" assured a *Publishers Weekly* critic. *School Library Journal* reviewer Patricia D. Lothrop felt that "readers looking for a romance novel set in ancient Greece . . . will be as pleased with *Ithaka* as they were with *Troy.*" According to Holly Koelling in *Booklist,* Geras's "visceral, lusty, tragic retelling will draw older teens," while *Horn Book* reviewer Anita L. Burkham concluded of the novel that "Geras gives this tale the epic treatment it deserves.

In addition to historical fiction, Geras has penned contemporary novels for both young teens and adults. *Other Echoes* draws from the author's own childhood spent in North Borneo (now Malaysia). The novel's narrator, nineteen-year-old Flora, is recovering from exhaustion at her boarding school, and recalls the events that shaped her childhood. According to Janis Flint-Ferguson in *Kliatt,* Geras "tells the story of a girl learning to fit in, of finding her own way and coming to appreciate the role that writing plays in such growth and development."

The author's love of both opera and ballet figure into much of her writing, and her "Magic of Ballet" series helps young audiences understand well-known dance productions by narrating the stories behind four ballets: *Sleeping Beauty, Giselle, Swan Lake,* and *The Nutcracker.* Geared for older readers, *The Random House Book of Opera Stories* presents the tales behind such productions as *Aïda, The Magic Flute, Turandot,* and *The Love for Three Oranges.* Geras also presents a picture-book introduction to the dance designed for young children in *Time for Ballet.* "As much about movement as ballet, this warm story aptly conveys a child's love of dance," wrote Susan Pine in *School Library Journal.*

Focusing on young readers, Geras's chapter books for beginning readers include the "Cats of Ku of Cuckoo Square" series. Comprising *Callie's Kitten, Geejay's Hero, Blossom's Revenge,* and *Picasso Perkins,* the tales feature four cats that share the same neighborhood. Blossom and her owner plot to get rid of an obnoxious human pest, while Perkins models for a painting, which he decorates with his own paw prints as a final touch. These chapter books are "just the right challenge for early chapter-book readers," according to Caroline Ward in *School Library Journal.* Geras has also contributed to the "Quick Reads" series with *Lily: A Ghost Story.* Quick Reads "are aimed at people who might be frightened of a fat book or of going into a conventional bookshop," Geras explained to a writer for *Europe Intelligence Wire.*

Geras has also written a collection of folk tales for younger readers. Originally published in 1990, *My Grandmother's Stories* received new life when it was re-illustrated by award-winning artist Anita Lobel. Susan Pine, writing in *School Library Journal,* noted that all the stories included "impart universal truths about everyday foibles and follies" and should be "shared and treasured." A *Publishers Weekly* critic predicted that "a treat is in store for readers of all faiths" with this book.

In 2003 Geras published her first adult novel, *Facing the Light,* a multi-layered story about a family over a time-span of seventy-five years. The novel describes the seventy-fifth birthday celebration of Leonora, during which some old family secrets emerge. Geras has followed this novel with several other works of fiction for adults, among them *Hester's Story,* a novel about a retired prima ballerina, and *Made in Heaven,* about a lavish family wedding. Of the former, *Kliatt* reviewer Nola Theiss commented: "The world of ballet . . . is interesting and the story is filled with some well-drawn characters."

When asked why she likes writing for children by a *Word Pool Online* interviewer, Geras explained: "Children read properly. They have the time. If they like a book, they live in it, and it becomes part of their lives." Whether intended for adults or children, Geras's books share similar themes. "Geras is interested in people and understands them, especially girls," Eccleshare wrote in *Twentieth-Century Children's Writers.* "Her books have an emotional integrity which makes them satisfying. Though not challenging or highly plotted they are all very well constructed and the fluent writing makes them easy to read and enjoy."

Biographical and Critical Sources

BOOKS

St. James Guide to Young-Adult Writers, St. James Press (Detroit, MI), 1999.
Twentieth-Century Children's Writers, 3rd edition, St. James Press (Detroit, MI), 1989.

PERIODICALS

Booklist, August, 1984, p. 1609; October 15, 1993; November 15 1996, Hazel Rochman, review of *Beauty and the Beast, and Other Stories,* p. 582; April 15 1997, Lauren Peterson, review of *From Lullaby to Lullaby,* p. 1436; October 15, 1998, Carolyn Phelan, review of *The Random House Book of Opera Stories,* p. 414; November 1, 1998, Michael Cart, review of *The Fabulous Fantoras, Book One: Family Files,* p. 490; June 1, 1999, review of *The Fabulous Fantoras, Book Two: Family Photographs,* p. 1829; April 1, 2001, Stephanie Zvirin, review of *Troy,* p. 1482; September 1, 2001, Zvirin, review of *The Cats of Cuckoo Square: Two Stories;* December 15, 2002, Lauren Peterson, review of *My Wishes for You,* p. 766; February 1, 2004, Carolyn Phelan, review of *Time for Bal-*
let, p. 975; May 1, 2004, Jennifer Mattson, review of *Sleeping Beauty,* p. 1556; December 15, 2005, Holly Koelling, review of *Ithaka,* p. 39.
Bookseller, November 5, 2004, "Royal Over-Seas League," p. 11.
Books for Keeps, May, 1996, review of *A Lane to the Land of the Dead, and Other Stories,* p. 17; September, 1996, review of *Beauty and the Beast, and Other Stories,* p. 32; March, 1999, review of *The Six Swan Brothers,* p. 21, and *Silent Snow, Secret Snow,* p. 27; May, 1999, review of *Beauty and the Beast, and Other Stories,* p. 27; July, 1999, review of *Sun Slices, Moon Slices,* p. 20; November, 1999, review of *Josephine and Pobble* and *Mimi; and Apricot Max,* p. 16.
Books for Your Children, autumn, 1992, p. 27.
Childhood Education, summer, 2003, Aaron Condon, review of *Troy,* p. 245.
Children's Bookwatch, May, 1997, review of *From Lullaby to Lullaby,* p. 3.
Christian Science Monitor, May 13, 1983.
Dance, December, 2001, review of "The Magic of Ballet" series, p. 77.
Emergency Librarian, May, 1998, review of *Beauty and the Beast, and Other Stories,* p. 51.
Europe Intelligence Wire, March 8, 2007, "Top Writer Shares Her Words of Wisdom with Schoolgirls"; March 23, 2007, "Renowned Author Inspires."
Guardian (London, England), March 28, 2000, review of *Troy,* p. 63; July 13, 2001, Julia Eccleshare, "Notes from an Accidental Career."
Horn Book, February, 1983, pp. 43, 44; August, 1983, p. 452; September-October, 1984, p. 596; March-April, 1993, p. 211; January-February, 2006, Anita L. Burkam, review of *Ithaka,* p. 78.
Junior Bookshelf, December, 1976, p. 326; June, 1994, p. 100; August, 1994, p. 134; June, 1996, review of *A Candle in the Dark,* p. 113; December, 1996, review of *Beauty and the Beast, and Other Stories,* p. 251.
Kirkus Reviews, September 1, 1984, p. J8; March 15, 1993; October 15, 1996, review of *Beauty and the Beast, and Other Stories,* p. 1532; April 1, 1997, review of *From Lullaby to Lullaby,* p. 554; May 1, 2001, review of *Sleep Tight, Ginger Kitten,* p. 659; October 1, 2001, review of *The Cats of Cuckoo Square,* p. 1423; February 1, 2004, review of *Time for Ballet,* p. 133; December 15, 2005, review of *Ithaka,* p. 1322.
Kliatt, March, 2005, Janis Flint-Ferguson, review of *Other Echoes,* p. 10.
New Statesman, December 4, 1998, review of *Beauty and the Beast, and Other Stories,* p. 60.
New York Times Book Review, July 15, 2001, Elizabeth Deveraux, review of *Troy,* p. 25.
Publishers Weekly, October 15, 1982, p. 66; November 25, 1996, review of *Beauty and the Beast, and Other Stories,* p. 74; March 17, 1997, review of *From Lullaby to Lullaby,* p. 82; August 10, 1998, review of *The Fabulous Fantoras, Book One,* p. 388; August 31, 1998, review of *The Random House Book of Opera Stories,* p. 78; May 7, 2001, reviews of *Sleep Tight, Ginger Kitten,* p. 245, and *Troy,* p. 248; August 25,

2003, review of *My Grandmother's Stories,* p. 51; March 1, 2004, review of *Time for Ballet,* p. 67; January 2, 2006, review of *Ithaka,* p. 63; June 26, 2006, review of *Happy Endings,* p. 54.

Ruminator Review, summer, 2001, Christine Alfano, review of *Troy,* pp. 53-54.

School Librarian, June, 1983, pp. 162, 165; November, 1992, p. 157; May, 1994, p. 60; May, 1995, p. 77; May, 1996, review of *A Candle in the Dark,* p. 62; winter, 1999, review of *Sun Slices, Moon Slices,* p. 185; summer, 1999, reviews of *Silent Snow, Secret Snow* and *The Six Swan Brothers,* pp. 79, 99.

School Library Journal, September, 1979, p. 138; February, 1997, Donna Scanlon, review of *Beauty and the Beast, and Other Stories,* p. 90; July, 1997, Sue Norris, review of *From Lullaby to Lullaby,* p. 67; October, 1998, Renee Steinberg, review of *The Random House Book of Opera Stories,* p. 153; January, 1999, Eva Mitnick, review of *The Fabulous Fantoras, Book One,* p. 127; May, 2001, Rosalyn Pierini, review of *Sleep Tight, Ginger Kitten,* p. 115; July, 2001, Patricia Lothrop-Green, review of *Troy,* p. 108; November, 2001, Amy Kellman, review of *Giselle* and *Sleeping Beauty,* p. 123; December, 2001, Caroline Ward, review of *The Cats of Cuckoo Square,* p. 102; December, 2002, Be Astengo, review of *My Wishes for You,* p. 96; August, 2003, Susan Pine, review of *My Grandmother's Stories,* p. 149; February, 2004, Susan Pine, review of *Time for Ballet,* p. 112; August, 2004, Susan Scheps, review of *Sleeping Beauty,* p. 107; October, 2004, review of *Time for Ballet,* p. S26; February, 2006, Patricia D. Lothrop, review of *Ithaka,* p. 131.

Times Educational Supplement, February 5, 1999, review of *Silent Snow, Secret Snow,* p. 27; September 24, 1999, review of *The Cats of Cuckoo Square,* p. 48.

Times Literary Supplement, September 29, 1978, p. 1083; March 27, 1981, p. 340; January 27, 1984; November 30, 1984; June 6, 1986.

Voice of Youth Advocates, December, 1992, p. 278.

ONLINE

Adèle Geras's Home Page, http://www.adelegeras.com/ (April 26, 2007).

Word Pool Web site, http://www.wordpool.com.

Autobiography Feature

Adèle Geras

Adèle Geras contributed the following autobiographical essay to *SATA:*

It is March 15, 1995, and my fifty-first birthday. It seems appropriate, somehow, to start an autobiography on a significant date. There's a symmetry about it which pleases me. One of the things I most enjoy about writing is the creation of patterns. I like putting things into an order; I like my work to have a structure. I'm also obsessed by all kinds of handiwork: embroidery, knitting, sewing, and so on, and images of threads, scissors, needles, and fabrics of one kind and another come up over and over again in what I write, and especially in my poems. One of my first books was called *Apricots at Midnight* and told the story of an old lady who had made a quilt in which each patch was the starting point for a tale. It seems to me that the principles of patchwork should govern the piece I am embarking on now. Please imagine, therefore, that my life is like a basket, full to overflowing with scraps of material in every possible color. Think of scarlets and blues, wool and silk, florals and stripes, checks and polka dots. What I plan to do is pick out one piece after another and stitch them together into a satisfying shape.

*

Before I begin a book or story, I choose a notebook. The choice is important. I love stationery. I am going to be writing in this notebook almost every day, sometimes for a couple of months, so it has to entice me, to enchant me. I've chosen an extra special one today. It has on the cover a picture of a cat, painted in India in about 1890. This saffron cat, with patches of black, has strange, human, pale blue eyes, and it's holding a glum-looking fish in its mouth. The notebook is ring-bound, and the paper is thick and white and unlined and luxurious. At the back of the book, there are with a few pages of music manuscript paper that make me wish I knew how to compose a song. I am writing with a black pen. I always do. I go back over what I've written with red, then turquoise, and only when I've corrected the manuscript about three times am I ready to put my

Geras at work on her sofa. (Photograph courtesy of Adèle Geras.)

words onto the word processor. I write lying down on my sofa, which is comfortable and upholstered in black velvet. I have a cushion at my back, and the notebook leaning on knees. I write very quickly, as though there were a time limit; as though I were in an xamination and the invigilator were about to stop me.

*

In 1944, on this day, I was born in Jerusalem. The world was still at war, and Jerusalem was still part of Palestine, under the authority of the British Government. The State of Israel was four years away. My father, Laurence Weston, was in the British Army in Egypt. I am an only child. My mother, Leah Hamburger, was one of nine children, so I have many cousins. One of these, Danny, became an honorary brother. When I first went to boarding school in England in 1955, I put his photo on my chest-of-drawers, next to a picture of my parents. I told anyone who asked that he was my brother, and my poor mother was quite disconcerted, when she came to visit me, to be asked how her son was.

*

My father's father died before I was born. He adored Gilbert and Sullivan operas, and my father always said

he would have loved me very much. When I was a child, I could never understand why he kept telling me this, but now I know exactly what he meant. My own father died when Sophie, my elder daughter, was one year old, and I find myself thinking very often of how much he would have loved her and her sister, Jenny, and being filled with a kind of frustration that he has missed knowing them, seeing them grow up. My paternal grandmother was called Messoda. She came from Morocco. She was a magnificent cook. She was a magical storyteller. I have memories of her in my aunt Vivienne's house in Cardiff, looking out of place in Wales: too exotic, too foreign, muttering under her breath, with something gypsylike and glamorous about her, even in old age.

*

My mother's mother was known to all her many grandchildren and great-grandchildren as Ima Gdola (Big Mother). She was quite an old lady by the time I was born, but according to family legend she had once been a fair-haired, blue-eyed beauty with an eighteen-inch waist. She married at sixteen; she was a widow before she was forty. My grandfather must have had raven-black hair, because all my aunts and uncles on my mother's side are either blonde, with a reddish tinge, or else dark, with straight eyebrows. I am named after an aunt who died before I was born. She was one of the dark ones. Her photograph much enlarged and in a wooden frame, hung in the dining room of Ima Gdola's apartment. The first Adèle is leaning on her hand. She is wearing a lace blouse, with a high collar, and staring soulfully into the distance.

*

When I was about two years old, we lived for a while in Rhodes. My father was in charge of a transit camp for men who had been German prisoners-of-war during World War II. The story goes that a man who used to be one of Hitler's cooks asked my mother whether he could teach me the words of "Lili Marlene" in German. She refused. I don't know how true this is, but it's a good story.

*

My cousin Danny and I played together all the time. He is four years older than I am and completely fearless. When we were small children, he was a climber-on-top-of-wardrobes, and a jumper-off-the-wardrobe-and-onto-the-bed. Once, he banged his mouth on the metal bedstead, and the pillows were covered with blood from his cut lip. He used to make a tent out of one of my grandmother's royal blue blankets, which was bound with wide, blue satin ribbon, and we'd lie in the blanket-tent and pretend the woolly blueness was the night sky.

*

From an early age, I knew exactly what I wanted to be when I grew up. My relations were constantly asking me to sing and admiring me greatly whenever I did. I loved dressing up in my aunt Sara's (tiny) shoes and my mother's scarves and jewels. Therefore, as soon as I saw my first movie, I knew at once that what I was going to be was "A Star." Musicals were my favorite kind of movie. When I was nine years old and we lived in North Borneo, my friend Monica and I used to go and gaze at Jane Powell, Ann Miller, Kathryn Grayson, and Esther Williams, and our games reflected what we saw. There was a beach at the bottom of our garden that looked much like the set for *Pagan Love Song,* so Esther Williams-type cavortings in the water went on a lot. The boys we knew always wanted to play cowboys, and once I was tied to a tree for hours while my friends disappeared to have a gunfight or organize a stampede somewhere else.

*

My aunt Sara was married to a crazy American journalist called Mike. He and my dad were great friends. Mike would come home late, late at night, sometimes in the early hours of the morning, after working in the offices of the *Jerusalem Post,* and he would always wake me up to play with me, sing to me, or read to me.

"With my mother, Leah Hamburger Weston," 1945. (Photograph courtesy of Adèle Geras.)

I guess my mother must have objected, but Mike was like a tornado of enthusiasm and he loved me so much! He and Sara never had children, so they shared me with my parents. I didn't mind. I was a terrible sleeper as a young child.

*

My children have lived in the same two streets throughout their childhood. They both went to local schools, and all the shopkeepers in the area have known them since birth. Until I was eleven, I never stayed at any school for longer than a year or two. This was because my father (after 1948, when the state of Israel came into being) joined the British Colonial Service and was sent to all kinds of places (Nigeria, North Borneo, The Gambia, Tanzania) as long as the British Empire lasted. When people asked him, towards the end of his life, why he didn't simply retire and live in England, he'd answer: "Oh, I couldn't live in England . . . the policemen don't salute me!" He was only partly joking. As a lawyer, and later a High Court judge, he enjoyed being quite a big fish in an exotic pond.

*

We spent some months in London before my father took up his first colonial post, in Nigeria. I remember almost everything as black and white, like an old movie, but one place was a monument to color and glamour and luxury and light. This was Lyons Corner House in Marble Arch. We used to go there to eat fish-and-chips and multicolored ice creams in silver dishes, or sundaes in tall glasses. I remember it as vast, and brightly lit, and were there really marble columns rising up to the ceiling? Certainly the waitresses wore black dresses and frilly white caps and starched white aprons, and tunes from Ivy Benson's All-Girl Band poured over us like musical maple syrup as we sat there. I thought Lyons Corner House was Paradise. Outside Lyons, London in the early fifties was a dark place. John Christie, the serial killer, was at large. My mother has always maintained that he, Christie, once spoke to her in the street. It's perfectly possible. We were living in a hotel in Notting Hill Gate, right round the corner from the infamous Rillington Place.

*

In my school in Ibadan, Nigeria, we read about English history from a fat book called *Our Island Story,* which concentrated on dramatic episodes like the execution of Mary, Queen of Scots. The ladies in the colored illustrations were dressed in wonderful costumes and looked noble and tragic. I don't recollect ever being taught mathematics at this age. My friends didn't believe me when I told them I was born in Jerusalem. "You can't have been," they'd say. "Jerusalem is in heaven."

*

My father read poetry aloud to me all the time. He never cared whether I understood it fully, but he would always explain if necessary. His brother, my uncle Reggie, was a painter living in Paris, and my father loved Paris better than anywhere else on earth. Every time my parents had home leave, we would spend some time there. We used to walk round art galleries for hours at a time. I had an exercise book into which I stuck postcards of paintings we had looked at together. All those galleries must have made an impression on me. Somewhere in my attic there is a story I wrote when I was nearly ten. It is about a mouse called Squeaker de Whiskers Blanches, who lived with his family of many baby mice behind a Cézanne in the Jeu de Paumes. I still love looking at paintings, and in Manchester we are lucky to have wonderful museums and art galleries. In the Whitworth there is a casket embroidered most beautifully by a young girl of twelve in 1644. Her name was Hannah Smith, and I've been obsessed by this casket since I first saw it, and I've written poems, stories, and even a play about it.

*

My father's work took him all around Nigeria. My mother and I followed him. In a place called Onitcha we lived in an enormous house with bats roosting in the roofspace. They came out at night and flopped around the cavernous rooms. We used to retire under the gauzy mosquito nets at twilight to hide from them. Around the house, blood red lilies grew in terrifying profusion.

*

In Kano, I fell ill with jaundice. My memory of the place is of somewhere very yellow, both because of my illness and because of the yellow walls of all the houses, and the general sandiness and desertlike feel of the town.

*

In Lagos, I had a friend called Alero, who had lots of brothers and sisters. I envied her and spent the night at her house as often as my parents would allow. We used to play a game called "What is the time, Mr. Wolf?" following Alero's big brother, Peter, until the horrifying moment when he turned around, crying "Dinner time!" and chased us into the hibiscus bushes. We knew the wolf was Peter, really, but there was always that heart-stopping second just before we saw his face when we thought: maybe he's changed . . . maybe his face has stretched and grown and become furry . . . maybe his teeth are sharp and white . . . maybe he truly will eat us up.

*

The house we live in now was built in 1911. It stands at the bottom of a cul-de-sac in a leafy suburb of

Adèle, about seven or eight. (Photograph courtesy of Adèle Geras.)

Manchester. We have been in this house for twelve years. The garden is tiny, but in it there is a wonderful spreading camellia which is now covered in pink flowers. In a couple of weeks, the yellow blossom on the laburnum tree will appear. All the rooms are well-proportioned, with high ceilings, and every window has a border of stained glass flowers at the top. The utility room (where the washing machine lives; where brooms and ironing boards are kept) has wooden walls. I have stuck hundreds and hundreds of pictures all over them: postcards, photographs, pictures cut from magazines. It's another kind of patchwork.

*

In North Borneo we lived in a town called Jesselton. Our house was a long bungalow with a verandah running along one side of it. There were halves of coconut shells hanging from the verandah roof, and in these orchids grew and grew, looking more like dragons than like flowers. The whole building was raised on stilts, because rain in Borneo means business, and roads turn into rivers overnight.

*

The school hut in Jesselton was a palm-thatched rickety affair, also up on stilts. Our teacher's name was Mrs. Arrowsmith, and she was married to a policeman, who drove her to school each day. Monica and I used to get to the hut especially early so that we could watch them kissing good-bye in the car. Mrs. Arrowsmith was delightful, but everyone over the age of eleven was at boarding school back in England. Monica and I were great readers of Enid Blyton's "Malory Towers" books and could hardly wait to sample midnight feasts and pleated tunics. My father thought that English food would put roses in my cheeks; that English teachers would teach me Latin and even manage to steer me through the mathematical rapids I'd been cheerfully avoiding all through my early childhood.

*

I may not have been any great shakes at arithmetic, but as a young child, I wrote up a storm. I wrote long poems about characters from Greek mythology; I wrote abut Helen of Troy. Behind our house, the purple mass of Mount Kinabalu rose into the clouds, and I wrote a story about a dragon who lived at the top of the mountain for a competition run by the local newspaper, the *Sabah Times*. I have always adored competitions and still go in for as many as I can. These days, it's mostly poetry competitions I favour, but I'm happy to turn my hand to stories as well. My dragon tale won first prize, and I was presented with a grey and gold Parker 51 pen-and-pencil set. I think it was the lustre of the dull gold, the sheen of the velvet lining the case, and above all the possibilities of all those words locked-up in the ink of the pen, the lead of the pencil that started my lifelong love affair with writing implements. Certainly having the story printed on the front page of the newspaper, with my name at the top, was a thrilling moment. I have no idea where that Parker set is now, although I can remember having it when I first arrived at my boarding school in January, 1955.

*

Dragons are everywhere in Borneo. Chinese shops had enormous dragon-masks hanging from the walls, and the creature is depicted on every available surface. I still have a silk dressing gown with a beautiful, twisting, blue dragon embroidered onto the back. The silk is brittle and yellowed, but the fabulous beast is as bright and vibrant as he was over forty years ago.

*

Wherever I go, I glance into windows. I've done it for as long as I can remember. Whether I'm walking, or on a bus or train, my head is permanently turned to one side, looking for the possibility of a glimpse, however brief, of other lives. When I write, the same process takes place in my head. I'm looking into imaginary windows, which I've devised for myself, and asking such questions as: who lives here? What's happening in their lives? What time of day is it? What season? Who, in particular, am I watching? What sort of story will it be? The most important question of all is: where am I going to situate myself as the writer in relation to the people in my story? It's as though I had a camera in my hand. What shall I focus on? Where will the edges of the picture come?

*

Where do ideas spring from? It's something which writers are asked over and over again. There are all sorts of answers to it, which can be reduced to one which sounds silly: ideas come from the writer. Well, OK, that's obvious enough, but what exactly does it mean? It means that our stories, our poems, come from our memories and our obsessions; from places we remember, from objects we are drawn to; from people who have interested or frightened or enchanted us; from the rooms of our childhood and the thick soup of everything in the world that we have read, seen, heard, smelled, eaten, and lived. A questioner might then say: fine, but what things in particular obsess and fascinate you? What is it that makes you want to write?

In my case, quite often, it's specific places. My own Ima Gdola's house in *My Grandmother's Stories* and *Golden Windows;* North Borneo in *Other Echoes;* my boarding school in *The Tower Room* and its sequels and so on. There are also places I see which ask for a story to be written about them. For instance, the old junk shop (now sadly closed) called J.F. Blood and Sons which begged for a vampire tale that I have now at last written, and which appears in a collection of ghost stories set in Manchester.

I love describing houses and rooms and enjoy reading books which pay proper attention to fixtures and fittings. I love describing almost anything: clothes, food, scenery—you name it. It's a substitute, I think, for not being able to paint. I try not to let this tendency hold up the narrative, and I've developed quite a critical eye and a fairly ruthless blue pencil which I hope sees to it that the descriptions don't go on too long or become too boring.

Here are some of the other things which appear again and again in my work: cats, sets of Russian nesting dolls, families with many children, older sisters (resourceful, clever) with younger, weaker brothers, Jerusalem, old women, photographs, jewellery, fabric, clothes, the sea, homelessness and exile, and every conceivable kind of handiwork, especially the ones (sewing, tapestry, embroidery) at which I am quite useless.

*

My English teachers at school, Miss Godfray and Miss Sturgis, stand like ghosts at my shoulder while I am going through my work, correcting it. They were eagle-eyed and swift to pounce on adjectives that were surplus to requirements, two words where one would do, redundant clauses, and anything at all they regarded as "showing off." Their red ink pens used to draw neat lines through entire paragraphs and write the damning word: "irrelevant" in the left-hand margin. Now I have to do their work for myself, and I hope I'm getting better at it. As well as my teachers, there was also my father. He was a great one for giving advice about what he considered to be Good English. It's thanks to him that I haven't dreamed of splitting an infinitive since I was ten years old, and I bet his shade is groaning somewhere every time someone uses the phrase: "at the end of the day" when they do not mean "evening."

*

But I *am* a show-off. I have always loved performing. I talk too much, in spite of eight years at a boarding school where teachers were forever saying: "Do be quiet, Adèle!" It seems I'm incapable of quiet. I am noisy. My daughter Sophie once referred to my "fluorescent voice," and I suppose that's accurate. I have the vocal equivalent of day-glo socks. This is a disadvantage most of the time, but used to be a terrific asset in the days when I was singing on stage. Microphones were unnecessary for the most part, and there wasn't a problem about the back row of the audience catching the words.

*

During World War II, North Borneo had been occupied by the Japanese. My friend Monica and her brother Ronnie had both been born in a prisoner-of-war camp. There was a thin volume on the top shelf of our bookcase called *Kinabalu Guerrillas,* which was the only book in the house my parents had forbidden me to read. It became in my mind something like the locked room in the Bluebeard story. I had to know what was in it. One day while they were busy somewhere else, I climbed up and found the book and opened it. It detailed all the atrocities of the recent Occupation and I put it back wishing I had never read it. But I did read it, all the way through to the end, even though I could have stopped at any time.

*

My first appearance in public was at a Red Cross concert in Jesselton in 1952. I sang "You Made Me Love You" and "Pretty Little Black-eyed Suzie" in a tent set up in the middle of a field. I realized then that there was no sound in the world like applause. Between 1952 and 1967, I sang at every possible opportunity. I sang in the choir at school; I sang (accompanied by a guitarist from Liverpool) in the streets of Paris in the summer of 1963, and made a fortune by passing a hat around

the assembled tourists. I sang all through my college years, in student reviews, and shows, and cabarets. I sang on stage in the West End of London, on the Edinburgh Festival Fringe, and even in the Royal Shakespeare Theatre at Stratford-upon-Avon. Later on, I continued to sing as I pushed my babies along the pavements in their buggies, but by then it was under my breath. I only let rip at the children's bedtime, when my husband and I would take it in turn to do the lullaby session. My specialties were "Bye-bye Blackbird," "Lulu's Back in Town" and, best of all, "Over the Rainbow." There's a tiny part of me still that imagines I'm really Judy Garland.

*

I was happy at Roedean, my boarding school. I was a noisy, exuberant child who was longing for the company of other people . . . the more the merrier. I was clever enough to do well, but not clever enough (dreadful, still, at math and science and appalling at all sporting activities) to intimidate anyone. I was a good chameleon, finding it easy to blend in with what was required to please a set of strangers. I am not obstinate, or single-minded, or brave, so I found it easy to accommodate myself to quite often silly rules and regulations. I was homesick at first, but not cripplingly so, and easily distracted by the next nice thing that happened. I've always been like that. I find it difficult to be unhappy for long, and count myself extremely fortunate that, for the most part, my life has proceeded smoothly. I think this incapacity for misery may be inherited. My father always maintained that he was allergic to unhappiness, and actually ran a temperature on some occasions when life was going badly for him.

*

All through my school days, I had no proper answer to the question: "Where do you live?" At boarding school, thoughts of home are very important, and there was much discussion of possessions, rooms, gardens, and so forth. There were photographs of parents and siblings standing next to flower beds and favourite trees, and references to dresses and shoes left behind in "my cupboard" because they were unsuitable for school. I had a home too, in the sense that my parents lived somewhere, but because that somewhere wasn't in Britain, I only went there once a year for the long summer holidays. Christmas and Easter holidays were spent moving round the country from one friend's home to another, and my base was my aunt Vivienne's house in Rhiwbina, a suburb of Cardiff. Vivienne was divorced. She lived with her mother, Messoda, and her two sons, Wyn and John. The house was small, in a long street of other small houses. I stayed there so often that I even had a circle of friends, and together we went to Saturday morning movies at the Monico cinema. Vivienne wore bright red lipstick and filled the house with laughter. Messoda cooked Moroccan dishes in the

"My father, Laurence Weston," about 1959. (Photograph courtesy of Adèle Geras.)

kitchen, and Wyn and John did little boy-stuff in the field behind the house.

*

I always enjoyed staying with friends. In one place, I went riding with Jillian, and discovered how terrifyingly high up a horse's back is. One of my friends was called Patricia, and she was the youngest daughter of the school doctor. Their house in Brighton seemed the perfect home to me, and their family (three daughters and a son) the perfect family. I suppose they must have been very well-off. The garden was huge and well-stocked with shrubs, and there were at least five bedrooms. I had another friend called Kaye, whose parents ran a public house in Portsmouth. Her mother had to get up at six o'clock to make sausage rolls and pies for the day. Kaye also had a very good-looking elder brother called Derek, with whom I was hopelessly infatuated.

*

My parents, living in The Gambia in a town that was then called Bathurst but is now called Banjul, were part of a circle that included many French expatriates, who had somehow slipped over the border from the neighbouring French colony of Senegal. My mother worked for a man called Marc, who was divinely handsome and more than twice my age. I fell in love with him, but an occasional dance at the Club was as close as I got. The summer after I was fourteen, I met another Frenchman, named Jean. He had the most extraordinary turquoise eyes, and he was the first man to kiss me properly. I returned to school after the summer holidays full of infor-

mation for my contemporaries, and with my French conversation greatly improved. It was also in The Gambia that I began to get some inkling of the pains of love. My parents had a good friend who was having an affair with someone who was not her husband. She broke up with her lover in the end, and I eavesdropped on long and tearful sessions between her and my mother, which often went on late into the night. My father used to drive me the five miles or so to the Club whenever there were dances. He used to sit in the Reading Room, looking at back numbers of the magazines from London, or else chatting to his friends at the bar. When the dance was over, he would drive me home. He didn't mind how late it was, but he would never let me come home with any of the young men, who were all, in his opinion "drunk as Bandusian goats." I do not know what a Bandusian goat is, and have never heard the expression from anyone but my father. After The Gambia, my parents went to Tanzania, which was then called Tanganyika. My father was a judge by then, and our house was next door to the home of Julius Nyerere, who later became president. In the evening the fragrance of cloves from the offshore island of Zanzibar drifted in on the sea breeze. I loved Dar es Salaam. I spent three summers there, and I was old enough by then to do some holiday work. I had a job in a dress shop one summer; I did some schools broadcasting for Tanganyika Radio, reciting long passages of nineteenth-century poetry onto tape for the benefit of students who were far from any teacher. I also showed tourists round the town. Many ships docked in Dar es Salaam, and I conducted excursions in both French and English to places of interest like the sisal factory. My chief memory of those days is of endless barbecues on the beach and dinners at the Aquarium Club. My mother spent a great deal of time turning up the hems of all her dresses so that they would be short enough for me. Then when she wanted to wear them herself, she would take them down again. During my last summer holiday in Tanzania, I took some driving lessons. I loved driving, but failed my test. From that day to this, cars have somehow never been conveniently at hand, so I still don't drive and we have never owned a car. We live in a city well-served by buses; I'm mad about trains, and I've always taken taxicabs at the drop of a hat.

*

I write and receive a great many letters. I wait for the postman every day. Getting mail in the morning makes me happy, and not getting any lowers my spirits in a quite irrational way. Fortunately, being a writer generates a lot of post, and I'm slightly dreading the day when everything becomes electronic. There's no delightful slitting open of envelopes on the Internet. This passion for the post dates from my days at Roedean. It was very important indeed to have frequent letters. Our House Mistress, Miss Ratcliffe, would bring the pile into breakfast with her, and after finishing her slice of toast and marmalade, she would read out the names of everyone who had a letter. We used to squint at the pile, trying to catch a glimpse of distinctive stationery, in my case the blue and red flashes along the edges of an airmail envelope. A writing case had been part of my equipment when I was first sent to school. It was a beautiful red affair with a gold zip, and it contained airletter cards, a pad of Basildon Bond paper, a packet of envelopes, and a book of stamps. Every Sunday morning, we sat in the prep room writing home. The prefect in charge used to chalk a list of "news items" on the board, for those who didn't otherwise have anything to tell their parents. As I grew older, I searched for more and more elaborate paper. I went through deckled edges, and all manner of fancy pastel colors, before settling at last on the austere (and I hoped elegant) combination of Three Candlesticks notepaper in cream, and always, always the blackest possible ink. I modelled my handwriting on that of a favourite teacher, and one of the reasons I like writing everything in longhand first is because I actually enjoy the way my handwriting looks.

*

Breaking friends with someone was what caused me the most misery during my school days. Not being picked for this or that gang was a tragedy, and one or other of my companions preferring someone else an absolute torment. Failures weren't too much fun, either. I failed all the math exams I ever took, and only managed to scrape a pass in my G.C.E. paper (which I had to have, to qualify for any college) after three attempts. I was also always the last to be picked for any team game whatsoever.

*

The author as she appeared in a show called "Four Degrees Over," 1966. (Photograph courtesy of Adèle Geras.)

I wanted to be an actress. I wanted to go to RADA, the Royal Academy of Dramatic Art. My parents and my teachers wanted me to go to university. My father was a dreadful snob when it came to universities. He had been at Oxford, so that was where he wanted me to go. The Sorbonne in Paris he also regarded as quite respectable, and Cambridge came a very poor third. No other places could even be considered. I agreed to stay on at school and take the entrance exams, partly because by then I had met a young man who was at Cambridge and was very much in love with him, and partly because I realized that one could do an enormous amount of acting along with the studying. The deal was, I could go to RADA if neither Oxford nor Cambridge accepted me. As it turned out, I went to St. Hilda's College, Oxford, and spent three wonderful years singing and acting and enjoying life and reading modern languages from time to time as well. I've written a memoir of that time, called *Yesterday,* but have so far resisted the temptation to produce yet another Oxford novel.

*

One evening, about a month after I arrived at St. Hilda's, I was in a pub called The Eastgate. We were on our way to a party. Then someone came in with the news of President Kennedy's assassination. We all went back to our colleges and watched those horrifying images blazing across our television screens for the very first time.

*

When I know what I want to write about, that's when the fun begins. First of all, I daydream about the story, turning it over and over in my mind while I'm cooking, or waiting at the bus stop, or pushing a trolley along the aisles of a supermarket. This part of the writing process is pure pleasure, like playing a game of dolls' houses in my head, and if I'm not careful, it can go on for months. Decisions have to be made now. Whose point of view should I use to tell this tale? Will it be in the first person (which is easier in some ways, but very limiting), or the third person, or a combination of the two? Even after I've decided, I may change my mind and have to rewrite chunks of the book, but I'm ready for this.

*

I started smoking when I was sixteen and didn't give it up until I was nearly forty. I come from a long line of dedicated smokers. My mother has smoked since her childhood; so has my aunt Sara. Their aunt, whom I remember as an ancient crone with prunelike wrinkles, used to exist on black coffee and fierce, untipped cigarettes. In Ima Gdola's apartment, on the Sabbath when smoking is forbidden, all the grown-ups used to make small excursions either to visit a neighbour, or go up to the roof for a quick puff.

From when I was about eight years old, one of my tasks, whenever my mother was dressing to go out, was to move her lipstick, powder compact, comb, and so on from her daytime bag to her evening one. She would sit at the dressing table and put her hair up with long, black pins and spray herself with "Arpege." My other duty was to put one of her cigarettes in my mouth and light it, and then hand it to her, making sure there was an ashtray nearby.

I can truthfully say that I enjoyed every single cigarette I ever smoked, but also that now that I've given it up, I don't miss it or even think about it.

*

After I gave up smoking, I took up knitting to keep my hands busy. I was clumsy at first, but I'm very proficient now, and do all sorts of complicated things: Fair Isle and Aran patterns and intarsia knitting and so forth. Kaffe Fassett, the knitwear genius who transformed the craft in the eighties is a hero of mine, and the character of Filomena (the grandmother in the Fantora books who can tell the future from her knitting) was inspired by

his example. He has also said something which I have adopted as a kind of motto. It works for almost everything: "If in doubt, add twenty more colors." I always have some knitting on the go, just as I'm always in the middle of a piece of writing, and the comparisons between the two processes are many. For instance, if you've made a mistake ten rows back, it's no good hoping that no one will notice. Nor is it any good trying to patch it up later. Much the best method is to unpick the work and start over again. This is what I do when I'm writing as well. I read yesterday's piece and fix it up before I go on.

*

When Sophie was five, we had a cat called Pobble. He was a beautiful tabby, with a funny, sideways sort of walk. He didn't live very long. Our house in those days was near a main road, and Pobble became a victim of the traffic. Toey's life was even shorter. He was a lovely ginger-and-white kitten. He used to follow me or my husband when we took Sophie to school. He, too, died on the road. Pobble and Toey were buried in the garden, with rose bushes to mark their graves. We all agreed that the misery of losing the cats was not something we wanted to go through again, so we spent several years with nothing more thrilling than a couple of stick insects to brighten our lives. Jenny was still a baby when Toey died, and as she grew older, she started to nag, gently, and say she wanted a cat. We agreed in the end. We no longer live near the main road, and Mimi has been with us for nearly five years. As she is a female, she is more home-loving than adventurous, and she is easily the most beautiful, clever, affectionate, and thoroughly wonderful cat in the whole world, and we are all devoted to her. She is usually called Meems. I have written about all three of our cats. Toey has a whole small book called after him, and Pobble appears in it as well. I've written many poems about Meems and also one about Pobble.

*

A person's writing style is largely unconscious, and it's almost impossible for a writer to analyse the elements of her own work. The main aim I have when I write is to find a suitable language for the story I'm telling. The right words depend on who the people in the story are. To put it at its most obvious: the words of a group of young male soldiers in an Army camp will be different from those of two old ladies in turn-of-the-century Cheltenham. The setting, the time, the characters—all these dictate the language, and it's almost as though, for each story, I put on a different costume, and different kinds of words come out. I regard writing as another form of acting and always see the action unfolding in my mind's eye as though it were a movie running in my head.

*

"My husband, Norm Geras, at his desk," 1994. (Photograph courtesy of Adèle Geras.)

I met my husband, Norman Geras, at Oxford. We were married on August 7th, 1967, and in the words of the music hall song: "It Don't Seem a Day Too Much." We came to live in Manchester because Norm had been appointed a junior lecturer in the Government Department of the university. We have lived here ever since. It's a handsome and exciting city with a long and illustrious history, and not at all the black hellhole we had been led to expect from rumours we'd heard in the south. I would have married Norm whatever he'd been called, but "Geras" is a wonderful name to have if you write for children. It puts you on the same shelf as Jane Gardam, Leon Garfield, and Alan Garner, and just a bit along from Anne Fine. "Geras" has not been an entirely trouble-free name, however. Hardly anyone pronounces it properly. It has a hard "G" and rhymes with "terrace," but I've had all sorts of variations from "giraffe" to "grass."

*

August 7th, 1967; June 28th, 1971; April 19th, 1977: these are the three best days of my life. The first was my wedding day, and the other two dates are Sophie's and Jenny's birthdays. I never write about my immediate family. First of all, I would have to tell the truth and I prefer invention. Secondly, real people are always much more complex and ungraspable than the richest of fictional characters. I have no such inhibitions about my

teachers. I've used them and their clothes and habits over and over again in many of my books. Creating characters is a little like playing with those old heads-bodies-legs books where pages are divided into three sections and you can turn them to make all sorts of combinations.

*

I wasn't a very good French teacher. I enjoyed having a captive audience, but I lacked any kind of authority. The only way I could manage to control the more unruly classes was by providing them with a kind of cabaret. I had had no training. In those days, a degree was considered to be enough of' a qualification. I couldn't think of any way to avoid the basic learning of vocabulary and grammar which everyone needed to know before they could go on to do the more pleasant things, like reading the literature. I met one of my old pupils in a school I visited last year. She was Deputy Head of History, which made me feel very ancient indeed. Another ex-pupil wrote to me recently, telling me her twelve-year-old child enjoyed my books. Where, as Villon used to say, are the snows of yesteryear?

*

I am a library junkie. If I can't go into my library on an almost daily basis, I become seriously twitchy and nervous. On Wednesday, when my local branch is closed, I'll go to the shops that lie in the opposite direction and take advantage of a branch that closes on Thursdays. My idea of Hell is living in the depths of the countryside, hours away from the nearest library—and cinema!

*

I never gave children's books a single thought until I started reading picture books to Sophie. I've been a voracious reader all my life, but as children we never had beautiful, full-color, specially designed volumes written just for us. Some of the books we discovered with Sophie and Jenny (*Where the Wild Things Are, The Sign on Rosie's Door, Mouse Tales, The Stone Doll of Sister Brute*) were magnificent, and Norm and I read them over and over again with enormous pleasure to ourselves. Not every book, however, was of this standard. Some were, quite frankly, dreadful. It's reciting stuff like that night after night, which makes many exasperated parents feel: "I could do so much better." Not everyone goes on actually to write a story, and I don't suppose I would have done so, either, were it not for a competition in the London *Times* newspaper. As soon as I saw the contest announced, memories of my wonderful Parker pen-and-pencil set flashed into my mind. I wrote a story and sent it off, and although it did not win, it did become the starting point for *Apricots at Midnight.* It's a ghost story called "Rose," and the moment I'd finished it, I knew that this was what I wanted to do from now on. It was completely pleasurable. You simply made things up; gave words to your best fantasies. You could do anything you wanted: travel in time and space, re-invent yourself, redesign the universe if you felt so inclined. You could do all this without any special equipment and without having to go to an office or factory. You could do it at the kitchen table, while your baby sucked on a rusk. You could pick your work up when your child was napping and put it down when she woke up. Best of all, you could tell yourself stories . . . once upon a time . . .

*

I am extremely lazy. Having failed to win the competition, I decided that as picture-book texts were very short, they would be an easy place to begin. I was wrong. Picture books are expensive to produce and are perhaps, the very worst way to start, particularly if the writer is not also the artist. It was only after two years of wall-to-wall rejection slips that I discovered the best place to begin was with what are called "series books." I wrote a story for a series called "Gazelles," published by Hamish Hamilton. It was called *Tea at Mrs. Manderby's.* They accepted it, and it appeared in 1976. Since then, I have published nearly fifty books, quite a

"Our daughter Sophie," 1989. (Photograph courtesy of Adèle Geras.)

number of which have also come out in the United-States. My novels and stories appear on the children's list. I write for very young children and also for what publishers call "young adults." If I am working on something I hope a five-year-old will like, I will not focus on the marital or financial difficulties of a sixty-year-old advertising executive. But—and I would like to emphasize this—I do not regard writing for children as an easier option or in any way inferior to writing for grown-ups. I try occasionally to think of an appropriate answer to the person who once asked me: "Will you write a real book when you've had the practice?" I was speechless at the time and I still am. The main differences between "grown-up" books and children's books are that the former are much longer and the latter generally (though not invariably) have children or teenagers as the main characters. Many writers of teenage novels are producing work that is infinitely more complicated and demanding than much of the fiction found on the adult lists. And (abracadabra! the magic of the movies!) the moment a book is metamorphosed into a film, it becomes perfect for every single member of the family.

*

When I'm writing for younger children, I try to keep my audience in mind, and often make life easier for myself by having the main character or narrator be the same age as the readers for whom the book is intended. Beyond a certain level of understanding (and I don't know at what biological age this takes place), I write to please myself. That sounds selfish, but what I mean is: I try to write the kind of book that I enjoy reading. I am the first person who has to be absorbed and interested, crying at all the sad bits and falling in love with the hero. I read every word I ever write aloud, and am amazed to discover that some people find this unnecessary. How they seek out clumsy rhythms and hideous repetitions is a mystery to me.

*

I try to put off writing as long as I possibly can. I think about the book constantly, imagining what the cover will look like, composing reviews, fantasising about interviews on the television—anything to push back the time when I actually have to put pen to paper. Starting to write is terrifying. It's like diving into a swimming pool, or like the first few seconds on stage, when every word you ever knew seems to have flown out of your head. But (and it's important to remember this) once the first sentence is written, the worst is over. This is true even if the words you have put down are the purest rubbish, and you're about to cross them out. All the other technical problems you meet (and there will be plenty of those) won't be anything like as bad, because by then you will be into the process of writing, anxious for your story to become the one you've envisaged during your daydreams.

*

The original "Girls in the Velvet Frame." The author's mother on the left, second row; her aunt Sara at the back. (Photograph courtesy of Adèle Geras.)

One thing led to another. When *Tea at Mrs. Manderby's* was published, the idea of writing a novel of about thirty-five thousand words never occurred to me. It was Linda Jennings, my first editor at Hamish Hamilton, who took a seven-thousand-word story I had written and pointed out to me that it would work much better as a novel. I reread the manuscript and saw at once that she was right. The result was *The Girls in the Velvet Frame.* The inspiration for this story comes from a real photograph of my mother and four of my aunts, taken when they were young girls. I used to look at it and wonder: what was the occasion? Why had these girls been dressed up and taken to the photographer's studio? I also wanted to write about sisters together. *Little Women* was my favourite book as a child, and this is the same sort of tale.

*

Short stories are pleasant to write simply because they are short. You can congratulate yourself on finishing

something after a few days instead of after a period of months. Collections of linked short stories (*Apricots at Midnight, Golden Windows, My Grandmother's Stories*) sometimes take longer to put together than a novel. I'm so delighted when story number one is done to my satisfaction that I'm quite likely to celebrate by taking a week off. It's sometimes said that a good short story is harder to achieve than a novel, and in many ways this is true. You have to ensure that nothing extraneous creeps in; that you have set the boundaries of the action in exactly the right place; that you enter the narrative at the precise moment that will ensure the maximum emotional punch; that you don't have too many characters jostling for attention and, above all, that your tale has a beginning, middle, and end (though not necessarily in that order, as someone once said). The short story is a restrictive form, but sometimes restrictions are liberating, and it's in a short story that you can experiment with such things as starting at the end and working through to the beginning, of braiding together different narrative strands.

*

I love writing ghost stories. I find them comforting. When so much of the real world is menacing and difficult, while there are real wars, real hunger, and real poverty all about us, it's pleasant to contemplate terrors that are happening to someone else, and which, moreover, couldn't posssibly be true. There . . . my secret is out. I don't believe in ghosts, but I do very strongly believe in the present-ness of the past in our lives, and also in the ability of places to convey atmosphere. Anywhere where people have suffered bears the imprint of their pain like damp. You don't have to visit goals to see the truth of this—just go into the home of any unhappy family.

*

A sense of place is important to me, both as a reader and as a writer. It's what remains with us long after we have forgotten the intricacies of the plot. Usually, I enjoy describing everything, but just recently, I have retold eight fairy tales for a wonderful British artist named Louise Brierley in 1996. These stories were exhilarating to write. On the one hand, I did not want, by so much as an adjective, to influence Louise's vision. On the other hand, I very much wanted to write the kind of words in the kind of order that would inspire her. I haven't yet seen the pictures, but I was happy writing a much sparer, leaner kind of prose for a change. I also felt that to do it in this way was much truer to the spirit of these old tales, which in their traditional forms give us almost no description at all. "There was once a merchant who had three daughters. . . ." What could you

"Our daughter Jenny and her favorite author," 1994. (Photograph courtesy of Adèle Geras.)

possibly add to that which would not remove some of its impact?

*

Whenever I write a book that is to be illustrated, the biggest treat is getting a first glimpse of the artwork. I've been very fortunate in most of my illustrators, and those of my books whose pictures I actually dislike are few and far between. Sometimes (as with the fairy tales) the bringing together of my words and someone's pictures is the publisher's idea, but sometimes I write a story and suggest illustrators whom I think might be suitable. I walk around bookstores looking at everything I can, and when the work of a particular artist catches my eye, I make a note of their name, just in case. . . .

*

I write a great many love stories. All my novels are in some sense love stories, and so are quite a few of my short fictions. I am quite unashamed about this. Writers of love stories are seen as even lower down the literary pecking order than children's writers, and children's

writers who write love stories . . . horrors! They (the scornful ones) think: "cheap romances" and "sloppy magazine stories" the minute the word "love" is uttered, but I throw *Wuthering Heights* and *Madame Bovary* and *Jane Eyre* and *Anna Karenina* at them, like a vampire-hunter hurling cloves of garlic at her prey.

*

I wish I could paint. All that walking round art galleries as a small child, all that closeness, in my uncle Reggie's studio in Paris, to the wonderful fragrances of turpentine and oils, has made me very conscious of how things look. The fact that I cannot draw so much as a cup and saucer that resemble what they're supposed to be is a sadness. I overcome this by writing poems, which I often think of as the pictures I'm incapable of painting. I don't write very many, but I have published one collection, work has appeared in magazines and anthologies, and I have won prizes in competitions. Someone once said that working on a poem was like having a secret bar of chocolate hidden in a drawer and taking little nibbles at it from time to time . . . that's exactly how I feel.

*

When I visit schools, boys will sometimes gaze at the covers of my books and I can see a kind of panic in their eyes. These, they can clearly see, are GIRLS' BOOKS. I try to calm them and generally steer them to the ghost stories, or to my two "Fantora" books, which are humorous. Sometimes I try to persuade them that it wouldn't kill them to read a book which had a heroine at its centre. We girls, I say, are perfectly happy to read about boys as heroes. The truth is that you can only write the kind of book that you can write, and much as I may wish to achieve a rip-roaring space adventure, or a tale of warring armies blasting one another to bits, it simply isn't in me. When you come right down to it, it's probably because those are not the kind of books I like to read.

*

I love all my books. I often say they are like children. The points of comparison are many, but the main one is: you love them. Once they go out into the world, there's very little you can do to influence what happens to them. Some succeed, others fail for no reason you can understand; but you love them. The one that preoccupies you (in very much the same way that a pregnancy preoccupies you) is this one . . . the one you're busy writing NOW.

*

The author at stage two of the writing process. (Photograph courtesy of Adèle Geras.)

After travelling a great deal all through my childhood, I suppose to many people my life at the moment may seem uneventful, but to me it is busy and packed with incident, and I'm not only talking about the things that go on in the books. I visit many schools and libraries and give talks about my work; I teach creative writing classes here and there to both adults and children; I go to conferences and book fairs; I write letters. We visit friends, they visit us; we go to the movies; I knit a lot, and I read a lot. . . . My family and friends would say I also never stop talking. There do not seem to be enough hours in the day.

*

Being a writer is such fun that it seems only fair to list some of the less pleasant aspects of the job. Here then is a list of HORRIBLE THINGS:

1) People who write a review of your book without having read it properly.

2) A book you have laboured over being completely ignored.

3) Being left off lists of "recommended reading."

4) Seeing a cover for one of your books that is not only ugly but WRONG.

5) Seeing a book already in the bookstore that is about something you were just going to write yourself.

6) Finding new mistakes in a published book that you never noticed at proof stage.

7) Spotting a misprint on the cover or in the blurb when it's too late to do anything about it.

8) Going to a school to discover that (a) they've never read any one of your books in the past, and (b) they clearly don't intend to read any in the future, since not one single copy has been provided for the children to buy or borrow.

9) Anyone who assumes you must be childish to write for children.

*

Beginnings are important. You have somehow to draw the reader into your words. You have to make them want to stay and listen for a while. Endings are even more important. You want everyone to go away happy. I'm a great believer in happy endings in fiction, and I try and fix it in such a way that everyone closes the book with some kind of satisfaction. In the case of this autobiographical piece, it's a little more difficult. I think I shall simply say "Goodbye" and close with a poem which expresses something of what I feel about writing, about patchwork, and about life. Good-bye. . . .

Adèle Geras contributed the following update to *SATA* in 2007:

I've just reread the entry I wrote in 1995 and now, a dozen years later, much of what I said in it still applies. I haven't changed my opinion about my own work, nor about the horrible things that sometimes attend it, though mostly it continues to be huge fun and something I still enjoy doing very much. I'm now nearly at an age when people begin to consider retirement, but I appear to have taken on even more work. This is the story of the last dozen years.

The first thing to say is that when looking at the photographs of our daughters, I see how time has passed. Sophie is now a published and acclaimed poet and novelist and writes under the name of Sophie Hannah. She has her own Web site, www.sophiehannah.com. Jenny works for Macmillan, the publisher, and both sisters are married—to two brothers! Sophie and her husband have two gorgeous children, so I've become a devoted granny too. No one tells you how marvellous that experience will be.

My husband has retired. He's now emeritus professor at the University of Manchester, but his main occupation these days is blogging and his site has acquired a world-wide reputation. He blogs at http://normblog.typepad.com/normblog/.

One thing that's gone are the notebooks. Alas and alack, I now have little excuse to buy them because I have gone over completely to computers. It happened like this. In 1999, I was commissioned to write my novel *Troy,* which I knew would be much longer than my previous books. I thought I'd risk typing it straight onto the computer, otherwise the whole handwriting/typing process would take much too long. It worked so well that I've never looked back and am now devoted to my laptop. *Troy* changed a lot for me. Since 1995, I've written something like forty new books, and it's true that some of those are quite short, and for quite young children. I have, however, taken a turn that's led me into writing longer YA books, like *Troy* and its follow-up (though not its sequel!), *Ithaka.*

One of the side effects of the Harry Potter phenomenon is that we're now allowed to write books of whatever length we feel is right for the story. Publishers can no longer say, *oh, but children can't read a book that long!* Before Harry, I was always told that forty thousand words was the maximum. Now, anything goes, length-wise, and I took full advantage of this with both *Troy* and *Ithaka.*

Troy tells the story of the last days of the Trojan War through the eyes of two young sisters. It was very successful indeed, both in the UK, where it was shortlisted for various prizes, and the USA, and also in some European countries. It is more than double the length of any of my previous novels for young adults and I loved writing it. So I was delighted to be asked to do a follow-up with *Ithaka.*

The writing of *Ithaka,* however, was interrupted by a life-changing turn of events. Late in 1999, a friend of mine in publishing suggested that it was time women's fiction stopped being dominated by chick lit. Why weren't there any good, solid novels for grown-up women? Did I have an idea for such a thing? By one of those flukes that sometimes does happen, the plot twist at the end of *Facing the Light* came to me, out of the blue. I wrote an email outlining my idea, was encouraged to write more, and an agent for adult novels asked to look at what I'd done. Laura Cecil, who's been (and still is!) a wonderful agent for my children's books since 1981, said, go for it! The long and the short of the story was that *Facing the Light* was sold to Orion in an extremely good two-book deal and also sold to twenty-two other countries. I had turned, almost overnight, into a Proper Writer for Grown-ups. *Facing the Light* was published in the USA, too, but it did very badly indeed. I cannot think why, but hey, you can't predict these things. It might have had a little to do with the lacklustre cover it was given, but I can't blame that entirely. Since then, I've written two more novels for adults (*Hester's Story* and *Made in Heaven),* and neither of these has been sold in the USA, I assume because the first one did so badly.

So what are my adult books like? Well, the best way to describe the first two is as novels where things that have happened in the past, and secrets that have been hidden for a long time, come back to affect characters in the present. *Facing the Light* takes place over one weekend in the summer at a beautiful house called Willow Court. Leonora is celebrating her seventy-fifth birthday and her family gathers for the party. Throughout the book, we have flashbacks to the past and we discover that all is not what it seems in this family.

Hester's Story is set in another big house, but this time we're in the middle of winter. Hester is a retired ballerina and has a theatre on the grounds of her house where each year a new ballet is premiered. The "let's do the show right here" story that takes place in the present alternates with the story of Hester's life . . . and there is a secret that is revealed during the course of the story.

My third novel, *Made in Heaven,* is entirely different as I didn't want to be typecast. It's about a grand family wedding. Zannah and Adrian are about to get married. There's a lunch party where the two families are going to meet for the first time. When Zannah's mother catches sight of Adrian's stepfather, she collapses and has to leave the party. So begins a story of romance,

Geras with committee members of the Oxford Women's Zionist Society, 2005. (Photograph courtesy of Adèle Geras.)

deception, and preparations for the wedding. My fourth novel is different again and deals with the effects of a malevolently drawn up will. It's called *A Hidden Life* and is due to be published in the UK in 2007.

I feel that any reader of my YA books won't find anything strange or difficult with these books. To me, they are all of a piece with the rest of what I've written. Books have your DNA whatever the age group they're intended for.

The main difference between writing for adults and writing for children, at least in that corner of the adult market that I inhabit, is that money is spent on publicity. So there are posters, advertisements in newspapers, and your novel is at the front of the store and in as many promotions as Orion can get it into. This contrasts with children's marketing, which usually means turning your book face out on the shelf yourself—if the store has stocked it! But it's interesting (and something that a few reviewers picked up on when *Facing the Light* first came out) that my adult books are of a kind that is scarcely ever reviewed in the serious press: women's fiction! The *Guardian* critic said something along the lines that I had leapt from one ghetto to another. The

first ghetto, of course, is children's books. It's also fascinating to me that my YA books are perceived as "literary" and my adult ones as "popular." I just try to write the stories as well as I can and I leave the categorization to others. My aim is still, as it always has been, to give pleasure to readers and to enjoy the process myself as much as I possibly can. I'm happy to say I still do. I don't feel jaded or as though I've got nothing to say, but I do dread the day coming when no more stories occur to me. I face this by refusing even to think about it till it happens. It may not and I hope very much it doesn't.

I haven't stopped writing for children, though, nor do I intend to. There have been several highlights over the last dozen years, apart from *Troy* and *Ithaka*. The artist Christian Birmingham asked me to provide the text for his most beautiful *Sleeping Beauty*. I wrote a YA book I'm very fond of called *Silent Snow, Secret Snow*. Another of my favourite books, *My Grandmother's Stories*, was reissued in the USA with gorgeous new illustrations by Anita Lobel. I wrote *The Orchard Book of Opera Stories* (*Random House Book of Opera Stories* in the USA) and *My First Ballet Stories*, both of which have wonderful artwork to accompany the text.

I also greatly enjoyed writing a series of books called "The Cats of Cuckoo Square" (*Blossom's Revenge, Picasso Perkins, Callie's Kitten,* and *Geejay the Hero),* in which the cats are the narrators, one for each story. A picture book called *Wishes for You (My Wishes for You* in the USA) has done very well indeed in Germany, where it's into its eighth reprint. Another picture book, *From Lullaby to Lullaby,* with illustrations by Kathryn Brown, was published by Simon and Schuster in the USA but never in the UK. Go figure! It's now long out of print.

More successful has been a book called *The Ballet Class,* with cute illustrations by Shelagh McNicholas (*Time for Ballet* in the USA). That's been through several reprints and a sequel is forthcoming, *Little Ballet Star* (in the USA, it will be called *Like a Real Ballerina*).

More recently, I've written two books in a series called the "Historical House," which imagines one house through time, with different girls living in it. My co-writers are Linda Newbery (www.lindanewbery.co.uk) and Ann Turnbull (www.annturnbull.com), and my own titles are *Lizzie's Wish,* and its sequel, *Cecily's Portrait.* It's been great fun to write books that allow you to be completely independent and yet also part of a team. Usborne published the books and further details of all the books in the series can be found on www.usborne.com.

I've also kept up my reviewing and write pieces for both the London *Guardian* and the *Times Educational Supplement,* and also for the online magazine *Armadillo* (www.armadillomagazine.com). I contribute occasional articles to the *Guardian* books blog at http://blogs.guardian.co.uk/books/.

In 2007 I'm one of the judges for the Costa Book Awards (which used to be called the Whitbread Awards) and that's been a terrific experience. I read about fifty children's books and now I've gone forward to be one of the panel deciding who gets the overall prize. This is is chosen from among five categories: First Novel, Novel, Children's Novel, Poetry, and Biography.

Look how scattered with Web addresses this piece is! I have become, instead of a postal junkie, an e-mail addict. I look at the little icon at the bottom of my screen all the time as I'm working, and I try to limit the number of times I go over and read messages or I'd be bobbing backwards and forwards constantly. But I do love the Internet—it's a mind-boggling resource and huge fun at the same time. I said back in 1995 that I love writing ghost stories. I've written one that was published by Orion on March 1, 2007, World Book Day. It's called *Lily: A Ghost Story* and it was written for a series called "Quick Reads," which aims to provide short books for people who find it hard to tackle long stories. I wrote it for adults but it's fine for YA readers as well.

The paperback of *Made in Heaven* is forthcoming, as is the hardback of *A Hidden Life*—and so it goes on. My next project is a YA book: something short and passionate this time, I reckon, but I've not decided yet exactly what it will be, so I shall say no more for the moment. Full details of my books can be found on my home page, www.adelegeras.com.

What else is different? I no longer go about to schools as much as I used to. Partly because I haven't the time (those adult novels take a lot of writing), but partly because I feel lazier and recognize that I'm now one of the Older Generation (see granny, above!). I've been doing it for years and now it's someone else's turn. But I do go out occasionally and love taking part in events with Linda and Ann for "The Historical House" series. I am also very fond of a good festival. I've been to Belgium a couple of times to speak at schools and that was great. If it weren't for my flying phobia, I'd be over in the States like a shot! Meanwhile, I sit in my study in the same house we've lived in since 1982 and hope I can continue to tell stories for many years to come.

*   *   *

GERAS, Adèle Daphne Weston
See GERAS, Adèle

*   *   *

GERSHATOR, David 1937-
(Jack Alchemy)

Personal

Born December 2, 1937, on Mount Carmel, Palestine (now Israel); immigrated to United States, 1945; son of Abraham (a teacher) and Miriam (a secretary) Gershator; married Phillis Manuela Dimondstein (a librarian and writer), October 19, 1962; children; Yonah, Daniel. *Education:* City College (now of the City University of New York), B.A., 1958; Columbia University, M.A., 1960; New York University, Ph.D., 1967.

Addresses

Home—Charlotte Amalie, St. Thomas, U.S. Virgin Islands.

Career

Rutgers University, New Brunswick, NJ, instructor in Romance languages, 1963-67; Adelphi University, Garden City, NY, assistant professor of Spanish, 1967-68; City University of New York, assistant professor of foreign languages, 1968-69; College of the Virgin Islands, St. Thomas, U.S. Virgin Islands, associate professor of English and modern languages, 1969-72; Brooklyn College of the City University of New York, associate professor of humanities, 1973-75; part-time teacher, writer, and small-press editor, 1975-79; Long Island University, Brooklyn Center, adjunct professor of English, 1979-82; writer and painter, 1982—. Lecturer.

Member

Poetry Society of America, Association for Poetry Therapy, Downtown Poets Co-Op (co-founder), New York Poets Co-op (co-founder).

Awards, Honors

Grant from National Endowment for the Humanities, 1971; poetry award from New York State Creative Arts Public Service, 1977-78.

Writings

FOR CHILDREN; WITH WIFE, PHILLIS GERSHATOR

Bread Is for Eating, illustrated by Emma Shaw-Smith, Holt (New York, NY), 1995.
Palampam Day, illustrated by Enrique O. Sanchez, Marshall Cavendish (New York, NY), 1997.
Greetings, Sun, illustrated by Synthia Saint James, DK Ink (New York, NY), 1998.
Only One Cowry: A Dhaomean Tale, Orchard Books (New York, NY), 2000.
Moon Rooster, illustrated by Megan Halsey, Marshall Cavendish (New York, NY), 2001.
Kallaloo!: A Caribbean Tale, illustrated by Diane Greenseid, Marshall Cavendish (New York, NY), 2005.
Summer Is Summer, illustrated by Sophie Blackall, Henry Holt (New York, NY), 2006.

OTHER

Elegy for Val (poetry), X Press Press, 1975.
(Under pseudonym Jack Alchemy) *For Sex and Free Road Maps* (poetry), Downtown Poets Co-Op, 1976.
Kanji: Poems of Japan, Downtown Poets Co-Op, 1977.
Play Mas (poetry), Downtown Poets Co-Op, 1981.
(Editor and translator) Federico García Lorca, *Selected Letters*, New Directions Publishing (New York, NY), 1983.
Sabra (poems), Cross-Cultural Communications, 1985.

Contributor to magazines, including *Roots, Antaeus, Occident, Confrontation,* and *Revista Interamericana.* Contributing editor of *Poets,* 1978; associate editor of *Home Planet News,* 1979.

Sidelights

Of European and American heritage, David Gershator was born on Mount Carmel and raised in Haifa and on a kibbutz—a communal farm—in Israel. He immigrated to New York from Egypt on the first civilian ship to cross the Atlantic after World War II. Raised in Brooklyn, he attended Boys High School and became a fan of the Brooklyn Dodgers. As an adult, he worked as a professor of foreign languages before retiring in the mid-1980s. In addition to publishing poetry in both periodi-

cals and collections, Gershator has also collaborated with his wife, author Phillis Gershator, on several books for young children. Beginning with *Bread Is for Eating,* a 1995 bilingual English/Spanish picture book featuring folk-style illustrations by Emma Shaw-Smith, the Gershators have created a number of original texts that draw on their experiences living and working in the Virgin Islands.

In *Palampam Day,* they bring to life a special day when every object is given the power of speech and the ability to speak its mind. Through the eyes of a young boy named Turo, readers enter the imaginary tale, in which all manner of things communicate, using the wide variety of languages heard in the Caribbean. While Turo goes hungry rather than bite into a coconut that has just requested that he be left alone, he also finds it difficult to deal with dogs, cats, and parrots with a lot on their minds. Fortunately, a trip to the local wise man, Papa Tata Wanga, provides the boy with a set of magic words that make the sun set quickly on this strange day. In *Caribbean Writer* online, Sarah F. Mahurt called *Palampam Day* an "enjoyable story that children can relate to," and *Booklist* writer Susan Dove Lempke dubbed the Gershators' story "rollicking."

Adapted from a West Indian version of "Stone Soup," *Kallaloo!: A Caribbean Tale* finds an elderly woman hungry but with nothing at home to eat. After a fruitless attempt to fish for lunch, she finds a colorful shell, runs to the busy town market, and claims that she can make gumbo soup—called kallaloo—from this shell, if others will each contribute something. In *School Library Journal,* Mary N. Oluonye praised the coauthors' "lilting language," adding that *Kallaloo!* serves as "a well-written, engaging, and gentle story about sharing and the power of working together."

Other books by the Gershators include *Moon Rooster, Greetings, Sun* and *Summer Is Summer,* both of which find young children enjoying time out of doors on a Caribbean island. Featuring stylized artwork by Synthia Saint James, *Greetings, Sun* is a "celebration of the ordinary," according to *Booklist* critic Susan Dove Lempke. From sun-filled skies, the Gershators move to nightfall with *Moon Rooster.* In this story, a rooster who can't sleep decides to crow the sun back into the sky. As each night sky brings an increasingly brighter, fuller moon, the rooster believes his crowing is working; he also assumes the objects thrown at him by those awakened by his nighttime crowing are gifts. When he finally realizes that a plot is underway to make rooster stew, he hides for a week and, the moon dwindles to a mere sliver without his attention. In typical porquoi fashion, Rooster is coaxed into returning for a few more weeks, thus explaining the monthly waxing and waning of the moon. In *School Library Journal* Susan Hepler enjoyed the coauthors' "humorous, tongue-in-cheek tone," dubbing *Moon Rooster* "a strong entry for storytimes." A "picture-book celebration of friends having fun in the summer," according to *Booklist* contributor

Hazel Rochman, *Summer Is Summer* features what a *Kirkus Reviews* writer deemed "short, rhyming text" in which "paired elements . . . convey the sights and sounds and tastes" of the festive season.

Biographical and Critical Sources

PERIODICALS

Booklist, June 1, 1995, Annie Ayres, review of *Bread Is for Eating,* p. 1784; August, 1997, Susan Dove Lempke, review of *Palampam Day,* p. 1905; March 15, 1998, Susan Dove Lempke, review of *Greetings, Sun,* p. 1247; April 15, 2006, Hazel Rochman, review of *Summer Is Summer,* p. 51.

Kirkus Reviews, May 15, 2006, review of *Summer Is Summer,* p. 518.

School Library Journal, December, 2001, Susan Hepler, review of *Moon Rooster,* p. 102; June, 2005, Mary N. Oluonye, review of *Kallaloo!: A Caribbean Tale,* p. 115; June, 2006, Marge Loch-Wouters, review of *Summer Is Summer,* p. 112.

ONLINE

Caribbean Writer Online, http://www.rps.uvi.edu/ CaribbeanWriter/volume12/ (May 15, 2007), Sarah F. Mahurt, review of *Palampam Day.**

*   *   *

GILLILAND, Judith Heide

Personal

Daughter of Florence Parry Heide (a writer); married; husband's name Kim; children: Win, Donny. *Education:* University of Wisconsin, B.A. (Russian and Arabic languages), 1970; University of Washington, M.A. (Near-Eastern languages), 1973.

Addresses

Home and office—Amherst, NH.

Career

Children's book author.

Awards, Honors

Children's Picture Book Award, Council of Wisconsin Writers, 1995, for *The Day of Ahmed's Secret*; Outstanding Children's Book Award, New Hampshire Writers and Publishers Project, 1995, for *Sami and the Time of Troubles*; Middle East Book Award, 2000, for *The House of Wisdom.*

Writings

(With mother, Florence Parry Heide) *The Day of Ahmed's Secret,* illustrated by Ted Lewin, Lothrop (New York, NY), 1990.

Judith Heide Gilliland (Photograph by Parry Heide. Courtesy of Judith Gilliland.)

(With Florence Parry Heide) *Sami and the Time of the Troubles,* illustrated by Ted Lewin, Clarion (New York, NY), 1992.

River, illustrated by Joyce Powzyk, Clarion (New York, NY), 1993.

Not in the House, Newton!, illustrated by Elizabeth Sayles, Clarion (New York, NY), 1995.

(With Florence Parry Heide) *The House of Wisdom,* illustrated by Mary GrandPré, Dorling Kindersley (New York, NY), 1999.

(With Florence Parry Heide and Roxanne Heide Pierce) *It's about Time!: Poems,* illustrated by Cathryn Falwell, Clarion (New York, NY), 1999.

Steamboat: The Story of Captain Blanche Leathers, illustrated by Holly Meade, Dorling Kindersley (New York, NY), 2000.

Strange Birds (novel), Farrar, Straus (New York, NY), 2006.

Sidelights

Judith Heide Gilliland had a good role model when she decided to become a children's book writer: her mother, Florence Parry Heide, has written more than one hundred books for children. Collaborating with Heide, Gilliland's first book put her master's degree in Near-Eastern languages and her experiences living in the Middle East to good use. The book, titled *The Day of Ahmed's Secret,* was one of two books to be ranked as a notable title about Arabs by the American Library Association. Other books by Gilliland include the story-hour favorite *Not in the House, Newton!* as well as *House of Wisdom,* the novel *Strange Birds,* and the picture-book biography *Steamboat: The Story of Captain Blanche Leathers.*

Cover of Gilliland' picture book **Not in the House, Newton!,** *which features artwork by Elizabeth Sayles.* (Clarion, 1995. Illustration © 1995 by Elizabeth Sayles. Reproduced by permission of Clarion Books, an imprint of Houghton Mifflin Company.)

The Day of Ahmed's Secret follows a young Egyptian as he completes his delivery work in the streets of Cairo. The story hints at a secret readers eventually discover: the young boy has learned how to write his name in Arabic. The text and pictures create "a sense of place so vivid that readers can almost hear the cry of vendors," according to a *Publishers Weekly* contributor. Another collaboration between mother and daughter, *The House of Wisdom,* is a picture book set in ninth-century Baghdad about Ishaq, a young would-be scholar who lives in the library—called the House of Wisdom. Although he aspires to become a respected scholar like his father, Ishaq also longs for adventure, a desire the Caliph channels by sending the young man across the known world on a mission to gather knowledge. The trip so inspires him that he eventually becomes one of the world's greatest translators of Aristotle. *The House of Wisdom* "is historically informative, [and] written in lyrical prose," according to Judith Gabriel in her review

for *Al Jadid* online. According to *Booklist* contributor Ilene Cooper, the coauthors "breathe new life into an event from an often neglected time and place." A note at the back of the book distinguishes the story's fiction from the facts about the real-life Ishaq.

Gilliland once again travels to the Middle East in her coauthored work *Sami and the Time of the Troubles,* a book about war in Lebanon, and spins an environmental tale about the Amazon in *River.* A *Publishers Weekly* contributor deemed *Sami and the Time of the Troubles* "valuable for its portrait of children caught in modern-day conflicts," while another reviewer in the same periodical noted that *River* "exemplifies the best sort of educational writing." The book's "narrative only implies its lessons," the critic added, explaining that in *River* the coauthors focus instead on giving readers a sensory experience of the Amazon basin region.

A solo book, Gilliland's *Steamboat!: The Story of Captain Blanche Leathers* is a picture-book biography about the Mississippi's first female steamboat captain. Starting her story in the late 1860s, Gilliland details Leathers' growing-up years and her dream of becoming a captain. "This beautifully written picture-book biography is filled with drama," wrote Michael Cart in his *Booklist* review of the work. Citing the illustrations by Holly Meade, a *Publishers Weekly* critic noted that author and illustrator "convincingly expose the mysteries of the Mississippi," while a *Horn Book* writer concluded of *Steamboat!* that "this lively book offers a ship-shape model of the best in picture-book biography."

Along with her picture books, Gilliland has also written the middle-grade novel, *Strange Birds*. In this story, eleven-year-old Anna, whose parents have disappeared at sea and whose guardian aunt is neglectful, discovers a nest of miniature, winged horses in the branches of a large tree. After discovering a diary, Anna is able to link the existence of the horses to her parents' mysterious disappearance. "Readers will be easily captured by the family secrets, whimsical magic, warm friendship, and brave, intrepid Anna," wrote Gillian Engberg in her *Booklist* review of the novel. Deirdre Root, writing in *Kliatt*, praised *Strange Birds* as "charming and timeless, inspiring without being overly moralistic."

Gilliland joins mother and fellow author Florence Parry Heide as well as illustrator Mary GrandPré in bringing to life a story of ancient Arabia in the picture book **House of Wisdom.** (DK Publishing, Inc., 1999. Illustration copyright © 1999 by Mary GrandPré. Reproduced by permission of DK Publishing, a division of Penguin Putnam Books for Young Readers.)

Biographical and Critical Sources

PERIODICALS

Booklist, April 1, 1992, Hazel Rochman, review of *Sami and the Time of the Troubles,* p. 1449; November 1, 1993, Julie Corsaro, review of *River,* p. 525; December 15, 1995, Susan Dove Lempke, review of *Not in the House, Newton!,* p. 708; September 15, 1999, review of *The House of Wisdom,* p. 261; March 15, 2000, Michael Cart, review of *Steamboat!: The Story of Captain Blanche Leathers,* p. 1374; March 1, 2001, Stephanie Avirin, review of *Steamboat!,* p. 1280; March 1, 2002, Ilene Cooper, review of *Steamboat!,* p. 1147; May 15, 2006, Gillian Engberg, review of *Strange Birds,* p. 58.

Bulletin of the Center for Children's Books, March, 2000, review of *Steamboat!,* p. 243; September, 2006, Karen Coats, review of *Strange Birds,* p. 14.

Horn Book, November-December, 1990, Ethel R. Twichell, review of *The Day of Ahmed's Secret,* p. 739; July-August, 1992, Ellen Fader, review of *Sami and the Time of the Troubles,* p. 445; March, 2000, review of *Steamboat!,* p. 211.

Kirkus Reviews, May 1, 2006, review of *Strange Birds,* p. 458.

Kliatt, May, 2006, Deirdre Root, review of *Strange Birds,* p. 9.

Publishers Weekly, August 10, 1990, review of *The Day of Ahmed's Secret,* p. 444; May 4, 1992, review of *Sami and the Time of the Troubles,* p. 56; October 4, 1993, review of *River,* p. 79; August 23, 1999, review of *The House of Wisdom,* p. 58; April 3, 2000, review of *Steamboat!,* p. 80.

School Library Journal, August, 1990, Luann Toth, review of *The Day of Ahmed's Secret,* p. 130; December, 1990, Trevelyn Jones and Luann Toth, review of *The Day of Ahmed's Secret,* p. 22; May, 1992, Ellen D. Warwick, review of *Sami and the Time of the Troubles,* p. 112; December, 1993, Ruth S. Vose, review of *River,* p. 104; January, 1996, review of *Not in the House, Newton!,* p. 83; January, 2000, Miriam Lang Budin, review of *The House of Wisdom,* p. 132; March, 2000, Susan Hepler, review of *Steamboat!,* p. 224; January, 2003, Alicia Eames, review of *The House of Wisdom,* p. 83; May, 2006, Carol Schene, review of *Strange Birds,* p. 124.

ONLINE

Al Jadid Online, http://leb.net/~aljadid/ (April 28, 2007), "Judith Heide Gilliland."

*   *   *

GORDON, David 1965-

Personal

Born January 22, 1965, in CO. *Education:* Parsons School of Design, B.F.A.

Addresses

Home and office—311 W. 84th St., Ste. 5F, New York, NY 10024. *E-mail*—daveygordon@mac.com.

Career

Author, illustrator, and concept artist. Visual developer, character designer, art director, director, and layout director for films and television programs, including *Robots, Cars, Monsters, Inc., A Bug's Life, Toy Story, Toy Story 2, Frankenstein, Curious George, Spongebob Squarepants, Back to the Future, El Kabong,* and *Locomotion.*

Awards, Honors

Broadcast Design Award Gold Medal, for *El Kabong*; Broadcast Design Award Bronze Medal, for *Loco Rodeo.*

Writings

SELF-ILLUSTRATED CHILDREN'S BOOKS

The Ugly Truckling, Laura Geringer (New York, NY), 2004.
The Three Little Rigs, Laura Geringer (New York, NY), 2005.
Hansel and Diesel, Laura Geringer (New York, NY), 2006.
Smitten, Atheneum (New York, NY), 2006.

ILLUSTRATOR

Laurie Halse Anderson, *The Big Cheese of Third Street,* Simon & Schuster (New York, NY), 2002.
Mike Dawns, *The Noisy Airplane Ride,* Tricycle Press (Berkeley, CA), 2003.
K.C. Olson, *Construction Countdown,* Holt (New York, NY), 2004.
Susan K. Leigh, *The Town That Forgot about Christmas,* Concordia (St. Louis, MO), 2006.

Contributor of illustrations to *Business Week, Entertainment Weekly, Forbes, Men's Journal, New York Times, Wall Street Journal,* and *Washington Post.*

Sidelights

Even readers unfamiliar with David Gordon's picture books know something of his art. Before becoming a picture-book author and illustrator, Gordon worked on animated films produced by Pixar Studios, among them *Toy Story, Monsters, Inc.,* and *Cars.* His work, which ranges from design to direction, has also appeared on television programs such as *Spongebob Squarepants.* In 2002, Gordon turned his hand to book illustration, creating art for Laurie Halse Anderson's *The Big Cheese of Third Street.* He has continued on to illustrate picture books, and has also paired his art with original stories in *Hansel and Diesel* and *The Three Little Rigs,* among others.

The illustrations for *The Big Cheese of Third Street* are done in "a style mixing Marc Simont and Dan Yaccarino," according to a *Kirkus Reviews* contributor. A *Publishers Weekly* reviewer commented that "Gordon picks up on the [story's] sly humor and fills his sturdy, uncomplicated cityscapes with comic touches." Of his illustrations for Mike Downs' *The Noisy Airplane Ride,* Todd Morning wrote in *Booklist* that "Gordon's vibrant, computer-generated illustrations help expand the words into a story." In *Construction Countdown* "Gordon achieves painterly effects through his series of digital illustrations," wrote Carolyn Phelan in her *Booklist* review.

Gordon "peoples" his original stories for children with airplanes, tractors, trucks, and construction equipment, and they are featured in the recast fairy tales *The Ugly Truckling, The Three Little Rigs,* and *Hansel and Diesel.* In *The Ugly Truckling* a young vehicle does not understand why she feels so out of place in her truck family: she only has three wheels instead of four, and she also has a strange beam on each side of her body. At the end, the vehicle discovers that she actually belongs to an airplane family. Jennifer Mattson commented in *Booklist* on Gordon's "felicitous rhyme," adding that his illustrations give the baby vehicles "high-octane cuteness." Though critical of the text, Wanda Meyers-Hines praised Gordon's artwork in *School Library Journal.* "Ranging from gloriously colored landscapes to vivid close-ups of the characters, the artwork is colorful and appealing," Meyers-Hines noted. A *Publishers Weekly* contributor wrote of the illustrations that they "will rev the engines of preschoolers obsessed with all things mechanical."

The Three Little Rigs features the youngsters of big rigs who are told to go out into the world to build garages. Instead of the wolf of the familiar "Little Pigs" saga, the danger in Gordon's story is the Big Bad Wrecking Ball. The author/illustrator "uses the familiar fairy tale as a framework to extol the virtues of teamwork," wrote a contributor to *Kirkus Reviews.* In *Booklist,* Jennifer Mattson remarked that the illustrations feature "headlights, bumpers, and rivets smoothly coalescing into expressive facial features," while Linda M. Kenton wrote in *School Library Journal* that Gordon's "accomplished artwork adds great drama to the story."

In *Hansel and Diesel* fuel runs low, prompting two young trucks to voyage deep into the junk yard, leaving behind them a trail of bolts to help them find their way home. They happen upon a brightly lit gas station, only to discover that the owner is a wicked winch. "Whether in a library or a bookstore, take the time to find this book," wrote a critic for *Curled up with a Good Kids Book* online. "The junkyard-as-forest is effectively rendered," noted Kathy Krasniewicz, the *School Library Journal* critic adding that children familiar with the original tale may miss the traditional ending; instead of Gretel coming to the rescue, the children's parents save the day in Gordon's book. "This story, though harrowing, applauds the ingenuity of youngsters and the embrace of a loving family," wrote a critic for *Kirkus Reviews,* and in *Booklist* Todd Morning concluded that "Gordon offers plenty for young children to look at and enjoy."

Biographical and Critical Sources

PERIODICALS

Booklist, December 1, 2001, Ilene Cooper, review of *The Big Cheese of Third Street,* p. 644; April 1, 2003, Todd Morning, review of *The Noisy Airplane Ride,* p. 1398; May 15, 2004, Carolyn Phelan, review of *Construction Countdown,* p. 1622; June 1, 2004, Jennifer Mattson, review of *The Ugly Truckling,* p. 1741; April 1, 2005, Jennifer Mattson, review of *The Three Little Rigs,* p. 1366; May 1, 2006, Todd Morning, review of *Hansel and Diesel,* p. 92.

Bulletin of the Center for Children's Books, July-August, 2004, Janice Del Negro, review of *The Ugly Truckling,* p. 465.

Kirkus Reviews, January 15, 2002, review of *The Big Cheese of Third Street,* p. 100; May 15, 2003, review of *The Noisy Airplane Ride,* p. 749; June 15, 2004, review of *The Ugly Truckling,* p. 576; April 15, 2005, review of *The Three Little Rigs,* p. 474; June 15, 2006, review of *Hansel and Diesel,* p. 633.

Publishers Weekly, November 19, 2001, review of *The Big Cheese of Third Street,* p. 67; July 26, 2004, review of *The Ugly Truckling,* p. 53; September 25, 2006, review of *The Town That Forgot about Christmas,* p. 71.

School Library Journal, February, 2002, Genevieve Gallagher, review of *The Big Cheese of Third Street,* p. 96; August, 2003, Joy Fleishhacker, review of *The Noisy Airplane Ride,* p. 148; July, 2004, Wanda Meyers-Hines, review of *The Ugly Truckling,* p. 76, Sally R. Dow, review of *Construction Countdown,* p. 95; June, 2005, Linda M. Kenton, review of *The Three Little Rigs,* p. 115; July, 2006, Kathy Krasniewicz, review of *Hansel and Diesel,* p. 78.

Tribune Books (Chicago, IL), July 16, 2006, Mary Harris Russell, review of *Hansel and Diesel,* p. 7.

ONLINE

Curled up with a Good Kids Book, http://www.curledupkids.com/ (April 28, 2007), review of *Hansel and Diesel.*

David Gordon Home Page, http://www.illustrationranch.com (April 28, 2007).

Out of Picture Web site, http://www.outofpicture.com/ (April 28, 2007), "David Gordon."*

H

HART, Philip S. 1944-

Personal

Born June 12, 1944, in Denver, CO; son of Judson and Murlee (an educator) Hart; married March 22, 1969; wife's name Tanya K. (a television/radio personality); children: Ayanna Hart-Beebe. *Ethnicity:* "African American." *Education:* University of Colorado, Boulder, B.A. (cum laude); Michigan State University, M.A., Ph.D., 1974. *Politics:* Democrat. *Religion:* Pentecostal, Church of Christ.

Addresses

Home and office—Los Angeles, CA; Edgartown, MA. *Office*—ULI-LA, 444 S. Flower St., Los Angeles, CA 90071. *E-mail*—hartpshow@aol.com; hart@uli-la.org.

Career

Educator, businessman, filmmaker, and author. University of Massachusetts, Boston, professor of sociology, 1974-2002, and director of William Monroe Trotter Institute for the Study of Black Culture; Tanya Hart Communications, Los Angeles, CA, vice president, 1995—; Hart Realty Advisors, Los Angeles, chief executive officer, 2002—; Urban Land Institute (nonprofit land-use organization), Los Angeles, member and advisor, 2006—. Federation of Boston Community Schools, former executive director; Greater Boston YMCA Black Achievers Branch, founder and co-chair; John W. McCormack Institute of Public Affairs, senior fellow; University of California—Los Angeles visiting research sociologist at Center for Afro-American Studies. AbilityFirst Housing Governance Board, Pasadena, CA, vice chair; Hollywood Wilshire YMCA, member of board of managers; American City Coalition, Boston, MA, chief executive officer, 1999-2002. Project manager on construction projects, including West Angeles Church. Documentary filmmaker; film, television, and radio commentator.

Philip S. Hart (Photograph courtesy of Philip S. Hart.)

Member

University of Colorado Alumni Association, Rotary Club of Los Angeles, Hollywood Chamber of Commerce, Los Angeles Library Foundation.

Awards, Honors

Notable Children's Trade Book in Social Studies designation, 2002, for *Flying Free;* Distinguished Alumni honor, University of Colorado; Human Dignitary Award, Metropolitan Los Angeles YMCA; February 2, 2002 declared "Philip S. Hart Day" by Commonwealth of Massachusetts.

Writings

FOR YOUNG READERS

Flying Free: America's First Black Aviators, Lerner Publications (Minneapolis, MN), 1992.
Up in the Air: The Story of Bessie Coleman, Carolrhoda Books (Minneapolis, MN), 1996, revised for younger readers as *Bessie Coleman: Just the Facts,* Lerner Publications (Minneapolis, MN), 2005.

FOR ADULTS

James Edward Blackwell, *Health Needs of Urban Blacks,* Solomon Fuller Institute (Cambridge, MA), 1978.
James Edward Blackwell, *Cities, Suburbs, and Blacks: A Study of Concerns, Distrust, and Alienation,* General Hall (Bayside, NY), 1982.
The Competitive Advantage of the Inner City: Does Race Matter?, William Monroe Trotter Institute (Boston, MA), 1995.

Contributor to anthologies, including *In Pursuit of Equality in Higher Education,* edited by Anne Pruit, General Hall Books, 1987; and *In the Vineyards: Churches and Community Development,* edited by Georgia Persons, 2005. Contributor of articles to periodicals, including *Sociological Practice* and *Urban Land.*

DOCUMENTARY SCREENPLAYS; AND DIRECTOR AND PRODUCER

Flyers in Search of a Dream, produced by Public Broadcasting Service, 1987.
Dark Passages, produced by Black Entertainment Television, 1990.

Adaptations

Hart's documentary films have been adapted for home video. *Up in the Air* was adapted as a television film.

Sidelights

Described by a *Boston Globe* interviewer as a "Renaissance" man due to his wide-ranging interests, his lifetime of public service, and his inspiring career as an educator, Philip S. Hart wears many hats: author, documentary filmmaker, educator, urban planner, and real-estate developer, among others. Working for over twenty-five years at the University of Massachusetts at Boston as a professor of sociology, Hart also directed the university's William Monroe Trotter Institute for the Study of Black Culture before retiring in 2002. Drawing on the history of his own family, he authored *Flying Free: America's First Black Aviators,* a book that inspired the History Channel production *Black Aviators: Flying Free.* Hart's own films, which include a documentary on pioneering black aviators titled *Flyers in Search of a Dream* that aired on public television, have led to other creative endeavors, including his children's book *Up in the Air: The Story of Bessie Coleman.*

In *Up in the Air* Hart chronicles the life of pioneering African-American pilot Bessie Coleman, a brave woman who gained renown in the early days of aviation. Determined to leave her life of poverty in Texas, Coleman traveled to France after being rejected from countless U.S. aviation schools due to her race, and she became a pilot in 1921. Hart's biography follows Coleman's eventful life up until her tragic death in 1926, in a plane crash. Drawing on detailed research to provide an accurate portray of Coleman's life, the author delves into both her personal and professional life and incorporates numerous photographs and original documents into the work. Reviewing *Up in the Air* for *Booklist,* Carolyn Phelan praised Hart for creating "a very readable account of Coleman's life."

As Hart recalled to *SATA,* "I began writing at an early age. My first published piece was when I was an undergraduate at the University of Colorado. I grew up in a family with ties to American aviation history.

"While in junior high school I began doing research on my mother's uncle, James Herman Banning, a pioneering black aviator in the 1920s. This research led to the Smithsonian Institute's 'Black Wings' exhibit which opened in 1982. My wife and I then produced a PBS documentary film *Flyers in Search of a Dream,* which aired in 1987.

"Reeve Lindbergh, a writer and the daughter of well-known early twentieth-century American aviator Charles Lindbergh, saw the PBS film, contacted me, and encouraged me to adopt some of these stories into children's books. Lerner Publishing subsequently published three of my children's books on the topic of America's first black aviators starting in 1992."

Biographical and Critical Sources

PERIODICALS

Booklist, October 15, 1992, Sheilamae O'Hara, review of *Flying Free: America's First Black Aviators,* p. 421; August, 1996, Carolyn Phelan, review of *Up in the Air: The Story of Bessie Coleman,* p. 1898.
Bulletin of the Center for Children's Books, December, 1992, review of *Flying Free,* p. 112.

Five Owls, September, 1993, review of *Flying Free,* p. 6.
School Library Journal, January, 1993, Eunice Weech, review of *Flying Free,* p. 113; August, 1996, Phyllis Graves, review of *Up in the Air,* p. 156.

ONLINE

Philip Hart Home Page, http://www.hartrealtyadvisors. com (May 14, 2007).*

*   *   *

HAUSMAN, Gerald 1945-
(Gerry Hausman)

Personal

Born October 13, 1945, in Baltimore, MD; son of Sidney (an engineer) and Dorothy (a teacher and homemaker) Hausman; married Loretta Wright (an author), June, 1968; children: Mariah, Hannah Hausman Greaux. *Education:* New Mexico Highlands University, B.A. (English literature), 1968. *Hobbies and other interests:* Reading, long-distance swimming, storytelling, qigong.

Addresses

Home and office—12699 Cristi Way, Bokeelia, FL 33922. *Agent*—George Nicholson, Sterling Lord Literistic, 65 Bleeker St., New York, NY 10012. *E-mail*—gerald@geraldhausman.com.

Career

Educator and author. Poetry teacher in Lenox, MA, 1969-72; Bookstore Press, Lenox, MA, editor, 1972-77; Sunstone Press, Santa Fe, NM, vice president, 1979-83; Santa Fe Preparatory School, Santa Fe, NM, teacher of English, 1983-94. Poet-in-residence in public schools, 1970-76, at Central Connecticut State College, 1973, and for city of Pittsfield, MA. Blue Harbour Creative Writing School, Port Maria, Jamaica, cofounder, 1986-93. Literary arts consultant for Berkshire County, MA.

Member

Authors Guild, Society of Children's Book Writers and Illustrators.

Awards, Honors

Union College poetry prize, 1965, for *Quebec Poems;* Children's Protective Services Award for performance art; Massachusetts Council on the Humanities teaching grant; Connecticut Commission on the Arts teaching grant; Gerald Hausman Scholarship established for Native-American high-school students at Santa Fe Preparatory School, 1985; Aesop Accolade Award, American Folklore Society (children's section), 1995, for *Duppy Talk: West Indian Tales of Mystery and Magic;*

Gerald Hausman (Photograph by Mariah Fox. Courtesy of Gerald Hausman.)

Notable Social Studies Book for Young People designation, Children's Book Council (CBC)/National Council for the Social Studies, 1996, and 1999, for *Doctor Bird: Three Lookin' Up Tales from Jamaica;* Americus Award honorable mention, 1998, for *Doctor Bird;* Pick of the Lists selection, American Booksellers Association, 1999, for *Dogs of Myth: Tales from around the World;* Bank Street College of Education Best Book selection, 2000, for *Tom Cringle: Battle on the High Seas* and *Cats of Myth: Tales from around the World;* Notable Social Studies Trade Books for Young People designation, and New York Public Library Best Books for the Teen Age designation, both 2001, both for *The Jacob Ladder;* Parents' Choice Silver Medal for Nonfiction, 2003, and New York Public Library Best Book for the Teen Age designation and CCBC Choice designation, both 2004, all for *Escape from Botany Bay;* National Social Studies Council/ CBC Best Book designation, 2007, for *A Mind with Wings.*

Writings

FOR CHILDREN

(Editor) *The Shivurrus Plant of Mopant, and Other Children's Poems,* Giligia, 1968.
The Boy with the Sun Tree Bow, Berkshire Traveller Press (Stockbridge, MA), 1973.

Beth: The Little Girl of Pine Knoll, Bookstore Press (Lenox, MA), 1974.

The Day the White Whales Came to Bangor, Cobblesmith, 1977.

Coyote Walks on Two Legs, Philomel (New York, NY), 1993.

Eagle Boy, illustrated by Cara and Barry Moser, HarperCollins (New York, NY), 1993.

Turtle Island Alphabet for Young Readers, HarperCollins (New York, NY), 1993.

(Reteller) *Duppy Talk: West Indian Tales of Mystery and Magic,* Simon & Schuster (New York, NY), 1994.

Doctor Moledinky's Castle: A Hometown Tale, Simon & Schuster (New York, NY), 1995.

(Collector and reteller) *How Chipmunk Got Tiny Feet: Native American Animal Origin Stories,* HarperCollins (New York, NY), 1995.

Doctor Bird: Three Lookin' Up Tales from Jamaica, illustrated by Ashley Wolff, Philomel Books (New York, NY), 1998.

(Reteller) *The Story of Blue Elk,* illustrated by Kristina Rodanas, Clarion Books (New York, NY), 1998.

(With Cedella Marley) *The Boy from Nine Miles: The Early Life of Bob Marley,* illustrated by Mariah Fox, Hampton Roads (Charlottesville, VA), 2002.

(With wife, Loretta Hausman) *Horses of Myth: Tales from around the World,* illustrated by Robert Florczak, Dutton (New York, NY), 2005.

(With Cedella Marley) *Three Little Birds* (board book), Tuff Gong Books (Miami, FL), 2006.

(With Loretta Hausman) *The Healing Horse* (middle-grade novel), Houghton Mifflin (Boston, MA), 2006.

FOR YOUNG ADULTS

Sitting on the Blue-Eyed Bear: Navajo Myths and Legends, Lawrence Hill (Westport, CT), 1975.

Turtle Dream (short fiction), Mariposa (Santa Fe, NM), 1989.

Ghost Walk (short stories), Mariposa (Santa Fe, NM), 1991.

Night Flight (novel), Philomel Books (New York, NY), 1996.

The Coyote Bead (novel), Hampton Roads (Charlottesville, VA), 1999.

(With Loretta Hausman) *Dogs of Myth: Tales from around the World,* illustrated by Barry Moser, Simon & Schuster (New York, NY), 1999.

(Coauthor) *Cats of Myth: Tales from around the World,* illustrated by Leslie Baker, Simon & Schuster (New York, NY), 2000.

Tom Cringle: Battle on the High Seas (novel), illustrated by Tad Hills, Simon & Schuster (New York, NY), 2000.

(With Loretta Hausman) *The Metaphysical Cat: Tales of Cats and Their Humans,* Hampton Roads (Charlottesville, VA), 2001.

(With Uton Hinds) *The Jacob Ladder* (novel), Orchard Books (New York, NY), 2001.

Tom Cringle: The Pirate and the Patriot (novel), Simon & Schuster (New York, NY), 2001.

Castaways: Stories of Survival, Greenwillow (New York, NY), 2003.

(With Loretta Hausman) *Escape from Botany Bay: The True Story of Mary Bryant,* Scholastic (New York, NY), 2003.

(With Loretta Hausman) *Napoleon and Josephine: The Sword and the Hummingbird* (novel), Scholastic (New York, NY), 2004.

(With Loretta Hausman) *A Mind with Wings: The Story of Henry David Thoreau,* Random House (New York, NY), 2006.

(With Loretta Hausman) *Leaves of Liberty* (novel), Scholastic (New York, NY), 2007.

POETRY AND SHORT FICTION; FOR ADULTS

(With David Kherdian) *Eight Poems,* Giligia, 1968.

New Marlboro Stage, Giligia, 1969, 2nd edition, Bookstore Press (Lenox, MA), 1971.

Circle Meadow, Bookstore Press (Lenox, MA), 1972.

(Editor with David Silverstein) *The Berkshire Anthology,* Bookstore Press, 1972.

Night Herding Song, Copper Canyon Press (Port Townsend, WA), 1979.

Runners, Sunstone Press (Santa Fe, NM), 1984.

Contributor to *Poets in the Schools,* edited by Kathleen Meagher, Connecticut Commission on the Arts, 1973. Contributor to anthologies, including *Contemporaries: Twenty-eight New American Poets,* Viking (New York, NY); *Desert Review Anthology,* Desert Review Press; *Poetry Here and Now,* edited by David Kherdian, Morrow (New York, NY); *Tales from the Great Turtle,* edited by Piers Anthony and Richard Gilliam, Tor (New York, NY), 1994; *Warriors of Blood and Dream,* edited by Roger Zelazny, Avon (New York, NY), 1995; *Wheel of Fortune,* edited by Zelazny, Avon, 1995; *The Gift of Tongues: Twenty-five Years of Poetry,* edited by Sam Hammill, Copper Canyon Press (Port Townsend, WA), 1996; *Lord of the Fantastic: Stories in Honor of Roger Zelazny,* edited by Martin H. Greenberg, Avon, 1998; and *Urban Nature: Poems about Wildlife in the City,* edited by Laure-Anne Bosselaar, Milkweed Editions (Minneapolis, MN), 2000.

OTHER

(With Loretta Hausman, under name Gerry Hausman) *The Pancake Book,* Persea Books (New York, NY), 1976.

(With Loretta Hausman, under name Gerry Hausman) *The Yogurt Book,* Persea Books (New York, NY), 1977.

No Witness (novel), Stackpole (Harrisburg, PA), 1980.

Meditations with Animals: A Native American Bestiary, Bear & Co. (Santa Fe, NM), 1986.

Meditations with the Navajo: Prayers, Songs, and Stories of Healing and Harmony, Bear & Co. (Santa Fe, NM), 1988.

Stargazer (novel), Lotus Press (Santa Fe, NM), 1989.

Turtle Island Alphabet (essays), St. Martin's Press (New York, NY), 1992.

(Reteller) *The Gift of the Gila Monster: Navajo Ceremonial Tales,* Simon & Schuster (New York, NY), 1993.

Tunkashila, St. Martin's Press (New York, NY), 1993.

(With Roger Zelazny) *Wilderness* (novel), Forge (New York, NY), 1994.

(Editor) *Prayer to the Great Mystery: The Uncollected Writings and Photography of Edward S. Curtis,* St. Martin's Press (New York, NY), 1995.

The Sun Horse (essays), Lotus Press, 1995.

(With Kelvin Rodrigues) *African-American Alphabet: A Celebration of African-American and West Indian Culture, Custom, Myth, and Symbol,* St. Martin's Press (New York, NY), 1996.

(Editor) *The Kebra Nagast: The Lost Bible of Rastafarian Wisdom and Faith from Ethiopia and Jamaica,* St. Martin's Press (New York, NY), 1997.

(Coauthor) *The Mythology of Dogs: Canine Legend and Lore through the Ages,* St. Martin's Press (New York, NY), 1997.

(With Loretta Hausman) *The Mythology of Cats: Feline Legend and Lore through the Ages,* St. Martin's Press (New York, NY), 1998.

(With Cedella Marley) *Fifty-six Thoughts from 56 Hope Road,* Tuff Gong Books (Miami, FL), 2002.

(With Loretta Hausman) *The Mythology of Horses: Horse Legend and Lore throughout the Ages,* Three Rivers Press (New York, NY), 2003.

Sixty Visions, Tuff Gong Books (Miami, FL), 2005.

Adaptations

Hausman's works have been recorded on audiotapes and released by Lotus Press (Santa Fe, NM), including *Navajo Nights,* 1987, *Stargazer,* 1989, *Native American Animal Stories,* 1990, and *Ghost Walk,* 1991. *The Boy with the Sun Tree Bow* was adapted as a short animated film by the University of Washington, 2006.

Sidelights

In addition to his work as a poet, editor, and educator, Gerald Hausman writes books for children and young adults that are inspired by his love of words and his interest in both history and Native-American and Caribbean lore. In *Duppy Talk: West Indian Tales of Mystery and Magic, Doctor Bird: Three Lookin' Up Tales from Jamaica,* and *The Story of Blue Elk* he retells tradition narratives, while *Castaways: Stories of Survival* includes six tales inspired by first-person accounts which combine courage and a touch of the supernatural. Collections of animal lore are compiled in a series of books Hausman has written in collaboration with his wife, Loretta Hausman. Focusing on older readers, Hausman has also written short fiction as well as novels such as *Tom Cringle: Battle on the High Seas* and its sequels. Collaborative works for teen readers include *The Jacob Ladder,* a novel coauthored with Jamaican writer Uton Hinds, as well as the history-centered *Napoleon and Josephine: The Sword and the Hummingbird, A Mind with Wings: The Story of Henry David Thoureau,* and *Escape from Botany Bay: The True Story of Mary Bryant,* all which were coauthored by Hausman and his wife..

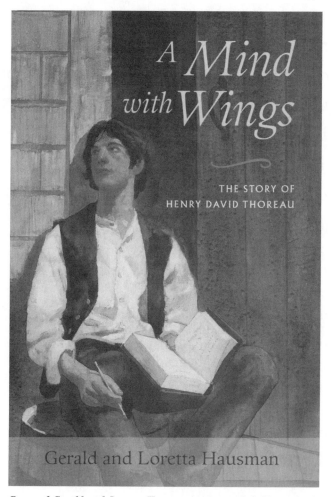

Cover of Gerald and Loretta Hausman's young-adult biography **A Mind with Wings,** *featuring artwork by Peter Fiore.* (Trumpeter, 2006. Cover art © 2002 by Peter Fiore. Reproduced by permission of Charlesbridge Publishing, Inc. All rights reserved.)

Praising *Escape from Botany Bay, Booklist* contributor Ed Sullivan dubbed it "an engrossing" account of the exploits of the nineteen-year-old woman who, in the late 1700s, led the first and only successful escape from Australia's notorious prison. In *School Library Journal,* Christina Stenson-Carey praised *A Mind with Wings* as "a well-researched novel [that] expertly captures Thoreau's character and life in mid-19th-century Massachusetts."

In *Duppy Talk* Hausman presents tales centering around the "Duppy", a West Indian term for a soul that has not yet settled peacefully in the spirit world and continues to haunt the living. The Duppy ghost has links to the indigenous African religions that were brought to the Caribbean region by African slaves. Also based on West Indian folklore, *Doctor Bird* introduces a figure allegedly native to the north coast of Jamaica: a top-hat-wearing, streamer-tailed hummingbird who helps other animals. This "Doctor" gives guidance to a little homeless mouse that finds shelter and nourishment in the trees, and helps a kleptomaniac mongoose realize that stealing is wrong. "Rather than write in dialect, Hausman lightly evokes oral cadences with a few scattered words or turns of phrase," noted *Booklist* critic John Peters in a review of *Doctor Bird*.

Navajo lore and stories from other indigenous peoples of the American Southwest have provided inspiration for several books by Hausman. He adapts several variants of one tale in *The Story of Blue Elk,* which begins as a baby is born in a Pueblo community on the same day a giant elk casts its shadow over the village. The shadow is an omen: the infant, named Blue Elk, will be mute for life. Although without the power of speech, the child is able to communicate with his namesake, which appears to the boy in animal form. When the giant elk dies, it falls to the ground next to a cedar tree, and its antlers merge with the cedar wood. The mute Blue Elk, now a grown man, uses that wood to carve a special flute. He then plays it to communicate with a woman whom he has loved from afar for many years. Reviewing the book for *School Library Journal,* Judith Gloyer commended Hausman's "beautiful, vivid language," and deemed *The Story of Blue Elk* "a lyrical tale from a gifted and experienced storyteller."

Hausman also mines Navajo history in the young-adult novel *The Coyote Bead*. The story is set in 1864, as Dineh, a young Tobachischin, is orphaned when his parents are slain by federal government troops. The backdrop of the story is the Long Walk, a tragic chapter in Navajo history that was ongoing during this time and involved the enforced migration of the tribe to Fort Sumner, New Mexico. Along with his grandfather, a medicine man, Dineh hides from the soldiers and also from a treacherous Ute named Two Face. When Dineh's grandfather is slain by one of Two Face's arrows—a death the man had prophesied for himself—Dineh saves the man's prized medicine bag and forges on alone. He comes across the site of an Ute massacre, and is shot at by Mary, a young woman who had been adopted by a sympathetic white family before her adoptive parents also became victims of Two Face. "Interestingly, the heroes and villains [of the Long Walk] aren't divided along racial lines," noted a critic writing for *Hungry Mind Review*. The reviewer wrote positively of the way Hausman portrays Navajo culture, noting that "cooking and eating, rituals, [and] interpreting nature . . . are astutely and painstakingly relayed, making the reader's transport back in time an effortless and worthwhile journey."

Hausman's other books for older readers include a series of novels that draw on eighteenth-and nineteenth-century English literature for their inspiration. *Tom Cringle: Battle on the High Seas* recounts, in fictional diary form, the adventures of a thirteen-year-old English boy who goes to sea. Living a life not uncommon for a boy of his age, Tom serves as a midshipman on board the *Bream,* a guard vessel trolling Caribbean waters during the War of 1812. Tom's direst hardships on board the *Bream* involve adjusting to life at sea, and he

and his young comrade are frequently nauseous. Soon, he finds his niche as an "eagle eye" who can spot an unfriendly ship far off on the horizon. While piracy is a danger, so are tropical storms, and when one wrecks the *Bream,* only Tom, his dog Sneezer, and two other crew members survive. Picked up by a pirate ship, they bribe the ship's captain into delivering them to a British naval base in the area by offering the gold buttons from their uniform as payment. Tom views the captain, a fierce Scot named Obediah Glasgow, with some fear, but the two forge an unlikely friendship, and Tom and his companions are ultimately delivered to safety. *School Library Journal* critic William McLoughlin wrote that the novel's opening pages are "brimming with colorful descriptions of life aboard the *Bream,* where Tom experiences drudgery, disease, thrilling naval battles, and the death of a companion."

Hausman's saga continues in *Tom Cringle: The Pirate and the Patriot*. A year older and promoted to first lieutenant, Tom is still sailing the Caribbean and still on the lookout for pirates. When his captain surprises a pirate ship and boards it by force, Tom and the crew discover that it carries slaves, taken from a plantation called Cinnamon Hill. Tom is assigned to return the slaves to their owner, but the mission presents a moral quandary for him as he believes slavery is wrong. After several more adventures, Tom is relieved when the Royal Navy agrees to take the slaves on as new conscripts. Although *School Library Journal* contributor Patricia B. McGee faulted *Tom Cringle: The Pirate and the Patriot* for presenting a pat solution to the slavery issue at a time when "Royal Navy life . . . was brutal," she also noted that the work's "lively plotting, picturesque language, and colorful setting make [*Tom Cringle: The Pirate and the Patriot*] . . . an exciting tale." Writing in *Booklist,* Roger Leslie praised the author for effectively employing an "epistolary format and *Treasure Island*-like dialogue" in his novel.

Set in Jamaica, the collaborative novel *The Jacob Ladder* is also geared for a young-adult readership. Based on coauthor Hinds's childhood, the work is set in the 1960s and narrated by a boy named Tall T. He reveals his troubled home life, with a father who gambles, drinks, and eventually abandons the family for a neighbor woman. Because Tall T cannot afford the uniform required to attend school, he spends his days at the local library, where a kindly librarian teaches him how to read. When his father offers him a chance to participate in a local festival in one of its coveted musician spots, Tall T is tempted by the offer. The biblical story of Jacob's ladder is like the cliff Tall T climbs in order to think about what he should do. *School Library Journal* reviewer Ellen Vevier found *The Jacob Ladder* "a compelling and vibrant book that will give young readers a real look into the Jamaica behind the postcard and cruise-ship images." Hazel Rochman, writing in

Booklist, termed it "a harsh story of poverty and betrayal. It's also about family love and faith."

Hausman's collaborations frequently involve his wife, and focus on the couple's joint interest in animals and folklore. *The Mythology of Dogs: Canine Legend and Lore through the Ages* is a collection of seventy folk tales, facts, and true stories, arranged in alphabetical order by breed. *The Mythology of Cats: Feline Legend and Lore through the Ages* is arranged along similar lines. In the latter volume, the Hausmans debunk the popular association of cats with negative spiritual forces. Both Buddha and Muhammad enjoyed feline companionship, they note, and in other cultures and at other points in time cats have been revered as harbingers of good luck and good harvests, or as healers and guides. *Library Journal* critic Florence Scarinci called the work "an entertaining compilation."

The Hausmans gather more folktales for *Dogs of Myth: Tales from around the World.* The stories here are divided into categories, including the trickster dog, the enchanted hound, and the guardian animal. One tale from Africa recounts how a clever dog stole fire and brought it to his human friend, even though it meant that he forever lost the ability to bark. The Hausmans also present a Celtic legend of a miniature bloodhound, "King Herla's Hound," as well as a Norse tale that explains why the Rottweiler's growl sounds like thunder. Others borrow from Japanese and Inuit culture. A *Publishers Weekly* reviewer praised the work, noting that the coauthors' "storytelling flows in an unbroken, lyrical stream, right from the poetic introduction."

Cats of Myth: Tales from around the World and *Horses of Myth: Tales from around the World* follow the same format as *Dogs of Myth.* In *Cats of Myth* the Hausmans present an East Indian tale that explains how the cat was domesticated, recount a Japanese martial-arts fable about a temple cat and a rat, and include an afterword that discusses each of the breeds depicted. In similar fashion, *Horses of Myth* include stories about five amazing horses, from the Arabian Abjer to the mustang named Snail that Crow chief Many Coups often raced to victory. *Booklist* contributor Ilene Cooper extolled *Cats of Myth* as "a treat for cat lovers [and] for readers who enjoy a good folktale," while *Booklist* reviewer John Peters dubbed *Horses of Myth* a "world-spanning set of horse stories, each one retold in an idiom evocative of its origins." Regarding the Hausmans' other foray into feline history, *The Metaphysical Cat: Tales of Cats and Their Humans,* a *Publishers Weekly* critic concluded that "anyone believing that cats live in another dimension will relish" the work.

"As a storyteller, I have always believed that the written word comes from the oral tradition," Hausman explained to *SATA.* "Therefore, my narrators are always talkers. When I write for adults or children, I concen-

Brought to life through Leslie Baker's art, Cats of Myth *is one of several collections of animal-related stories and traditions compiled by **Gerald and Loretta Hausman.*** (Simon & Schuster Books for Young Readers, 2000. Illustration © 2000 by Leslie Baker. Reprinted by permission of Simon & Schuster Books for Young Readers, an imprint of Simon & Schuster Children's Publishing Division.)

trate on the rhythms of the words, the flow, the pattern, the beauty of sentences. Yes, I have written books of poetry. And yes, I still do.

"As a teacher in the classroom for over eighteen years I have witnessed the power of the spoken word and how, when this becomes the written word, students only lose interest in a story when the narrator doesn't sound like someone they know, or perhaps someone they might *want* to know. Keeping it real is an understatement.

"As an editor I have always been passionate, putting in as many years helping others get their manuscripts into print as writing books for myself. I have worked with many Native American, West Indian, and European authors. Many—and I would hope through my efforts—have gone on to successful writing careers. A number of writers I mentored have produced books that have sold widely. Some of these books are still in print after twenty years.

"As a writer I love what I do. At the age of sixty, and with some sixty books written, I am still very much in love with writing. I dance when a new book comes out. I don't believe I will ever lose sight of the fact that writing, like life, is a joyous expression, a gift that makes each day a transcendent treasure, freshly opened to the eye and ear."

Biographical and Critical Sources

PERIODICALS

Booklist, December 1, 1995, Janice Del Negro, review of *Doctor Moledinky's Castle: A Hometown Tale,* p. 618; February 1, 1996, Carolyn Phelan, review of *Eagle Boy,* p. 934; February 15, 1996, Brad Hooper, review of *African-American Alphabet,* p. 985; March 1, 1996, Hazel Rochman, review of *Night Flight,* p. 1174; October 1, 1997, Mike Tribby, review of *The Kebra Nagast,* p. 284; May 15, 1998, Ilene Cooper, review of *The Story of Blue Elk,* p. 1628; June 1, 1998, John Peters, review of *Doctor Bird,* p. 1754; November 1, 1999, Michael Cart, review of *Dogs of Myth: Tales from around the World,* p. 520; November 1, 2000, Carolyn Phelan, review of *Tom Cringle: Battle on the High Seas,* p. 526; December 15, 2000, Ilene Cooper, review of *Cats of Myth: Tales from around the World,* p. 813; May 1, 2001, Hazel Rochman, review of *The Jacob Ladder,* p. 1678; September 15, 2001, Roger Leslie, review of *Tom Cringle: The Pirate and the Patriot,* p. 222; March 1, 2003, Ed Sullivan, review of *Escape from Botany Bay: The True Story of Mary Bryant,* p. 1206; September 15, 2003, GraceAnne A. DeCandido, review of *Castaways: Stories of Survival,* p. 233; October 1, 2005, John Peters, review of *Horses of Myth,* p. 54; March 1, 2006, Todd Morning, review of *A Mind with Wings: The Story of Henry David Thoreau,* p. 79.
Bulletin of the Center for Children's Books, March, 2003, review of *Escape from Botany Bay,* p. 276; July, 2003, review of *Castaways,* p. 449.
Hungry Mind Review, winter, 1999, review of *The Coyote Bead,* p. 50.
Kirkus Reviews, November 1, 1997, review of *Dogs of Myth,* p. 1742; May 15, 2003, review of *Castaways,* p. 751; September 15, 2004, review of *Napoleon and Josephine: The Sword and the Hummingbird,* p. 914; September 15, 2005, review of *Horses of Myth,* p. 1027.
Kliatt, March, 2006, Claire Rosser, review of *A Mind with Wings,* p. 11.
Library Journal, October 1, 1997, L. Kriz, review of *The Kebra Nagast,* p. 88; July, 1998, Florence Scarinci, review of *The Mythology of Cats: Feline Legend and Lore through the Ages,* p. 121.
Publishers Weekly, December 18, 1995, review of *Eagle Boy,* p. 54; May 11, 1998, review of *Doctor Bird,* p. 67; November 8, 1999, review of *Dogs of Myth,* p. 68; September 3, 2001, review of *The Metaphysical Cat,* p. 82; June 9, 2003, review of *Castaways,* p. 54.
School Library Journal, August, 1998, Judith Gloyer, review of *The Story of Blue Elk,* pp. 150-151; March, 2000, Cheri Estes, review of *Dogs of Myth,* p. 254; November, 2000, William McLoughlin, review of *Tom Cringle: Battle on the High Seas,* p. 154; December, 2000, Nancy Call, review of *Cats of Myth,* p. 133; April, 2001, Ellen Vevier, review of *The Jacob Ladder,* p. 140; October, 2001, Patricia B. McGee, review of *Tom Cringle: The Pirate and the Patriot,* p. 160; April, 2003, Carolyn Janssen, review of *Escape from Botany Bay,* p. 162; June, 2003, review of *Castaways,* p. 161; October, 2004, Ann W. Moore, review of *Napoleon and Josephine,* p. 166; December, 2005, Coop Renner, review of *Horses of Myth,* p. 128; September, 2006, Christina Stenson-Carey, review of *A Mind with Wings,* p. 208.
Tribune Books (Chicago, IL), February 9, 1997, Robert Rodi, review of *The Mythology of Dogs: Canine Legend and Lore through the Ages,* pp. 1, 11.
Voice of Youth Advocates, June, 2003, review of *Escape from Botany Bay,* p. 130; October, 2004, Cynthia Winfield, review of *Napoleon and Josephine,* p. 298.

ONLINE

Gerald Hausman Home Page, http://www.geraldhausman. com (May 15, 2007).

*   *   *

HAUSMAN, Gerry
See HAUSMAN, Gerald

*   *   *

HAWES, Louise 1943-
(Jamie Suzanne)

Personal

Born June 21, 1943, in Boulder, CO; daughter of Maurice (an economic consultant) and Isabel (a homemaker) Hawes; married Stephen Jacobson, December 26, 1965 (divorced, 1978); children: Marc, Robin. *Education:* Swarthmore College, B.A., 1965; attended Lehigh University, 1971-73, and Barnes Foundation, 1977-78. *Hobbies and other interests:* Drawing, sculpting, long walks.

Addresses

Home—Pittsboro, NC. *E-mail*—mail@louisehawes.com.

Career

Children's book author and educator. State of New Jersey Department of Community Affairs, Division on Aging, Trenton, public information director, 1967-69; Supermarkets General Corp., Woodbridge, NJ, assistant editor of *Pathmark News,* 1970-72; Barbizon School, Paramus, NJ, instructor in advertising and writing, 1978-79; Stanley H. Kaplan Educational Centers, New York, NY, advertising manager, beginning 1980; freelance writer, 1985—. Spalding University, KY, instructor in M.F.A. writing program; Vermont College M.F.A. Writing for Children program, cofounder and member of faculty; lecturer at schools; teacher at writing workshops.

Awards, Honors

New Jersey Authors Award, New Jersey Institute of Technology, 1987, for *Nelson Malone Meets the Man from Mush-Nut;* two New Jersey writing fellowships; South Carolina Young-Adult Book of the Year nomination and YALSA Popular Paperback designation, both 2002, both for *Rosey in the Present Tense;* New York Public Library Books for the Teen Age designation, 2003, for *Waiting for Christopher;* Children's Book Council/International Reading Association Choice designation; New York Public Library Books for the Teen Age designation and Bank Street College of Education choice, both 2004, both for *The Vanishing Point.*

Writings

FOR CHILDREN

Nelson Malone Meets the Man from Mush-Nut (middle-grade novel), illustrated by Bert Dodson, Lodestar (New York, NY), 1986.

Nelson Malone Saves Flight 942 (middle-grade novel), illustrated by Jacqueline Rogers, Lodestar (New York, NY), 1986.

Rosey in the Present Tense, Walker (New York, NY), 1999.

Willem de Kooning: The Life of an Artist, Enslow (Berkeley Heights, NJ), 2002.

Waiting for Christopher, Candlewick Press (Cambridge, MA), 2002.

The Vanishing Point: A Story of Lavinia Fontana, Houghton Mifflin (Boston, MA), 2004.

Muti's Necklace: The Oldest Story in the World (picture book), illustrated by Rebecca Guay-Mitchell, Houghton Mifflin (Boston, MA), 2006.

Anteaters Don't Dream, and Other Stories, University Press of Mississippi (Jackson, MS), 2007.

Short fiction included in anthologies *Love and Sex: Ten Stories of Truth,* 2001; *Such a Pretty Face,* 2007; and *Be Careful What You Wish,* 2007.

"SWEET VALLEY TWINS" SERIES; UNDER PSEUDONYM JAMIE SUZANNE

Stretching out the Truth, Bantam (New York, NY), 1987.

Outcast, Bantam (New York, NY), 1987.

New Girl Bantam (New York, NY), 1987.

Sneaking Out, Bantam (New York, NY), 1987.

OTHER

Also author of filmstrips for Time-Life and Educational Reading Services, 1973-74. Author of monographs for State of New Jersey, 1969-86. Contributor of articles and short fiction to periodicals, including *Mademoiselle, Scholastic Voice, Extension Journal,* and *Midnight.*

Sidelights

Louise Hawes writes for children and teens, as well as for adults. Her award-winning novels for older readers include *Rosey in the Present Tense, Waiting for Christopher* and *The Vanishing Point: A Story of Lavinia Fontana.* In addition to longer works, Hawes has published nonfiction, has produced the short-story anthology *Anteaters Don't Dream, and Other Stories,* and has had her short fiction included in several anthologies. She has also authored the picture book *Muti's Necklace: The Oldest Story in the World,* an adaptation of an ancient Egyptian tale about a young woman who risks everything to recover a prized family possession, the book was praised by *School Library Journal* reviewer Coop Renner as "an original fairy tale about familial love and its power to thwart even the majesty of Pharaoh." In addition to writing, Hawes dedicates much of her time to teaching. In addition to serving on the faculty at Spalding University's graduate-level writing program, she was a cofounder and instructor at Vermont College's innovative M.F.A. program in writing for children.

Praised by *Booklist* contributor Shelle Rosenfeld as "a multifaceted, insightful exploration of heartbreak and loss," *Rosey in the Present Tense* focuses on Franklin, a seventeen year old who is having difficulty dealing with

Louise Hawes draws on an ancient Egyptian story in Muti's Necklace, *which features detailed illustrations by Rebecca Guay-Mitchell.* (Houghton Mifflin Company, 2006. Illustration © 2006 by Rebecca Guay-Mitchell. All rights reserved. Reproduced by permission of Houghton Mifflin Company.)

the recent death of his girlfriend. When Rosey appears to him as a ghost, called back by his grief, Franklin is at first glad. With the help of Rosey's grandmother Lin, who can also see the ghostly teen, he eventually comes to realize that, just as Rosey's spirit must move on, so must he. Rosenfeld praised Hawes's decision to compose her novel in both first-and third-person narratives, going on to write that Hawes creates an "appealing" teen protagonist whose story is told in an evocative, "lyrical" text.

Concerns over child abuse justify kidnapping, in the opinion of the two young teens that star Hawes' young-adult novel *Waiting for Christopher.* When readers meet fourteen-year-old Feena Harvey, she has just moved from New England to Florida with her depressed single mother. Shy, lonely, and friendless, and still grieving the death of infant brother Christy from SIDS nine years before, Feena becomes emotionally involved with an unhappy young child she has seen crying in a city park near her home. Rather than turn the situation over to authorities, however, Feena comforts the sobbing toddler and hides him in a secret place. The logistics of caring for him is made easier when classmate Raylene figures out what is going on and decides to help. As they plan a life focused on the toddler, the girls also create a bond of friendship, but are eventually forced to confront the realities of the situation they have created. Hawes' "simple, eloquent words reveal complex truths of family love and sorrow," noted Hazel Rochman in *Booklist,* while in *Kliatt* Paula Rohrlick described *Waiting for Christopher* as "emotionally convincing and suspenseful."

An historical novel based on the life of late sixteenth-century Italian painter Lavinia Fontana, *The Vanishing Point* brings to life a talented young woman as she attempts to overcome social obstacles in order to follow her calling as an artist. Taught to paint by her portrait-painter father Prospero while growing up in Bologna, Lavinia marries an artist who also supports her painting. Hawes tells Lavinia's story through a first-person narration that finds the young protagonist, at age fourteen, eliciting the aid of her father's apprentices in getting paper; meeting Paolo, the young man who will become her husband; battling the measles; and obtaining clandestine critiques of her work. "Hawes deftly blends history and invention" in her fictional biography, noted *Booklist* contributor Jennifer Mattson, while in *School Library Journal* Ginny Gustin deemed the novel "a fascinating glimpse into the life of a Renaissance artist." Praising *The Vanishing Point* as "well-written" and "unique," Claire Rosser added in *Kliatt* that Hawes successfully "immerse[s] her readers into life in Italy so long ago."

"Before I was ten years old, I had decided to be a writer," Hawes once told *SATA.* "Not that there weren't detours along the way to this happy outcome. Both my parents were gifted, bright people who enjoyed painting as well as writing. For years, I painted and drew as

Cover of Hawes' inspiring novel The Vanishing Point, *featuring artwork by Cynthia von Buhler.* (Houghton Mifflin Company, 2004. Jacket art copyright © 2004 by Cynthia von Buhler. Reproduced by permission of Houghton Mifflin Company.)

much as I wrote. I also tried my hand at acting and even had a sculpture studio for several years before I returned to that rock-hard place at the pit of my soul, the place where a very calm, sure voice told me, 'You can flirt with all these exciting modes of expression, you can wriggle and twist and carry on, but the way you're meant to be you is by writing. It's lonely, it's frustrating, and you can't do it at parties to the amusement and delight of your friends. But it's you.'

"*Nelson Malone Meets the Man from Mush-Nut* was written for my children when they were very close to Nelson's age, eleven. I wanted to make sure they were exposed to some stories that didn't teach or preach or serve any other nefarious, 'useful' purpose. I wanted Nelson's adventures to be what children crave most and get least: silliness and fun.

"*Nelson Malone Saves Flight 942* is a sixth-grade curtain call for Nelson's fifth-grade foolishness and carryings-on. He may have gained a grade in this sequel, but he's lost none of his propensity for crazy adventure—with preening rock idols, has-been magicians, newly hatched pterodactyls, not to mention pint-size ghosts and a teacher who takes her class on field trips to horror movies and amusement parks.

"Whenever anyone asks me how on earth I come up with such off-beat stories, I have a ready excuse: my mother. In fact, Nelson's wonderful teacher, Sylvia Tuckman, is patterned after the woman who used to beg my sisters and me to skip school in favor of shadow shows, talking animals, and life-size paper dolls. Because she didn't have an 'outside' job and because she was endlessly creative, lonely, and loving, she was forever bursting with exciting projects and plans. Physically, she's a small woman who lacks 'Terrible Tuckman''s imposing girth, but emotionally she was unquestionably the largest influence in my childhood.

"Perhaps the most rewarding part of writing for young readers is the mail. I have received letters from all over, letters from girls and boys I'd never met, but who had met me! What a wonderful, life-redeeming feeling to be told that, because of a book of mine, some youngster wants to be a writer, too!"

Biographical and Critical Sources

PERIODICALS

Booklist, April 1, 1999, Shelle Rosenfeld, review of *Rosey in the Present Tense,* p. 1398; July, 2002, Hazel Rochman, review of *Waiting for Christopher,* p. 1838; November 1, 2004, Jennifer Mattson, review of *The Vanishing Point: A Story of Lavinia Fontana,* p. 496; July 1, 2006, Jennifer Mattson, review of *Muti's Necklace: The Oldest Story in the World,* p. 66.

Bulletin of the Center for Children's Books, May, 1999, review of *Rosey in the Present Tense,* p. 314; September, 2002, review of *Waiting for Christopher,* p. 41.

Horn Book, September-October, 2002, Kitty Flynn, review of *Waiting for Christopher,* p. 573.

Journal of Adolescent and Adult Literacy, March, 2003, Pamela Osback, review of *Waiting for Christopher,* p. 527.

Kirkus Reviews, April 1, 1986, review of *Nelson Malone Meets the Man from Mush-Nut;* May 1, 2002, review of *Waiting for Christopher,* p. 655; September 1, 2004, review of *The Vanishing Point,* p. 866; May 15, 2006, review of *Muti's Necklace,* p. 518.

Kliatt, March, 2002, Paula Rohrlick, review of *Waiting for Christopher,* p. 11; September, 2004, Claire Rosser, review of *The Vanishing Point,* p. 10.

New York Times Book Review, March 12, 1989, p. 37.

Publishers Weekly, June 27, 1986, review of *Nelson Malone Meets the Man from Mush-Nut;* March 8, 1999, review of *Rosey in the Present Tense,* p. 69; May 20, 2002, review of *Waiting for Christopher,* p. 66; November 15, 2004, review of *The Vanishing Point,* p. 61.

School Library Journal, August, 1986, review of *Nelson Malone Meets the Man from Mush-Nut;* May, 1988, review of *Nelson Malone Saves Flight 942;* May,

1999, Alison Follos, review of *Rosey in the Present Tense,* p. 125; June, 2002, Connie Tyrrell Burns, review of *Waiting for Christopher,* p. 140; March, 2003, Mary Elam, review of *Willem de Kooning: The Life of an Artist,* p. 251; December, 2004, Ginny Gustin, review of *The Vanishing Point,* p. 146; June, 2006, Coop Renner, review of *Muti's Necklace,* p. 119.

Voice of Youth Advocates, April, 2002, review of *Waiting for Christopher,* p. 655; December, 2004, Gale Giles, review of *The Vanishing Point,* p. 382.

ONLINE

Wordswimmer, http://wordswimmer.blogspog.com/ (February, 2007), Bruce Black, interview with Hawes.

Louise Hawes Home Page, http://www.louisehawes.com (May 10, 2007).*

*   *   *

HAYCAK, Cara 1961-

Personal

Born 1961; married J. Miller Tobin (a television director). *Education:* Attended Reed College, Cornell University, University of California, Los Angeles Extension, and Bennington College; Columbia University, M.F.A. *Hobbies and other interests:* Travel.

Addresses

Home—Los Angeles, CA. *Agent*—Dan Mandel, Sanford J. Greenburger Associates, 55 5th Ave., New York, NY 10003. *E-mail*—redpalms@earthlink.net.

Career

Writer, editor, and Web-site programmer. Formerly worked in films as set decorator, documentary film production, script reader, and story editor.

Member

Society of Children's Book Writers and Illustrators.

Awards, Honors

Society of Children's Book Writers and Illustrators works-in-progress grant, 2000, for *Red Palms.*

Writings

Red Palms (young-adult novel), Wendy Lamb Books (New York, NY), 2004.

Contributor to periodicals, including *Kliatt* and *First for Women.*

Sidelights

A former set designer and story editor in the motion-picture industry, Cara Haycak worked in Web and print editing before making her fiction debut with the young-adult novel *Red Palms.* The book draws readers back in time to the early 1930s and introduces fourteen-year-old Benita. Financially ruined by the worldwide economic collapse known as the Great Depression, Benita's bankrupt father is forced to give up the family's lavish city home in Guayaquil, Ecuador. Although the man is determined to do the best he can for his family, his response to the crisis is drastic: he moves Betina and the rest of the family to the remote tropical island where he intends to start a coconut plantation. A stubborn man, Betina's father refuses to let go of his dream despite his lack of farming knowledge; only with the help of Paita Island's kindhearted local residents does the plantation have any chance of success. Unfortunately, Benita's father openly expresses contempt for the unsophisticated natives, and this antagonism grows as the situation deteriorates. When Benita falls in love with a handsome, Spanish-speaking islander named Raul, she makes the fateful choice to move from girlhood into womanhood, leaving behind all vestiges of her comfortable, civilized life in the process.

Reviewing *Red Palms* in *Booklist,* Gillian Engberg called Haycak's fiction debut "fascinating," describing the work as a "captivating, insightful" tale with well-drawn protagonists and a "vividly evoked setting." In *Kliatt* Claire Rosser noted the novelist's "experience working with tribal people in South America," adding that "Benita is a highly intelligent and sensitive young woman, who learns to survive a bad relationship and a difficult family situation." Remarking on the "overtones of magical realism" that characterize the second part of the novel, *School Library Journal* critic Bruce Anne Shook deemed *Red Palms* "an absorbing tale," while a *Kirkus Reviews* critic praised Haycak's story as "unique and beautiful." In *Publishers Weekly* a critic concluded that the young heroine's "unquenchable thirst for knowledge and ultimate liberation" provides Haycak's coming-of-age tale with "an uplifting" ending.

In an essay for *Kliatt,* Haycak described the genesis of her debut novel. Although *Red Palms* started out with an adult focus when Haycak began writing it as her M.F.A. thesis, she noted that "creative works always take on a life of their own, despite all your intentions and labor to shape them a particular way." "The book I found myself writing was a tale of high adventure," the author soon realized, "with perils, pitfalls and personal triumphs." As Haycak explained, she soon realized that her novel-in-progress "would more thoroughly entertain a younger reader."

Although *Red Palms* was inspired by the wealth of childhood memories Haycak's mother shared with her only daughter, its central story is grounded in a good deal of research. As the author explained in her *Kliatt* essay, "topics as wide-ranging as water systems of medieval monasteries, ancient priestesses and their rituals, the habits of jaguars in the wild, and languages of ancient South American people filled out the story in ways I could not possibly invent all on my own."

Cover of Cara Haycak's debut novel **Red Palms,** *featuring artwork by Marci Senders.*

Biographical and Critical Sources

PERIODICALS

Booklist, November 15, 2004, Gillian Engberg, review of *Red Palms,* p. 595.

Bulletin of the Center for Children's Books, January, 2005, Timnah Card, review of *Red Palms,* p. 210.

Kirkus Reviews, November 1, 2004, review of *Red Palms,* p. 1044.

Kliatt, January, 2005, Cara Haycak, "Writing *Red Palms,*" p. 4; May, 2006, Claire Rosser, review of *Red Palms,* p. 19.

Publishers Weekly, December 6, 2004, review of *Red Palms,* p. 60.

School Library Journal, December, 2004, Bruce Anne Shook, review of *Red Palms,* p. 147.

Voice of Youth Advocates, December, 2004, review of *Red Palms,* p. 404.

ONLINE

Red Palms Web site, http://www.red-palms.com/ (May 10, 2007).

*   *   *

HOPKINSON, Deborah 1952-

Personal

Born February 4, 1952, in Lowell, MA; daughter of Russell W. (a machinist) and Gloria D. Hopkinson; married Andrew D. Thomas (a teacher); children: Rebekah, Dimitri. *Education:* University of Massachusetts—Amherst, B.A., 1973; University of Hawaii, M.A., 1978. *Hobbies and other interests:* Reading, hiking, gardening, history.

Addresses

Home—Corvallis, OR. *Office*—Oregon State University Foundation, 850 SW 35th St., Corvallis, OR 97333.

Career

Manoa Valley Theater, Honolulu, HI, marketing director, 1981-84; University of Hawaii Foundation, Honolulu, development director, 1985-89; East-West Center, Honolulu, development director, 1989-94; Whitman College, Walla Walla, WA, director of grants, 1994-2004; Oregon State University Foundation, director of foundation relations, 2004—.

Member

Society of Children's Book Writers and Illustrators.

Awards, Honors

Merit award, Society of Children's Book Writers and Illustrators, 1991; work-in-progress grant, Society of Children's Book Writers and Illustrators, 1993; International Reading Association Award for Young People, 1994, for *Sweet Clara and the Freedom Quilt;* Golden Kite Award for Picture-Book Text, 1999, for *A Band of Angels,* 2004, for *Apples to Oregon;* American Library Association Notable Children's Books designation, 2000, for *A Band of Angels,* 2005, for *Apples to Oranges,* 2007, for *Up before Daybreak* and *Sky Boys;* National Council of Teachers of English/Orbis Pictus Award Honor Book designation, and Jane Addams Children's Book Award Honor Book designation, both 2004, both for *Shutting out the Sky; Boston Globe/Horn Book* Award Honor Book designation, 2006, for *Sky Boys.*

Writings

Bluebird Summer, illustrated by Bethanne Andersen, Greenwillow (New York, NY), 2001.

Deborah Hopkinson, with her dog, Pea, 2007. (Photograph courtesy of Deborah Hopkinson.)

Contributor of short stories to periodicals, including *Cricket.*

NONFICTION FOR CHILDREN

Pearl Harbor, Dillon Press/Macmillan (New York, NY), 1991.
Shutting out the Sky: Life in the Tenements of New York, 1880-1915, Orchard Books (New York, NY), 2003.
Up before Daybreak: Cotton and People in America, Scholastic (New York, NY), 2006.

HISTORICAL FICTION FOR CHILDREN

Sweet Clara and the Freedom Quilt, illustrated by James E. Ransome, Knopf (New York, NY), 1993.
Birdie's Lighthouse, illustrated by Kimberly Bulcken Root, Atheneum (New York, NY), 1996.
A Band of Angels: A Story Inspired by the Jubilee Singers, illustrated by Raúl Colón, Atheneum (New York, NY), 1999.
Maria's Comet, illustrated by Deborah Lanino, Atheneum (New York, NY), 1999.
Fannie in the Kitchen: The Whole Story from Soup to Nuts of How Fannie Farmer Invented Recipes with Precise Measurements, illustrated by Nancy Carpenter, Atheneum (New York, NY), 2001.
Under the Quilt of Night, illustrated by James E. Ransome, Atheneum (New York, NY), 2002.
Girl Wonder: A Baseball Story in Nine Innings, illustrated by Terry Widener, Atheneum (New York, NY), 2003.
Apples to Oregon: Being the (Slightly) True Narrative of How a Brave Pioneer Father Brought Apples, Peaches, Plums, Grapes, and Cherries (and Children) across the Plains, illustrated by Nancy Carpenter, Atheneum (New York, NY), 2003.
A Packet of Seeds, illustrated by Bethanne Anderson, Greenwillow (New York, NY), 2004.
Hear My Sorrow: The Diary of Angela Denoto, a Shirtwaist Worker, Scholastic (New York, NY), 2004.

Billy and the Rebel: Based on a True Civil War Story, illustrated by Brian Floca, Atheneum (New York, NY), 2005.

Saving Strawberry Farm, illustrated by Rachel Isadora, Greenwillow (New York, NY), 2005.

From Slave to Soldier: Based on a True Civil War Story, illustrated by Brian Floca, Atheneum (New York, NY), 2005.

Sky Boys: How They Built the Empire State Building, illustrated by James E. Ransome, Schwartz & Wade, 2006.

Into the Firestorm: A Novel of San Francisco, 1906, Knopf (New York, NY), 2006.

Sweet Land of Liberty, illustrated by Leonard Jenkins, Peachtree (Atlanta, GA), 2007.

"PRAIRIE SKIES" SERIES; CHAPTER BOOKS

Pioneer Summer, illustrated by Patrick Faricy, Aladdin (New York, NY), 2002.

Cabin in the Snow, illustrated by Patrick Faricy, Aladdin (New York, NY), 2002.

Our Kansas Home, illustrated by Patrick Faricy, Aladdin (New York, NY), 2003.

"KLONDIKE KID" SERIES; CHAPTER BOOKS

Sailing for Gold, illustrated by Bill Farnsworth, Aladdin (New York, NY), 2004.

Adventure in Gold Town, illustrated by Bill Farnsworth, Aladdin (New York, NY), 2004.

The Long Trail, illustrated by Bill Farnsworth, Aladdin (New York, NY), 2004.

BIOGRAPHIES; FOR CHILDREN

Susan B. Anthony: Fighter for Women's Rights, illustrated by Amy Bates, Aladdin (New York, NY), 2005.

Who Was Charles Darwin?, illustrated by Nancy Harrison, Grosset & Dunlap (New York, NY), 2005.

John Adams Speaks for Freedom, illustrated by Craig Orback, Aladdin (New York, NY), 2005.

Deborah Hopkinson and You (autobiography), Libraries Unlimited (Westport, CT), 2007.

Sidelights

When Deborah Hopkinson was in school, she thought learning about history was boring, and often hid a novel inside her history text during class. "But eventually it did make me curious about all the missing parts," she wrote in an essay for *Horn Book*. "For one thing, where were the women? . . . And what about everyone else: African Americans, Asian Americans, Latinos, children? What were the rest of us doing all that time, anyway?" Questions such as these Hopkinson explores in her historical fiction for young readers, as well as in her nonfiction titles.

Hopkinson's first book, *Pearl Harbor,* was published in 1991 as part of Dillon Press's "Places in American History" series. Aimed at older children, the book tells the story of the surprise Japanese bombing of Pearl Harbor during World War II and includes photographs showing the Hawaiian harbor both during and after the war.

For her second book, Hopkinson decided to try her hand at fiction. *Sweet Clara and the Freedom Quilt* is about a slave girl who is separated from her mother and sent to work in the fields. While living with an elderly woman named Aunt Rachel, who teaches her to sew, Clara becomes a seamstress. Preoccupied with thoughts of her mother and freedom, Clara overhears other slaves discussing the "underground railroad," and decides to use her sewing skills to help herself and other slaves escape. In her spare time, she sews a quilt; but instead of patchwork, Clara's quilt is a map detailing an escape route. When she finally does escape the plantation, she leaves the quilt for other slaves.

Hopkinson commented: "The idea for *Sweet Clara and the Freedom Quilt* came to me while listening to an NPR radio story about African American quilts. I consider this story a wonderful gift, and feel very happy that I was able to tell it." The story "brings power and substance to this noteworthy picture book," according to a reviewer for *Publishers Weekly,* the critic concluding that Hopkinsons's "first-rate book is a triumph of the heart."

Hopkinson gave her readers another exciting story about a brave young girl with *Birdie's Lighthouse.* Set in the mid-nineteenth century, the book takes the form of a ten-year-old girl's diary. Bertha "Birdie" Holland, the main character, moves to a lighthouse island in Maine with her father after he gives up life as a sailor. Birdie's brother is more interested in fishing than in the workings of the beacon light, but Birdie herself becomes fascinated with the job. Eventually, she learns enough about the lighthouse to man it herself when her father falls gravely ill.

Although Birdie is a fictional character, she is closely based on real-life girls whose heroic lighthouse adventures are well documented. The book is illustrated with watercolor and pen and ink, and these pictures were remarked upon by several reviewers as an important part of the book. Praising the work as a whole, Mary M. Burns wrote in *Horn Book* that, "with an exemplary assemblage of genre paintings perfectly attuned to the flow of the text," *Birdie's Lighthouse* "is restrained yet charged with emotion." A *Kirkus Reviews* contributor enthused that "period details and a spirited heroine with a clear voice make this book a genuine delight." A *Publishers Weekly* reviewer found *Birdie's Lighthouse* "atmospheric" and Birdie herself "brave and likable." While noting that the narrative "is unlikely to be mistaken for the voice of an actual young girl," the critic went on to praise Hopkinson's "careful attention to period and setting," concluding that the "nuances of feeling and historical detail shine through" in the novel. Anne Parker, writing in *School Library Journal,* called *Birdie's Lighthouse* "a shining bit of historical fiction."

Several of Hopkinson's picture books return to the issues discussed in *Sweet Clara and the Freedom Quilt.* In *A Band of Angels: A Story Inspired by the Jubilee Singers,* the author tells a tale based on pianist Ella Sheppard's experience at the Fisk School, which took freed slaves on a performance tour to raise money. When singing classical music, they could not draw a crowd, but when they started to sing spirituals, audiences flocked to hear them perform. Hopkinson's "lilting text interweaves subtle details about racial tensions . . . emphasizing the importance of education and of being true to oneself," wrote a *Publishers Weekly* contributor of the title. *Under the Quilt of Night,* which is considered to be a companion to *Sweet Clara and the Freedom Quilt,* follows five families as they escape from slavery, watching for the message, through a quilt, that they have reached a safe house. "Hopkinson captures the fear of the escaping slaves, but tempers their fear with the bravery and hope that spurred them on," wrote a contributor to *Kirkus Reviews.* According to Marianne Saccardi in *School Library Journal,* "the narrative is told in a series of poems, . . . and the language is lovely."

Told through the eyes of young Marcia Shaw, *Fannie in the Kitchen: The Whole Story from Soup to Nuts of How Fannie Farmer Invented Recipes with Precise Measurements* introduces young readers to an important woman in history. "Hopkinson fashions her clever narrative after her subtitle, presenting the book as seven courses-cum-chapters," explained a *Horn Book* critic. Although Marcia at first resents Fannie's invasion of the kitchen, she soon becomes mystified by the magic of the young woman's cooking. It's not magic, Fannie explains, but science. A *Publishers Weekly* contributor called the book "prepared to perfection and served up with style," while Genevieve Ceraldi commented in *School Library Journal* that, "in a time of celebrity chefs on television, this is a whimsical look back to when it all began."

Though less famous that Fannie Farmer, Alta Weiss also serves as an historical role model for young women in Hopkinson's retelling of her story: *Girl Wonder: A Baseball Story in Nine Innings.* Weiss manages to convince a coach of a semi-professional baseball team to let her play with the men, because watching the spectacle of a girl playing baseball is sure to sell tickets. "Cleverly organized into nine brief 'innings,' this graphically rich, rewarding tale will inspire readers," a *Publishers Weekly* critic wrote of the book. In order to help readers understand the actual history behind the story, "Hopkinson enriches her burnished prose with an author's note about the real Alta Weiss," according to GraceAnne A. DeCandido in *Booklist.*

Hopkinson has also approached historical fiction through chapter books for beginning readers. Her "Prairie Skies" trilogy follows Charlie and Ida Jane Keller's move to Kansas from Massachusetts in the 1850s. In *Pioneer Summer,* the Keller family makes the long jour-

ney west, leaving behind Charlie's grandfather, who comforts Charlie by explaining that they will both still be under the same sky. Several adventures, including a fall through a frozen pond and a battle with a prairie wildfire, mark the journey. "Distinguished by taut sentences well tailored to the audience, this informative tale rolls at a promising clip," according to a *Publishers Weekly* contributor.

In the second entry in the series, *Cabin in the Snow,* Charlie must decide whether to sympathize with the Morgans, a family they once traveled with who support slavery, or stand with his family, who are abolitionists. The final book in the trilogy, *Our Kansas Home,* deals with the Underground Railroad, and the dangers that the Keller family must face in order to stay true to their abolitionist beliefs. "Hopkinson tells a good story, steeped in rich history and research," wrote a *Kirkus Reviews* contributor of *Cabin in the Snow.* A *Kirkus Reviews* contributor wrote of *Our Kansas Home* that "dramatic cliffhanging chapters, brisk action, and exciting historical situations mesh together into a memorable, exciting tale." Susan Shaver, writing in *School Library Journal,* noted that the trilogy "brings an era of history alive, and will pique children's interest." Hopkinson used the same trilogy format in her "Klondike Kids" series, recounting the adventures of Davey Hill, the Klondike Kid, set in Alaska during the early 1800s.

Apples to Oregon: Being the (Slightly) True Narrative of How a Brave Pioneer Father Brought Apples, Peaches, Plums, Grapes, and Cherries (and Children) across the Plains sets the pioneer journey in picture-book format. A family journeys from Iowa to Oregon, keeping Daddy's fruit trees from being damaged on the journey. "The flavor is in the folksy telling of this clever tall tale," wrote a *Kirkus Reviews* critic. *Booklist* contributor Kay Weisman found the tale to be "rich in language that begs to be read out loud."

In *Saving Strawberry Farm* Hopkinson tells the story of how young Davy got a whole community together during the Great Depression to help Miss Elsie save her strawberry farm. "Hopkinson's graceful text [is] filled with colloquial dialogue," wrote Gillian Engberg in *Booklist.* Kristine M. Casper, reviewing the book for *School Library Journal,* considered the picture book "an excellent introduction to this time period." *Sky Boys: How They Built the Empire State Building,* shows another aspect of the Great Depression: how the construction of the tallest building in the world gave hope to the people of New York. Engberg complimented Hopkinson's "crisp, lyrical free verse" and suggested that the "unique, memorable title" would "enhance poetry and history units." According to a critic for *Publishers Weekly,* "the drama of the building's rise makes for a literally riveting account."

Along with her historical fiction, Hopkinson has also written contemporary picture books. *Bluebird Summer* is the story of how two young children help bluebirds return to their grandfather's yard after their grandmother dies. "Hopkinson's prose expresses the tightly knit love of the family," wrote a contributor to *Publishers Weekly.* Noting that the book has an open conclusion, John Peters added in *Booklist* that "youngsters will understand that the work, and the feelings behind it, are more important than the ostensible goal."

Two of Hopkinson's tales, *Billy and the Rebel* and *From Slave to Soldier,* invite readers to imagine life during the U.S. Civil War. The latter follows Johnny, a young African American who, when released from slavery, quickly joins the Union army. Unlike many slaves who became soldiers, Johnny is welcomed by the unit he joins, and, in a dire situation, he manages to save the entire company. "Young Civil War buffs will welcome something they can read themselves," wrote a *Kirkus Reviews* contributor, and Peters maintained that Hopkinson's chapter book "will bring the era and people to life for modern young readers."

Into the Firestorm: A Novel of San Francisco, 1906 is the story of Nick Dray, a Texas farm boy who moved to San Francisco to make his way in the world. When the 1906 earthquake and subsequent great fire strikes, Nick's quick thinking helps save his employer's business and the lives of two of his neighbors. "Characterization and action are strong in this memorable tale," commented a *Kirkus Reviews* contributor, while Kristen Oravec wrote in *School Library Journal* that "the terror of the 1906 disaster is brought powerfully alive" by Hopkinson.

Inspired by the research she gathered for her "Dear America" title, *Hear My Sorrow: The Diary of Angela Denoto, a Shirtwaist Worker,* Hopkinson's *Shutting out the Sky: Life in the Tenements of New York* helps young readers imagine what life would have been like for youn immigrants in America near the turn of the twentieth century. "Hopkinson's enthusiasm for research, primary sources, and individual stories that make history come alive is evident," noted a contributor to *Kirkus Reviews.* A *Publishers Weekly* critic found the book to be "a highly readable discussion of change and reform with a look at the culture, joy and play" of the era. Another nonfiction title, *Up before Daybreak: Cotton and People in America,* helps young readers understand how cotton and the economics of the cotton trade helped shape the culture of the Americas. "The prose is clear, the documentation excellent . . . the voices of the children vivid and personal," noted a *Kirkus Reviews* contributor. Jennifer Mattson, writing in *Booklist,* felt that the complexity of America's cotton industry is "skillfully distilled for this audience," and *School Library Journal* critic Ann Welton recommended the book as "a first-rate report and research source."

Speaking with an interviewer for the *Down Home Books* Web site regarding the stylistic differences among her many picture books, Hopkinson explained: "I have tried, as much as possible, to experiment with both writing style and structure," making each book unique. As for her goal as a writer, she told Sharon L. McElmeel of *Talk* that she hopes "to write stories good enough, important enough, that if a library didn't have much money, they would still want to have them."

Biographical and Critical Sources

BOOKS

Hopkinson, Deborah, *Deborah Hopkinson and You* (autobiography), Libraries Unlimited (Westport, CT), 2007.

PERIODICALS

Booklist, June 1, 1997, p. 1718; April 15, 1999, Ilene Cooper, review of *A Band of Angels: A Story Inspired by the Jubilee Singers,* p. 1529; September 15, 1999, Carolyn Phelan, review of *Maria's Comet,* p. 268; April 15, 2001, John Peters, review of *Bluebird Summer,* p. 1564; May 15, 2001, Shelle Rosenfeld, review of *Fannie in the Kitchen: The Whole Story from Soup to Nuts of How Fannie Farmer Invented Recipes with Precise Measurements,* p. 1751; February 15, 2002, Cynthia Turnquest, review of *Under the Quilt of Night,* p. 1034; May 1, 2002, Susan Dove Lempke, review of *Pioneer Summer,* p. 1526; December 15, 2002, Susan Dove Lempke, review of *Cabin in the Snow,* p. 759; January 1, 2003, GraceAnne A. DeCandido, review of *Girl Wonder: A Baseball Story in Nine Innings,* p. 880; March 1, 2003, Susan Dove Lempke, review of *Our Kansas Home,* p. 1197; November 1, 2003, Hazel Rochman, review of *Shutting out the Sky: Life in the Tenements of New York, 1880-1915,* p. 492; January 1, 2004, Hazel Rochman, review of *Sailing for Gold,* p. 856; May 15, 2004, Gillian Engberg, review of *A Packet of Seeds,* p. 1625; September 1, 2004, Kay Weisman, review of *Apples to Oregon: Being the (Slightly) True Narrative of How a Brave Pioneer Father Brought Apples, Peaches, Plums, Grapes, and Cherries (and Children) across the Plains,* p. 132; February 1, 2005, Hazel Rochman, review of *Billy and the Rebel,* p. 965; May 1, 2005, Gillian Engberg, review of *Saving Strawberry Farm,* p. 1590; December 1, 2005, Gillian Engberg, review of *Sky Boys: How They Built the Empire State Building,* p. 66; January 1, 2006, John Peters, review of *From Slave to Soldier,* p. 116; February 1, 2006, Ilene Cooper, review of *Susan B. Anthony: Fighter for Women's Rights,* p. 52; April 15, 2006, Jennifer Mattson, review of *Up before Daybreak: Cotton and People in America,* p. 46; September 1, 2006, John Peters, review of *Into the Firestorm: A Novel of San Francisco, 1906,* p. 129.

Black Issues Book Review, May-June, 2003, Adrienne Ingrum, review of *Sweet Clara and the Freedom Quilt,* p. 58; January-February, 2004, Kitty Flynn, review of *Shutting out the Sky,* p. 101.

Bulletin of the Center for Children's Books, July-August 1993, p. 346.

Children's Bookwatch, April, 2006, review of *Sky Boys.*

Horn Book, July-August, 1997, p. 443; March, 1999, Joanna Rudge Long, review of *A Band of Angels,* p. 190; May, 2001, review of *Fannie in the Kitchen,* p. 312; July-August, 2002, Susan P. Bloom, review of *Under the Quilt of Night,* p. 447; November-December, 2002, Deborah Hopkinson, "The Missing Parts," p. 812; March-April, 2003, Martha V. Parravano, review of *Girl Wonder,* p. 204; March-April, 2006, Susan Dove Lempke, review of *Sky Boys,* p. 172; May-June, 2006, Kathleen Isaacs, review of *Up before Daybreak,* p. 343.

Kirkus Reviews, May 1, 1997, p. 722; November 1, 2001, review of *Under the Quilt of Night,* p. 1550; April 15, 2002, review of *Pioneer Summer,* p. 570; August 1, 2002, review of *Cabin in the Snow,* p. 1133; December 15, 2002, review of *Our Kansas Home,* p. 1850; February 1, 2003, review of *Girl Wonder,* p. 232; September 15, 2003, review of *Shutting out the Sky,* p. 1175; February 1, 2004, review of *Sailing for Gold,* p. 134; March 1, 2004, review of *A Packet of Seeds,* p. 223; August 15, 2004, review of *Apples to Oregon,* p. 807; June 15, 2004, review of *The Long Trail,* p. 577; January 15, 2005, review of *Billy and the Rebel,* p. 121; April 15, 2005, review of *Saving Strawberry Farm,* p. 475; September 1, 2005, review of *From Slave to Soldier,* p. 974; January 15, 2006, review of *Sky Boys,* p. 85; March 1, 2006, review of *Up before Daybreak,* p. 231; August 15, 2006, review of *Into the Firestorm,* p. 2006.

New York Times Book Review, June 17, 2001, Alida Becker, review of *Fannie in the Kitchen,* p. 25; December 21, 2003, review of *Shutting out the Sky,* p. 16; January 16, 2005, Stephanie Deutsch, review of *Apples to Oregon,* p. 14.

Publishers Weekly, February 8, 1993, p. 87; July 12, 1993, pp. 25-26; April 14, 1997, p. 74; January 4, 1999, review of *A Band of Angels,* p. 90; October 11, 1999, review of *Maria's Comet,* p. 75; April 23, 2001, review of *Fannie in the Kitchen,* p. 77, review of *Bluebird Summer,* p. 78; November 26, 2001, review of *Under the Freedom Quilt,* p. 61; April 15, 2002, review of *Pioneer Summer,* p. 65; December 23, 2002, review of *Girl Wonder,* p. 71; December 1, 2003, review of *Shutting out the Sky,* p. 58; August 30, 2004, review of *Apples to Oregon,* p. 54; January 9, 2006, review of *Sky Boys,* p. 52.

School Library Journal, June 1993, p. 76; June, 1997, pp. 90-92; May, 2001, Karen Land, review of *Bluebird Summer,* p. 123; May, 2001, Genevieve Ceraldi, review of *Fannie in the Kitchen,* p. 143; January, 2002, Marianne Saccardi, review of *Under the Quilt of Night,* p. 102; October, 2002, Kristen Oravec, review of *Pioneer Summer,* p. 112; January, 2003, Be Astengo, review of *Cabin in the Snow,* p. 97; March, 2003, Susan Shaver, review of *Our Kansas Home,* p. 196; March, 2003, Blair Christolon, review of *Girl Wonder,* p. 193; Decmeber, 2003, Carol Fazioli, review of *Shutting out the Sky,* p. 169; April, 2004, Marian Creamer, review of *A Packet of Seeds,* p. 114; July, 2004, Anne Knickerbocker, review of *Sailing for Gold,* p. 77; September, 2004, Roxanee Burg, review of *Apples to Oranges,* p. 162; November, 2004, Anne Knickerbocker, review of *The Long Trail,* p. 107; February, 2005, Joyce Adams Burner, review of *Fannie in the Kitchen,* p. 57; April, 2005, Sharon R. Pearce, review of *Adventure in Gold Town,* and Bethany L.W. Hankinson, review of *Billy and the Rebel,* both p. 98; August, 2005, Kristine M. Casper, review of *Saving Strawberry Farm,* p. 97; October, 2005, Anne Knickerbocker, review of *From Slave to Soldier,* p. 116; February, 2006, Grace Oliff, review of *Sky Boys,* p. 120; March, 2006, John Peters, review of *Girl Wonder,* p. 88; May, 2006, Julie R. Ranelli, review of *Susan B. Anthony,* p. 112; June, 2006, Ann Welton, review of *Up before Daybreak,* p. 178; December, 2006, Kristen Oravec, review of *Into the Firestorm,* p. 146.

Talk, November-December, 1998, "Author Profile: Deborah Hopkinson."

Teacher Librarian, December, 2005, GraceAnne A. DeCandido, "Food, Glorious Food," p. 13.

ONLINE

Deborah Hopkinson Home Page, http://www. deborahhopkinson.com (April 24, 2007).

Down Home Books Web site, http://www.downhomebooks. com/hopkinson.htm (June, 2004), interview with Hopkinson.

Rutgers University Web site, http://www.scils.rutgers.edu/ (January, 1999), "Words from Deborah Hopkinson."

Scholastic Web site, http://www.scholastic.com/ (April 24, 2007), profile of Hopkinson.

Autobiography Feature

Deborah Hopkinson

Deborah Hopkinson contributed the following auto-biographical essay to *SATA:*

Did you ever have dreams for your future that seemed far away and impossible to reach?

Maybe you wanted to see the Great Wall of China, scale Mt. Everest, be an astronaut, or just go surfing in Waikiki. Or perhaps you had daydreams about being a singer, playing professional sports, winning a gold medal in the Olympics, or receiving an Oscar.

Many of us have dreams like this. But often they change over time as we grow up. We end up making different choices, or find that while we love music, we can't carry a tune. We might come to realize that it's just not in the cards—someone who's five feet tall, like me, is simply not going to have what it takes to play basketball!

But every once in a while, those early childhood dreams stay with us no matter what. They don't go away, even if our life seems to be on a totally different course. And so we come to a point where we decide that after all, we have to at least try.

That's what happened to me, anyway. My fourth-grade teacher was named Miss Grace. She was silver-haired, round, and soft-spoken. She seemed very old, at least to a nine year old. We often had cold, snowy winters in my hometown of Lowell, Massachusetts. I remember that well, because like most of my classmates, I walked to school, which was probably a mile away. (I didn't know anyone whose family had more than one car.)

Now, it's fun to play in the snow, but my elementary school had a strict dress code: girls had to wear skirts or dresses. That's right: no pants or jeans, even in the winter. (This dress code didn't change until I was leaving high school!) We were allowed to wear snow pants under our skirts, so long as we took them off at school.

Perhaps Miss Grace felt sorry for all of us little girls arriving each morning with cold legs as bright red as lobsters. Or maybe she worried that we'd get sick and miss a lot of homework. In any case, what I remember most about the winter of fourth grade was that Miss Grace had a huge campaign to get each and every one of us to eat a hot breakfast every day—especially oatmeal.

Young Deborah, growing up in Lowell, Massachusetts (Photograph courtesy of Deborah Hopkinson.)

If you came to school in the morning and told her you'd had oatmeal for breakfast, you'd get a gold star on a big chart on the board. I think there was probably some kind of prize for the most stars. I wouldn't know. The thing was, I hated oatmeal—no matter how much brown sugar my mom let me sprinkle on it. I just could not eat it! (I love oatmeal now, though.)

Every morning Miss Grace would ask me if I ate some good, hot oatmeal, and every morning I hung my head and mumbled, "No, Miss Grace." She'd shake her head, disappointed in my lack of gold stars. She expected more from me, she said.

The thing was, Miss Grace was used to my being a model student. I was polite. I got good grades. I didn't talk, giggle, or cause any disruption in class. I always seemed to mind my own business.

Except for the oatmeal, Miss Grace probably figured I was just about the best kind of fourth grader she could have. But what Miss Grace didn't know was that there a reason I was always so quiet in class. I wasn't being good—I was being sneaky.

It happened like this: whenever we took out our big history or geography book, I'd prop it up open on my desk, hiding my face as much as possible. Then, being careful not to make a sound, I'd open my desk, and slip out whatever chapter book I happened to be reading. I'd hide it behind the big textbook. Somehow I managed to follow along in class—and read my favorite stories at the same time!

Even now, whenever I see a kid with her head buried in a book, I see myself. To tell the truth, I haven't changed much over the years: if I'm at an airport engrossed in a good book, I'll sometimes walk right onto the plane still reading, oblivious to my surroundings.

Sometime during elementary school, I decided I wanted to be a writer when I grew up. Now, I didn't really know what I wanted to write, or what being a writer actually meant. I only knew one thing: I loved to read. I loved how stories let me slip off into other worlds. I liked reading about real-life adventures or mysteries that made me keep turning the page. I especially loved staying up late to find out how the story ended.

Reading helped me find a world that seemed so much bigger than the one I knew. I might not fit in at recess (I was horrible at jump rope and way too short for Red Rover!), but somehow I belonged in the world of books, ideas, stories, and imagination—if only I could find a way to get there.

Someday, I determined, I would write a book myself. But that someday took a long time in coming.

You've probably already figured out that I was a pretty boring kid. Just ask my sisters. I'm the oldest of three girls. My sister Bonnie is almost three years younger, and my sister Janice five years younger. And, no surprise, what they remember most is that I always seemed to be walking around with my nose in a book, or holed up in my room reading until the middle of the night.

We did play together sometimes, though. We liked to wander in the fields and meadows near our house. One of my favorite places as a kid was Polliwog Pond. Once, my sister Bonnie fell in while we were out exploring. I wouldn't let her go home until she sat on a rock and her clothes dried, because otherwise I knew I'd be in big trouble. After all, as the oldest I was supposed to be watching out for her.

Although I wasn't very good at sports like kickball, we did live near the town tennis courts. My friends and sisters and I played a lot as we were growing up. I never

had formal lessons, but that didn't stop me from entering tournaments and playing on our school's team. Unfortunately, I don't think we won very much—if at all!

Our family didn't have a lot of extra money. My father worked hard: his job as an automotive machinist kept him working on his feet five days a week and half of each Saturday. My mom stayed home until my littlest sister was in school, but then she went to work to help make ends meet.

We did take one family vacation each summer, though. You see, my dad was an avid fly fisherman. He used to tie his own flies, and I loved to go down into the basement to watch him. He had set up a workbench there, with hooks and little containers full of soft, brightly colored feathers that he ordered from a specialty catalogue. Somehow, even though his hands were large, rough, and often oil-stained, he managed to create tiny imitations of real flies and insects, perfect for attracting trout.

Each summer, during my dad's two weeks of vacation, we went where the fishing was good—a small town called Rangeley in the northwest corner of Maine. It's a beautiful place, with thick forests, ponds, rivers, and several large lakes. In the winter, skiers flock to Saddleback Mountain. The Appalachian Trail passes through there, and hikers often stop in town to do laundry, buy groceries, and have a hot meal.

Rangeley is far north, close to the Canadian border, and some summers the lake was cold and it rained. But no matter what the weather, there was always something to do. And what my sisters and I remember most is going to the dump.

The dump? Yup, that's right. The Rangeley town dump was like the parking lot of a drive-in movie. And the feature attraction? Scavenging bears! On evenings when we didn't go to the dump to watch the bears, we drove along backwoods roads to find overlooks over marshy areas, perfect for viewing moose, who love to feed on water plants. . . .

Like my dad, I fell in love with Maine. After college I spent one summer in Rangeley, working as a waitress at a place called Saddleback Lake Lodge, which sat alone on a tiny lake at the foot of Saddleback Mountain. I lived in a log cabin with a wood stove. I had to wait tables three meals a day—starting at seven in the morning until nine o'clock, when dinner ended.

The best part was my days off. I went canoeing by myself on the quiet lake, looking for families of loons. Sometimes I took long bicycle trips. It was downhill into town, but boy, what a steep climb back up to the lodge!

Once, while walking my bike back along a logging road, a large animal crossed directly in front of me. It was the closest to a moose I'd ever been. Luckily, I

The author's daughter, Rebekeh, at age five, picking blueberries while on vacation in Maine (Photograph courtesy of Deborah Hopkinson.)

stopped short because a little while later a tall, gangly calf came by, following its mother. You do *not* want to get between a mama moose and her baby!

Over the years, I tried to time my visits back home to coincide with the annual Rangeley vacation, and my daughter, Rebekah, can still remember picking Maine blueberries when she was little. I've also tried to bring my love of Maine into my work.

My second picture book, *Birdie's Lighthouse,* is based on the story of a real-life Maine lighthouse keeper named Abigail Burgess Grant, who lived on Matinicus Rock, off the coast of Maine. She moved to the island with her family when she was a girl, and later married a light keeper.

In addition, one of my very first published stories, titled "The Bread Trough," was inspired by a harrowing incident that happened to the first white family who settled in Rangeley. As they trekked through the woods on their way to Rangeley Lake, the wooden bread trough (sort of like a large tray) with the baby of the family strapped onto it, somehow fell off the sled. The scary part was that no one in the family even noticed that the baby was gone until they stopped to rest farther up the trail. Luckily, when they backtracked, they found the baby safe and sound, with her "cradle" wedged between two trees.

Often when I visit schools, kids ask me about the kinds of books I liked to read when I was a girl. We didn't have a lot of money to buy books, so mostly I went to the library. But I do still own a few of the same books I had then. One is a copy of Robert McClusky's wonderful picture book, *Make Way for Ducklings,* which my grandmother gave me on my second birthday.

Some of my other favorites were *The Secret Garden* and *The Little Princess* by Frances Hodgson Burnett. I devoured series. We didn't have as many then as we do now, but I especially liked the "Trixie Belden" and the "Happy Hollisters" books (I think you can find old copies on eBay!). I can still remember how excited I was one Christmas morning when I got a whole box of books as a present. (Are you starting to see a pattern here? I *really, really* liked to read!)

When I was older, I read lots of historical fiction, such as *Hawaii,* by James Michener, or *Arundel,* by Kenneth Roberts. By the time I was in middle school, I was reading (though maybe not fully understanding) classical British literature such as Jane Austen's *Pride and Prejudice* and Charlotte Brontë's *Jane Eyre,* which are still two of my all-time favorites. I also read the novels of Charles Dickens, and liked *Great Expectations* and *David Copperfield* the best. At the same time, I liked real-life adventure books like Sir Edmund Hillary's *The Conquest of Everest.*

Although I love to read (and write) nonfiction now, back then I preferred to read fiction. I think part of the reason was that there simply weren't as many excellent nonfiction works and biographies for young readers as there are now. There was, however, one nonfiction series I remember well. It was called "Childhood of Famous Americans."

Over the years I've talked to lots of people (especially "baby boomers" like me) who recall this series, too. And what everyone remembers most is that all the books had bright orange covers. Most people just call them the "the orange biographies." The books were fictionalized stories about real people: Clara Barton, Helen Keller, Eleanor Roosevelt, Thomas Jefferson, and George Washington.

Most of the orange biographies in our school library were about famous men. I couldn't help wondering, *why aren't there more books about girls?* That was probably the first time I seriously began thinking about the role of women in history. It's no surprise, then, that many of the books I've gone on to write have been about girls and women, especially those whose stories aren't very well known.

One of these women was Maria Mitchell, America's first woman astronomer. Maria Mitchell was born in Nantucket, Massachusetts in the early 1800s, and she became the first American woman to discover a comet. She used to watch the stars from her family's rooftop with her father. Later she taught astronomy at Vassar College. There's even a crater on the moon named after her! When I first heard about the life of Maria Mitchell, I thought, "Wow. I grew up in Massachusetts and went to school there, but I never learned anything about this pioneer in American science." That's one of the reasons I wrote my picture book *Maria's Comet,* to make sure that other kids—who might want to study the stars someday—could find out about this fascinating woman.

Another book I wrote about a woman of the past is titled *Fannie in the Kitchen.* This story is about another Massachusetts woman named Fannie Merritt Farmer. When Fannie Farmer was about sixteen or seventeen, or so the story goes, she went to work as a mother's helper in the home of Mrs. Charles Shaw. While she was there, Fannie taught young Marcia Shaw, the daughter of the household, to cook. My story tells how Fannie decided to use exact measurements in recipes to make cooking easy for little Marcia.

Fannie Farmer later went on to write *The Boston Cooking School Cookbook,* one of the most popular cookbooks ever published. (I wish I could say that I'm a good cook, but, unfortunately, nothing could be further from the truth. But that's one of the best things about being an author. You can write about things, like cooking, singing, sewing, or climbing the Chilkoot Pass, without actually having to be good at them in real life.)

If you've read any of my books, you've probably noticed that I write a lot about history. The fact is, though, that when I was growing up I never thought of myself as someone who was interested in the past. I found history books pretty boring. I mean, does anyone really *enjoy* memorizing the dates of battles or the names of presidents?

But something happened back in Miss Grace's fourth-grade class that makes me think that I probably would have liked history better if I'd been able to learn about it differently. It was one of those times when we reading that big old history textbook. Only this time, I was actually paying attention to it rather than my own book!

And I can actually remember sitting at my desk and coming across a short description of the Underground Railroad. It wasn't much, just a few sentences about enslaved people escaping on the Underground Railroad, with those two words in bold. (If the term was bolded, of course, this meant we had better learn what it was, because it might be on a test.)

But the truth was, I actually did *want* to know what it was! "Trying to escape from slavery must have been so hard to do," I remember thinking. "How did people have the courage? What was it actually like?"

At the time, that one mention of the Underground Railroad was about all I could find in our textbook. Back then, we didn't have the Internet. "There just has to be more about this Underground Railroad," I thought. "If I only knew where to find it."

When I finally became a children's writer, I remembered that feeling of sitting in class and being curious about something. I remembered wanting to know more. I guess in a way, I'm still that kind of person who loves to discover something new.

And that's how I came to write about history.

"Skiing around town as a kid," Lowell, Massachusetts, 1960 (Photograph courtesy of Deborah Hopkinson.)

I didn't like middle school much at all. But things definitely began to look up in high school. On the very first morning in my homeroom, a friendly red-haired girl in the seat in front of me turned around to introduce herself.

"I'm Vicki Hemphill," she said. Well, we've been friends since. In high school we worked part time at the same ice cream parlor. Later we were roommates in college, hiked the Appalachian Trail, went on vacations together with our families, and for the past three years have lived with our families about an hour away from one another in Oregon.

I wanted to go to college, but I knew money was limited. So as soon as I turned sixteen I got a job. I worked twenty hours a week during the school year and full time in the summer. Luckily, I got at least one scholarship, too. After I graduated from high school at age seventeen, I entered the University of Massachusetts at Amherst. I'd thought about being a writer, but I didn't think I could actually support myself writing. I wasn't sure what else to do, though. So I became an English major because—you guessed it—it gave me the chance to read lots of books!

The University of Massachusetts was about eighty miles away. College became my first experience away from my home. Still, maybe because I loved reading about adventures, I was restless to travel even farther. Since I couldn't afford to attend a college out of state, in my sophomore year I took part in a one-year domestic exchange program. I decided to go as far from Massachusetts as I could—and that meant going to the University of Hawai'i at Manoa, in Honolulu. It was my first real adventure.

I'd been on an airplane only once before—now I was flying thousands of miles away. Stepping off the plane in Honolulu, I can still remember how magical everything looked and smelled: plumeria blossoms perfumed the air, the ocean sparkled a deep, warm, blue, and the green hills of Oahu boasted luscious plants and trees I'd never imagined.

That year in Honolulu was life-changing in many ways. I'd never lived in such a diverse city before, with people from Japan, China, Samoa, the Philippines, and many small Pacific islands. I felt very much at home among Hawaii's diverse cultures and made lots of friends. I went swimming in the ocean, visited other islands, and was even invited to a real luau. And, of course, after years of New England winters, I liked the warm, sunny weather, too.

When the year was up I returned to Massachusetts to finish my degree. After I graduated, it was difficult to find a job. I wasn't sure what I wanted to do for a career. I still liked to read and occasionally thought about writing, but I had no idea how to begin—or how I would be able to support myself.

After about a year of working as a waitress, I decided to go back to school. I'd gotten interested in Japan and Japanese literature in college. And what better place to study Asia than Honolulu? So I returned to the University of Hawai'i and entered the Asian Studies graduate program. It took three years, but eventually I earned a master's degree with a focus on Japanese language, philosophy, and history.

The longer I lived in Honolulu, the more I loved it. And it wasn't just the food. In graduate school I met my husband, Andy Thomas, who was earning a degree in fine arts from the university. We both were interested in Zen Buddhism and practiced under Roshi Robert Aitken in the Diamond Sangha for a number of years. I've found that the creative process of writing and meditation are much alike. Just sitting quietly and counting your breaths from one to ten takes attention and practice. And I have used this quality of attention in my writing also.

Sometimes people end up in careers they didn't really plan for, and that's what happened to me. After graduate school I had two degrees—but no job! After a long search, I found my first professional position—as a staff writer for the American Red Cross in Honolulu. My job required me to write grant proposals, press releases, newsletter articles, and fundraising letters. I realized there were many more kinds of writing than I'd ever imagined.

I also discovered that I liked working in nonprofit organizations. Somehow I'd manage to stumble into the field of development: a career that fit well with my skills. People who work in development help to raise money for nonprofit organizations, such as schools, theatres, museums, symphonies, universities, wildlife conservation groups, and public radio stations.

After the American Red Cross, I took a job at a small theatre, the Manoa Valley Theatre, doing similar work. The theatre was a very unusual place to work. Many years before, the building had been a church. It was quite small; the theatre itself only fit about one hundred people. The theatre office came with two cats. It wasn't unusual to walk into work in the morning and find a cat sitting on the papers you'd left on your desk the night before.

I love cats, but I didn't like some of the other creatures we often came across in Hawaii's tropical climate: cockroaches and centipedes. In fact, centipedes are just about my least favorite thing in the world. I've been bitten twice, and let me tell you, centipedes can really cause pain.

Our daughter, Rebekah, was born while I was working at the theatre. While both Andy and I worked part time when she was a baby, eventually I took a full time position in development at the University of Hawai'i Foundation, writing grant proposals to raise money for scholarships, research, and other university programs. Ever since then, all my jobs have been on university or college campuses. I like meeting students and professors—and I'm always learning new things.

A lot of writers don't have a day job, but I still do. My current job is director of foundation relations at Oregon State University Foundation. I help raise money to do a lot of different things at the university, such as allow scientists to do research on energy, health, and climate change; buy a new piece of equipment; build a new facility for classrooms or research; and help get more scholarships so students who want to attend college can afford to do so.

You may be wondering, how did this person *ever* get to be a children's author? After all, there hasn't been much yet about writing books for kids.

Well, the truth is that although I'd *thought* about wanting to be a writer for a long time, I didn't actually do any creative writing for many years. I took one creative writing class in college, but I didn't like it very much. In high school I wrote one short story, but that was about it.

Now, this doesn't mean I wasn't writing at all. I was—I was writing every day at work, although I didn't really think of that as the kind of writing I really wanted to do. But as it turned out, the writing I was doing for my job played an important part in leading me to become a children's author—and so did my daughter, Rebekah.

Each week Rebekah and I went to the library to choose some books to take home. I couldn't help noticing that there seemed to be many more picture books than when I was a girl. And that's when I began to think again about my old dream. Maybe, I thought, I could write stories for children. After all, picture books were short, short enough for a working mom to try. I wouldn't have to worry about starting a three-hundred-page novel and never getting the chance to finish it.

At first, I was scared of being rejected. But that's where my job came in. When you write a grant proposal to a private foundation, such as the Ford Foundation or the Gates Foundation, you frequently get turned down. That's just the way it is. Fundraisers know that the competition is fierce. Sometimes there are projects that just fit better than yours. Sometimes your proposal isn't as good as it could be.

I had already learned that when a proposal got rejected, it didn't mean I should stop trying. I knew it was just part of the competitive world of fundraising, and I didn't let it stop me from doing my job. No, I would just get back to work, writing a new proposal. So, why should I be afraid of being rejected as a children's author? There was only one way to find out if I could really become a writer and publish a book: I had to begin. I had to try.

As it turned out, it's a good thing I was really determined to be a writer, because it took a lot longer to get published than I ever expected. Every weekend, I'd get up at six in the morning to write stories. Then I'd send them out regularly to publishers. The result? Rejection letter after rejection letter—soon I had a file full of rejections!

Curiosity may be one of the most important things a writer needs to succeed. But you also need perseverance. If you want to be a writer, you simply can't give up. Still, after two years of trying, I didn't seem to be getting anywhere. Maybe I wasn't meant to be a writer after all.

Then I got lucky. One Saturday, I attended a writers' workshop. The presenter gave us a great piece of advice. "Start by sending your stories to magazines," she told us. "If you can get published there, you'll get practice working with editors, and you can also include your publication credits when you submit your stories to book publishers."

I was happy to take her advice since I certainly wasn't getting anywhere on my own. And to my amazement, it worked! The very first story I sent to *Cricket* magazine, "Skate, Kirsten, Skate," was accepted.

I still faced many challenges though. Over the next couple of years I was able to sell several stories to magazines, but I didn't seem any closer to my dream of publishing a real book. Those rejection letters from publishers just kept coming.

Then one day I heard a piece on National Public Radio about African-American quilts, and the legend that quilts were once associated with the Underground Railroad. There does not appear to be any actual historical evidence for this. But the idea made me think about one of the questions I'd had back in Miss Grace's classroom: "What would it have been like to travel on the Underground Railroad?"

Hearing that piece on the radio inspired me to write a story about a slave girl who sews a map to escape on the Underground Railroad. It was called *Sweet Clara and the Freedom Quilt.* I sent it to ten or twelve different publishers. But I still kept getting rejection letters.

Then one day at work my phone rang. I picked it up and a voice said, "My name is Anne Schwartz, I'm an editor at Random House. We'd like to publish your book."

At last! *Sweet Clara and the Freedom Quilt* was published in 1993 and has been my most successful book. In 1994, I sold my second picture book, *Birdie's Lighthouse.* That same year, we left Hawai'i. In addition to Rebekah, we now had a son, Dimitri, who was adopted from Russia in May of 1992, when he was six years old.

Adopting Dimitri, who was living in an orphanage north of Moscow, was a challenging adventure for all of us. Rebekah, who was eight years old, my husband, Andy, and I flew from Honolulu to New York City to meet Dimitri, who was brought to the United States with some other children by the director of his orphanage.

Of course at the time Dimitri didn't speak or understand any English. At six years old he must have been very confused as to who these new people actually were! Dimitri had never ridden in cars or gone to restaurants. He certainly had never seen a swimming pool or the ocean. He'd never gone trick-or-treating on Halloween. And probably he'd never had a birthday party. We all had a lot of challenges to face in the years ahead. But Dimitri had a wonderful, patient sister and dedicated teachers who helped him adjust to a new life.

With two children, we found that our tiny rental house in Honolulu was too crowded. Reluctantly, we decided to move back to the mainland. I found a job at Whitman College, a small college in Walla Walla, Washington. The town of Walla Walla, which is in the southwest corner of Washington state, was quite a change from living in Hawai'i. It was a lot colder, for one thing! Walla Walla is surrounded by wheat fields and rolling hills. It's four or five hours from the ocean.

Autographing books while on a school visit in Oregon, 1999 (Photograph courtesy of Deborah Hopkinson.)

No more beaches or palm trees. Rebekah, who had grown up in Hawaii, now was going sledding and skiing for the first time.

"We may not be able to go to the beach anymore, but if we have our own house, we can get a dog," my husband and I promised the kids. One night, some friends called us. They'd found a young dog abandoned in a ditch by their farmhouse. "We'll take her!" we decided.

As it turned out, Zoe was just the first of many pets. We'd already brought two cats with us from Hawaii. But now that we had lots of space, Dimitri was able to indulge his growing love of animals.

Thanks to Dimitri, at one time or another our family has had just about every kind of pet you can imagine: dogs, cats, finches, canaries, chickens, pigeons, doves, a ferret, chinchillas, frogs, snakes, quail, turkeys, geese, and even sheep and a couple of peacocks.

Not all the animals got along, though, and we had our share of disasters, especially when our dogs got loose

and chased Dimitri's chickens. It's no surprise that Dimitri has been working in pet stores since he was fifteen and also does a lot of pet sitting and dog walking.

Although Zoe is no longer with us, we now have two cats, including a calico who is about seventeen years old and who has been with us since Honolulu, when Rebekah was in kindergarten. We have a young Golden Retriever named Kona. And then there is my dog, Pea (a Hawaiian word meaning bear and is pronounced *pay-uh*), who really does look like a bear sometimes!

When Dimitri was in elementary and middle school, he sometimes traveled with me around Washington and Oregon as I visited schools to talk about writing and books with kids. Since my presentation also included slides of my family and pets, most of the students were a lot more interested in asking questions about Dimitri's animals than they were about my books. And, of course, they wanted his autograph.

Whenever I visit schools, kids always ask me where I get the ideas for my books. The answer is, really, I get them from everywhere: from things I read, hear on the radio, from something I see on television or in a film, something that's happened in my own life, or even just from an idea in my own head. Story ideas are all around us: in newspapers, books, museums, library and museum exhibits; on the radio, roadside markers, the Internet; and, of course, in our personal experiences.

How does it actually work? Well, for example, *Apples to Oregon,* a tall tale based on the true story of a pioneer family who brought the first apple trees to Oregon on the Oregon Trail, came about because I saw one note about it in a magazine article.

I couldn't help thinking, "What would it have been like to be a pioneer and carry seven hundred fruit trees across the plains?" Instead of telling the story exactly as it happened, though, it seemed more fun to make it a tall tale about the ups and downs of this incredible family. That's why the subtitle is *Being the (Slightly) True Narrative of How a Brave Pioneer Father Took Apples, Peaches, Pears, Plums, and Cherries (and Children) across the Plains.*

Thanks to Anne Schwartz, my editor, and Nancy Carpenter, the illustrator, this picture book has won several

awards, including a prize for storytelling from the Western Writers of America.

Sometimes the ideas for stories come from other people. James E. Ransome, who illustrated two of my books, *Sweet Clara and the Freedom Quilt* and *Under the Quilt of Night,* both stories about the Underground Railroad, once told me that he really wanted to paint the Empire State Building.

"That sounds interesting," I said.

And so I researched the building and in 2006 we published the award-winning picture book *Sky Boys: How They Built the Empire State Building.* The book gets it title from the men who climbed high up on the steel frame. They were called "sky boys." The book gave me the chance to include fascinating facts about the Empire State Building itself.

I also like writing stories that come out of my personal experience, even though the finished book is usually a lot different from what actually happened. For instance, when we lived in Walla Walla, I loved to go to the U-pick strawberry farm near our house.

With daughter, Rebekeh, age eighteen, 2002 (Photograph courtesy of Deborah Hopkinson.)

I love the way fresh strawberries smell in the early summer—and the way they taste, too. I'd often go early in the morning and pick a whole flat of berries. I'd stoop or kneel in the hay between the rows. By the time I got home my fingers would be bright red from the juice. I liked picking strawberries so much I wanted to find a way to put it into a story. And eventually I did, in a book about a sister and brother during the Great Depression of the 1930s. The title is *Saving Strawberry Farm.*

Once, when we were going for a walk in the countryside around Walla Walla, I saw a bluebird for the very first time. Now, just seeing a bluebird wasn't enough to write a whole story about. But eventually I found a way to create a story around that experience. *Bluebird Summer* is about two kids who go stay with their grandpa after their grandmother's death. Their grandmother loved bluebirds, and by the end of the story the kids have decided to build bluebird houses in her honor—and to help bluebirds find safe places to nest, too.

I also like to choose topics I know a little bit about. Both my kids loved playing soccer, baseball, and softball. For several years, Rebekah was a pitcher for her softball team. Watching my daughter play ball made me curious about the history of women in baseball and softball, so I went to the library and found a book about the history of women in baseball. One story about Alta Weiss, who pitched for a men's minor league team in 1907, caught my eye. She was such a good player she got the nickname "Girl Wonder." That seemed like a great name for a book, and so I turned Alta's story into a picture book called Girl *Wonder: A Baseball Story in Nine Innings.*

When I visit schools, I often get asked why I like to write about history. It's true that a lot of my books are historical fiction, while others are nonfiction, or informational books, about the past. There are many different genres, or types, of books to write. Some people love science fiction, or fantasy, or mysteries. While it's not always the case, many times authors like to write the same kinds of stories they enjoy reading. After all, if you love science fiction and you've read it all your life, chances are you know what makes this kind of story good.

Each kind of writing is a bit different. For example, although many parts of an historical fiction story are made up, usually it's also based on something that actually happened, or the story might be set in a certain time period.

I sometimes take liberties with the historical facts to make stories more exciting or dramatic. But even if I'm making up a part of the story, I still need to do a lot of research. I want my readers to feel as if they are actually there, whether the story is set on the streets of New York City or on the Chilkoot Pass in the midst of a driving snowstorm.

Do you like doing research? Not everyone does, but I happen to love it. To me, research is a bit like solving a puzzle. It's a chance to make a discovery and learn something new. Research helps me understand history better, especially what life was like for ordinary people.

When I look at newspapers from the era, listen to interviews with real people, and read contemporary journals and letters, I can begin to understand a bit more about a certain time period or event. And that makes it a lot easier to write about.

Research Tips

More than likely, you'll have to do research papers in school now and then. Here are a few tips that have worked for me:

• It's great to get as many books and articles as possible about your topic. But it's just as important to know how to evaluate your source. Does it have good footnotes? Is the person writing it an expert? And if you are reading something written by a person who was involved in an event, what is their point of view? For instance, think about a U.S. Civil War battle. If you had two newspapers—one in the North and one in the South—how might their reporting on the battle be different?

• Don't be afraid to contact an expert to get help with a question. Many scholars are happy to answer questions by email, especially if you identify yourself as a student.

• If you're writing about something in your own town, don't be shy about interviewing someone in person to get information.

• Be careful when using the Internet! Understand where your information is coming from. Yes, you can Google just about everything, but unless you look carefully at the Web site, you don't know if the information on it is reliable. Don't take the easy way out—check your source! Developing good "information literacy" skills now will help you throughout high school and college—and in future jobs also.

• It's not always possible, but if you ever have the chance to do research in person, try to do it. Going there and seeing a place you are writing about with your own eyes is invaluable. For example, suppose you are writing about the history of your town. You might find some old pictures. But it's even more fun to go to the center of town and look around. Imagine what you would see and hear if you were standing on the same street corner a hundred years ago.

Writing Tips

Researching a book can take a long time. But when I finally finish my research, the next challenge is actually sitting down to write the story. No matter how many

Son, Dimitri, age twenty, with his dog, Kona, 2006 (Photograph courtesy of Deborah Hopkinson.)

books I have published (and I have sold more than thirty), this part never seems to get easier. All writers need perseverance and determination. But I will give you a tip—the most important thing about being a good writer is being able to revise your work. The best writers keep working, and are willing to try something and fail, until their story is the best it can be.

Now, you might think that the word revision just means correcting spelling and grammar or polishing "sloppy copy" to a final paper. Not! When we go to the doctor to get our vision tested, we're getting our eyes checked. And so I like to think of the word revision very literally: "re-vision" means "to see again."

To revise your writing means looking at all parts of your story or paper with new eyes—as if you are somehow looking at it for the first time. This is sometimes hard to do after you've struggled with it for a long time. Reading it aloud helps a lot, and also getting feedback from other people.

Another important part of revision is to look not only at what you've written, but at what's NOT there. In other words, is something important missing?

I learned this lesson the hard way. Once, as part of my job, I had to write a speech for the president of the University of Hawai'i. The president was giving away teaching awards to a number of professors. Well, I gathered all the information about each professor who was getting an award. I made the speech perfect. But then, when the awards were announced, someone was missing! It was so embarrassing to be sitting in a room with two hundred people and realize that I had made such a big mistake. Worse, I had made the president look bad also. You see, I had forgotten to go back and check each name in the final speech against the original list of winners, to make sure that I had not forgotten anyone. In other words, I had looked at and corrected everything in the speech itself—but not what wasn't there.

Looking at what might be missing from a piece of writing is an essential part of revising. Needless to say, I learned this lesson well and I use it not only when writing my books, but also in my job.

Writing is a little bit like baking bread. It takes time for the yeast to grow and the dough to rise. In the same way, revision takes time. Stories, like bread dough, seem to come alive as they sit and when we knead them. New ideas, connections, and possibilities appear. And then, somehow, it feels done. With bread, you pop it into the oven and when it's ready you have the satisfaction of sharing something you made with your family and friends.

Stories are like this, too. When we are done with the writing and revising, the editor and publisher put everything together and produce a finished product—something that you made that you can now share with the world.

About My Books

Sometimes kids ask me which of the books I've written are my favorites. That's a little like asking which pet you like best. Still, I thought I'd share with you a little about some of my most recent books and how I came to write them.

Into the Firestorm: A Novel of San Francisco, 1906

For a second, the shaking let up. Then it started in again, violent and more twisting, An image flashed through Nick's mind of Gran wringing clothes over the wash tin with her tough, strong hands. That was it. The earth was being wrung out of shape.

Into the Firestorm was published in 2006, one hundred years after the great San Francisco earthquake and fire. It's my first middle-grade novel and I had a wonderful time writing it.

The San Francisco earthquake occurred at 5:13 A.M. on Wednesday, April 18, 1906. It's estimated that about three thousand people died in this disaster, primarily as a result of collapsing buildings. Most of the physical damage to the city occurred not from the quake itself, but in three days of raging fires.

One newspaper account of stories of the disaster was of a boy named Nicholas Dray, who had apparently escaped from a poor county farm and had been taken in by a local merchant just a few days before the fire. Left alone while his new employer was away on business, Nick braved a soldier's gun to rescue his employer's retriever, Brownie. Supposedly the boy said, "He is a very good dog."

To research *Into the Firestorm,* I relied on excellent primary sources, including letters, photographs, and eyewitness accounts. I also traveled to San Francisco to walk around Jackson Square, the story's setting, to help me imagine Nick, his friend Annie, and their journey to safety. I also changed the dog's name to Shakespeare—Shake for short!

If, like me, you like adventure stories, I hope you'll read this book!

The "Prairie Skies" Series

Grandpa pulled Charlie close. "I hear they've got big skies our there in Kansas Territory. But it's the same sky that covers us here. If you aks me, the sky's a lot like love. It just spreads out over folks no matter how far apart they are."

I first became interested in the period just before the U.S. Civil War while helping Dimitri and Rebekah with their history homework. The books in the "Prairie Skies" series are: *Pioneer Summer, Cabin in the Snow,* and *Our Kansas Home.*

The stories follow Charlie Keller and his family as they leave from Massachusetts in 1855 for Lawrence, Kansas. This was a time when people were debating whether slavery should spread to America's territories in the West. The Kansas-Nebraska Act of 1854 created the territories of Kansas and Nebraska. It ended the Missouri Compromise, an agreement in 1820 that forbid slavery in the lands of the Louisiana Purchase except for Missouri, and it changed the law about whether slavery could spread to the territories.

The Kansas-Nebraska Act established that Kansas would be a free state or a slave state based on how the people in Kansas voted. People from pro-slavery Missouri and free-soil Northerners, like the fictional Keller family, flocked to Kansas to have a voice in the territory's future. Since the groups wanted different things, they soon clashed. To research these books I went to Kansas and read lots of letters, memoirs, and books. Mostly I think readers will like the story of one family's struggles to make a new life in a new place.

The "Klondike Kid" Series

It wasn't even noon, but it seemed we had been climbing for hours. The day was so overcast and gray, it felt like late afternoon. My breath came in ragged gasps. Five more steps before resting, I told myself. Now five more.

The "Klondike Kid" series includes three short books: *Sailing for Gold, The Long Trail,* and *Adventure in Gold Town.* The Klondike Gold Rush took place at the very end of the nineteenth century. Word of a gold discovery on the Yukon River in Canada's Klondike Valley reached the "outside" in 1897. When the steamer *Portland* docked in Seattle in July of that year, returning miners had to drag their suitcases down the gangplank because they were so weighted down with gold! Thousands of people caught gold fever, drawn by the promise of riches and adventure.

But it wasn't easy to get to the Klondike. Men and women journeyed thousands of miles in harsh conditions. Most people never made any money at all. Many gave up before they reached the boom town of Dawson City. Those who made it that far learned that the richest stakes had been claimed long ago.

The "Klondike Kid" series follows the adventures of an eleven-year-old boy named Davey Hill, who is living in Seattle when the book begins. Orphaned, he is staying in the boarding house where he and his widowed mother lived before she died. There he is treated like a servant by Mrs. Tinker, the owner. Davey eventually makes his way to the Klondike, and through his adventures we see not only the world of the prospectors, but that of the pioneering frontier photographers whose pictures capture the hope—and, in many cases, the heartbreak—of the men, women, children, and animals who made the long, harrowing trek into the wilderness.

Hear My Sorrow: The Diary of Angela Denota, a Shirtwaist Worker

> *It was dark and wet this morning, almost as if the skies had decided to cry . . . and the rain streamed on top of my head and into my eyes. No one spoke. As one, we began to follow behind the hearse. Along the way, in the tenements, women leaned out their windows and waved white handkerchiefs. They were silent at first. But as we passed, low mourning moans burst from their lips.*

This book is the story of a fourteen-year-old girl named Angela who works in a factory in New York City. The story is about the tragedy of the Triangle Waist Company fire, which took place on March 25, 1911, and killed one hundred-forty-six people, mostly teenaged girls.

But I also wanted to write about the lives of the girls and their families who worked at that time in the garment industry in New York. Not long before the fire, in the fall of 1909, the workers had gone on strike for improved conditions. This strike is called the Uprising of the Twenty Thousand. Although the workers made some gains, conditions didn't really improve until after the Triangle disaster. Finally, then, people realized that things had to change.

Like many children at the time, the girl in my story, Angela Denoto, must leave school at the age of fourteen to go to work to help her family. We see the strike and the fire through her eyes. Most workers in the garment industry were young Jewish and Italian immigrants living on New York City's Lower East Side. The women usually worked very long hours, earning between seven and fourteen dollars a week.

To research this story, I read many books about the strike and the fire. I also read newspapers of the time. And I went to New York City. I visited the Lower East Side Tenement Museum and stood on the sidewalk outside the building where the fire took place. There is a

Working at the computer with her cat, Sophie, 2000 (Photograph courtesy of Deborah Hopkinson.)

Hopkinson and her husband, Andy Thomas, 2006 (Photograph courtesy of Deborah Hopkinson.)

small plaque on the wall there. Standing on the same sidewalk where many young girls fell to their deaths made me want to do as good a job as I could writing this book so that their stories would not be forgotten.

I did so much research for *Hear My Sorrow* that it made me want to write a nonfiction book about the same time period. And so I wrote a book called *Shutting out the Sky: Life in the Tenements of New York, 1880-1924.* The book includes actual photographs and stories of real people who came to America as immigrants during this time. Like my other recent nonfiction book, *Up before Daybreak: Cotton and People in America,* this book is how I am trying to make history interesting to kids.

These books are about the lives of ordinary children and their families—the people whose names never appeared in that big history textbook I read so long ago in Miss Grace's fourth-grade classroom.

Do you remember the question I asked at the beginning of this essay: Did you ever have dreams for your future that seemed far away and impossible to reach? My dream of being a writer seemed that way to me for a long time. It takes hard work, luck, lots of support from others, and determination to make any dream come true. I'm still working on my dream, and still trying to become a better writer.

I hope you have the courage to follow your dreams, too.

*   *   *

HORNE, Richard 1960-2007
(Richard George Anthony Horne, Harry Horse)

OBITUARY NOTICE—

See index for *SATA* sketch: Born May 9, 1960, in Earlsdon, Coventry, Warwickshire, England; died of an apparent suicide, January 10, 2007. Illustrator, cartoonist, musician, and author. Horne was an award-winning author and illustrator of children's books who was also a prize-winning political cartoonist. After attending Wrekin College, he struggled as a musician but began gaining commissions as an illustrator in the late 1970s.

His first self-illustrated children's story, *The Ogopogo; or, My Journey with the Loch Ness Monster,* was published in 1981 and earned him a Writer of the Year Award from the Scottish Arts Council. Horne would go on to write over half a dozen other children's titles, and he illustrated works by such authors as Dick King-Smith, Margaret Mahy, Stuart McDonald, and Robert Louis Stevenson. As a political cartoonist, Horne was known for his intelligent humor. A staff cartoonist for the *Scotland on Sunday* from 1987 to 1993, he also regularly contributed to such newspapers as the London *Independent, Guardian,* and *Observer,* as well as to the *New Yorker.* Among his most popular children's books was *The Last Polar Bears* (1996), which won the Kinderjury Award and was adapted to television in 2000. His *The Last Gold Diggers* (1998) won the Smarties Gold Award, and *Little Rabbit Lost* (2002) earned a children's book of the year award from the Scottish Arts Council. Also a musician, Horne played the banjo and was an aficionado of bluegrass and Cajun music. In 1985, he founded a mock bluegrass band called Swamptrash. In more recent years, Horne was increasingly troubled by his beloved wife's advancing multiple sclerosis, which confined her to a wheelchair. When the couple was found dead in their Burra Isle home, it was believed to be the result of a suicide pact between husband and wife.

OBITUARIES AND OTHER SOURCES:

PERIODICALS

Times (London, England), January 19, 2007, p. 63.

ONLINE

Scotsman Online, http://news.scotsman.com/ (January 11, 2007).

*   *   *

HORNE, Richard George Anthony
See HORNE, Richard

*   *   *

HORSE, Harry
See HORNE, Richard

*   *   *

HUNTINGTON, Amy

Personal

Married; children: two. *Education:* Attended Swain School of Design and University of Florida; University of Vermont, B.A.

Addresses

Home and office—Williston, VT. *Agent*—Portfolio Solutions, 136 Jameson Hill Rd., Clinton Corners, NY 12514.

Career

Author and illustrator.

Writings

(Self-illustrated) *One Monday,* Orchard Books (New York, NY), 2001.

ILLUSTRATOR

Katie Clark, *Grandma Drove the Garbage Truck,* Down East Books (Camden, ME), 2006.
Katie Clark, *Seagull Sam,* Down East Books (Camden, ME), 2007.
Martin Brennan, *Three Lessons for Astair the Bear,* Mitten Press (Ann Arbor, MI), 2007.
Jacqueline Jules, *No English,* Mitten Press (Ann Arbor, MI), 2007.

Sidelights

A love for drawing and words was instilled in Amy Huntington at a very early age. As the author and illustrator recalled on her home page: "My favorite memories as a child are of painting on bumpy paper with watercolors. . . . I would color my way into a world of my own." Huntington's interest in children's books was heightened when she became the mother of two young children, and her career as an illustrator began in 1996 when *Ladybug* magazine published her first illustrated story. Primarily a children's book illustrator, Huntington expanded into writing with *One Monday.* Her work as an artist has been paired with texts by other writers, such as Katie Clark's engaging multigenerational picture book *Grandma Drove the Garbage Truck* and *Seagull Sam,* as well as Jacqueline Jules' *No English.*

In *One Monday* Huntington follows a young farm girl named Annabelle as she is awakened on a Monday morning by a noisy, gusty wind storm. The storm sends all of the animals into a "barnyard hoopla" as described by *School Library Journal* reviewer Kathy Piehl. Written in verse and illustrated with warm-toned watercolor, Huntington's self-illustrated title humorously caricatures how the wind storm affects the farm animals during each day of the week. On Tuesday the wind blows the hens' feathers inside out and by Friday there are frogs riding the wind-blown waves of the troughs. In her text, the author uses "metaphors [that] are as charm-

Amy Huntington portrays a close relationship between a grandmother and grandchild in her illustrations for Katie Clark's picture book Grandma Drove the Garbage Truck. (Down East Books, 2005. Illustrations copyright © 2005 by Amy Huntington. All rights reserved. Reproduced by permission.)

ing as the pictures," according to a *Kirkus Reviews* critic. A *Publishers Weekly* reviewer also cited the "light, elegant touch and dry wit" apparent in Huntington's text. Though many books share similar themes with *One Monday*, "Huntington's originality is never in doubt," the critic added.

Biographical and Critical Sources

PERIODICALS

Booklist, February 1, 2002, Kathy Broderick, review of *One Monday,* p. 946.

Five Owls (annual), 2002, review of *One Monday,* p. 76.

Kirkus Reviews, October 1, 2001, review of *One Monday,* p. 1425; March 15, 2006, review of *Grandma Drove the Garbage Truck,* p. 287.

Publishers Weekly, October 22, 2001, review of *One Monday,* p. 74.

School Library Journal, December, 2001, Kathy Piehl, review of *One Monday,* p. 104; November, 2006, Alexa Sandmann, review of *Grandma Drove the Garbage Truck,* p. 87.

ONLINE

Amy Huntington Home Page, http://www.amyhuntington. com (April 30, 2007).

Children's Bookwatch Online, http://www. midwestbookreview.com/ (April, 2006), review of *Grandma Drove the Garbage Truck.**

*　　*　　*

HURWIN, Davida Wills 1950-

Personal

Born 1950, in San Francisco, CA; married; husband's name Gene; children: Frazier Malone (daughter).

Addresses

Home and office—Southern CA.

Career

Dancer, actor, educator, and writer. Crossroads School for Arts and Sciences, Santa Monica, CA, instructor in drama.

Awards, Honors

Iowa Teen Award nomination, 1998-99, for *A Time for Dancing*; New York Public Library Best Book for the Teen Age selection, 2003, for *The Farther You Run*.

Writings

A Time for Dancing, Little, Brown (Boston, MA), 1995.
The Farther You Run, Viking (New York, NY), 2003.
Circle the Soul Softly, HarperCollins (New York, NY), 2006.

Adaptations

A Time for Dancing was adapted as a film, released in 2000.

Sidelights

In her fiction for young adults, Davida Wills Hurwin focuses on young women coming of age. Her debut novel, *A Time for Dancing,* draws on Hurwin's experiences as a dancer, while *Circle the Soul Softly* benefits from Hurwin's insight as a high-school drama instructor.

A Time for Dancing is a story of grief and loss. Samantha and Juliana are best friends, and have been since childhood. They perform together in the same dance company and attend the same school. However, when Juliana is diagnosed with cancer, their friendship changes, and Samantha has to learn to say goodbye. "Few YA dramas deal with the issue of terminal illness as intimately as this gripping first novel," wrote a *Publishers Weekly* contributor, while Anne O'Malley noted in *Booklist* that *A Time for Dancing* "will hold fans of this genre glued to the page." Samantha and Juliana "are likable, fully drawn characters who immediately engage the reader," Maeve Visser Knoth maintained in her *Horn Book* review of the novel, which was also adapted as a film.

The Farther You Run begins six months after *A Time for Dancing,* and continues to focus on Samantha as she struggles through her grief, refusing to dance. Her new friend, Mona, tries to get close, but Samantha pushes her away, unwilling to accept emotional support. "The emotional intensity and vibrant characters will hook readers from the first page," wrote O'Malley in *Booklist.* While feeling that the book would mainly appeal to fans of the first novel, Miranda Doyle noted in *School Library Journal* that "the friendship between the

Cover of Davida Wills Hurwin's teen novel The Farther You Run, *featuring a photograph by Jim Erickson.* (Speak, 2003. Reproduced by permission of Speak, a division of Penguin Putnam Books for Young Readers.)

two girls is convincing." A *Kirkus Reviews* contributor found *The Farther You Run* "immensely appealing and slightly unrealistic in the depiction of life on one's own."

In *Circle the Soul Softly,* Kate O'Connor suffers from post-traumatic stress disorder following the death of her father. After a move to a Los Angeles suburb with her family several years later, Kate is terrified of literally running into things and people. She is also sure she is being stalked by a presence she calls the Monster. As school progresses, however, she begins to connect with the other teens in her drama group. When Kate begins to suspect that one of her new friends is being abused, the act of helping someone else in need helps Kate face issues from her own past. "Hurwin's creation is tender, thought-provoking, and emotionally profound, with an inescapable crescendo," wrote J.A. Kaszuba Locke in a review of *Circle the Soul Softly* for *Book Loons* online. Myrna Marler, writing in *Kliatt,* described Kate's narrative voice as "likeable and believable," and *School Li-*

brary Journal critic Susan Riley predicted that "teen girls will strongly relate to the protagonist's feelings."

Biographical and Critical Sources

PERIODICALS

Booklist, November 1, 1995, Anne O'Malley, review of *A Time for Dancing,* p. 470; August, 2003, Anne O'Malley, review of *The Farther You Run,* p. 1980.

Bulletin of the Center for Children's Books, October, 1995, review of *A Time for Dancing,* p. 58; April, 2006, Loretta Gaffney, review of *Circle the Soul Softly,* p. 357.

Horn Book, January-February, 1996, Maeve Visser Knoth, review of *A Time for Dancing,* p. 78.

Journal of Adolescent and Adult Literacy, November, 1997, review of *A Time for Dancing,* p. 215.

Kirkus Reviews, June 15, 2003, review of *The Farther You Run,* p. 859; February 1, 2006, review of *Circle the Soul Softly,* p. 133.

Kliatt, March, 2006, Myrna Marler, review of *Circle the Soul Softly,* p. 12.

Publishers Weekly, October 9, 1995, review of *A Time for Dancing,* p. 87; December 22, 1997, review of *A Time for Dancing,* p. 61; June 30, 2003, review of *The Farther You Run,* p. 82.

School Library Journal, August, 2003, Miranda Doyle, review of *The Farther You Run,* p. 160; March, 2006, Susan Riley, review of *Circle the Soul Softly,* p. 223.

Voice of Youth Advocates, December, 1995, review of *A Time for Dancing,* p. 302; August, 2003, review of *The Farther You Run,* p. 225; February, 2006, Laura Woodruff, review of *Circle the Soul Softly,* p. 487.

ONLINE

Book Loons, http://www.bookloons.com/ (April 28, 2007), J.A. Kaszuba Locke, review of *Circle the Soul Softly.*

HarperCollins Web site, http://www.harpercollins.com/ (April 28, 2007), "Davida Wills Hurwin.*

J-K

JOHNSTON, Tony 1942-

Personal

Born January 30, 1942, in Los Angeles, CA; daughter of David Leslie (a golf professional) and Ruth Taylor; married Roger D. Johnston (a banker), June 25, 1966; children: Jennifer, Samantha, Ashley. *Education:* Stanford University, B.A. (history), 1963, M.Ed., 1964. *Hobbies and other interests:* Archaeology, collecting dance masks and Latin American textiles, collecting children's books and children's book art, Western history, especially of California.

Addresses

Home—San Marino, CA.

Career

Children's book author. Fourth-grade teacher in public elementary school, Altadena, CA, 1964-66; McGraw-Hill Publishing Company, New York, NY, editing supervisor, 1966-68; Harper & Row Publishers, Inc., New York, NY, copy editor of children's books, 1969. University of California—Los Angeles Extension, teacher of picture-book writing. Active member, Friends of the Adobes.

Awards, Honors

Children's Choice Award, Harris County Public Library, 1979, for *Four Scary Stories;* Children's Choice designation, 1986, for *The Quilt Story;* Outstanding Literary Quality in a Picture Book honor, Southern California Council on Literature for Children and Young People, 1989, for *Yonder;* Parents' Choice Award for Children's Books, 1992, for *Slither McCreep and His Brother, Joe;* named Honorary Texan, 1993, for *The Cowboy and the Black-eyed Pea;* award from Southern California Council on Literature for Children and Young People (now California Literature Council), 1997, for body of work; Simon Wiesenthal Once upon a World Award, and City

of Los Angeles plaque, both 1997, both for *The Wagon;* American Society for the Prevention of Cruelty to Animals Henry Bergh Honor, 2000, for *It's about Dogs;* John and Patricia Beatty Award, Southern California Bookseller's Association, and Golden Dolphin Award, Southern California Booksellers Association, both 2003, both for *Any Small Goodness;* Sigurd F. Olson Nature Writing Award, Sigurd Olson Environmental Institute, 2004, for *Isabel's House of Butterflies.*

Writings

FOR CHILDREN

The Adventures of Mole and Troll, illustrated by Wallace Tripp, Putnam (New York, NY), 1972.

Fig Tale, illustrated by Giulio Maestro, Putnam (New York, NY), 1974.

Mole and Troll Trim the Tree, illustrated by Wallace Tripp, Putnam (New York, NY), 1974.

Odd Jobs, illustrated by Tomie dePaola, Putnam (New York, NY), 1977.

Five Little Foxes and the Snow, illustrated by Cyndy Szekeres, Putnam (New York, NY), 1977.

Night Noises, and Other Mole and Troll Stories, illustrated by Cyndy Szekeres, Putnam (New York, NY), 1977.

Four Scary Stories, illustrated by Tomie dePaola, Putnam (New York, NY), 1978.

Little Mouse Nibbling, illustrated by Diane Stanley, Putnam (New York, NY), 1979.

Dedos de luna (title means "Moon Fingers"), illustrated by Leonel Maciel, Secretaría de Educación Pública (Mexico City, Mexico), 1979.

Conchas y caracoles (title means "Shells and Snails"), Secretaría de Educación Pública (Mexico City, Mexico), 1979.

Animales fantásticas (title means "Fantastic Animals"), Secretaría de Educación Pública (Mexico City, Mexico), 1979.

Happy Birthday, Mole and Troll, illustrated by Cindy Szekeres, Putnam (New York, NY), 1979.

Odd Jobs and Friends, illustrated by Tomie dePaola, Putnam (New York, NY), 1982.

The Vanishing Pumpkin, illustrated by Tomie dePaola, Putnam (New York, NY), 1983.

Mi Regalo (title means "My Present"), Secretaría de Educación Pública (Mexico City, Mexico), 1984.

The Witch's Hat, illustrated by Margot Tomes, Putnam (New York, NY), 1984.

The Quilt Story, illustrated by Tomie dePaola, Putnam (New York, NY), 1985.

Farmer Mack Measures His Pig, illustrated by Megan Lloyd, Harper (New York, NY), 1986.

Whale Song, illustrated by Ed Young, Putnam (New York, NY), 1987.

Yonder, illustrated by Lloyd Bloom, Dial Books for Young Readers (New York, NY), 1988, reprinted, Gibbs Smith (Salt Lake City, UT), 2002.

Pages of Music, illustrated by Tomie dePaola, Putnam (New York, NY), 1988.

My Friend Bear, Ladybird Books (London, England), 1989.

The Badger and the Magic Fan: A Japanese Folktale, illustrated by Tomie dePaola, Putnam (New York, NY), 1990.

The Soup Bone, illustrated by Margot Tomes, Harcourt (San Diego, CA), 1990.

I'm Gonna Tell Mama I Want an Iguana (poems), illustrated by Lillian Hoban, Putnam (New York, NY), 1990.

Grandpa's Song, illustrated by Brad Sneed, Dial Books for Young Readers (New York, NY), 1991.

Goblin Walk, illustrated by Bruce Degen, Putnam (New York, NY), 1991.

Little Bear Sleeping, illustrated by Lillian Hoban, Putnam (New York, NY), 1991.

The Promise, illustrated by Pamela Keavney, Harper (New York, NY), 1992.

The Cowboy and the Black-eyed Pea, illustrated by Warren Ludwig, Putnam (New York, NY), 1992.

Slither McCreep and His Brother, Joe, illustrated by Victoria Chess, Harcourt (San Diego, CA), 1992.

Lorenzo, the Naughty Parrot, illustrated by Leo Politi, Harcourt (San Diego, CA), 1992.

The Last Snow of Winter, illustrated by Friso Henstra, Tambourine (New York, NY), 1993.

The Tale of Rabbit and Coyote, illustrated by Tomie dePaola, Putnam (New York, NY), 1994.

(Translator) *My Mexico = Mexico mío,* illustrated by F. John Sierra, Putnam (New York, NY), 1994.

Three Little Bikers, illustrated by G. Brian Karas, Knopf (New York, NY), 1994.

The Old Lady and the Birds, illustrated by Stephanie Garcia, Harcourt (San Diego, CA), 1994.

Little Rabbit Goes to Sleep, illustrated by Harvey Stevenson, HarperCollins (New York, NY), 1994.

Amber on the Mountain, illustrated by Robert Duncan, Dial Books for Young Readers (New York, NY), 1994.

Alice Nizzy Nazzy: The Witch of Santa Fe, illustrated by Tomie dePaola, Putnam (New York, NY), 1995.

The Iguana Brothers, illustrated by Mark Teague, Blue Sky Press (New York, NY), 1995.

Very Scary, illustrated by Douglas Florian, Harcourt (San Diego, CA), 1995.

How Many Miles to Jacksonville?, illustrated by Bart Forbes, Putnam (New York, NY), 1995.

Little Wild Parrot, Tambourine Books (New York, NY), 1995.

The Bull and the Fire Truck, illustrated by R.W. Alley, East West Books (New York, NY), 1996.

Fishing Sunday, illustrated by Barry Root, Tambourine Books (New York, NY), 1996.

The Ghost of Nicholas Greebe, illustrated by S.D. Schindler, Dial Books for Young Readers, (New York, NY), 1996.

The Magic Maguey, illustrated by Elisa Kleven, Harcourt (San Diego, CA), 1996.

Once in the Country: Poems of a Farm, illustrated by Thomas B. Allen, Putnam (New York, NY), 1996.

The Wagon, illustrated by James E. Ransome, Tambourine Books (New York, NY), 1996.

Day of the Dead, illustrated by Jeanette Winter, Harcourt (San Diego, CA), 1997.

We Love the Dirt, illustrated by Alexa Brandenberg, Cartwheel Books (New York, NY), 1997.

Sparky and Eddie: The First Day of School, illustrated by Susannah Ryan, Scholastic Press (New York, NY), 1997.

The Chizzywink and the Alamagoozlum, illustrated by Robert Bender, Holiday House (New York, NY), 1998.

Boo!: A Ghost Story That Could Be True, Cartwheel Books (New York, NY), 1998.

Sparky and Eddie: Trouble with Bugs, illustrated by Susannah Ryan, Scholastic (New York, NY), 1998.

Sparky and Eddie: Wild, Wild Rodeo!, illustrated by Susannah Ryan, Scholastic (New York, NY), 1998.

Bigfoot Cinderrrrrella, illustrated by James Warhola, Putnam (New York, NY), 1998.

An Old Shell: Poems of the Galápagos, illustrated by Tom Pohrt, Farrar, Straus (New York, NY), 1999.

Big Red Apple, illustrated by Judith Hoffman Corwin, Cartwheel Books (New York, NY), 1999.

It's about Dogs, illustrated by Ted Rand, Harcourt (San Diego, CA), 2000.

Uncle Rain Cloud, illustrated by Fabricio Vanden Broeck, Charlesbridge (Watertown, MA), 2000.

The Barn Owls, illustrated by Deborah Kogan Ray, Charlesbridge (Watertown, MA), 2000.

Any Small Goodness: A Novel of the Barrio, illustrated by Raúl Colón, Blue Sky Press (New York, NY), 2000.

Desert Song, illustrated by Ed Young, Sierra Club Books for Children (San Francisco, CA), 2000.

The Whole Green World, illustrated by Elsa Kleven, Farrar, Straus (New York, NY), 2001.

Angel City, illustrated by Carole Byard, Philomel Books (New York, NY), 2001.

Alien and Possum: Friends No Matter What, illustrated by Tony DiTerlizzi, Simon & Schuster Books for Young Readers (New York, NY), 2001.

Cat, What Is That?, illustrated by Wendell Minor, HarperCollins (New York, NY), 2001.

My Best Friend Bear, illustrated by Joy Allen, Rising Moon (Flagstaff, AZ), 2001.

Clear Moon, Snow Soon, illustrated by Guy Porfirio, Rising Moon (Flagstaff, AZ), 2001.

Desert Dog, illustrated by Robert Weatherford, Sierra Club Books for Children (San Francisco, CA), 2001.

Gopher up Your Sleeve, illustrated by Trip Park, Rising Moon (Flagstaff, AZ), 2001.

Sticky People, illustrated by Cyd Moore, HarperCollins (New York, NY), 2002.

That Summer, illustrated by Barry Moser, Harcourt (San Diego, CA), 2002.

Sunsets of the West, illustrated by Ted Lewin, Putnam (New York, NY), 2002.

Alien and Possum Hanging Out, illustrated by Tony DiTerlizzi, Simon & Schuster (New York, NY), 2002.

Go Track a Yak!, illustrated by Tim Raglin, Simon & Schuster (New York, NY), 2003.

The Mummy's Mother, Sky Blue Press (New York, NY), 2003.

A Kenya Christmas, illustrated by Leonard Jenkins, Holiday House (New York, NY), 2003.

Isabel's House of Butterflies, illustrated Susan Guevara, Sierra Club Books for Children (San Francisco, CA), 2003.

The Ancestors Are Singing, illustrated by Karen Barbour, Farrar, Straus (New York, NY), 2003.

The Worm Family, illustrated by Stacy Innerst, Harcourt (San Diego, CA), 2004.

The Harmonica, illustrated by Ron Mazellan, Charlesbridge (Watertown, MA), 2004.

Ten Fat Turkeys, illustrated by Rich Deas, Cartwheel Books (New York, NY), 2004.

The Spoon in the Bathroom Wall, Harcourt (San Diego, CA), 2005.

Noel, illustrated by Cheng-Khee Chee, Carolrhoda (Minneapolis, MN), 2005.

Chicken in the Kitchen, illustrated by Eleanor Taylor, Simon & Schuster (New York, NY), 2005.

Off to Kindergarten, illustrated by Melissa Sweet, Cartwheel Books (New York, NY), 2007.

Bone by Bone by Bone, Roaring Brook Press (New Milford, CT), 2007.

Contributor to textbooks. Contributor to periodicals, including *Cricket.* Contributor to numerous poetry anthologies.

Author's papers are housed in the Tony Johnston Collection, Huntington Library, San Marino, CA.

Adaptations

The Last Snow of Winter and *Fishing Sunday* were adapted as electronic books by iPictureBooks (New York, NY), 2001.

Sidelights

Tony Johnston, named for the cowboy Tom Mix's horse, is a versatile author of books for preschool-and grade-school-aged children whose works include fiction and nonfiction, picture books, poetry, and early readers. Johnston's novels are for middle-grade, young-adult, and older audiences. A number of her books, which include the picture books *Go Track a Yak!* and *The Worm Family* as well as the middle-grade Arthurian spoof *The Spoon in the Bathroom Wall,* feature quirky characters—both human and animal—in a variety of unusual situations. Other books, such as *The Quilt Story,* focus on historical or contemporary themes, while still others feature bilingual texts in which Spanish words intermingle with a largely English text. In appraising the many books to her credit, it is difficult to pin Johnston down to a specific focus, in part due to her wide-ranging interests. "I am curious about everything," she said in an interview for the Harcourt Web site. "Since grammar school, I've been collecting newspaper articles about archaeology, legendary beings (Bigfoot, the Hodag, Yeti), bugs, history, dinosaurs, coelacanths,. . .—you name it. Maybe curiosity killed the cat, but it sure sustains this writer."

Johnston was born in Los Angeles and grew up in nearby San Marino. As a child, she loved reading and books, and was most impressed by the fantasies of J.R.R. Tolkien. As she recalled to a *Junior Literary Guild* contributor, her interest in writing was "partly a desire to be in that other world of fantasy and partly an attempt to transfer to paper the traces that keep popping up from time to time to take me back—traces of childhood." Johnston's fascination with T.H. White's novel quartet about King Arthur inspired her novel *The Spoon in the Bathroom Wall,* in which fourth grader Martha Snapdragon discovers that her science teacher is raising dragons. As the school bully takes on the role of Martha's arch nemesis and school principal Mr. Klunk sets his evil designs on ruling the world (at least, the world of Horace E. Bloggins Elementary School), Martha finds her destiny in the prophecy surrounding a spoon that is wedged in the tile wall of the school's boy's bathroom. In *School Library Journal,* Terrie Dorio dubbed *The Spoon in the Bathroom Wall* an "entertaining story," and a *Publishers Weekly* critic concluded that, "with duly preposterous pomp, [Johnston's] . . . comically written caper builds to a crowning scene of glory."

After graduating from Stanford University, Johnston taught for two years at a public school in Altadena, California. When her husband's job required them to relocate, Johnston moved east to New York City, where she worked for a number of years as an editing supervisor and a copy editor for children's books. While working at Harper & Row, Johnston benefited from her job as private secretary to legendary editor Ursula Nordstrom. In 1972 Putnam published her first children's book, *The Adventures of Mole and Troll.*

Everyday childhood situations were the inspiration for the first of Johnston's popular "Mole and Troll" stories, while the second, *Mole and Troll Trim the Tree,* was based on the author's memories of her own real-life Christmases. Other books in the series include *Night Noises, and Other Mole and Troll Stories* and *Happy Birthday, Mole and Troll.* A *Booklist* reviewer, describing Johnston's endearing protagonists as "two of the more worthwhile recurring easy-reader actors," went on to call Mole and Troll "ingenious and distinct, and they regularly show evidence of a remarkable likeness-of-soul to their audience."

Tony Johnston depicts family life in the early 1800s in **The Quilt Story,** *a picture book featuring illustrations by award-winning artist Tomie dePaola.*
(Penguin Putnam, 1985. Illustration copyright © 1985 by Tomie dePaola. Reproduced by permission of Penguin Putnam, a division of Penguin Putnam Books for Young Readers.)

Animals are also cast in the title role of *Five Little Foxes and the Snow,* which was inspired by a Christmas the author spent in New Hampshire. In *Little Mouse Nibbling* Johnston introduces a very shy mouse who stays inside nibbling at this and that until a cricket brings Christmas carolers to her door, while *The Worm Family* finds a squirmy seven-member family proud of their worminess, despite the disdain of their less-twisty neighbors. A *Publishers Weekly* contributor wrote of *Little Mouse Nibbling* that Johnston's "unabashedly sentimental Christmas fantasy should find its way under

many a Yuletide tree for years to come," while *School Library Journal* writer John Sigwald praised *The Worm Family* as "a unique take on prejudice."

In her picture-book texts, Johnston often uses a rhythmic, poetic style. *Whale Song,* which a *Kirkus Reviews* contributor deemed "a stunningly beautiful evocation of the gentle giants of the deep," is a paen to Nature; the numbers only represent the song that travels from whale to whale. Children will "respond to the chanting beat" of *Chicken in the Kitchen,* predicted *Booklist* contributor Gillian Engberg, the reviewer adding that Johnston's "folksy language is appealing." *Yonder* is based on a Johnston family tradition in which trees are planted to commemorate the births and deaths of family members. "With the eloquent simplicity of a Shaker hymn, Tony Johnston's words capture the cyclical pattern of a farming way of life," Hanna B. Zeiger stated in a review of *Yonder* for *Horn Book.* The author's other poetry books include *I'm Gonna Tell Mama I Want an Iguana,* which includes mostly humorous poems on such diverse subjects as sunset, frogs' eggs, skeletons, and jellyfish. The collection was described by Tiffany Chrisman in *Children's Book Review Service* as a collection that "does much to stretch the imaginative powers" of its readers.

It's about Dogs is a collection of forty short poems, including rhymed quatrains, haiku, and blank verse, while *Cat, What Is That?* finds Johnston taking a similar poetic look at felines. According to Margaret Bush in *School Library Journal, It's about Dogs* includes both contains "poignant . . . as well as funny" moments, resulting in a "richly rendered tribute" to man's best friend. "Johnston's compact rhymes [are] often aston-

Johnston takes readers on a fantastic journey in her middle-grade adventure **The Spoon in the Bathroom Wall,** *featuring a cover illustration by Brett Helquist.* (Harcourt, Inc., 2005. Cover illustration © 2005 by Brett Helquist. Reproduced by permission of Harcourt.)

ishingly apt," a *Publishers Weekly* critic wrote in a review of *Cat, What Is That?*

Johnston profiles a fascinating creature in *The Barn Owls,* which focuses on a family of owls living in an old barn in California, while *An Old Shell: Poems of the Galápagos* presents young readers with a poetic look at the remarkable creatures of these isolated islands. Johnston offers over thirty very short poems in *Gopher up Your Sleeve,* a verse collection that features all manner of creatures: from caterpillars and parrots to quetzals and sloths. Citing the "outlandish, computer-generated illustrations" by Trip Park, *School Library Journal* contributor Kathleen Kelly MacMillan wrote that in *Gopher up Your Sleeve* Johnston "plays with language and rhyme in a way that will draw kids in."

In the more humorous *Slither McCreep and His Brother, Joe* two siblings deal with the usual problems of fighting and sharing. Rather than human children, however, Slither and Joe are boa constrictors, and they go around squeezing, swallowing, and ruining each other's possessions. *Wilson Library Bulletin* reviewers Donnarae MacCann and Olga Richard commented that *Slither McCreep and His Brother, Joe* "offers family realism plus one of the most zany, surreal settings imaginable." Similarly, *The Chizzywink and the Alamogoozlum,* a story featuring the letter "z", presents the tale of a marauding giant mosquito whose intentions are foiled by a healthy dose of maple syrup. Writing in *Booklist,* Susan Dove Lempke complimented Johnston's use of "rich language and a rhythm" in the book, adding that *The Chizzywink and the Almagoozlum* is amply suited to reading aloud.

Not all of Johnston's stories cast animals as main characters. For example, *Odd Jobs* focuses on an enterprising young man who will take on any job that is offered, including washing the dirtiest dog in town, standing in for a friend at dance class, and guarding a balloon from a bratty child brandishing a sharp pin. A critic for *Booklist* praised the fact that in *Odd Jobs* Johnston has "created a resilient, inventive character and put him into laughable situations." In what *Booklist* contributor Gillian Engberg described as "moving lines that read like free-verse poetry," Johnston tells a more poignant story in *Angel City,* a tale about an old man who finds a baby abandoned in a dumpster. *Any Small Goodness: A Novel of the Barrio* is also set in Los Angeles, and finds Arturo and his family working to diminish the impact of gang violence on their lives.

In the more lighthearted *The Vanishing Pumpkin* a seven-hundred-year-old woman and an eight-hundred-year-old man meet a ghoul, a rapscallion, and a varmint as they search for their missing Halloween pumpkin. The headgear featured in *The Witch's Hat*—a tale *School Library Journal* contributor Kay McPherson dubbed "fresh and funny"—falls into the witch's magic pot and turns into a bat, a rat, and a cat before Johnston's entertaining Halloween tale winds to a close; while a less-

Cover of Johnston's coming-of-age novel **Any Small Goodness,** *featuring a cover illustration by Raúl Colón.* (Scholastic Signature, 2001. Illustrations © 2001 by Raúl Colón. All rights reserved. Reproduced by permission of Scholastic, Inc.)

helpful witch send a frustrated father on a foolish errand in *Go Track a Yak!* According to *Horn Book* contributor Ann A. Flowers, *The Ghost of Nicholas Greebe* is a "not too spooky story" about a man whose bones are dug up by a dog and how, as a ghost, he must retrieve them. *Bigfoot Cinderrrrrella* follows Ella the Bigfoot and her romance with a prince, presenting youngsters with a "silly twist on a favorite fairy tale" that deals with the romance question "with humor and style," according to a *Publishers Weekly* contributor. Also praising Johnston's quirky tale, Ellen Mandel, in her *Booklist* review, deemed *Bigfoot Cinderrrrrella* a "howlingly funny take on the original."

Readers are introduced to life during different periods of history in several books by Johnston. She takes readers back to ancient Egypt in *The Mummy's Mother,* a humorous story that finds a boy mummy determined to track down his mummy mother, stolen by grave robbers. Including art by award-winning illustrator Tomie dePaola, *The Quilt Story* introduces readers to Abigail, a young girl who finds comfort and companionship in the midnight-blue appliquéd quilt her mother made especially for her. Abigail and her family travel West via covered wagon and make a new home on the American frontier. As the girl grows up, her treasured quilt is

eventually stored away in the attic, where, a century later, it is discovered by another little girl, who also finds it a comfort when her family moves. The true-life experience of Holocaust survivor Henryk Rosmaryn is the focus of *The Harmonica,* in which a Polish boy shares his musical gifts with others during a dark time.

Setting is an important component of *Amber on the Mountain,* a novel for older elementary-grade readers. Amber lives in an isolated mountain community that has no school or teacher; she has never even learned to read. However, when a man comes to build a mountain road (a seemingly impossible task), his daughter sets herself the just-as-impossible task of teaching Amber to read. When the road is completed and the man and his daughter leave, Amber teaches herself to write so that she can keep in touch with her new friend. A *Kirkus Reviews* critic stated that "Johnston's beautifully honed narrative glows with mountain imagery and the warmth of the girls' friendship," and a reviewer in *Publishers Weekly* called the novel a "heartwarming story" with "lyrical images and picturesque and convincing dialogue."

The setting for several of Johnston's books, including *Lorenzo, the Naughty Parrot, The Old Lady and the Birds, My Mexico = Mexico mío, Uncle Rain Cloud, Day of the Dead, The Ancestors Are Singing,* and *Isabel's House of Butterflies,* reflects the fact that the author and her family lived in Mexico for fifteen years. Featuring a bilingual text, *My Mexico = Mexico mío* contains eighteen short poems in English and Spanish versions, while *Uncle Rain Cloud* and *Day of the Dead* insert Spanish vocabulary within a mostly English text. In *Uncle Rain Cloud* Johnston introduces a man who needs his nephew to translate for him, although this dependency causes him embarrassment. *Booklist* reviewer Hazel Rochman called *Uncle Rain Cloud* "funny" and "touching," adding that "Johnston's text is clear and poetic." "Brisk pacing, sympathetic characters, and clear prose . . . effectively make a winner," concluded Ann Welton in her *School Library Journal* of the same book. In *Day of the Dead* the customs surrounding a well-known Mexican tradition of celebrating ancestors are incorporated into a "dazzling little volume," according to a *Publishers Weekly* reviewer, while *Isabel's House of Butterflies* introduces children to the annual monarch butterfly migration into the mountains of Mexico.

In addition to picture books, Johnston has also written beginning readers such as *Alien and Possum: Friends No Matter What* and the "Sparky and Eddie" series: *Sparky and Eddie: The First Day of School, Sparky and Eddie: Wild, Wild Rodeo,* and *Sparky and Eddie: Trouble with Bugs.* In *Alien and Possum* a possum sees a spaceship crash near his home, then befriends his alien visitor and learns about tolerance. The characters return in *Alien and Possum Hanging Out,* which follows the growing friendship between the unlikely duo in three short stories. According to a *Publishers Weekly* contributor, the "springy pace, lively dialogue and

Alien's silly sound effects" in *Alien and Possum* will appeal to the younger set. In *Booklist,* Carolyn Phelan cited Johnston's "ready wit and understanding of a child's perspective" in the two books, while a *Kirkus Reviews* writer noted that Johnston's "droll and expressive language helps to add a little humor" to each story. In *Sparky and Eddie: The First Day of School* two close friends are looking forward to the first day of school until they learn they will be in different classrooms, while *Sparky and Eddie: Wild, Wild Rodeo,* find the siblings competing in the class rodeo. In *Booklist,* Rochman described Johnston's text in the series opener as "exuberant," while Phelan judged *Sparky and Eddie: Wild, Wild Rodeo* a "highly entertaining entry in a fine series."

Johnston once explained to *SATA,* "I write because I'd rather not iron (and also because I love to). My work habits are lousy. I sit either with a dog in my lap or a dog underneath me if she gets to the chair first. My goal in writing is simply to entertain—myself and someone else. If I manage to stir up a little love of language or make someone laugh or feel good about himself or go back to the library for another book along the way, well, that's all pink frosting on the cake." In addition to her writing, Johnston adopted Del Rey School, in King City, California, in 1999, with the ongoing goal of providing books for both classroom and library use. Her interest in California history has also inspired her active interest in Friends of the Adobes, a San Miguel-based volunteer organization dedicated to restoring and keeping up ancient adobe structures in the region.

Biographical and Critical Sources

BOOKS

Authors of Books for Young People, Scarecrow Press (Metuchen, NJ), 1990.

PERIODICALS

Booklist, October 15, 1974, review of *Mole and Troll Trim the Tree,* p. 244; March 15, 1977, review of *Night Noises and Other Mole and Troll Stories,* p. 1097; November 15, 1977, review of *Odd Jobs,* p. 559; May 15, 1996, Kay Weisman, review of *Fishing Sunday,* p. 1592; July, 1996, Stephanie Zvirin, review of *The Ghost of Nicholas Greebe,* p. 1829; October 15, 1996, Annie Ayres, review of *The Magic Maguey,* pp. 435-436, and Michael Cart, review of *How Many Miles to Jacksonville?,* p. 435; January 1, 1997, Carolyn Phelan, review of *The Wagon,* p. 869; February 1, 1997, Carolyn Phelan, review of *The Bull and the Fire Truck,* p. 949; August, 1997, Carolyn Phelan, review of *Sparky and Eddie: The First Day of School,* p. 1910; September 15, 1997, Hazel Rochman, review of *Day of the Dead,* p. 242; February 1, 1998, Hazel

Rochman, review of *Sparky and Eddie: The First Day of School,* p. 926; May 1, 1998, Carolyn Phelan, review of *Sparky and Eddie: Wild, Wild Rodeo,* p. 1524; June 1, 1998, Susan Dove Lempke, review of *The Chizzywink and the Alamagoozlum,* pp. 1779-1780; December 1, 1998, Ellen Mandel, review of *Bigfoot Cinderrrrrella,* p. 668; December 1, 1999, GraceAnne A. DeCandido, review of *An Old Shell: Poems of the Galápagos,* p. 700; February 15, 2000, Todd Morning, review of *The Barn Owls,* p. 1118; March 15, 2000, John Peters, review of *It's about Dogs,* p. 1383; October 1, 2000, Gillian Engberg, review of *Desert Song,* p. 336; January 1, 2004, Hazel Rochman, review of *The Harmonica,* p. 857; February 15, 2001, Hazel Rochman, review of *Uncle Rain Cloud,* p. 1134; July, 2001, Carolyn Phelan, review of *Alien and Possum: Friends No Matter What,* p. 2023; November 1, 2001, Ilene Cooper, review of *Clear Moon, Snow Soon,* p. 482; April 1, 2003, Gillian Engberg, review of *The Ancestors Are Singing,* p. 1406; September 1, 2003, Hazel Rochman, review of *A Kenyan Christmas,* p. 134; November 1, 2003, Ed Sullivan, review of *The Mummy's Mother,* p. 497, and Carolyn Phelan, review of *Isabel's House of Butterflies,* p. 600; January 1, 2005, Gillian Engberg, review of *Chicken in the Kitchen,* p. 870; June 1, 2006, Gillian Engberg, review of *Angel City,* p. 84.

Bulletin of the Center for Children's Books, December, 1974, review of *Mole and Troll Trim the Tree,* p. 64; November, 2003, Deborah Stevenson, review of *A Kenya Christmas,* p. 109; January, 2004, Elizabeth Bush, review of *The Mummy's Mother,* p. 195; September, 2004, Deborah Stevenson, review of *The Worm Family,* p. 23.

Catholic Library World, March, 1973, review of *Mole and Troll,* p. 512.

Children's Book Review Service, December 19, 1990, Tiffany Chrisman, review of *I'm Gonna Tell Mama I Want an Iguana,* p. 39.

Horn Book, July-August, 1988, Hanna B. Zeiger, review of *Yonder,* p. 480; May-June, 1996, Nancy Vasilakis, review of *My Mexico = Mexico mio,* p. 345; November-December, 1996, Ann A. Flowers, review of *The Ghost of Nicholas Greebe,* pp. 725-726; January-February, 1997, Anne Deifendeifer, review of *Once in the Country: Poems of a Farm,* p. 74.

Junior Bookshelf, April, 1975, review of *Mole and Troll Trim the Tree,* p. 98.

Junior Literary Guild, September, 1974, review of *Mole and Troll Trim the Tree,* p. 23.

Kirkus Reviews, December 15, 1974, review of *Mole and Troll Trim the Tree,* p. 1302; August 15, 1987, review of *Whale Song,* p. 1241; June 15, 1994, review of *Amber on the Mountain,* p. 847; August 1, 2001, review of *Alien and Possum: Friends No Matter What,* p. 1126; March 15, 2003, review of *The Ancestors Are Singing,* p. 469; June 15, 2003, review of *Go Track a Yak!,* p. 860; September 1, 2003, review of *Isabel's House of Butterflies,* p. 1126; October 1, 2003, review of *The Mummy's Mother,* p. 1225; November 1, 2003, review of *A Kenya Christmas,* p. 1317; December 15, 2003, review of *The Harmonica,* p. 1451; October 1,

2004, review of *The Worm Family,* p. 963; January 1, 2005, review of *Chicken in the Kitchen,* p. 53; March 15, 2005, review of *The Whole Green World,* p. 353; April 15, 2005, review of *The Spoon in the Bathroom Wall,* p. 475; November 1, 2005, review of *Noel,* p. 1194; May 1, 2006, review of *Sticky People,* p. 461; May 15, 2006, review of *Angel City,* p. 518.

Publishers Weekly, May 7, 1979, review of *Little Mouse Nibbling,* p. 83; June 16, 1994, review of *Amber on the Mountain,* p. 63; October 9, 1995, review of *Little Wild Parrot,* p. 85; October 21, 1996, review of *The Magic Maguey,* p. 82; September 1, 1997, review of *Day of the Dead,* p. 103; March 30, 1998, review of *The Chizzywink and the Alamogoozlum,* p. 81; November 2, 1998, review of *Bigfoot Cinderrrrrella,* p. 81; October 4, 1999, review of *The Ghost of Nicholas Greebe,* p. 77; November 8, 1999, review of *An Old Shell,* p. 67; January 31, 2000, review of *The Barn Owls,* p. 105; September 11, 2000, review of *Day of the Dead,* p. 93; September 25, 2000, review of *Desert Song,* p. 118; October 30, 2000, review of *Bigfoot Cinderrrrrella,* p. 78; February 26, 2001, review of *My Best Friend Bear,* p. 84; July 30, 2001, review of *Cat, What Is That?,* p. 83; September 24, 2001, review of *Clear Moon, Snow Soon,* p. 52, review of *Alien and Possum: Friends No Matter What,* p. 93; June 23, 2003, review of *Go Track a Yak!,* p. 66; September 22, 2003, review of *A Kenya Christmas,* p. 70; November 24, 2003, review of *The Mummy's Mother,* p. 65; January 26, 2004, review of *The Harmonica,* p. 254; May, 2004, Cris Riedel, review of *The Harmonica,* p. 116; December 6, 2004, review of *The Worm Family,* p. 58; February 28, 2005, review of *Chicken in the Kitchen,* p. 66; May 23, 2005, review of *The Spoon in the Bathroom Wall,* p. 79; September 26, 2005, review of *Noel,* p. 89.

Quill & Quire, September, 1992, p. 78.

School Library Journal, October, 1978, review of *Four Scary Stories,* p. 135; December, 1984, Kay McPherson, review of *The Witch's Hat,* p. 72; March, 2000, Sue Sherif, review of *The Barn Owls,* p. 208; June, 2000, Margaret Bush, review of *It's about Dogs,* p. 167; December, 2000, Daryl Grabarek, review of *Desert Song,* p. 112; April, 2001, Ann Welton, review of *Uncle Rain Cloud,* p. 113; August, 2001, Susan Marie Pitard, review of *My Best Friend Bear,* p. 154; October, 2001, review of *Clear Moon, Snow Soon,* p. 66; November, 2001, Ruth Semaru, review of *Desert Dog,* p. 126; August, 2002, Kristin de Lacoste, review of *Alien and Possum Hanging Out,* p. 158; November, 2002, Kathleen Kelly MacMillan, review of *Gopher up Your Sleeve,* p. 127; April, 2003, Sharon Korbeck, review of *The Ancestors Are Singing,* p. 183; October, 2003, Virginia Walter, review of *A Kenya Christmas,* p. 64, and Jennifer Ralston, review of *Any Small Goodness,* p. 98, and Angela J. Reynolds, review of *The Mummy's Mother,* p. 168; November, 2003, Catherine Threadgill, review of *Go Track a Yak!,* p. 102; December, 2003, Ann Welton, review of *Isabel's House of Butterflies,* p. 117; February, 2005, John Sigwald, review of *The Worm Family,* p. 104; April, 2005, Nina Lindsay, review of *The Ancestors Are Singing,* p. 56, and Bethany L.W. Hankinson, review of *The*

Whole Green World, p. 99; May, 2005, Corrina Austin, review of *Chicken in the Kitchen,* p. 86; June, 2005, Terrie Dorio, review of *The Spoon in the Bathroom Wall,* p. 117; June, 2006, Wendy Lukehart, review of *Angel City,* p. 120; July, 2006, Julie Roach, review of *Sticky People,* p. 79.

Teacher Librarian, March, 1999, Shirley Lewis, review of *Bigfoot Cinderrrrrella,* p. 44.

Wilson Library Bulletin, September, 1992, Donnarae MacCann and Olga Richard, review of *Slither McCreep and His Brother, Joe,* p. 90.

ONLINE

Harcourt Web site, http://www.harcourtbooks.com/ (June 1, 2007), "Tony Johnston."

Children's Literature, http://www.childrenslit.com/ (February 3, 2002), Marilyn Courtot, "Tony Johnston."

*   *   *

KADOHATA, Cynthia 1956-

Personal

Born 1956, in Chicago, IL; married (divorced, 2000); children: Sammy (adopted). *Education:* Attended Los Angeles City College; University of Southern California, B.A. (journalism); graduate study at University of Pittsburgh and Columbia University.

Addresses

Home—Long Beach, CA. *Agent*—Andrew Wylie, Wylie, Aitken & Stone, Inc., 250 W. 57th St., Ste 2106, New York, NY 10107. *E-mail*—cynthia@kira-kira.us.

Career

Writer. Worked variously as a department-store clerk and waitress.

Awards, Honors

Whiting Writer's Award, Mrs. Giles Whiting Foundation; Chesterfield Writer's Film Project screenwriting fellowship; National Endowment for the Arts grant; Newbery Medal, 2005, and APALA Award for Young-Adult Literature, 2006, both for *Kira-Kira.*

Writings

The Floating World, Viking (New York, NY), 1989.

In the Heart of the Valley of Love, Viking (New York, NY), 1992.

Kira-Kira, Atheneum (New York, NY), 2004.

Weedflower, Atheneum (New York, NY), 2006.

Cracker!: The Best Dog in Vietnam, Atheneum (New York, NY), 2007.

Contributor of short stories to periodicals, including *New Yorker, Grand Street, Ploughshares,* and *Pennsylvania Review.*

Adaptations

Author's novels have been adapted as audiobooks.

Sidelights

Cynthia Kadohata is an award-winning novelist and short-story writer. Her short fiction has appeared in the *New Yorker, Grand Street,* and the *Pennsylvania Review,* and her novels, including *The Floating World* and *In the Heart of the Valley of Love,* have been generally well received. In 2005 Kadohata received the prestigious Newbery Medal for her young-adult title *Kira-Kira,* a semi-autobiographical tale about a Japanese-American girl growing up in a small town in rural Georgia.

Like writers such as Amy Tan, Kadohata is frequently cited as a literary spokesperson for Asian Americans. However, this is a position about which she is

Cynthia Kahodata focuses on a young-adult audience in her award-winning Kira-Kira, *a novel featuring a cover photograph by Julia Kuskin.* (Aladdin Paperbacks, 2004. Cover photo copyright © 2005 by Julia Kuskin. Jacket design by Russell Gordon (NY, 2005). Reprinted by permission of Aladdin Paperbacks, an imprint of Simon & Schuster Children's Publishing Division.)

ambivalent. As she told *Publishers Weekly* interviewer Lisa See, "there's so much variety among Asian-American writers that you can't say what an Asian-American writer is." Kadohata's novels contain many clearly autobiographical features and have frequently been lauded for their striking imagery and their hauntingly lyrical narrative. Her writing has been compared to that of Raymond Carver, Bobbie Ann Mason, Mark Twain, and J.D. Salinger.

Although Kadohata was born in Chicago, Illinois, she and her family lived in Michigan, Georgia, Arkansas, and California while searching for work. A voracious reader but an indifferent student, she dropped out of high school during her senior year, opting instead to go to work in a department store and a restaurant before enrolling in Los Angeles City College. From there, Kadohata transferred to the University of Southern California, where she earned a degree in journalism in 1977. After an automobile jumped the curb and severely injured her arm, Kadohata moved to Boston where she concentrated on her writing career. "I started looking at short stories," the author told See. "I had always thought that nonfiction represented the 'truth.' Fiction seemed like something that people had done a long time ago, and wasn't very profound. But in these short stories I saw that people were writing now, and that the work was very alive. I realized that you could say things with fiction that you couldn't say any other way."

Kadohata set herself the goal of writing one story each month, using money from temp jobs and her insurance settlement to support herself. After receiving numerous rejections, she sold a story to the *New Yorker* in 1986; that tale, along with two others also published by that prestigious magazine, would later become part of her debut novel, *The Floating World.* After briefly attending graduate-level writing courses at the University of Pittsburgh, Kadohata transferred to Columbia University's writing program. However, after finding a publisher for *The Floating World,* she abandoned her program at Columbia.

The Floating World is narrated by twelve-year-old Olivia and follows the journey of a Japanese-American family searching for economic and emotional security in post-World War II America. Kadohata uses Olivia's character to portray the family dynamics and interactions that occur as they travel, eat, and even sleep in the same room together. In a passage that reveals the significance of the book's title, Olivia explains this itinerant life: "We were traveling then in what she [Obasan, Olivia's grandmother] called *ukiyo,* the floating world. The floating world was the gas station attendants, restaurants, and jobs we depended on, the motel towns floating in the middle of fields and mountains. In old Japan, ukiyo meant the districts full of brothels, tea houses and public baths, but it also referred to change and the pleasures and loneliness change brings. For a long time, I never exactly thought of us as part of any of that, though. *We* were stable, traveling through an unstable world while my father looked for jobs."

In addition to the physical journey, Kadohata illustrates Olivia's internal journey in *The Floating World*. Due to the close quarters of her family's living arrangements, Olivia is exposed to adult issues at an early age. She witnesses the tension that exists between her parents, their quiet arguments, and even their love making. In addition, she is constantly subjected to her eccentric grandmother's frequently abusive behavior. Finally the family finds a stable home in Arkansas where Olivia matures from a young teen to a young adult. It is during this time that she learns to understand the ways of her parents and grandmother and to develop her own values. *Los Angeles Times Book Review* contributor Grace Edwards-Yearwood commended this portrayal, pointing out that "Kadohata writes compellingly of Olivia's coming of age, her determination to grow beyond her parents' dreams."

Reviewing *The Floating World,* Diana O'Hehir wrote in the *New York Times Book Review* that Kadohata's "aim and the book's seem to be one: to present the world affectionately and without embroidery. To notice what's there. To see it as clearly as you can." Caroline Ong, a *Times Literary Supplement* contributor, described Olivia's narrative as "haunting because of its very simplicity and starkness, its sketchy descriptions fleshing out raw emotions and painful truths." Susanna Moore, writing in the *Washington Post Book World,* judged that *The Floating World* would be more effective had it been written in the style of a memoir. However, the critic also conceded that "Kadohata has written a book that is a child's view of the floating world, a view that is perceptive, unsentimental and intelligent." *New York Times* critic Michiko Kakutani praised the first-time novelist's ability to handle painful moments with humor and sensitivity, concluding that such "moments not only help to capture the emotional reality of these people's lives in a delicate net of images and words, but they also attest to Ms. Kadohata's authority as a writer." Kakutani concluded the review by noting that *The Floating World* marks the debut of a luminous new voice in fiction."

In the Heart of the Valley of Love concerns survival and quality of life in Los Angeles in the year 2052. In her fictional future world Kadohata pits the haves and have-nots against one another. Both are gun-toting communities without morals, law, or order. Amid this chaos, the main character, a nineteen-year-old orphan of Asian and African descent named Francie, relates her story of endurance.

Some critics found Kahodota's sophomore effort to be relatively disappointing. Barbara Quick, writing in the *New York Times Book Review,* criticized *In the Heart of the Valley of Love* for its lack of conviction and imagination, and further noted that main character Francie, with only a few alterations, is identical to Kadohata's earlier protagonist. In a similar vein, Kakutani argued that "Kadohata's vision of the future is not sufficiently original or compelling," resulting in "an uncomfortable hybrid: a pallid piece of futuristic writing, and an unconvincing tale of coming of age." The reviewer noted, however, that "the writing in this volume is lucid and finely honed, often lyrical and occasionally magical." Praising *In the Heart of the Valley of Love, Los Angeles Times Book Review* contributor Susan Heeger lauded Kadohata as "masterful in her evocation of physical, spiritual and cultural displacement," adding that "the message of this marvelous though often painful book is that our capacity to feel deep emotion . . . just might bind us together, and save us from ourselves."

The Newbery Medal-winning *Kira-Kira,* Kadohata's first book for a young-adult audience, "tells the tender story of a Japanese-American family that moves from Iowa to rural Georgia in the 1950s," according to *School Library Journal* contributor Susan Faust. The work concerns the complex relationship between Katie Takeshima and her older sister, Lynn, who often cares for Katie while their parents work long hours at the town's poultry plants. Katie worships her older sister, who taught Katie the Japanese word "kira-kira," which means "glittering" and which Katie uses to describe everything she loves. When Lynn falls ill and is diagnosed with lymphoma, the sisters' roles are reversed; Katie becomes Lynn's caretaker, an exhausting and heart-wrenching ordeal that ends with her sister's death. Through Katie's narration, *Kira-Kira* "stays true to the child's viewpoint," the "plain, beautiful prose . . . barely containing the [narrator's] passionate feelings," noted *Booklist* critic Hazel Rochman. "The family's devotion to one another, and Lynn's ability to teach Katie to appreciate the 'kira-kira,' or glittering, in everyday life makes this novel shine," added a *Publishers Weekly* critic.

Also for a young-adult readership, *Weedflower* is set in the aftermath of Pearl Harbor and chronicles the growing friendship between Sumiko Yamaguchi, a Japanese-American girl living in an internment camp, and a Native-American boy who lives on nearby reservation lands. Noting that the work is loosely based on the childhood experiences of her father, Kadohata explained on her home page: "My father and his family were interned in the Poston camp on the Colorado River Indian Reservation in the Sonoran desert. One source claims the thermometer in 1942 hit more than 140 degrees in the Poston area." In the novel, Sumiko's uncle and grandfather are sent to North Dakota after the United States declares war on Japan, while the rest of her family is transported to a camp in the Arizona desert. Despite the harsh living conditions and her frustrations at being imprisoned, "Sumiko finds hope and a form of salvation" by creating a garden, observed a contributor for *Publishers Weekly.* A reviewer in *Kliatt* praised *Weedflower,* calling it "a haunting story of dramatic loss and subtle triumphs."

A high school dropout turned award-winning novelist, Kadohata believes that, as it did for her, literature has

Cover of Kadohata's young-adult novel Weedflower, *featuring a cover photograph by Kamil Vojnar.* (Atheneum Books for Young Readers, 2006. Jacket photographs and photo-illustration copyright © 2006 by Kamil Vojnar. Jacket design by Russell Gordon (NY, 2006). Reproduced by permission of Atheneum Books for Young Readers, an imprint of Simon & Schuster Children's Publishing Division.)

the power to nurture and transform an individual. After she left school, the author explained in her Newbery acceptance speech (as published in *Horn Book*), "I sought out the library near my home. Seeking it out was more of an instinct, really, not a conscious thought. I didn't think to myself, I need to start reading again. I felt it. I rediscovered reading—the way I'd read as a child, when there was constantly a book I was just finishing or just beginning or in the middle of. I rediscovered myself." She continued, "I look back on 1973, the year I dropped out of school, with the belief that libraries can not just change your life but save it. Not the same way a Coast Guardsman or a police officer might save a life, not all at once. It happens more slowly, but just as surely."

Biographical and Critical Sources

BOOKS

Kadohata, Cynthia, *The Floating World,* Viking (New York, NY), 1989.

Notable Asian Americans, Thomson Gale (Detroit, MI), 1995.

PERIODICALS

Amerasia Journal, winter, 1997, Lynn M. Itagaki, review of *In the Heart of the Valley of Love,* p. 229.

America, November 18, 1989, Eve Shelnutt, review of *The Floating World,* p. 361.

Antioch Review, winter, 1990, review of *The Floating World,* p. 125.

Belles Lettres, spring, 1993, review of *In the Heart of the Valley of Love,* p. 46.

Booklist, June 15, 1992, Gilbert Taylor, review of *In the Heart of the Valley of Love,* p. 1807; January 1, 2004, Hazel Rochman, review of *Kira-Kira,* p. 858.

Globe & Mail (Toronto, Ontario, Canada), August 5, 1989.

Horn Book, March-April, 2004, Jennifer M. Brabander, review of *Kira-Kira,* pp. 183-184; July-August, 2005, Cynthia Kadohata, "Newbery Medal Acceptance," pp. 409-417, and Caitlyn M. Dlouhy, "Cynthia Kadohata," pp. 419-427.

Kliatt, March, 2006, Janis Flint-Ferguson, review of *Weedflower,* pp. 12-13.

Library Journal, June 15, 1992, Cherry W. Li, review of *In the Heart of the Valley of Love,* p. 102.

Los Angeles Times Book Review, July 16, 1989, p. 12; August 23, 1992, pp. 1, 8; May 2, 1993, review of *The Floating World,* p. 10.

New York Times, June 30, 1989, Michiko Kakutani, review of *The Floating World,* p. B4; July 28, 1992, Michiko Kakutani, review of *In the Heart of the Valley of Love,* p. C15.

New York Times Book Review, July 23, 1989, Diana O'Hehir, review of *The Floating World,* p. 16; August 30, 1992, Barbara Quick, review of *In the Heart of the Valley of Love,* p. 14.

Publishers Weekly, May 12, 1989, review of *The Floating World,* p. 279; June 1, 1992, review of *In the Heart of the Valley of Love,* p. 51; August 3, 1992, Lisa See, "Cynthia Kadohata," pp. 48-49; February 9, 2004, review of *Kira-Kira,* pp. 81-82; February 27, 2006, review of *Weedflower,* p. 62.

School Library Journal, January, 1990, Anne Paget, review of *The Floating World,* p. 127; March, 2004, Ashley Larsen, review of *Kira-Kira,* pp. 214-215; May, 2005, Susan Faust, "The Comeback Kid," pp. 38-40.

Time, June 19, 1989, review of *The Floating World,* p. 65.

Times Literary Supplement, December 29, 1989, Caroline Ong, review of *The Floating World,* p. 1447.

U.S. News & World Report, December 26, 1988, Miriam Horn and Nancy Linnon, "New Cultural Worlds," p. 101.

Washington Post Book World, June 25, 1989, pp. 5, 7; August 16, 1992, p. 5.

ONLINE

Cynthia Kadohata Web site, http://www.kira-kira.us (June 8, 2007).

Time for Kids Web site, http://www.timeforkids.com/ (February 28, 2005), Aminah Sallam, "TFK Talks with Cynthia Kadohata."*

OTHER

Good Conversation! A Talk with Cynthia Kahodata (film), Tim Podell Productions, 2005.

* * *

KANN, Elizabeth

Personal

Born in New York, NY; married; children: two. *Education:* Graduate of Vassar College, Columbia University, and Albany Medical College.

Addresses

Home and office—Reading, PA. *E-mail*—elizabethkann@hotmail.com.

Career

Physician and children's book author.

Writings

(With sister, Victoria Kann) *Pinkalicious,* illustrated by Victoria Kann, HarperCollins (New York, NY), 2006.
(With Victoria Kann) *Pinkalicious the Musical* produced in New York, NY, 2007.
(With Victoria Kann) *Purplicious,* illustrated by Victoria Kann, HarperCollins (New York, NY), 2007.

Contributor to periodicals, including *Pittsburgh Post-Gazette, Go World Travel,* and *Forum.* Contributor to books, including *Chocolate for the Woman's Soul, Volume II.*

Sidelights

Elizabeth Kann coauthored the children's book *Pinkalicious* with her sister, illustrator Victoria Kann. In the playful tale, Pinkalicious is a young girl who absolutely adores the color pink. Her clothes are pink, her room is pink, and when her mother makes pink cupcakes, even her food can be pink! Although Pinkalicious finds the pink confection decidedly to her taste, she ignores her mother's warnings and eats so many cupcakes that her skin actually turns pink! Overjoyed at the family doctor's diagnosis of Pinkitis, the girl continue munching on pink cupcakes until her pink tinge darkens to red. When the only cure is to eat green foods, Pinkalicious realizes that there is, indeed, such a thing as too much pink, as well as too much broccoli and cabbage, and too many brussel sprouts, green beans, and peas. "Kann's snappy prose is filled with subtle puns and jokes," remarked one *Kirkus Reviews* critic in a review of *Pinkalicious,* while GraceAnne A. DeCandido wrote in *Booklist* that the Kann sisters bring to life a "fun premise" that will "guarantee an audience" for their pink-crazed young protagonist.

Biographical and Critical Sources

PERIODICALS

Booklist, June, 2006, GraceAnne A. DeCandido, review of *Pinkalicious,* p. 84.
Bulletin of the Center for Children's Books, July-August, 2006, Deborah Stevenson, review of *Pinkalicious,* p. 504.
Kirkus Reviews, May 15, 2006, review of *Pinkalicious,* p. 518.
School Library Journal, August, 2006, Erlene Bishop Killeen, review of *Pinkalicious,* p. 90.

ONLINE

Elizabeth Kann Home Page, http://www.elizabethkann.com (May 14, 2007).
Pinkalicious Web site, http://www.cupcakesforall.com/ (July 10, 2007).

* * *

KANN, Victoria

Personal

Born in New York, NY. *Education:* Rhode Island School of Design, graduate.

Addresses

Home and office—Westport, CT.

Career

Illustrator and children's book author.

Awards, Honors

Award of Design Excellence, *Print;* Award of Distinction, Creativity 26; *Applied Arts* Magazine Award in Best Magazine Spread Category; Bronze and silver awards, Dimensional Illustrator Awards Show; Award of Merit, Society of Illustrators of Los Angeles.

Writings

(With sister, Elizabeth Kann; and illustrator) *Pinkalicious,* HarperCollins (New York, NY), 2006.

(With Elizabeth Kann) _Pinkalicious the Musical_ produced in New York, NY, 2007.

(With Elizabeth Kann; and illustrator) _Purplicious,_ Harper-Collins (New York, NY), 2007.

Biographical and Critical Sources

PERIODICALS

Booklist, June, 2006, GraceAnne A. DeCandido, review of _Pinkalicious,_ p. 84.

Bulletin of the Center for Children's Books, July-August, 2006, Deborah Stevenson, review of _Pinkalicious,_ p. 504.

Kirkus Reviews, May 15, 2006, review of _Pinkalicious,_ p. 518.

School Library Journal, August, 2006, Erlene Bishop Killeen, review of _Pinkalicious,_ p. 90.

ONLINE

AltPick Web site, http://altpick.com/spot/ (April 29, 2007), "Victoria Kann."

Pinkalicious Web site, http://www.cupcakesforall.com/ (July 10, 2007).

Victoria Kann Home Page, www.ilikeart.com (April 29, 2007).

*   *   *

KIMMELMAN, Burt 1947-
(L.V. Mack)

Personal

Born May 6, 1947, in Brooklyn, NY; son of David Brown (a physician) and Sylvia (a teacher) Kimmelman; married LaVonne Mack, June 6, 1970 (divorced, 1974); married Diane Maureen Ellis Simmons (a professor and novelist), December 28, 1989; children: Jane. _Ethnicity:_ "Jewish." _Education:_ State University of New York College at Cortland, B.A., 1983; Hunter College of the City University of New York, M.A., 1987; Graduate School of the City University of New York, Ph.D., 1991. _Politics:_ "Independent."

Addresses

Office—Department of Humanities, New Jersey Institute of Technology, Newark, NJ 07102. _E-mail_—kimmelman@jit.edu.

Career

New Jersey Institute of Technology, Newark, professor of humanities, 1988—. _Poetry New York_ (journal), senior editor and publisher, 1988-2001.

Member

Modern Language Association of America, Association of Literary Scholars and Critics, Society for Textual Scholarship.

Awards, Honors

Mary Fay Poetry Award, 1982; fellow-in-residence, Cummington Community of the Arts, 1988; finalist, Rainer Maria Rilke National Poetry Competition, 1984.

Writings

Musaics (poems), Spuyten Duyvil Books (New York, NY), 1992.

The Poetics of Authorship in the Later Middle Ages: The Emergence of the Modern Literary Persona, Peter Lang (New York, NY), 1996.

(With others) _Environmental Protection: Solving Environmental Problems from Social Science and Humanities Perspectives_ (textbook), Kendall/Hunt (Dubuque, IA), 1997.

The "Winter Mind": William Bronk and American Letters, Fairleigh Dickinson University Press (Madison, NJ), 1998.

First Life (poems), Jensen Daniels, 2000.

The Pond at Cape May Point, paintings by Fred Caruso, Marsh Hawk Press (New York, NY), 2002.

(Author of foreword) Steven Carter, _Bearing Across: Studies in Science and Literature,_ 2nd edition, International Scholasr Publications (Washington, DC), 2002.

(Author of introduction) Martha King, _Imperfect Fit,_ Marsh Hawk Press (New York, NY), 2004.

(Editor and contributor) _The Facts on File Companion to 20th-Century American Poetry,_ Facts on File (New York, NY), 2005.

Somehow (poetry), Marsh Hawk Press (New York, NY), 2005.

There Are Words (poetry), Dos Madres Press (Loveland, OH), 2007.

Contributor to books, including: Joseph Conte, editor, _Dictionary of Literary Biography,_ Volume 165: _American Poets since World War II, Fourth Series,_ Thomson Gale (Detroit, MI), 1996; Michael Heller, editor, _Carl Rakosi: Man and Poet,_ National Poetry Foundation (Orono, ME), 1993; Albrecht Classen, editor, _The Medieval Book and the Magic of Reading,_ Garland Publishing (New York, NY), 1999; Joel Shatzky and Michael Taub, editors, _Jewish-American Dramatists and Poets: A Bio-Critical Sourcebook,_ Greenwood Press (Westport, CT), 1999; David Clippinger, editor, _The Body of This Life: Essays on the Work of William Bronk,_ Talisman House (Jersey City, NJ), 2000; John M. Hill and Deborah Sinnreich-Levi, editors, _Rhetorical Poetics of the Middle Ages: Reconstructive Polyphony; Essays in Honor of Robert O. Payne,_ Fairleigh Dickinson University Press, 2000; _The World in Time and Space: Toward a History of Innovative American Poetry, 1970-2000,_

Talisman House, 2002; and *Chaucer Encyclopedia.* Work represented in anthologies, including *American Poetry Anthology,* American Poetry Association (Santa Cruz, CA), 1987; and *The Second Word Thursdays Anthology,* Bright Hill Press (Treadwell, NY), 1999. Contributor of poems, articles, and reviews to periodicals, including *Sagetrieb, Journal of the Early Book, Terra Nova, Sycamore, Mudfish, Trumpeter, Re Visions, Newark Review, Apostrophe, Pequod, Journal of Imagism,* and *Arkansas Quarterly.* Some writings appear under pseudonym L.V. Mack.

Sidelights

The senior editor and publisher of the journal *Poetry New York* from 1988 to 2001, Burt Kimmelman is professor of humanities at New Jersey Institute of Technology, Newark. In addition to his work as a poet, he is also the author of several scholarly and reference works, and edited *The Facts on File Companion to 20th-Century American Poetry.* Praising the anthology, which includes 500 entries covering the styles, schools, and other topics related to twentieth-century poetics, *Booklist* contributor Diana Kirby cited Kimmelmann's "eclectic approach" and recommended the work as a "valuable companion to standard reference sources."

Kimmelman once commented: "I write poetry out of a deep need. When I am writing I am communing with both my self and the world in a fundamental way unattainable otherwise. All writing is greatly pleasurable to me, but poetry most of all. My poetry has primarily been influenced by poets in the imagist/objectivist tradition. When I was younger I used to work a lot on paper with a pencil. Nowadays I wait until the poem is a kind of complete statement, then I begin to put words on paper. I work on paper for a number of drafts, after which I continue to work on the computer.

"Nowadays I am involved in writing syllabic poetry that concentrates on nouns and verbs and their interplay. The play of language *per se* is most important to me."

Biographical and Critical Sources

PERIODICALS

Booklist, May 15, 2005, Diana Kirby, review of *The Facts on File Companion to 20th-Century American Poetry,* p. 1700.
Choice, December, 1998, review of *The "Winter Mind:" William Bronk and American Letters,* p. 687; July-August, 2005, N. Knipe, review of *The Facts on File Companion to 20th-Century American Poetry,* p. 1958.
Library Journal, March 1, 2005, review of *The Facts on File Companion to 20th-Century American Poetry,* p. 114.
School Library Journal, Julie Web, review of *The Facts on File Companion to 20th-Century American Poetry,* p. 76.

ONLINE

New Jersey Institute of Technology Web site, http://web.njit.edu/ (June 1, 2007), "Bert Kimmelman."*

*   *   *

KLISE, M. Sarah 1961-

Personal

Born December 31, 1961, in Peoria, IL; daughter of Thomas S. (a writer and film producer) and Marjorie A. (president of Thomas S. Klise Co.) Klise. *Education:* Marquette University, graduate.

Addresses

Home and office—2830 8th St., Berkeley, CA 94710. *Agent*—William Corsa, Specialty Book Marketing, Inc., 443 Park Ave. S., Ste. 806, New York, NY 10016. *E-mail*—msklise@pacbell.net.

Career

Illustrator and designer of books. Chinatown Young Artist Program, San Francisco, CA, founder and teacher.

Illustrator

FOR CHILDREN; WITH SISTER, KATE KLISE

Regarding the Fountain: A Tale, in Letters, of Liars and Leaks, Avon Books (New York, NY), 1998.
Letters from Camp, Avon Books (New York, NY), 1999.
Trial by Journal, HarperCollins (New York, NY), 2001.
Shall I Knit You a Hat?: A Christmas Yarn, Henry Holt (New York, NY), 2004.

M. Sarah Klise (Photograph courtesy of M. Sarah Klise.)

Regarding the Sink: Where, Oh Where, Did Waters Go?, Harcourt (Orlando, FL), 2004.

Regarding the Trees: A Splintered Saga Rooted in Secrets, Harcourt (Orlando, FL), 2005.

Why Do You Cry?: Not a Sob Story, Henry Holt (New York, NY), 2006.

Regarding the Bathrooms: A Privy to the Past, Harcourt (San Diego, CA), 2006.

Imagine Harry, Harcourt (Orlando, FL), 2007.

Regarding the Bees: A Lesson, in Letters, on Honey, Dating, and Other Sticky Subjects, Harcourt (Orlando, FL), 2007.

Little Rabbit and the Nightmare, Harcourt (Orlando, FL), 2008.

43 Old Cemetery Road: The First Summer, Harcourt (Orlando, FL), 2008.

Sidelights

M. Sarah Klise and her sister Kate Klise share a love of writing and receiving letters, and this is at the heart of their novels for middle-grade students. In their first book, *Regarding the Fountain: A Tale, in Letters, of Liars and Leaks,* the simple job of replacing the drinking fountain at Missouri's Dry Creek Middle School becomes preternaturally complicated once local fountain designer Florence Waters is called in. Flo invites Mr. Sam N.'s fifth-grade class—including Tad Poll, Gil, Lily, and Paddy—to help design the new fountain, and various members of the community must also be consulted and pacified. As Flo moves through the town like a force of nature, the story morphs into a romp told via the letters, memos, faxes, postcards, and newspaper clippings circulating among school principal Walter Russ, members of Mr. Sam N.'s class, school board president Sally Mander, and Mr. D. Eel, owner of the municipal water company. Soon the mystery behind why the town is permanently in a state of drought is revealed, as is the role played by the old, leaky school water fountain in keeping it so.

In *Regarding the Fountain* "the hilarious shenanigans are unremitting; the puns flow faster than the leaks in the old fountain," observed Nancy Vasilakis in *Horn Book.* M. Sarah Klise's contribution lies in creating the graphic design of the various items of correspondence that comprise each page. Though the mystery may not be too difficult to unravel, according to Rita Soltan in *School Library Journal,* "it is still fun to continue reading the diverse pages, all in different fonts with eclectic drawings, just to see how the mystery will be revealed and solved." Susan Dove Lempke, reviewing *Regarding the Fountain* for *Booklist,* likewise wrote that while the scheme for the novel is "a trifle gimmicky," author and illustrator "carry it off extraordinarily well," and the graphic presentation of the story will attract even reluctant readers.

Using their unique format, the Klise sisters continue the adventures of Mr. Sam N's class in *Regarding the Sink: Where, Oh Where, Did Waters Go?, Regarding the Trees: A Splintered Saga Rooted in Secrets, Regarding the Bathrooms: A Privy to the Past,* and *Regarding the Bees: A Lesson, in Letters, on Honey, Dating, and Other Sticky Subjects.* Dry Creek Middle School has been renamed Geyser Creek Middle School in *Regarding the Sink,* and in a graphically engaging mix of letters, memos, school announcements, e-mails, and drawings readers follow Flo Waters' efforts to design a new sink for the school cafeteria until her sudden disappearance—and its links to the machinations of the evil Senator Sue Ergass—prompts the members of Sam N.'s sixth-grade class to uncover her whereabouts. In *Horn Book* Susan P. Bloom had special praise for M. Sarah Klise's "inventive layouts and typography," while in *Booklist* Francisca Goldsmith noted that "the array of nicely designed documentation" combine with a surprise ending to "keep many young bibliophiles content."

In *Regarding the Trees* "the puns fall faster than autumn leaves," according to *Horn Book* contributor Susan P. Bloom. Worried over an upcoming school evaluation, Principal Russ asks Flo to assist in trimming the school trees, sparking student protests, a town uprising, and a cooking face-off between two local chefs. All ends well, however, and romance even blooms. Police reports take their place among letters, newspaper articles, and other communications in *Regarding the Bathrooms,* as the principal's hope of renovating a basement bathroom during summer session is stalled when several escaped convicts are found hiding in the building, along with a cache of stolen Roman antiquities. The action moves to seventh grade in *Regarding the Bees,* as budding student romances, stresses over standardized tests, and difficulties surrounding the school mascot's appearance at a regional spelling bee result in a flurry of humorous visual communication.

Calling *Regarding the Trees* as "filled with humor and whimsical characters," Shelle Rosenfeld added in *Booklist* that "kids will enjoy the peppy, multiformat read." In her *School Library Journal* review, Cheryl Ashton noted that "each page" of the book "is painstakingly laid out in scrapbook form," and a *Kirkus Reviews* writer dubbed *Regarding the Trees* "consistently clever and often hilarious."

In addition to *Regarding the Fountain* and its sequels, the Klise sisters use letters, notes, newspaper articles, and other missives to tell the story in *Letters from Camp* and *Trial by Journal.* In *Letters from Camp,* three pairs of siblings suffer from more than a little rivalry. Frustrated, their parents ship them off to Camp Harmony, there to get a lesson in getting along from the Harmony siblings, a former family singing act and now owners of the camp. As the children suffer through endless chores and terrible food, they begin to realize that the Harmonys are secretly trying to kill each other off. Their own squabbling diminishes as the siblings join forces to solve the mystery that lies at the heart of the Harmony family ranch, in the process learning how to get along,

Cover of Kate Klise's **Regarding the Trees,** *a middle-grade novel that gains much of its humor and energy from the illustrations of sister M. Sarah Klise.* (Gulliver Books, 2005. Jacket illustration copyright © 2005 by M. Sarah Klise. All rights reserved. Reproduced by permission of Harcourt.)

just as the camp brochure promised! Like *Regarding the Fountain, Letters from Camp* features M. Sarah Klise's graphic art, and "each page is a collage of written evidence through which the story unfolds," according to Connie Tyrrell Burns in *School Library Journal.* Burns went on to predict that *Letters from Camp* will appeal most to "students with a wacky sense of humor."

In *Trial by Journal* twelve-year-old Lily Watson faces a difficult choice: either attend summer school or become a jury member in a murder trial and write a report about the experience. (Because of a fictional state law in Missouri, juveniles can participate on juries in cases where a juvenile was the victim of the crime.) Lily decides to take the second option and help decide the fate of Bob White, a zoo employee accused of killing eleven-year-old Perry Keet. Using their trademark puns and humor, the Klises create what a *Publishers Weekly* critic called a "three-ring circus" that "will set in motion readers' flights of fancy from beginning to end." According to a *Horn Book* reviewer, in *Trial by Journal* "Klise matches her sister's sense of fun with outrageous layouts and sketches throughout the text."

While most of their books are geared toward middle-grade readers, the Klise sisters also turn their attention to younger children in the picture books *Shall I Knit You a Hat?: A Christmas Yarn* and *Why Do You Cry?: Not a Sob Story.* In *Shall I Knit You a Hat?* Mother Rabbit decided to knit a warm blue hat to cover Little Rabbit's ears. The bunny loves his hat so much that he wants all his friends to have one to, and his doting mother begins a flurry of knitting that results in custom-made caps for horse, goose, and others, all in time for Christmas. Little Rabbit turns five in *Why Do You Cry?,* and when he decides to invite only friends too big to burst into tears, the bunny learns that crying can be appropriate at certain times, no matter what one's age. Calling *Shall I Knit You a Hat?* "a promising picture-book debut," *Booklist* reviewer Ilene Cooper wrote that M. Sarah Klise's "acrylic artwork glows with humor and radiates warmth," while in *Kirkus Reviews* a contributor praised the artist for "incorporat[ing] . . . clever, whimsical details into her paintings." The "warm acrylic illustrations" she contributes to *Why Do You Cry?* "have a retro quality and are full of humor and detail," noted Robin L. Gibson in a *School Library Journal* review of the picture-book collaboration, while in *Publishers Weekly* a critic wrote that M. Sarah Klise "sidesteps preciousness" in bringing to life her sister's gentle story "by virtue of her crisp shapes and radiant, saturated colors."

Klise once told *SATA:* "As a child, I wondered if adults were paid to work or if one was required to pay for the opportunity TO work. I never could remember which way it went. Many years later, I sometimes feel the same way. It is such an honor to be able to draw pictures for children's books that I think I would PAY to do it—please don't tell our publisher this. I have to feed my three cats! I get to be part-architect, part-inventor, part-designer, and part-just-about-anything-else-you-can-think-of.

"I am also lucky to get to collaborate with my sister, Kate Klise, author. Because there are four states in between our homes, we rely on letters, packages, e-mail, phone calls, and visits to create our books. We have collaborated on books since we were children, knowing early on that Kate had a knack for telling funny stories and that I could draw pictures that sort of looked how they were supposed to. In a pinch, she would write a short story for me and I would illustrate research papers for her.

"Over the years we became great pen pals. These many, many letters and the many letters from our parents and siblings became the framework for our books. Everyone loves to get a piece of mail. Correspondence can be secret and very personal. We both hope that writing letters, like making valentines and Christmas cards and sending postcards from across town, never becomes a thing of the past but remains a part of our daily lives."

M. Sarah Klise and sister Kate Klise team up on their engaging and imaginative picture books despite the fact that they live in different states. (Illustration by M. Sarah Klise, 2007. Courtesy of illustrator.)

Biographical and Critical Sources

PERIODICALS

Booklist, August, 1998, Susan Dove Lempke, review of *Regarding the Fountain: A Tale, in Letters, of Liars and Leaks,* p. 2006; September 1, 2001, Shelle Rosenfeld, review of *Trial by Journal,* p. 106; September 1, 2004, Francisca Goldsmith, review of *Regarding the Sink: Where, Oh Where, Did Waters Go?,* p. 124; December 1, 2004, Ilene Cooper, review of *Shall I Knit You a Hat?: A Christmas Yarn,* p. 659; November 1, 2005, Shelle Rosenfeld, review of *Regarding the Trees: A Splintered Saga Rooted in Secrets,* p. 47; May 1, 2006, Kathleen Odean, review of *Why Do You Cry?: Not a Sob Story,* p. 92; September 1, 2006, Shelle Rosenfeld, review of *Regarding the Bathroom: A Privy to the Past,* p. 129.

Horn Book, May-June, 1998, Nancy Vasilakis, review of *Regarding the Fountain,* p. 345; May-June, 2001, Susan P. Brabander, review of *Trial by Journal,* p. 328; September-October, 2004, Susan P. Bloom, review of *Regarding the Sink,* p. 588; September-October, 2005, Susan P. Bloom, review of *Regarding the Trees,* p. 582.

Kirkus Reviews, July 15, 2004, review of *Regarding the Sink,* p. 688; November 1, 2004, review of *Shall I Knit You a Hat?,* p. 1051; July 15, 2005, review of *Regarding the Trees,* p. 792; May 15, 2006, review of *Why Do You Cry?,* p. 519; July 15, 2006, review of *Regarding the Bathrooms,* p. 725.

New York Times Book Review, December 19, 2004, J.D. Biersdorfer, review of *Shall I Knit You a Hat?,* p. 26.

Publishers Weekly, April 30, 2001, review of *Trial by Journal,* p. 78; September 27, 2004, review of *Shall I Knit You a Hat?,* p. 61; May 1, 2006, review of *Why Do You Cry?,* p. 62.

School Library Journal, June, 1998, Rita Soltan, review of *Regarding the Fountain,* p. 147; June, 1999, Connie Tyrrell Burns, review of *Letters from Camp,* p. 132; June, 2001, Sharon McNeil, review of *Trial by Journal,* p. 152; October, 2004, Jean Gaffney, review of *Regarding the Sink,* p. 170; November, 2005, Cheryl Ashton, review of *Regarding the Trees,* p. 138; July, 2006, review of *Why Do You Cry?,* p. 80; August, 2006, Wendy Woodfill, review of *Regarding the Bathrooms,* p. 123.

Tribune Books (Chicago, IL), July 16, 2006, Mary Harris Russell, review of *Why Do You Cry?,* p. 7.

ONLINE

Kate and M. Sarah Klise Home Page, http://www.kateandsarahklise.com (May 10, 2007).

L

LJUNGKVIST, Laura

Personal

Born in Gothenburg, Sweden. *Education:* Attended Grundis, RMI-Berghs Communication Arts School (Stockholm, Sweden), 1988.

Addresses

Home and office—Brooklyn, NY. *Agent*—c/o George Nicholson, Sterling Lord Literistic, 65 Bleecker St., New York, NY 10012. *E-mail*—laura@followtheline. com.

Career

Author and illustrator. Worked variously as an instructor and freelance illustrator.

Awards, Honors

Nominated twice for Swedish Golden Egg Award.

Writings

Toni's Topsy-Turvy Telephone Day, Harry N. Abrams (New York, NY), 2001.
Snow White and the Seven Dwarves, Harry N. Abrams (New York, NY), 2003.
Follow the Line, Viking (New York, NY), 2006.
Follow the Line through the House, Viking (New York, NY), 2007.

Authors work has been translated into Korean and Japanese.

Sidelights

Swedish-born author and illustrator Laura Ljungkvist once commented in an interview with Nathalie Beeck for *Publishers Weekly* that she considers herself a "vi-

Laura Ljungkvist (Photograph © 2006. Courtesy of Laura Ljungkvist.)

sual problem solver." Ljungkvist originally began her career as a freelance illustrator before becoming a children's book author and illustrator, creating designs for such esteemed publications as the *New Yorker, Harper's Bazaar* and the *New York Times.* She especially enjoys illustrating and writing children's books because it allows her to "solve my own problem," an aspect that is unique to Ljungkvist. While Ljungkvist initially had no

The uniquely modern style of illustrator and author Ljungkvist pairs well with her spare text in picture books such as **Follow the Line.** (Viking, 2006.
Illustration copyright © 2006 by Laura Ljungkvist. All rights reserved. Reproduced by permission of Viking, a division of Penguin Putnam.)

intention of pursuing a profession as a children's book author and illustrator, a serious accident in 1997 caused her to think twice about her career decision. "It took a hit on the head to make me decide, I'm going to do this again," she noted in her *Publishers Weekly* interview.

Ljungkvist is known for creating stylized gouache images which feature bold colors and straight, geometric lines. Her simple yet vibrant artwork, modernistic in its effect, has been compared by some reviewers to the work of Spanish surrealist painter Joan Miró. In a review of the artist's body of work for *Print* magazine, Katherine Nelson described Ljungkvist's artistic method

as "contemporary yet nostalgic" and capturing a style that is both "vibrant and playful." The use of bright, dramatic colors pairs with her bold line throughout her illustrated works. Karin Snelson, in a review for *Booklist,* noticed the author/illustrator's unique use of color in her retelling of the childhood fairy-tale classic *Snow White and the Seven Dwarves.* According to the critic, Ljungkvist's "ultraclean artwork" and her "use [of] color and form" combine "to communicate mood and meaning."

Discussing her craft, Ljungkvist told *SATA:* "I resisted going digital for a long time, and continued to mix my beloved Windsor & Newton gouache paints. Now, since getting a power Mac, I either draw on my Wacom pen tablet or paint or draw on paper, and then scan my work into the computer. Then I add color and pattern elements using Adobe Photoshop."

Biographical and Critical Sources

PERIODICALS

Books, May 14, 2006, Mary Harris Russell, review of *Follow the Line,* p. 7.

Booklist, June 1, 2001, Amy Brandt, review of *Toni's Topsy-Turvy Telephone Day,* p. 1892; April 15, 2003, Karin Snelson, review of *Snow White and the Seven Dwarves,* p. 1473.

Bulletin of the Center for Children's Books, July, 2003, review of *Snow White and the Seven Dwarves,* p. 454.

Child, May, 2007, Julie Yates Walton, "Books: The Best New Stories to Inspire Young Minds," p. 38.

Kirkus Reviews, April 1, 2003, review of *Snow White and the Seven Dwarves,* p. 536; April 15, 2006, review of *Follow the Line,* p. 409.

Print, Katherine Nelson, January-February 1999, "Lifeline: Evaluation of Laura Ljungkvist's Works," p. 50.

Publishers Weekly, June 25, 2001, Nathalie Beeck, "Laura Ljungkvist," p. 23; March 31, 2003, review of *Snow White and the Seven Dwarves,* p. 66; May 15, 2006, review of *Follow the Line,* p. 71.

School Library Journal, May, 2001, John Peters, review of *Toni's Topsy-Turvy Telephone Day,* p. 128; July, 2003, Susan Hepler, review of *Snow White and the Seven Dwarfs,* p. 114; May, 2006, Mary Elam, review of *Follow the Line,* p. 92.

ONLINE

Laura Ljungkvist Home Page, http://www.followtheline. com (April 30, 2007).

Penguin Group Web site, http://www.penguingroup.com/ (April 30, 2007), "Laura Ljungkvist."

*　　*　　*

LOOK, Lenore

Personal

Born in Seattle, WA. *Education:* Princeton University, bachelor's degree, 1984.

Career

Journalist and author. Worked as a journalist for *L.A. Times,* and *Trenton Times,* Trenton, NJ.

Awards, Honors

Notable Book for Children selection, *Smithsonian* magazine, 2001, for *Henry's First-Moon Birthday*; Manoa Award for Best American Essays, 2001, for "Facing the Village"; Notable Resources selection, Young-Adult Library Services Association, 2007, for both *Uncle Peter's Amazing Chinese Wedding* and *Ruby Lu, Empress of Everything.*

Writings

Love as Strong as Ginger, illustrated by Stephen T. Johnson, Atheneum (New York, NY), 1999.

Henry's First-Moon Birthday, illustrated by Yumi Heo, Atheneum (New York, NY), 2001.

Ruby Lu, Brave and True, illustrated by Anne Wilsdorf, Atheneum (New York, NY), 2004.

Ruby Lu, Empress of Everything, illustrated by Anne Wilsdorf, Atheneum (New York, NY), 2006.

Uncle Peter's Amazing Chinese Wedding, illustrated by Yumi Heo, Atheneum (New York, NY), 2006.

Contributor of essays and articles to *Princeton Alumni Weekly, Publishers Weekly,* and *Race and Races: Cases for a Diverse America.*

Adaptations

Henry's First-Moon Birthday was adapted for videocassette.

Sidelights

Author Lenore Look draws on her experiences growing up as a Chinese American, as well as those as an American visiting China, to tell stories that balance the ideas of individuality and tradition. Each of her picture books "emphasizes its main character's attempt to achieve a healthy balance between independence and connection to family, often through traditions such as the celebration of first-moon birthdays and adherence to the elaborate Chinese wedding ceremony rules," wrote April Spisak in the *Bulletin of the Center for Children's Books* online. Along with her picture books, Look is also the author of the "Ruby Lu" chapter-books, where readers can follow the adventures of enigmatic protagonist Ruby and her cousin and kindred spirit, Flying Duck.

Look's first picture book, *Love as Strong as Ginger,* draws on memories of the author's grandmother, who worked in a factory in Seattle during the 1960s and 1970s. Set in that era, the story focuses on the relationship between young Katie and her grandmother, GninGnin, and Katie's understanding of the hard work GninGnin must perform in order to earn a living. "The words are simple. The facts are stark," wrote Hazel Rochman in her *Booklist* review, concluding that *Love as Strong as Ginger* "is a fine addition to the realistic stories of coming to America." A *Horn Book* critic called the book a "powerfully felt evocation of the dreams that can sustain one generation with hope of a better life for the next." While Look "doesn't flinch from describing the harsh conditions . . . her story focuses on the strength and dreams of the women who work there," wrote a *Publishers Weekly* contributor of the work, which features illustrations by Stephen T. Johnson.

Henry's First-Moon Birthday and *Uncle Peter's Amazing Chinese Wedding* both follow Jen's struggles to deal with the changes occurring in her life. In *Henry's First-Moon Birthday* Jen helps prepare for her baby brother's one-month birthday celebration and, although feeling jealous that the baby receives all the attention, realizes by day's end that he will one day be glad she was in charge of his party. "Jen's chatty narration infuses the book with . . . cozy immediacy," wrote Gillian Engberg in *Booklist. Uncle Peter's Amazing Chinese Wedding* finds Jen once again jealous, this time because Uncle Peter's fiancée is taking all her usually doting uncle's attention. Initially intending to disrupt the celebration, Jen changes her plans after she is invited to help coordinate wedding plans by both bride and groom. As Jennifer Mattson noted in her *Booklist* review, "references to Chinese traditions emerge naturally throughout," giving readers an insight into Chinese-American culture. Though a *Publishers Weekly* critic also noted the cultural appeal of the book, the reviewer added that the real draw comes from Jen's narrative voice: "With her true-to-life voice, Jen conveys real feeling."

Ruby Lu, almost eight years old, has her first adventure in *Ruby Lu, Brave and True*. With a mother who studies Chinese fan dancing, a dad who loves board games, and a mischievous little brother named Oscar, Ruby's family life is as important to her story as her time at Chinese school. Considered "plucky" by a *Publishers Weekly* critic and "refreshingly feisty" by a contributor to *School Library Journal*, Look's protagonist fills "the need for a recurring Asian American character," according to *Booklist* contributor Terry Glover. Debbie Stewart, writing in *School Library Journal*, called *Ruby Lu, Brave and True* "funny and charming," adding that a favorite magic trick of Ruby's is featured in flip-book format on the corner pages. Look also provides a glossary, enabling readers to research terms related to Chinese culture.

Ruby's cousin Flying Duck is visiting from China in *Ruby Lu, Empress of Everything*. Although she immediately feels a kinship with her cousin, the changes the boy brings to the Lu household make her feel out of place: the family begins to speak Cantonese at home and eats with chopsticks. When Flying Duck teaches Oscar Chinese sign language and begins to understand the toddler faster than does Ruby, the girl's jealously peaks. Ruby is "as spunky as Ramona and as moody as Judy," according to *Horn Book* critic Jennifer M. Brabander, comparing Look's heroine to the beloved fictional heroines of Beverly Cleary and Megan McDonald respectively. "Ruby Lu invites readers into a contemporary world that honors differences while ultimately celebrating universal moments of childhood," wrote Julie

Cover of Lenore Look's chapter book Ruby Lu, Brave and True, *featuring artwork by Anne Wilsdorf.* (Aladdin Paperbacks, 2004. Cover illustration copyright © 2004 by Anne Wilsdorf. Reproduced by permission of Aladdin Paperbacks, an imprint of Simon & Schuster Children's Publishing Division.)

R. Ranelli in her *School Library Journal* review of *Ruby Lu, Empress of Everything.*

Although Look covers a variety of themes in both her picture books and chapter books, Spisak found a unifying factor: "It's clear that her books reflect her own understanding," she wrote of Look's work in the *Bulletin of the Center for Children's Books* online, "and yet with their focus on home, family, and culture they manage to be universal as well as personal."

Biographical and Critical Sources

PERIODICALS

Booklist, October 15, 1999, Hazel Rochman, review of *Love as Strong as Ginger,* p. 443; April 1, 2001, Gillian Engberg, review of *Henry's First-Moon Birthday,* p. 1470; January 1, 2002, review of *Henry's First-Moon Birthday,* p. 768; January 1, 2004, Terry Glover, review of *Ruby Lu, Brave and True,* p. 878; December 15, 2005, Jennifer Mattson, review of *Uncle Peter's Amazing Chinese Wedding,* p. 47; February 15, 2006, Cindy Dobrez, review of *Ruby Lu, Empress of Everything,* p. 104.

Bulletin of the Center for Children's Books, April, 2004, Karen Coats, review of *Ruby Lu, Brave and True,* p. 336; January, 2006, Elizabeth Bush, review of *Uncle Peter's Amazing Chinese Wedding,* p. 215; May, 2006, Karen Coats, review of *Ruby Lu, Empress of Everything,* p. 410.

Childhood Education, winter, 2001, Debora Wisneski, review of *Henry's First-Moon Birthday,* p. 111, annual, 2006, Lea Lee, review of *Uncle Peter's Amazing Chinese Wedding,* p. 303.

Horn Book, May, 1999, review of *Love as Strong as Ginger,* p. 318; May-June, 2006, Jennifer M. Brabander, review of *Ruby Lu, Empress of Everything,* p. 322.

Kirkus Reviews, December 1, 2005, review of *Uncle Peter's Amazing Chinese Wedding,* p. 1277; March 1, 2006, review of *Ruby Lu, Empress of Everything,* p. 234.

Publishers Weekly, May 24, 1999, review of *Love as Strong as Ginger,* p. 79; April 9, 2001, review of *Henry's First-Moon Birthday,* p. 73; January 19, 2004, review of *Ruby Lu, Brave and True,* p. 76; December 5, 2005, review of *Uncle Peter's Amazing Chinese Wedding,* p. 54.

School Library Journal, July, 1999, Margaret A. Change, review of *Love as Strong as Ginger,* p. 76; June, 2001, Alice Casey Smith, review of *Henry's First-Moon Birthday,* p. 126; February, 2004, Debbie Stewart, review of *Ruby Lu, Brave and True,* p. 116; March, 2005, Kathleen T. Isaacs, review of *Ruby Lu, Brave and True,* p. 68; January, 2006, Maura Bresnahan, review of *Uncle Peter's Amazing Chinese Wedding,* p. 106; July, 2006, Julie R. Ranelli, review of *Ruby Lu, Empress of Everything.*

ONLINE

Asian American Books Web site, http://www.asianamericanbooks.com/ (April 28, 2007), "Lenore Look."

Bulletin of the Center for Children's Books Online, http://bccb.lis.uiuc.edu/ (April 28, 2007), April Spisak, "Rising Star: Lenore Look."*

*   *   *

LOVE, D. Anne 1949-

Personal

Born January 12, 1949, in Selmer, TN; daughter of Oscar W. and Elsie M. Catlett; married Ronald W. Love, June 8, 1974. *Education:* Lamar University, B.S., 1972; University of North Texas, M.Ed., 1976, Ph.D., 1984. *Politics:* "Independent." *Religion:* Protestant. *Hobbies and other interests:* Jazz music, travel.

Addresses

Home—Austin, TX. *Agent*—Maria Carvainis, Maria Carvainis Agency, Inc., 1270 Avenue of the Americas, Ste. 2320, New York, NY 10020. *E-mail*—doro7@insight.rr.com.

Career

Educator and writer. School administrator in Richardson, TX, 1974-88; University of North Texas, Denton, professor, 1989-91; full-time writer, 1989—. Western Hills Area Education Agency, Sioux City, IA, consultant, 1994-96; speaker at schools.

Member

Society of Children's Book Writers and Illustrators.

Awards, Honors

Prize for Juvenile Fiction, Friends of American Writers, 1997, for *My Lone Star Summer;* American Library Association Amelia Bloomer listee, International Reading Association Notable Book in Language Arts designation, William Allen White Award nomination, Children's Book Award, Writers League of Texas, and several other state book award nominations, all 2003, all for *The Puppeteer's Apprentice;* New York Public Library Book for the Teen Age selection, 2007, for *Semiprecious;* nominations for several state reading awards.

Writings

Bess's Log Cabin Quilt, illustrated by Ronald Himler, Holiday House (New York, NY), 1995.

Dakota Spring, illustrated by Ronald Himler, Holiday House (New York, NY), 1995.

My Lone Star Summer, Holiday House (New York, NY), 1996.

Three against the Tide, Holiday House (New York, NY), 1998.

I Remember the Alamo, Dell Yearling (New York, NY), 1999.

A Year without Rain, Holiday House (New York, NY), 2000.

The Puppeteer's Apprentice, Margaret K. McElderry Books (New York, NY), 2003.

The Secret Prince, Margaret K. McElderry Books (New York, NY), 2005.

Semiprecious, Margaret K. McElderry Books (New York, NY), 2006.

Of Numbers and Stars: The Story of Hypatia, illustrated by Pam Papparone, Holiday House (New York, NY), 2006.

Picture Perfect, Margaret K. McElderry Books (New York, NY), 2007.

Contributor to magazines, newspapers, and educational journals.

Sidelights

A former educator, D. Anne Love writes novels in which resourceful young adults rise to the occasion when faced with severe challenges. While her novels *Bess's Log*

Cabin Quilt, Dakota Spring, and *Three against the Tide* draw readers into the past, Love deals with modern life in novels such as *My Lone Star Summer* and *Semiprecious.* In addition to coming-of-age tales, Love is also the author of the award-winning historical novel *The Puppeteer's Apprentice* and well as the fantasy novel *The Secret Prince* and the picture-book biography *Of Numbers and Stars: The Story of Hypatia.* In the last, a story about the fourth-century Alexandrian mathematician and scholar that *School Library Journal* reviewer Julie R. Ranelli dubbed a "fascinating read" due to its "clear and captivating text," Love introduces the brillian young woman whose unconventional life was cut tragically short by a murderous mob. Praised by a *Kirkus Reviews* writer as "an attractive and engaging" work, *Of Numbers and Stars* presents young readers with "a worthy contribution to women's history," according to the critic.

Love's first book for younger readers, *Bess's Log Cabin Quilt,* tells the story of a ten-year-old girl who single-handedly comes to the rescue of her pioneer family. When her father fails to return from his work on the Oregon Trail and her mother falls ill, Bess must handle the incursions of local Indians and the visits of a money-lender who threatens to seize the family farm. Melissa McPherson, a contributor to *Voice of Youth Advocates,* applauded Love's detailed description of frontier life, going on to claim that "readers of historical fiction will definitely enjoy this."

In *Dakota Spring,* Caroline and her brother rely on the help of a neighbor to manage their family's Dakota farm after their father breaks his leg. When their strait-laced grandmother arrives to help out, the children must learn to deal with the elderly woman's cold personality while also coming to terms with their own mother's untimely death. Comparing *Dakota Spring* to Patricia MacLachlan's classic children's story *Sarah, Plain and Tall* in her review for *Voice of Youth Advocates,* Susan Steinfirst maintained that Love's novel "should appeal to kids who love these tame wild west sagas." *Booklist* contributor Carolyn Phelan also recommended *Dakota Spring,* praising the author's "well drawn and intriguing" characters, consistent point of view, and ability to create a strong sense of place and historical period. "This book will please youngsters looking for good historical fiction," Phelan concluded.

The U.S. Civil War sets the stage for *Three against the Tide,* which finds twelve-year-old Susannah caring for her younger brothers after her father leaves their South Carolina island home to join the war effort. As the war continues and the family's slaves and neighbors depart, the children struggle to survive on their own, then make a perilous journey down river to Charleston, where they hope to find their father. Charleston offers no shelter, however, after the town is burnt to the ground by Union troops, and the children once again set off in search of their father. Along the way, tomboyish Susannah learns the value of some of the womanly arts she had earlier

spurned. She also finds her unthinking support for the Confederate war effort weakened when she encounters her family's former slaves on their quest for freedom, a quest Susannah can now understand. Although some critics found *Three against the Tide* occasionally marred by sentimentality, Kathleen Squires wrote in *Booklist* that "the fast pace, historical detail, and well-drawn heroine . . . will help readers overlook" the novel's flaws. A contributor to *Publishers Weekly* reached a similar conclusion, predicting that despite Love's nostalgic portrayal of "Southern gentility," "readers will revel in the three protagonists' bravery and spirit."

Love turns to a pivotal moment in Texas history in *I Remember the Alamo.* The novel centers on the McCann family, recently arrived in Texas from Kentucky. Soon Jessie McCann's father and older brother become caught up in the escalating battle that will culminate in the bloody siege and final rout at the Alamo Mission, leaving the region's women and children to seek a brief refuge at the doomed and battered building. "The strength of the novel . . . lies in its setting and sense of history," observed a contributor to *Horn Book.* Although the realism of Love's period piece is aided by the appearance of several historical figures, an important theme—the relationship between the Mexican residents of San Antonio and the recent North American settlers—is symbolized by Jessie's tempestuous friendship with a Mexican girl named Angelina. While noting that the novel's "ending is pretty pat after so much blood and tragedy," John Peters concluded in *Booklist* that fans of historical novels "will enjoy [Love's] . . . perceptive view of this American turning point." Likewise, a contributor to *Kirkus Reviews* cited the novel's implausible characterizations, yet nevertheless concluded of *I Remember the Alamo* that "the pacing is fast, and the historical details [are] captivating."

A drought-stricken South Dakota provides the setting for Love's young-adult historical novel *A Year without Rain.* It is the late 1800s, and twelve-year-old Rachel lives on the prairie with her widowed father and her younger brother, her mother having passed away four years earlier. When a drought extends through the long, hot summer, Rachel's father sends the children to the home of their aunt's sister in Savannah, Georgia. There the two siblings reminisce with family and servants who remember their mother, and read through the late woman's letters. When Rachel's father arrives to bring his children back home, he announces that he plans to marry Rachel's teacher. Rachel now hatches a scheme to foil the nuptials that has disastrous results. All is forgiven in the end, however, as the girl accepts that change is inevitable. A contributor to *Horn Book* concluded that preteens who "enjoy this kind of 'touched by an angel' comfort . . . will find the book a pleasing diversion." In *School Library Journal* Valerie Diamond called *A Year without Rain* "simply yet artfully told with characters both realistic and endearing."

In her first work of contemporary fiction, *My Lone Star Summer,* Love focuses on twelve-year-old Jill. Each

Cover of D. Anne Love's middle-grade novel Semiprecious, *featuring a cover photograph by Simon Weller.* (Margaret K. McElderry Books, 2006. Jacket photograph copyright © 2006 by Simon Weller/nevstock.com. Reproduced by permission of Margaret K. McElderry Books, an imprint of Simon & Schuster Children's Division.)

summer, Jill visits her grandmother's Texas ranch, where she enjoys spending time with good friend B.J. This year, B.J. insists on being called Belinda; no longer a tomboy, she has also started wearing make-up and flirting with boys, leaving little time for Jill. *My Lone Star Summer* "is a fairly standard girl-coming-of-age novel for the youngest of YAs," Alice F. Stern remarked in a review for *Voice of Youth Advocates.* While admitting that Love's "story's a bit formulaic," Deborah Stevenson wrote in the *Bulletin of the Center for Children's Books* that the protagonist's "narration is unforced, honest, and touching in its examination of the gains and losses of growing up."

Readers are introduced to life in 1960s Oklahoma in *Semiprecious,* which finds twelve-year-old Texans Garnet Hubbard and her older sister Opal dealing with a difficult school year. Their father has been hospitalized following a disfiguring work-related accident and their mom is more focused on her singing career in Nashville than her family. Now the sisters are sent to live with an aunt in rural Oklahoma, where they must deal with their sense of abandonment while building independent lives for themselves. In *Booklist,* Carolyn Phelan called *Semiprecious* "an involving novel of hurt, healing, and adjustment," while in *School Library Journal* Catherine Ensley maintained that "the intriguing questions [Love] . . . poses . . . make her an author to watch." "Tugging at the heart with painful truths" and featuring a resilient narrator, *Semiprecious* "is Love's best yet," concluded a *Kirkus Reviews* writer.

Another case of parental abandonment is at the core of *Picture Perfect.* Things for fourteen-year-old Phoebe Trask have been tricky enough due to typical adolescent concerns. When her mother's a dream job with a cosmetic company requires that she relocate to Las Vegas, the teen must navigate her difficult year as a high school freshman solo. When a lonely widowed neighbor begins to insinuate herself into the family as a motherly caretaker, Phoebe becomes resentful, and her anger soon turns on her own mom. As Phoebe learns to deal with peer pressure as well as a budding romance, she grows emotionally, and a tragedy ultimately forges stronger relationships among family members. Writing that Love "has a knack for capturing the essence of what it's like to be young and burdened by life," a *Publishers Weekly* contributor wrote of *Picture Perfect* that the author's "rendition of family trauma is ultimately both uplifting and realistic." A *Kirkus Reviews* critic also praised the novel, dubbing it "a rewarding read, despite a vaguely soap-ish plot," and *Voice of Youth Advocates* critic Kathleen Beck deemed *Picture Perfect* "a refreshing book" in which, through its upbeat message, "Love demonstrates that characters coping successfully with challenges can make a good story too."

In *The Puppeteer's Apprentice* Love departs from her usual American setting and takes readers back in time to medieval England. Her heroine, Mouse, is a girl so downtrodden that she lacks even a formal name. Drawing on her strength, determination, and perseverance, Mouse overcomes being brutalized by the manor cook for whom she works as a scullery maid and strikes out on her own. Coming to a fair, she is mesmerized by the puppet show and volunteers to serve as the puppet master's apprentice. Tension builds as Mouse becomes aware of the mysteries surrounding the puppet master's identity and finally forges her own identity, along with a proper name. "Love sketches an eclectic cast and packs in plenty of historical details as she portrays the freedoms and perils of the puppeteer's vagabond life," explained a *Publishers Weekly* contributor in a review of *The Puppeteer's Apprentice.* Calling the book a "wonderfully written tale," Kit Vaughan added in *School Library Journal* that the novel focuses on "mystery, suspense, and the realism that comes with a battle fought and won." Describing Mouse as a likable character whose heart, ingenuity, and spunk will win readers' hearts, some critics also found Love writing in top form, offering a tight, suspenseful plot and many realistic period details. As a contributor to *Kirkus Reviews* concluded of *The Puppeteer's Apprentice,* "colorful, lively, rhythmic language and a strong sense of medieval England make this a great read-aloud."

History merges with fantasy in *The Secret Prince,* which introduces a world evocative of the age of King Arthur. In Love's novel, a foundling born under a blood-red sunset is raised by Morwid, an exiled warrior who follows the prophecies set down in the Book of the Ancients. The child, Thorn, is actually of royal birth, and as he grows up he is trained in the ways of battle and diplomacy. When Thorn comes of age he follows his destiny: to locate the lost amulet of the kingdom of Kelhadden. This token will help Thorn free his people from the rule of his own father, Ranulf, whose lust for power prompted him to steal the throne from his son years before. Although Saleena L. Davidson described Love's plot as somewhat "predictable," she added in her *School Library Journal* review of the novel that the "twist at the end comes as a complete surprise." "Readers looking for adventure in a medieval fantasy world will find it here," predicted Phelan, while *Kliatt* reviewer Michele Winship wrote that *The Secret Prince* yields "all of the requisite elements of the quest fantasy, including fantastic creatures, surprising twists, and a variety of roadblocks along the way."

Cover of Love's historical novel The Puppeteer's Apprentice, *featuring artwork by John Rowe.* (Aladdin Paperbacks, 2003. Cover illustration copyright © 2004 by John Rowe. Reprinted by permission of Aladdin Paperbacks, an imprint of Simon & Schuster Children's Publishing Division.)

Discussing her career as a writer, Love once commented: "I left public school administration in order to devote more time to writing and teaching at the university level. For me, the writing process usually begins with visualizing the last scene and working backward. I am a collector of information and often find that a postcard, brochure, or photograph collected somewhere along the way can spark story ideas. Inspiration flows from my love of history and a strong sense of place."

"As life grows more complicated," Love more recently noted to *SATA,* "future novels will examine topics of interest to modern teens, including bullying and obsessive relationships. As with *Semiprecious* and *Picture Perfect,* I hope to show teens confronting real situations in ways that are uplifting and realistic."

Biographical and Critical Sources

PERIODICALS

Booklist, February 15, 1995, Kay Weisman, review of *Bess's Log Cabin Quilt,* p. 1085; November 15, 1995, Carolyn Phelan, review of *Dakota Spring,* p. 559; May 1, 1996, Susan DeRonne, review of *My Lone Star Summer,* p. 1506; December 1, 1998, Kathleen Squires, review of *Three against the Tide,* p. 667; January 1, 2000, John Peters, review of *I Remember the Alamo,* p. 926; April 1, 2000, GraceAnne A. DeCandido, review of *A Year without Rain,* p. 1477; March 15, 2003, Carolyn Phelan, review of *The Puppeteer's Apprentice,* p. 1327; January 1, 2005, review of *The Secret Prince,* p. 859; April 15, 2006, Carolyn Phelan, review of *Of Numbers and Stars: The Story of Hypatia,* p. 49; July 1, 2006, Carolyn Phelan, review of *Semiprecious,* p. 55.

Bulletin of the Center for Children's Books, July, 1996, Deborah Stevenson, review of *My Lone Star Summer,* pp. 378-379; May, 2003, review of *The Puppeteer's Apprentice,* p. 367; February, 2005, Timnah Card, review of *The Secret Prince,* p. 257; October, 2006, Karen Coats, review of *Semiprecious,* p. 81.

Childhood Education, fall, 2000, Jeanie Burnett, review of *I Remember the Alamo,* p. 45.

Horn Book, March, 2000, review of *I Remember the Alamo,* p. 197; July, 2000, review of *A Year without Rain,* p. 461.

Florida Times-Union, May 11, 2004, Brandy Hilboldt Allport, "Read Lots, Get a Life, and Stay Focused" (interview), p. C1.

Kirkus Reviews, November 1, 1998, review of *Three against the Tide,* p. 1601; November 15, 1999, review of *I Remember the Alamo,* p. 1812; March 15, 2003, review of *The Puppeteer's Apprentice,* p. 472; February, 2005, Timnah Card, review of *Of Numbers and Stars,* p. 235; June 15, 2006, review of *Semiprecious,* p. 635; March 1, 2007, review of *Picture Perfect,* p. 226.

Kliatt, March, 2005, Michelle Winship, review of *The Secret Prince,* p. 13.

Publishers Weekly, April 17, 1995, review of *Bess's Log Cabin Quilt,* p. 60; December 7, 1998, review of *Three against the Tide,* p. 60; April 10, 2000, review of *A Year without Rain,* p. 99; March 17, 2003, review of *The Puppeteer's Apprentice,* p. 77; February 26, 2007, review of *Picture Perfect,* p. 91.

School Library Journal, June, 1995, Lucinda Snyder Whitehurst, review of *Bess's Log Cabin Quilt,* p. 111; November, 1995, Rita Soltan, review of *Dakota Spring,* p. 103; March, 1996, Susan Oliver, review of *My Lone Star Summer,* p. 196; January, 1999, Cindy Darling Codell, review of *Three against the Tide,* p. 128; January, 2000, Coop Renner, review of *I Remember the Alamo,* p. 134; September, 2000, Valerie Diamond, review of *A Year without Rain,* p. 233; May, 2003, Kit Vaughan, review of *The Puppeteer's Apprentice,* p. 156; June, 2005, Saleena L. Davidson, review of *The Secret Prince,* p. 162; May, 2006, Julie R. Ranelli, review of *Of Numbers and Stars,* p. 114; September, 2006, Catherine Ensley, review of *Semiprecious,* p. 211.

Voice of Youth Advocates, October, 1995, Melissa McPherson, review of *Bess's Log Cabin Quilt,* p. 220; April, 1996, Susan Steinfirst, review of *Dakota Spring,* p. 27; October, 1996, Alice F. Stern, review of *My Lone Star Summer,* pp. 211-212; April, 2005, Karen Sykeny, review of *The Secret Prince,* p. 58; June, 2007, Kathleen Beck, review of *Picture Perfect,* p. 146.

ONLINE

D. Anne Love Home Page, http://www.dannelove.com (June 1, 2007).

*   *   *

LUTZ, John 1939-
(John Thomas Lutz)

Personal

Born September 11, 1939, in Dallas, TX; son of John Peter (a photographer) and Jane (a homemaker) Lutz; married Barbara Jean Bradley, March 25, 1958; children: Steven, Jennifer Lutz-Bauer, Wendy Murray. *Education:* Attended Meramec Community College, 1966. *Politics:* "Reasonable."

Addresses

Home and office—Webster Groves, MO; Sarasota, FL. *Agent*—Dominick Abel Literary Agency Inc., 146 W. 82nd St., Ste 1B, New York, NY 10024. *E-mail*—JLutz65151@aol.com.

Career

Writer. Has worked in construction, as a civilian police employee, and as a truck driver.

Member

Mystery Writers of America (former president), Private Eye Writers of America (former president).

John Lutz (Photograph courtesy of John Lutz.)

Awards, Honors

Mystery Writers of America scroll, 1981, for short story "Until You Are Dead," Edgar Allan Poe Award, 1986, for short story "Ride the Lightning," and Edgar Allan Poe Award nomination for best paperback original, 2003, for *The Night Watcher;* Private Eye Writers of America Shamus Award, 1982, and 1989, for *Kiss,* and Shamus Award for lifetime achievement, 1995; Gold Derringer Life Achievement Award, Short Mystery Fiction Society, 2001; Trophee 813 Award, for best mystery collection translated into French; honorary degree from University of Missouri, 2007.

Writings

MYSTERY NOVELS

The Truth of the Matter, Pocket Books (New York, NY), 1971.
Bonegrinder, Putnam (New York, NY), 1976.
Lazarus Man, Morrow (New York, NY), 1979.
Jericho Man, Morrow (New York, NY), 1980.
The Shadow Man, Morrow (New York, NY), 1981.
(With Steve Greene; uncredited) *Exiled,* Fawcett (New York, NY), 1982.
(With Bill Pronzini) *The Eye,* Mysterious Press (New York, NY), 1984.

Shadowtown, Mysterious Press (New York, NY), 1988.
SWF Seeks Same, St. Martin's Press (New York, NY), 1990.
Dancing with the Dead, St. Martin's Press (New York, NY), 1992.
The Ex, Kensington (San Diego, CA), 1996.
(With David August) *Final Seconds,* Kensington (San Diego, CA), 1998.
The Night Caller, Pinnacle Books (New York, NY), 2001.
The Night Watcher, Pinnacle Books (New York, NY), 2002.
The Night Spider, Pinnacle Books (New York, NY), 2003.
Darker than Night, Pinnacle Books (New York, NY), 2004.
Fear the Night, Pinnacle Books (New York, NY), 2005.
Chill of Night, Pinnacle Books (New York, NY), 2006.
In for the Kill, Pinnacle Books (New York, NY), 2007.

Author's works have been translated into numerous languages.

"NUDGER" SERIES; MYSTERY NOVELS

Buyer Beware, Putnam (New York, NY), 1976.
Nightlines, St. Martin's Press (New York, NY), 1984.
The Right to Sing the Blues, St. Martin's Press (New York, NY), 1986.
Ride the Lightning, St. Martin's Press (New York, NY), 1987.
Dancer's Debt, St. Martin's Press (New York, NY), 1988.
Time Exposure, St. Martin's Press (New York, NY), 1989.
Diamond Eyes, St. Martin's Press (New York, NY), 1990.
Thicker than Blood, St. Martin's Press (New York, NY), 1993.
Death by Jury, St. Martin's Press (New York, NY), 1995.
Oops!, St. Martin's Press (New York, NY), 1998.

"CARVER" SERIES; MYSTERY NOVELS

Tropical Heat, Holt (New York, NY), 1986.
Scorcher, Holt (New York, NY), 1987.
Flame, Holt (New York, NY), 1989.
Kiss, Holt (New York, NY), 1990.
Bloodfire, Holt (New York, NY), 1991.
Hot, Holt (New York, NY), 1992.
Spark, Holt (New York, NY), 1993.
Torch, Holt (New York, NY), 1994.
Burn, Holt (New York, NY), 1995.
Lightning, Holt (New York, NY), 1996.

SHORT-STORY COLLECTIONS

Better Mousetraps, edited by Francis M. Nevins, St. Martin's Press (New York, NY), 1988.
Shadows Everywhere, Mystery Scene Press, 1994.
Until You Are Dead, Five Star (Waterville, ME), 1998.
The Nudger Dilemmas, Five Star (Waterville, ME), 2001.
Endless Road, and Other Stories, Five Star (Waterville, ME), 2003.

OTHER

Author (with Larry Cohen) of screenplay adaptation *The Ex,* based on Lutz's novel of the same title. Contributor to anthologies, including *Alfred Hitchcock's*

Tales to Make Your Blood Run Cold, edited by Eleanor Sullivan, Dial (New York, NY), 1978; *Ellery Queen's Circumstantial Evidence,* edited by Queen, Dial, 1980; *Arbor House Treasury of Mystery and Suspense,* edited by Martin Greenberg, Malzberg, and Pronzini, Arbor House (New York, NY), 1981; *Arbor House Treasury of Horror and the Supernatural,* Arbor House, 1981; *Creature,* edited by Pronzini, Arbor House, 1981; and *Irreconcilable Differences,* edited by Lia Matera, HarperCollins (New York, NY), 1999. Contributor of hundreds of stories to magazines.

Adaptations

SWF Seeks Same was adapted as the film *Single White Female,* starring Bridget Fonda and Jennifer Jason Leigh. *The Ex* was adapted as a film produced by Home Box Office. Several of Lutz's novels have been adapted as audiobooks.

Sidelights

In popular novels such as *SWF Seeks Same, The Night Watcher,* and *Chill of Night,* award-winning writer John Lutz experiments with the limits of the thriller genre. A typical Lutz outing is tense and tightly plotted, but the author also emphasizes character and theme as he makes even the most despicable villains well-rounded and believable individuals. As the novelist himself noted in a *Writer* article, "The modern mystery should be much more than a simple deductive puzzle; it should mean something." According to *New York Times Book Review* contributor Newgate Callendar, Lutz achieves his end. In his review of *Tropical Heat,* Callendar asserted that "professionalism marks every page." As the critic added, "the plotting is tight, the characterizations are sharp, the police work has an authentic feeling, and there is an ending that may make the reader gulp once or twice."

Lutz began his career as a short-story writer, selling his first story to *Alfred Hitchcock's Mystery Magazine* in 1966. His many stories, which include suspense, humor, the occult, and espionage, have been published in magazines and anthologies ever since and have also been translated into many languages. According to Francis M. Nevins in the *St. James Guide to Crime and Mystery Writers,* Lutz's stories are characterized by "the wildest premises [and] . . . a strong anti-business viewpoint with imaginative bizarrerie, as if Kafka had come back from the grave to collaborate on fiction with Ralph Nader." The best of the author's short fiction has been collected in several volumes, among them *Better Mousetraps, Shadows Everywhere,* and *Endless Road, and Other Stories.*

Among Lutz's best-known novels are those featuring Florida detective Fred Carver. Forced out of police work when a street punk shoots him in the knee, Carver turns to private detection—cane in hand—and solves a series of dark and twisted crimes in the Florida Keys. A *Publishers Weekly* reviewer wrote of the "Carver" series:

"Tense and relentless tales, they are essentially linear stories in which the reader is drawn along in the wake of brutal and seemingly unrelated events." The same reviewer described Carver as "a believably heroic guy, tough, scarred and able to exhibit fear and courage at the same time."

First introduced to readers in the 1986 novel *Tropical Heat,* the "Carver" series plays out in *Kiss, Bloodfire, Torch,* and *Lightning.* Some critics have commended the "Carver" books for their evocation of the Florida environs. As a *Publishers Weekly* reviewer noted in a review of *Burn,* "Lutz's eye for Florida noir (fast food joints, trailer parks and 'local criminals' who 'view tourists as game animals') is impeccable," and "it's easy to see why [he] . . . has won an Edgar and two Shamuses." Reviewing *Torch* in the *New York Times Book Review,* Marilyn Stasio stated her admiration for "the palpable sense of place in this series, and especially the author's bottomless stock of heat imagery." In a review of the same novel for *Publishers Weekly,* a contributor dubbed the series "tense and relentless . . . linear stories in which the reader is drawn along in the wake of brutal and seemingly unrelated events." As Stasio concluded of the "Carver" books, "the dialogue is brisk and brittle, the action gets nasty when it must, and the characters are as shady as the sunny climate allows. For a long-running series, this one is still hot."

Another favorite Lutz character is Alo Nudger, a St. Louis, Missouri-based private eye who stars in his own series of mystery novels. Nevins characterized Nudger as "one of the most fascinating protagonists in recent detective fiction, a near-total loser plagued by overdue bills, deadbeat clients, and a bloodsucking ex-wife but most of all by his near-paralyzing unaggressiveness and compassion." Lutz's ironic protagonist "shares the word with Charlie Chaplin's tramp," the critic added: "whatever can go wrong for him, will." A *Publishers Weekly* contributor cited Nudger for his "piranha of an ex-wife and an office above a shop selling the world's greasiest doughnuts," claiming that in a typical "Nudger" novel "the pieces all fit and the fade from humor to homicide is never less than convincing." *Death by Jury* finds Lutz's "tough-as-push-pins hero" hired by a sleazy lawyer to trail a local banker about to stand trial for murder, resulting in what *Booklist* contributor Wes Lukowsky characterized as "an intricate masterpiece" of suspense plotting. In *Thicker than Blood* the PI is hired to track down a swindling securities salesman but winds up in a tangle involving incest, blackmail, drug deals, and even murder, resulting in what Lukowsky dubbed "a fine addition to an outstanding series." Bearing a title appropriate to the plot, *Oops!* finds the cash-strapped sleuth taking on a client convinced that his daughter's death was not an accident. When his client dies, Nudger persists, true to form, fueled by what Lukowsky characterized as "loyalty, a sense of justice, morality, and a desire to fix the world."

In addition to his "Nudger" and "Carver" mysteries, Lutz has authored a number of stand-alone novels. In *SWF Seeks Same* Allie tells her live-in boyfriend to hit the road, then finds a new roommate in Hedra. At first quiet and likeable, Hedra eventually shows her less-agreeable nature as she slowly begins infiltrating Allie's personal life and ruthlessly eliminates a number of human obstacles in the process. Retired and recently widowed New York City detective Artemis Beam trails a serial killer targeting former jury foremen in *Chill of Night,* while in *Fear the Night* a lone sniper terrorizes Manhattan. Another retired cop is on the case in the latter novel, the story strengthened by Lutz's creation of "layered and three-dimensional characters," according to a *Publishers Weekly* contributor. Described by another *Publishers Weekly* writer as a "gritty psychological thriller" featuring "a fully realized villain who simultaneously inspires the reader's sympathy and revulsion," *The Night Watcher* returns readers to the mean streets of the Big Apple, as former NYPD homicide detectives Rica Lopez and Ben Stack trail a murderous arsonist who targets wealthy individuals living in high-rise apartments.

Discussing his decision to become a writer, Lutz once noted: "It would be difficult for me to say exactly what motivated me to begin writing; it's possible that the original motivation is gone, much as a match that starts a forest fire is consumed in the early moments of the fire. I continue writing for selfish reasons. I thoroughly enjoy it."

Biographical and Critical Sources

BOOKS

St. James Guide to Crime and Mystery Writers, 4th edition, St. James Press (Detroit, MI), 1996.

PERIODICALS

Booklist, May 1, 1992, Peter Robertson, review of *Dancing with the Dead,* p. 1586; December 15, 1992, Bill Ott, review of *Spark,* p. 717; October 15, 1993, Wes Lukowsky, review of *Thicker than Blood,* p. 421; March 15, 1994, Bill Ott, review of *Torch,* p. 1331; June 1, 1994, Bill Ott, review of *Spark,* p. 1779; March 1, 1995, Wes Lukowsky, review of *Burn,* p. 1182; October 1, 1995, Wes Lukowsky, review of *Death by Jury,* p. 254; June 1, 1996, Thomas Gaughan, review of *Lightning,* p. 1679; August, 1996, Wes Lukowsky, review of *The Ex,* p. 1886; February 1, 1998, Wes Lukowsky, review of *Oops!,* p. 903; March 15, 1998, Wes Lukowsky, review of *Final Seconds,* p. p. 1205; May 1, 2001, Bill Ott, review of *Spark,* p. 1602, and Wes Lukowsky, review of *The Nudger Dilemmas,* p. 1636; September 15, 2001, Wes Lukowsky, review of *The Night Caller,* p. 199; September 15, 2003, Wes Lukowsky, review of *Endless Road, and Other Stories,* p. 216.

New York Times Book Review, August 17, 1980, review of *Lazarus Man,* p. 27; May 5, 1985, review of *Nightlines,* p. 35; September 21, 1986, Newgate Callendar, review of *Tropical Heat,* p. 36; January 19, 1992, Marilyn Stasio, review of *Hot,* p. 20; January 3, 1993; April 3, 1994, Marilyn Stasio, review of *Torch,* p. 22.

Publishers Weekly, November 22, 1985, review of *The Right to Sing the Blues,* p. 49; May 23, 1986, review of *Tropical Heat,* p. 92; September 7, 1992, review of *SWF Seeks Same,* p. 30; September 6, 1993, review of *Thicker than Blood,* p. 85; January 24, 1994, review of *Torch,* p. 42; February 6, 1995, review of *Burn,* p. 79; July 17, 1995, review of *Death by Jury,* p. 223; May 6, 1996, review of *Lighning,* p. 72; July 8, 1996, review of *The Ex,* p. 75; March 9, 1998, review of *Final Seconds,* p. 49; June 25, 2001, review of *The Nudger Dilemmas,* p. 55; October 7, 2002, review of *The Night Watcher,* p. 58; August 11, 2003, review of *Endless Road, and Other Stories,* p. 262; October 3, 2005, review of *Fear the Night,* p. 52; September 4, 2006, review of *Chill of Night,* p. 44.

Writer, December, 1994, John Lutz, "Beyond Good and Evil," pp. 9-13.

*   *   *

LUTZ, John Thomas
See LUTZ, John

M

MACK, L.V.
See KIMMELMAN, Burt

* * *

MATTHESON, Jenny

Personal
Female. *Education:* Art Institute of Boston, B.F.A. (illustration).

Addresses
Home and office—Berkeley, CA. *E-mail*—jenny@jennymattheson.com.

Career
Illustrator. Malcolm X Elementary School, Berkeley, CA, art teacher.

Member
Society of Children's Book Authors and Illustrators (Northern CA chapter).

Illustrator
Nancy Willard, *The Mouse, the Cat, and Grandmother's Hat,* Little, Brown (Boston, MA), 2003.
Cheryl Ryan, *Christmas Morning,* Scholastic (New York, NY), 2004.
Sarah Davies, *Happy to Be Girls,* G.P. Putnam's Sons (New York, NY), 2005.
Beth Wagner Brust, *The Great Tulip Trade,* Random House (New York, NY), 2005.
Shirley Smith Duke, *No Bows!,* Peachtree (Atlanta, GA), 2006.
MaryAnn Hoberman, *Mrs. O'Leary's Cow,* Little, Brown (Boston, MA), 2007.

Sidelights
Growing up in Pennsylvania, children's book illustrator Jenny Mattheson maintained a sketchbook that included all of the things she was fascinated by: drawings of her friends, depictions of evil stepmothers, as well as illustrations of princesses and mermaids. As she noted on her home page, as an adult Mattheson continues to have "a strong appreciation of whimsical situations and characters." In addition to working as a freelance children's book illustrator, Mattheson also teaches art to elementary-grade children in Berkeley, California. On the Alphabet Books Web site, she explained that one reason she enjoys teaching art to children is that she enjoys her students' wonderful imaginations: "I love seeing how kids interpret stories! . . . It's a trade—I teach them and they teach me."

In her first picture-book collaboration, Mattheson created oil paintings for Newbery Award-winning author Nancy Willard's *The Mouse, the Cat, and Grandmother's Hat* that "add both a feeling of intimacy and side-splitting details" to Willard's story, in the opinion of a *Kirkus Reviews* writer. Also enthusiastic, a *Publishers Weekly* contributor wrote that the first-time illustrator "rises to the challenges in Willard's text," employing "a slightly quirky, retro but representational style that encourages readers to" accept the story's string of amazing coincidences without question. Other titles have followed from this 2003 book, among them *Happy to Be Girls* by Sarah Davies and *No Bows!* by Shirley Smith Duke. In *No Bows!* Mattheson uses oil paint on primed paper to depict the independence and identity of the book's independent-minded young heroine, a tom boy who prefers braids over bows, lizards over puppies, and stories over quiet time. As a *Publishers Weekly* contributor noted, Mattheson's images "juxtapose the girl's rejections in small-scale, often framed images with full-bleed, full-page paintings of her chosen alternatives." A *Kirkus Reviews* critic commented on Mattheson's use of color in the book, noting that her illustrations are

Jenny Mattheson's stylized artwork for **No Bows!** *emphasizes the rambunctious energy of author Shirley Smith Duke's happy-go-lucky protagonist.* (Peachtree, 2006. Illustration © 2006 by Jenny Mattheson. All rights reserved. Reproduced by permission of Peachtree Publishers.)

"rendered in handsome, burnished colors that nonetheless have an element of dazzle to them."

Biographical and Critical Sources

PERIODICALS

Booklist, April 15, 2003, GraceAnne A. DeCandido, review of *The Mouse, the Cat, and Grandmother's Hat,* p. 1479; May 1, 2005, Shelle Rosenfeld, review of *The Great Tulip Trade,* p. 1819; June 1, 2005, Ilene Cooper, review of *Happy to Be Girls,* p. July 1, 2006, Randall Enos, review of *No Bows!,* p. 64.

Bulletin of the Center for Children's Books, June, 2003, review of *The Mouse, the Cat, and Grandmother's Hat,* p. 428.

Kirkus Reviews, March 15, 2003, review of *The Mouse, the Cat, and Grandmother's Hat,* p. 482; February 15, 2006, review of *No Bows!,* p. 181; March 1, 2007, review of *Mrs. O'Leary's Cow,* p. 223.

Publishers Weekly, April 7, 2003, review of *The Mouse, the Cat, and Grandmother's Hat,* p. 65; September 27, 2004, review of *Christmas Morning,* p. 60; May 30, 2005, "Girl Talk," p. 63; April 10, 2006, review of *No Bows!,* p. 70.

School Library Journal, May, 2003, Laurie Edwards, review of *The Mouse, the Cat, and Grandmother's Hat,* p. 132; June, 2005, Rachel G. Payne, review of *Happy*

to Be Girls, p. 108; April, 2006, Amelia Jenkins, review of *No Bows!,* p. 99; March, 2007, Mary Elam, review of *Mrs. O'Leary's Cow,* p. 173.

ONLINE

Alphabet Books Web site, http://www.alphabetbooksonline.com/ (May 1, 2007), "Jenny Mattheson."

Jenny Mattheson Home Page, http://www.jennymattheson.com (May 1, 2007).*

*   *   *

MATTHEWS, Aline
See De WIRE, Elinor

*   *   *

MENOTTI, Gian Carlo 1911-2007

OBITUARY NOTICE—

See index for *SATA* sketch: Born July 7, 1911, in Cadegliano, Italy; died February 1, 2007, in Monaco. Menotti was a Pulitzer Prize-winning composer of operas popular on Broadway and on television and radio, including *The Consul, Amahl and the Night Visitors,* and *The Saint of Bleecker Street.* The son of a coffee merchant, he was taught by his mother to play the violin, piano, and cello. The young Menotti proved very capable and even composed his own opera, *The Death of Pierrot,* when he was just eleven years old. After his father died in 1928, Menotti's mother took her son to Philadelphia and enrolled him at the Curtis Institute of Music. Though he did not speak English at the time, his letter of recommendation from Arturo Toscanini easily impressed the school. He graduated in 1933, then moved to Vienna, Austria, where he had a home with fellow composer Samuel Barber. Menotti's first opera to be performed was *Amelia Goes to the Ball.* It was produced in Philadelphia in 1937 and at the Metropolitan Opera House in 1938. Next, he notably composed the first opera written expressly for the radio, *The Old Maid and the Thief* (1939), which was also produced on the stage two years later. Menotti's *The Island God* (1942) was panned by critics, but the composer felt the problem was with staging, and so he thereafter insisted he be allowed to have a say on how his operas were produced. When the United States entered World War II, Menotti offered his services to the Office of War Information, and became a broadcaster for Italian-language radio. After the war, Menotti was a part-time composition teacher at the Curtis Institute of Music for several years and briefly worked as a script writer for Metro-Goldwyn Mayer. He continued to write operas, such as *The Medium* (1946), which he adapted himself to film, and *The Consul* (1950), which earned him his first Pulitzer. His *The Saint of Bleecker Street* (1955) also won a Pulitzer, as well as a Drama Critics' Circle Award, even though it proved unpopular with audiences. One of Menotti's greatest popular operas, *Amahl and the Night Visitors* (1951), was written for television and became a standard Christmas season program. Known for creating romantic melodies that reminded many theater reviewers of the works of Puccini, Menotti was a traditionalist. Thus, when a modern movement to create experimental, atonal works began in the 1960s, he was increasingly criticized for lack of innovation. The composer, nevertheless, refused to cater to critics; he did very well financially because of income from television rights to his operas. He continued to compose, too, though a number of critics consider his later works to be minor achievements. Among these are *The Egg* (1976), *Juana, la Loca* (1979), *Goya* (1986), and *Giorino di Nozze* (1988). He also composed many symphonies, chamber music, and vocal/choral works. Among his other accomplishments, Menotti was composer and artistic director of the Spoleto Festival in Charleston, South Carolina, and cofounder of the Festival of Two Worlds in Spoleto, Italy, which he helped run from 1958 until 1999, when he turned it over to his adopted son, Francis Phelan.

OBITUARIES AND OTHER SOURCES:

BOOKS

Contemporary Composers, St. James Press (Detroit, MI), 1992.
Contemporary Musicians, Thomson Gale (Detroit, MI), 2002.

PERIODICALS

Chicago Tribune, February 2, 2007, section 1, p. 14.
New York Times, February 2, 2007, p. C11.
Times (London, England), February 3, 2007, p. 68.
Washington Post, February 2, 2007, p. B7.

*   *   *

MLYNOWSKI, Sarah 1977(?)-

Personal
Born c. 1977, in Montreal, Quebec, Canada; married. *Education:* McGill University, B.A. (English).

Addresses
Home—New York, NY. *E-mail*—sarah@sarah mlynowski.com.

Career
Writer. Harlequin Publishers, Toronto, Ontario, Canada, formerly worked in marketing.

Writings

ADULT NOVELS

Milkrun, Red Dress Ink (Don Mills, Ontario, Canada), 2001.
Fishbowl, Red Dress Ink (Don Mills, Ontario, Canada), 2002.
As Seen on TV, Red Dress Ink (Don Mills, Ontario, Canada), 2003.
Monkey Business, Red Dress Ink (Don Mills, Ontario, Canada), 2004.
Me vs. Me, Red Dress Ink (Don Mills, Ontario, Canada), 2006.

YOUNG-ADULT NOVELS

Bras and Broomsticks, Delacorte (New York, NY), 2005.
Frogs and French Kisses, Delacorte (New York, NY), 2006.
Spells and Sleeping Bags, Delacorte (New York, NY), 2007.

OTHER

(Editor with Lauren Henderson and Chris Manby, and contributor) *Girls' Night In,* Red Dress Ink (Don Mills, Ontario, Canada), 2004.
(Editor with Carole Matthews and Chris Manby, and contributor) *Girls' Night Out* (fiction anthology) Red Dress Ink (Don Mills, Ontario, Canada), 2006.
(With Farrin Jacobs) *See Jane Write: A Girl's Guide to Writing Chick Lit,* Quirk, 2006.

Contributor of short fiction to anthologies, including *21 Proms, Sixteen: Stories about That Sweet and Bitter Birthday,* and *American Girls about Town.*

Adaptations
Bras and Broomsticks was adapted as an audiobook, read by Aradne Meyers, Listening Library, 2005, and was optioned as a feature film by Fox 2000. Author's short story "Know It All" was considered for film adaptation.

Sidelights
Sarah Mlynowski began her career writing what has come to be known as "chick lit": novels that focus on the emotional lives, loves, relationships, and careers of contemporary younger women. Aimed at young women just starting out on their own, her first two books—both published while the author was herself in her early twenties—were fresh, stylish romances geared for a fashion-and-media-oriented generation. "I love exploring and satirizing the anxieties of today's twentysomething woman," Mlynowski told *Heartstrings* contributor Lori A. May with regard to these books. While she has continued her focus on chick lit—Mlynowski shares her

Cover of Sarah Mlynowski's young-adult novel **Bras and Broomsticks,** *featuring artwork by Robin Zingone.* (Delacorte Press, 2005. Cover hand-lettering and illustration by Robin Zingone. Copyright © 2005 by Learning in Focus, Inc. All rights reserved. Used by permission of Random House Children's Books, a division of Random House, Inc.)

knowledge of the popular genre in the nonfiction title *See Jane Write: A Girl's Guide to Writing Chick Lit*— she has also moved into young-adult fiction with the novels *Bras and Broomsticks, Frogs and French Kisses,* and *Spells and Sleeping Bags.*

Mlynowski was born and raised in Montreal, Quebec, Canada, where she attended a Jewish high school. After graduating with a degree in English from McGill University, where she served as fiction editor for the school's literary journal and contributed a biweekly column to the newspaper, she got a job in Toronto, Ontario, in Harlequin's marketing department. Since the publication of *Milkrun*—the first novel published by Harlequin's Red Dress Ink imprint, which offers an alternative take on traditional romance novels—she has relocated to New York City, where she now writes full time.

Milkrun was described by a *Publishers Weekly* reviewer as an "entertaining debut" with "both humor and substance." The novel centers on the life of twenty-four-

year-old Jackie, a copyeditor for a romance publishing company. Shortly after she relocates to Boston with her boyfriend, Jackie is told that her beloved intends to go on a long trip to Thailand—without her. She decides not to waste time being emotionally distraught about the breakup; instead, she resolves to get back out into the dating scene right away. She enlists the help of her friends, buys some sexy boots, and hangs out at a trendy singles bar called Orgasm; finding the right guy, though, turns out to be harder than Jackie ever expected. "Mlynowski is acutely aware of the plight of the twentysomething single woman," the *Publishers Weekly* reviewer noted. While finding Jackie "at times annoyingly neurotic," *Booklist* reviewer Kristine Huntley nonetheless described the young woman as "a likable heroine." Reviewers also admired Mlynowski's upbeat, offbeat style, May writing in *Heartstrings* that "her style of flirty dialogue and quick-wit narrative is both touching and humorous, hitting every beat dead on."

Mlynowski has followed *Milkrun* with several other chick-lit novels, including *Fishbowl, Monkey Business,* and *Me vs. Me.* In *Fishbowl* three strangers find themselves roommates when they enter a rental contract on an apartment in Toronto. Allie is a perky but naïve twenty-two year-old; Jodine is a perfectionistic law student; and Emma is a beautiful fashion editor's assistant with a penchant for partying. Although their personalities clash, the women must work together after a fire damages their kitchen and they need to earn money to cover the uninsured damage. A series of money-making schemes—including throwing parties at a local bar and presenting a "How to Pick Up Women" seminar—teach them about each other and also about themselves. "Mlynowski delivers a solid if formulaic roommate caper," a *Publishers Weekly* reviewer commented of *Fishbowl,* while a *Scribes World* online contributor noted that "personality clashes, fight scenes and sex make this a perfect book for the MTV generation."

Monkey Business introduces Kimmy, Jamie, Layla, and Russ, friends who meet in business school. Over the year, romantic entanglements form among Kimmy and Layla and the two young men, but time, career goals, and a growing maturity eventually cause the four to move on. The choice between the love of her life an a dream job in New York City is facing Arizona native Gabby Wolf in *Me vs. Me*—that, is, until something magical happens and Gabby can experience the lifestyle each choice would create for her. "The shifts in the group's loyalties and friendships . . . keep [*Monkey Business*] . . . fresh and riveting," noted Huntley in *Booklist,* the contributor also calling *Me vs. Me* "a clever look at what happens to one woman when her wish comes true."

Geared for a younger readership, *Bras and Broomsticks* takes place in New York City and introduces fourteen year old Rachel Weinstein. While she deals with typical adolescent concerns, Rachel has somewhat of an advantage over most teens: her younger sister, Miri, is a witch! Although Miri is still learning how to use her powers, with the help of the sisters' ultrabusy single mom—also a witch—Rachel gets the help she needs to win popularity at school and derail her divorced dad's impending marriage to a woman the sisters both dislike. Noting that the novel "offers plenty of laughs and some deliciously complicated predicaments," a *Publishers Weekly* contributor added that the sisters are realistic enough "to draw sympathy from readers and keep events interesting." "Rachel is sassy, self-absorbed, shy and insecure," wrote *Booklist* contributor Chris Sherman, the critic adding that "her concerns will be comfortably familiar to readers." In *School Library Journal,* Sarah Couri deemed *Bras and Broomsticks* "a breezy read that is sure to be popular."

A freshman in high school when readers reconnect with her in *Frogs and French Kisses,* Rachel hopes to win the love of the über-gorgeous Raf Kosravi. Of course, such a dream requires the help of her little sister, who is very much a novice when it comes to both love AND casting spells. Miri's work as an environmental caretaker, for example, creates several potential disasters,

and when Rachel seeks her aid, it is no surprise that nothing turns out as planned. Noting the novel's unexpected ending, *Booklist* contributor Jennifer Hubert wrote of *Frogs and French Kisses* that "Mlynowski's sassy text surpasses a chick-lit label by being wonderfully fast-paced and clever." "Less frantic and more mature than *Bras and Broomsticks,*" according to a *Kirkus Reviews* writer, the second novel in the series finds "Mlynowski's prose style . . . improved without sacrificing any humor." The sisters' saga continues in *Spells and Sleeping Bags,* which finds the two sisters summering at Camp Wood Lake, where Rachel uncovers some powers of her own.

Discussing the inspiration for her characters, Mlynowski noted on her home page: "My ideas come from everyday feelings and experiences. For example, [*Bras and Broomsticks*] . . . was based on my little sister Aviva. Unfortunately, not the witchcraft part. What inspired the book is the always complicated love, jealousy, and pride involved in a sister relationship. . . . In my opinion, the key to writing is to take what you know and go wild with it."

Biographical and Critical Sources

PERIODICALS

Cover of See Jane Write, *a guide to writing for the "Chick Lit" market coauthored by Mlynowski and Farrin Jacobs.* (Quirk Books, 2006. Reproduced by permission.)

Booklist, December 15, 2001, Kristine Huntley, review of *Milkrun,* p. 708; October 1, 2002, Kristine Huntley, review of *Fishbowl,* p. 305; September 15, 2003, Kristine Huntley, review of *As Seen on TV,* p. 224; September 15, 2004, review of *Monkey Business,* p. 224; January 1, 2005, Chris Sherman, review of *Bras and Broomsticks,* p. 846; July 1, 2006, Kristine Huntley, review of *Me vs Me,* p. 40, and Jennifer Hubert, review of *Frogs and French Kisses,* p. 51.

Bulletin of the Center for Children's Books, January, 2005, Timnah Card, review of *Bras and Broomsticks,* p. 221.

Kirkus Reviews, January 15, 2005, review of *Bras and Broomsticks,* p. 123; May 1, 2006, review of *Frogs and French Kisses,* p. 463.

Library Journal, August 1, 2006, Stacey Rae Brownlie, review of *See Jane Write: A Girl's Guide to Writing Chick Lit,* p. 99.

Publishers Weekly, October 29, 2001, review of *Milkrun,* p. 34; August 26, 2002, "One of the Most Successful Authors at Harlequin's 'Chick Lit' Imprint," p. 13; October 28, 2002, review of *Fishbowl,* pp. 52-53; August 23, 2004, review of *Girls' Night In,* p. 37; February 7, 2005, review of *Bras and Broomsticks,* p. 60.

School Library Journal, September, 2006, Kelly Czarnecki, review of *Frogs and French Kisses,* p. 212; January, 2005, Sarah Couri, review of *Bras and Broomsticks,* p. 134; September, 2006, Marcie Mann, review of *See Jane Write,* p. 233.

Voice of Youth Advocates, February, 2005, Julie Scordato, review of *Bras and Broomsticks,* p. 497.

ONLINE

Sarah Mlynowski Home Page, http://www.sarahmlynowksi. com (May 15, 2007).

Heartstrings, http://romanticfiction.tripod.com/ (October 15, 2002), Lori A. May, review of *Milkrun* and interview with Mlynowski.

Red Dress Ink Web site, http://www.reddressink.com/ (May 31, 2003), interview with Mlynowski.

Romantic Times, http://www.romantictimes.com/ (May 15, 2007), Christine Chambers, review of *Milkrun;* Samantha J. Gust, review of *Fishbowl.*

Scribes World, http://www.scribesworld.com/ (May 31, 2003), review of *Fishbowl.**

*   *   *

MORALES, Yuyi 1968-

Personal

Born 1968, in Xalapa, Veracruz, Mexico; immigrated to United States, 1994; married; husband's name Tim; children: Kelly (son). *Education:* University of Xalapa, B.A.; graduate study in creative writing.

Addresses

Home—San Francisco, CA. *E-mail*—yuyi@pacbell.net.

Career

Children's writer and illustrator. Swimming coach in Mexico; KPOO radio, San Francisco, CA, host of children's radio show, 1997-2000.

Awards, Honors

Don Freeman Memorial grant-in-aid, Society of Children's Book Writers and Illustrators, 2000; Americas Award for Children's and Young-Adult Literature, Consortium of Latin American Studies programs, Parent's Choice Award, Northern California Book Award nomination, named to Best of the Best List, Children's Literature, Chicago Public Library, and named to Best Children's Books of the Year list, Bank Street College of Education, all 2003, all for *Just a Minute: A Trickster Tale and Counting Book;* Pura Belpré Illustrator Award, California Book Award Silver Medal for juvenile fiction, Tomás Rivera Mexican-American Children's Book Award, Golden Kite Honor Book Award, Picture Book Illustration, Latino Book Award, Latino Literary Award for best children's book, Notable Books for Children list of Younger Readers, Cooperative Children's Book Center (CCBC), and *Choice* selection, Notable Books for a Global Society, all 2004, all for *Just a Minute;* Americas Award honorable mention, *School Library Journal* Best Books list, *San Francisco Chronicle* Best of Year list, Lasting Connections, Best of the Year, *Book Links,* and Best of the Year designation, *Child* magazine, all 2003, and Christopher Award, Jane Add-

Yuyi Morales (Photograph courtesy of Yuyi Morales.)

ams Children's Book Award, Pura Belpré Illustrator Award, CCBC Choices Selection, Notable Social Studies Trade Books for Young People, National Council for Social Studies, and Blue Bonnet Award nomination, all 2004, all for *Harvesting Hope.*

Writings

SELF-ILLUSTRATED

Just a Minute: A Trickster Tale and Counting Book, Chronicle Books (San Francisco, CA), 2003.

Little Night, Roaring Brook Press (New Milford, CT), 2006.

ILLUSTRATOR

Kathleen Krull, *Harvesting Hope: The Story of Cesar Chavez,* Harcourt (San Diego, CA), 2003.

Amanda White, *Sand Sister,* Barefoot Books (Cambridge, MA), 2004.

Marisa Montes, *Los Gatos Black on Halloween,* Holt (New York, NY), 2006.

Also illustrator of *Todas las buenas manos,* by F. Isabel Campoy, Harcourt (San Diego, CA).

Sidelights

Yuyi Morales is an award-winning illustrator and author of children's books whose original self-illustrated picture books include *Just a Minute: A Trickster Tale and Counting Book* and *Little Night.* Noted for her bright, child-friendly art, Morales has twice won the Pura Belpré Illustrator Award, which honors "Latino authors and illustrators whose work best portrays and celebrates Latino cultural experience in a children's book."

Morales was born in 1968 in Xalapa, Mexico, the eldest of four children. As a child she loved drawing, and often paired her pictures with stories. As she recalled in an interview for *Authors and Artists for Young Adults* (*AAYA*), "I . . . copied from family photographs, but mostly I looked at myself in the mirror and copied my face again and again until I memorized the shapes, the lines, and the shadows my face was made of. During these years I often dreamed of telling stories like in the books we had at home. . . . [and] the illustrated encyclopedia that my Mama bought from a door-to-door salesman, was among my favorites." "Yet, as much as I liked drawing and dreaming of stories," Morales added, "it never occurred to me, or to my parents or teachers, that I could choose to be an artist when I grew up." Although her father recognized her talent for drawing, he encouraged her to follow a career in architecture, but Morales felt no inspiration there. Instead, drawing on her skill as a competitive swimmer, she decided to major in physical education at the University of Xalapa and worked as a swimming coach for two years following graduation.

While coaching, Morales met her future husband, Tim, an American, got married, and had a son, Kelly. When her husband's grandfather became seriously ill, they went to visit him in San Francisco and decided to stay there. Recalling her first months in the United States, Morales noted in her *AAYA* interview that "the transition was long and arduous; I spoke almost no English, I had no job, I knew no friends, and I missed my family. At first . . . I felt as if there was no place for me here in this country, and I only longed to go back to the land I loved. Then one day, my mother-in-law . . . brought my son and me to the most incredible place I was going to know in the USA. She brought us to the Public Library." Inspired by the collection of children's books, Morales rekindled her love of bookmaking, and soon she was busy creating handmade picture books for Kelly. She then learned to read English along with her son, using library picture-book illustrations to decipher the simple texts. While attending writers' and illustrators' conferences, Morales began to learn the skills of the trade, and a meeting with author F. Isabel Campoy resulted in an offer to illustrate Campoy's next book, *Todas las buenas manos.*

Morales's first English-language picture-book project was Kathleen Krull's text for *Harvesting Hope: The Story of Cesar Chavez.* Chavez, a labor organizer who worked on behalf of California's migrant farm workers, made gains in the mid-1960s by organizing boycotts and strikes that ultimately won concessions from growers to improve the working conditions and pay rates for farm workers. Reviewing Morales's work for the volume, *School Library Journal* contributor Sue Morgan praised her "beautifully rendered earth-tone illustrations," while Traci Todd, writing in *Booklist,* cited the book's "gorgeous paintings, with their rounded, organic forms and lush, gemstone hues." *Horn Book* contributor Susan Dove Lempke noted that the illustrator "suffused" her acrylic paintings "with a variety of emotions, especially fear and sorrow," while a *Kirkus Reviews* critic compared Morales's artwork to that of noted twentieth-century Mexican muralist Diego Rivera.

Morales's first self-illustrated title, *Just a Minute,* was published in 2003. In the book, an old woman is summoned by Death to the afterlife. Death, a skeleton who calls himself Señor Calavera, arrives at Grandma Beetle's door and requests that she come with him. Although the old woman agrees, she has one small task to complete, then another, and then another, leaving Death increasingly impatient and frustrated. The reason for all the woman's work is soon revealed: Grandma Beetle's nine children are on their way to her house to celebrate her birthday. After the party, the woman prepares to go, but Señor Calavera has enjoyed himself so much during the festivities that he decides not to take her right now; instead, he leaves her a note saying that he is looking forward to coming to her next birthday party. "Morales's personification of death is never forbidding or scary," Catherine Threadgill commented in the *School Library Journal,* while a *Publishers Weekly* critic wrote that Death's "ghoulish, goofy gallantry would make him the comic lead of any Day of the Dead festivity."

In her original picture book *Little Night,* Morales presents "a tribute to mothers and the loving bond with their children through playing," as she explained in her *AAYA* interview. In the story, Little Night hides from Mother Sky, and readers follow the mother's search for her child across dusky hills and in dark caves. Ultimately, Little Night is discovered, and must bathe in falling stars, pin glowing planets in her hair, and have a bedtime glass of milk from the Milky Way before playing games with the moon at bedtime. Noting the book's "mystical effect," a *Kirkus Reviews* writer dubbed *Little Night* "lovely" while Enos Randall wrote in *Booklist* that Morales presents readers with "a sumptuous feast of metaphors," both in her serene text and "equally splendid illustrations." "Creating what amounts to a new myth may seem an ambitious project," noted a *Publishers Weekly* reviewer in appraising *Little Night,* "but Morales succeeds by combining intimacy and grandeur."

In addition to her self-illustrated books, Morales also takes on illustration duties for Amanda White's *Sand Sister* and *Los Gatos Black on Halloween,* a holiday-themed picture book with an English/Spanish text by Marisa Montes. *Sand Sister* finds a shy child wishing for a playmate at the beach while other children play with their brothers and sisters. When the lonely girl finds a stick and draws a picture of a playmate in the wet sand, her drawing magically comes alive. The two play together for the rest of the day, but when the tide turns the "sand sister" must leave and go back to the sea. Moving from the sunlit seashore to a shadow-filled haunted house, *Los Gatos Black on Halloween* invites readers to join a Halloween party where witches, skeletons, vampires, and black cats join in the scary fun. Reviewing *Sand Sister* for *Booklist,* Jennifer Mattson noted that Morales's "sun-drenched paintings," are filled with "vigor and fantastical sensibility," while her illustrations for *Los Gatos Black on Halloween* make the book "an atmospheric, bilingual romp" according to a *Publishers Weekly* contributor. Noting that the frightening creatures depicted in the illustrations might be too scary for smaller readers, Ilene Cooper wrote in *Booklist* that Morales's "soft-edged paintings glow with the luminosity of jewels." The illustrator's "dark, glowing pictures of inventively proportioned ghosts and other sinister night creatures provide the ideal accompaniment" for Montes' tale, concluded a *Kirkus Reviews* critic.

Describing how she creates characters for her books, Morales explained in her *AAYA* interview that "some . . . are modeled on people I know. My son Kelly appears in a couple of my books. . . . *Los Gatos Black on Halloween* is filled with people I know. My lovely dog Chacho is there, except he is a skeleton dog, frolicking and rattling his bones. My husband and I are the skeleton couple admiring the moon and dancing together, and my son is the dead boy who comes out from his coffin to join the dance." Creating such characters is a two-part process, according to the artist. "One is the conceptual part, and the other one the technical. Usually I like to have an idea of who my characters are. What do they feel, what emotions they portray, and how do they behave (are they playful, solemn, stern, silly, hard working?). Having this in mind, yes, sometimes I remember people I know, and that helps. Or sometimes they might remind me of a certain animal. . . . Then comes the technical part; I have to draw my characters. Sometimes I have an idea of how they might look, but quiet often I don't. Nevertheless, the next step is to start drawing. Perhaps I would start with a simple circle . . . , or a thin line if I am going to make somebody skinny like a skeleton. After I put down my first lines, I need to continue drawing, erasing and retracing, many, many times, because that is how I will eventually find what my characters will look like. There is a lot of experimentation, a lot of trying on different shapes, different sizes, different eyes, mouth, nose, etc, until I find the image I like for that specific character. My first attempts never come out right. They take a long time before I like them, sometimes even after I have sketched the whole book, I might go back and change one of my characters. I am always looking for the moment when I see what I have done and I say, 'Yes, that is him/her!'

"What I am trying to do through my books is mostly to surround myself with the things I love, the stories that bring me closer to my homeland, the colors that make me vibrate, the tales and customs I want my son to know," Morales explained in her *AAYA* interview. "When I came to the USA, there were so many things I missed! I missed the colorful houses, because the little apartment we rented was cream color inside and gray on the outside like many other houses in San Francisco, and I couldn't change that. And I missed my family and friends and the many things we did together, like having birthday parties with piñatas and yummy food. And I missed my mother and my sisters and my father and my brother and the many stories we told together, and when I couldn't have any of that near me anymore, I decided to put it in my books."

Biographical and Critical Sources

PERIODICALS

Booklist, June 1, 2003, Traci Todd, review of *Harvesting Hope: The Story of Cesar Chavez,* p. 1795; December 1, 2003, Jennifer Mattson, review of *Just a Minute: A Trickster Tale and Counting Book,* p. 668; March 15, 2004, Jennifer Mattson, review of *Sand Sister,* p. 1311; February 1, 2007, Randall Enos, review of *Little Night,* p. 46.

Horn Book, July-August, 2003, Susan Dove Lempke, review of *Harvesting Hope,* p. 480; March-April, 2004, "Pura Belpré Illustrator Award," p. 220; July-August, 2004, "Jane Addams Children's Book Award," p. 492.

Kirkus Reviews, July 1, 2003, review of *Harvesting Hope,* p. 911; October 15, 2003, review of *Just a Minute,* p. 1274; August 15, 2006, review of *Los Gatos Black on Halloween,* p. 848; April 1, 2007, review of *Little Night.*

Publishers Weekly, May 5, 2003, review of *Harvesting Hope,* p. 221; December 1, 2003, review of *Just a Minute,* p. 55; August 14, 2006, review of *Los Gatos Black on Halloween,* p. 204; March 26, 2007, review of *Little Night,* p. 93.

School Library Journal, June, 2003, Sue Morgan, review of *Harvesting Hope,* p. 129; December, 2003, Catherine Threadgill, review of *Just a Minute,* p. 136; October, 2004, Maryann H. Owen, review of *Sand Sister,* p. 136; July, 2005, Coop Renner, review of *Just a Minute,* p. 44; September, 2006, Joy Fleishhacker, review of *Los Gatos Black on Halloween,* p. 180; May, 2007, DoAnn Okamura, review of *Little Night,* p. 106.

ONLINE

PaperTigers, http://www.papertigers.org/ (October, 2005), Aline Pereira, interview with Morales.

Society of Children's Book Writers and Illustrators Web site, http://www.scbwi.org/ (June 10, 2007), "Yuyi Morales."

Yuyi Morales Home Page, http://www.yuyimorales.com (June 10, 2007).*

*　　　*　　　*

MORGAN, Michaela

Personal

Born in Manchester, England; children: Edward. *Education:* Universities of Warwick, B.A. (English; with honors); University of Leicester, Postgraduate Certificate (Education); Cambridge University, educational studies.

Addresses

Home and office—Brighton, England; Villefranche sur Mer, France. *E-mail*—info@michaelamorgan.com.

Career

Author. Worked variously as a teacher, shop owner, writer-in-residence, and public speaker.

Awards, Honors

Children's Choice designation, International Reading Association, 1991; United Kingdom Reading Association Award, 1993; Children's Book Award shortlist, 1995; Blue Peter Book Award shortlist, 2003, for *Words to Whisper, Words to Shout.*

Writings

FOR CHILDREN

Edward Buys a Pet, illustrated by Sue Porter, Dutton (New York, NY), 1987.
Visitors for Edward, illustrated by Sue Porter, Dutton (New York, NY), 1987.
Edward Hurts His Knee, illustrated by Sue Porter, Dutton (New York, NY), 1988.
Edward Loses His Teddy Bear, illustrated by Sue Porter, Dutton (New York, NY), 1988.
The Monster Is Coming!, illustrated by Sue Porter, Harper & Row (New York, NY), 1990.
Dinostory, illustrated by True Kelley, Dutton (New York, NY), 1991.
(With Colin S. Milkins) *The Introductory Encyclopedia of British Wild Animals,* Longman (Harlow, England), 1994.
Pudding, Longman (Harlow, England), 1994.
Tiger, Longman (Harlow, England), 1994.
Pickles Sniffs It Out, illustrated by Dee Schulman, A. & C. Black (London, England), 1994.
Snowflake, Longman (Harlow, Vongland), 1994.
The Not So Famous Four, illustrated by Mick Reid, Longman (Harlow, England), 1994.

Catnapped, Longman (Harlow, England), 1994.
Helpful Betty Solves a Mystery, illustrated by Moira Kemp, Carolrhoda Books (Minneapolis, MN), 1994, published as *Betty Solves a Mystery,* Mathew Price (Sherborne, England), 2005, published as *Hippo Solves a Mystery,* Koala Books (Australia), 2005.
Helpful Betty to the Rescue, illustrated by Moira Kemp, Carolrhoda Books (Minneapolis, MN), 1994, published as *Betty to the Rescue,* Mathew Price (Sherborne, England), 2005 published as *Hippo to the Rescue,* Koala Books (Australia), 2005.
The Only Child in Hamelin Town, illustrated by Llewelyn Thomas, Longman (Harlow, England), 1995.
Cool Clive, illustrated by Dee Shulman, Oxford University Press (Oxford, England), 1995.
Loyalty and Royalty: Two Tales from Wales, illustrated by Sarah Warburton, Collins Educational (London, England), 1996.
Clive Keeps His Cool, illustrated by Dee Shulman, Oxford University Press (Oxford, England), 1996.
Robbie Woods and His Merry Men, illustrated by Doffy Weir, Oxford University Press (Oxford, England), 1996.
Spooky!, illustrated by Stephen Lewis, Oxford University Press (Oxford, England), 1996.
Sick as a Parrot, illustrated by Trevor Dunton, Collins (London, England), 1997.
Invasion of the Dinner Ladies, illustrated by Dee Shulman, A. & C. Black (London, England), 1997.
The First Snow of Winter, illustrated by Sue Tong, BBC (London, England), 1998.
Dexter's Dinosaurs, illustrated by Guy Parker-Rees, Oxford University Press (Oxford, England), 1998.
Monster Mysteries: The Loch Ness Monster, illustrated by Colin Sullivan, Martin Remphry and Karen Hiscock, Ginn (Aylesbury, England), 1998.
Cool Clive and the Little Pest, illustrated by Dee Shulman, Oxford University Press (Oxford, England), 1998.
Shelley Holmes, Ace Detective, illustrated by Dee Shulman, Oxford University Press (Oxford, England), 1998.
Leela's Secret Plan, illustrated by Ian Newsham, Oxford University Press (Oxford, England), 1999.
Cool Clive and the Bubble Trouble, illustrated by Dee Shulman, Oxford University Press (Oxford, England), 2000.
Pompom, illustrated by Dee Shulman, Barrington Stoke (Edinburgh, Scotland), 2000.
The Magic Puppet, illustrated by Ian Newsham, Oxford University Press (Oxford, England), 2000.
Shelley Holmes, Animal Trainer, illustrated by Dee Shulman, Oxford University Press (Oxford, England), 2000.
The Songbird, illustrated by Ian Newsham, Oxford University Press (Oxford, England), 2000.
Spike and the Footy Shirt, illustrated by Rob Lee, Egmont World (Handforth, England), 2000.
Sports Day, illustrated by Ian Newsham, Oxford University Press (Oxford, England), 2000.
A Year at Duck Green, illustrated by Ian Newsham, Oxford University Press (Oxford, England), 2000.

Sausage in Trouble, illustrated by Dee Shulman, A. & C. Black (London, England), 2001.

Cool Clive, the Coolest Kid Alive: Two Books in One, illustrated by Dee Shulman, Oxford University Press (Oxford, England), 2001.

Watch the Birdie!, illustrated by Ian Newsham, Oxford University Press (Oxford, England), 2001.

Dinosaur Danger!, illustrated by Ian Newsham, Oxford University Press (Oxford, England), 2001.

School for Sausage, illustrated by Dee Shulman, A. & C. Black (London, England), 2001.

Sausage and the Spooks, illustrated by Dee Shulman, A. & C. Black (London, England), 2001.

Sausage and the Little Visitor, illustrated by Dee Shulman, A. & C. Black (London, England), 2001.

Words to Whisper, Words to Shout: and Other Poems to Read Aloud, illustrated by Chloe Cheese, Belitha (London, England), 2002.

The Beast, illustrated by Chris Mould, Barrington Stoke (Edinburgh, Scotland), 2004.

Brave, Brave Mouse, illustrated by Michelle Cartlidge, Albert Whitman & Co. (Morton Grove, IL), 2004.

Buffalo Bert: The Cowboy Grandad, illustrated by Ian Newsham, A. & C. Black (London, England), 2004.

Letter from America, illustrated by Ros Asquith, Barrington Stoke (Edinburgh, Scotland), 2004.

Respect!, illustrated by Karen Donnelly, Barrington Stoke (Edinburgh, Scotland),2005.

Dear Bunny: A Bunny Love Story, illustrated by Caroline Jayne Church, Scholastic (New York, NY), 2005.

Buffalo Bert: The Cowboy Grandad, illustrated by Ian Newsham, Picture Window Books (Minneapolis, MN), 2006.

Buddies, illustrated by Ros Asquith, Barrington Stoke (Edinburgh, Scotland), 2006.

Silly Sausage and the Little Visitor, illustrated by Dee Schulman, Picture Window Books (Minneapolis, MN), 2006.

Silly Sausage and the Spooks, illustrated by Dee Schulman, Picture Window Books (Minneapolis, MN), 2006.

Silly Sausage Goes to School, illustrated by Dee Schulman, Picture Window Books (Minneapolis, MN), 2006.

Silly Sausage in Trouble, illustrated by Dee Schulman, Picture Window Books (Minneapolis, MN), 2006.

The Thing in the Basement, illustrated by Doffy Weir, Picture Window Books (Minneapolis, MN), 2006.

The Spooks, illustrated by Daniel Postgate, Oxford University Press (Oxford, England), 2006.

Author's works have been translated into French, Korean, and Dutch.

OTHER

"Oxford Reading Tree" series (readers), thirty-six books, Oxford University Press (London, England), 1998–2006.

How to Teach Poetry Writing at Key Stage 2, David Fulton (London, England), 2001.

How to Teach Poetry Writing at Key Stage 1, David Fulton (London, England), 2003.

Also author of phonics books, teacher's resource books, and other books for educational publishers.

Sidelights

A teacher as well as the author of numerous books for beginning readers, Michaela Morgan has always been a writer. As she noted in an interview for the Chicken House Publishing Web site, "before I could actually write, I made up stories and rhymes in my head." With over a hundred books to her credit, many for the education markets, Morgan shifts her focus between picture books and series titles such as her "Silly Sausage" and "Cool Clive" books for primary-grade readers. On Stories from the Web online, Morgan remarked that the most enjoyable aspect of being a writer is "is getting a new idea and capturing it." Aspiring writers should

Michaela Morgan introduces readers to an engaging and imaginative young pup in **Silly Sausage Goes to School,** *a picture book featuring illustrations by Dee Shulman.* (Picture Window Books, 2001. Illustrations copyright © Dee Shulman 2001. All rights reserved. Reproduced by permission.)

"just do it," she added. "Every day sit down somewhere and write. Anything. For practice in finding words, finding your voice. Don't think about 'being a writer.' Just write."

Among Morgan's books for younger children are the picture books *Dear Bunny: A Bunny Love Story* and *Brave, Brave Mouse*. *Dear Bunny* centers on two bunnies that are smitten with each other but too shy to openly express their feelings. For Valentine's Day, Valentino and Valenteeny each pen a love letter, then leave them in a hollow log, each hoping that the other will find their token of affection. A twist is added to the love story when a family of mice finds the letters and use them for nesting purposes. Mice also star in *Brave, Brave Mouse*, as a young mouse shows more caution than many of his friends, and also shies from dark corners, loud noises, and strangers. Despite the fact that he is sometimes teased, the creature learns to trust his inner voice: sometimes it tells him to be brave and sometimes it tells him to hold back despite the pressure to do them. A critic for *Kirkus Reviews* dubbed *Dear Bunny* a "sweet and simple story [that] offers a fresh idea for Valentine's Day." Elaine Lesh Morgan, writing in *School Library Journal*, described the book as a "charming story, perfect for Valentine's Day." Also reviewing for *School Library Journal*, Kelley Rae Unger noted of *Brave, Brave Mouse* that Morgan's "gentle words of encouragement are presented in rhyming verses," and that Michelle Cartlidge's finely drawn pen-and-ink and watercolor images "match the text's reassuring message." Noting the book's "powerful message" for younger children, Ilene Cooper wrote in *Booklist* that "there's a place for [*Brave, Brave Mouse*] . . . in every preschool and kindergarten library."

Biographical and Critical Sources

PERIODICALS

Booklist, January 1, 2005, Ilene Cooper, review of *Brave, Brave Mouse*, p. 872; February 1, 2006, Karin Snelson, review of *Dear Bunny: A Bunny Love Story*, p. 56.

Bulletin of the Center for Children's Books, September, 1994, review of *Helpful Betty Solves a Mystery*, p. 20; September, 1994, review of *Helpful Betty to the Rescue*, p. 20.

Kirkus Reviews, January 1, 2006, review of *Dear Bunny*, p. 44.

Library Journal, March, 1989, Virginia Opocensky, review of *Edward Loses His Teddy Bear*, p. 166.

Publishers Weekly, August 16, 1991, review of *Dinostory*, p. 58.

School Library Journal, September, 1988, Nancy Seiner, review of *Visitors for Edward*, p. 172; September, 1988, Nancy Seiner, review of *Edward Gets a Pet*, p. 172; March, 1989, Virginia Opocensky, review of *Edward Hurts His Knee*, p. 166; May, 1989, Carol Mc-

Michael, review of *The Monster Is Coming*, p. 90; October, 1991, Gail C. Ross, review of *Dinostory*, p. 102; October, 1994, Pamela K. Bomboy, review of *Helpful Betty Solves a Mystery*, and *Helpful Betty to the Rescue*, p. 95; November, 2004, Kelley Rae Unger, review of *Brave, Brave Mouse*, p. 113; January, 2006, Elaine Lesh Morgan, review of *Dear Bunny*, p. 108.

Times Educational Supplement, March 8, 1986, Elaine Williams, review of *Tales Told within Walls*, p. 3; December 20, 1996, p. 26; January 24, 1997, "Fruitful Exercises," p. 15; November 14, 1997, review of *Sick as a Parrot*, and *Colour Jets*, p. 14; June 30, 2000, review of "Happy Kids" series, p. 23; October 22, 2004, Jan Mark, "Touching Tales and Alluring Fables," p. 19.

ONLINE

Chicken House Publishing Web site, http://www.doublecluck.com/ (May 1, 2007), "Michaela Morgan."

Michaela Morgan Home Page, http://www.michaelamorgan.com (May 1, 2007).

Oxford University Press Web site, http://www.oup.com/ (May 1, 2007), "Michaela Morgan."

Stories from the Web, http://www.storiesfromtheweb.org/ (May 1, 2007), "Michaela Morgan."

*　　　*　　　*

MURPHY, Rita

Personal

Married; children: one son.

Career

Author and educator.

Awards, Honors

Delacorte Press Prize for First Young-Adult Novel, 1999, for *Night Flying*.

Writings

Night Flying, Delacorte (New York, NY), 2000.
Black Angels, Delacorte (New York, NY), 2001.
Harmony, Delacorte (New York, NY), 2002.
Looking for Lucy Buick, Delacorte (New York, NY), 2005.

Adaptations

Night Flying was adapted as an audiobook.

Sidelights

There was a time when author Rita Murphy literally wrote in the closet. Writing was hobby then, and in order to keep from bothering her husband and son in the family's one-room apartment, "I pulled a lamp and my computer into a closet where I wouldn't disturb them," Murphy explained to *Publishers Weekly* contributor Shannon Maughan. Murphy's writing habits changed after her first novel, *Night Flying,* was selected for the Delecorte Press Prize for First Young-Adult Novel. "Murphy's work station has moved from the closet to a desk near the kitchen, where she now writes for about four hours each morning," Maughan explained.

Night Flying introduces almost-sixteen-year-old Georgia Hansen. Like all of the women in her family, Georgia can fly. Of course, she must obey the rules of her domineering grandmother, the same rules the whole family must obey. Then Georgia meets her Aunt Carmen, who was cast out of the family years before. As Georgia begins to uncover old family secrets and lies, she must ultimately decide whether to honor family tradition or choose her own path. Murphy "infuses Georgia's narrative voice with a naïve lyricism that beautifully captures the human desire to soar," wrote Debbie Carton in a review of *Night Flying* for *Booklist.* A *Publishers Weekly* critic commented that the novelist "seamlessly links the metaphor of flying with Georgia's rite of passage."

In *Black Angels,* Murphy moves from fantasy to the real-life town of Mystic, Georgia. The year is 1961, when Celli, who lives on the white side of town, discovers that her father is half black and passing for white. Confused by the racial tensions erupting in her town, Celli must now decide where she will stand along the racial divide. While Hazel Rochman wrote in *Booklist* that parts of the plot are contrived, "what will hold readers is the young girl's viewpoint of politics coming to town and right into her home."

In *Harmony* Murphy returns to the fantastic; Harmony is a young girl who came to her parents from the stars. She has incredible powers, and is able to make things happen with only a thought. Fitting into her small mountain community is a challenge for Harmony, however, and she has to learn how to use her gifts for the good of the community. "Once again, Murphy introduces us to strong female characters and adds a touch of the super-natural as well," wrote Paula Rohrlick in *Kliatt.* A *Kirkus Reviews* contributor dubbed the novel "a magical story written with a light, lyrical touch" that is "always rooted in the particulars of the mountain setting," and GraceAnne A. DeCandido wrote in *Booklist* that Murphy uses "sweet, sharp language as clear as the scent of pine."

Looking for Lucy Buick is a contemporary novel about a girl who grows up among a family of surrogate aunts and uncles. The reason?: Lucy was discovered, as an infant, in the back seat of a Buick won by an "aunt" in a bet. Lucy grows up determined to find her birth family, who she refers to as the Buicks, and when she turns eighteen, a fire allows her to fake her own death and make her way from New York to Iowa. There, Lucy

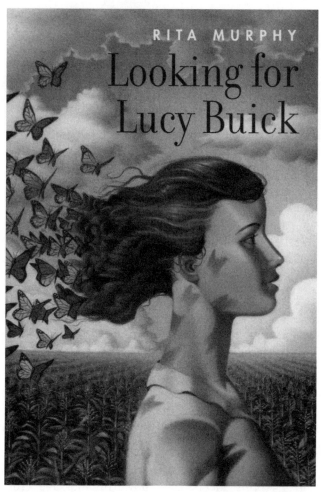

Cover of Rita Murphy's young-adult novel Looking for Lucy Buick, *featuring artwork by Jim Tsinganos.* (Delacorte, 2005. Jacket illustration copyright © 2005 by Jim Tsinganos. All rights reserved. Copyright © 2005 by Learning in Focus, Inc. All rights reserved. Used by permission of Dell Publishing, a division of Random House, Inc.)

finds, not her birth family, but a colorful cast of people who become a real family to her. Nicole Marcuccilli, writing in *School Library Journal,* considered Murphy's novel "an excellent read about a teen searching for her identity and where she belongs," while a *Kirkus Reviews* contributor dubbed *Looking for Lucy Buick* "sweet and light as a feather but with the substantial charm of music or a summer's day."

Biographical and Critical Sources

PERIODICALS

Booklist, December 15, 2000, Debbie Carton, review of *Night Flying,* p. 809; February 15, 2001, Hazel Rochman, review of *Black Angels,* p. 1149; March 15, 2001, review of *Night Flying,* p. 1366; September 15, 2002, GraceAnne A. DeCandido, review of *Harmony,* p. 222; October 15, 2005, Ilene Cooper, review of *Looking for Lucy Buick,* p. 47.

Book Report, May, 2001, Heather Hepler, review of *Night Flying,* p. 61.

Bulletin of the Center for Children's Books, January, 2001, review of *Night Flying,* p. 190; March, 2001, review of *Black Angels,* p. 272; January, 2006, Deborah Stevenson, review of *Looking for Lucy Buick,* p. 243.

Horn Book, September, 2000, Lauren Adams, review of *Night Flying,* p. 577; January-February, 2003, Lauren Adams, review of *Harmony,* p. 81; January-February, 2006, Philip Charles Crawford, review of *Looking for Lucy Buick,* p. 85.

Kirkus Reviews, September 1, 2002, review of *Harmony,* p. 1316.

Kliatt, July, 2002, Paula Rohrlick, review of *Night Flying,* p. 31; November, 2002, Paula Rohrlick, review of *Harmony,* p. 14; November, 2005, Myrna Marler, review of *Looking for Lucy Buick,* p. 9.

Publishers Weekly, November 27, 2000, review of *Night Flying,* p. 77; December 18, 2000, Shannon Maughan, "Rita Murphy," p. 28; February 5, 2001, review of

Black Angels, p. 89; April 22, 2002, review of *Night Flying,* p. 73; September 23, 2002, review of *Harmony,* p. 73.

School Library Journal, November, 2000, Sharon Grover, review of *Night Flying,* p. 160; July, 2001, Louise L. Sherman, review of *Black Angels,* p. 111; October, 2002, Saleena L. Davidson, review of *Harmony,* p. 169; November, 2005, Nicole Marcuccilli, review of *Looking for Lucy Buick,* p. 143.

Voice of Youth Advocates, October, 2000, review of *Night Flying,* p. 277; December, 2002, review of *Harmony,* p. 400.

ONLINE

Crescent Blues Book Views Online, http://www.crescentblues.com/ (April 28, 2007), Lynne Marie Pisano, review of *Night Flying.*

Random House Web site, http://www.randomhouse.com/ (April 28, 2007), interview with Murphy.

N

NAIDOO, Beverley 1943-

Personal

Born May 21, 1943, in Johannesburg, South Africa; daughter of Ralph (a composer and music copyright manager) and Evelyn (a broadcaster and theater critic) Trewhela; married Nandhagopaul Naidoo (a solicitor), February 1, 1969; children: Praveen, Maya. *Education:* University of Witwatersrand, South Africa, B.A., 1963; University of York, B.A. (with honors), 1967, Certificate of Education, 1968; University of Southampton, Ph.D., 1991.

Addresses

Home—Dorset, England. *Agent*—Gary Carter, Roger Hancock Ltd., 4 Water Lane, London NW1 8NZ, England.

Career

Educator and author. Kupugani Non-Profit Nutrition Corporation, Johannesburg, South Africa, field worker; primary and secondary teacher in London, England, 1969; writer, 1985—, and researcher, 1988-91. Advisory teacher of cultural diversity and English in Dorset, England, beginning 1988; visiting fellow, University of Southampton.

Member

British Defence and Aid Fund for Southern Africa's Education Committee, Writers' Guild for Great Britain, National Association for Teachers of English.

Awards, Honors

Other Award, *Children's Book Bulletin,* 1985, Children's Book Award, Child Study Book Committee at Bank Street College of Education, 1986, Children's Books of the Year selection, Child Study Association of America, 1987, Parents' Choice Honor Book for Paperback Literature, Parents' Choice Foundation, 1988, and

Beverley Naidoo (Photograph by David Mallett. Reproduced by permission of Beverley Naidoo and David Mallett.)

Notable Children's Trade Book in the Field of Social Studies, National Council for the Social Studies/Children's Book Council (NCSS/CBC), all for *Journey to Jo'burg;* Notable Children's Trade Book in the Field of Social Studies, NCSS/CBC, 1990, and Best Book for Young Adults selection, American Library Association (ALA), 1991, both for *Chain of Fire;* Carnegie Medal and Nestlé Smarties Book Prize Silver Awards, both 2000, *Booklist* Top of the List winner for Youth Fiction,

2001, Jane Addams Book Award and IBBY Honor Book, both 2002, and Sankei Children's Book Award (Japan), 2003, all for *The Other Side of Truth;* honorary D.Litt., University of Southampton, 2002; honorary D.Univ., Open University, 2003; Parents' Choice Silver Honor Award, 2003, and Jane Addams Peace Association Book Award, African Studies Association Children's Africana Book Award, *Riverbank Review* Children's Book of Distinction designation, and ALA Best Book for Young Adults designation, all 2004, all for *Out of Bounds; Time Out* Critics Choice designation for Best Plays for Children and Young People, 2004, for *The Playground;* New York Public Library Book for the Teen Age designation, 2007, for *Web of Lies.*

Writings

YOUNG-ADULT NOVELS

Journey to Jo'burg: A South African Story, illustrated by Eric Velasquez, Longman (London, England), 1985, Lippincott (Philadelphia, PA), 1986.

Chain of Fire (sequel to *Journey to Jo'burg*), Collins (London, England), 1989.

No Turning Back: A Novel of South Africa, Viking (London, England), 1995, HarperCollins (London, England), 1997.

The Other Side of Truth, Puffin (London, England), 2000, HarperCollins (New York, NY), 2001.

Web of Lies (sequel to *The Other Side of Truth*), Penguin (London, England), 2004, Amistad (New York, NY), 2006.

Burn My Heart, Penguin (London, England), 2007.

PICTURE BOOKS

Letang's New Friend, illustrated by Petra Röhr-Rouendaal, Longman (London, England), 1994.

Letang and Julie Save the Day, illustrated by Petra Röhr-Rouendaal, Longman (London, England), 1994.

Trouble for Letang and Julie, illustrated by Petra Röhr-Rouendaal, Longman (London, England), 1994.

Where Is Zami?, illustrated by Petra Röhr-Rouendaal, Macmillan (London, England), 1998.

(With daughter, Maya Naidoo) *Baba's Gift,* illustrated by Karin Littlewood, Puffin (London, England), 2004.

The Great Tug of War, and Other Stories, illustrated by Piet Grobleer, Frances Lincoln (London, England), 2006.

OTHER

Censoring Reality: An Examination of Books on South Africa, ILEA Centre for Anti-Racist Education and British Defence/Aid Fund for Southern Africa, 1985.

(Editor) *Free as I Know,* Bell & Hyman (London, England), 1987.

Through Whose Eyes? Exploring Racism: Reader, Text and Context, Trentham Books (London, England), 1992.

Out of Bounds: Seven Stories of Conflict and Hope, foreword by Archbishop Desmond Mpilo Tutu, Puffin (London, England), 2001, HarperCollins (New York, NY), 2003.

The Playground (play), produced 2004.

(Author of introduction) *Making It Home: Real-Life Stories from Children Forced to Flee,* Puffin (London, England), 2004, Dial (New York, NY), 2005.

Contributor to academic journals, including *English in Education* and *Researching Language and Literature.*

Sidelights

Born in Johannesburg, South African, Beverley Naidoo witnessed the evils of the apartheid system first hand, but as a white in that segregated society she did not understand such evils until years later. Eventually rejecting the country's racist policies, she relocated to England. There, through her writing—including the young-adult novels *Journey to Jo'burg: A South African Story* and *Chain of Fire,* the short-story collection *Out of Bounds: Seven Stories of Conflict and Hope,* and as several picture books for younger children—she has worked to educate young people on the evils of racism in her homeland. Since apartheid was dismantled in South Africa with the rise to power of black leader Nelson Mandella in the mid-1990s, Naidoo has turned her attentions to more general concerns. She discusses the plight of homeless street children in *No Turning Back: A Novel of South Africa* and covers the issue of racism in her adopted country, England, in *The Other Side of Truth* and its sequel, *Web of Lies.* In addition, she has taken time to join her daughter, Maya Naidoo, in writing a more uplifting work, the picture book *Baba's Gift.*

Born into an affluent family, Naidoo grew up in a world of privilege where whites patronizingly referred to African males of all ages as "boys" and females as "girls." In the care of a black nanny whom she called Mary, she was oblivious to the fact that her caregiver had three young children of her own who lived nearly two hundred miles away. Mary seldom saw her own family because she had to work in town to support them. One particular incident, which occurred when Naidoo was eight or nine, still resonates, and she recalled it in her acceptance speech for the 1986 Child Study Children's Book Award (reprinted in *School Library Journal*): "Mary received a telegram and collapsed. The telegram said that two of her three young daughters had died. It was diphtheria—something for which, I as a white child, had been vaccinated." It took Naidoo years to realize the significance of that event. She continued, "I must have continued to spout with the arrogance of white youth the customary rationalizations—that Mary and those who followed her, were lucky because we gave them jobs, sent presents to their children at Christmas, and so on. I still feel intensely angry about the racist

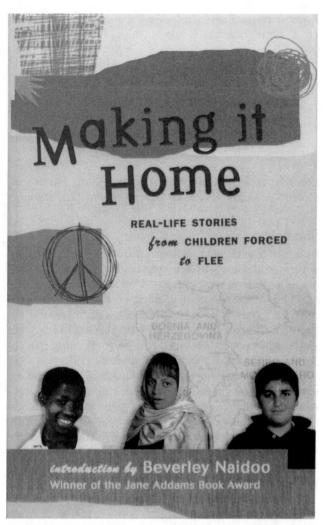

Cover of Making It Home, *a collection of stories written by young refugees that features an introduction by noted author Naidoo.* (Puffin Books, 2004. Reproduced by permission of Puffin Books, a division of Penguin Putnam Books for Young Readers.)

deceptions and distortions of reality which the adult society passed on to me as a child."

Following high school, Naidoo attended the University of Witwatersrand, but most of her learning took place outside of the classroom. "As I gradually began to see for the first time some of the stark reality all around me, I became intensely angry not only at the narrowness of my schooling, but at its complicity in perpetuating apartheid through not previously challenging my blinkered vision," she wrote in her book *Through Whose Eyes? Exploring Racism: Reader, Text, and Context.* Politicized, she joined in the anti-apartheid movement, where her activism resulted in a 1964 police detainment under the "Ninety Days" solitary confinement law. That experience forever changed the way Naidoo viewed life in South Africa.

Although Naidoo had always resisted her mother's suggestion that she become a teacher, she now realized the impact of education as a tool in the fight against apartheid. In 1965 she moved to England to pursue a

teaching degree at the University of York while also teaching school part time. She also continued to expand her own horizons by following the continuing events in South Africa. Inspired by two books—*The African Child* by Camara Laye and *Roaring Boys* by Edward Blishen—Naidoo earned a B.A. with honors from York in 1967 and received her teaching certificate the following year. For the next decade, she taught primary and secondary school in London. She also became involved with an anti-apartheid group and began to look for ways to educate young people about the dangers of racism in general and of the South African apartheid system in particular.

During the early 1980s, Naidoo began doing research for the Education Group of the British Defence and Aid Fund for Southern Africa, an activist organization that aided victims of apartheid and worked to raise the world's awareness of human-rights abuses in South Africa. Her efforts helped make people aware of the alarming shortage of suitable teaching materials about apartheid and resulted in the publication of a critical bibliographical study called *Censoring Reality: An Examination of Books on South Africa,* which Naidoo edited. When the Education Group decided to commission a work of "informed and helpful fiction" on apartheid, she volunteered to write it. "I wrote the text simply, quite deliberately," she explained. Naidoo penned the story as if she were telling it to her own children, she recalled, because "it seemed important to be able to explain at their level what was happening in South Africa."

The fruit of Naidoo's efforts was the young-adult novella *Journey to Jo'burg,* which follows the adventures of Naledi, a young black girl, and her younger brother Tiro when they travel to Johannesburg in search of their mother, a domestic servant in a white household. The children set out on the three-day journey because their baby sister is critically ill and their grandmother, who cares for them in their mother's absence, has no money for medicine or a doctor. During their journey, the children encounter the ugly realities of life for black people under apartheid.

In *School Library Journal* JoAnn Butler Henry called Naidoo's short work a "well-written piece [that] has no equal," and *Times Educational Supplement* contributor Gillian Klein deemed it a work of "uncompromising realism." In *Booklist,* however, Hazel Rochman faulted Naidoo's strong message. "This is not great fiction," she contended: "story and characters are thinly disguised mechanisms for describing the brutal social conditions and the need for change." While disagreements sparked over the literary value of *Journey to Jo'burg*, Naidoo's subject was as powerful as it was shocking and her book achieved the desired effect: it helped to draw the world's attention to the anti-apartheid struggle. Although *Journey to Jo'burg* was banned by the South African government, it won several children's book awards in the United States and the United Kingdom.

In *Chain of Fire,* a sequel to *Journey to Jo'burg,* Naidoo revisits Naledi, who is now fifteen years old, as her family and neighbors face eviction and enforced resettlement to a "black homeland" called Bophuthatswana. Because apartheid laws prevented Naidoo from living in South Africa, she researched *Chain of Fire* by interviewing other South African expatriates and by reading whatever books and articles she could find about the government's ethnic cleansing policies. "I immersed myself in the devastating data on the mass destruction of the homes and lives of millions of South Africans by the apartheid regime through its program of 'Removals' to [these] so-called 'Homelands,'" she later explained.

According to Marcia Hupp, writing in *School Library Journal, Chain of Fire* "flows effortlessly, with power and grace, as it succeeds in making a foreign culture immediate and real." The novel "is not easy reading, nor should it be," noted a *Publishers Weekly* contributor; "it tackles tough issues head-on and presents them with superb dramatic tension." The novel's "chief strength lies in the moving representation of family and village life," wrote Peter Hollindale in the *Times Educational Supplement,* and *Kliatt* contributor Sherri Forgash Ginsberg found the story "uplifting," due to its focus on teens "who have the courage to stand up for what they believe."

A stark, uncompromising look at the plight of abused and homeless street children, *No Turning Back* focuses on a twelve-year-old African boy named Sipho. Fleeing an abusive stepfather, he runs runs away, hoping to find a better life on the streets of Johannesburg. Tragically, Sipho quickly learns about survival in the "new South Africa." He gets involved with a street gang, sleeps in the gutters, begs for food, and experiments with glue sniffing in an effort to escape his misery. In the end, he finds refuge in a shelter where he has the chance to go to school.

Amy Chamberlain praised *No Turning Back* in her *Horn Book* review as "a can't put down account of an impoverished South African boy." In *Publishers Weekly,* a reviewer noted that Naidoo's novel seems written "effortlessly from the boy's point of view, so that his confusion, eagerness and naive wishes unfold naturally." A contributor to *Kirkus Reviews* was less impressed, describing the book as "bland" and "uninvolving" and noting "the story lacks the fire that made *Journey to Jo'burg* so compelling." Elizabeth Bush, reviewing the novel for the *Bulletin of the Center for Children's Books,* also felt that Naidoo "toned down" Sipho's struggles "for middle-grade consumption," shepherding the youth through street danger like a "literary guardian angel." However, Rochman remarked in *Booklist* that *No Turning Back* shares the power of Naidoo's earlier novels, and something more. "This time the social realism is just as authentic," asserted the critic, "but there is more personal focus." In *Voice of Youth Advocates* Beth E. Anderson also noted that Naidoo "brings to her readers the reality of homeless children," and ends her tale with a "glimmer of hope," and *Magpies* contributor Nola Allen deemed the novel "eloquent and compassionate."

Naidoo moves beyond the boundaries of South Africa both politically and geographically with *The Other Side of Truth,* which was honored with the United Kingdom's prestigious Carnegie Medal. In this novel, set in Nigeria during the political unrest of the 1990s, twelve-year-old Sade Solaja and her younger brother Femi find themselves in great danger after assassins accidentally shoot their mother. The assassins meant to kill their father, outspoken journalist Forlarin Solaja. Shipped off to London to life with their father's brother, the children soon discover that their university professor uncle has abandoned them and gone into hiding after being threatened himself. Detained and interviewed by the police and British immigration authorities, the two siblings remain silent, afraid that revealing anything about themselves might put their father in jeopardy. Sade and Femi eventually find kindness in a foster home, but experience harassment at school. When their father rejoins them after entering England illegally, their jubilation turns to fear when Forlarin is arrested and subsequently goes on a hunger strike. Sade now finds a way to act: she manages to tell her father's story on the evening news, and once public attention is drawn to the case the man is released. With freedom, the Solaja family is left to make a home in their new country.

Reviewing *The Other Side of Truth* for *School Library Journal,* Gerry Larson wrote that Naidoo effectively "captured and revealed the personal anguish and universality of the refugee experience." In *Horn Book* Nell D. Beram dubbed the novel a "scrupulously well-observed narrative," further commenting that it not only "honors its political and ethical engagements," but also "succeeds as a first-rate escape-adventure story." *Booklist* reviewer Hazel Rochman similarly noted that *The Other Side of Truth* "brings the news images very close," while Stephanie Zvirin noted in the same periodical that Naidoo "raises tough questions."

Readers rejoin the Solaja family in *Web of Lies,* as they attempt to make a life for themselves in the strange and volatile culture of South London. Femi, now age twelve, is having the most difficulty, and like many teens his age has become involved with a gang. As the half-truths and evasions mount, fourteen-year-old Sade begins to suspect, but hopes, in the journal entries that weave throughout the novel, that she can help her brother without troubling her father. As the family hangs in limbo, unsure whether the British government will grant them political asylum, Femi's new friends escalate their destructive behavior. Now Femi faces a crisis: should he follow the gang, or follow his conscience. And if he comes clean, will his family lose their chance to be granted the asylum they have long hoped for? Praising *Web of Lies* as "a riveting sequel," *Horn Book* contributor Susan P. Bloom noted that Naidoo's story "powerfully clarif[ies] . . . the seductive power the violent gang holds for the lonely, grief-stricken boy." As Sue Giffard maintained in *School Library Journal,* the author "integrates Nigerian culture seamlessly into the British context, revealing the complex social world inhabited by [the country's] immigrants." According to *Kliatt* contributor KaaVonia Hinton, Naidoo's "ability to weave political unrest and social issues into characters' lives" is one of the book's strengths, making *Web of Lies* "ideal for social studies classrooms."

As she has throughout her career, Naidoo continues to balance her writing with teaching and social activism. Although confronting social injustices such as racism and poverty can be disheartening, as she explained on the British Council's Crossing Borders Web site, through her writing she both illuminates problems and shares her optimism that such problems can be solved. "Stories are a way of making sense, first of all for myself, and then for others," she explained. "I believe that if a writer can find the truths in a specific human situation, the meaning will carry across time, place, at least to some readers if not to all."

Biographical and Critical Sources

BOOKS

Children's Literature Review, Volume 29, Thomson Gale (Detroit, MI), 1993.

Gallo, Donald R., editor and compiler, *Speaking for Ourselves, Too,* National Council of Teachers of English (Urbana, IL), 1993.

Naidoo, Beverley, *Through Whose Eyes? Exploring Racism: Reader, Text, and Context,* Trentham Books (London, England, 1992.

Twentieth-Century Young-Adult Writers, St. James Press (Detroit, MI), 1994.

PERIODICALS

Booklist, March 15, 1986, Hazel Rochman, review of *Journey to Jo'burg: A South African Story,* p. 1086; March 15, 1990, review of *Chain of Fire,* p. 1430; December 15, 1996, Hazel Rochman, review of *No Turning Back: A Novel of South Africa,* p. 724; December 15, 2001, Hazel Rochman, review of *The Other Side of Truth,* p. 723; January 1, 2002, Hazel Rochman, interview with Naidoo, p. 830; February 15, 2002, Stephanie Zvirin, review of *The Other Side of Truth,* p. 1034; February 15, 2003, Hazel Rochman, review of *Out of Bounds: Seven Stories of Conflict and Hope,* p. 1080; February 1, 2006, Hazel Rochman, review of *Web of Lies,* p. 60.

Book Report, September-October, 1997, Karen Sebesta, review of *No Turning Back,* pp. 38-39.

Bulletin of the Center for Children's Books, May, 1986, review of *Journey to Jo'burg,* p. 175; May, 1990, review of *Chain of Fire,* p. 223; February, 1997, Eliza-beth Bush, review of *No Turning Back,* p. 217; February, 2003, review of *Out of Bounds,* p. 246; June, 2006, Loretta Gaffney, review of *Web of Lies,* p. 464.

English Journal, September, 1986, review of *Journey to Jo'burg,* p. 81.

Five Owls, May, 1990, review of *Chain of Fire,* p. 90; March, 1991, p. 70.

Horn Book, September-October, 1990, review of *Journey to Jo'burg,* p. 607; March-April, 1997, Amy Chamberlain, review of *No Turning Back,* p. 203; November-December, 2001, Nell D. Beram, review of *The Other Side of Truth,* pp. 756-757; March-April, 2003, Susan P. Bloom, review of *Out of Bounds,* p. 214; July-August, 2006, Susan P. Bloom, review of *Web of Lies,* p. 447.

Kirkus Reviews, March 15, 1990, review of *Chain of Fire,* p. 428; December 1, 1996, review of *No Turning Back;* December 1, 2002, review of *Out of Bounds,* p. 1771.

Kliatt, May, 1993, Sherri Forgash Ginsberg, review of *Chain of Fire,* p. 10; May, 2003, Rebecca Rabinowitz, review of *The Other Side of Truth,* p. 20; August 15, 2005, review of *Making It Home: Real-Life Stories from Children Forced to Flee,* p. 919; May, 2006, KaaVonia Hinton, review of *Web of Lies,* p. 12.

Magpies, March, 1996, Nola Allen, review of *No Turning Back,* p. 36; September, 2002, Sophie Masson, "Know the Author: Beverley Naidoo," pp. 10-12.

Publishers Weekly, May 30, 1986, review of *Journey to Jo'burg,* p. 67; March 30, 1990, review of *Chain of Fire,* p. 64; December 16, 1996, review of *No Turning Back,* p. 60; November 5, 2001, review of *The Other Side of Truth,* p. 36; December 16, 2002, review of *Out of Bounds,* p. 68.

School Librarian, May, 1989, review of *Chain of Fire,* p. 75; February, 1996, review of *No Turning Back,* p. 31; winter, 2004, Sue Roe, review of *Web of Lies,* p. 216.

School Library Journal, August, 1986, JoAnn Butler Henry, review of *Journey to Jo'burg,* p. 96; May, 1987, Beverly Naidoo, "The Story behind 'Journey to Jo'burg,'" p. 43; May, 1990, Marcia Hupp, review of *Chain of Fire,* pp. 108, 113; September, 2001, Gerry Larson, review of *The Other Side of Truth,* p. 231; January, 2003, Sue Giffard, review of *Out of Bounds,* p. 141; May, 2006, Sue Giffard, review of *Web of Lies,* p. 132.

Times Educational Supplement, April 26, 1985, Gillian Klein, review of *Journey to Jo'burg,* p. 26; May 20, 1988, Bill Deller, "Breadth of Vision," p. B21; March 10, 1989, Peter Hollindale, "Bound to Protest," p. B15; July 5, 1996, review of *No Turning Back,* p. R8.

Voice of Youth Advocates, August, 1986, review of *Journey to Jo'burg,* p. 148; June, 1990, review of *Chain of Fire,* p. 108; October, 1997, Beth E. Anderson, review of *No Turning Back,* p. 246; June, 2003, review of *Out of Bounds,* p. 141.

ONLINE

Beverley Naidoo Home Page, http://www.beverleynaidoo.com (June 10, 2007).

British Council Crossing Borders Web site, http://www. crossingborder-africanwriting.org/writersonwriting/ (June 10, 2007), "Beverley Naidoo."*

*   *   *

NELSON, Marilyn 1946-
(Marilyn Nelson Waniek)

Personal

Born April 26, 1946, in Cleveland, OH; daughter of Melvin M. (in the U.S. Air Force) and Johnnie (a teacher) Nelson; married Erdmann F. Waniek, September, 1970 (divorced, 1979); married Roger R. Wilkenfeld, November 22, 1979 (divorced, 1998); children: (second marriage) Jacob, Dora. *Education:* University of California, Davis, B.A., 1968; University of Pennsylvania, M.A., 1970; University of Minnesota, Ph.D., 1978. *Politics:* "Yes." *Religion:* "Yes." *Hobbies and other interests:* Quilting, traveling.

Addresses

Home—East Haddam, CT. *Office*—Department of English, University of Connecticut, Box U-4025, 215 Glenbrook Rd., Storrs, CT 06269-4025. *E-mail*—nelson@frontstreetbooks.com.

Career

National Lutheran Campus Ministry, lay associate, 1969-70; Lane Community College, Eugene, OR, assistant professor of English, 1970-72; Norre Nissum Seminariam, Norre Nissum, Denmark, English teacher, 1972-73; Saint Olaf College, Northfield, MN, instructor in English, 1973-78; University of Connecticut, Storrs, CT, assistant professor, 1978-82, associate professor, 1982-88, professor of English, 1988-2002, professor emeritus, 2002—; University of Delaware, Newark, professor of English, 2002-04; Soul Mountain Retreat, East Haddam, CT, director, 2002—. Visiting assistant professor, Reed College, 1971-72, and Trinity College (Hartford, CT), 1982-83; visiting professor, University of Hamburg, spring, 1977, New York University, spring, 1988, spring, 1994, and Vermont College, spring, 1991; Elliston Professor, University of Cincinnati, spring, 1994; U.S. Military Academy, visiting faculty, spring, 2000.

Member

Society for the Study of Multi-Ethnic Literature of the United States, Society for Values in Higher Education, Modern Language Association, American Literary Translators Association, Poetry Society of America, Associated Writing Programs, Third World Villanelle Society, Phi Kappa Phi.

Awards, Honors

Kent fellowship, 1976; National Endowment for the Arts fellowships, 1981, 1990; Connecticut Arts Award, 1990; National Book Award finalist for poetry, 1991;

Marilyn Nelson (Photograph by Fran Funk. Courtesy of Marilyn Nelson.)

Annisfield-Wolf Award, 1992; Fulbright teaching fellowship, 1995; National Book Award finalist for poetry, 1997; Poets' Prize, 1999, for *The Fields of Praise: New and Selected Poems;* Contemplative Practices fellowship, American Council of Learned Societies, 2000; named Poet Laureate for the State of Connecticut, Connecticut Commission on the Arts, 2001; J.S. Guggenheim Memorial Foundation fellowship, 2001; *Boston Globe/Horn Book* Award and National Book Award finalist in young-people's literature category, both 2001, and Coretta Scott King Honor Book designation, Flora Stieglitz Straus Award for Nonfiction, and Newbery Honor designation, all 2002, all for *Carver: A Life in Poems;* Coretta Scott King Book Award, 2005, for *Fortune's Bones: The Manumission Requiem;* two Pushcart prizes; Michael L. Printz Award honor book designation, Lee Bennett Hopkins Poetry Award honor book designation, and Coretta Scott King Honor Award, all 2006, all for *A Wreath for Emmett Till;* Lifetime Achievement honor, Connecticut Book Awards, 2006.

Writings

(Translator) Pil Dahlerup, *Literary Sex Roles,* Minnesota Women in Higher Education (Minneapolis, MN), 1975.

(As Marilyn Nelson Waniek) *For the Body* (poems), Louisiana State University Press (Baton Rouge, LA), 1978.

(Translator, with Pamela Espeland) Halfdan Rasmussen, *Hundreds of Hens, and Other Poems for Children,* Black Willow Press (Minneapolis, MN), 1982.

(As Marilyn Waniek, with Pamela Espeland) *The Cat Walked through the Casserole, and Other Poems for Children,* Carolrhoda (Minneapolis, MN), 1984.

(As Marilyn Nelson Waniek) *Mama's Promises* (poems), Louisiana State University Press (Baton Rouge, LA), 1985.

(As Marilyn Nelson Waniek) *The Homeplace* (poems), Louisiana State University Press (Baton Rouge, LA), 1990.

(As Marilyn Nelson Waniek) *Magnificat* (poems), Louisiana State University Press (Baton Rouge, LA), 1994.

The Fields of Praise: New and Selected Poems, Louisiana State University Press (Baton Rouge, LA), 1997.

Carver: A Life in Poems (young adult), Front Street (Asheville, NC), 2001.

Fortune's Bones: The Manumission Requiem (young adult), Front Street (Asheville, NC), 2004.

(Translator) Inge Pederson, *The Thirteenth Month* (poems), Oberlin College Press, Oberlin, OH), 2005.

The Cachoeira Tales, and Other Poems, Louisiana State University Press (Baton Rouge, LA), 2005.

A Wreath for Emmett Till (fpr young adults), illustrated by Philippe Lardy, Houghton Mifflin (Boston, MA), 2005.

(Translator) Halfdan Rasmussen, *Ladder* (picture book), illustrated by Pierre Pratt, Candlewick Press (Cambridge, MA), 2005.

The Freedom Business: Connecticut Landscapes through the Eyes of Venture Smith: Poems, Lyme Historical Society/Florence Griswold Museum (Old Lyme, CT), 2006.

(With Elizabeth Alexander) *Miss Crandall's School for Young Ladies and Little Misses of Color: Poems* (for young readers), illustrated by Floyd Cooper, Wordsong (Honesdale, PA), 2007.

Contributor of poetry to numerous anthologies, including *A Formal Feeling Comes: Contemporary Women Formalist Poets,* 1993, and *The New Breadloaf Anthology of Contemporary American Poetry,* 1999. Contributor to literary journals and periodicals, including the *Gettysburg Review, Obsidian II, Southern Review, MELUS, Minority Voices, Field,* and *Studies in Black Literature.* Manuscripts by Nelson and other archives relevant to her writing are held in the Kerlan Collection at the University of Minnesota and in the archives of the University of Connecticut.

Sidelights

Poet Marilyn Nelson, who published her early work under the name Marilyn Nelson Waniek, writes in a variety of styles about many subjects, often dealing with topics involivng the African diaspora. She has also written verses for children and translated poetry from the Danish and German. As fellow poet Yusef Komunyakaa wrote of Nelson's work in *Prime Zone Media Network:* "Rooted in the basic soil of redemptive imagination, the voices in Marilyn Nelson's poems seek a lyrical foothold in our daily lives. Her words teach us how to praise ourselves by praising each other."

Nelson's first poetry collection, *For the Body,* focuses on the relationships between individuals and the larger social groupings of family, extended family, and society. Using domestic settings and memories of her own childhood, she fashions poetry that "sometimes sings, sometimes narrates," as a *Dictionary of Literary Biography* essayist described it. In *Mama's Promises* Nelson continues to experiment with poetic forms in verses about a woman's role in marriage and society, but she utilizes stanzaic division more than in her previous work. The poems in *Mama's Promises* also bear a cumulative theological weight, as the "Mama" named in each poem is revealed in the last poem to be God.

In *The Homeplace* Nelson turns her attention to the history of her own family, telling its story from the time of her great-great-grandmother to the present via a series of interconnected poems ranging in style from traditional forms to colloquial free verse. Some critics praised the variety of poetic expression Nelson displays. "The sheer range of [Nelson's] voice," Christian Wiman wrote in *Shenandoah,* "is one of the book's greatest strengths, varying not only from poem to poem, but within individual poems as well." Suzanne Gardinier, reviewing the book for *Parnassus,* found that through her poems Nelson "reaches back through generations hemmed in on all sides by slavery and its antecedents; all along the way she finds sweetness, and humor, and more complicated truth than its disguises have revealed."

In her poetry for children, Nelson also writes of family situations, although in a more humorous manner. Her collection *The Cat Walked through the Casserole and Other Poems for Children,* written with Pamela Espeland, contains poems about domestic problems and pleasures. The title poem, for example, tells of the family dog and cat and the trouble they cause throughout the neighborhood. Such poems as "Grampa's Whiskers" and "When I Grow Up" also focus on family life in a light-hearted manner.

Although biblical allusions appear in even her earliest poems, only with the collection *Magnificat* does Nelson write directly of spiritual subjects. Inspired by her friendship with a Benedictine monk, Nelson tells of her religious awakening to a more profound sense of Christian devotion. Writing in *Multicultural Review,* Mary Walsh Meany found Nelson's voice—"humorous, earthy, tender, joyous, sorrowful, contemplative, speculative, attached, detached, sometimes silent"—to be what "makes the poems wonderful." A *Publishers Weekly* contributor noted that Nelson's "passion, sincerity and self-deprecating humor will engage even the most skeptical reader."

In *The Fields of Praise: New and Selected Poems* Nelson's poems embrace numerous themes, including the changing nature of love, racism, motherhood, marriage, and domesticity. A *Publishers Weekly* contributor called the collection "stirring," noting that the verses in Section III, "grappling with evil and filled with biblical and philosophical references, demonstrate a luminous power." Writing in *America,* Edward J. Ingebretsen commented that he was drawn to Nelson's humorous poems. "Nelson is at her best when she is wry and comic," Ingebretsen wrote. "Many of her narrative scenes are Swiftian indignities observed with compassion." Miller Williams, writing in the *African American Review,* called Nelson's voice "quietly lyrical" and her poems ones "of simple wisdom and straightforward, indelible stories."

The Cachoeira Tales, and Other Poems is a more recent collection of poems by Nelson that explores travel from an African-American historical and social point of view. Nelson writes about an encounter with a cab driver, a trip to a Creole village, and a strange journey to Brazil's Bahia. A *Black Issues Book Review* contributor asserted that "Nelson's gift as a poet is her simple, fluid mastery of poetic forms."

In 2001 *Carver: A Life in Poems* was published to critical acclaim, notable nominations, and awards. In this volume Nelson provides a lyrical rendering through forty-four poems of the life of George Washington Carver, a renowned and revered African-American botanist and inventor who was widely respected for his scholarly mind, hard work, and humility. As head of the agricultural department at the Tuskegee Institute, Carver specialized in crop research and was especially noted for his work with peanuts, including developing peanut butter. Nelson's poems tell Carver's story within the political and cultural milieu of his time, and the book includes prose summaries of the events in Carver's life and numerous photographs. Ray Olson, reviewing *Carver* in *Booklist,* noted that "Nelson beautifully and movingly revives his reputation." As Cathryn M. Mercier commented in *Horn Book,* "each poem stands as a finely wrought whole of such high caliber that one can hardly name a favorite," and *School Library Journal* critic Herman Sutter remarked that Nelson's verses "are simple, sincere, and sometimes so beautiful that they seem not works of artifice, but honest statements of pure, natural truths."

In *Fortune's Bones: The Manumission Requiem* Nelson writes about the real-life Fortune, a slave whose master preserved his bones for anatomical research after Fortune died. The poems are based on information gathered by the Mattatuck Museum, which stored the bones. A *Kirkus Reviews* contributor called the verse collection a "slim funeral mass, moving from grief to joy," adding that the author likens the slave's "death as his deliverance from slavery to the ultimate freedom." "Moved by the poetry and the history," Hazel Rochman wrote in *Booklist,* "readers will want to join the debate." *School Library Journal* critic Nancy Palmer concluded of *For-*

tune's Bones that "this volume sets history and poetry side by side and, combined with the author's personal note on inspirations, creates a unique amalgam."

Nelson writes about another notorious incident in her book *A Wreath for Emmett Till.* Till was a young African American from Chicago who was brutally beaten and murdered in Mississippi in 1955 after whistling at a white woman. A *Kirkus Reviews* contributor praised the author's ability to "take one of the most hideous events of the 20th century and make of it something glorious," while *School Library Journal* critic Cris Riedel referred to the book as being "in the Homeric tradition of poet-as-historian." As a *Publishers Weekly* contributor further remarked, "for those readers who are ready to confront the evil and goodness of which human beings are capable, this wise book is both haunting and memorable."

Halfdan Rasmussen, a Danish poet who died in 2002, is among the writers whose works have been translated by Nelson for English-speaking audiences. His works *Hundreds of Hens and Other Poems for Children* and *The Ladder* feature rhyming couplets, the latter telling the story of an independent-minded ladder that travels the countryside. "Not every translated rhyme is felicitous, but most are jaunty and light," wrote Abby Nolan of Nelson's translations in her *Booklist* review. Nelson has also cowritten several books of poetry, including collaborating with Elizabeth Alexander on *Miss Crandall's School for Young Ladies and Little Misses of Color.*

Nelson served as poet laureate of the State of Connecticut from 2001 through 2006. Also in 2006, she was honored with a Lifetime Achievement award at the Connecticut Book Awards. In her speech accepting the honor, she said she felt strange for receiving an award for something that came so naturally. "Poets are dreamers and live in the imagination," Nelson said, as quoted by Carol Goldberg for the *Hartford Courant.* "My achievements are really blessings for being in the right place at the right time. It's odd to be honored for being blessed." Along with continuing to write poetry, Nelson continues to teach her craft at the University of Connecticut and at Soul Mountain, a poet's retreat she helped establish. She also contributes as a writer and performer to the Poetry Foundation's podcasts, which introduce poetry as an oral tradition to students.

Biographical and Critical Sources

BOOKS

Dictionary of Literary Biography, Volume 120: *American Poets since World War II, Third Series,* Thomson Gale (Detroit, MI), 1992.

PERIODICALS

African American Review, spring, 1999, Miller Williams, review of *The Fields of Praise: New and Selected Poems,* p. 179.

America, April 25, 1998, Edward J. Ingebretsen, review of *The Fields of Praise,* p. 27.

Black Issues Book Review, March-April, 2006, review of *The Cachoeira Tales, and Other Poems,* p. 18.

Booklinks, January-February, 2006, Chris Liska Carger and Mayra Carillo-Daniel, review of *A Wreath for Emmett Till,* p. 49.

Booklist, May 1, 2001, Ray Olson, review of *Carver: A Life in Poems,* p. 1658; November 15, 2004, Hazel Rochman, review of *Fortune's Bones: The Manumission Requiem,* p. 573; February 1, 2005, Gillian Engberg, review of *A Wreath for Emmett Till,* p. 970; January 1, 2006, review of *A Wreath for Emmett Till,* p. 12; June 1, 2006, Abby Nolan, review of *The Ladder,* p. 88.

Christian Century, December 14, 2004, review of *Fortune's Bones,* p. 24.

Christianity and Literature, summer, 1998, Anne West Ramirez, review of *The Fields of Praise,* p. 510.

Georgia Review, winter, 1997, Judith Kitchen, review of *The Fields of Praise,* p. 756.

Hartford Courant, December 4, 2006, Carole Goldberg, "Poet's 'Blessed' Life Honored at Connecticut Book Awards."

Horn Book, September, 2001, Cathryn M. Mercier, review of *Carver,* p. 606; January-February, 2002, Cathryn M. Mercier, review of *Carver,* p. 41; January-February 2005, Sue Houchins, review of *Fortune's Bones,* p. 105; May-June, 2005, Betsy Hearne, review of *A Wreath for Emmett Till,* p. 339; May-June, 2006, "Lee Bennett Hopkins Poetry Award," p. 365.

Hudson Review, spring, 1998, R.S. Gwynn, review of *The Fields of Praise,* p. 257; summer, 2005, David Mason, "The Passionate Pursuit of the Real," pp. 319-328.

Kirkus Reviews, October 15, 2004, review of *Fortune's Bones,* p. 1011; March 1, 2005, review of *A Wreath for Emmitt Till,* p. 292.

Los Angeles Times, December 30, 2001, Carol Muske Dukes, review of *Carver,* p. R10.

Multicultural Review, March, 1995, Mary Walsh Meany, review of *Magnificat.*

Newsweek, April 17, 2006, Raina Kelley, "Poetry in Motion," p. 66.

New York Times Book Review, July 15, 2001, review of *Carver,* p. 24.

Parnassus, Volume 17, number 1, 1992, Suzanne Gardinier, review of *The Homeplace,* pp. 65-78.

Poetry, May, 2006, D.H. Tracy, review of *The Cachoeira Tales, and Other Poems,* p. 159.

Publishers Weekly, November 16, 1990, review of *The Homeplace,* p. 52; August 29, 1994, review of *Magnificat,* p. 67; May 26, 1997, review of *The Fields of Praise,* p. 82; April 11, 2005, review of *A Wreath for Emmett Till,* p. 54.

Reading Today, December, 2005, David L. Richardson, review of *A Wreath for Emmett Till,* p. 34.

School Library Journal, July, 2001, Herman Sutter, review of *Carver,* p. 129; December, 2004, Nancy Palmer, review of *Fortune's Bones,* p. 166; April, 2005, Nina Lindsay, review of *Fortune's Bones,* p. 57; May, 2005, Cris Riedel, review of *A Wreath for Emmett Till,* p. 156.

Shenandoah, winter, 1992, Christian Wiman, review of *The Homeplace.*

Women's Review of Books, May, 1998, Marilyn Hacker, review of *The Fields of Praise,* p. 17.

ONLINE

Academy of American Poets Web site, http://www.poets. org/ (March 16, 2007), "Marilyn Nelson."

African American Literature Book Club Online, http:// aalbc.com/ (March 16, 2007), "Marilyn Nelson."

Connecticut State Poet Laureate Web site, http://vvv.state. ct.us/emblems/poet.htm (March 16, 2007), "Marilyn Nelson."

Marilyn Nelson Home Page, http://web.uconn.edu/ mnelson/ (March 16, 2007).

Poetry Foundation Web site, http://www.poetryfoundation. org/ (March 16, 2007), "Marilyn Nelson."

University of Connecticut Web site, http://uconn.edu/ (March 16, 2007), "Marilyn Nelson."*

Autobiography Feature

Marilyn Nelson

Marilyn Nelson contributed the following autobiographical essay to *SATA:*

In the Southern and black tradition, I like to start telling of myself by telling who my people are. My mother's mother was an Atwood, the eldest of a family of seven children, some of whose names are remembered in the little town of Hickman, Kentucky, even now, long after their deaths. Their parents were mulattos born into slavery; later their father, Pomp Atwood, co-owned a little

The Atwood family, 1943: (from left) Great-uncle Rufus (president of Kentucky State College; all seated on the steps of his house), Annisue (Mildred's daughter), Geneva, Story (in front, Mildred's husband), Annie, Mildred, Blanche, Rose, Ray (my maternal grandmother), Mabel (Rufus's wife), Julian Hale (Annie's husband) (Photograph courtesy of Marilyn Nelson.)

grocery store in Hickman, had a coal and oil business, and sold real estate. There's an Atwood Street in a black neighborhood of Hickman. I met a woman from Hickman in California once, who told me that if anyone ever stood in my way, I should "tell them you're an Atwood woman, and go right on to the top." My grandmother's sisters and brother were teachers and preachers and darers. In the nineteen-teens, Aunt Blanche won an essay contest whose prize was a full-tuition scholarship to a major Southern university. When she showed up to claim her prize and it was discovered that she was "colored," the committee decided not to award the scholarship that year. The Atwoods fought the decision. The committee finally compromised and gave her a full scholarship to a Negro college. She taught for a while at Fisk University. For some thirty years Uncle Rufus was president of Kentucky State College. I found his name in a Negro history textbook when I was in college: he won the Bronze Star for bravery in World War I. Aunt Rose once stuck a hat pin—she always kept one

in the lapel of her coat, to be used in such circumstances—into a haughty white woman who snorted something insulting when Aunt Rose sat down next to her on a city bus. The Hickman woman I met in California told me her high school graduation ceremony was interrupted when my grandmother entered the auditorium with her walker, after decades of living elsewhere teaching school. The high school principal said, "Wait; is that Miss Ray? Miss Ray, would you like to say something to our graduates?" Meema, who must have been in her late seventies then, followed her clunking walker down the middle aisle, and at the stage turned to face the audience and recited a soliloquy from a Shakespeare play. She played the piano by ear—but only on the black keys—and was so proud, the story goes, that "she was the only woman in the county who bought shoes without looking at them: she refused to lower her head in front of a white shoe salesman."

The other half of Mama's side of our family was her father, John Mitchell, who was born into slavery.

His father ran away to fight for the Union. After the war he rejoined his family in Tennessee, and with his severance pay bought a piece of land to farm. Night riders attacked the farm when my grandfather was a little boy and set the cabin on fire. His mother told him to run north, and he ran away with his younger brother, Will. He lost Will; I've never heard the story of that loss. My grandfather was found by a white family, the Bryants, in Dorena, Missouri. They took him in and raised him with their own son, Cullen. They were never able to find his birth family. As a young man, he farmed with the Bryants and ran their Mississippi River ferry. One day a bunch of rednecks from out of town insulted him on the ferry, and he threw them overboard. He left town that night, on a train with a ticket paid for by the Bryants, and with farm animals they had given him as a premature inheritance. He went west, to the all-black town of Boley, Oklahoma, and farmed there for the rest of his life. Mama said he talked so often about "ol' Cull," his boyhood friend and surrogate brother, that at last her exasperated mother said he should write Cullen a letter. He did. A few weeks later they received a reply: Cullen was dead. His wife said Cullen had spoken of my grandfather often and with love, even on his deathbed. A few years ago my uncle was in Hickman, which is near Dorena, so he drove into Dorena for the first time in his life and stopped at a little department store called Bryant's. He asked to speak with the owner, and when he did, told Mr. Bryant that he thought perhaps Mr. Bryant's parents might have raised his father. Mr. Bryant remembered hearing of John Mitchell when he was a boy; he invited my uncle home with him to meet his family, and he accompanied my uncle to our family reunion the following day. My uncle says that when I was an infant he and my mother, having received the news that their father was dying, drove with me all night from Cleveland to Boley. They got there in the morning, went into their father's room, and Mama held me up: "Here's your first grandbaby, Papa." He opened his eyes and said, "My grandbaby." He died later that day.

My father never talked much about his family. His people came from Tennessee, but Daddy was born and raised in St. Louis. His father was a cook on a paddle-wheel steamboat. Somewhere there's a photograph of the steamboat crew, in which my grandfather is wearing a long white apron and a white chef's hat. My grandmother's German shepherd once grabbed the shirt of a child who was teetering on the edge of their upper-story tenement balcony and held the child in the air until she could haul the child up. When she died, the dog lay down and refused to move or eat until it died. When my eleventh-grade history teacher told us to ask our parents about the Great Depression, Daddy's eyes filled with tears. All he said was that he used to walk along the railroad tracks, looking for pieces of coal. His parents died when he was a young man, and he attended Wilburforce College on scholarship. He had wanted to be a doctor, but wasn't able to afford medical school. He went to law school for a while, but made his career

in the air force. He was in the last class to graduate from the experimental military Negro cadet school which produced the Tuskegee Airmen. His class graduated too late to fly in World War II, but they were of that first generation of Negro military aviators.

Daddy was a navigator, and my childhood was splendid with pride in the fact that he flew, and that because he was an officer, men in uniform saluted him right and left. Our car was saluted whenever we passed the checkpoint leaving or entering an air force base, and Daddy's magisterial military bearing commanded respect wherever he went. One foggy New Year's Eve, on our way to Mexico from our home in northern California, we were stopped by a white highway patrolman. The policeman walked up to our car, shined his flashlight on us, and asked Daddy, "What do you think you're flying, boy?" Daddy, who was wearing his uniform, said with great dignity, "B-52's." The policeman looked shocked, then laughed and said, "Well, I guess you know what you're doing, then. But please be careful." They exchanged New Year's wishes and waved as we drove away.

This background provided me with the security and courage implied by the proverb which advises us to give two things to our children: roots and wings. Mama,

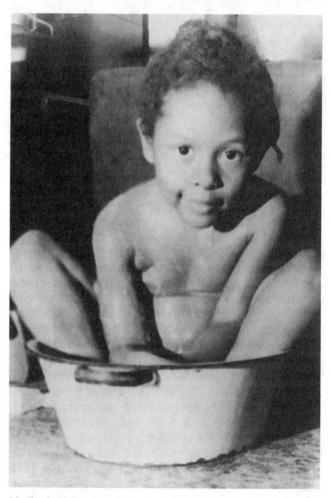

Marilyn in 1948 (Photograph courtesy of Marilyn Nelson.)

with her proud stories of her family, gave us roots; Daddy, who used to drive us out into the country at night, park the car and point out constellations and name stars, gave us wings. They encouraged us to dream big, and they had confidence in our ability to be what we dreamed. My sister, Jennifer, is an actor/director; our brother, Mel, is a musician/composer. These are my people, and this is where I start.

Mama and Daddy met in Cleveland; I was born there in 1946. Daddy was driving a taxi and going to law school; Mama had graduated from Kentucky State and was working on a master's degree in music theory at Case Western Reserve. I foiled her plans: she didn't get her master's for another twenty years. Jennifer was born two years after I was. We lived in an apartment on, I think, Euclid Avenue. The one surviving photograph of the neighborhood shows me on a tricycle, in outsized, shabby overalls (Mama said I used to embarrass her by announcing, when someone admired my clothes, that we had bought them "to the Goodwill"). Behind me are the wooden fire escapes of a ghetto tenement. And with me are a few other children; we look like the Dead End Kids. One of Mama's cousins, George Freeman, lived in Cleveland. We called him Uncle George; his wife, Aunt Carma, was my godmother. Their daughter, Oneida, died of childhood leukemia. Uncle George's mother, Aunt Rose (Mama's aunt, my great-aunt), lived in Cleveland, too, and was for years the housekeeper of the Jeloff family. One day Aunt Rose was talking to her minister on the telephone when the elastic in her "bloomers" broke and they fell off. She did a little dance for me, laughing with her eyes, the "bloomers" around her ankles, as she continued her serious conversation. She was my favorite aunt.

Jennifer and I shared a double bed and told each other stories or played a game we called "footsies" until Daddy banged on the door and old us to "pipe down in there!" I started kindergarten in Cleveland, but all I remember of school there is a plague of head lice (I didn't get them) and snacks of graham crackers and milk. Mama was teaching school and Daddy was working and taking law school courses, and acting and taking photography classes at the Karamu settlement house, when he was recalled into the service for the Korean conflict.

He stayed in the air force for sixteen years. We lived in Waco, Texas; Salina, Kansas; Denver, Colorado; Sacramento, California; Portsmouth, New Hampshire; Kittery Point, Maine; Sacramento again; Fort Worth, Texas; Burns Flat, Oklahoma; and Sacramento again, permanently. We usually lived in base housing, which meant we lived in the "better" neighborhoods of a society which segregated officers and enlisted men. Daddy was often the only Negro officer on a base, and even when he wasn't, we were often the only Negro officer's children, and more often the only Negro children in our classes. Jennifer and I were studious to the point of bookishness, though I was more of a "tomboy" than

she. We rode bicycles, roller-skated, caught frogs and lizards, and climbed trees. My knees and elbows are permanently scarred from being skinned so often. In second or third grade at an air force base near Salina, Kansas, I read all the books in the school library, and Mrs. Leibel brought in books from the high school to keep me occupied. My best friend was Tommy Avery. Tommy's mother was British; they had a little Winston Churchill statue next to their radio, and a box of teensy cigars it could actually smoke when Tommy's mother lit them. Tommy got sprayed by a skunk one day when we were out playing in a dry drainage ditch. His mother made him take off all his clothes outside and washed him with a hose. I couldn't look into his eyes for a long time after that.

In fourth grade at Mather Field, near Sacramento, California, the boy I liked best was Sammy Hartley. He had red hair and freckles, and looked like he could have been invented by Mark Twain. My best friend that year was Helene Straker, whose father had known mine when they were Tuskegee cadets. Helene and Jennifer and I had lots of slumber parties during which we pretended we were orphans lost in the woods, or made up stories about our futures. One of the few racial incidents I remember from childhood happened with Helene: we were walking in another neighborhood of base housing when a little white girl called us the N-word. Helene said, "What did you say?" The girl repeated the word. Helene hauled off and hit her with her fist, right in the middle of her forehead. A big lump formed. Then Helene and I walked on home. I guess the girl's father was an enlisted man; we never heard anything more about the incident.

My brother, Mel Junior, was born in 1956. He was just a few weeks old when Daddy was transferred to Portsmouth, New Hampshire. A few weeks later Daddy was sent to England on temporary duty, and Mama, who wasn't happy in the apartment we had found, moved us across the river to Kittery Point, Maine. There we rented a big old colonial house a block from the ocean, between Miss Lydia Pinkham, a sweet old spinster-lady, and Ed and Flossie Bayliss, an old childless couple who soon became our surrogate grandparents. There were fruit trees in their overgrown yard, and in the barn a Model-T Ford which hadn't been driven in years. Daddy convinced Uncle Ed that it should be driven, so we took them for rides in it, Aunt Flossie pointing out medicinal herbs by the roadside. A poultice of Queen Anne's lace flowers is good against psoriasis. They had a dark parlor they never used, with photographs of dead relatives, in their coffins, on the tables and mantel. Uncle Ed used to sit in their bay window with binoculars and watch the town. Once or twice he said, with his broad Maine accent, "I saw you had steak last night." We were the first Negroes ever to live in Kittery Point. My sixth grade teacher, Mrs. Dorothy Gray, had never had a Negro student before. Some of the other children—temporary immigrants from the South whose fathers worked at the Kittery Naval Yard—snubbed me, but I had many more friends than enemies.

Marilyn (right) with sister, Jennifer, about 1951 (Photograph courtesy of Marilyn Nelson.)

My best friend that year, Ellie Mitchell, has been my friend for almost forty years.

That year was a turning point for me: our house was only a few doors from the library, and I read almost every book in it. I loved A.J. Cronin's *The Green Years,* which I read over and over. And I discovered poetry, reading anthologies of old nineteenth-century chestnuts. I decided I wanted to be a poet, and I wrote my first poem about my baby brother. "Little Sir Melvin, in knighthood is he, / Rides on a brown charger (it's really my knee)," and so on. Mama kept a copy of it, and Mrs. Gray predicted that I'd grow up to be a famous writer. I was heartbroken when we had to leave Kittery Point; I'd planned to become a Mariner Scout the next year and learn to sail.

We were transferred three times the following year, back to Sacramento, then to Fort Worth, Texas, then to Burns Flat, Oklahoma. In Fort Worth we lived in a black neighborhood called "Stop Six" and went to segregated schools. The teachers I liked best there were Miss Lee and Mr. Lee. Miss Lee taught English and read poems to us by Paul Laurence Dunbar (the school was named for him). Mr. Lee taught string quartet. Since we were only to be in Fort Worth for a short time, Mama had put the piano into storage. She told me to continue to practice, however, by fingering on my school desk the pieces

I'd been learning. My homeroom teacher noticed this, thought I must be "musical," and had me put into Mr. Lee's class. He gave me the viola. Daddy made me go out on the balcony to practice: he couldn't stand the screeching. How humiliating it was to stand in the open air, scratching out scales, while the cutest boys in the school, I was sure, were watching and hearing me. But I loved the class: Mr. Lee would start the three of us girls sawing notes that must have made several great composers groan in their graves, then he'd crack us up by plucking out jazz accompaniments on his bass. I was famous in the school because I had "a California accent." Kids stopped me in the hall, asking me to talk for them. Before I could capitalize on my fame by exchanging words with the boy I'd noticed, whose first name was Major, we were transferred again, this time to Oklahoma. By now I had known and forgotten so many people that I was half convinced that they permanently disappeared after we left them. I'd learned not to look back.

On one of those cross-country trips, which we made driving all night, stopping at dusk-to-dawn drive-in theatres where Mama and Daddy snored while we children watched movies until we couldn't help giving up, Daddy drove as we slept and parked the car on the edge of the Grand Canyon. We awoke to that grandeur at dawn. Daddy was like that. He loved the sound of rain on the car's roof at night, and once or twice he invited me to sleep in the car so I could hear it. I slept in the backseat, he in the front. Rain sounds like wren's wings beating against a parked car's roof at night. Or like a cascade of coins made of moonlight. Or like a raging stampede of chipmunks. Daddy could pull coins out of our ears. I remember thinking as a young child that as long as he could do that, we would never be poor. He could also execute a standing back-flip, which for years endeared him to my friends. When I was little, children used to knock on our door after school and ask whether Mr. Nelson could come out and play. Once or twice he drove into a midwestern farmyard because the mailbox said "Nelson." He introduced us as "Nelsons, too," and asked if we could look around. The Nelsons never turned us away. Mama was a trained and intuitive pianist with perfect pitch. She could identify all of the notes in a chord heard once, and often called from the kitchen when we were practicing the piano, to say, "Not B-flat; B-natural!" Severe storms were always a treat because when the electricity went out our neighbors came to our house, and Mama played and everyone sang along by candlelight. When the civil rights movement started in earnest, Mama made up a joke: "Knock knock." "Who's there?" "Eyes." "Eyes, who?" "Eyes yo' new neighbor." We sang and laughed and played games, driving across the country eating fried chicken and sandwiches of raisin bread and bologna.

I finished seventh and eighth grade and part of ninth at Burns Flat High School. There were three Negro students, all from air force families, in the school. Though we lived on base, the school was in town, and the high school townies made life miserable for us. The boys teased each other at lunch by calling me across the caf-

"Mama with her class at Shilling Air Force Base," Saline, Kansas, 1955 (Photograph courtesy of Marilyn Nelson.)

eteria, then pointing at each other and saying, "He says he likes you." Two of the teachers, Mr. and Mrs. Purdy, resented my presence in their classrooms. Though my grades were excellent, Mr. Purdy gave me a D in math. I went home in tears. Daddy said, "He's a redneck cracker, Marilyn; he knows you're better than he is. Just do the work and be proud. We'll be out of here soon." Mrs. Purdy once made me read a racist black dialect poem aloud in English class. She had the smile of a viper. But the other teachers encouraged me and treated me with respect and affection. I had three best friends: Kim McCauley, Cheryl Wesson, and John Henry Brand III. Kim and I wrote a novel, "The Case of the Fabulous Belt Buckle Monster," passing a notebook back and forth in Mr. Purdy's class. Kim told me only years later that her mother had disapproved of our friendship. The civil rights movement was in the daily news, with lunch counter sit-ins and police dogs and fire hoses. Kids whose fathers had been transferred to Burns Flat from Little Rock had terrible stories to tell. Even in Oklahoma, Negroes couldn't try on clothes in the local department stores, or eat in ice cream parlors (you had to buy your soda and drink it outside). My class voted not to take a field trip to a local movie the-

atre because I wouldn't have been able to sit with the class: Negroes had to sit in the balcony.

One day I was roller-skating near our house when I ran into Sammy Hartley, who had been in my fourth grade class. I'd never met a classmate from my past before, and I was stunned. Sammy's life had gone on, as mine had, and our paths had crossed twice! This changed some heavy thinking I was doing at the time, about being and—shall we say—nothingness. I was trying to decide whether I was Catholic or Mohammedan. Though my parents had been raised in black AME and CME churches, we usually attended nondenominational Protestant services in the base chapel. But after seeing *The Nun's Story* and reading a book about Albert Schweitzer, I imagined that I might someday be called, so I was reading everything I could find about saints. And, after reading an article about him in *Life* magazine, I'd developed a crush on Karim, the Aga Khan (at that time a dashing Harvard undergraduate), so I was also reading everything I could find about Islam. I spent one whole summer believing I was born to unite Christianity and Islam.

In 1958 Mama had another baby, a boy we named Peter Michael, but called Michael. When he was a few months old, the doctors informed us that he had Down's Syndrome. Daddy, who chain-smoked Salems, was flying twenty-four-hour missions for the Strategic Air Command then, and under a great deal of cold war, civil rights, and family stress. One night while flying a mission he had a heart attack. After leaving the hospital, he was grounded, with a large reduction in pay, and transferred to California for retraining.

In the middle of my ninth-grade year we moved back to Sacramento, to Glen Elder, the black neighborhood of tract houses in which we had lived for a short time three years earlier. After several years of financial difficulties caused by his loss of flight pay, Daddy took a medical discharge from the air force and entered civilian life. The family stayed in Sacramento, while he moved from a position as technical writer for a large corporation, then to one as technical editor, then finally to a job teaching English in a junior high school. I went to high school in Sacramento. Having lived for so long in a predominantly white world, I was a social dud in the neighborhood and with the black kids at school. I couldn't dance, I "talked white," I read books for pleasure and enjoyed studying: I was as square as they come.

But my best friend, Marjorie Gibson, was as awkward a black girl as I. Hiram Johnson High had a substantial black student population, though the student body was predominantly white, with a lot of Chicanos and a sprinkling of Asians. We were "tracked" in three levels: most of the white and Asian students took accelerated college-prep classes; some of the whites, some of the Asians, and one or two Chicanos and blacks took the "normal" curriculum; and most of the blacks and Chicanos and a few whites took vocational classes. When I told my high-school counselor that my junior-high-school counselor had told me that I would be put into accelerated classes, he said I must have been mistaken. I was finally accelerated in my senior year, after my father demanded to know why, since I was almost a straight-A student, I hadn't been given more challenging courses.

In my junior year I fell in love. He was a sophomore, an athlete; his name was Walt Slider. During our two years as a couple, Walt excelled in everything he did: he was the star of our varsity basketball team; he played third base on the varsity baseball team; he lettered in football and track, winning several second or third place medals in long jump in state-wide competitions. And he got good grades, he was funny

The author's father (front row, far right) with his crew, about 1954 (Photograph courtesy of Marilyn Nelson.)

and sweet and more than six feet tall and brown-skinned, with sleepy-looking eyes and a faint, downy moustache. Walt and I became one of the "campus couples," his popularity winning me a place in the coveted inner circle of high school society. We had friends in all of the racial groups at school. I was elected homeroom representative to the student council and selected for rally committee. I was yearbook editor, sang in the choir, and marched in the drill team at football and basketball games. I was in several clubs, and was our school's representative to California Girls' State. But Walt was my focus in those years. He taught me a great deal about tenderness. I wore his medal-festooned letter-sweater. We held hands in the hall. Because of him, my high school years were virtually painless. In his senior year Walt was student body president, the first black student the history of the school to be elected to that office. He maintained a B average throughout high school, yet when he graduated in 1965 his counselor suggested he apply only to the local junior college.

Our youngest brother began to have spells during which he stopped breathing and turned blue. My years as a Girl Scout had included a first aid badge, and several times I resuscitated Michael mouth-to-mouth. When he was three years old he contracted pneumonia, was hospitalized, died. People outside the family said it was for the best. Maybe it was. But his presence among us was one of total trust and love.

I was in civics class when we got the news about President Kennedy's assassination. In gym one rainy winter afternoon playing "floor volleyball," I suddenly realized that I was me, here, alive; that the other girls were themselves, alive and here, too; and that the meaning of life is love. It came to me suddenly and powerfully, in midst of the noise. I graduated in 1964 and gave a commencement speech about "Today's Woman." And behind my father's back (he wanted me to go to Sacramento State College and live at home) and with Mama's blessing, I applied to University of California at Davis. To my delight, I was accepted.

At our Lutheran church the summer after graduation, I met Drew Blackwell, a Harvard student, a white Canadian boy in Sacramento on a summer youth project. We began to correspond. During that year I outgrew Walt and dumped him as gently as I could, though we remained close. The following summer, at a national Lutheran youth conference, Drew and I became "engaged to be engaged." Our romance lasted for four years, fed by long letters and expensive phone calls and half-fare standby airline tickets. Drew was the son of a Lutheran pastor and at Harvard on scholarship. He had been a Fabian Socialist since the age of fourteen and planned to go into politics in the Canadian New Democratic Party after finishing his studies. His studies enhanced my own, in which I was flourishing with wide-eyed wonder.

There were only five of us black American students at Davis, in a student body of approximately twelve

Marilyn (right) with her mother, sister, Jennifer, and brother, Mel, New Year's Day, Mexico, 1961 (Photograph courtesy of Marilyn Nelson.)

thousand. We joked that I was "the English department nigger," while others were the "niggers" of their major departments. But I was in my element at Davis, with a social life in some ways more rewarding (and interesting) than I'd had in high school.

Though I loved Drew, I liked lots of other boys: I dated boys from Nigeria, Guinea, India, Australia, and Guatemala, a couple of black American students from Stanford and California Polytechnical Institute, and several white Americans, one an Orthodox Jew. I worked in the library, paying my way through college. Drew and I saw each other at holidays, sometimes in Sacramento and Davis, sometimes in Cambridge or Drew's hometown in Ontario.

We spent the summer of 1965 in Chicago, Drew at the Urban Training Center in an experiential course on poverty (in its "plunge," students were given five dollars and sent out to live for a weekend in Chicago), and I on a YMCA/ YWCA summer project which placed college students with community-development projects. At the orientation for the YMCA/YWCA project, we students were asked to introduce ourselves and our interests. I told my name, and that I liked to read and write poems. The director of the program said sternly, "Baby, you gone have a hard time." Drew and I lived on the west side. Not together. He shared an apartment with a bunch of seminary students; I lived with six students from various colleges and countries in the large home of a black family. The Southern Christian Leadership Conference (SCLC) brought the movement to Chicago that summer in a struggle for equal housing. We did volunteer office work, "tested" real estate agencies, handed out leaflets, and marched. We celebrated the day one of my roommates was asked to clean Dr. King's house. The city erupted with riots that summer, and with the nastiest, most virulent racism I've personally experienced. But, in a bubble of love, I wasn't afraid. Attacks and insults came from all sides. Police cars slowed, sometimes even stopped, when Drew and I walked together. When we marched with SCLC in white neighborhoods, we were spat at and called vile names. I was passing out leaflets on a corner one day, when a group of young black men circled me, jeering and hooting obscenities. Suddenly, a black man in a suit and tie said in a firm voice, "That's my daughter. Now, you leave her alone!" When I turned to thank him, he was gone.

I went back to Davis. Drew spent the year as a Student Nonviolent Coordinating Committee volunteer doing voter registration in Pine Bluff, Arkansas. I marched for equal rights and farm workers and peace, helped to organize the new Black Students' Union (the number of black students at Davis increased with affirmative action), was a fellow-traveler of Students for a Democratic Society, participated in activities sponsored by our activist campus ministry, learned to dance High Life at parties hosted by West African graduate students, and represented Davis as a poet at an all-University of California student artist conference. My sister had joined me at UC-Davis, and in the apartment we shared, with another black girl and one white girl, we held a little ongoing "salon." I'd started writing more seriously, encouraged by a new graduate student, Jack Vernon, who offered a poetry workshop through our student-initiated "experimental college." Jack, who is now a novelist (*Peter Doyle, All for Love*), was my first and best poetry-writing teacher.

My father had another heart attack the day after Christmas. He had taken up acting again and had played Othello at UC-Davis and many roles in the Sacramento State College theatre and various community theatres. His death came the day he returned from a whirlwind drive to Los Angeles, where he had been invited to audition for the National Repertory Theatre. He died after the celebratory party. We never knew whether he would have been invited to join the company, but he thought the audition had gone well. I felt the bottom had fallen out of my world.

I met a boy that year who made me question my commitment to Drew, but nothing happened except with our eyes, so I flew off to Cambridge, Massachusetts, that summer, to work as a secretary at the Massachusetts Institute of Technology, live with Drew, who taught that summer in Upward Bound program. Our Harvard/Radcliffe friends were all English majors; most of us dreamed of being writers. We had lobster feasts in our apartment on Pearl Street and roasted legs of lamb in the fireplace of a friend's room in Adams House, drinking Greek wine, reciting poetry, and talking politics. We went to Red Sox games and to the beach, we took long walks along the Charles. It was a wonderful idyll; every girl should have a summer like that. Drew and I planned live in Vancouver on the Commonwealth fellowship he had won (which would pay for his Ph.D. studies in any country in the British Commonwealth), while we worked toward graduate degrees at the University of British Columbia. He planned after completing his Ph.D. to run for office with the NDP. We also planned names for our children and our Irish setter. But I was somehow numb at the center, and that numbness lasted through the following year.

We graduated in 1968. Drew decided that summer that we should go to Venezuela for two years, with a sort of Lutheran Peace Corps called Prince of Peace Volunteers. He signed us up, then called to tell me. Suddenly a loud voice in my mind said, "Whoa!" I had turned down a graduate fellowship at Davis, planning to take courses at UBC. I turned to my advisor for help and wound up with a tuition fellowship at his alma mater, the University of Pennsylvania. Drew and I drove from California to Pennsylvania, then he left. I called him once from a pay phone in Philadelphia with about twenty-five pounds of quarters. But it was over between us.

In Philadelphia I lived in a one-room apartment in a running-down building in Rittenhouse Square. It was a neighborhood of expensive boutiques and fancy little dogs, and I believe I was the only black person living there. On several occasions, in the real estate office paying my rent, I overheard conversations between an agent and a black person looking for an apartment: the agent always said the only apartments available were in the ghetto. I knew there were vacancies in my building, and I wondered how I had slipped through the net. My apartment was a short walk across the Schuylkill River to the Penn campus. I mourned my father, missed the rest of my family and Drew, and floundered in required courses which seemed absolutely irrelevant to what was going on in the world. John Lyly, for heaven's sake! The only professor I got to know slightly was the poet Daniel Hoffman, with whom I studied modern American poetry. The only student who was in all of my classes was a handsome young German, Erdmann Waniek, who seemed brilliant. We met when we literally bumped into each other on the street, both of us reading and walking at the same time. Thus thrown together we rapidly became friends, then, much more slowly and with trepidation, lovers. He passed his M.A. exam; I failed mine. At the end of the year we decided to let our brief romance become a beautiful memory. He left to work toward a Ph.D. in German at the University of Oregon. I accepted a position as lay associate in campus ministry with the Lutheran church at Cornell University. He telephoned a few weeks later, having decided to risk losing his family and his ability to feel comfortable living in Germany to ask me to marry him.

I spent the summer of 1969 teaching in an Upward Bound program at Franklin and Marshall College, with wonderful black high-school kids. I've often wondered what happened to one of them, Lance Edward Jones. He told me once that he knew he wouldn't be dead when he died, if I remembered him. Then I spent a year in campus ministry at Cornell, as a gadfly in the congregation and an off-campus housemother for the Lutheran student community. I worked with the Reverend Lee Snook, a fine, funny, and wonderfully intelligent man. I had an office on campus, in a big building which housed Cornell United Religious Work (CURW). Father Daniel Berrigan was one of our colleagues there. I counseled would-be drop-outs and pregnant undergraduates, played matchmaker, argued with born-again students, and worked for peace, racial equality, and the environment. I marched on Washington. I drove down to Penn and passed the M.A. exam. I counseled draft-dodgers. One day someone called from New York City, asking how he could avoid the draft. After a long conversation, I suggested he might talk to others in CURW. Two days later he arrived on a bus, a tall, cadaverous young man with a duffle bag, wearing a black, ankle-length coat. He looked exactly like Bartleby, the Scrivener. He wanted me to help him find a job as a librarian in Canada. He was clearly out of his mind. I turned to Lee for help. He said, "You got him here; he's yours." The other ministers and priests at CURW said he was my cross to bear. So I was stuck with him. I persuaded a Lutheran fraternity boy to let him sleep in the frat house, and he arrived at my apartment promptly at 6:00 every morning: he had to eat at 6:00, and he had to eat oatmeal. He had to have a tuna sandwich for lunch, and a large glass of grapefruit juice. I no longer remember what he had to have for dinner. He spent days in my office laboriously hand-writing job application letters to Canadian libraries, offering as professional experience the fact that he had read many library books. He never took off his coat. He never said thank you. I finally bought him a one-way ticket to Toronto and put him on a bus. I figured somebody else could carry that cross for a while.

That year, in a letter responding to a sheaf of poems I had sent him, my great-uncle Rufus asked, "Why is it that young *poets* nowadays don't write poems people like me can understand?" His question shook me then and has stayed with me. Uncle Rufus wasn't exactly a literary man, but he did earn a master's degree in the twenties from Iowa State, and he was, after all, a college president. Why, indeed?

Walt was killed in an automobile accident that year, shortly after his college graduation. A drunk driver hit his car from behind, and he was thrown through the windshield. He left a twenty-two-year-old widow pregnant with their first child.

After another summer at Franklin and Marshall's Upward Bound program, I joined Erdmann in Eugene, Oregon. We married that fall, in the backyard of the beautiful little house we had rented for its view of the Cascade Mountains. Erdmann took graduate courses

Marilyn Nelson and Erdmann Waniak, 1969 (Photograph courtesy of Marilyn Nelson.)

and was a teaching assistant; I taught English at Lane Community College (LCC). We hiked, skied, walked on the beach, and went camping. We had two Irish setters, a fireplace, and homemade plywood furniture. I was appointed to a committee which was preparing a new Lutheran hymnal; periodically over the next few years I was flown to other cities to pore over mountains of hymn texts, looking for racism, sexism, and militarism. The committee edited, retranslated, or rewrote many hymns. There's a small chance that any Lutheran in America may one Sunday sing one of my words. In our second year in Eugene I taught full-time at LCC (four courses each semester) and half-time (two courses) at Reed College, in Portland. Then Erdmann finished his degree and, because he had come to the U.S. on a Fulbright fellowship, had to leave the country. He thought life would be difficult for us in Germany. My dean at LCC wrote to some of his friends at a college in Denmark, and we were hired.

We spent a year teaching German and English at Norre Nissum Seminarium in Jutland. During visits to his home in Germany, I got to know and love Erdmann's family. Our Danish friends were Inge and Bent Pedersen, both of them now writers, and my special friends were Niels Jacob Nielsen and Jan Holtegaard. Niels Jacob and Jan and I took a camping tour of Denmark that summer. We must have been a sight for villagers: Niels Jacob with dark-tinted glasses and a goatee; Jan with a bright red beard; and me. The owner of one campground asked us to play one night; when we asked what she meant, she asked whether we weren't a rock and roll band. *Og jeg kan taler Dansk.* On a driving hiking vacation in Norway with Erdmann's sister and brother-in-law at the end of the year, we walked through a grocery store in a tiny, remote mountain village, discussing in English and German which meats we wanted to buy. When we had decided, I told the butcher in Danish (which is Norwegian with a mouthful of mashed potatoes) what we wanted. He wrapped our packages, gave them to us, and followed us to the cashier. The cashier asked him in Norwegian how he had known what we wanted. The butcher, pointing at me with an expression of absolute wonder, said in Norwegian: "*SHE* speaks Norwegian!"

One of my colleagues on the Lutheran Hymn Text Committee was the head of the English department at St. Olaf College in Minnesota. He wrote that there was an opening and suggested I apply. We said we could only come if there were two positions. There was an opening in German, too. We were interviewed in Copenhagen by Howard and Edna Hong, the translators Kierkegaard. They liked us. We liked them. And who'd be crazy enough to turn down jobs? Vowing to return, we left Denmark in fall of 1972, though the whole country felt like home.

St. Olaf (not St. Olaf's) is a small Lutheran college in the town of Northfield, Minnesota. On its beautiful hilltop stone campus all of the students, except for a handful of black students recruited from northern cities and small towns down south, were blond midwestern Norwegian Americans. I liked my colleagues and my students, and was delighted to have a black friend and colleague in the English department, John Edgar Tidwell. I taught composition, American literature, and black literature, and invented courses in minority literature and Native American literature. My friends, the theologian/philosophers Mary and David Pellauer, lived across the street. I nursed a sourdough starter, made all of our bread and granola, and cooked dinners for my minority literature classes, with smoked salmon and homemade bagels, corn bread and fried chicken, or roast rabbit and succotash. I had given up writing and politics and the church, and led a rather hedonistic life with Erdmann, going to parties, making fancy dinners, camping and hiking and cross-country skiing, attending the theatre, discussing books. I enrolled in graduate courses at the University of Minnesota, eventually taking a leave from St. Olaf to finish course work toward a Ph.D. in English with an emphasis on American minority literature.

I took courses in the English department and in the Afro-American and Latin American studies programs, and studied Native American culture with an anthropologist. One day, arriving at the anthropologist's office for my weekly tutorial, I was told our meeting had to be cancelled: a Sioux singer had stopped by to say hello. My professor introduced me to a tall, white-haired Indian who looked into my eyes for a long moment, then told me to wait: he wanted to sing for me. My professor whispered that this singer was famous nation-wide; that it was a very great personal honor to be invited to be his private audience. I hung around in the hall until they had finished their conversation in Sioux, then the old singer ushered me into the office and closed the door. What followed was strange, magical, and transporting. For the next hour or so, I sat and listened as he introduced each song by its tribal origin, explained what it signified, closed his eyes and sang, shaking a feathered gourd rattle and slowly dancing from one foot to the other. Natachee Momaday, the Pulitzer Prize-winning Kiowa novelist, often writes of times when his grandmother, by telling him ancient stories, opened him the door to the timelessness of the oral

tradition. Momaday calls it being "invited into her presence." I know exactly what he means.

Erdmann and I traveled a lot, usually to spend holidays with our families in California and Germany. One summer, having heard from friends who had camped out there, we visited Churchill, a town on the southern shore of Hudson's Bay. The trip required a day of driving to the end of the highway, then a long train ride across the flat summer tundra. We arrived in Churchill in the afternoon, got off the train with our camping gear, and walked into town. Several townspeople asked whether we seriously intended to camp out *now.* It was polar bear migration season; one person after another told us polar bear stories; the size of a paw print; the time a bear ripped out the side of a panel truck to get at the dressed goose inside. We walked around for a couple of hours in a constant swarm of biting gnats. We visited a museum of Inuit art. Then we got on the train again and went home. But we did see a distant pod of Beluga whales and a sky ablaze with the northern lights.

One year we flew to Venezuela to visit my former fiancé, Drew, and his wife and child. Drew was teaching in Caracas, at an experimental national university based on the teachings of Paulo Freire. His family and friends called him Andres. We spent several days in Caracas, then flew off to explore the rest of the country. Luckily, I'd studied Spanish in high school and college. Everywhere we went, brown and black men surrounded me to ask where I was from, or called *"Ay, negrita!"* admiringly from busses and cars. And they called Erdmann *gringo,* and threw bottles and stones at his side of our little rented car. I've often thought since that visit that I'd like someday to teach in Venezuela, at the University of the Andes in Merida. We drove there, passing almost vertical fields divided by stone walls, here and there a farmer leading a laden ox. At every place we stopped, children with runny noses and cheeks red with cold, barefoot and wearing rough woven ponchos, ran up to the car, crying, *"Señor Nosotros somos pobres! Danos algo!"*—"We are poor! Give us something." White children. Blond, with blue eyes. In Merida we happened, completely by chance, into an international festival of New Song, where for the first time I heard Inti-Illimani sing the rousing and tender melody of Latin American liberation: *"El pueblo unido jamas sera vencido!"*—"The people united will never be conquered!" It is as memorable and heartwarming an anthem as "We Shall Overcome." We visited a village settled more than one hundred years ago by German immigrants, where an archaic Black Forest dialect is still spoken. We flew with "Jungle Rudy" (whose age and German accent—not to mention the dueling scar on his cheek—made us wonder whether someone in Israel might be looking for him) over Angel Falls. We spent a week on the island of Margarita, watching pelicans snatch fish from the fishermen's nets, eating fish fried so fresh they retained their tropical colors, and lying in hammocks and waving the oysterman over to pull an oyster out of his bucket, open it with his knife, take a lemon from his pocket, slice it, squeeze the juice over the oyster, and sell it to us for a coin. I spent the first part of the week lying in a hammock and drinking down tart, sweet oysters. I spent the last part of the week in the necessary room.

In my last year of course work at the University of Minnesota, I gave myself a gift: though I hadn't tried to write a poem in several years, I enrolled in a graduate poetry workshop taught by Michael Dennis Browne. David Wojahn, who was also in the workshop, became a good friend; as a lark we invented a Danish poet and his biography, and David wrote fake "translations" of several of his poems, which I translated into clumsy Danish. We planned to send them to a major poetry journal, but as I remember we chickened out. Later we enrolled in a workshop offered privately by Etheridge Knight, which promised occasional visits by Etheridge's friend, Robert Bly. Under Etheridge's tutelage we sweated over drafts of our poems and regularly presented unannounced group readings at sites he picked: restaurants, bars. Bly came to a few of our readings; an approving grunt from him was a special sign of honor. One evening we were reading in a bar when a drunk held out a piece of paper and asked the poet at the microphone to read it aloud. It was a letter from his wife on the reservation, asking him to come home, saying the children missed him, promising they could make their marriage work. Our poems seemed suddenly very trivial.

Erdmann and I taught one semester in Germany at the University of Hamburg. We became friends with two other couples mixed racially and nationally like ourselves, who seemed to be perfectly content living in Germany. But when I walked alone in the city, North African "guest-workers" ran up to me to tell me that they knew, after living for some time in Germany, what it was like to be an American Negro. Germans look you up and down, and then stare right into your eyes. I know it's a cultural, rather than a personal characteristic, but it made me feel as I'd felt marching through pristine white neighborhoods in Chicago. I was several times discussing a product with a shop clerk who addressed me politely as *"Sie,"* when a Turkish guest-worker entered the shop and she turned and addressed him contemptuously as *"du."* All of the university students in Germany went on a long strike a couple of weeks into the semester, so I spent much of that period working on my dissertation and writing poems. I read *Leaves of Grass* that spring and walked in the park along the Alster River charged with Whitman's magnificence. We went to the opera. I love Mozart's operas. I became friends with Ralf Thenior, a young German poet. I saw a rainbow which straddled the Alster one foot on each bank.

We went to Innsbruck, Austria, during that spring, to visit my friend, Michael Ihlenfeldt, whom I had met at Cornell. Michael loaned us his Volkwagon for a trip through Umbria, the northe part of Italy. We picked up a young American hitchhiker on the way, near Garmisch Partenkirchen, high in the Alps. When he was settled in the backseat, we asked him where he was headed. He said he thought he'd go to a city Erdmann knew to be far distant. Erdmann him he'd have to get out of the Alps first. My countryman responded flatly, "Oh. Are these Alps?" In Italy—Ah, Italy!—we visited cathedrals and museums and castles and art and art and art (My now-husband, Roger, calls such trips "the grim march through culture"). But on the other hand, Italian men called *"Ciao, bella!"* when passed and threw me kisses. In the first part of the trip we ate pasta in workers' restaurants we'd found in *Europe on Ten Dollars a Day.* We ran out of money early in the trip, so for the rest of the time we traveled high on the hog, eating truffle-laced sauces in fancy restaurants that took American credit cards. I can close my eyes and see the morning landscapes dotted with sunlit hilltop villages sticking up over thickly misted vineyards. The Umbrian light seemed, somehow, different from any other light I've ever seen. I walked in that light in Assisi, it seemed no wonder, I thought, there are so many Italian saints.

My commitment to writing grew steadily; poems came to me with a frequency that frightened me. I saw that the muse can be a terrible task-master. When we returned to Minnesota, I lived part-time in Minneapolis with my friend, Pamela Espeland, with whom I later translated several poems for children written by the Danish poet, Halfdan Rasmussen (published as a chapbook called *Hundreds of Hens, and Other Poems for Children*), and still later wrote a book of verse called *The Cat Walked through the Casserole, and Other Poems for Children.* My time was given to writing my dissertation, going to readings, and finding my voice. I gave my first big reading in Minneapolis with Mary Karr, to a surprisingly large and appreciative audience. I sent some of my poems to Daniel Hoffman, who had been my professor at Penn, and Dan suggested I send him a manuscript, which he would submit to a publisher.

When Erdmann came up for tenure at St. Olaf, it was denied—more, we believed, because of the years-long feud he'd had with the head his department (who once told me at a dinner at our house that it was too bad it had been made illegal to ask a candidate's race, but that he'd compensated by deciding that if a candidate's letter was ungrammatical, the candidate must black) than because of his work. We decided to seek other positions. I felt freed. I was struggling accept the new identity which had come with a serious commitment to poetry, and our marriage was too small to hold my emerging wings. Erdmann went one direction; I went another. Though we've both looked back, that decision was for the best.

I've been at the University of Connecticut since 1978. By the end of my first year here, I had finished my dissertation, gotten my Ph.D., had a book published, and decided to marry one of my colleagues. Milton scholars know my husband, Roger Wilkenfeld, for some essays he published when he was in his twenties. He can recite much of "Paradise Lost" by heart, and does so at most opportunities. He's a sports fan, an old-movie buff, a collector of beautiful objects, a voracious reader, and an excellent poetry critic. He has an aggravatingly intractable opinion about any topic you name. Like most men, he's impossible. He may, as a matter of fact, be more impossible than most. Our son Jacob was born in 1980; our daughter Dora in 1986. Lest this essay dissolve into a bath of motherly anecdotes, I'll change its direction now and talk about my work.

For the Body was published in 1978. Daniel Hoffman, who submitted its manuscript for me to LSU Press, was its godfather. The first poem after its "Dedication" was the last one I worked on as a grad student at Penn; Dan had seen the earlier draft and written to me with suggestions. I finished it five years later and felt it might be good enough to send to him. I was, frankly, surprised that he remembered me. I'd been as colossally undistinguished a student in his class as in my other classes at Penn: I'd spent much of my time wondering where my next meal would be coming from (my fellowship paid only for tuition), and then falling in love. My book is clearly autobiographical, and anyone long-suffering enough to have read thus far will recognize people and places if she or he has read that book. My former father-in-law, who served briefly in the German cavalry toward the end of World War II, is the old soldier in "War-horses." "April Rape" started not with a rape, but with the whistles and catcalls I provoked when I walked across the bridge to Penn. At that point they raised my feminist hackles; later I came to accept them with pleasure. I think now I'd be flattered to death. The "Mary" of several poems is Mary Pellauer, my theologian friend in Northfield. I wrote "Emily Dickinson's Defunct" after she told me she'd like to make theology out of women's poetry and asked me where I thought she should start. When I suggested Emily Dickinson, Mary said she'd always been intimidated by Emily Dickinson. I found very funny the idea that the reclusive maid of Amherst could intimidate anyone, and wrote a poem about her in which all of her intimidating features are true. "Wanda S." was my roommate, Wanda Smith, at UC-Davis in 1965. We shared an apartment in a trailer park and mailed each other long letters, although we saw each other every day. She recently moved back to the U.S. after living for a while in Chile. The young women in "Silver Earrings" and "For Karen" were St. Olaf students. I wrote "The Life of a Saint" after seeing Giotto's frescoes of the life of St. Francis in the cathedral of Assisi. "The Perfect Couple" is one of several poems I wrote during the time I first began to wrestle with the muse; it's about finally accepting that sense of being possessed. Several of the poems started with reading I was doing for my courses in Native American culture, immigration history, and speech-act theory. I wrote "Fish Poem" after a friend asked me whether I'd noticed that several of my poems contained fish and told me fish are a phallic symbol. My friend Pamela gave me a jade fish on a gold chain to remind

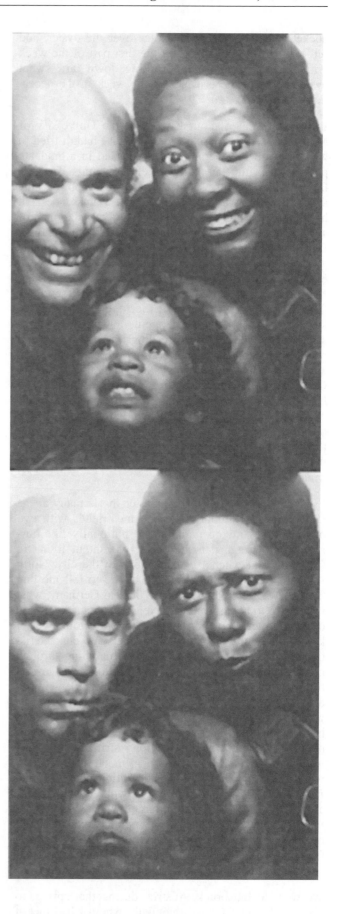

Posing in a photo booth with Roger Wilkenfeld and their son, Jacob, 1982 (Photograph courtesy of Marilyn Nelson.)

me that my fish was a muse. "Dedication" and "The Source of the Singing" are intended to mirror each other, and to claim the body (not just the mind) as the source of consciousness and creativity.

Like most first-book poets, I fully expected my first book to catapult me to the stars. What it did instead was make me want to be a better writer.

I hoped *Mama's Promises* would be read as a book of black feminist theology. I wanted to proclaim a "Mama" God, a black working-mother God, whose stress might be greater than my own (I came up for tenure when Jacob was a nine-month-old toddler), and who might be too wrung-out (as I was every night) to answer our prayers. I had originally wanted to call Her "Mammy," remembering an offensive joke I heard a comedian tell years ago on the Johnny Carson show: an astronaut came back from orbit with good news and bad news— the good news was that he'd seen God; the bad news was that "She's black!" Unfortunately, my own life dominates the book. Our house had a very strange layout; my desk was right beside Jacob's crib. Though my self-correcting electric typewriter (God, I loved that machine!) was quiet, Jacob was a very light sleeper. We experimented, and found that just our talking about him in low voices two or three rooms or even a floor away woke him from his version of a sound sleep. Until we partitioned the space and enclosed my desk in a tiny, cork-lined cubicle study, I could only write when he was in day-care or with a babysitter, and even with the study I had to spend most of my not-mommying time preparing classes and grading papers. I wrote most of the poems in this book by getting up before dawn and writing for the hour or two before Jacob woke. It's good to hear the birds begin their day's business, and to watch the sun rise.

The titles of the first few poems in this book were written by Amanda Jordan, who was eight years old when we met in the public library, reaching for the same book. We discovered we were both writers; I wrote poems, and Mandy wrote titles of poems she planned to write someday. She had several notebooks full of titles; she agreed to give me some of them, and I agreed to write poems for them. For several months we had regular "writers' lunches." I have a book of poems she wrote and stapled together in a little illustrated book to give me for Christmas. The porcelain fawn in the title poem was a birthday present my friend Kim bought for me in seventh grade: just as she handed it to me, it fell and shattered; Kim was mortified. There are several dragons in this book, in my mind modeled after the dragons of Anne McCaffrey's "Pern" science fiction novels. Between 1978 and 1980 I had worked unsuccessfully on a blank-verse adaptation of Rilke's first and second "Duino Elegies," turning them into dialogues between myself and a dragon-muse. My "Dragon Dialogues" never got off the ground, but McCaffrey's fierce and benevolent flying dragons stayed with me. Roger and

Pamela and Jennifer gave me dragons to wear while I was working on the book. The dragon-muse in "Levitation with Baby" flies off with my next-door neighbor, Bob Burkinshaw, who's always out working in his yard. Bob likes this poem a lot.

"It's All in Your Head" is dedicated to Deborah Muirhead, who teaches art here at the University of Connecticut. Deborah's abstract paintings explore her roots in the black South; her genealogical research inspired my own. Readers of this essay will recognize most of the names poem. Zilphia was the daughter of one of my grandmother's sisters; I love her name. Jamie Crowl who is mentioned in "Mama's Murders," was from one of the southern families stationed at Kittery Yard when I was in sixth grade. At recess one day we were throwing her end of the seesaw so that it banged against the blacktop; she realized we were trying to hurt her and tried to get off. Her arm was caught under the seat. It was an accident, but accidentally on purpose.

"I Dream the Book of Jonah" antedates the other poems in the book. I began working on it in 1977 when Pamela, who works as a freelance editor, edited a book about the Bible, and called me in Northfield to say she found Jonah very funny. She suggested I tell his story. The poem grew very slowly, as I discovered a voice for Jonah, moving from a Standard English voice through several levels of folksy colloquial ones before finally arriving at a Jonah I could see clearly. He looks like the great blues artist, Mississippi John Hurt. At that point I thought the poem was finished. But Mary Pellauer said it couldn't be finished unless I included a Blues. I wrote the last draft of the poem while visiting Pamela in Minneapolis. I was looking for a way to end the poem. Pamela and I discussed at length what I had in mind and mused over it together for several days. One morning she came out of the bathroom, her toothbrush out of her mouth, and said the last seven lines of my poem. *Our* poem. Pamela's son, by the way, is named Jonah.

I dreamed a phrase early in the writing this book: "Rhymed free-verse" (I also dreamed the phrase "Iago powder"), so I worked very hard making several poems rhyme. I hid the rhymes by making them slant-rhymes; they are so slant that even I can only find two or three of them now. There's not much else to say about the book except that the cover is a portrait of me, drawn by Jacob. Note the big earrings.

Like many second-book poets, I began to realize that maybe it was time for me to learn something about poetry. I began to study traditional prosody. I had long admired the work of Marilyn Hacker, and I followed with mild interest passionate debates in literary journals about the so-called "new formalism." I began to include Paul Fussell's *Poetic Meter and Poetic Form* as a text my graduate workshops, and to experiment with fixed forms in my own work. For about a year I was busy writing a sequence of fifty therapeutic sonnets about my first marriage, modeled after George Meredith's *Mod-*

ern Love, and not intended for publication. A couple of years after they were finished, I showed some of them to my friend Margaret Gibson, who asked me if she could include them in an issue of the *New Virginia Review,* which she was guest-editing. I hesitated, but finally agreed to publish them under a pseudonym. To my astonishment and chagrin, they won a Pushcart prize and were reprinted, still under a pseudonym, in the *Pushcart Prize Anthology.* In 1992 Emily Strayer of the Kutenai Press offered to publish a chapbook for me. I had no work at the time to give her, except the sonnets. She published fourteen of them, with two illustrations by Eric Spencer. The book, *Partial Truth,* is designed by Emily and printed with handset Californian type on Japanese Wahon paper and sewn with linen into covers of Duchene Mouchette from the Moulin du Pombie in France and endsheets of banana paper, handmade in the Philippines. The edition is limited to two hundred numbered copies signed by Eric and myself. It's a beautiful book; it even smells good. The rest of my sonnets are gathering dust.

There's not much to say about *The Homeplace* that hasn't been said earlier in this essay. The book is a family history. For several years my mother had been slowly disappearing into the fog of Alzheimer's disease; the last time I came home from visiting her in California, my husband said he thought I should go to my grandmother's hometown. I don't know what made him suggest that: I don't think I'd talked of Hickman often. But I made airplane reservations the day after I got back to Connecticut, and wound up flying to Kentucky on that reservation only a few days after coming home from my mother's funeral in Sacramento. (Entering the cemetery, the cortege passed four young white men in an open convertible. Jennifer, Mel, and I rode in the funeral parlor limousine. My eyes met those of the driver of the convertible as we passed it, and he yelled, "Good! Another dead nigger!") I spent several days in Hickman with my second cousin, Annisue Briggs, sleeping in "the homeplace" that's been in the family since 1862, and prowling through records in the county courthouse. I planned to write a book in Mama's memory, just for the family, but gradually, as far-flung relatives and local historians, black and white, eagerly gave me anecdotes and information, the book "jest growed." The first part of the book, poems about my mother's family, was much influenced by my earlier work with fixed forms.

Since I know so little about my father's family, I decided to include a section about his second family, the Tuskegee Airmen. Some of the stories I tell about them were given to me by my uncle, Rufus Mitchell, who was a member of the ground crew of the Tuskegee Airmen, or by Edward Woodward, an old family Air Force friend. Ed Woodward and my father were among the men who were almost court-martialed after the incident at Freeman Field, when black officers refused the order to use the NCO Club instead of the Officers' Club. Most of the stories came from my fortuitously meeting Bert

Wilson, a black retired lieutenant colonel, formerly a pilot in the famed ninety-ninth Squadron, who lives not far from me in Connecticut. Over lunch one day Bert told me his World War II experiences; the best line in the book ("I was sleeping on his breath") quotes him directly. I did not tape record these men's stories, but I did try in the poems to capture their voices as authentically as I could.

The photograph of Tuskegee cadets, which introduces the last section of the book, came to me in such an odd way that I wrote a poem about it ("The True Magic" in *Magnificat*). But I'll tell the story again here. I had given up on finding a photograph of my father as a cadet, and settled for a photograph of three cadets I did not recognize. A few days before the manuscript was due to arrive at the press, one of my cousins, Roy Mitchell, telephoned from Ohio. He had recently joined the fraternal organization known as "The Tuskegee Airmen" and attended his first meeting. Since in order to become a member one must be related to one of the original Tuskegee Airmen, the man sitting next to Roy asked what his relationship was to the original group, and Roy told him my father's name. The man, Bob Hunter, had brought to the meeting a large black-and-white photograph of a group of cadets; he said, "Well, I guess this is for you." The photograph shows Bob Hunter second in line in a group of cadets getting ready to climb into a plane. My father is first in line, in the center of the picture, looking directly into the camera. On the phone Roy said, "Marilyn, there's no question about it: there's something divine in this."

The Homeplace was a finalist for the 1991 National Book Award, and it won the Annisfield-Wolf Award in 1992. I've been amazed by the warmth with which readers of all racial grounds have received the stories of my family, which I'd thought of as private and personal, as if my family were theirs.

Like *The Homeplace, Magnificat* is a narrative made up of individual poems. When I confessed, before sending it in to the press, that I was uncomfortable about the possibility that it might inadvertently reveal the identity and location of the monk/priest it presents, my friend, the poet Theodore Deppe, assured me there was nothing to worry about: nobody would believe the story anyway. And it is, I think, an extraordinary story. At the end of fall semester in 1989, as I commented on a story written by a student in my undergraduate creative course, I suddenly remembered the boy for whom I would have broken off my engagement when we were undergraduates. I couldn't get of my mind. At last I told my husband about him. I'd never told anyone the entire story, or confronted it inwardly for more than a minute or two. When we were introduced at a party, I had offered my hand for him to shake, and he had lifted it and kissed it, looking into my eyes and saying, again and again, that he would never cease loving me. I remember thinking, "Is he the one?" I looked around us, asking if someone could tell me his name. He never took his eyes off of me, never stopped murmuring his promise. At last I took a long look into his brown eyes, and, wishing it possible to see in someone's eyes whether was serious or not, I promised to love him forever. He smiled at that and turned away. Then friends surrounded him and took him home. I looked back once, and we exchanged a shy, wondering smile. Though we later became friends, we never mentioned that momentous meeting. He told me at another party that he had a strong feeling that we would someday write some books of poems together. My flirting, flippant response was to laugh and say maybe they would be pornagraphic. I don't think we ever had another serious conversation, though we did have one disastrous date. I've told the story in the first poem in *Magnificat* of how and why he ran away. When I told Roger about him, I hadn't seen him in twenty years, though I had heard that he had entered a Benedictine monastery some ten years later.

Roger said we had to find him. Our search lasted for almost a year, during which I pored over books about the monastic life and contemplative prayer and Catholic theology and spiritual poverty and desert spirituality and Divine Union. Roger trusted my memory of this man to be accurate enough to ensure that our finding him would bring joy to all of us. When we found him, he wrote to us that he had finished a doctorate at Cambridge University, worked for seven years, then felt the call. After seven years in a monastery he had left, with the blessings his Father Abbot, to live as a hermit and build a new monastery.

My list of acknowledgments for the book includes medievalists, Catholic and Episcopal priests, Protestant ministers, monks, and nuns. The monks are the brothers of the Weston Priory, a small Benedictine community in Vermont. When I went to priory to find out something about contemporary Benedictinism, the brothers welcomed me like a long-lost sister. The nuns I thank are the Guadalupans, a Mexican Benedictine community, the "sister community" of the Weston Priory, with whom I participated in a two-week long "hospitality experience" in which *gringos* are invited to receive the hospitality of the poor, and which deepened my understanding of poverty and of the radical interior changes demanded by Christ's proclamantion of liberation. The Weston monks (R.R. 50, Weston, Vermont, 05161) organize several such "experiences" each year, for groups of ten or fifteen people. The several priests to whom I turned for advice assured me that I was not doing wrong in trying to find my friend again. One told me that "You're probably perfectly matched: a mystic and a poet. To the rest of the world, you're *both* nuts!" These new connections have very much altered my life: I once overheard Dora telling a playmate that "my mom is a monk."

I meant *Magnificat* to reflect spiritual struggle and growth. The longest poem in the book, "Letter to a Benedictine Monk," tells of the beginning of humility and renunciation. I wanted to write an ode, but couldn't find a clear enough definition, so I "deconstructed" Wordsworth's "Immortality" ode, patterning my lines and rhyme scheme after his. The sequence of prayers which follows is intended to demonstrate a development from humor to seriousness, from selfish requests and gratitude for personal blessings to awe at the mysteries of time and death, and finally to compassion. The title of "The Dream's Wisdom" was left over from Mandy Jordan's notebooks. And, after, in "Gloria," I receive the first answering letter from my friend (in real life, he sent a telegram), my prayers open to profound and thankful silence.

Most of the anecdotes of the book's second section, "A Desert Father," are things that happened, more or less, the first time I visited my friend's hermitage. "A Canticle for Abba Jacob" is modeled on "The Canticle of the Soul" by St. John of the Cross. I don't think there's much else to say here about this section of the book, except that when I showed one priest a photograph of my friend, he said, "Oh! He's not a nerd-monk; he's a matinee-idol monk!" And that I hope it's read, if it's read at all, less as an impossible love story than as an invitation to understand those who choose solitude and renunciation in order to be witnesses to love, and to offer unceasing prayer.

My poem, "Payday Evening at My Desk," in the book's third section, remembers Mariano Serano Cirilo, an eight-year-old boy I met with the Guadalupan sisters in a Cuernavaca slum. I had asked Jacob, who was then also eight years old, whether he wanted me to bring him something special from Mexico; he had written his name on a slip of paper, asked me to give it to a Mexican kid, and said he'd like me to bring him back the Mexican kid's name. I gave it to Mariano, who took it solemnly, then wrote his own name for Jacob. His grandmother was so pleased by our visit that she insisted we accept the rolls a baker had given her when the market closed earlier that day. They were the only food in her bare, clean, one-room house. This is the hospitality of the poor.

"The Sacrament of Poverty" and "Valentine for a Bride Bereaved" were written for Judy Maines-LaMarre, who is one of the "Ladymonks," my friends who committed several years ago to work together toward self-understanding and spiritual growth. Judy, a widow, had been married to her second husband for only one month when he died suddenly, while away at a-conference, of a heart attack. Judy is a nurse and has given herself to working with families of critically ill babies; every year since I've known her, she has spent her vacations holding Haitian babies who are dying of AIDS, or assisting in portable eye-clinics in Honduras, or inoculating children in remote villages in Papua New Guinea.

For three years I offered a poem-to-order at the annual fund-raising auction of the Congregational church. One year bidding for my poem was fast and furious; it was finally sold for, I think, 73 dollars. A few months after the auction I asked one of the women who had bought it whether they didn't want me to write their poem. They told me they were lesbians; they had found a minister willing to marry them in the church; they wanted me to write a poem to be used in their wedding. When I told Roger of their request, he said, "Boy, this one has to be *good!*" Linda and Debbie and the minister (also a woman) and I met one evening to discuss the service, which they were writing themselves. They wanted the poem to include the idea that lovers are loaned to each other by God, and that, in love, one solitude embraces another. Judy told me over lunch one day, as I was struggling with the poem, that we take such a risk in loving that it's like walking out on a tightrope into the unknown. Another of my "Lady-monks" friends, Kathy Jambeck, who is a medievalist, told me that St. Bernard once wrote something about religious people and lovers being "holy fools." The fools' song in the poem is an echo of an ecstatic poem by Rumi, whom I was reading avidly at the time. Linda and Debbie have a houseful of cats and dogs—Linda works as a dog-catcher—so I put cats and dogs into their poem. I read it—"Epithalamium and Shivaree"—at their wedding, which was very beautiful. Linda's father, who had for years refused to acknowledge their love, and who had told Linda that he would not attend her so-called wedding, gave her away with tears in his eyes.

I must confess here that I did not read Plotinus. But Roger did and copied on slips of paper passages he thought to be crucial or beautiful. Each of the poems of "The Plotinus Suite" started with the italicized passage from Plotinus; the poems grew around the quotes.

My life has been full of blessings. As Mama would have said, "Knock on wood." I don't think I'm a good teacher, but I have tenure. I've spent semesters teaching in M.F.A. programs at the Vermont College, the University of Cincinnati, and NYU. I've studied briefly with Seamus Heaney. I've had writing time purchased for me by the National Endowment for the Arts. Since finishing *Magnificat* I've spent another two weeks in Mexico with the Guadalupan sisters and Mexican poor, traveled in Zimbabwe (where I spent several days in Harare with an independent community of African nuns and visited the ruins of Great Zimbabwe and Victoria Falls), and lived with my family in the south of France, on a Fulbright teaching fellowship. I am nourished by family and friends, both old and new. Last week I legally changed my name back to Marilyn Nelson and spent 176 dollars on three little jars of creams which promise to make my face twenty younger. I'm sitting in front of my computer right now, at five minutes to midnight, on Sunday 10, 1995. Roger and Jacob and Dora (and Sydney, our dog) are asleep upstairs. I'll spend tomorrow running errands and preparing for Tuesday's classes. Our lakeside house is small, but there's only one small leak in the roof, and it hasn't rained here for thirty-seven days. This afternoon Dora and our neighbors' boys put on a show for us—"The Harley Davison Show," their placard read—of look, Mom, no-hands bicycle riding (one of the showpeople had training

wheels). Our dogs tussled and growled ar our legs; the sky was a deep and cloudless blue.

Meanwhile, people are dying of age and illness, and killing each other and themselves, starving, and devising new ways to humiliate and degrade each other, and making love and giving birth and being lonely and closing their eyes and wishing, all over the planet. The first time I sat in the little oratory of Abba Jacob's hermitage on my low stool to the left of the door, while he sat on his on the right side, his head bowed, his eyes closed, his hands still and relaxed in lap, I listened to the wind in the cane and knew that we are the only way God's light can enter this darkness. I hope my poems are windows. So many people have been windows for me.

Marilyn Nelson contributed the following update to *SATA* in 2007:

So much has changed between the point at which my original essay stopped—September 10, 1995—and the present, that I might as well be living a different life. In April, 1996, I was fifty years old. That year I gave myself myself as a birthday present. I dropped the last name I had been carrying since my first marriage, though my first husband and I had been divorced for years, and took my birth name again. My impossible second husband and I agreed to an amicable divorce.

David Slavitt, the general editor of the Penn Greek Drama series, for which several American poets were commissioned to retranslate the great classics, asked me to translate Euripides' "Hecuba." David's request came late in the summer of 1996, just before I was to teach a graduate seminar on African-American women's slave narratives, and there was a tight deadline. Having never studied Greek or read "Hecuba," I went to the library and checked out every English translation of the play. And during the course of the fall semester I worked through the play speech by speech, with the six or seven translations before me, careful not to use any phrasing that had been used by any of the earlier translators, trying to figure out from differing translations what Euripides was saying. At the same time, I was reading slave narratives with my graduate students. I spent the entire semester weeping, reading of Hecuba's descent from the throne of Troy into slavery, and of African-American women in the throes of slavery. I made this translation as homage to Euripides, filled with deepening respect for his genius. The first production of the play, performed in 1998 by the African Continuum Theatre Company of Washington, DC, was directed by my sister, Jennifer Nelson, who was for many years the artistic director of that company. I happened to see the play on an evening when the actors were terrified because the toughest theatre critic for one of the city's newspapers had arrived unannounced. He was pointed out to me just before the play began. It was a theatre in the round, and by pure chance, I was seated directly across the stage from the critic, so I was able to watch him wiping his eyes throughout the play. He gave it a rave review, and selected it at the end of the year as one of the best productions of the year in the city. Another newspaper, however, sent a third-string reviewer who, under the

Son, Jacob, and daughter, Dora, 1989 (Photograph courtesy of Marilyn Nelson.)

impression that he was seeing a *different* Euripides play ("The Trojan Women") slammed the translator, director, and actors for changing the plot! The only review I've seen of the *Euripides I* volume in which the play appears was published in the *New York Times Book Review.* The reviewer, Daniel Mendelsohn, a classics professor at Princeton, dismissed the play in three sentences, referring to—and misunderstanding—something I had said in the translator's introduction to the play. His review gave no indication that he had bothered to read the play itself.

It seemed time to publish a "new and selected." My friend Pamela Espeland sorted through every poem I

had ever written and put together a volume for me. *The Fields of Praise* was published in 1997. The new poems in this collection are "Thus Far by Faith," a crown of sonnets written during a visit to the hermitage of my dear friend Abba Jacob; several new Abba Jacob poems based on conversations I had with my friend during my visits in 1990 and 1993; and a sequence of poems about radical evil. Writing the Abba Jacob poems gave me the courage to write the others. Since I included notes to the poems in that book, I shall not discuss the poems here.

As it happened, *Fields* was a finalist for the 1997 National Book Award. At the gala I ran into Stephen

Roxburgh, whom I had known years earlier as the children's book editor at a large publishing firm. I had tried then to write something he would publish, but he hadn't liked anything I wrote. Now, in our brief conversation at the National Book Award gala, he told me that he had started his own publishing house, Front Street Books, that one of the books he had published was a finalist for Young People's Literature, and that we should make a book together. In the next several months I sent him everything I had written for children those years ago. He still didn't like any of it.

Having learned from my struggle with those poems about evil in *Fields,* that there is apparently no limit to our human capacity for evil, I decided to explore the opposite question: whether there is a limit to our capacity for good. I thought I'd try to write a saint's life. For some reason I no longer remember, I decided to write about Hildegard von Bingen (1098–1179). I got a research grant, went to Germany, visited every site related to that remarkable woman. I was back home, sitting at my desk in the house I had rented, preparing to sort through my notes and books and CDs, when the telephone rang. It was Al Price, Jr., a pilot friend of my late father, whom I had not heard from or of since I was twelve. He said he was in the area, had heard I was there, and would like to stop by to say hello. He came, drank a glass of lemonade, then said he had to go. I walked him to his car. He opened his trunk, gave me a copy of Emerson's essay "On Self-Reliance," which he carried around in case he wanted to give it to someone, and then he gave me a brochure. "I visited this George Washington Carver museum a few days ago," he said, handing me the brochure. "You should go there. I think you should write a book about George Washington Carver."

I took the brochure inside, looked through it, remembered how much I had loved Carver when I was a child. For many years I had wanted to be a scientist because of Carver. And, no question: Carver *was* a saint. The Real Thing. I set Hildegard aside and started reading about Carver. That decision was something of a turning point. I spent the next few years doing serious research and slowly writing a book about Carver.

In 1997, with the help of several friends, I was able to buy a house. I learned a great deal from the process. In Connecticut, where I live, it is not possible to use money loaned by friends as a down payment: one can only use financial *gifts,* which must come from relatives. And apparently the state looks into one's bank accounts, and those of one's closest relatives, for several months before the house buying, to make sure no large amounts have been deposited. I argued with my mortgage broker that this is a racist policy: though it is quite likely in *some* families that relatives might be able to give one a largish amount of money, in most African American families that I know, including my own (and my family is quite well-off, considering; my siblings are starving artists, and my first cousins are upstanding citizens),

rarely is there a relative well-off enough to *give* one thousands of dollars. We went back and forth, around and around; finally the broker suggested a way we might launder my friends' gifts so they could come to me as gifts via several members of my family . . . I suppose he broke the law. And it was a great kindness. By taking on some extra readings I was able to repay my friends within a year. The house was on Candide Lane. Shortly after we moved in, I found, while walking the dog (still Sydney, our Dalmatian; neurotic as all getout) I discovered a flourishing clover plant on which about one-fifth of all the leaves had four lobes. There were worries, financial and familial, but gradually life stopped wobbling, and it really did feel like Jacob, Dora, and I were living in "the best of all possible worlds."

I should mention here the writing programs in which I worked for several years: at the William Joiner Center at UMass Boston, at West Chester University in Pennsylvania, and at the Vermont Studio Center. Each of these played its part in my growth as a poet: the Joiner Center by demonstrating an unwavering commitment to a literature of peace and social justice; West Chester by encouraging my slow move toward coming out of the closet as a formalist; and VSC for giving me writing time in a beautiful space, and modeling for me what an intentional community of artists might look like.

I loved the house on Candide Lane. It was almost perfect for us. And I enjoyed modifying it to our needs over the next few years. In my study, which looked out over the woods of the backyard, I enjoyed a thriving virtual social life, getting to know a fascinating, pleasant, and humorous community of friends who subscribed to an online discussion of the poetry of Emily Dickinson, called Emweb. Somebody ought to print excerpts of our discussions; it would make a wonderful Dickinson book, and I'll bet it would make some significant contributions to Dickinson scholarship. Several members of the community are highly respected scholars in the field. It's archived online. Man, I miss Emweb. I learned so much from those folks. It lasted for several years, and finally fell apart when it was invaded by a nasty s.o.b. who flamed everything everybody wrote. Grrrr! Emweb's online archives are full of information, insight, and good humor.

In 1999 I was invited to be the writer-in-residence at Vanderbilt University just as my son Jake graduated from high school. For teaching one workshop for one semester, the position paid something like fifteen thousand dollars more than I was currently paid for a semester of two courses. It looked like first-year tuition at Jake's first choice, an expensive private university, was in the bag. The dean at Vanderbilt explained that Vanderbilt would pay my salary and the cost of my benefits to my home institution, and I could retain all of my benefits as usual and receive one semester of increased pay. Wonderful! So I said yes, thinking I could fly to Nashville for a couple of days a week without changing joint custody of my daughter. However, just before the semester began, my home institution refused to allow me to receive the increased salary. I could accept the job and keep my benefits, but my home institution would absorb the extra fifteen thousand dollars as a sort of payment for allowing Vanderbilt to use my services. I could receive only my regular salary, and not a penny more. By the time it was clear there would be absolutely no way around this deadlock, I was already well into the semester of commuting to teach a really wonderful group of young poets. It was too late for me to back out. The very nice dean at Vanderbilt told me, after weeks of wrangling, that my home institution was the most difficult institution he had ever dealt with in his twenty-odd years of administering this honorary poet-in-residence position. Because of the weekly commute by air, the honorary semester of being poet-in-residence at Vanderbilt cost me several thousand dollars instead of helping me financially. By the time my home institution had figured out a way for me to do summer busywork to earn the Vanderbilt money, Jake had fallen ill and moved back home. Ironically, his ill health was a godsend: I wouldn't have been able to pay his second-semester tuition. I determined then that I would retire from my home institution—the University of Connecticut—as soon as I could.

I got a lot of research done on Carver that semester. Meanwhile, Stephen Roxburgh, my children's book publisher acquaintance, was reading my kiddy manuscripts, one or two at a time, and sending them back with NO stamped on their poor little pale foreheads. Finally, I told him that all I had left was the Carver book I was working on, but that it wasn't for children. He asked to see it; I sent what I had at the time and he said, "This is it." For the first time, I was given the opportunity to have a beautifully illustrated book of poems. And to receive a book advance (something I knew only from novels about novelists) as well! Despite my fear that publishing my book as one for young adults might mean it would be lost in the world of children's books, I accepted Stephen's offer to publish it. That was another turning point, for which I am unendingly grateful.

Until now, everything I'd written had been written on its own schedule, and I hadn't sent a manuscript to my home-publisher, Louisiana State University Press, until I was sure it was finished. But Stephen's advance came with a kicker: I received half of it upon signing the contract, and the second half when the completed manuscript was accepted. My manuscript was about half finished when I left for a visit at Abba Jacob's hermitage. Several talks with him were crucial in the development of several poems.

My visit with Abba Jacob gave me another project: a chapbook called *Triolets for Triolet*. It's a long story, involving his taking me to a Creole village called Triolet (Abba J. lives in a distant island nation) which was just starting to rebuild the school and several homes damaged by fires set in an outbreak of racist violence. I

said I'd try to do something to help the village. When I got home, I discovered, quite by accident, the poetic form called the triolet. It seemed obvious. I wrote some, and paid Curbstone Press to print them for me as a chapbook, the proceeds from which I donated to a literacy program there.

One day I received a telephone call from the head of the English department at the U.S. Military Academy at West Point, Colonel Stromberg, whom I had met when I read at the academy shortly before. He asked me whether I would like to teach there. Completely taken aback, I told him I'd have to think about it. The following day I received notification that I had won a fellowship I had applied for, a contemplative practices fellowship, that would pay me to develop a course which incorporated some teaching about contemplation/meditation. I called Colonel Stromberg back and told him I'd received the fellowship, and I really wanted to develop the course, so I couldn't accept his invitation. He said, "Bring the course here!" So in spring, 2000 I taught two sections of a course called "Poetry and Meditation" at the U.S. Military Academy at West Point. My essay about that experience, "Aborigine in the Citadel," was first published in the *Hudson Review* and has been reprinted several times. I love my cadets. Several of them are still in my life now, seven years later.

But what a pain that semester was! I had convinced Dora she'd enjoy the experience of going to school with military kids. Hey, I was a military kid! But we both suffered serious culture shock, getting through five days, then driving home to live for a couple of days before returning to the long gray straitjacket. I loved so much of it, the lives so different from mine, the camaraderie, the respect, the humor. Late that spring I got permission to have a labyrinth-maker chalk the design of the Chartres labyrinth on one of the football fields. Rain quickly obliterated it, but I have pictures.

Carver: A Life in Poems was published by Front Street Books in 2001 and almost immediately began to win prizes, most of which I had never heard of before, but which Stephen assured me meant something. It was a National Book Award finalist, a Newbery Honor Book, a Coretta Scott King Honor Book, won the *Boston Globe-Horn Book* Award, was named one of the 2002 Best Book for Young Adults by the Young Adult Library Services Association/American Library Association . . . I'm still pinching myself.

At the National Book Award gala a young African American woman introduced herself to me as a literary agent, and asked whether she could represent me. I laughed: an agent? Goodness, I'm a *poet*! Poets don't have agents! But she—Regina Brooks, Serendipity Literary Agency—insisted. So I told her I'd let her try.

September 11, 2001 was my first ever day of jury duty. Several days later, as we were all still reeling, I received a call from the director of the Mattatuck Museum in Waterbury, Connecticut. It seemed the museum owned a skeleton and had recently done research which proved without question that it was the skeleton of an

Marilyn with her friend Abba Jacob (Photograph courtesy of Marilyn Nelson.)

eighteenth-century slave named Fortune, who lived and died in Waterbury and whose owner, a Doctor Preserved Porter, dissected Fortune's body at his death (apparently as the result of a fall), removing the flesh from the bones, boiling them, and reassembling the skeleton to hang in his office to be used as a teaching tool. The city would like to honor Fortune by commissioning a piece of music to be premiered by the Waterbury Symphony. Would I be willing to write a text for the piece? They would give me all of their research findings. I accepted the commission, patterning my "Manumission Requiem" after the many orchestral and choral requiems which were being played every day in churches, schools, and on the radio. The poem came rather quickly, after the research; I wrote most of it in friends' cottage on Cape Cod. At one point I attended a lecture by Thich Nhat Hanh, the great Zen master, at the end of which someone in the audience asked what Thich Nhat Hanh suggested we say to comfort the dying and the bereaved. He said, "We have found the most comforting thing we can say is 'you are not this body which is dying here now.'" I used his suggestion in my poem, hoping my words might offer some comfort to our bereaved nation.

True to my earlier promise to myself, I retired from the University of Connecticut at the earliest opportunity, as soon as I turned fifty-five, and took what I thought would be a permanent position at the University of Delaware, at a larger salary than I had ever dreamed of. But before I could go, I received a Guggenheim fellowship. The wonderful people at the University of Delaware (no kidding: I have only positive things to say about all of my dealings with faculty and administration there) agreed to let me take off what would have been my first year there. So I had a year of freedom, a large salary, and a pension. I paid off my debts and started saving.

Jake, who had decided to stay at the University of Connecticut, studied abroad in programs at McGill University in Montreal, then at a university in Salvador do Bahia in Brazil. Dora's friend Dan moved out of his father's home and spent his senior year of high school living with us.

I was named poet laureate of the State of Connecticut in 2001. Many people were under the impression that this meant the state was paying me to give readings. Some people were downright rude when I suggested they pay me to drive across the state to read in their public libraries or schools. One literary club wrote to inform me that it planned to hold a large formal dinner in my honor, after which I would be allowed to read a few poems. Finally I told the Connecticut Commission on the Arts that the intended honor was threatening to turn into an unpaid part-time job. They sent me a check for one thousand dollars. I used the money to hold a "Poet's Lounge," featuring readings by several very different Connecticut poets. Several friends helped with the arrangements, and our evening was held in a Latino restaurant in Hartford, standing room only, a wonderful occasion. The mayor of Hartford was there. I was given one thousand dollars again the following year and used it to have bookplates printed ("Waiting Room Poems, brought to you by the CT Commission for the Arts and CT's Poet Laureate, Marilyn Nelson"), and to pay for postage and packaging for poetry books which I donated to waiting rooms and hospitals around the state. I started by downsizing my own poetry library, and the response was so positive that I solicited donations from publishers (several donated books; Copper Canyon was especially generous). For several months Dora, Dan, and I had a little business on the ping-pong table in the basement, distributing, packing, and addressing books. (I don't know why, but I did not receive another check from the commission until the end of my five-year term, when I received a check for three thousand dollars.)

I was given a three-week residency at the Heinrich Boll Cottage on Achill Island, Ireland, a barren and beautiful place. I had not expected to be so deeply touched by the still-visible history of Ireland, or to feel so deeply our commonality. I was joined on Achill by my German "sister," Sabine Waniek Jentsch, and by my Danish poet friend, Inge Pedersen. Inge and I spent some time every morning translating each other's poems, just for fun. When I returned to the United States I sent my translations to journals, one of which was Oberlin College's *Field.* Some time later the directors of the Oberlin College Press asked whether I had a complete manuscript of these translations, as they would be interested in publishing them as a book.

Another visit with Abba Jacob. He and I spent time inventing a story about a little dog marooned on an uninhabited island. Abba Jacob has spent a great deal of time in solitude on an uninhabited island, and he made a map of the island and described what the dog would see and experience. I wrote the story when I got home. It's an allegory for contemplation/meditation. It will soon be published as a children's picture book called *Snook Alone.*

I decided to use part of my Guggenheim grant to go to Brazil. I went twice: once alone to visit Jake and get an idea of what it was like, and later with my sister, Jennifer, my brother, Mel, and friends Mercedes Arnold and Albert Price, Jr. The second trip was undertaken as part of my Guggenheim project, to write a book about a group of African-American "pilgrims" who tell stories as they travel on their pilgrimage. This book became *The Cachoeira Tales, and Other Poems.*

For five thousand dollars my carpenter-friend, Rich Rustmann, built a tower—something I had always wanted—for me in the woods behind the house. I had originally envisioned a little tree house, but the town didn't see things my way. Instead, Rich built me a little square room on stilts, with two windows and a lovely stairway with a landing. With siding on the stilts, it really *was* a tower, a sweet little building. Dora teased that it looked like a sniper's tower. But with a buried extension cord for light and an electric oil heater, a table, a chair, a pen, a bottle of ink, and some legal pads, my tower was perfect. No telephone, no Internet. And, until he understood that I was out there and could be disturbed by constant barking, Sydney the Dalmatian, who had been ruining my work in my wonderful study in the house with his neurotic noises, left me alone, and I could sit out there and write. Sometimes, in the winter, I wrote with mittens on.

In June, 2002 I joined the Cave Canem family by leading a week-long workshop at its summer workshop retreat designed to counter the under-representation and isolation of black poets. Founded by African-American poets Toi Derricotte and Cornelius Eady in 1996, Cave Canem has become a powerful movement, influencing American literature's present and future: graduates from Cave Canem's arduous summer poetry boot camp are publishing books, winning prizes, and teaching in M.F.A. programs all over the country. Like every Cave Canem student and faculty member, I was, from the first evening's confessional community circle, in which each of us told why we were there, touched to my very core. This was the first time I had ever been in a community of African-American artists. Though our life experiences were very diverse, there was that *something* which each of us could recognize in each of the others. I had never had that experience before. I imagine a gathering of one hundred young American women, each of whom had been adopted as an infant from China, might have similar feelings. No matter what their adoptive families were like, or where they grew up in this country, they would inevitably share some deep things. At the end of the second or third day of my first summer workshop (Cave Canem faculty and fellows commit to three years of summer workshops), I told the directors that I was going to try to buy a house which could be a retreat for Cave Canem graduates; a place where they could replicate, on a much smaller scale, that intense, trust-based workshop community. In my mind, I was already calling the place "Soul Mountain."

Then Scholastic bought reprint rights to *Carver,* and published a book-fair edition, sold at middle-and high-school book fairs all over the country. And I got a nice chunk of change from that. I don't think I'd ever made more than a couple of hundred dollars on a book before, so this was something of a shock.

Regina sold two manuscripts of verse by the very great children's poet Halfdan Rasmussen, which I had translated from the Danish. Each of these contracts came with an advance. Then Regina called to tell me that a publisher had an idea for me and wanted me to come to her office to discuss it. We made an appointment, which, as it turned out, was the day of a bad ice storm. I managed to get into New York city, and to Regina as planned in the outer office of Andrea Pinkney, senior editor and publisher of children's books at Houghton Mifflin. We sat, exchanged niceties, and then Andrea said she thought I was the writer who might be able to fulfill her childhood dream of publishing a book for children about lynching. I almost fell off my chair. But I went home and thought about it, while Regina and Andrea discussed a contract, and when Regina told me about the advance, I decided it might be possible to write a book for children about lynching.

So here I was, with money in the bank. I became obsessed with real estate, looking for the right house in which to plant Soul Mountain. I looked in Delaware, in Pennsylvania, in West Virginia. I found the house in Connecticut: nine bedrooms, three living rooms, three kitchens, and a large deck, on six acres of lawn, meadow, and woods, with a large pond. Only fifteen minutes from a train station. I bought the house in 2003. Stephen Roxburgh's advance for my "Manumission Requiem" was the last piece of the down payment.

I couldn't move for a year, until Dora finished her last year of high school. For one year I paid two large mortgages and commuted by train to my new position at the University of Delaware. Because I wasn't entirely sure I'd be able to manage two mortgages and the expense of maintaining two houses, in addition to the cost of the wearying commute, I also accepted an invitation to teach in the New England College low-residency M.F.A. program. Just to be on the safe side.

On the days when I wasn't in Delaware, I sat in my tower working on my Guggenheim project, *The Cachoeira Tales.* I interrupted that project to write the book Andrea Pinkney had commissioned: a heroic crown of sonnets called *A Wreath for Emmett Till.* Meanwhile, the Bush administration was pushing the country toward war. While I was working on the sonnets I received an invitation from First Lady Laura Bush to a literary luncheon at the White House. I pondered, asked my friends, asked my Abba. Some friends said don't go. Some said go. Abba Jacob said I should go. So I asked a local fabric artist to make a peace scarf for me, something I could wear as a gesture against the movement toward war. As my sonnet sequence began to be a not-too-thinly veiled cry against the war in Iraq, the pace of my writing shifted into fifth gear.

Sometimes I wrote all night, slept a few hours, and went back to my desk to write again. I planned to present the finished poem to Mrs. Bush, hoping she might be moved to stop her husband's misguided vengeance. The event was cancelled because several poets publicly proclaimed their refusal to enter the Bush White House; one of the invited poets made public his plan go there to protest. A movement called Poets against the War sprang into being. Because I had decided to accept the invitation, and because of my peace scarf, I received an inordinate amount of publicity, both positive and negative, for the non-event. The most interesting publicity was a taped interview for a German television news magazine. They photographed me standing on the top landing of my little tower.

Jake came home from Brazil with Rita, who is sweet and funny and brilliant and beautiful. They lived with Dora and me while Jake finished his senior year of college.

The commute between Connecticut and Delaware required me to drive one hour to the train, then sit for four and a half hours in a sort of zombie state (I had rationalized the commute by telling myself I'd get a lot of work done on the train, but it turned out to be impossible) until Wilmington, where I rented a car to drive to Newark, parked the car on campus, went to my late afternoon office hours, grabbed something to eat in the student union, and taught a three-hour workshop. For the first weeks I slept in motels, or on the couch at the home of two of my former students. Then Lois Potter, the kind and charming Shakespearean scholar in the department, invited me to use her guest room every week. So I arrived at her home after class, sat with her over a glass of sherry, and fell, exhausted, into bed. Got up early to teach another three-hour workshop, then raced to return the car and get the train back to Connecticut. Have I mentioned menopause? Readers who are women of a certain age will understand my saying I don't know how I survived that year.

When the new head of the English department at the University of Connecticut asked whether there was anything the university could do to convince me to come back, I said hmmm, maybe. He and the dean of the College of Arts and Science suggested I come back as a "special payroll lecturer," teaching one semester a year, two courses. I would be paid one-half of the salary I had received before I left UConn, but UConn would make a fifty-thousand-dollar donation to my artists' colony, if it became a nonprofit entity. Months of negotiations followed. I created a nonprofit entity. The administration had to be convinced that it would not be helping me much if the university's donation could be used to pay to publish my guests' books and send them to literary conferences but not to *feed* them and heat the house. Finally, as we neared our final agreement, an anti-affirmative action decision at the University of Michigan made the administrators at the University of Connecticut decide that UConn could not support any program intended exclusively for African Americans. So my dream of providing a haven for Cave Canem graduates shriveled, like a raisin in the sun, so to speak. It was too late by then to back out of the UConn agreement: I had already submitted my letter of resignation to the University of Delaware. There was nothing I could do, except to retain the house for one month only for African-American poets, and to pay for that month—utilities, telephone, Internet, food, stipends—out of my own pocket.

I sold the Candide Lane house and moved to Soul Mountain in the summer of 2004. Dora had graduated from high school and was about to leave for college. But instead of having an empty nest, I now had a huge nest waiting to be filled. Tonya Hegamin, a young woman I had met at a Cave Canem workshop, joined me soon afterward, to be the first program director of Soul Mountain. Even though we knew there could be no salary involved, we made a pact to dream this dream together for a while, and to help it come true. We invited our first guests, two Cave Canem poets. And Soul Mountain was off and running.

Jake and Rita were married that summer, first in Brazil, then in the United States. My dear Abba came for a brief visit in the early fall. One of the first things our first Soul Mountain community did together was to share in a wedding-blessing celebration for Jake and Rita held under a big tent in the yard and conducted by Abba Jacob.

He and I collaborated on a little book while he was here: *The Baobab Room,* a picture book. My Danish friend Inge Pedersen and her husband, Bent, also a writer, arrived soon after Abba Jacob left. She and I completed the translation of a book of her poems, which has been published as *The Thirteenth Month.* I invited Elizabeth Alexander to collaborate with me on a book of sonnets about the girls who were students in Prudence Crandall's short-lived school for "young ladies and little misses of color" in a Connecticut town in 1833. We visited the Crandall Museum and came back to Soul Mountain to begin writing. That book, *Miss Crandall's School for Young Ladies and Little Misses of Color,* was published in 2007 as a young-adult book. And our guests were working on their own writing.

Seasons changed, new guests arrived. I wrote *The Freedom Business,* a sequence of poems based on the life of Venture Smith, an eighteenth-century Connecticut slave/freeman whose grave is in the same small town as Soul Mountain.

In 2003, at the first conference of state poets laureate, I spoke with Dana Gioia, chairman of the National Endowment for the Arts and an old friend, about my experience teaching at West Point, and about the wars in Iraq and Afghanistan. Chairman Gioia has generously credited that conversation as being the seed of what was to become the NEA's "Operation Homecoming" initiative. It invited military personnel and their families to write about their wartime experiences, and offered writing workshops on military bases, led by visiting writers. The first workshops were so well received that the NEA was forced to expand its program, and in 2006

Random House published an anthology called *Operation Homecoming,* edited by Andrew Carroll, containing eyewitness accounts, excerpts from private journals, short stories, and other writing by soldiers and those who love them. I am very proud to have played a part in this important contribution.

Seasons changed, new guests arrived. I began to realize how ill-equipped I am to direct a nonprofit business, and how much I enjoy hosting the poets who have been our guests.

In September of 2005, with an advance from Stephen Roxburgh for "an unspecified book of poems," Abba Jacob and I traveled into the Kalahari in Botswana, in search of Bushmen, hoping to be able to write a book which might sensitize readers to their tragic plight. I fell in love with a little girl named N!hunka!, whom we met in a village near the sacred Tsolido Hills.

We plan to go back to Botswana soon, because the book we had planned has not yet materialized. But I did write a little picture-book text to be the vehicle for illustrations made by Bushmen artists we encountered elsewhere, so the artists will earn some money from their art. That book will be called *Ostrich and Lark.*

Seasons changed, I taught in the spring semester, guests came and went. The year 2006 saw the publication of *The Cachoeira Tales, The Thirteenth Month, A Wreath for Emmett Till,* and *The Ladder,* the last my translation of a verse narrative for children by Halfdan Rasmussen. To my profound astonishment, Professor David Wallace, president of the New Chaucer Society, took it upon himself to champion *The Cachoeira Tales* as one of a handful of "neo-Chaucerian topographies."

Seasons changed, I taught again, guests came and went. In the summer of 2006 I taught a five-week workshop in Florence for UConn's Study-Abroad program. That was fun. Dora and Tonya joined me for part of the time. Dora and I made a side trip to Berlin to visit our German "family." Later that summer Tonya and I collaborated on a ghost story in poems, a young-adult book with the working title *Pemba: Song of Present Existence.*

And now it's January of 2007. I've been looking toward the future by writing a strategic plan for Soul Mountain, trying to figure out how to raise enough money so that it can be self-sufficient (its operating budget still depends upon my teaching at UConn, and I would like to retire) and hire a director to take from me the burden of trying to turn my brain into one that can do feasibility studies and budgets. If that happens, I will move into a smaller home (if I can cajole some bank into giving me a mortgage) and let Soul Mountain expand. Abba Jacob and I plan to go back to Botswana again next summer, still hoping to write "our Bushman book." I have a couple more writing projects simmering on back burners. I understand that quantum physics indicates that we can move backward in time as well as forward. I hope someone will figure out how to do that during my lifetime. I'd like to go back and tell my past self to live in the moment, that everything is going to be all right. I wonder how far back I'd have to go to be able to do something to make the current chaos in the Middle East and North Africa not come to pass.

*   *   *

NICHOLSON, William 1948-

Personal

Born 1948, in England; married Virginia Bell (a writer); children: three. *Education:* Christ's College, Cambridge, B.A., 1973.

Addresses

Home—Sussex, England. *Agent*—Sally Wilcox/Carin Sage, Creative Artists Agency, 9830 Wilshire Blvd., Beverly Hills, CA 90212-1825.

Career

Writer, playwright, and screenwriter. Former director and producer of documentary films for the British Broadcasting Corporation. Executive producer of *Everyman,* 1979-82, and *Global Report,* 1983-84; director, *Firelight,* Carnival/Wind Dancer, 1997.

Awards, Honors

Best Television Play, British Academy of Film and Television Arts (BAFTA), 1985, for *Shadowlands;* Best Television Film designation, New York Film Festival, 1987, Best Television Drama award, BAFTA, 1987, and ACE Award for best picture, 1988, all for *Life Story;* Banff Festival Best Drama designation, 1988, ACE Award for Best International Drama, 1990, and Royal Television Society's Writer's Award, 1987-88, all for *Sweet as You Are;* Best Play of 1990, London *Evening Standard,* for *Shadowlands;* Emmy Award nomination for best screenplay, Academy of Television Arts and Sciences, 1992, for *A Private Matter;* Golden Globe and Emmy Award nominations for best screenplay, both 1996, both for *Crime of the Century;* Nestlé Smarties Prize Gold Award, 2000, and Blue Peter Book of the Year Award, 2001, both for *The Wind Singer;* Academy Award nomination for best screenplay, Academy of Motion Picture Arts and Sciences, 2000, for *Gladiator;* Antoinette Perry ("Tony") Award nomination for best play, 2004, for *The Retreat from Moscow.*

Writings

"WIND ON FIRE" JUVENILE NOVEL SERIES

The Wind Singer: An Adventure, illustrations by Peter Sis, Hyperion Books for Children (New York, NY), 2000.
Slaves of the Mastery, illustrations by Peter Sis, Hyperion Books for Children (New York, NY), 2001.

Firesong: An Adventure, illustrations by Peter Sis, Hyperion Books for Children (New York, NY), 2002.

"NOBLE WARRIORS" JUVENILE NOVEL SERIES

Seeker, Harcourt (Orlando, FL), 2006.
Jango, Harcourt (Orlando, FL), 2007.

ADULT NOVELS

The Seventh Level: A Sexual Progress, Stein & Day (New York, NY), 1979.
The Society of Others, Nan A. Talese (New York, NY), 2005.
The Trial of True Love, Nan A Talese (New York, NY), 2005.

TELEPLAYS

Martin Luther, British Broadcasting Corporation (BBC), 1983.
New World BBC, 1986.
Life Story BBC, 1987.
Sweet as You Are BBC, 1988.
The Vision BBC, 1988.
The March BBC, 1990.
A Private Matter, Home Box Office (HBO), 1992.
Crime of the Century HBO, 1996.

Author's work has been translated into German.

SCREENPLAYS

Double Helix (a.k.a. Life Story), Films for the Humanities and Sciences, 1987.
Sarafina, Distant Horizon/Disney, 1992.
Shadowlands (based on the author's television play), Savoy, 1993.
(With Mark Handley) *Nell,* Twentieth Century-Fox, 1994.
First Knight, Columbia, 1995.
(And director) *Firelight,* Disney, 1998.
Grey Owl, Allied Pictures, 2000.
(With David Franzoni and John Logan) *Gladiator,* DreamWorks, 2000.
Long Walk to Freedom, 2004.
The Golden Age, 2007.

PLAYS

Shadowlands (produced in London, England, 1989), Plume (New York, NY), 1990.
Map of the Heart (produced in London, England, 1991), Samuel French (New York, NY), 1991.
Katherine Howard (produced in Chichester, England, 1998), Samuel French (New York, NY), 1999.
The Retreat from Moscow: A Play about a Family (produced in Chichester, England, 1999), Anchor Books (New York, NY), 2004.

Adaptations

The film *Shadowlands* was adapted as a television film broadcast in England, 1985, as a novel of the same name by Leonore Fleishcer, Signet (New York, NY), 1993, and also as a sound recording by LA Theatre Works (Los Angeles, CA), 2001. *Gladiator* was adapted into a book by Dewey Gra, Onyx (New York, NY), 2000. The "Wind on Fire" trilogy was adapted for audiobook by BBC Audiobooks America. *Seeker* was adapted as an audiobook, read by Michael Page, by Brilliance Audio, 2006.

Sidelights

William Nicholson has written screenplays for television and film, plays performed in both England and the United States, and novels, including the "Wind on Fire" trilogy for young-adult readers. Beginning his career in British television, Nicholson gained wide notice in 1985 for his television play *Shadowlands,* which is about the real-life love affair between British writer and Christian apologist C.S. Lewis and American Joy Davidman. His screenplays include *Double Helix (a.k.a. Life Story),* a dramatization of the discovery of Deoxyribonucleic acid (DNA), and *Nell,* which tells the story of a woman who is discovered, living in virtual isolation in the woods of North Carolina by a local psychologist. As a playwright, Nicholson received the prestigious Tony award for his 2004 stage production, *The Retreat from Moscow: A Play about a Family.*

In addition to his work for stage and screen, Nicholson is also an accomplished novelist. His young-adult "Wind on Fire" fantasy trilogy features the male-female twins Bowman and Kestrel, who must save the Manth people from slavery in a dystopian world. In the first book, *The Wind Singer: An Adventure,* the twins set out to recover a pipe organ known as the Wind Singer after they are targeted by the Chief Examiner, who thinks they are misfits. Writing in *School Library Journal,* John Peters felt that while many of the plot devices read as conveniences, "fans of such barbed journey tales . . . will enjoy the social commentary." *Booklist* contributor GraceAnne A. DeCandido asserted that Nicholson's plot lacks "imagination" and "depth . . . in the heavy-handed portrayal of caste systems, warrior tribes, and smarmy villains," but she admitted that "the background is well delineated" and that *The Wind Singer* has "comic relief" and a "thrilling denouement."

As the trilogy continues in *Slaves of the Mastery,* Bowman and Kestrel are once again fighting evil after five years of peace. This time they and their family are made slaves and taken to the city of the Mastery, where the twins use both their cunning and magical abilities to fight back. Writing in *Booklist,* DeCandido called the book "an astonishing mishmash of lore, myth, and magicking" and noted that Nicholson includes some "splendid battle scenes." Eva Mitnick, writing in *School Library Journal,* called *Slaves of the Mastery* a "masterful sequel" in which "every character . . . is compelling

Cover of William Nicholson's young-adult fantasy **The Wind Singer,** *featuring artwork by Peter Sis.* (Hyperion Paperbacks for Children, 2000. Copyright © 2000 by William Nicholson. Artwork copyright © 2000 by Peter Sis. All rights reserved. Reprinted by permission of Hyperion Books for Children.)

and full of life." The final installment in the trilogy, *Firesong: An Adventure,* finds the twins leading their people back home after the fall of the Mastery, facing both a grueling journey and dissent from within. *School Library Journal* contributor Beth L. Meister wrote that the trilogy's "concluding volume . . . features fast-paced action, poetic language, and carefully constructed characters."

Also geared for teen readers, Nicholson's "Noble Warriors" series begins with *Seeker,* described by *School Library Journal* reviewer June H. Keuhn as "a novel of friendship, loyalty, and accomplishment." A fantasy with a quest at its core, *Seeker* transports readers to the fictional Island of Anacrea, where an order of warrior monks known as the Nomana are dedicated to defending and serving the one god. Known as the All and Only, the god is revered despite a prophecy that predicts its death at the hands of an assassin. Hoping to follow in the footsteps of his older brother and become a warrior for his god, sixteen-year-old Seeker sets out for Anacrea. Also hoping to prove their worthiness—and following similar and ultimately connecting paths—are a devout girl named Morning Star and a thief named Wildman. At first rejected by the Nomana, the three teens nonetheless fear for the monks' safety when they discover a plot to destroy the island and the All and Only. Together, they embark on a journey to the cosmopolitan city of Radiance, where the worship of a jealous pantheon of competing gods requires human sacrifices. There the three traveler learn of Soren Similin and his plot to both destroy the meek Nomana and end worship of the All and Only. Harnessing the power of terror, Similin's scheme is to send suicide bombers to the remote island and destroy Anacrea's beauty forever. In a review of *Seeker* for *Booklist,* Jennifer Mattson cited Nicholson's "tight plotting" as well as his ability to interweave the "numerous perspectives" that "lend the novel a cinematic breadth." *Kliatt* contributor Deirdre Root dubbed *Seeker* "an astoundingly beautiful book," and added that the novel's "simplicity belies a complex world" that seems vivid and real due to Nicholson's skill with character and setting.

Cover of Seeker, *the first installment in Nicholson's "Noble Warriors" series, featuring artwork by Douglas Mullen.* (Harcourt, Inc., 2005. Jacket illustration copyright © 2006 by Douglas Mullen. Reproduced by permission of Harcourt.)

In addition to his books for young adults, Nicholson has also addressed older readers with novels such as *The Society of Others* and *The Trial of True Love,* the latter described by *Booklist* reviewer Allison Block as a "thought-provoking tale about lives transformed in the blink of an eye." In *The Society of Others* he introduces a recent college graduate who, becoming disillusioned, flees his family in England and ends up in a totalitarian Eastern bloc country. Accused of terrorism, the young man is paraded on television, then bullied into answering questions while films of brutal torture are played on nearby monitors. The man's ultimate goal is to escape, a task that will require both his wits and the kindness of strangers. Reviewing the novel, Sarah Weinman wrote in the *Chicago Tribune* that in *The Society of Others* Nicholson "doesn't skimp on novelistic essentials in his pursuit of intellectual ones," and Piers Paul Read concluded in a *Spectator* review that with the book Nicholson "has to my mind established himself . . . as one of the best novelists around."

Biographical and Critical Sources

PERIODICALS

Booklist, October 15, 2000, GraceAnne A. DeCandido, review of *The Wind Singer: An Adventure,* p. 438; October 15, 2001, GraceAnne A. DeCandido, review of *Slaves of the Mastery,* p. 389; January 1, 2005, Allison Block, review of *The Society of Others,* p. 821; January 1, 2006, Allison Block, review of *The Trial of True Love,* p. 58; June 1, 2006, Jennifer Mattson, review of *Seeker,* p. 63.

Bulletin of the Center for Children's Books, June, 2006, April Spisak, review of *Seeker,* p. 465.

Chicago Tribune, September 4, 1998, Michael Wilmington, review of *Firelight,* p. A; February 3, 2005, Sarah Weinman, review of *The Society of Others,* p. 2.

Guardian (London, England), May 31, 2000, Lyn Gardner, review of *The Wind Singer,* p. 9.

Kirkus Reviews, October 15, 2004, review of *The Society of Others,* p. 981; January 15, 2006, review of *The Trial of True Love,* p. 58; May 1, 2006, review of *Seeker,* p. 464.

Kliatt, July, 2004, Hugh Flick, Jr., review of *Firesong,* p. 51; July, 2004, review of "Wind on Fire" trilogy, p. 32; May, 2006, Deirdre Root, review of *Seeker,* p. 12.

Library Journal, November 1, 2004, Lawrence Rungren, review of *The Society of Others,* p. 76.

New Republic, February 7, 1994, Stanley Kauffmann, review of *Shadowlands* (film), p. 26; October 12, 1998, Stanley Kauffmann, review of *Firelight,* p. 30.

New York Times Book Review, February 13, 2005, Tobin Harshaw, review of *The Society of Others,* p. 13.

Publishers Weekly, August 28, 2000, review of *The Wind Singer,* p. 84; November 19, 2001, review of *The Wind Singer,* p. 70; August 26, 2002, review of *Firesong,* p.

70; September 29, 2003, review of the "Wind in the Fire" trilogy, p. 67; January 17, 2005, review of *The Society of Others,* p. 36; January 9, 2006, review of *The Trial of True Love,* p. 32; June 19, 2006, review of *Seeker,* p. 63.

School Library Journal, December, 2000, John Peters, review of *The Wind Singer,* p. 146; December, 2001, Eva Mitnick, review of *Slaves of the Mastery,* p. 141; January, 2003, Beth L. Meister, review of *Firesong,* p. 141; August, 2006, June H. Keuhn, review of *Seeker,* p. 126.

Science Fiction Chronicle, February, 2001, Don D'Ammassa, review of *The Wind Singer,* p. 38.

Spectator, March 20, 2004, Piers Paul Read, review of *The Society of Others,* p. 50.

Voice of Youth Advocates, April, 2006, Leslie McCombs, review of *Seeker,* p. 63.

ONLINE

Achuka Web site, http://www.achuka.co.uk/ (February 24, 2005), "William Nicholson."

Spectrum Web site, htt://www.incwell.com/ (February 25, 2005), interview with Nicholson.

William Nicholson Home Page, http:///www. williamnicholson.co.uk (June 10, 2007).*

*   *   *

NIKOLA-LISA, W. 1951-

Personal

Born June 15, 1951, in Jersey City, NJ; son of William Henry (an engineer) and Dorothy Ethel (a nurse) Nikola-Lisa; married June 6, 1975; wife's name Joan (divorced); married Barbara Cooper (a sculptor), August 12, 1988; children: (first marriage) Ylla, Larissa. *Education:* University of Florida, B.A. (religion), 1974, M.Ed., 1976; Montana State University, Ed.D., 1986. *Politics:* "Independent." *Religion:* "Agnostic."

Addresses

Home—Chicago, IL. *E-mail*—nikolabooks@gmail.com.

Career

Educator and author. World Family School, Bozeman, MT, head teacher, 1976-78; Irving Elementary School, Bozeman, second-grade teacher, 1978-82; National-Louis University, Evanston, IL, associate professor of education, 1986—.

Member

International Reading Association, National Council of Teachers of English, Society of Children's Book Writers and Illustrators.

Awards, Honors

Jane Addams Honor Book Award, and *Parents* magazine Best Book designation, both 1994, both for *Bein' with You This Way;* Indiana Hoosier Book Award Mas-

W. Nikola-Lisa (Photograph by Eileen Ryan. Courtesy of W. Nikola-Lisa.)

ter List inclusion, and Bank Street School of Education Best Book of the Year designation, both 2002, both for *Summer Sun Risin';* Christopher Award, 2007, for *How We Are Smart.*

Writings

FOR CHILDREN

Night Is Coming, illustrated by Jamichael Henterly, Dutton (New York, NY), 1991.

1, 2, 3, Thanksgiving, illustrated by Robin Kramer, Albert Whitman (Morton Grove, IL), 1991.

Storm, illustrated by Michael Hays, Atheneum (New York, NY), 1993.

Bein' with You This Way, illustrated by Michael Bryant, Lee & Low (New York, NY), 1994.

No Babies Asleep, illustrated by Peter Palagonia, Atheneum (New York, NY), 1994.

Wheels Go Round, illustrated by Jane Conteh-Morgan, Doubleday (New York, NY), 1994.

One Hole in the Road, illustrated by Dan Yaccarino, Henry Holt (New York, NY), 1996.

Tangletalk, illustrated by Jessica Clerk, Dutton (New York, NY), 1997.

Shake Dem Halloween Bones, illustrated by Mike Reed, Houghton Mifflin (Boston, MA), 1997.

Till Year's Good End: A Calendar of Medieval Labors, illustrated by Christopher Manson, Atheneum (New York, NY), 1997.

America: My Land, Your Land, Our Land, Lee & Low (New York, NY), 1997.

(Selector and contributor) *The Year with Grandma Moses,* illustrated by Grandma Moses, Henry Holt (New York, NY), 2000.

Hallelujah!: A Christmas Celebration, illustrated by Synthia Saint James, Atheneum (New York, NY), 2000.

Can You Top That?, illustrated by Hector Viveros Lee, Lee & Low (New York, NY), 2000.

America: A Book of Opposites (bilingual English/Spanish text), Lee & Low (New York, NY), 2001.

Summer Sun Risin', illustrated by Don Tate, Lee & Low (New York, NY), 2002.

To Hear the Angels Sing: A Christmas Poem, illustrated by Jill Weber, Holiday House (New York, NY), 2002.

My Teacher Can Teach—Anyone!, illustrated by Felipe Galindo, Lee & Low (New York, NY), 2004.

Setting the Turkeys Free, illustrated by Ken Wilson-Max, Hyperion Books for Children (New York, NY), 2004.

How We Are Smart, illustrated by Sean Qualls, Lee & Low (New York, NY), 2006.

Magic in the Margins: A Medieval Tale of Bookmaking, illustrated by Bonnie Christensen, Houghton Mifflin (Boston, MA), 2007.

Contributor to periodicals, including *Children's Literature in Education, Horn Book, Language Arts, Lion and the Unicorn, New Advocate,* and *Teaching and Learning Literature.*

Author's works have been translated into Spanish.

Sidelights

In addition to teaching education on the college level, W. Nikola-Lisa has produced a number of picture books that have been praised for their multicultural focus and promotion of a gender-and race-neutral storyhour experience. In *Summer Sun Risin'* he shares the life of an African-American farming family in a text that gains "a compelling, comforting rhythm from the accumulation of small details," according to a *Publishers Weekly* contributor. A *Kirkus Reviews* critic described *Summer Sun Risin'* as a "cheery introduction to farm life and simple poetry." In another rural-themed offering, *Night Is Coming,* Nikola-Lisa and illustrator Jamichael Henterly produce a "gentle, wistful book that captures the piercing beauty of a rural sunset," according to a *Publishers Weekly* reviewer. Other picture books by Nikola-Lisa include the holiday-themed *Shake Dem Halloween Bones,* featuring a sing-song text and art by Mike Reed, and *One Hole in the Road,* a counting book that uses a road construction project and the attendant barricades, engineers, police, and street pavers to introduce number sequences.

In *Bein' with You This Way,* which *Booklist* contributor Julie Corsaro described as a "joyfully illustrated" story about "racial tolerance," Nikola-Lisa creates a cumulative rhyme focusing on physical differences. In a city park playground, a youngster creates a cumulative game that ultimately draws together all the children playing there. Reviewing the work for *Publishers Weekly,* a critic wrote that Nikola-Lisa's "bouncy, well-intentioned text" pairs with Michael Bryant's pencil and watercolor art to create a story of "buoyancy and warmth." As the author explained in a *Horn Book* essay, in writing the book "I wanted children to know that although we are all physically different—and certainly different in other ways as well—still we are all the same, or at least simi-

Nikola-Lisa's picture book **America: A Book of Opposites,** *combines a basic concept lesson with images that reflect the diversity of a vast nation.* (Lee & Low Books Inc., 1997. Illustration copyright © 1997. All rights reserved. Reproduced by permission of Lee & Low Books, Inc.)

The bold graphic art of Ken Wilson-Max pairs perfectly with Nikola-Lisa's story of a young child's developing creativity in **Setting the Turkeys Free.**
(Jump at the Sun/ Hyperion Books for Children, 2004. Illustration copyright © 2004 by Ken Wilson-Max. All rights reserved. Reproduced by permission of Hyperion Books for Children.)

lar in that we share the same sense of human identity." Nikola-Lisa draws an analogy between the physical and racial landscape in *America: My Land, Your Land, Our Land,* which features illustrations from over a dozen well-known artists that reflect diverse cultural and stylistic backgrounds, and continues to explore the American identity in *America: A Book of Opposites.*

Setting the Turkeys Free finds a young African-American boy and his loyal pup working on a Thanksgiving craft project that is unleashed through the boy's active imagination. In his text, "Nikola-Lisa keeps sentences simple and enthused," according to *School Library Journal* contributor Gay Lynn Van Vleck, noting the book's year-round appeal. Calling *Setting the Turkeys Free* an "unusual story about art and imagination," a *Kirkus Reviews* writer deemed the work a "fresh, original offering" that is enhanced by Ken Wilson-Max's boldly colored art.

Tangletalk draws on the wordplay and upside-down logic of Victorian writers such as Edward Lear and Lewis Carroll, creating what a *Publishers Weekly* critic dubbed "funny and flippant rhymed couplets fueled by inherent contradictions and role reversals." Paired with pen-and-ink drawings by Jessica Clerk, Nikola-Lisa's story shares his narrator's silly, backward view of a beautiful day, when birds bloom, daisies sing, and the best way to enjoy the sunshine is to go indoors. Calling *Tangletalk* "an upside-down tale in verse," Ilene Cooper also praised Clerk's art, writing in her *Booklist* appraisal that the detailed illustrations will fascinate young children. Nikola-Lisa takes a tall-tale approach in *Can You Top That?,* in which one boy's sidewalk drawing sparks a series of ever-more-boastful stories from his friends.

In a more-serious vein, Nikola-Lisa's *How We Are Smart* features poems, quotations, and prose. The book introduces young children to a dozen men and women who,

although pursuing very different careers, are also similar in that their lives illustrate one of eight forms of intelligence: "Body Smart," "Logic Smart," and "Nature Smart," among others. The individuals profiled by Nikola-Lisa span races and cultures: Native-American Maria Tallchief was a prima ballerina, African American jurist Thurgood Marshall was an honored member of the U.S. Supreme Court, and Asian American I.M. Pei is a world-renowned architect. Although the book's subject is complex, it is made appealing to children due to its straight-forward layout and engaging artwork by Sean Qualls. As Joy Fleishhacker wrote in her *School Library Journal* review of the book, Nikola-Lisa's "creative blend of poetry, biography, and psychology" will "inspire youngsters to view themselves and others from a fresh perspective."

While most of his books are contemporary in their setting, both *Till Year's Good End: A Calendar of Medieval Labors* and *Magic in the Margins: A Medieval Tale of Bookmaking* bring readers back to the middle ages. *Magic in the Margins* takes place at a monastery, where an orphaned boy named Simon is being trained in the art of creating illuminated manuscripts. A talented apprentice, Simon is chosen by the monastery's Father Anselm for a special and somewhat unusual task. The life of the medieval peasantry scrolls through all four seasons in *Till Year's Good End,* Nikola-Lisa's text bringing to light the crucial importance of agriculture to these hard-working people. In a *Publishers Weekly* review a critic praised the author's "succinct but informative prose," adding that Christopher Manson's "handsome . . . pen-and-ink and watercolor" illustrations give *Till Year's Good End* a sense of "solidity and grace." The author provides a different perspective on the seasons with *The Year with Grandma Moses,* a picture book that organizes the image of the well-known American primitive painter into a season-spanning vision highlighted by selections from the artist's memoirs.

"Nikola-Lisa's careful selections and spare approach effectively convey the spirit of this self-taught, spirited woman," noted *School Library Journal* contributor Wendy Lukehart.

Nikola-Lisa once told *SATA:* "I like writing about human relationships in the context of both everyday life and special occasions. I think my strongest writing comes when I allow myself to sink way down into my feelings and explore the world when I was young. There's something intensely intimate about those moments, few and far between as they sometimes are." As he wrote in a *Horn Book* article, "American life is riddled with un-paralleled duality—between rich and poor, young and old, black and white." "Most of my writing . . . involves multicultural issues," Nikola-Lisa added: "it is the belief that we must first recognize our differences, and indeed celebrate them, but ultimately we must transcend them as well—though without sacrificing our own personal and cultural sense of identity. It is in the act of transcendence, of finding a new, even higher level of synthesis, that our future as a multiethnic, multiracial nation lies—but we have a long way to go."

Biographical and Critical Sources

PERIODICALS

Booklist, February 15, 1992, Quraysh Ali, review of *Storm,* p. 1068; July, 1994, Julie Corsaro, review of *Bein' with You This Way,* p. 1951; October 1, 1996, Michael Cart, review of *One Hole in the Road,* p. 359; May 1, 1997, Ilene Cooper, review of *Tangletalk,* p. 1500; September 1, 1997, Julie Corsaro, review of *America: My Land, Your Land, Our Land,* p. 134; October 1, 1997, Hazel Rochman, review of *Shake Dem Halloween Bones,* p. 338; October 15, 1997, Susan Dove Lempke, review of *Till Year's Good End: A Calendar of Medieval Labors,* p. 409; September 1, 2000, Hazel Rochman, review of *Hallelujah!: A Christmas Celebration,* p. 130, and Kathy Broderick, review of *Can You Top That?,* p. 250; October 15, 2000, Randy Meyer, review of *The Year with Grandma Moses,* p. 433; November 1, 2004, Ilene Cooper, review of *Setting the Turkeys Free,* p. 490; November 15, 2004, Connie Fletcher, review of *My Teacher Can Teach . . . Anyone!,* p. 591; April 1, 2006, Hazel Rochman, review of *How We Are Smart,* p. 38.

Bulletin of the Center for Children's Books, December, 1997, review of *Shake Dem Halloween Bones,* p. 135; November, 2000, review of *The Year with Grandma Moses,* p. 115.

Horn Book, May-June, 1998, W. Nikola-Lisa, "'Around My Table' Is Not Always Enough," p. 315.

Kirkus Reviews, April 15, 2002, review of *Summer Sun Risin',* p. 575; November 1, 2002, review of *To Hear the Angels Sing: A Christmas Poem,* p. 1623; August 1, 2004, review of *Setting the Turkeys Free,* p. 747; October 15, 2004, review of *My Teacher Can Teach . . . Anyone!,* p. 1011; April 15, 2006, review of *How We Are Smart,* p. 413.

Indian Life, July-August, 2006, Brenlee Longclaws, review of *We Are Smart,* p. 13.

Los Angeles Times Book Review, May 26, 1991, p. 7.

Publishers Weekly, December 7, 1990, review of *Night Is Coming,* p. 81; February 8, 1993, review of *Storm,* p. 85; February 21, 1994, review of *Bein' with You This Way,* p. 251; August 12, 1996, review of *One Hole in the Road,* p. 82; March 17, 1997, review of *Tangletalk,* p. 82; May 5, 1997, review of *America,* p. 209; October 6, 1997, review of *Shake Dem Halloween Bones,* p. 49; October 13, 1997, review of *Till Year's Good End,* p. 75; September 25, 2000, review of *Hallelujah!,* p. 69, and review of *Can You Top That?,* p. 116; October 9, 2000, review of *The Year with Grandma Moses,* p. 87; June 11, 2001, review of *America: A Book of Opposites,* p. 87; April 22, 2002, review of *Summer Sun Risin',* p. 68; September 23, 2002, review of *To Hear the Angels Sing,* p. 32.

School Library Journal, April, 1991, p. 100; July, 1997, Barbara Elleman, review of *America,* p. 72; October, 2000, review of *Hallelujah!,* p. 62, and Wendy Lukehart, review of *The Year with Grandma Moses,* p. 150; December, 2000, Alicia Eames, review of *Can You Top That?,* p. 119; May, 2002, Anna DeWind Walls, review of *Summer Sun Risin',* p. 124; October, 2002, Eva Mitnick, review of *To Hear the Angels Sing,* p. 62; September, 2004, Gay Lynn Van Vleck, review of *Setting the Turkeys Free,* p. 176; December, 2004, Linda L. Walkins, review of *My Teacher Can Teach . . . Anyone!,* p. 116; June, 2006, Joy Fleishhacker, review of *How We Are Smart,* p. 182.

Smithsonian, November, 1991, p. 183.

ONLINE

W. Nikola-Lisa Home Page, http://www.nikolabooks.com (May 8, 2007).

P

PFEFFER, Susan Beth 1948-

Personal

Born February 17, 1948, in New York, NY; daughter of Leo (a lawyer and professor) and Freda (a secretary) Pfeffer. *Education:* New York University, B.A., 1969. *Hobbies and other interests:* Old movies, baseball, shopping for used books, working with Friends of the Library.

Addresses

Home—Middletown, NY. *Agent*—Marilyn E. Marlow, Curtis Brown Agency, 10 Astor Pl., New York, NY 10003. *E-mail*—Susanpfeffer@lycos.com.

Career

Children's book author.

Awards, Honors

Dorothy Canfield Fisher Award, 1979, and Oklahoma Library Association Sequoyah Young Adult Book Award, 1980, both for *Kid Power;* South Carolina Library Association Young Adult Book Awards, 1983, for *About David,* and 1990, for *The Year without Michael;* Parents' Choice Award, 1983, for *Courage, Dana;* American Library Association (ALA) Best Books for Young Adults citation, 1993, for *Family of Strangers;* inclusion among 100 Best Books for Young Adults, 1969-1994, ALA Young Adult Services, for *The Year without Michael;* honorary doctorate from Mount St. Mary College; Andre Norton Award for Best Young-Adult Science Fiction/Fantasy nomination, Hal Clement Award nomination, Quill Award nomination, and nominations for five state awards, all 2007, all for *Life as We Knew It.*

Writings

FOR CHILDREN

Awful Evelina, illustrated by Diane Dawson, Albert Whitman (Morton Grove, IL), 1979.

Susan Beth Pfeffer (Photograph by Donal Holway. Reproduced by permission.)

Twin Surprises, illustrated by Abby Carter, Holt (New York, NY), 1991.
Twin Troubles, illustrated by Abby Carter, Holt (New York, NY), 1992.

FOR MIDDLE-GRADE READERS

Kid Power, illustrated by Leigh Grant, Franklin Watts (New York, NY), 1977.

Just Between Us, illustrated by Lorna Tomei, Delacorte (New York, NY), 1980.

What Do You Do When Your Mouth Won't Open?, illustrated by Lorna Tomei, Delacorte (New York, NY), 1981.

Courage, Dana, illustrated by Jenny Rutherford, Delacorte (New York, NY), 1983.

Truth or Dare, Macmillan (New York, NY), 1983.

Kid Power Strikes Back, illustrated by Leigh Grant, Franklin Watts (New York, NY), 1984.

The Friendship Pact, Scholastic (New York, NY), 1986.

Rewind to Yesterday, illustrated by Andrew Glass, Delacorte (New York, NY), 1988.

(Self-illustrated) *Dear Dad, Love Laurie,* Scholastic (New York, NY), 1989.

Future Forward, illustrated by Andrew Glass, Delacorte (New York, NY), 1989.

April Upstairs, Holt (New York, NY), 1990.

Darcy Downstairs, Holt (New York, NY), 1990.

Make Believe, Holt (New York, NY), 1992.

The Riddle Streak, illustrated by Michael Chesworth, Holt (New York, NY), 1993.

Sara Kate, Superkid, illustrated by Suzanne Hankins, Holt (New York, NY), 1994.

Sara Kate Saves the World, illustrated by Tony DeLuna, Holt (New York, NY), 1995.

The Trouble with Wishes, illustrated by Jennifer Plecas, Holt (New York, NY), 1996.

YOUNG-ADULT NOVELS

Just Morgan, Walck, 1970.

Better than All Right, Doubleday (New York, NY), 1972.

Rainbows and Fireworks, Walck, 1973.

The Beauty Queen, Doubleday (New York, NY), 1974.

Whatever Words You Want to Hear, Walck, 1974.

Marly the Kid, Doubleday (New York, NY), 1975.

Starring Peter and Leigh, Delacorte (New York, NY), 1978.

About David, Delacorte (New York, NY), 1980.

A Matter of Principle, Delacorte (New York, NY), 1982, reprinted, 2002.

Starting with Melodie, Four Winds (New York, NY), 1982.

Fantasy Summer, Pacer, 1984.

Paperdolls, Dell (New York, NY), 1984.

Getting Even, Pacer, 1986.

The Year without Michael, Bantam (New York, NY), 1987.

Turning Thirteen, Scholastic (New York, NY), 1988.

Head of the Class, Bantam (New York, NY), 1989.

Most Precious Blood, Bantam (New York, NY), 1991.

Family of Strangers, Bantam (New York, NY), 1992.

The Ring of Truth, Bantam (New York, NY), 1993.

Twice Taken, Delacorte (New York, NY), 1994.

Nobody's Daughter, Delacorte (New York, NY), 1995.

The Pizza Puzzle, Delacorte (New York, NY), 1996.

Justice for Emily (sequel to *Nobody's Daughter*), Delacorte (New York, NY), 1997.

Devil's Den, Walker (New York, NY), 1998.

Revenge of the Aztecs, Jamestown Publishers (Lincolnwood, IL), 2000.

Life as We Knew It, Harcourt (New York, NY), 2006.

"MAKE ME A STAR" NOVEL SERIES

Prime Time, Berkley (New York, NY), 1985.

Take Two and Rolling, Berkley (New York, NY), 1985.

Wanting It All, Berkley (New York, NY), 1985.

On the Move, Berkley (New York, NY), 1985.

Love Scenes, Berkley (New York, NY), 1986.

Hard Times High, Berkley (New York, NY), 1986.

"SEBASTIAN SISTERS" NOVEL SERIES

Evvie at Sixteen, Bantam (New York, NY), 1988.

Thea at Sixteen, Bantam (New York, NY), 1988.

Claire at Sixteen, Bantam (New York, NY), 1989.

Sybil at Sixteen, Bantam (New York, NY), 1989.

Meg at Sixteen, Bantam (New York, NY), 1990.

"PORTRAITS OF LITTLE WOMEN" NOVEL SERIES

Meg's Story, Delacorte (New York, NY), 1997.

Jo's Story, Delacorte (New York, NY), 1997.

Beth's Story, Delacorte (New York, NY), 1997.

Amy's Story, Delacorte (New York, NY), 1997.

Meg Makes a Friend, Delacorte (New York, NY), 1998.

Jo Makes a Friend, Delacorte (New York, NY), 1998.

Christmas Dreams: Four Stories, Delacorte (New York, NY), 1998.

Beth Makes a Friend, Delacorte (New York, NY), 1998.

Amy Makes a Friend, Delacorte (New York, NY), 1998.

A Gift for Meg, Delacorte (New York, NY), 1999.

A Gift for Jo, Delacorte (New York, NY), 1999.

A Gift for Beth, Delacorte (New York, NY), 1999.

A Gift for Amy, Delacorte (New York, NY), 1999.

Birthday Wishes: Four Stories, Delacorte (New York, NY), 1999.

Ghostly Tales: Four Stories, Delacorte (New York, NY), 2000.

OTHER

You Can Write Children's Books in Your Spare Time, Mine Book Press, 1993.

Who Were They Really?: The True Stories behind Famous Characters, Milbrook Press (Brookfield, CT), 1999.

Contributor of short stories to *Sixteen,* *Visions,* and *Connections.* Contributor of one-act play to *Center Stage,* edited by Ronald R. Gallo, and an essay to *Vital Signs 1,* edited by James L. Collins.

Adaptations

A Year without Michael was adapted as an audiobook, 1998. *Life as We Knew It* was adapted as an audiobook, read by Emily Bauer, Listening Library, 2006.

Sidelights

A chronicler of adolescent middle-class America, Susan Beth Pfeffer has created an impressive list of publications for young adults that include the novels *The Year without Michael, The Pizza Puzzle, Devil's Den,* and *Life as We Knew It.* Her themes run the gamut, from serious emotional problems resulting from suicidal thoughts or divorce and typical teen fantasies of modeling or acting to historical fiction and science fiction that addresses an apocalyptic future. Pfeffer's protagonists deal with issues ranging from censorship to speaking in public, and they meet challenges with spunk and not a small degree of humor. Skilled at realistically depicting emotional states, Pfeffer concentrates on story rather than scene; on realistic dialogue rather than characterization. According to a *Publishers Weekly* reviewer, Pfeffer's body of work shows her to be "a natural storyteller with an acute ear."

Raised in a well-off family, Pfeffer grew up in the suburbs of New York City, and her family vacationed at a summer house in the Catskill Mountains. Her childhood experiences inform her writing, especially her focus on young people growing up in the suburbs. Pfeffer decided she wanted to be a writer at age six when her father, a law professor, was writing a book on constitutional law. When the published book was dedicated to her, she felt huge pride in seeing her name in print on the title page. Pfeffer began writing that same year, crafting a story about the love between an Oreo cookie and a pair of scissors. "I know I defined myself as a writer at least by third grade," she later recalled in a sketch for *Something about the Author Autobiographical Series (SAAS),* "because it was in third grade that I used a semicolon in a book report and felt it was an important occasion, my first semicolon."

Pfeffer started on her career course while she was finishing up her degree in radio and television at New York University. During a writing course, she used chapters of a juvenile book she was working on as class assignments, writing five pages a day, and by mid-year she had a completed manuscript. Helped by a professor with finding a publisher, Pfeffer became a professional author at age twenty with the young-adult novel *Just Morgan.* The story of an orphaned girl, *Just Morgan* delighted Robin Davies, who wrote in the *New York Times Book Review* that "there's lots of fast, fresh, often very funny dialogue in this . . . funny, worthwhile novel." Encouraged by such positive critical praise, there was no turning back for Pfeffer, and in the dozens of books she has written since she has earned the luxury of being a full-time writer.

The award-winning middle-grade novel *Kid Power* was born of Pfeffer's wish that an enterprising neighborhood kid would take on the onerous job of mowing her lawn; it focuses on just that sort of girl. In her other books for middle-grade readers, such as *Just between Us, Darcy Downstairs,* and *What Do You Do When Your Mouth Won't Open?,* Pfeffer turns other personal foibles—such as not being able to keep a secret, or a fear of public speaking—to her advantage. The main character in *Sara Kate Saves the World* finds that superpowers are a boon in her battle with a school bully, while third-grader

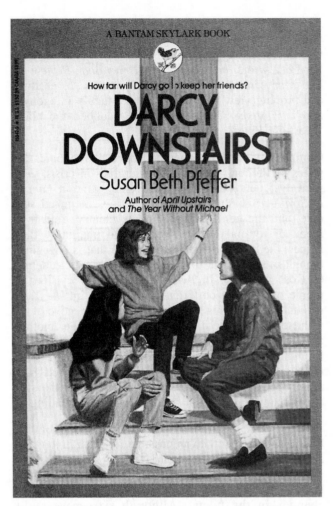

Cover of Pfeffer's 1993 middle-grade novel **Darcy Downstairs,** *featuring artwork by Rick Mujica.* (Bantam Books, 1993. Cover art copyright © 1992 by Rick Mujica. Used by permission of Bantam Books, a division of Random House, Inc.)

Kate finds the opportunity to have a wish granted is more of a burden than a joy in *The Trouble with Wishes.* According to several reviewers, Pfeffer's light and breezy texts make such chapter books attractive and accessible to young readers, and Susan Dove Lempke praised the author's "skilled use of point of view and humor" in her *Booklist* review of *The Trouble with Wishes.*

In her books for older readers, Pfeffer tackles more serious issues. Told in diary form, *About David* focuses on a boy who kills his parents and then takes his own life. According to John Lansingh Bennett in a review for *Best Sellers,* the grim story also provides "a measure of empathy, some slight understanding of grief and how it passes, a touch of humanity, to its teen readers." In *Devil's Den* seventh-grader Joey Browne comes to terms with his feelings of abandonment while helping his caring stepfather caretake the grave site of a forgotten Civil War soldier. With *The Year without Michael* Pfeffer addresses the tragedy of missing children through the story of the Chapman family: the missing son, Michael, the parents who are stumbling along through a strained marriage, and sixteen-year-old sister

Jody, who is trying to keep it all together. Like life, the novel is somewhat unsettling in that the reader does not find out what happened to Michael in the end. As Elinor Lenz wrote in the *New York Times Book Review,* in *The Year without Michael* Pfeffer presents "a sensitive and probing view of a contemporary family in agony," and a *Publishers Weekly* reviewer dubbed the book "heart-breaking."

Complicated and unexpected characters people the pages of Pfeffer's novels, as do families in crisis. One such dysfunctional family takes center stage in *Family of Strangers,* a story of drug addiction, attempted suicide, and the curative power of psychiatry. Told in a blend of journal entries, letters, and imaginary dialogues, the book provides a "narrative that is engaging, though often painful to read," according to Jacqueline C. Rose in *Kliatt.* In *Twice Taken* Pfeffer revisits the theme of missing children she explored in *The Year without Michael,* this time through the perspective of an abducted child whose father took her from her mother eleven years before. Despite the novel's serious theme, Pfeffer avoids becoming maudlin; as Margaret Cole noted in *School Library Journal,* the book's "lively narration, peppered with wry, insightful wit, and the story's balanced resolution make it enjoyable reading if not a strong literary achievement."

Pfeffer takes a leap into an unstable future in *Life as We Knew It,* a novel that combines coming-of-age themes with an apocalyptic future. In the story, Earth's moon is knocked out of its orbit by a meteor, causing drastic changes in the planet. Although sixteen-year-old Miranda questions her mom's panicked stockpiling of food and other supplies, as news of earthquakes, volcanoes, and atmospheric disturbances soon filters in she realizes that her family is better off than many of their neighbors. As the globe plunges into perpetual winter, the family's lack of electricity and the discomfort of living in a single room, huddled around a wood stove, give way to more significant worries. By designing her book as Miranda's diary, Pfeffer brings to life the unfolding catastrophe from a teen's perspective and makes the girl's growing acceptance of pain and death that much more visceral." Each page is filled with events both wearying and terrifying," noted *Booklist* reviewer Ilene Cooper, the critic adding that Pfeffer's text is "infused with honest emotions." As a *Publishers Weekly* reviewer noted, the teen's "undying love for her family and heightened appreciation of simple pleasures will likely provoke discussion and inspire gratitude" for the comforts they enjoy, while John Peters explained in his *School Library Journal* review that *Life as We Knew It* will leave readers "stunned and thoughtful."

Pfeffer turns to the past in several of her books for young readers, such as the novel *Nobody's Daughter* and the short-fiction collection *Ghostly Tales: Four Stories.* Taking place in 1913 in a New England mill town, *Nobody's Daughter* introduces Emily, an eleven-year-old orphan living at the Austen Home for Orphaned

Girls. With the help of a caring librarian and several close friends, Emily copes with the prejudice that exists against the poor and determines to remain hopeful despite her daunting circumstances. Dubbing the book "a wrenching story," a *Publishers Weekly* contributor called *Nobody's Daughter* a "compassionate exploration of what happens to those who fall between the cracks." A sequel, *Justice for Emily,* finds the girl determined to bring three well-to-do preteens to justice when she witnesses their involvement in a tragic accident that left another girl dead. Reviewing the novel for *Booklist,* Lauren Peterson noted that Pfeffer's heroine shows "dignity in the face of . . . bullying," adding that Emily's bravery in "stand[ing] up for the truth will arouse empathy and admiration" in young readers.

In addition to her stand-alone novels for children and older teens, Pfeffer has also won fans for her novel series "Sebastian Sisters," "Make Me a Star," and "Portraits of Little Women," the last based on the beloved books by nineteenth-century novelist Louisa May Alcott. While the "Portraits of Little Women" books fo-

The scratchy pen-and-ink art of Marcy Ramsey adds a nostalgic element to Pfeffer's spine-tingling story collection **Ghostly Tales.** (Delacorte Press 2000. Illustration copyright © 2000 by Marcy Ramsey. Reproduced by permission of Dilys Evans Fine Illustrations, on behalf of the illustrator.)

cus, in turn, on sisters Meg, Beth, Jo, and Amy, each of Pfeffer's "Sebastian Sisters" books feature a different daughter of the Sebastian clan as they reach age sixteen, and the series concludes with an historical look at the mother's sixteenth year. The "Sebastian Sisters" series gave Pfeffer the opportunity to stick with one subject for six years. "Writing those five books was like living with a whole other family, but a family that had to do what I wanted them to—enormous fun to write," she recalled in her *SAAS* essay. In *School Library Journal*, Merilyn S. Burrington called the Sebastians "some of the most complicated, intriguing people in contemporary [young adult] literature."

A fast writer, Pfeffer typically writes a chapter a day when her book is fully researched and thought out. On several occasions, she has written a book in two weeks, which leaves time for speaking to young readers and presenting workshops for budding writers. "I think everybody has a creative mind," she told an interviewer in *Authors and Artists for Young Adults*. "I tell people to start with a situation that appeals to them, and they can get that anywhere—from their favorite novel or TV show or fairy tale or just something that has been eating away at them for a long time. Then you ask, 'Who would be in that situation, what would their ages be, how did they get in this situation,' and so on. That leads in to the plot, what is going to happen. Then I teach people how to outline, which is remarkably easy." "What I love best about being a writer," she added, "is that people actually pay me for making up stories."

Biographical and Critical Sources

BOOKS

Authors and Artists for Young Adults, Volume 12, Thomson Gale (Detroit, MI), 1994.
Children's Literature Review, Volume 11, Thomson Gale (Detroit, MI), 1986.
Something about the Author Autobiography Series, Volume 17, Thomson Gale (Detroit, MI), 1994.

PERIODICALS

Best Sellers, November, 1980, John Lansingh Bennett, review of *About David*, p. 303.
Booklist, September 1, 1995, Mary Harris Veeder, review of *Sara Kate Saves the World*, p. 78; May 1, 1996, Susan Dove Lempke, review of *The Trouble with Wishes*, p. 1507; October 1, 1996, Chris Sherman, review of *The Pizza Puzzle*, p. 352; January 1, 1997, Lauren Peterson, review of *Justice for Emily*, p. 862; May 15, 1998, Hazel Rochman, review of *Devil's Den*, p. 1627; December 15, 1999, Ilene Cooper, review of *Who Were They Really?: The True Stories behind Famous Characters*, p. 781; September 1, 2006, Ilene Cooper, review of *Life as We Knew It*, p. 127.

Bulletin of the Center for Children's Books, May, 1980, review of *Just between Us*, p. 180; January, 1995, review of *Sara Kate, Superkid*, p. 174; June, 1996, review of *The Trouble with Wishes*, p. 349; May, 1998, review of *Devil's Den*, p. 335.
Children's Book Review Service, July, 1973; August, 1974; October, 1974; October, 1977; August, 1979; May, 1983; winter supplement, 1985.
English Journal, January, 1972, John W. Conner, review of *Just Morgan*, p. 138.
Horn Book, December, 1980, Mary M. Burns, review of *About David*, p. 649; August, 1982, Karen M. Klockner, review of *A Matter of Principle*, p. 416; August, 1984; March-April, 1988, Nancy Vasilakis, review of *The Year without Michael*, p. 204; May-June, 1992, Maeve Visser-Knoth, review of *Family of Strangers*, p. 345; November-December, 2006, Christine M. Heppermann, review of *Life as We Knew It*, p. 723.
Kirkus Reviews, September 15, 2006, Susan Beth Pfeffer, review of *Life as We Knew It*, p. 963.
Kliatt, March, 1994, Jacqueline C. Rose, review of *Family of Strangers*, p. 11.
New York Times Book Review, May 24, 1970, Robin Davies, review of *Just Morgan*, pp. 16, 18; November 8, 1987, Elinor Lenz, review of *The Year without Michael*, p. 38; May 15, 1993, Ilene Cooper, review of *The Ring of Truth*, p. 29.
Publishers Weekly, September 23, 1974, review of *Whatever Words You Want to Hear*, p. 155; January 8 1988, review of *The Year without Michael*, p. 45; July 5, 1991, review of *Most Precious Blood*, p. 66; February 10, 1992, review of *Family of Strangers*, p. 82; April 12, 1993, review of *Ring of Truth*, p. 64; September 20, 1993, review of *Make Believe*, p. 73; January 2, 1995, review of *Nobody's Daughter*, p. 77; June 3, 1996, review of *Twice Taken*, p. 85; June 24, 1996, review of *The Pizza Puzzle*, p. 61; January 6, 1997, review of *Justice for Emily*, p. 74; November 24, 1997, review of *Amy's Story*, p. 75; March 2, 1998, review of *Devil's Den*, p. 69, and *Justice for Emily*, p. 70; September 28, 1998, review of *Christmas Dreams: Four Stories*, p. 64; October 16, 2006, review of *Life as We Knew It*, p. 53.
School Library Journal, February, 1980, Sandra S. Ridenour, review of *Kid Power*, p. 32; May, 1981, Nordhielm Wooldridge, review of *What Do You do When Your Mouth Won't Open?*, p. 68; March, 1983, Susan Rosenkoetter, review of *Starting with Melodie*, p. 196; October, 1984, review of *Truth or Dare*, p. 160; November, 1984, Miriam Lang Budin, review of *Fantasy Summer*, p. 136; October, 1985, Constance Allen, review of *Prime Time*, p. 186; October, 1986, review of *The Friendship Pact*, p. 181; November, 1986, Kathleen D. Whalin, review of *Getting Even*, p. 107; June 26, 1987, review of *The Year without Michael*, p. 74; October, 1988, Carolyn Noah, review of *Rewind to Yesterday*, p. 147; November, 1988, Libby K. White, review of *Thea at Sixteen*, p. 130; June, 1989, Anne Connor, review of *Future Forward*, p. 108; September, 1989, Merilyn S. Burrington, review of *Sybil at Sixteen*, p. 276; August, 1990, Lucinda Snyder Whitehurst, review of *Meg at Sixteen*, p. 164; September,

1991, Bonnie L. Raasch, review of *Most Precious Blood,* p. 283; April, 1993, Alice Casey Smith, review of *The Ring of Truth,* p. 143; December, 1993, Nancy P. Reeder, review of *Make Believe,* p. 116; June, 1994, Margaret Cole, review of *Twice Taken,* p. 152; December, 1994, Christina Dorr, review of *Sara Kate, Superkids,* pp. 79-80; June, 1996, Christina Dorr, review of *The Trouble with Wishes,* p. 107; February, 1997, Sally Margolis, review of *Justice for Emily,* p. 104; January, 1998, review of *Jo's Story,* p. 90; June, 1998, Carolyn Noah, review of *Devil's Den,* p. 151; December, 1999, Anne Chapman Callaghan, review of *Who Were They Really?,* p. 158; October, 2006, John Peters, review of *Life as We Knew It,* p. 166.

Voice of Youth Advocates, October, 1984, review of *Fantasy Summer,* p. 198; February, 1985, review of *Paper Dolls,* p. 330; August, 1988, review of *Evvie at Sixteen,* p. 134; June, 1989, review of *Claire at Sixteen,* p. 105; April, 1990, review of *Meg at Sixteen,* p. 33; June, 1991, review of *Meg at Sixteen,* p. 141; June, 1992, review of *Family of Strangers,* p. 99; February, 1994; June, 1994, Donna Houser, review of *Twice Taken,* pp. 89-90; August, 1996, review of *The Pizza Puzzle,* p. 160; August, 2002, review of *A Matter of Principle,* p. 176.

ONLINE

SciFi.com, http://www.scifi.com/ (March 19, 2007), John Joseph Adams, review of *Life as We Knew It.*
Susan Beth Pfeffer Blog Site, http://susanbethpfeffer.blogspot.com/ (June 4, 2007).*

*   *   *

POLACCO, Patricia 1944-

Personal

Born July 11, 1944, in Lansing, MI; daughter of William F. (a traveling salesman and television talk-show host) and Mary Ellen (a teacher) Barber; married c. 1962 (marriage ended); married Enzo Mario Polacco (a chef and cooking instructor), August 18, 1979; children: (first marriage) Traci Denise, Steven John. *Education:* Attended Ohio State University, California College of Arts and Crafts, and Lancy College; Morash University (Melbourne, Australia), B.F.A. (painting), 1974; Royal Melbourne Institute of Technology, M.A., Ph.D. (art history), 1978; also studied in England, France, and Russia *Hobbies and other interests:* Travel, running, pets, painting, sculpture, egg art.

Addresses

Home—Union City, MI. *Agent*—Edythea Selman, 14 Washington Pl., New York, NY 10003.

Career

Author and illustrator, 1986—. Consultant on icon restoration; Babushka, Inc., founder. Speaker for school and reading organizations.

Patricia Polacco (Photograph by Al Guiteras. Reproduced by permission of Guiteras Photography.)

Member

Society of Children's Book Writers and Illustrators.

Awards, Honors

International Reading Association Award for Younger Readers, 1989, for *Rechenka's Eggs;* Sydney Taylor Book Award for Picture Books, 1989, for *The Keeping Quilt;* Commonwealth Club of California Award, 1990, for *Babushka's Doll,* and 1992, for *Chicken Sunday;* Boston Area Education for Social Responsibility Award, 1992; Golden Kite Award for Illustration, 1992, for *Chicken Sunday;* Jane Addams Award Honor Book designation, 1993 for *Mrs. Katz and Tush;* American Book of the Year Award nomination, 1995, and West Virginia Children's Book Award, 1997, both for *Pink and Say;* Jo Osborne Award for Humor, 1996; North Dakota Library Association Children's Book Award, 1996, and Missouri Show Me Readers' Award, 1997, both for *My Rotten Redheaded Older Brother;* Parents' Choice honor designation, 1998, and Gold Award, 1999, both for *Thank You, Mr. Falker;* Mid-South Independent Booksellers Humpty Dumpty Award, 1998.

Writings

PICTURE BOOKS; SELF-ILLUSTRATED, EXCEPT AS NOTED

Meteor!, Dodd, Mead (New York, NY), 1987.
Rechenka's Eggs, Philomel (New York, NY), 1988.

Boat Ride with Lillian Two Blossom, Philomel (New York, NY), 1988.

(With Ernest Lawrence Thayer) *Casey at the Bat,* Putnam (New York, NY), 1988.

The Keeping Quilt, Simon & Schuster (New York, NY), 1988, tenth anniversary edition with eight new drawings, 1998.

Uncle Vova's Tree, Philomel (New York, NY), 1989.

Babushka's Doll, Simon & Schuster (New York, NY), 1990.

Just Plain Fancy, Bantam (New York, NY), 1990.

Thunder Cake, Philomel (New York, NY), 1990.

Some Birthday!, Simon & Schuster (New York, NY), 1991.

Appelemando's Dreams, Philomel (New York, NY), 1991.

Chicken Sunday, Philomel (New York, NY), 1992.

Mrs. Katz and Tush, Bantam (New York, NY), 1992.

Picnic at Mudsock Meadow, Putnam (New York, NY), 1992.

The Bee Tree, Putnam (New York, NY), 1993.

Babushka Baba Yaga, Philomel (New York, NY), 1993.

My Rotten Redheaded Older Brother, Simon & Schuster (New York, NY), 1994.

Pink and Say, Philomel (New York, NY), 1994.

Tikvah Means Hope, Doubleday (New York, NY), 1994.

Babushka's Mother Goose (collection of stories and poems), Philomel (New York, NY), 1995.

My Ol' Man, Philomel (New York, NY), 1995.

The Trees of the Dancing Goats, Simon & Schuster (New York, NY), 1996.

Aunt Chip and the Great Triple Creek Dam Affair, Philomel (New York, NY), 1996.

I Can Hear the Sun: A Modern Myth, Philomel (New York, NY), 1996.

In Enzo's Splendid Gardens, Philomel (New York, NY), 1997.

Uncle Isaaco, Philomel (New York, NY), 1997.

Mrs. Mack, Philomel (New York, NY), 1998.

Thank You, Mr. Falker, Philomel (New York, NY), 1998.

Welcome Comfort, Philomel (New York, NY), 1999.

Luba and the Wren, Philomel (New York, NY), 1999.

The Calhoun Club, Philomel (New York, NY), 2000.

The Butterfly, Philomel (New York, NY), 2000.

Betty Doll, Philomel (New York, NY), 2001.

Mr. Lincoln's Way, Philomel (New York, NY), 2001.

When Lightning Comes in a Jar, Philomel (New York, NY), 2002.

A Christmas Tapestry, Philomel (New York, NY), 2002.

The Graves Family, Philomel (New York, NY), 2003.

G Is for Goat, Philomel (New York, NY), 2003.

An Orange for Frankie, Philomel (New York, NY), 2004.

Oh, Look!, Philomel (New York, NY), 2004.

John Philip Duck, Philomel (New York, NY), 2004.

Mommies Say Shhh!, Philomel (New York, NY), 2005.

The Graves Family Goes Camping, Philomel (New York, NY), 2005.

Emma Kate, Philomel (New York, NY), 2005.

Something about Hensley's, Philomel (New York, NY), 2006.

Rotten Richie and the Ultimate Dare, Philomel (New York, NY), 2006.

Ginger and Petunia, Philomel (New York, NY), 2007.

Several of Polacco's works have been translated into Spanish.

OTHER

Firetalking (autobiography), photographs by Lawrence Migdale, Richard C. Owen (Katonah, NY), 1994.

Adaptations

Spoken Arts video adaptations of Polacco's books include *Rechenka's Eggs,* 1991, *Chicken Sunday,* 1992, *The Keeping Quilt,* 1993, *Aunt Chip and the Great Triple Creek Dam Affair,* 1996, *Pink and Say,* 1996, *Thank You, Mr. Falker,* 1999, *Christmas Tapestry,* 2004, and *John Philip Duck,* 2005, *Rechenka's Eggs,* and *Thunder Cake.* Sound recordings of author's works include *Chicken Sunday,* Scholastic, 1993; *Just Plain Fancy,* Bantam Doubleday Dell Audio, 1994; *Casey at the Bat,* Spoken Arts, 1994; *The Keeping Quilt,* Spoken Arts, 1998; *Meteor!; Thunder Cake;* and *Thank You, Mr. Falker.* Several of Polacco's works have been issued in book/cassette combinations.

Sidelights

Author and illustrator Patricia Polacco is "as natural a storyteller as they come," according to Shannon Maughan in *Publishers Weekly.* The highly praised, award-winning Polacco has over thirty picture books to her credit, quite a feat in light of the fact that she did not start publishing until 1987, at the age of forty-one. A popular writer and artist, Polacco is lauded for transforming childhood memories, favorite episodes from

One of Polacco's most popular children's books, **The Keeping Quilt** *brings to life the traditions of a close-knit family.* (Simon & Schuster, 1988. Copyright © 1988 by Patricia Polacco. Reproduced by permission of Simon & Schuster Books for Young Readers, an imprint of Simon & Schuster Children's Publishing Division.)

family history, and elements from her Russian, Ukrainian, Jewish, and Irish heritage into books that are noted for their freshness, originality, warmth, panache, and universality. The characters in books such as *The Keeping Quilt, Uncle Vova's Tree, Pink and Say, My Ol' Man, In Enzo's Splendid Gardens, Welcome Comfort,* and *The Butterfly* reflect a variety of races, religions, and age groups, celebrating both diversity and commonality, while *My Rotten Redheaded Older Brother* is drawn directly from her own childhood. Several of Polacco's works retell family stories that have been handed down for generations; while often including Russian and Jewish customs and folklore, she has also written about African and Native Americans, the Irish, and the Amish. Her stories are noted for clear, fluid language that makes them suitable for reading aloud. As an illustrator, she works in watercolor, gouache, charcoal, and collage, and characteristically offsets images penciled on a stark white field with bright colors and patterned backgrounds. Praising Polacco's renderings of facial expressions as "priceless," *School Library Journal* reviewer Grace Oliff wrote in her review of *John Philip Duck* that the picture book's "artwork is simply beautiful as the artist orchestrates a harmonious symphony of color."

Polacco was born in Lansing, Michigan, in 1944, the daughter of William Barber, a salesman who became a television talk-show host, and Mary Ellen Gaw Barber, a teacher. Her father was of Irish descent and her mother was from a Russian and Ukrainian background. After her parents' divorce when she was three years old, Polacco and her older brother spent their school years with their mother and summers with their father. The author spent her early childhood on a farm in Union City, Michigan. When she was five, her beloved Babushka (grandmother) passed away, after which Polacco, her mother, and brother moved to Coral Gables, Florida, for three years before settling in Oakland, California. Writing on her home page, Polacco recalled that living on the farm in Union City "was the most magical time of my life" and "my Babushka and other grandparents were some of the most inspirational people in my life."

Polacco inherited a natural storytelling voice from both sides of the family. Although stories—both oral and read from books—fascinated the introspective girl, she had problems reading on her own. At age fourteen Polacco was finally diagnosed with dyslexia; by this time, however, she had already suffered her classmates' taunts due to her lackluster progress in reading and math. Sketching and illustrating became her focus; her classmates were speechless when confronted with her fluid artwork. The world created by her own imagination became Polacco's refuge during adolescence.

Graduating from high school, Polacco received a college scholarship, but instead she decided to marry at age eighteen. She attended Ohio State University for a couple of terms, but eventually dropped out to go to

Polacco recounts her memories of a rambunctious older brother in **My Rotten Redheaded Older Brother,** *which features the author's engaging artwork.* (Aladdin Paperbacks, 1994. Copyright © 1994 by Patricia Polacco. Reproduced by permission of Simon & Schuster Books for Young Readers, an imprint of Simon & Schuster Children's Publishing Division.)

work and have two children, Traci and Steven. After she and her first husband were divorced, Polacco completed her undergraduate studies in California. She went to Australia for further education, earning an M.F.A. in painting from Morash University in Melbourne and a Ph.D. in Russian and Greek iconographic history from the Royal Melbourne Institute of Technology. While studying in Australia, Polacco met her second husband, Enzo Polacco, an Italian Jew from Trieste, Italy, who is a chef and cooking instructor as well as a Holocaust survivor.

Throughout her life, Polacco has been a maker of books. As she told Maughan in *Publishers Weekly,* "I've always made rough dummies, like thick greeting cards, for people in my life to celebrate any occasion." At the insistence of a friend who admired these efforts, Polacco joined her local chapter of the Society of Children's Book Writers and Illustrators and began adapting her family stories as picture books. In 1987, she and her mother went to New York City to shop around Polacco's eighty-pound portfolio, visiting sixty publishers in a single week. "I was too stupid to be frightened, and I just loved it," she recalled to Maughan. The same year, Polacco sold her first book, *Meteor!*

Meteor! is the "mostly true" tale about the events that occur after a fallen star crashes in the backyard of

Grampa and Gramma Gaw in Union City, Michigan. After the meteor lands, the news buzzes through town, more detailed with every telling. Soon the farm becomes a carnival ground complete with a circus. When the festivities end, the townspeople who have touched the meteor feel that it has changed their lives. Called "an affectionate poke at small-town life" by a critic in *Kirkus Reviews, Meteor!* was praised by a *Publishers Weekly* critic as "an enchanting book [that] overwhelmingly expresses the magic that suddenly pervades a small town, from the funny, folksy way the story is told to the imaginative, full-color illustrations." Polacco produced *The Calhoun Club,* a sequel to *Meteor!,* in 2000. In this book, children's author Petra Penwrite sets out to prove that the meteorite in her hometown of Union City is real and that it grants wishes to children.

Rechenka's Eggs is a folkloric tale set in Russia before the communist revolution of 1917. In this work, old Babushka, who lives alone in her small country home, paints beautiful, prize-winning eggs that always win first place at the Easter Festival. Babushka rescues Rechenka, a goose shot by a hunter, nurses her back to health, and in so doing receives the gift of beautifully colored eggs which the goose lays for her. Noting the book's "beauty and authenticity," Shaun Traynor, reviewing the work for the *Times Educational Supplement,* called *Rechenka's Eggs* "the perfect Easter book for all seasons." Leonard Marcus stated in the *New York Times Book Review* that Polacco's book "is as much about friendship and the workmanlike small things of this life as it is about faith," while Marcus Crouch concluded in *Junior Bookshelf* that "this lovely book introduces a new and outstanding talent to the field of children's books. . . . It is a picture-book of outstanding quality."

In one of Polacco's most popular books, *The Keeping Quilt,* little Patricia narrates the story of a quilt that has been in her family for many years. The quilt ties together four generations of an immigrant Jewish family and becomes a symbol of their love and faith. Writing in *School Library Journal,* Lee Bock called *The Keeping Quilt* a "beautifully conceived book" and a "lovely story," while Denise M. Wilms concluded in *Booklist* that, in addition to being "useful for the sense of history it presents to young viewers (especially in discussions of genealogy), this tale also carries a warm message on the meaning of family." In 1998, Polacco produced a revised, tenth-anniversary edition of *The Keeping Quilt.* The first edition ended with a picture of Polacco holding her newborn daughter; the revised edition expands the story with five new pages of text and paintings that depict the author's two children and their use of the keeping quilt.

A story from Polacco's childhood was the inspiration behind her self-illustrated picture book **Chicken Sunday.** (Philomel Books, 1992. Copyright © 1992 by Patricia Polacco. Reproduced by permission of Philomel Books, a division of Penguin Putnam Books for Young Readers.)

Polacco has published several other books that deal with her Jewish heritage and the history of Jews in the United States and abroad. In *Tikvah Means Hope,* a Jewish family exhibits resilience after a devastating fire occurs in the hills of Oakland, California. A reviewer for *Publishers Weekly* wrote that Polacco's drawings "skillfully and emotionally convey the anguish and suffering of the community, as well as its resilience and hopefulness." In *The Trees of the Dancing Goats* Polacco once again draws on family memory and stories to tell the tale of how a Jewish family in Michigan helps make their neighbors' Christmas memorable during an outbreak of scarlet fever. "Polacco's brightly colored, detailed paintings in marking pens and pencil show a child in a close, loving home that is bursting with energy and joy," wrote *Booklist* contributor Hazel Rochman in a review of *The Tree of the Dancing Goats.*

With *Uncle Isaaco,* Polacco focuses on the events surrounding World War II and the Holocaust. In the book she tells how her husband, Enzo, was expelled from his home in Trieste, Italy, by the Nazis as a little boy and how he missed his beloved uncle most of all. She also details the suffering of the Jews in World War II and the bravery of the French Resistance in *The Butterfly,* a story originally told to her by her Aunt Monique. Monique's mother hides a Jewish family in her basement and tries to help them escape. Wendy Lukehart, writing in *School Library Journal,* called *Uncle Isaaco* a "perfect blend of art and story," while *Booklist* reviewer Rochman concluded that "what will hold grade-school kids is the truth of the friendship story and the tension of hiding to survive."

Polacco deals with issues of race in several of her books. In *Chicken Sunday,* neighborhood children help get Miss Eula the Easter bonnet she likes and in so doing win over a local Jewish shopkeeper. Carolyn Phelan wrote in *Booklist* that in Polacco's "moving picture book, the hatred sometimes engendered by racial and religious differences is overpowered by the love of people who recognize their common humanity." Calling *Chicken Sunday* "an authentic tale of childhood friendship," Dorothy Houlihan noted in *School Library Journal* that Polacco's tale "resonates with the veracity of a personal recollection and is replete with vivid visual and visceral images."

Polacco blends questions of race with another family tale that stands among her most highly regarded books. *Pink and Say* relates a poignant story set during the U.S. Civil War that was told by the author's great-great-great-grandfather on her father's side. In this book, fifteen-year-old Sheldon Russell Curtis (Say), an Ohio boy left for dead in a Georgia battlefield, is rescued by gravedigger Pinkus Sylee (Pink), an African-American teen who is a fellow Union soldier. Pink drags Say to his home a few miles away. While the boy convalesces, he and Pink become friends and share their secrets: Pink can read—a knowledge forbidden to slaves—and

wants to fight slavery, while Say admits that he is a deserter. Say also shook the hand of U.S. President Abraham Lincoln, and this becomes a talismanic handshake between Pink and Say. Pink teaches Say to read, and his fervor against slavery inspires Say to rejoin his regiment. However, both boys are taken prisoners by the Confederates, who kill Pink's mother and send the friends to the notorious Andersonville prison camp. Due to his skin color, Pink is hung a few hours after entering the prison, while Say is released several months later. As a reviewer noted in *Publishers Weekly, Pink and Say* "stands as a testament to [Pink's] life," and Polacco's "gripping story resonates with emotion as she details the chilling and horrible reverberations of war and social injustice." Praising the book's illustrations as "a spectacular achievement," a *Kirkus Reviews* critic added that Polacco tells her story "carefully and without melodrama so that it speaks for itself." Writing in the *New York Times Book Review,* Henry Mayer concluded that Polacco "has addressed the theme of interracial friendship in previous books with heartfelt sentiment, but *Pink and Say* has a resonance that these contemporary stories lack. It is rare to find a children's book that deals so richly, yet gently, with the sober themes of slavery and freedom, martyrdom, and historical memory."

Thank You, Mr. Falker is based heavily on Polacco's own life. In this story, ten-year-old Trisha yearns to read, but has been teased constantly by her classmates because she stumbles over words and numbers. Although she has won respect for her artistic talent, Trisha still hides the fact that she cannot read. Finally, her fifth-grade teacher, Mr. Falker, turns a sympathetic eye to the girl's difficulty. Using his own money, he pays a reading specialist to work with Trisha until she overcomes her problem. Rochman, writing in *Booklist,* noted in a review of *Thank You, Mr. Falker* that Polacco's young heroine "isn't idealized; we see her messy and desperate, poring over her books. This will encourage the child who feels like a failure and the teacher who cares."

The eponymous protagonist of *Welcome Comfort,* a lonely, overweight foster child, is taken under the wing—or rather in the sleigh—of a rather plump school custodian. Comfort has never known the joys of Christmas until the mysterious custodian and his wife initiate him. A reviewer for *Publishers Weekly* noted that "this warm blend of fantasy and reality delivers a satisfying surprise ending," and that Polacco's artwork "is even more vibrant than usual." Reviewing the same title in the *Washington Post Book World,* Michael Patrick Hearn called *Welcome Comfort* "as warm as a down comforter and told with the conviction and cadences of a tall tale."

Other tales that draw from Polacco's Midwest family traditions include *When Lightning Comes in a Jar, Betty Doll, My Rotten Redheaded Older Brother, Christmas Tapestry,* and *An Orange for Frankie.* Two reunions of

A handmade doll that brings joy to many generations of a family is the thread running through Polacco's story in **Betty Doll.** (Puffin Books, 2001. Reproduced by permission of Puffin Books, a division of Penguin Putnam Books for Young Readers.)

extended family are the focus of *When Lightning Comes from a Jar,* as relatives come from all over Michigan to gossip, share food, and talk about the latest news, both in the early twentieth century and again, three generations later. In *Betty Doll* Polacco's sensitive graphite drawings bring to life the story of a beloved handmade doll that, cherished by its first owner, is eventually packed away, only to be discovered by future generations. A poignant Christmas Eve from generations past is the setting for *An Orange for Frankie,* which finds a young boy looking forward to waking up on Christmas morning to find the highly prized citrus perched on the family home's fireplace mantel. "With her usual narrative flair Polacco weaves a story of family remembrances and traditions," wrote Wanda Meyers-Hines in her *School Library Journal* review of *When Lightning Comes in a Jar,* while a *Publishers Weekly* contributor predicted that adult readers will "appreciate the [book's] . . . warm message of the importance of heritage." Similar praise was accorded the nostalgic holiday story *Christmas Tapestry,* which finds a boy and his minister father patching up a hole in the crumbling wall of their Detroit church with a wall-hanging that has unexpected tied to the past of an elderly friend. Reviewing the story, GraceAnne A. DeCandido wrote in *Booklist* that "Polacco is a master at intergenerational, interfaith stories that bring comfort and joy," and

a *Kirkus Reviews* writer wrote that in *Christmas Tapestry* the author/illustrator "succeeds as always with her watercolor-and-pencil illustrations in creating unique, expressive characters."

In a family story with a twist, Polacco describes the experiences of two children who meet some interesting new neighbors in *The Graves Family.* The wife, Shalleaux Graves, kills every plant she touches and her Venus Fly trap gobbles up the hats of nearby ladies when she participates in a garden club tea, while husband Doug Graves distributes a hair restorative that causes its user to behave like the cats which serve as the concoction's secret ingredient. When it seems like the new family will never be accepted by the town, their spooky, blood-red house finds favor with a well-known interior decorator, spider webs and all. A trip to Lake Bleakmire, with its assorted creepy crawlies, is in store for both Doug and Shalleaux Graves, as well as readers of *The Graves Family Goes Camping,* until a pastry-loving, fire-breathing dragon cuts the couple's gruesome holiday short. Noting that Polacco's tale mixes "a little light horror" with "over-the-top hilarity," a *Publishers Weekly* reviewer added that in *The Graves Family* the author/illustrator "mines the theme of children nourished by unexpected friendships." Uncharacteristic of Polacco, *The Graves Family* "is lighter and less emotionally resonant than many of her other works," according to *School Library Journal* reviewer Rachel G. Payne, although Payne also noted that the author's "creative puns, and over-the-top descriptions" pair well with her "comic, cartoon" art.

Another imaginative tale by Polacco, *Ginger and Petunia,* introduces a pianist who teaches students in the home she shares with a pig named Petunia. When a solo performance required Ginger's absence, the pet sitter is a not-show, forcing the clever swine to masquerade as the fashion-conscious Ginger until the woman's return. Praising the "droll text and playfully hyperbolic art," a *Publishers Weekly* reviewer dubbed "Polacco's porcine protagonist" the star of an "endear[ing] and "lighthearted caper," while a *Kirkus Reviews* writer praised the author/illustrator's "vibrant signature artwork," which features "expressive cameo portraits" as well as "more expansive compositions that spill over from one page to the next."

Whether writing about inter-generational relationships, cross-cultural friendships, Russian witches, or Jewish quilts, Polacco is happily at home in her created worlds and makes such worlds accessible for her readers as well. As she noted in *Firetalking,* her autobiography, "I am lucky . . . so very lucky! I love my life. Can you imagine doing what you love every day? . . . My thoughts boil in my head. They catch the air and fly. The images and stories come back with fury and energy. . . . My heart sings whenever I am drawing."

Unlike most of Polacco's books, the text and dramatic pictures in **The Graves Family** *bring a shiver to the spine of young readers.* (Philomel Books, 2003. Illustration copyright © 2003 by Babushka, Inc. All rights reserved. Reproduced by permission of Philomel Books, a division of Penguin Putnam Books for Young Readers.)

Biographical and Critical Sources

BOOKS

Children's Literature Review, Volume 40, Thomson Gale (Detroit, MI), 1996, pp. 175-201.

Polacco, Patricia, *Firetalking,* Richard C. Owen (Katonah, NY), 1994.

PERIODICALS

Booklist, December 1, 1988, Denise M. Wilms, review of *The Keeping Quilt,* p. 654; March 15, 1992, Carolyn Phelan, review of *Chicken Sunday,* p. 1388; November 1, 1996, Hazel Rochman, review of *The Trees of the Dancing Goats,* p. 509; May 1, 1998, Hazel Rochman, review of *Thank You, Mr. Falker,* p. 1522; November 15, 1998, Susan Dove Lempke, review of *Mrs. Mack,* p. 597; May 15, 1999, review of *Luba and the Wren,* p. 1700; April 4, 2000, Hazel Rochman, review of *The Butterfly,* p. 1479; August, 2000, Isabel Schon, review of *The Keeping Quilt,* p. 155; August, 2002, Julie Cummins, review of *When Lightning Comes in a Jar,* p. 1975; September 1, 2002, GraceAnne A. De-Candido, review of *Christmas Tapestry,* p. 138; May 1, 2003, GraceAnne A. DeCandido, review of *G Is for Goat,* p. 1606; September 15, 2003, Kay Weisman, review of *The Graves Family,* p. 248; March 1, 2004, Linda Perkins, review of *Oh, Look!,* p. 1198; August, 2004, Lauren Peterson, review of *John Philip Duck,* p. 1944; December 1, 2004, Terry Glover, review of *An Orange for Frankie,* p. 662; May 15, 2005, Ilene Cooper, review of *The Graves Family Goes Camping,* p. 1666; September 15, 2005, Gillian Engberg, review of *Emma Kate,* p. 75; April 15, 2006, Jennifer Mattson, review of *Rotten Richie and the Ultimate Dare,* p. 54.

Horn Book, March-April, 2004, Susan Dove Lempke, review of *Oh, Look!,* p. 174.

Grand Rapids Press, September 18, 2005, Maranda, interview with Polacco, p. J2.

Junior Bookshelf, June, 1988, Marcus Crouch, review of *Rechenka's Eggs,* p. 131.

Kirkus Reviews, April 1, 1987, review of *Meteor!,* p. 557; April 15, 1993, p. 535; June 1, 1994, p. 779; September 15, 1994, review of *Pink and Say,* p. 1279; April 15, 1997, p. 647; May 1, 1999, p. 726; May 1, 2002, review of *When Lighting Comes in a Jar,* p. 665; November 1, 2002, review of *Christmas Tapestry,* p. 1624; April 15, 2003, review of *G Is for Goat,* p. 610; August 15, 2003, review of *The Graves Family,* p. 1077; February 1, 2004, review of *Oh, Look!,* p. 137; May 1, 2004, review of *John Philip Duck,* p. 446; November 1, 2004, review of *An Orange for Frankie,* p. 1052; January 15, 2005, review of *Mommies Say Shhh!,* p. 124; April 15, 2005, review of *The Graves Family Goes Camping,* p. 479; August 1, 2005, review of *Emma Kate,* p. 856; April 15, 2006, review of *Rotten Richie and the Ultimate Dare,* p. 414; July 1, 2006, review of *Something about Hensley's,* p. 68; April 1, 2007, review of *Ginger and Petunia.*

New York Times Book Review, April 3, 1988, Leonard Marcus, review of *Rechenka's Eggs,* p. 16; November 13, 1994, Henry Mayer, review of *Pink and Say,* p. 42; May 31, 1998, p. 40; December 19, 1999, p. 31; July 18, 1999, p. 24.

Publishers Weekly, April 10, 1987, review of *Meteor!,* p. 95; February 15, 1993, Shannon Maughan, interview with Polacco, pp. 179, 185; August 15, 1994, review of *Pink and Say,* p. 95; September 12, 1994, review of *Tikvah Means Hope,* p. 90; September 2, 1996, p. 130; September 30, 1996, p. 87; October 12, 1998, review of *Mrs. Mack,* p. 76, and *My Rotten Redheaded Older Brother,* p. 79; September 27, 1999, review of *Welcome Comfort,* p. 56; June 12, 2000, review of *The Butterfly,* p. 72; May 13, 2002, review of *When Lighting Comes in a Jar,* p. 70; March 29, 2004, review of *Oh, Look!,* p. 61; September 27, 2004, review of *An Orange for Frankie,* p. 63; August 8, 2005, review of *Emma Kate,* p. 232; July 5, 2004, review of *John Philip Duck,* p. 56; February 7, 2005, review of *Mommies Say Shhh!,* p. 58; April 9, 2007, review of *Ginger and Petunia,* p. 52.

School Library Journal, October, 1988, Lee Bock, review of *The Keeping Quilt,* p. 136; May, 1992, Dorothy Houlihan, review of *Chicken Sunday,* p. 92; August, 1994, Pamela K. Bomboy, review of *Firetalking,* p. 150; November, 1996, review of *The Trees and the*

Dancing Goat, pp. 90-91; December, 1998, Christy Norris Blanchette, review of *Mrs. Mack,* p. 89; June, 1999, review of *Meteor!,* p. 119; May, 2000, Wendy Lukehart, review of *The Butterfly,* p. 151; June, 2002, Wanda Meyers-Hines, review of *When Lighting Comes in a Jar,* p. 108; October, 2002, Virginia Walter, review of *Christmas Tapestry,* p. 62; May, 2003, Nancy Call, review of *G Is for Goat,* p. 128; August 4, 2003, review of *The Graves Family,* p. 79; September, 2003, Rachel G. Payne, review of *The Graves Family,* p. 187; February, 2004, Gay Lynn Van Vleck, review of *Oh, Look!,* p. 121; June, 2004, Grace Oliff, review of *John Philip Duck,* p. 116; March, 2005, Rachel G. Payne, review of *Mommies Say Shhh!,* p. 186; June, 2005, Kathleen Kelly MacMillan, review of *The Graves Family Goes Camping,* p. 124; November, 2005, Kristine M. Casper, review of *Emma Kate,* p. 103; May, 2006, Eve Ottenberg Stone, review of *Rotten Richie and the Ultimate Dare,* p. 97; August, 2006, Kathleene Pavin, review of *Something about Hensley's,* p. 94.

Times Educational Supplement, March 25, 1988, Shaun Traynor, review of *Rechenka's Eggs,* p. 31.

Washington Post Book World, December 12, 1999, Michael Patrick Hearn, "Picturing the Holidays," p. 15.

ONLINE

Patricia Polacco Web site, http://www.patriciapolacco.com (June 1, 2007).

OTHER

Drawing with Patricia Polacco (short film), Art'SCool, 2005.*

*   *   *

PRINCE, April Jones 1975-

Personal

Born April 17, 1975; married; children: two sons. *Education:* University of North Carolina at Chapel Hill, B.A. (journalism and mass communications), 1997; Radcliffe Publishing Course, graduate, 1997.

Addresses

Home and office—Shrewsbury, MA. *E-mail*—april@ apriljonesprince.com.

Career

Author and freelance editor. Lothrop, Lee & Shepard, New York, NY, former editorial assistant; HarperCollins Children's Books, New York, NY, former assistant editor.

Writings

Meet Our Flag, Old Glory, illustrated by Joan Paley, Little, Brown (New York, NY), 2004.

April Jones Prince (Photograph courtesy of April Jones Prince.)

Who Was Mark Twain?, illustrated by John O'Brien, Grosset & Dunlap (New York, NY), 2004.

Twenty-one Elephants and Still Standing, illustrated by François Roca, Houghton Mifflin (Boston, MA), 2005.

What Do Wheels Do All Day?, illustrated by Giles Laroche, Houghton Mifflin (Boston, MA), 2006.

Valentine Friends, illustrated by Elisabeth Schlossberg, Scholastic (New York, NY), 2007.

Jackie Robinson: He Led the Way, illustrated by Robert Casilla, Grosset & Dunlap (New York, NY), 2008.

Sidelights

April Jones Prince uses poetry to share interesting facts and stories with hidden lessons in her books for young children. Her verses, comprised of a straight-forward prose using a simple vocabulary, also engage readers, creating a sense of anticipation through guessing games in *What Do Wheels Do All Day?* and presenting an exciting tale of derring do in *Twenty-one Elephants and Still Standing.* Prince also introduces intriguing character from America's past in her picture-book biographies *Who Was Mark Twain?* and *Jackie Robinson: He Led the Way,* and tells a story about the nation's flag in *Meet Our Flag, Old Glory.*

What Do Wheels Do All Day? explains to children the many functions of wheels and provides examples of what wheels do. Several different types of wheels are covered: Prince includes descriptions of a ferris wheel, car wheels, and windmills. In *School Library Journal* Janet S. Thompson remarked that the "anticipatory quality of the rhymes" works together with the visual images supplied by illustrator Giles Laroche to "help children to guess the next word, making this a fun choice for storytime." Carolyn Phelan, reviewing *What Do Wheels Do All Day?* for *Booklist,* summarized the picture book as "simply written" and "well-illustrated."

Another rhyming picture book, *Twenty-one Elephants and Still Standing* moves back in time and reveals how famous American circus showman Phineas T. Barnum concocted an elaborate event to win over the skeptics of New York City's newly built Brooklyn Bridge in 1884. After the bridge was completed, its height and span was such that many New Yorkers were afraid to traverse it for fear it would collapse. Enter Barnum, who proved the sturdiness and reliability of the Brooklyn Bridge by

Cover of Prince's picture-book biography **Who Was Mark Twain?,** *featuring artwork by John O'Brien.* (Grosset & Dunlap, 2004. Illustrations copyright © 2004 by John O'Brien. All rights reserved. Reproduced by permission of Grosset & Dunlap, a division of Penguin Putnam.)

parading twenty-one elephants across the magnificent structure. Prince expands her story of Barnum and the Brooklyn Bridge by incorporating a number of interesting facts in her poetic verses. *School Library Journal* reviewer Barbara Auerbach praised *Twenty-one Elephants and Still Standing* as "well researched," noting that Prince's text is "sparse, yet powerful." Equally enthusiastic, *Booklist* reviewer Karin Snelson called the real-life story one that is "told with real poetry."

Prince loves writing about history for young people. "I grew up fascinated by the details of the past: what people did, ate, and wore. Today I love taking tantalizing people or 'nuggets' from history and weaving them into stories that are exciting and engaging for children. As I like to tell students when I visit schools, I have wanted to be a children's book author since I was in third grade. I feel lucky that I can combine my passions into a job that I'm crazy about."

Biographical and Critical Sources

PERIODICALS

Booklist, October 15, 2005, Karin Snelson, review of *Twenty-one Elephants and Still Standing,* p. 58; April 15, 2006, Carolyn Phelan, review of *What Do Wheels Do All Day?,* p. 50.

Horn Book, May-June 2006, Lolly Robinson, review of *What Do Wheels Do All Day?,* p. 299.

Kirkus Reviews, September 1, 2005, review of *Twenty-one Elephants and Still Standing,* p. 981; May 1, 2006, review of *What Do Wheels Do All Day?,* p. 465.

Library Media Connection, January, 2005, Barbara Feehrer, review of *Meet Our Flag, Old Glory,* p. 68.

School Library Journal, August, 2004, Sheilah Kosco, review of *Meet Our Flag, Old Glory,* p. 112; November, 2005, Barbara Auerbach, review of *Twenty-one Elephants and Still Standing,* p. 104; June, 2006, Janet S. Thompson, review of *What Do Wheels Do All Day?,* p. 140.

ONLINE

Children's Bookwatch, http://www.midwestbookreview.com/ (November, 2005), review of *Twenty-one Elephants and Still Standing.*

R

REISER, Lynn 1944-
(Lynn Whisnant Reiser)

Personal

Born July 28, 1944, in Charlotte, NC; daughter of Ward William (a businessman) and Susan Richardson (a college professor) Whisnant; married Morton F. Reiser (a physician, professor, psychoanalyst, and author), December 19, 1976. *Education:* Duke University, B.S., 1966; Yale Medical School, M.D., 1970, psychiatric residency, 1970-75; Western New England Institute for Psychoanalysis, psychoanalytic training, 1976-85. *Hobbies and other interests:* Watercolor painting, gardening, cats and dogs, nature.

Addresses

Office—Department of Psychiatry, Yale Medical School, 25 Park St., New Haven, CT 06511.

Career

Educator and author. Yale University School of Medicine, New Haven, CT, assistant clinical professor, 1975-84, associate clinical professor, 1984-94, clinical professor, 1994—, director of undergraduate education in psychiatry, 1985—. Private practice in psychiatry and psychoanalysis, beginning 1975; author and illustrator of children's books, 1991—. Research fellow under Dr. Myrna Weissman, Yale University School of Epidemiology and Public Health, 1976-77; Western New England Psychoanalytic Institute, member of clinic committee, 1988—, faculty, 1991—, and board of trustees, 1993—. Member, Center for Advanced Psychoanalytic Studies at Aspen, 1992—, and at Princeton, 1993—. Member, Muriel Gardiner Program in Psychoanalysis and the Humanities, and fellow, Davenport College, both at Yale University.

Member

International Psychoanalytic Association, American Psychiatric Association (fellow, 1986), American Psychoanalytic Association, American College of Psychoanalysts (fellow, 1990; board of regents, 1992—), Association of Academic Psychiatry, American Board of Psychiatry and Neurology (examiner, 1980—), Western New England Psychoanalytic Society (treasurer, 1989-91), Sigma Xi.

Awards, Honors

Peter Parker Research fellowship, 1968; Connecticut Heart Association Research Award, 1968; Falk fellowship, American Psychiatric Association, 1972-74; Lustman Research Prize, Yale University Department of Psychiatry, 1974; Child Study Children's Book Committee List of Children's Books of the Year, 1991, for *Dog and Cat*; Picture Book Honor Book, Parent's Choice Award, 1992, for *Any Kind of Dog*; Nancy C.A. Roeske, M.D., Certificate of Recognition for Excellence in Medical Student Education, American Psychiatric Association, 1992.

Writings

PICTURE BOOKS; SELF-ILLUSTRATED, EXCEPT AS NOTED

Dog and Cat, Greenwillow (New York, NY), 1991.
Bedtime Cat, Greenwillow (New York, NY), 1991.
Any Kind of Dog, Greenwillow (New York, NY), 1992.
Christmas Counting, Greenwillow (New York, NY), 1992.
Tomorrow on Rocky Pond, Greenwillow (New York, NY), 1993.
Margaret and Margarita/Margarita y Margaret, Greenwillow (New York, NY), 1993.
The Surprise Family, Greenwillow (New York, NY), 1994.
Two Mice in Three Fables, Greenwillow (New York, NY), 1995.
Night Thunder and the Queen of the Wild Horses, Greenwillow (New York, NY), 1995.
Beach Feet, Greenwillow (New York, NY), 1996.
Best Friends Think Alike, Greenwillow (New York, NY), 1997.

Cherry Pies and Lullabies, Greenwillow (New York, NY), 1998.

(With translator Rebecca Hart) *Tortillas and Lullabies/ Tortillas y cancioncitas,* illustrated by Corazones Valientes, Greenwillow (New York, NY), 1998.

Little Clam, Greenwillow (New York, NY), 1998.

Earthdance, Greenwillow (New York, NY), 1999.

My Dog Truffle, Greenwillow (New York, NY), 2000.

My Cat Tuna: A Book about the Five Senses, Greenwillow (New York, NY), 2000.

(With M.J. Infante) *The Lost Ball/La pelota perdida,* Greenwillow (New York, NY), 2002.

Ten Puppies, Greenwillow (New York, NY), 2003.

Two Dogs Swimming, Greenwillow (New York, NY), 2005.

Hardworking Puppies, Harcourt (Orlando, FL), 2006.

You and Me, Baby, photographs by Penny Gentieu, Knopf (New York, NY), 2006.

Play Ball with Me!, Knopf (New York, NY), 2006.

My Way/A mi manera, Greenwillow (New York, NY), 2007.

OTHER

Contributor of "Two Mice," to *First Grade Reading Program,* D.C. Heath, 1994. Illustrator of *Making Yourself at Home in Charlotte, North Carolina,* by Susan Whisnant, published annually since 1972. Author, as Lynn Whisnant Reiser, of medical and professional articles on psychiatry, psychoanalysis, and medical education.

Adaptations

Margaret and Margarita/Margarita y Margaret was adapted for audiocassette, read by Chloe Patellis, with music by Jeff Wasman, Scholastic, 1993. *Any Kind of Dog* was adapted for audiocassette, Live Oak Media, 1996.

Sidelights

A respected psychiatrist and educator, Lynn Reiser is also a prolific author of children's picture books. In addition to her work at Yale University School of Medicine, where she is a clinical professor of psychiatry and active in numerous departmental activities, Reiser has managed to find the time to both write and illustrate an average of two children's books per year since beginning to write in the early 1990s. As one might expect of a person in Reiser's field, some of her books focus on the interpersonal relationships most important to young children: those among family and friends, as brought to life in her collaborative photo essay with Peggy Gentieu, *You and Me, Baby.* Reiser also shares her love of animals in many of her works, such as *Dog and Cat, Hardworking Puppies,* and *Two Dogs Swimming.* Reiser is an illustrator as well as an author, and she varies her artistic medium from simple line drawings to watercolor paintings to photograph/painting hybrids. Her illustrations reflect the maturity of her intended audience, whether it be a toddler or a grade-school student.

Book cover of Lynn Reiser's You and Me, Baby, **which pairs Reiser's text with photographs by Penny Gentieu.** (Alfred A. Knopf, 2006. Photographs copyright © 2006 by Penny Gentieu. All rights reserved. Used by permission of Alfred A. Knopf, an imprint of Random House Children's Books, a division of Random House, Inc.)

In her first published book for children, *Dog and Cat,* Reiser depicts the meeting of a restless dog and his neighbor, a drowsy cat. The dog gets more than he bargains for when he heeds his instinct and chases the cat. The cat jumps on the pup's back and, with a trick, teaches the hapless canine a lesson he is unlikely to forget. Reiser "deftly presents this bustling confrontation in a cheerful style," noted a *Publishers Weekly* reviewer. In *Horn Book* Mary M. Burns noted the author/illustrator's emphasis on "shape and movement," adding that the book's illustrations are sure to "attract the attention" of young readers. *School Library Journal* contributor Joan McGrath described *Dog and Cat* as a picture book "enlivened by wild and woolly artwork" which reflects the cat-dog synergy.

Reiser's other animals stories include *Bedtime Cat,* which describes the nightly ritual of a young girl and her cat, and *Any Kind of Dog,* which focuses on the love many people have for dogs, no matter what the breed. All goes well in *Bedtime Cat* until bedtime, when the cat, who usually sleeps with the little girl, cannot be found. The anxiety builds as the girl and her parents search for the cat, without success. The child returns to her bed, only to find the cat under a blanket, ready and waiting for lights out all along. Reviewers of the book cited the appealing text and pen-and-ink and watercolor illustrations, Carolyn K. Jenks remarking in *Horn Book* that "the simple, childlike pictures and text are just right for this small but universal drama." A *Kirkus Reviews* writer credited *Bedtime Cat* with "real sensitivity to the child's world," remarking on the sense of security it evokes in its recitation of the child's nighttime routine. Similarly, Liza Bliss commended Reiser's simplified artwork, dubbing it "just right" in her *School Library Journal* review.

In *Any Kind of Dog* Richard begs his mom for a dog. When a series of substitute pets are suggested, none satisfy the boy; instead they remind him of the many different dog breeds. In Reiser's humorous tale, after each alternative pet—both real and imaginary—is determined to cause its own brand of trouble, Richard's mom gives in. The "boldly colored pictures filled with funny details embellish the text nicely," wrote Anna Biagioni Hart in *School Library Journal,* while a *Kirkus Reviews* critic called the art "unpretentious but amusingly expressive." Other dog-cat books for the pre-reader include Reiser's lift-the-flap books *My Cat Tuna: A Book about the Five Senses* and *My Dog Truffle,* both of which treat the same topic. Another interactive book, *Play Ball with Me!,* features a frisky kitten whose toys and sports accouterments are visible through die-cut pages.

Counting and differences are explored in the concept books *Ten Puppies* and *Ten Hardworking Puppies.* In *Ten Puppies* Reiser illustrates basic addition by grouping ten dogs, some sharing similar characteristics, such as coat color, floppy ears, and pink tongues. Noting that the dogs' "clearly differentiated characteristics offer all kinds of opportunities for observation and the exercise of logic," *Horn Book* contributor Joanna Rudge Long concluded of *Ten Puppies* that "there's much here to discover, . . . learn, and enjoy." A similar focus is employed in *Ten Hardworking Puppies,* as Reiser follows ten unique dogs as they match their skills with jobs ranging from firehouse dog to water-rescue puppy to beloved family pet. Counting and subtraction are the concepts explored in Reiser's simple text and engaging art. Noting that the book "successfully" meets its intended goal, Roger Sutton added in *Horn Book* that *Ten Hardworking Puppies* "honors both the puppies and the [young] audience, who will know about being small but craving responsibility. "Even if kids aren't ready for the arithmetic concepts, they'll coo over the wriggling pups" and the "underlying messages" about praising a job well done and "balancing work and play," predicted *Booklist* contributor Jennifer Mattson.

Relationship books form an important part of Reiser's oeuvre. In *The Surprise Family* she describes how a chick is cared for by a human boy, grows up, then adopts a clutch of ducklings in turn. Although the plot has particular appeal for adoptive families, Reiser's theme is universal: Love transcends boundaries and labels. *School Library Journal* reviewer Beth Tegart praised *The Surprise Family* as a "delightful story," and *Booklist* critic Mary Harris Veeder dubbed it a "graceful fable" that is "well served by" the author's signature

illustrations. The same caring bond is the focus of *You and Me, Baby,* in which Reiser collaborates with photographer Gentieu in creating a simple book that *School Library Journal* contributor Catherine Callegari deemed "engaging." Noting the effective repetitive text, a *Kirkus Reviews* writer wrote that author and illustrator focus on "the bond that forms between baby and caregiver as they imitate each other, the simplest form of communication."

Reiser further simplifies her artwork in *Best Friends Think Alike,* which features line drawings of red and blue marker, each color representing the thoughts of best friends Beryl (blue) and Ruby (red). Describing the technique in *Booklist,* Susan Dove Lempke dubbed it "ingenious." During a play date, both Beryl and Ruby want to be the horse in their game of horse and rider; the negotiation and resolution that follow is one that, according to Sutton, preschoolers "should appreciate." The boundaries of language can also be overcome for the sake of friendship, as Reiser illustrates in *Margaret and Margarita/Margarita y Margaret.* In this bilingual story two children visit the park with their mothers, their budding friendship told in mirror images, the English text in red ink, and the Spanish text in blue. As the girls cement their friendship, the text merges over the double-page spread.

Reiser has made bilingual children's books an increasing focus as her writing career has progressed, and she honors cultural traditions as well as exploring expressions of affection in several of these works. In *The Lost Ball/La pelota perdida* two boys play ball with their respective dogs, until their balls become switched, leading each boy to a new friend. *Cherry Pies and Lullabies* shares a focus with its Spanish-English analog, *Tortillas and Lullabies: Tortillas y cancioncitas,* in depicting generations of women showing their affection for their families through cooking and caretaking. Readers can see that, over time, while everyday tasks may change, the love behind these efforts remains. Although *Horn Book* reviewer Sutton maintained that the author's artwork for *Cherry Pies and Lullabies* lack "emotional resonance," Mirta Ojito praised them in the *New York Times Book Review,* citing the author/illustrator's "gorgeous" and "exquisitely detailed full-page illustrations." Impressed by a Peace Corps exhibit of work by Costa Rican artists cooperative Valiant Hearts (Corazones Valientes), Reiser asked this group to illustrate *Tortillas and Lullabies* with their colorful, stylized paintings.

Reiser gives young armchair travelers the opportunity to enjoy nature in several of her books. In *Tomorrow on Rocky Pond* she explores a young girl's anticipation on the eve of a family vacation, when the family will fish at Rocky Pond. This ritual includes a special breakfast, clothes, the journey to the pond, and finally the fishing. The story's text "aptly portrays the eagerness of the girl," wrote *Booklist* reviewer Christie Sylvester, while in *School Library Journal* Susan Hepler remarked that "Reiser's precise watercolor and black line illustrations

In Reiser's self-illustrated concept book **Hardworking Puppies** *a gang of frisky young dogs illustrates a number of basic spatial concepts.* (Harcourt, Inc., 2006. Reproduced by permission of Harcourt.)

clarify details and evoke emotions." Reiser also brings the seashore home with *Beach Feet,* which focuses on sea creatures with different kinds of feet, and *Little Clam,* which concerns the clam' self-defense mechanisms.

Nature is celebrated by Reiser in *Earthdance,* a lyrical introduction to the solar system. In verse and illustrations that combine drawings and photographs of Earth as seen from outer space, she tells of how a girl named Terra dances the lead role in the school production of a play titled *Earthdance,* while Terra's astronaut mother takes to the skies. Although *Booklist* contributor Susan

Dove Lempke noted errors in the scientific content, a *Kirkus Reviews* writer dubbed *Earthdance* "charming." Finding the work successful over all, Tina Hudak praised Reiser's "imaginative approach" in her *School Library Journal* review.

Biographical and Critical Sources

PERIODICALS

Booklist, May 1, 1992, Denia Hester, review of *Any Kind of Dog,* pp. 1609-1610; August, 1993, Christie

Sylvester, review of *Tomorrow on Rocky Pond,* p. 2071; September 15, 1993, Janice Del Negro, review of *Margarita y Margaret/Margaret and Margarita,* p. 160; June 1, 1994, Mary Harris Veeder, review of *The Surprise Family,* p. 1844; March 1, 1995; Lauren Peterson, review of *Two Mice in Three Fables,* p. 1249; October 15, 1995, Kay Weisman, review of *Night Thunder and the Queen of the Wild Horses,* p. 90; June 1, 1997, Susan Dove Lempke, review of *Best Friends Think Alike,* p. 1721; March 1, 1998, Shelley Townsend-Hudson, review of *Cherry Pies and Lullabies,* p. 1141; April, 1998, Susan Dove Lempke, review of *Tortillas and Lullabies/Tortillas y cancioncitas,* p. 1333; August, 1998, John Peters, review of *Little Clam,* p. 2016; December 1, 1999, Susan Dove Lempke, review of *Earthdance,* p. 713; June 1, 2006, Jennifer Mattson, review of *Hardworking Puppies,* p. 88.

Horn Book, May-June, 1991, Carolyn K. Jenks, review of *Bedtime Cat,* p. 321, Mary M. Burns, review of *Dog and Cat,* p. 321; September-October, 1993; March-April, 1997, Roger Sutton, review of *Best Friends Think Alike,* pp. 194-195; May, 1998, Roger Sutton, review of *Cherry Pies and Lullabies,* pp. 335-336; September-October, 1998, Susan P. Bloom, review of *Little Clam,* pp. 599-600; March, 2001, Joanna Rudge Long, reviews of *My Dog Truffle* and *My Cat Tuna,* p. 201; May-June, 2003, Joanna Rudge Long, review of *Ten Puppies,* p. 335; May-June, 2006, Roger Sutton, review of *Hardworking Puppies,* p. 301.

Kirkus Reviews, February 1, 1992, review of *Any Kind of Dog*; February 15, 1992, review of *Bedtime Cat,* p. 251; June 1, 1994; April 1, 1998, review of *Cherry Pies and Lullabies,* p. 500, and review of *Tortillas and Lullabies/Tortillas y cancioncitas,* p. 501; July 15, 1999, review of *Earthdance,* p. 1138; March 15, 2003, review of *Ten Puppies,* p. 476; April 15, 2005, review of *Two Dogs Swimming,* p. 480; May 1, 2006, review of *Hardworking Puppies,* p. 466; September 15, 2006, review of *You and Me, Baby,* p. 965.

Language Arts, November, 1996, Miriam Martinez and Marcia Nash, review of *Beach Feet,* p. 522.

New York Times Book Review, September 20, 1998, Mirta Ojito, reviews of *Cherry Pies and Lullabies* and *Tortillas and Lullabies/Tortillas y cancioncitas,* p. 32.

Publishers Weekly, January 18, 1991, review of *Dog and Cat,* p. 57; March 9, 1992, review of *Any Kind of Dog,* p. 56; September 7, 1992, Elizabeth Devereaux, review of *Christmas Counting,* p. 67; May 31, 1993, review of *Tomorrow on Rocky Pond,* p. 53; September 25, 1995, review of *Night Thunder and the Queen of the Wild Horses,* p. 56; February 2, 1998, review of *Cherry Pies and Lullabies,* p. 90; September 14, 1998, review of *Little Clam,* p. 68; January 22, 2001, "Experience the Seasons," p. 326; May 26, 2003, review of *Ten Puppies,* p. 72.

School Library Journal, May, 1991, Liza Bliss, review of *Bedtime Cat,* p. 82; June, 1991, Joan McGrath, review of *Dog and Cat,* pp. 88-89; June, 1992, Anna Biagioni Hart, review of *Any Kind of Dog,* p. 102; October, 1992; September, 1993, Susan Hepler, review of *Tomorrow on Rocky Pond,* p. 218; July, 1994, Beth

Tegart, review of *The Surprise Family,* pp. 87-88; August, 1994, Rose Zertuche Trevino, review of *Margarita y Margaret,* p. 182; April, 1995, Jane Marino, review of *Two Mice in Three Fables,* pp. 114, 116; December, 1995, Meg Stackpole, review of *Night Thunder and the Queen of the Wild Horses,* p. 90; May, 1997, Marianne Saccardi, review of *Best Friends Think Alike,* pp. 111-112; April, 1998, Denise E. Agosto, review of *Tortillas and Lullabies/Tortillas y cancioncitas,* p. 108; September, 1998, Lisa S. Murphy, review of *Cherry Pies and Lullabies,* p. 180; November 1, 1998, Shelley Woods, review of *Little Clam,* p. 92; October, 1999, Tina Hudak, review of *Earthdance,* p. 123; March, 2001, DeAnn Tabuchi, reviews of *My Cat Tuna* and *My Dog Truffle,* p. 219; November, 2002, Ann Welton, review of *The Lost Ball/ La Peolta Perdida,* p. 153; April, 2003, Andrea Tarr, review of *Ten Puppies,* p. 137; May, 2005, Kathleen Meulen, review of *Two Dogs Swimming,* p. 94; April, 2006, Linda Zeilstra Sawyer, review of *Hardworking Puppies,* p. 116; August, 2006, Linda Ludke, review of *Play Ball with Me!,* p. 110; October, 2006, Catherine Callegari, review of *You and Me, Baby,* p. 124.

Science Books and Films, December, 1996, Frank M. Truesdale, review of *Beach Feet,* p. 275.

Teaching Children Mathematics, David J. Whitin, review of *Beach Feet,* p. 294.*

*   *   *

REISER, Lynn Whisnant
See REISER, Lynn

*   *   *

REYNOLDS, Jan 1956-

Personal

Born 1956. *Education:* Attended college.

Addresses

Home and office—4856 Mountain Rd., Stowe, VT 05672. *E-mail*—janreynolds@pshift.com.

Career

Photographer, journalist, skier, mountaineer, and writer. Expeditions include first circumnavigation of Mt. Everest, solo crossing of the Himalayas, camel crossing of the Sahara, ballooning over the Himalayas, and cross-country ski tour of Toubkal, North Africa Southern Alps, New Zealand, and many others. Speaker at schools and other assemblies. *Exhibitions:* Photographs have been exhibited at United Nations, Asian Society, New York, NY, and elsewhere.

Awards, Honors

Member, U.S. World Cup biathlon team; World High Altitude Skiing Record for Women, American Friendship Expedition to China; other high-altitude skiing and

Jan Reynolds (Photograph courtesy of Jan Reynolds.)

climbing records; Mountain Man Triathlon Champion (Vail, CO); Freedman Foundation grant, for film *Cultural Adventure with Jan Reynolds.*

Writings

AND PHOTOGRAPHER

(With Ned Gillette) *Everest Grand Circle: A Climbing and Skiing Adventure through Nepal and Tibet,* Mountaineers (Seattle, WA), 1985.

Sahara: Vanishing Cultures, Harcourt, Brace, Jovanovich (San Diego, CA), 1991.

Himalaya: Vanishing Cultures, Harcourt, Brace, Jovanovich (San Diego, CA), 1991.

Down Under: Vanishing Cultures, Harcourt, Brace, Jovanovich (San Diego, CA), 1992.

Far North: Vanishing Cultures, Harcourt, Brace, Jovanovich (San Diego, CA), 1992.

Amazon Basin: Vanishing Cultures, Harcourt, Brace, Jovanovich (San Diego, CA), 1993.

Frozen Land: Vanishing Cultures, Harcourt, Brace, Jovanovich (San Diego, CA), 1993.

Mongolia: Vanishing Cultures, Harcourt, Brace, Jovanovich (San Diego, CA), 1994.

Mother and Child: Visions of Parenting from Indigenous Cultures, Inner Traditions International (Rochester, VT), 1997.

Celebrate!: Connections among Cultures, Lee & Low (New York, NY), 2006.

Author and narrator of documentary film *Cultural Adventure with Jan Reynolds,* 2002. Contributor to periodicals, including *National Geographic* and *Cross Country Skier.*

Sidelights

A photographer, mountaineer, skier, and world traveler, Jan Reynolds has dedicated much of her life to exploring and documenting the vestiges of traditional cultures that still remain throughout the globe. A former member of the U.S. World Cup biathlon team, Reynolds holds high-altitude skiing and climbing records, was a member of the first team to circumnavigate Mt. Everest, has manned a hot-air balloon over the Himalayas, and has sought out native people living in the most remote locations on earth. Attesting to Reynolds' dedication, Heather Frederick wrote in *Publishers Weekly* that, "whether clinging by her fingers to a glacier wall while crossing a Himalayan mountain pass, paddling solo down the Amazon river in a collapsible boat or launching into the Sahara desert on camelback in search of a tiny nomadic tribe, this intrepid woman—world-class athlete, successful freelance writer and photographer and now children's book author—will do whatever it takes to get the material she needs for her stories." In addition to her extreme adventures, Reynolds is also a highly respected writer and photojournalist whose work includes the "Vanishing Cultures" series as well as *Celebrate!: Connections among Cultures.*

The "Vanishing Cultures" books had an interesting genesis. Although Reynolds began working on the series while recuperating from a back injury, the series has its roots in her experiences during the 1980s when, as a newly minted college graduate, she began participating in athletic challenges throughout the globe. Returning to places such as Nepal and the Sahara several times throughout that decade, Reynolds began to notice that the lives of the native people who welcomed her in each of these regions was slowly being altered. As new roads connected these remote areas, traditional trade routes traversed by yaks or camels were abandoned. Many residents of remote villages were now lured by the promise of jobs into metropolitan areas. With roads have also come those in search of natural resources, such as timber and minerals, with unfortunate environmental and economic impacts. "I realized that the things that I was seeing, my children won't," the photojournalist told Frederick. "They'll be gone. I wanted to capture what was there before it's gone, because it is part of us, part of the entire human family."

The "Vanishing Culture" series includes seven children's books that capture traditional cultures before they disappear. In *Sahara: Vanishing Cultures* Reynolds profiles the nomadic Tuaregs, who inhabit the world's

As Reynolds shows through her picture book Celebrate!, *people share many of the same simple joys everywhere around the globe.* (Lee & Low Books, Inc., 2006. Photograph copyright © 2006 by Jan Reynolds. All rights reserved. Reproduced by permission of Lee & Low Books, Inc.)

largest desert, while a typical day in the life of a large, extended family of herders living in Mongolia—including two young children who dream of owning their own horses and carrying on family traditions—is the focus of *Mongolia: Vanishing Cultures*. In revealing photographs, Reynolds introduces the aboriginal Tiwi people in *Down Under: Vanishing Cultures,* and reveals the traditions that have sustained their primitive island culture. The Yanomama, who live in Venezuela's Amazon Territory, is the focus of *Amazon Basin: Vanishing Cultures.*

Moving to more chilly climes, *Far North* also features Reynolds' revealing text and photographs. Here she documents the culture of the reindeer herders known as the Samis, who make their home in Finmark, while *Frozen Land: Vanishing Cultures* profiles the Inuit people who attempt to preserve their traditions in the face of the encroachment of "civilization" into Canada's Northwest Territories. Moving to a higher elevation, *Himalaya: Vanishing Cultures* profiles customs and day-to-day life of a family living in the Himalaya Mountains.

Although Reynolds initially found a publisher for the "Vanishing Cultures" series, her decision to keep the book's focus on younger readers prompted her to complete the project independently. "I really wanted them to seem like storybooks, so that children would be entertained but learn at the same time," she explained to Frederick. Although financing was a problem, she found a way to continue the project, and with the help of children's author Nancy Willard, the series eventually found a publisher. The "Vanishing Cultures" books, first published in the early 1990s, have been more recently released due to their timely multicultural and environmental focus.

In addition to her "Vanishing Cultures" books, Reynolds captures the myriad ways that people mark life passages and moments of profound joy and grief in *Celebrate!* The book was compiled of Reynolds' experiences living among families throughout the world during her many travels. From the Australian Aborigines and Balinese of South Asia to the North American Inuit, Arctic Sami, Himalayan-dwelling Tibetians and Sherpas, Saharan Tuareg, and Amazonian Yanomami, the text and pictures cover such things as the passage of seasons, birth and death rituals, coming-of-age ceremonies and weddings, and the passage of history. In what *School Library Journal* contributor Alexa Sandmann described as "colorful, inviting" photographs, the author details the common threads that run through the colorful patchwork of traditional celebrations, her "brief, engaging text" supplemented by maps, a pronunciation guide, and an author's note. Citing Reynolds' "fascinating photographs" as "the strong point" in the volume, a *Kirkus Reviews* writer added that *Celebrate!* "will tantalize readers to find out more." In addition to her photoessays, Reynolds has also produced the documentary film *Cultural Adventures with Jan Reynolds,* in which she introduces the culture and traditions of the Sherpa who live on the southern slopes of the Himalayan mountains.

Biographical and Critical Sources

PERIODICALS

Backpacker, March, 1986, Jim Chase, "Not One of the Guys: Jan Reynolds Can Compete with the Best of Them," p. 42.

Booklist, March 15, 1992, Denia Hester, review of *Down Under: Vanishing Cultures,* p. 1353; April 1, 1992, Hazel Rochman, review of *Far North: Vanishing Cultures,* p. 1444; December 1, 1993, Carolyn Phelan, reviews of *Frozen Land: Vanishing Cultures,* p. 114, and *Amazon Basin: Vanishing Cultures,* p. 688; November 15, 2002, Candace Smith, review of *Cultural Adventure with Jan Reynolds,* p. 614; March 15, 2006, Hazel Rochman, review of *Celebrate!: Connections among Cultures,* p. 48.

Bulletin of the Center for Children's Books, October, 1991, review of *Himalaya: Vanishing Cultures,* p. 112; November, 1991, review of *Sahara: Vanishing Cultures,* p. 73; April, 1992, review of *Far North* and *Down Under,* p. 220; November, 1993, reviews of *Frozen Land* and *Amazon Basin,* p. 97.

Esquire, June, 1984, Geoffrey Norman, "She Shoots to Conquer: The Breathtaking Adventures of Jan Reynolds," p. 130.

Kirkus Reviews, May 1, 2006, review of *Celebrate!,* p. 466.

New York Times Book Review, March 15, 1992, Suzanne Fisher Staples, review of *Himalaya,* p. 23.

Publishers Weekly, August 23, 1991, review of *Sahara,* p. 64; October 25, 1991, Heather Frederick, "Visionary Globetrotter," p. 34.

School Library Journal, October, 1991, Eva Elisabeth von Ancken, review of *Sahara* and *Himalaya,* p. 112; May, 1992, Mollie Bynum, review of *Far North,* and Jeanette Larson, review of *Down Under,* both p. 126; October, 1993, Ellen Fader, review of *Amazon Basin,* p. 146; February, 1994, Roz Goodman, review of *Frozen Land,* p. 114; April, 1994, Dot Minzer, review of *Mongolia: Vanishing Cultures,* p. 145; August, 2006, Alexa Sandmann, review of *Celebrate!,* p. 110.

Science Books and Film, October, 1993, review of *Amazon Basin,* p. 205.

Wilson Library Bulletin, November, 1991, Frances Bradburn, review of *Sahara,* p. 131.

Women's Sports and Fitness, March, 1986, Judy Mills, "Living on the Edge," p. 25.

ONLINE

Jan Reynolds Home Page, http://www.janreynolds.com (May 8, 2007).

OTHER

Cultural Adventures with Jan Reynolds (film), Jan Reynolds Productions, 2003.

RODRÍGUEZ, Rachel
(Rachel Victoria Rodríguez)

Personal

Born in Ann Arbor, MI. *Education:* University of California, Berkeley, graduate.

Addresses

Home and office—San Francisco, CA. *E-mail*—mail@ RachelRodriguezBooks.com.

Career

Educator and author. Former park ranger; former high school teacher and K-12 teacher trainer. Workshop facilitator and speech coach. Contributor to programming for National Public Radio.

Member

Society of Children's Book Writers and Illustrators, National Art Education Association, Northern California Children's Booksellers Association.

Writings

Through Georgia's Eyes, illustrated by Julie Paschkis, Henry Holt (New York, NY), 2006.

Contributor of articles to *Los Angeles Times.*

Sidelights

A speech coach and workshop facilitator based in northern California, Rachel Rodríguez attained her lifelong dream of becoming a writer when her picture book *Through Georgia's Eyes* was published in 2006. Featuring evocative illustrations by Julie Paschkis, the book is its author's way of honoring legendary painter Georgia O'Keeffe, an early-twentieth-century artist who Rodríguez credits as one of her primary inspirations. A short biography, *Through Georgia's Eyes* reveals the experiences of the creative child who would grow up to painting images that are considered early examples of abstract modernism.

Born in 1887 and raised on a Wisconsin dairy farm, O'Keeffe learned to paint using water colors as a child, and determined to become a painter at a young age. Although her decision attracted disapproval from some, O'Keeffe moved to Chicago in 1905, and went on to study with numerous well-known artists of her day. Pairing her fact-laced text with Paschkis's brightly colored cut-paper-collage illustrations, Rodríguez helps readers understand the woman behind O'Keeffe's paintings, as well as the world she painted in. "It is not often that author, illustrator and subject come together so

seamlessly" remarked a *Kirkus Reviews* critic in discussing *Through Georgia's Eyes,* while *School Library Journal* Carolyn Janssen cited "the clarity of text and illustrations." Carolyn Phelan praised the work as "written and illustrated with directness and sensitivity," concluding in her *Booklist* review that *Through Georgia's Eyes* "is a fresh, original portrait of the artist."

Biographical and Critical Sources

PERIODICALS

Booklist, February 15, 2006, Carolyn Phelan, review of *Through Georgia's Eyes,* p. 109.
Bulletin of the Center for Children's Books, April, 2006, Deborah Stevenson, review of *Through Georgia's Eyes,* p. 371.
Horn Book, May-June, 2006, Lolly Robinson, review of *Through Georgia's Eyes,* p. 347.
Kirkus Reviews, February 1, 2006, review of *Through Georgia's Eyes,* p. 136.
Publishers Weekly, February 20, 2006, review of *Through Georgia's Eyes,* p. 156.
School Library Journal, March, 2006, Carolyn Janssen, review of *Through Georgia's Eyes,* p. 212; October, 2006, review of *Through Georgia's Eyes,* p. 37.

ONLINE

Rachel Rodríguez Home Page, http://www. rachelrodriguezbooks.com (May 14, 2007).

*   *   *

RODRÍGUEZ, Rachel Victoria
See RODRÍGUEZ, Rachel

*   *   *

ROTH, Julie Jersild

Personal

Born in WI; married; children: two. *Education:* University of Minnesota, B.A. (fine arts and art history). *Hobbies and other interests:* Knitting, travel, gardening, painting.

Addresses

Home and office—Minneapolis, MN. *E-mail*—julie@ juliejersildroth.com.

Career

Author, illustrator, and artist.

Writings

(And illustrator) *Knitting Nell,* Houghton Mifflin (Boston, MA), 2006.

Sidelights

While growing up in Wisconsin, Julie Jersild Roth found many ways to express her creative side: dancing, writing poetry and songs, and drawing. In her picture-book debut, *Knitting Nell,* she combines many of these creative endeavors, and also shares her enthusiasm for the spirit and energy guiding the women in her neighborhood knitting group, who managed to keep up with knitting assignments despite their busy lives. "I started imagining how they could accomplish [so many] . . . things," Roth noted on her home page. "Do they knit while walking the dog? Do they knit in the bathtub? I decided to explore this with a little character . . . Nell."

In *Knitting Nell* a shy young girl enjoys knitting for her family, friends, and especially for charities that can use baby blankets, warm mittens, and scarves. Although a run-in with a school bully who teased the girl about her voice has left Nell reticent, she gains a boost in confidence when a special knitting project, a sweater, wins first prize at the local county fair. Soon Nell is talking freely, and teaching her skill to others as well. In *Booklist* Ilene Cooper cited Roth's ability to focus "in on common kid traits such as shyness and a propensity to help others," and added that "the story is illustrated with spunk and charm." Linda Staskus, reviewing *Knitting Nell* for *School Library Journal,* wrote that with its "soft and bright" art, Roth's self-illustrated picture book

Julie Jersild Roth's love of knitting inspired her self-illustrated picture book **Knitting Nell.** (Houghton Mifflin Company, 2006. Copyright © 2006 by Julie Jersild Roth. All rights reserved. Reproduced by permission of Houghton Mifflin Company.)

will be especially useful to children like Nell, who deal with shyness, while a *Kirkus Reviews* writer wrote that the heroine's "unusual tenacity and generous way of coping with a bully add enlightenment to an all-too-common occurrence in children's lives.

Biographical and Critical Sources

PERIODICALS

Booklist, September 1, 2006, Ilene Cooper, review of *Knitting Nell,* p. 140.

Kirkus Reviews, June 15, 2006, review of *Knitting Nell,* p. 637.

School Library Journal, July, 2006, Linda Staskus, review of *Knitting Nell,* p. 86.

ONLINE

Houghton Mifflin Web site, http://www.houghton mifflinbooks.com/ (May 15, 2007).

Julie Jersild Roth Home Page, http://www.juliejersildroth. com (May 15, 2007).

S

SARAH, DUCHESS OF YORK
See FERGUSON, Sarah

* * *

SCAMELL, Ragnhild 1940-

Personal

Given name pronounced "Roundhill"; born March 20, 1940, in Copenhagen, Denmark; immigrated to Great Britain, c. 1960; daughter of Viggo (in business) and Karin Marie (a homemaker) Holdt; married Ernest Harold Scamell (an attorney), September 11, 1977; children: Cleere; (stepchildren) Grant, Adrian, Joanna, Amanda. *Education:* Attended commercial college; attended Institute of Linguists, London, 1985. *Politics:* Conservative. *Religion:* Church of England. *Hobbies and other interests:* Painting, reading, classical music.

Addresses

Home and office—Woldingham, Surrey, England.

Career

Freelance translator, 1985—; author of books for children.

Member

Society of Authors, Institute of Linguists (London), Ashford Art Society.

Awards, Honors

Mother Goose Award runner up, 1993, for *Three Bags Full.*

Writings

FOR CHILDREN

Solo, illustrated by Elizabeth Martland, ABC (London, England), 1992, published as *Solo Plus One,* Little, Brown (Boston, MA), 1992.

Woof! Woof!, illustrated by Genevieve Webster, ABC (London, England), 1993, published as *Buster's Echo,* HarperCollins (New York, NY), 1993.

Three Bags Full, illustrated by Sally Hobson, Orchard Books (New York, NY), 1993.

The Dawn Chorus, illustrated by Judith Riches, ABC (London, England), 1994, published as *Rooster Crows,* Tambourine Books (New York, NY), 1994.

Who Likes Wolfie?, illustrated by Tim Warnes, Little, Brown (Boston, MA), 1995.

The Big Prints, illustrated by Sally Hobson, ABC (London, England), 1996.

Toby's Doll House, illustrated by Adrian Reynolds, Levinson Books (London, England), 1998.

Fat Cats, illustrated by Doffy Weir, Anderson (London, England), 2000.

Jake and the Red Bird, illustrated by Valeria Petrone, Red Fox (London, England), 2001.

The Wish Cat, illustrated by Gaby Hansen, Little Tiger (London, England), 2001, published as *The Wish Come True Cat,* Barron's Educational (Hauppauge, NY), 2001.

Jed's Really Useful Poem, illustrated by Jane Gray, Heinemann (Oxford, England), 2003.

Ouch!, illustrated by Michael Terry, Good Books (Intercourse, PA), 2006.

Contributor of short fiction to periodicals.

Sidelights

Although she first worked as a translator, Ragnhild Scamell turned to writing in the early 1990s, and her first book for children was published in 1992. Scamell's stories for younger children, which feature illustrations from such artists as Sally Hobson, Doffy Weir, and Tim Warnes, often focus on animal characters and include *Rooster Crows, Who Likes Wolfie?,* and *Ouch!* "Although my first book was published only in 1992, I have, in fact, always been writing for children," Scamell once explained to *SATA.* "Short stories published in magazines and longer stories clutter every drawer in my study," she also admitted.

Ouch!, *Ragnhild Scamell's story about true friendships, is brought to life in comforting illustrations by Michael Terry.* (Good Books, 2006. Illustrations copyright © 2006 by Michael Terry. Reproduced by permission.)

Scamell was born in Denmark, and grew up as the oldest of four sisters in a large, close-knit family. Relocating to England as a young woman, she worked for a shipping company before completing her education and finding work as a professional translator. For her first story, she drew on her love of animals in a tale about the relationship between a duckling and a barnyard cat. *Solo*—published in the United States as *Solo Plus One*—"was inspired by my own Siamese cat, whose ferocious behavior belies his need for unconditional ten-

derness and who takes cover under our Labrador dog when all else fails," the author later recalled. "The story was based on the findings of Konrad Lorenz, whose theory of imprinting states that a newly hatched gosling will follow the first object it sees, be it a cardboard box, a man, or a balloon—or a bad cat? I turned the gosling into a duckling, and the story began." In Scamell's book, after a duckling hatches, the first creature it sees is the cat who had been eyeing the hatching egg as a potential meal. After the duckling mistakes the cat for its mother and follows the feline everywhere, the perceptive kitty finds a way to introduce the baby duckling to its real mother. A *Horn Book* contributor noted of *Solo* that Elizabeth Martland's "bold illustrations of the substantial black cat and the little, misinformed duckling lend color to an amusing story."

In *Buster's Echo*—published in England under the title *Woof! Woof!*—Scamell presents young readers with what *Horn Book* contributor Lolly Robinson praised as a "spirited story ideal for reading aloud." In this tale, Buster the dog joins a cow, rooster, and mouse in mistaking the echo of his own bark for the aggressive response of a larger and fiercer counterpart. Banding together, the animals bravely cross the valley to face their foes, and their pride builds when they find that their (nonexistent) enemies have fled. In *Three Bags Full*, one of Scamell's own favorites, a generous sheep named Millie gives away her heavy coat of wool during the warm summer months, forgetting that it will be useful when the seasons change and cooler weather arrives. A feathered fowl takes center stage in *Rooster Crows*, as foolish Rooster is confused by his place in dawn's cause-and-effect sequence. Believing that he alone initiates the sun's rise through his crowing, the bird boasts to Bluebird that his powerful song can perform the same feat in the dark of night. In *Publishers Weekly* a writer noted that the text of *Rooster Crows* "has a slightly biting tone which keeps pace with her haughty, bickering characters."

An animal suffering from a bad reputation tries to win over new friends in Scamell's *Who Likes Wolfie?* A young wolf finds it hard to gain the trust of his fellow forest residents because most fear his sharp teeth and keen glance. The advice of a friendly bird—that Wolfie try singing—only results in an ear-splitting howl. Although Wolfie's song does not endear him to rabbits, chipmunks, or squirrels, it does attract a companion—a white-coated she-wolf—in a story *Booklist* reviewer Ilene Cooper described as perfect "for anyone who has been left out in the cold and then warmed by love." In *Ouch!* Scamell introduces prickly brown Hedgehog, who is aided by a friendly goat while trying to dislodge an apple from her spiny coat so that she can curl up in her cozy den. Praising the story as "animal problem-solving at its best," a *Kirkus Reviews* critic described Michael Terry's humorous illustrations as "perfectly suited" to Scamell's story extolling the benefits of cooperation.

Human characters are featured in several of Scamell's picture books, among them *The Wish Come True Cat* and *Toby's Doll's House*. Described by a *Publishers Weekly* reviewer as a "simple tale" containing several "droll observations" about "the tendency of gift givers to give what they want," *Toby's Doll's House* finds a resourceful birthday boy constructing the doll house he had hoped for from the boxes containing his birthday presents. Another young child—this time a girl named Holly—hopes for a new friend in *The Wish Come True Cat*, but when her wish on a star generates a scruffy stray rather than a cuddly kitten, Holly learns a lesson about compassion as well.

Biographical and Critical Sources

PERIODICALS

Booklist, July, 1993, Stephanie Zvirin, review of *Three Bags Full,* p. 1777; October 15, 1993, Janice Del Negro, review of *Buster's Echo,* p. 454; April 15, 1996, Ilene Cooper, review of *Who Likes Wolfie?,* p. 1447.

Horn Book, May, 1992, review of *Solo Plus One,* p. 334; September-October, 1993, Mary M. Burns, review of *Three Bags Full,* p. 590l; March-April, 1994, Lolly Robinson, review of *Buster's Echo,* p. 192.

Kirkus Reviews, March 15, 1992, review of *Solo Plus One,* p. 398; May 1, 2006, review of *Ouch!,* p. 466.

New York Times Book Review, July 11, 1993, review of *Three Bags Full,* p. 27.

Publishers Weekly, May 11, 1992, review of *Solo Plus One,* p. 71; August 30, 1993, review of *Buster's Echo,* p. 95; September 19, 1994, review of *Rooster Crows,* p. 69; April 8, 1996, review of *Who Likes Wolfie?,* p. 68; June 14, 1999, review of *Toby's Doll's House,* p. 69.

School Library Journal, October, 1993, Trev Jones, review of *Three Bags Full,* p. 112; September, 1994, Christine A. Moesch, review of *Rooster Crows,* p. 192; January, 2002, Anne Knickerbocker, review of *The Wish Come True Cat,* p. 109; July, 2006, Maryann H. Owen, review of *Ouch!,* p. 87.

School Librarian, winter, 2006, Lynda Jones, review of *Ouch!,* p. 184.

Smithsonian, November, 1993, review of *Three Bags Full,* p. 190; February, 1994, Lesley McKinstry, review of *Buster's Echo,* p. 91.

ONLINE

Word Pool Online, http://www.wordpool.co.uk/ (May 15, 2007), interview with Scamell.*

*   *   *

SCHEFFLER, Axel 1957-

Personal

Born 1957, in Hamburg, Germany; immigrated to England, 1982. *Education:* Attended University of Hamburg; Bath Academy of Art, graduated, 1985. *Hobbies and other interests:* Walking, cooking, reading, beadwork.

Addresses

Home and office—London, England.

Career
Illustrator. Has worked in advertising.

Awards, Honors
Nestlé Smarties Gold Medal Award for picture books, and Kate Greenaway Medal nominee, both 1999, and Blue Peter Award for Best Book to Read Aloud, and Experian Big Three Book Prize, both 2000, all for *The Gruffalo,* by Julia Donaldson; Kate Greenaway Medal nomination, 2002, for *Monkey Puzzle;* Blue Peter Award for Best Book to Read Aloud, Children's Book Award shortlist, Sheffield Children's Book Award shortlist, and Scottish Children's Book Award, all 2002, all for *Room on the Broom* by Donaldson; W.H. Smith Children's Book of the Year honor, 2005, for *The Gruffalo's Child* by Donaldson; Blue Peter Award for Best Book to Read Aloud, 2005, for *The Snail and the Whale..*

Writings

SELF-ILLUSTRATED

Proverbs from Far and Wide, Macmillan (London, England), 1997, published as *Let Sleeping Dogs Lie and Other Proverbs from around the World,* Barron's Educational (Hauppauge, NY), 1997.

Jingle Jangle Jungle, Macmillan (London, England), 2003.

Muddle Farm, Macmillan (London, England), 2004, Barrons Educational (Hauppauge, NY), 2007.

Lizzy the Lamb (board book), Campbell (London, England), 2005.

Pip the Puppy (board book), Campbell (London, England), 2005.

Katie the Kitten (board book), Campbell (London, England), 2005.

Freddy the Frog (board book), Campbell (London, England), 2006.

ILLUSTRATOR

Helen Cresswell, *The Piemakers,* Faber & Faber (London, England), 1988.

Bernard McCabe, *The Bottle Rabbit,* Faber & Faber (Boston, MA), 1988.

Bernard McCabe, *Bottle Rabbit and Friends,* Faber & Faber (Boston, MA), 1989.

Jon Blake, *Daley B.,* Walker (London, England), 1992, published as *You're a Hero, Daley B.!,* Candlewick Press (Boston, MA), 1992.

Robert Leeson, *Smark Girls,* Walker (London, England), 1993.

Julia Donaldson, *A Squash and a Squeeze,* Margaret K. McElderry Books (New York, NY), 1993.

Phyllis Root, *Sam Who Was Swallowed by a Shark,* Candlewick Press (Cambridge, MA), 1994, published as *Sam Who Went to See,* Walker Books (London, England), 2005.

Robert Leeson, *The Amazing Adventures of Idle Jack,* Walker (London, England), 1995.

David Henry Wilson, *Do Gerbils Go to Heaven?,* Macmillan (London, England), 1996.

David Henry Wilson, *Do Goldfish Play the Violin?,* Macmillan (London, England), 1996.

David Henry Wilson, *Please Keep Off the Dinosaur,* Macmillan (London, England), 1996.

David Henry Wilson, *Never Say Moo to a Bull,* Macmillan (London, England), 1996.

David Henry Wilson, *Can a Spider Learn to Fly?,* Macmillan (London, England), 1996.

David Henry Wilson, *How the Lion Lost His Lunch,* Macmillan (London, England), 1996.

Ian Whybrow, *The Bedtime Bear,* Macmillan (London, England), 1996.

Martine Oborne, *Juice the Pig,* Holt (New York, NY), 1996.

Keto von Waberer, *Vom Gluck, eine Leberwurst zu lieben: und andere kulinarische Glossen,* Kiepenheuer & Witsch, 1996.

Kate Petty, *Sam Plants a Sunflower: A Lift-the-Flap Nature Book with Real Seeds,* Andrews McMeel (Kansas City, MO), 1997.

Kate Petty, *Rosie Plants a Radish: A Lift-the-Flap Nature Book with Real Seeds,* Andrews McMeel (Kansas City, MO), 1997.

Bernard McCabe, *Pongle!: A Week with the Bottle Rabbit,* Fibre & Fibre (Ludlow, England), 1997.

Robert Leeson, *Lucky Lad!,* Walker (London, England), 1997.

Ian Whybrow, *The Christmas Bear,* Macmillan (London, England), 1998.

Kate Petty, *Ben Plants a Butterfly Garden,* Macmillan (London, England), 1998.

Robert Leeson, *Why's the Cow on the Roof?,* Walker (London, England), 1998.

Julia Donaldson, *The Gruffalo,* Dial Books for Young Readers (New York, NY), 1999.

Ian Whybrow, *The Tickle Book,* Macmillan (London, England), 2000.

Julia Donaldson, *Tales from Acorn Wood: Rabbit's Nap,* Campbell (London, England), 2000.

Julia Donaldson, *Tales from Acorn Wood: Fox's Sox,* Campbell (London, England), 2000.

Julia Donaldson, *Tales from Acorn Wood: Hide and Seek Pig,* Campbell (London, England), 2000.

Julia Donaldson, *Tales from Acorn Wood: Postman Bear,* Campbell (London, England), 2000.

Julia Donaldson, *Monkey Puzzle,* Dial Books for Young Readers (New York, NY), 2000.

David Henry Wilson, *Never Steal Wheels from a Dog,* Macmillan (London, England), 2001.

Julia Donaldson, *Room on the Broom,* Dial Books for Young Readers (New York, NY), 2001.

Julia Donaldson, *The Smartest Giant in Town,* Macmillan Children's (London, England), 2002, published as *The Spiffiest Giant in Town,* Dial Books for Young Readers (New York, NY), 2003.

Julia Donaldson, *The Snail and the Whale,* Macmillan Children's Books (London, England), 2003.

Julia Donaldson, *The Gruffalo's Child,* Macmillan (London, England), 2004, Dial Books for Young Readers (New York, NY), 2005.

Brian Moses, selector, *Monster Poems,* Macmillan (London, England), 2005.

Julia Donaldson, *Charlie Cook's Favorite Book,* Macmillan (London, England), 2005, Dial Books for Young Readers (New York, NY), 2006.

(Alison Green, reteller) *Mother Goose's Nursery Rhymes, and How She Came to Tell Them,* Macmillan (London, England), 2007, published as *Mother Goose's Storytime Nursery Rhymes,* Arther A. Levine Books (New York, NY), 2007.

Martine Oborne, *Hamilton's Hats,* Macmillan (London, England), 2007.

Adaptations

The Gruffalo has been translated into over twenty languages.

Biographical and Critical Sources

PERIODICALS

Booklist, May 1, 1993, Janice Del Negro, review of *A Squash and a Squeeze,* p. 1602; July, 1997, Michael Cart, review of *Juice the Pig,* p. 1822; July, 1999, Stephanie Zvirin, review of *The Gruffalo,* p. 1950; September 1, 2001, GraceAnne A. DeCandido, review of *Room on the Broom,* p. 120; March 1, 2003, Carolyn Phelan, review of *The Spiffiest Giant in Town,* p. 1201; May 1, 2006, Carolyn Phelan, review of *Charlie Cook's Favorite Book,* p. 88.

Bookseller, January 20, 2006, Caroline Horn, review of *The Gruffalo,* p. 9.

Horn Book, January-February, 2005, Jennifer M. Brabander, review of *The Gruffalo's Child,* p. 75.

Kirkus Reviews, August 1, 2001, review of *Room on the Broom,* p. 1121; January 1, 2003, review of *The Spiffiest Giant in Town,* p. 60; February 15, 2004, review of *The Snail and the Whale,* p. 176; May 1, 2006, review of *Charlie Cook's Favorite Book,* p. 455.

Publishers Weekly, May 30, 1994, review of *Sam Who Was Swallowed by a Shark,* p. 55; June 21, 1999, review of *The Gruffalo,* p. 67; September 10, 2001, review of *Room on the Broom,* p. 92; January 6, 2003, review of *The Spiffiest Giant in Town,* p. 59; December 13, 2004, review of *The Gruffalo's Child,* p. 68; May 15, 2006, review of *Charlie Cook's Favorite Book,* p. 71.

School Library Journal, July, 1997, Marsha McGrath, review of *Juice the Pig,* p. 72; September, 2001, Pamela K. Bomboy, review of *Room on the Broom,* p. 187; March, 2003, Bina Williams, review of *The Spiffiest Giant in Town,* p. 191; February, 2004, Kathleen Kelly MacMillan, review of *The Snail and the Whale,* p. 111; March, 2005, Marge Loch-Wouters, review of *The Gruffalo's Child,* p. 170; July, 2006, Jill Heritage Maza, review of *Charlie Cook's Favorite Book,* p. 71.

ONLINE

Images of Delight Web site, http://www.imagesofdelight. com/ (April 29, 2007), "Axel Scheffler."*

*   *   *

SCOTT, Jessica
See De WIRE, Elinor

*   *   *

SHAW, Mary 1965-

Personal

Born March 20, 1965, in Oshawa, Ontario, Canada; married Brad Shaw (a hockey coach and former professional hockey player), 1988; children: Taylore, Brady, Caroline. *Education:* Attended University of Guelph; Wilfrid Laurier University, B.A. (history and English).

Addresses

Office—Brady Brady, Inc., P.O. Box 367, Waterloo, Ontario N2J 4A4, Canada. *E-mail*—mary@bradybrady. com.

Career

Author.

Writings

"BRADY BRADY" BEGINNING READER SERIES

Brady Brady and the Great Rink, illustrated by Chuck Temple, Stoddart Kids (Toronto, Ontario, Canada), 2001.

Brady Brady and the Runaway Goalie, illustrated by Chuck Temple, Stoddart Kids (Toronto, Ontario, Canada), 2001.

Brady Brady and the Twirlin' Torpedo, illustrated by Chuck Temple, Stoddart Kids (Toronto, Ontario, Canada), 2002.

Brady Brady and the Singing Tree, illustrated by Chuck Temple, Stoddart Kids (Toronto, Ontario, Canada), 2002.

Brady Brady and the Big Mistake, illustrated by Chuck Temple, Fitzhenry & Whiteside (Markham, Ontario, Canada), 2003.

Brady Brady and the Great Exchange, illustrated by Chuck Temple, Fitzhenry & Whiteside (Markham, Ontario, Canada), 2003.

Brady Brady and the Most Important Game, illustrated by Chuck Temple, Fitzhenry & Whiteside (Markham, Ontario, Canada), 2004.

Brady Brady and the MVP, illustrated by Chuck Temple, Fitzhenry & Whiteside (Markham, Ontario, Canada), 2004.

Brady Brady and the Super Skater, illustrated by Chuck Temple, Brady Brady Inc. (Waterloo, Ontario, Canada), 2005.

Brady Brady and the Puck on the Pond, illustrated by Chuck Temple, Brady Brady Inc. (Waterloo, Ontario, Canada), 2005.

Brady Brady and the Cranky Kicker, illustrated by Chuck Temple, Brady Brady Inc. (Waterloo, Ontario, Canada), 2006.

Brady Brady and the B Team, illustrated by Chuck Temple, Brady Brady Inc. (Waterloo, Ontario, Canada), 2007.

Brady Brady and the Ballpark Bark, illustrated by Chuck Temple, Brady Brady Inc. (Waterloo, Ontario, Canada), 2007.

The "Brady Brady" series has been translated into French, and older series titles have been reprinted by Brady Brady Inc.

Sidelights

As the wife of a former professional hockey player and the mother of three enthusiastic young hockey fanatics, it is not surprising that Canadian author Mary Shaw channeled her interest in writing in a direction that has resulted in a children's-book series about children and hockey. The "Brady Brady" beginning readers series, which had its debut in 2001 with *Brady Brady and the Great Rink* has expanded to include such titles as *Brady Brady and the Puck on the Pond, Brady Brady and the Cranky Kicker,* and *Brady Brady and the Twirlin' Torpedo.* Shaw's title character is based on her own hockey-obsessed son. According to *School Library Journal* critic Carol Schene, the "Brady Brady" novels each contain "messages about honesty, sportsmanship, and friendship," all of which "are clear but woven nicely into the simple plots." Reviewing *Brady Brady and the Great Rink, Resource Links* contributor Elaine Rospad noted that Shaw's "delightful" story keeps the focus on "determination and sportsmanship," while Shannon Danylko wrote in the same periodical that Shaw's young protagonist would make a good friend. "A unique, sensitive" boy, Brady Brady puts "the feelings and needs of his friends" first, according to the critic.

In an interview with Dave Jenkinson for *Canadian Review of Materials,* Shaw discussed how she gets ideas for her books, explaining that she often finds inspiration in the lives of her three children. "I always carry a little note pad, and I'm always listening for some little thing that I can include," she admitted. "I'll write stuff down about what's happening with Brady's team in the dressing room or when we're at tournaments." Her writing process has changed and evolved since the series began; with over a dozen novels to her credit, she now spends less time editing while writing than she used to. Shaw gets a great deal of satisfaction from seeing how children respond to her titles, explaining in her inter-

view: "I love seeing the reactions of kids that are flipping through the books . . . and I just like seeing them chuckle at the drawings. It really makes me happy that these books are being received so well."

Biographical and Critical Sources

PERIODICALS

Canadian Book Review Annual, 2001, review of *Brady Brady and the Great Rink,* p. 467; 2002, reviews of *Brady Brady and the Runaway Goalie,* p. 467, and of *Brady Brady and the Singing Tree* and *Brady Brady and the Twirlin' Torpedo,* both p. 469.

Resource Links, December, 2001, Elaine Rospad, review of *Brady Brady and the Great Rink,* and Elaine Rospad, review of *Brady Brady and the Runaway Goalie,* both p. 10; June, 2002, Shannon Danylko, reviews of *Brady Brady and the Singing Tree,* p. 5, and *Brady Brady and the Twirlin' Torpedo,* p. 6; December, 2004, Joanne de Groot, review of *Brady Brady and the MVP,* p. 10.

School Library Journal, October, 2002, Linda M. Kenton, review of *Brady Brady and the Great Rink,* p. 130; August, 2003, Carol Schene, reviews of *Brady Brady and the Big Mistake, Brady Brady and the Singing Tree,* and *Brady Brady and the Twirlin' Torpedo,* all p. 143.

ONLINE

Canadian Review of Materials Online, http://www.umanitoba.ca/cm/ (October 19, 2001) review of *Brady Brady and the Runaway Goalie* and *Brady Brady and the Great Rink;* (November 16, 2001) Dave Jenkinson, interview with Shaw.

Mary Shaw Home Page, http://www.bradybrady.com (May 1, 2007).

* * *

STEIN, David Ezra

Personal

Born in Brooklyn, NY; married; wife's name Miriam. *Education:* Attended Parsons School of Design. *Hobbies and other interests:* Playing 'cello, rock climbing, walking in the woods.

Addresses

Home—Queens, NY. *Agent*—Rebecca Sherman, Writers House, 21 W. 26th St., New York, NY 10010. *E-mail*—david@davidezra.com.

Career

Author and illustrator.

Writings

SELF-ILLUSTRATED PICTURE BOOKS

Cowboy Ned and Andy, Simon & Schuster Books for Young Readers (New York, NY), 2006.
Cowboy Ned's New Friend, Simon & Schuster Books for Young Readers (New York, NY), 2007.
Leaves, Putnam (New York, NY), 2007.
Monster Hug!, Putnam (New York, NY), 2007.

Biographical and Critical Sources

PERIODICALS

Kirkus Reviews, June 15, 2006, review of *Cowboy Ned and Andy,* p. 638.
Publishers Weekly, July 31, 2006, review of *Cowboy Ned and Andy,* p. 74.
School Library Journal, July, 2006, Joy Fleishhacker, review of *Cowboy Ned and Andy,* p. 87.

ONLINE

David Stein Home Page, http://www.davidezra.com (May 14, 2007).

* * *

STIEGEMEYER, Julie

Personal

Born in Denver, CO; married; husband's name Scott (a Lutheran minister); children: Jacob. *Education:* B.A. (English); M.A. (English education) *Hobbies and other interests:* Walking in the woods, spending time with family, watching movies, doing puzzles, reading, writing.

Addresses

Home and office—IN.

Career

Author and freelance writer. Worked previously as an educator.

Member

Society of Children's Book Writers and Illustrators.

Writings

Faith at Work, Concordia Pub. House (St. Louis, MO), 2001.

Colors I See in Church, illustrated by Kathey Mitter, Concordia Pub. House (St. Louis, MO), 2002.
Things I Do in Church, illustrated by Kathey Mitter, Concordia Pub. House (St. Louis, MO), 2002.
Things I Hear in Church, illustrated by Kathey Mitter, Concordia Pub. House (St. Louis, MO), 2002.
Things I See in Church, illustrated by Kathey Mitter, Concordia Pub. House (St. Louis, MO), 2003.
Saint Nicholas: The Real Story of the Christmas Legend, illustrated by Chris Ellison, Concordia Pub. House (St. Louis, MO), 2003.
Thanksgiving: A Harvest Celebration, illustrated by Renné Benoit, Concordia Pub. House (St. Louis, MO), 2003.
Baby in a Manger, illustrated by Nicole Wong, Concordia Pub. House (St. Louis, MO), 2004.
Things I See at Easter, illustrated by Kathy Mitter, Concordia Pub. House (St. Louis, MO), 2004.
Bethlehem Night, illustrated by Gina Capaldi, Concordia Pub. House (St. Louis, MO), 2005.
Bright Easter Day, illustrated by Susan Spellman, Concordia Pub. House (St. Louis, MO), 2005.
Cheep! Cheep!, illustrated by Carol Baicker-McKee, Bloomsbury Children's Books (New York, NY), 2006.
Mommy Promises, illustrated by Wilson Ong, Concordia Pub. House (St. Louis, MO), 2006.
Things I See at Baptism, illustrated by Kathryn Mitter, Concordia Pub. House (St. Louis, MO), 2007.
Merry Christmas, Cheeps!, illustrated by Carol Baicker-McKee, Bloomsbury Children's Books (New York, NY), 2007.

Contributor to *Christian Parenting Today* magazine.

Sidelights

Julie Stiegemeyer has always had two loves in her life: reading and writing. She began her writing career at a very young age, completing her first children's book—recounting the adventures of a helicopter—while she was still in kindergarten and moving into poetry in fourth grade. As a writer for children, Stiegmeyer's focus has been primarily on religious-themed books for pre-readers, although the board book *Cheep! Cheep!* and its sequel, *Merry Christmas, Cheeps!,* are published by a mainstream press. Deemed "irresistible" and "inventive" by a *Publishers Weekly* reviewer, *Cheep! Cheep!* uses one-syllable words to express the anticipation of three newly hatched chicks as they anxiously await the arrival of a sibling who has yet to emerge from his egg. Linda Zeilstra Sawyer, reviewing the board book for *School Library Journal,* cited the simplicity of both text and illustrations and added that, "together they strike the perfect balance to create a charming picture book." Citing the engaging illustrations by Carol Baicker-McKee as depicting "cuteness in action," a *Kirkus Reviews* critic called *Cheep! Cheep!* "one to keep."

As a professional writer and children's-book author, Stiegemeyer has made it a habit to keep a journal capturing daily events and thoughts, and she often refers to this book for her story ideas. On her home page, she

Julie Stiegemeyer's simple counting book Cheep! Cheep! *features collage artwork by Carol Baicker-McKee.* (Bloomsbury Publishing, PLC, 2006. Illustrations copyright © Carol Baicker-McKee, 2006. Reproduced by permission.)

encourages aspiring writers to read as much as they can in the genre that they would like to write for. While beginning writers often neglect the value of reading, she added, "reading in your specialty helps you learn the basics of style, tone, length, pacing, character development, plot development, and a whole host of other things."

Biographical and Critical Sources

PERIODICALS

Bulletin of the Center for Children's Books, March, 2006, Loretta Gaffney, review of *Cheep! Cheep!,* p. 327.

Child, March, 2006, Julie Yates Walton, review of *Cheep! Cheep!,* p. 36.

Kirkus Reviews, January 1, 2006, review of *Cheep! Cheep!,* p. 45.

Publishers Weekly, September 22, 2003, review of *Saint Nicholas: The Real Story of the Christmas Legend,* p. 71; September 22, 2003, review of *Cheep! Cheep!,* p. 66.

School Library Journal, March, 2006, Linda Zeilstra Sawyer, review of *Cheep! Cheep!,* p. 202.

ONLINE

Julie Stiegemeyer Home Page, http://juliestiegemeyer.com (May 1, 2007).*

STOLZ, Mary 1920-2006
(Mary Slattery Stolz)

OBITUARY NOTICE—

See index for *SATA* sketch: Born March 24, 1920, in Boston, MA; died December 15, 2006, in Longboat Key, FL. Author. Stolz was an award-winning author of books for children and young adults. Educated at Columbia University Teacher's College and the Katharine Gibbs School in the 1930s, she first worked as a secretary at Columbia University. Stolz, unfortunately, suffered from arthritis at an early age. During one severe bout with the ailment, she decided to work on her first book. This was released in 1950 as *To Tell Your Love.* Many more works of fiction would follow, and Stolz developed a reputation for writing novels that appealed to young girls. Her stories were frequently on American Library Association notable book lists, and several titles were award winners. Her *In a Mirror* (1953), for example, won the Children's Book Award from Bank Street College; she was a National Book Award finalist for *The Edge of Next Year* (1974), and her *Belling the Tiger* (1961) and *The Noonday Friends* (1965) were both Newbery Honor books. Praised for her strong characterizations of teenagers facing troubles in love and with family, Stolz penned such other memorable young adult titles as *Leap before You Look* (1972), *Go and Catch a Flying Fish* (1979), and *Coco Grimes* (1994). Her titles for younger children include favorites like *Emmett's Pig* (1959), *The Bully of Barkham Street* (1963), and *Bartholomew Fair* (1990).

OBITUARIES AND OTHER SOURCES:

PERIODICALS

Chicago Tribune, January 23, 2007, section 2, p. 10.
New York Times, January 22, 2007, p. A18.

*   *   *

STOLZ, Mary Slattery
See STOLZ, Mary

*   *   *

STURTEVANT, Katherine 1950-

Personal

Born December 14, 1950, in Oakland, CA; daughter of Royal William (a carpenter and teacher) and Leisa (a school) Sturtevant; married Ronald Stuart (a software engineer), December 18, 1971; children: Joseph, Peter (twins). *Education:* San Francisco State University, B.A. (creative writing; magna cum laude), 1976, M.A. (creative writing), 1993. *Politics:* Democrat. *Religion:* Roman Catholic. *Hobbies and other interests:* Movies, theatre, the San Francisco Giants.

Addresses

Home—Berkeley, CA. *E-mail*—author@katherine sturtevant.com.

Career

Writer. Writer-in-residence at MacDowell Colony, and others.

Member

Society of Children's Book Writers and Illustrators, Authors Guild.

Awards, Honors

Booklist Editor's Choice designation, Bay Area Book Reviewers Association finalist for best children's book, Association of Children's Librarians of Northern California Notable Book designation, New York Public Library Best Books for the Teen Age citation, Bank Street College Best Books for Children designation, and silver medal (young adult literature), Commonwealth Club/California Book Awards, all 2000, all for *At the Sign of the Star; School Library Journal* Best Books designation, and *Booklist* Top Ten Historical Fiction for Youth designation, both 2006, both for *A True and Faithful Narrative.*

Writings

YOUNG-ADULT NOVELS

At the Sign of the Star, Farrar, Straus & Giroux (New York, NY), 2000.
A True and Faithful Narrative, Farrar, Straus & Giroux (New York, NY), 2006.

FOR ADULTS

A Mistress Moderately Fair, Alyson Publications (Boston, MA), 1988.
Our Sisters' London: Feminist Walking Tours, Chicago Review Press (Chicago, IL), 1990, published with additional material by Kate Murphy as *Our Sisters' London: Nineteen Feminist Walks,* Women's Press, 1991.

Adaptations

At the Sign of the Star was adapted for audiobook, read by Emily Gray, Recorded Books, 2002.

Sidelights

Katherine Sturtevant was a writer for many years before turning to young-adult fiction with *At the Sign of the Star.* Drawing on the author's interest in the history of Restoration-era England, *At the Sign of the Star* is set in 1677 London and tells the story of twelve-year-old Meg Moore. Living with her widowed, bookseller father, Meg loves books and writing and has little interest in needlework, cooking, and the other activities that are traditionally the domain of women. Because she is the sole heir of her prosperous father's estate, the girl looks forward to a life of relative independence: her family's affluence will allow her the freedom to write, select a suitable husband, and continue to be immersed in London's stimulating literary culture. However, Meg's dream of inheriting and running her father's bookshop and publishing business is threatened when Mr. Moore remarries. Her inheritance in jeopardy after her stepmother, Susannah, gives birth to a son, Meg now finds her freedom curtailed as Susannah attempts to teach the headstrong preteen the homemaking skills that will win her a suitable husband.

At the Sign of the Star was praised for successfully introducing readers to life as it was lived in a bygone era. As Carolyn Phelan wrote in her *Booklist* review, Sturtevant draws on "vocabulary, speech patterns . . . as well as the many details" of daily life to create a "lively backdrop" for her coming-of-age tale. In *School Library Journal* Connie Tyrrell Burns noted that the novel "paints a lively picture" of seventeenth-century London life, weaving in such fascinating details as "medical procedures, food, and wedding rituals." A *Publishers Weekly* critic noted that Sturtevant avoids "simplistic devices" in illustrating Meg's maturation, instead showing that her heroine's accomplishments are "achieved through perseverance and genuine growth." In *Horn Book,* Anita L. Burkam lauded Sturtevant for her "portrayal of the struggles of a blended family" as well as for incorporating historically accurate vignettes that illustrate women's attitudes and opportunities during the Restoration. Concluding her review, Burns praised Sturtevant for creating a strong female protagonist and for setting Meg "in a time and place not often portrayed in books" intended for a teen readership.

When readers rejoin Meg in *A True and Faithful Narrative,* the girl is now sixteen years old and courted by two suitors: Will is her father's apprentice, while Edward is the adventurous brother of Meg's best friend. Although the choice of a husband is an important one for Meg, she puts this quandary on the back burner when she learns that Edward has been captured by Barbary pirates and sold into slavery, along with the rest of his trading ship's crew. Meg had ridiculed the young man's decision to go to sea, and now she must enlist Will's help, and use her skill at writing, to amass the funds needed to secure Edward's release. In her first-person narrative, Meg is portrayed as "a strong-willed yet vulnerable young woman," according to Phelan, the critic adding that Sturtevant frames her novel with "great clarity" and the incorporation of "vivid details." Noting the pragmatism demonstrated by Sturtevant's teen heroine, Vicky Smith added in *Horn Book* that this installment in Meg's story serves as "a quietly meticulous" illustration "of the collision between East and West as well as a musing on the mutability of destiny." In a *Kirkus Reviews* appraisal, a critic described *A True and Faithful Narrative* as "beautifully detailed" and "authentically voiced," adding that "readers will root" for Sturtevant's "lively heroine."

Sturtevant once told *SATA:* "I grew up in the Santa Clara Valley, which was at that time filled with fruit orchards. I wrote my first story when I was in the second grade, and from then on I never wanted to be anything except a writer of fiction. And, in spite of much clerical and secretarial work, and a few other miscellaneous jobs, it's really all I have ever been. In spite of that fact, it took me a long time to discover exactly what *kind* of fiction I wanted to write. After many years of experimentation, I happened, in one my periodic raids on the children's section of the library, to come across Karen Cushman's wonderful novel, *Catherine, Called Birdy.* As I read I found myself thinking: *This* is the kind of book I want to write. And so I began a historical novel for young readers, set in Restoration London, a time period that has always fascinated me.

"I love history, especially the details of daily life. I've always loved reading historical novels, or, for that matter, reading any kind of novels. (Short stories are another matter.) My favorite authors of literature for adults include Jane Austen, Anthony Trollope, Virginia Woolf, E.M. Forster, Henry James, Edith Wharton, Iris Murdoch, Toni Morrison, David Lodge, and Rose Tremain. I like novels in which people talk to each other, novels with lots of interesting dialogue. Landscapes generally bore me.

"My roots are English and I have always loved English literature and history as much as that of the United States. But I am less interested in royalty or nobility than I am in the lives of merchants or tradespeople, apprentices and servants. In the future, I hope to divide my time between writing literature for children and for adults. I imagine that most of my work will be set at least partly in the past.

"When I'm not reading, writing, or researching, I enjoy movies, the San Francisco Giants, and an occasional play or ballet. But most of all—in my life as in my favorite novels—I find that nothing can equal the pleasure of good conversation."

Biographical and Critical Sources

PERIODICALS

Booklist, October 15, 2000, Carolyn Phelan, review of *At the Sign of the Star,* p. 436; April 1, 2001, Stephanie Zvirin, review of *At the Sign of the Star,* p. 1486; March 1, 2006, Carolyn Phelan, review of *A True and Faithful Narrative,* p. 90.

Bulletin of the Center for Children's Books, January, 2001, review of *At the Sign of the Star,* p. 199.

Horn Book, September, 2000, Anita L. Burkam, review of *At the Sign of the Star,* p. 583; May-June, 2006, Vicky Smith, review of *A True and Faithful Narrative,* p. 332.

Kirkus Reviews, April 15, 2006, review of *A True and Faithful Narrative,* p. 417.

Kliatt, September, 2002, Rebecca Rabinowitz, review of *At the Sign of the Star,* p. 22.

Library Journal, July, 1990, Paula M. Zieselman, review of *Our Sisters' London: Feminist Walking Tours,* p. 116.

New York Times Book Review, June 10, 1990, Thomas Swick, review of *Our Sisters' London,* p. 49.

Publishers Weekly, August 26, 1988, Penny Kaganoff, review of *A Mistress Moderately Fair,* p. 81; October 23, 2000, review of *At the Sign of the Star,* p. 76.

School Library Journal, September, 2000, Connie Tyrrell Burns, review of *At the Sign of the Star,* p. 237; October, 2006, review of *A True and Faithful Narrative,* p. 559.

Voice of Youth Advocates, December, 2000, review of *At the Sign of the Star,* p. 355.

Women's Review of Books, October, 1990, Anna Davin, review of *Our Sisters' London,* p. 11.

ONLINE

Katherine Sturtevant Home Page, http://www.thesignofthestar.com (May 15, 2007).*

*   *   *

SUZANNE, Jamie
See HAWES, Louise

*   *   *

SWIATKOWSKA, Gabi 1971(?)-

Personal

Surname pronounced "Svee-at-KOVE-ska"; born c. 1971, in Cracow, Poland; immigrated to United States, 1988; daughter of Michal and Lidia Swiatkowska; children: Zak (daughter). *Education:* Attended Lyceum of Art (Bielsko, Poland); Cooper Union, degree; studied at Parson's School of Design.

Addresses

Home—Pszczyna, Poland. *E-mail*—gabi.swiat@gmail.com.

Career

Illustrator and painter. *Exhibitions:* Paintings have been exhibited in galleries in the United States and Europe.

Awards, Honors

Ezra Jack Keats New Illustrator Award, 2004.

Illustrator

FOR CHILDREN

Sally Derby, *Hannah's Bookmobile Christmas,* Henry Holt (New York, NY), 2001.

Helen Recorvits, *My Name Is Yoon,* Farrar, Straus & Giroux (New York, NY), 2003.

Lola M. Schaefer, *Arrowhawk,* Henry Holt (New York, NY), 2004.

Nina Payne, *Summertime Waltz,* Farrar, Straus & Giroux (New York, NY), 2005.

Kimberly Willis Holt, *Waiting for Gregory,* Henry Holt (New York, NY), 2006.

Helen Recorvits, *Yoon and the Christmas Mitten,* Farrar, Straus & Giroux (New York, NY), 2006.

Ilene Cooper, *The Golden Rule,* Harry Abrams (New York, NY), 2007.

Helen Recorvits, *Yoon and the Jade Bracelet,* Farrar, Straus & Giroux (New York, NY), 2008.

Sidelights

Illustrator Gabi Swiatkowska moved to the United States in 1988, joining her parents who had arrived eight years earlier, and attended art school in New York City as well as in her native Poland. Although her ability to create interesting characters had prompted many of her friends to suggest a career as a children's book illustrator, Swiatkowska did not immediately pursue this option, preferring to focus on her painting. In 2000 she finally put together a portfolio that attracted interest from the first publisher she submitted it to. In addition to the steady stream of illustration assignments she has received since, Swiatkowska has also been awarded the prestigious Ezra Jack Keats Award for New Illustrator, given to her in 2004.

Swiatkowska's first illustration project, creating artwork for Sally Derby's *Hannah's Bookmobile Christmas,* was praised by Gillian Engberg, who noted in her *Booklist* review that the illustrator's "beautiful, atmospheric paintings with spot-on details" help give Derby's holiday story about a woman who runs a rural school-bus library a "subdued, unusual" feel. Praising Swiatkowska's contributions to Kimberly Willis Holt's *Waiting for Gregory,* a *Publishers Weekly* contributor cited in particular the illustrator's sophisticated and well-schooled approach. "In her artwork, Swiatkowska . . . elegantly muses on the elasticity of time and the mystery of gestation," the critic noted. "She unmoors her characters from geography and gravity; they float in austere, brush-stroked spaces." The poetic text of Nina Payne's *Summertime Waltz* "launches" Swiatkowska on a "flight of fancy," added another *Publishers Weekly* reviewer; despite alternating between pen-and-ink drawings and acrylics applied in "thickly layered brush-

In addition to appearing in picture books, Gabi Swiatkowska's evocative paintings have been exhibited around the world. (Painting, "Angel," © 2006, by Gabi Swiatkowska. Courtesy of the artist.)

strokes," the artist establishes continuity in the whole through her focus on "the recurring details of the characters' clothing and activities." In her profile on the illustrator for *School Library Journal,* Andrea Glick wrote that "Swiatkowska brings to Payne's poem about childhood summers a virtuoso drawing and painting technique, coupled with a gleefully unorthodox use of space and a gift for creating funny, surreal imagery. All in all, it's a strikingly innovative work."

Swiatkowska has collaborated with author Helen Recorvits on several books that feature a young Korean girl named Yoon, whose family has moved to the United States. Introduced in *My Name Is Yoon,* the young immigrant and her adventures are also detailed in *Yoon and the Christmas Mitten* and *Yoon and the Jade Bracelet.* While noting that *Yoon and the Christmas Mitten* is "a sweet and subtle holiday story" that finds the girl learning about the traditions surrounding the Christmas season in her adopted country, Gregory Cowles had special praise for Swiatkowska's contribution to Yoon's adventures. Within "rich, textured illustrations" that are "impressionistic and drenched in color," Cowles noted in his *New York Times Book Review* appraisal, Swiatkowska embeds "a wealth of art history"; for example, the heroine's visions of Santa's home at the North Pole are portrayed "like something from the Byzantine Empire, while [Yoon's] . . . teacher resembles a Raphael Madonna and her classroom might have been decorated by [nineteenth-century Pre-Raphaelite painter] William Morris." Appraising the illustrator's work for *My Name Is Yoon,* Teri Markson and Stephen Samuel Wise concluded in *School Library Journal* that "Swiatkowska's stunningly spare, almost surrealistic paintings enhance the . . . message" underlying Rocorvits' "powerful and inspiring" story.

Biographical and Critical Sources

PERIODICALS

Booklist, September 15, 2001, Gillian Engberg, review of *Hannah's Bookmobile Christmas,* p. 234; March 1, 2003, Hazel Rochman, review of *My Name Is Yoon,* p. 1333; May 15, 2004, GraceAnne A. DeCandido, review of *Arrowhawk,* p. 1626; May 15, 2005, Gillian Engberg, review of *Summertime Waltz,* p. 1652; December 1, 2006, Gillian Engberg, review of *Yoon and the Christmas Mitten,* p. 55.

Bulletin of the Center for Children's Books, April, 2003, review of *My Name Is Yoon,* p. 328; July-August, 2004, Timnah Card, review of *Arrowhawk,* p. 482; February 1, 2006, Hazel Rochman, review of *Waiting for Gregory,* p. 55; November, 2006, Elizabeth Bush, review of *Yoon and the Christmas Mitten,* p. 142.

Kirkus Reviews, March 1, 2003, review of *My Name Is Yoon,* p. 396; May 1, 2004, Lola M. Schaefer, *Arrowhawk,* p. 448; April 15, 2005, review of *Summertime Waltz,* p. 479; April 1, 2006, review of *Waiting for Gregory,* p. 348; November 1, 2006, review of *Yoon and the Christmas Mitten,* p. 1133.

New York Times Book Review, Gregory Cowles, review of *Yoon and the Christmas Mitten,* p. 66.

Publishers Weekly, September 24, 2001, review of *Hannah's Bookmobile Christmas,* p. 50; January 20, 2003, review of *My Name Is Yoon,* p. 81; November 10, 2003, review of *My Name Is Yoon,* p. 36; May 16, 2005, review of *Summertime Waltz,* p. 62; April 24, 2006, review of *Waiting for Gregory,* p. 59.

School Library Journal, October, 2001, review of *Hannah's Bookmobile Christmas,* p. 64; May, 2003, Teri Markson and Stephen Samuel Wise, review of *My Name Is Yoon,* p. 128; December, 2003, review of *My Name Is Yoon,* p. 48; May, 2004, Susan Oliver, review of *Arrowhawk,* p. 122; July, 2004, Lisa G. Kropp, review of *My Name Is Yoon,* p. 44; July, 2005, Genevieve Gallagher, review of *Summertime Waltz,* p. 80; November, 2005, Andrea Glick, "Gabi's World," p. 46; March, 2006, Marianne Saccardi, review of *Waiting for Gregory,* p. 194; October, 2006, Eva Mitnick, review of *Yoon and the Christmas Mitten,* p. 100.

ONLINE

New York Public Library Web site, http://www.nypl.org/ (February 19, 2004), "2004 Ezra Jack Keats Book Award Winners Announced."

T-V

TAYLOR, Kim

Personal

Born in Denver, CO. *Education:* University of California, Irvine, B.A. (drama); California State University, Los Angeles, M.A. (special education).

Addresses

Home and office—Salinas, CA. *E-mail*—kimtaylor@kimtaylor.net.

Career

Educator and author. Heald College, Salinas, CA, instructor; RISE (nonprofit job-training program), lead faculty. Singular Productions, Los Angeles, CA, former actor and founding member.

Awards, Honors

Willa Literary Award for Best Young Adult Novel, Women Writing the West, 2002, for *Cissy Funk.*

Writings

Cissy Funk (young-adult fiction), HarperCollins (New York, NY), 2001.
Bowery Girl (young-adult novel), Viking (New York, NY), 2006.

Also author of two-act play *Not So Quiet,* adapted from the novel by Helen Zenna Smith.

Sidelights

In addition to teaching at the college level, Kim Taylor is the author of several young-adult novels, as well as a stage adaptation of Helen Zenna Smith's World War I novel *Not So Quiet. Cissy Funk,* which earned Taylor

the 2002 Willa Cather Award from Women Writing the West, is set in Colorado during the depression years of the 1930s, and follows a fourteen-year-old girl as she copes with an abusive mother, a runaway father, and the loving aunt who attempts to rescue her. Taylor's second novel, *Bowery Girl,* was inspired by the author's love of history and her reading of Jacob Riis's famous 1890 social documentary history *How the Other Half Lives: Studies among the Tenements of New York.*

Set in the late nineteenth century, *Bowery Girl* shows teen readers that the modern realities of city life—gang violence, crime, unplanned pregnancy, and poverty—are nothing new: they were shared by teens of previous generations. In the novel, street-smart, sixteen-year-old Mollie Flynn relies on her wits and thieving ways to survive in nineteenth-century Manhattan. Dreaming of the better life that could be hers across the newly erected Brooklyn Bridge, Molly and her roommate Annabelle decide to save up enough money to make this shared dream a reality. However, Annabelle works as a prostitute, and when she winds up pregnant the dream is threatened. Hoping to find a way to keep their plan alive, the teens enroll in a series of self-improvement classes, despite the pressure of those around them to accept their station as Bowery dwellers. In *Kliatt,* Janis Flint-Ferguson called *Bowery Girl* "a gritty, realistic look" at life in the nineteenth century, while Jennifer Mattson commented in *Booklist* that the author "allows her characters to behave mostly unhampered" by any overarching message. In *Voice of Youth Advocates,* Mary E. Heslin called Taylor's young characters "complex" and concluded that *Bowery Girl* "is not just fine historical fiction; it is also splendid writing with mega teen appeal."

For Taylor, the research she did while writing *Bowery Girl* was one of the most compelling parts of the writing process. As she noted on her home page: "To research 1883 Manhattan is to conjure ghosts, to dig through contemporary and historical accounts that sometimes glorify and exaggerate both rich and poor, both goodness and evil. The specifics in research, be-

Cover of Kim Taylor's young-adult novel Bowery Girl, *featuring an illustration by Larry Rostant.* (Viking, 2006. Jacket illustration copyright © 2006 by Larry Rostant. Reproduced by permission of Viking, a division of Penguin Putnam Books for Young Readers.)

yond dates and places and streets, came from studying the photographs of the time. To look for the dimness of the gaslights, the children playing in a street and blithely unaware of the dead horse laying ten feet away, the thick layer of grease on a tenement wall, a momentary smile. To walk, for a moment, with two young women who wanted only a bit of sunshine and a chance for something better."

Biographical and Critical Sources

PERIODICALS

Booklist, August, 2001, Frances Bradburn, review of *Cissy Funk,* p. 2109; March 1, 2006, Jennifer Mattson, review of *Bowery Girl,* p. 83.
Bulletin of the Center for Children's Books, May, 2001, review of *Cissy Funk,* p. 354; May, 2006, Elizabeth Bush, review of *Bowery Girl,* p. 425.
Journal of Adolescent & Adult Literacy, October, 2006, Judith A. Hayn, review of *Bowery Girl,* p. 159.
Kirkus Reviews, April 1, 2006, review of *Bowery Girl,* p. 358.

Kliatt, March, 2006, Janis Flint-Ferguson, review of *Bowery Girl,* p. 17.
Publishers Weekly, May 28, 2001, review of *Cissy Funk,* p. 89.
School Library Journal, May, 2001, Cindy Darling Codell, review of *Cissy Funk,* p. 160; March, 2006, Kelly Czarnecki, review of *Bowery Girl,* p. 230.
Voice of Youth Advocates, August, 2001, review of *Cissy Funk,* p. 207; April, 2006, Mary E. Heslin, review of *Bowery Girl,* p. 52.

ONLINE

Kim Taylor Home Page, http://www.kimtaylor.net (May 16, 2007).

* * *

TODD, Anne Ophelia
See DOWDEN, Anne Ophelia Todd

* * *

TULLOCH, Richard 1949-
(Richard George Tulloch)

Personal

Born September 1, 1949, in Melbourne, Victoria, Australia; son of Ian Mitchell (a doctor) and Cecily Muriel (a social worker) Tulloch; married Agnes Blaauw (a drug and alcohol counselor), October, 1977; children: Telma, Bram. *Education:* Melbourne University, B.A., 1972, LL.B., Dip.Ed., 1973.

Addresses

Home—Sydney, New South Wales, Australia; Amsterdam, Netherlands. *Agent*—Cameron's Management, 163 Brougham St., Woolloomooloo, New South Wales 2011, Australia.

Career

Actor, director, teacher, and writer. Freelance actor and musician in Melbourne, Victoria, Australia, and Europe, 1975-78; National Theatre, Perth, Western Australia, Australia, associate director, 1979-80; Toe Truck Theatre, Sydney, New South Wales, Australia, artistic director, 1981-83; freelance actor, theater director, and writer, 1984—. Teacher of children and adults at Center Europeen d'Ecriture Audiovisuelle, Paris, France, and at University of New South Wales, Thammasat University, Bangkok, Thailand; Unitec, New Zealand; and Australian Film, Television, and Radio School.

Member

International Theatre Institute (member, Australian committee, 1990-92), Australian Writers Guild (member, management committee, 1990-92), Actors Equity (Australia).

Awards, Honors

Australian Writers Guild AWGIE awards, for stage adaptations of *Hating Alison Ashley* and *Talking to Grandma While the World Goes By,* both 1988, and for *Body and Soul;* Annie Award nomination for best screenplay, for *Ferngully II: The Magical Rescue;* Kids Own Australian Literature Award nominations, for *Danny in the Toybox, Being Bad for the Babysitter,* and *Barry the Burglar,* and shortlist, 2001, for *Cocky Colin.*

Writings

FOR CHILDREN

Stories from Our House, illustrated by Julie Vivas, Cambridge University Press (Cambridge, England), 1987.

Stories from Our Street, illustrated by Vivas, Cambridge University Press (Cambridge, England), 1989.

Rain for Christmas, illustrated by Wayne Harris, Cambridge University Press (Cambridge, England), 1989.

The Strongest Man in Gundiwallanup, illustrated by Sue O'Loughlin, Cambridge University Press (Cambridge, England), 1990.

The Brown Felt Hat, illustrated by Craig Smith, Omnibus Books (Norwood, South Australia, Australia), 1990.

Danny in the Toybox, illustrated by Armin Greder, Scholastic (New York, NY), 1990.

Being Bad for the Babysitter, illustrated by Coral Tulloch, Omnibus Books (Norwood, South Australia, Australia), 1991, Scholastic (New York, NY), 1992.

Barry the Burglar's Last Job, illustrated by Coral Tulloch, Omnibus Books (Norwood, South Australia, Australia), 1992.

Our New Old House, illustrated by Sue O'Loughlin, Macmillan Australia (South Melbourne, Victoria, Australia), 1992.

Barry the Burglar's Big Mistake, illustrated by Coral Tulloch, Omnibus Books (Norwood, South Australia, Australia), 1995.

Wishes and Dreams, illustrated by Kris Wyld, Random House (New York, NY), 1996.

Mr. Biffy's Battle, illustrated by Andrew McLean, Puffin (Ringwood, Victoria, Australia), 1997.

Parpity-Parp!: A Road Safety Book, illustrated by Fiona Quigley, ABC Books (Sydney, New South Wales, Australia), 1997.

Scruffy's Way Home, illustrated by Craig Smith, ABC Books (Sydney, New South Wales, Australia), 1997.

Dorothy's Garden, illustrated by Peter Townsend, Golden Press (Pymble, New South Wales, Australia), 1998.

Cocky Colin, illustrated by Stephen Axelsen, Omnibus Books (Norwood, South Australia, Australia), 1999.

Mixy's Mixed-up Rhymes, illustrated by Jonathan Bentley, ABC Books (Sydney, New South Wales, Australia), 1999.

Rodney's Runaway Nose, ABC Books (Sydney, New South Wales, Australia), 1999.

Luke's Amazing Smell, illustrated by Stephen Axelsen, ABC Books (Sydney, New South Wales, Australia), 2000.

Tortoise the Hero, ABC Books (Sydney, New South Wales, Australia), 2000.

Barry the Burglar's Bumper Book, illustrated by Coral Tulloch, Omnibus Books (Norwood, New South Wales, Australia), 2001.

Dash in a Flash, illustrated by Steve Moltzen, Funtastic Publishing (South Oakleigh, Victoria, Australia), 2004.

Noisy Night, illustrated by Steve Moltzen, Funtastic Publishing (South Oakleigh, Victoria, Australia), 2004.

Weird Stuff, illustrated by Shane Nagle, Random House Australia (Milsons Point, New South Wales, Australia), 2004, Walker Books (New York, NY), 2006.

Windy Wash Day, illustrated by Steven Moltzen, Funtastic Publishing (South Oakleigh, Victoria, Australia), 2004.

Awesome Stuff, illustrated by Shane Nagle, Random House Australia (Milson's Point, New South Wales, Australia), 2005.

Freaky Stuff, illustrated by Shane Nagle, Random House Australia (Milson's Point, New South Wales, Australia), 2005, Walker Books (New York, NY), 2006.

Beastly Tales, illustrated by Terry Denton, Random House Australia (Milson's Point, New South Wales, Australia), 2006.

"BANANAS IN PYJAMAS" SERIES; BASED ON THE TELEVISION SERIES

Dr Bananas, ABC Books (Sydney, New South Wales, Australia), 1993.

Magic Carpet, ABC Books (Sydney, New South Wales, Australia), 1993.

Bananas in Pyjamas Storybook, ABC Books (Sydney, New South Wales, Australia), 1994.

Café Rat, ABC Books (Sydney, New South Wales, Australia), 1994.

Pyjama Party: A Bananas in Pyjamas Counting Book, illustrated by Felicity Meyer, ABC Books (Sydney, New South Wales, Australia), 1994.

Wishing Pool, ABC Books (Sydney, New South Wales, Australia), 1994.

Circus Time, ABC Books (Sydney, New South Wales, Australia), 1995.

Play Time, ABC Books (Sydney, New South Wales, Australia), 1995.

Pony Ride, ABC Books (Sydney, New South Wales, Australia), 1995.

(With Simon Hopkinson) *Bananas in Pyjamas: Wish Fairies,* illustrated by Peter Townsend, ABC Books (Sydney, New South Wales, Australia), 1996.

Magic Mystery, illustrated by Simon Hopkinson, Random House (New York, NY), 1996.

Adventures with Bananas in Pajamas, illustrated by Simon Hopkinson, Random House (New York, NY), 1996.

The Dinner Party, illustrated by Leonie Worthington, ABC Books (Sydney, New South Wales, Australia), 1997.

Space Bananas, illustrated by Leonie Worthington, ABC Books (Sydney, New South Wales, Australia), 1997.

News Bananas, illustrated by Leonie Worthington, ABC Books (Sydney, New South Wales, Australia), 1998.

Banana Zoo, illustrated by Paul Pattie, ABC Books (Sydney, New South Wales, Australia), 1998.

The Bananas and the Beanstalk, illustrated by Paul Pattie, ABC Books (Sydney, New South Wales, Australia), 1999.

Cinder Bananas, illustrated by Paul Pattie, ABC Books (Sydney, New South Wales, Australia), 1999.

Little Red Riding Banana, illustrated by Paul Pattie, ABC Books (Sydney, New South Wales, Australia), 1999.

Banana Farm, illustrated by Paul Pattie, ABC Books (Sydney, New South Wales, Australia), 2001.

PLAYS

Year 9 Are Animals, Heinemann (Richmond, Victoria, Australia), 1983, published as *The Fourth Year Are Animals,* [England], 1988.

If We Only Had a Cat, Currency Press (Sydney, New South Wales, Australia), 1985.

Face to Face: Five Australian Plays, Cambridge University Press (Cambridge, England), 1987.

(Adaptor) *Moving On* (based on the play by Dave Williams), Cambridge University Press (Cambridge, England), 1988.

(Adaptor) *Hating Alison Ashley* (based on the novel by Robin Klein), Penguin Books (Ringwood, Victoria, Australia), 1988.

(Adaptor) *Space Demons* (based on the novel by Gillian Rubinstein), Omnibus Books (Norwood, South Australia, Australia), 1990.

The Cocky of Bungaree, illustrated by Peter Tierney, Currency Press (Sydney, New South Wales, Australia), 1990.

Could Do Better, Currency Press (Sydney, New South Wales, Australia), 1992.

(Adaptor) *Stage Fright!: Plays Based on the Stories of Paul Jennings,* Puffin Books (Ringwood, Victoria, Australia), 1996.

(Adaptor) *Midnight* (based on the novel by Randolph Stow), Penguin (Ringwood, Victoria, Australia), 1997.

Body and Soul: A Musical Play, music by Saxon Francis, Currency Press (Sydney, New South Wales, Australia), 1998.

OTHER

Letter to Santa (screenplay), Nine Network, 1986.

The Miraculous Mellops (television series), Ten Network, 1991.

Author of television series, including *Bananas in Pyjamas,* 150 episodes beginning 1991; *The Magic Mountain;* and *Playschool,* all for Australian Writers' Guild. Author of screenplays, including of animated film *FernGully II: The Magical Rescue.* Author of radio plays for *Kindergarten.* Also author of *Talking to Grandma while the World Goes By.*

Adaptations

The *Bananas in Pyjamas* television series was the basis of picture books by other authors, all published by ABC Books for the Australian Broadcasting Corporation.

Sidelights

One of Australia's most popular children's book authors, Richard Tulloch has won over legions of loyal young fans as author of the long-running *Bananas in Pyjamas* television series, which has aired around the globe. Among the dozens of book he has written for younger children, *Danny in the Toy Box, Being Bad for the Babysitter,* and *Cocky Colin* have been honored with awards. Tulloch's books for middle-grade readers, which include *Weird Stuff* and *Freaky Stuff,* share the humorously outlandish adventures of likable and sometimes amazing narrator Brian Hobbie. In addition to writing for young people, Tulloch is also an award-winning playwright as well as an actor, director, and storyteller. His many talents have also made him an inspiring educator; Tulloch teaches creative writing at schools both in his native country and elsewhere.

Readers first meet Brian in *Weird Stuff,* as the young soccer buff gains an inkling that he is someone special. A superstar on the soccer field, Brian is less at home in the classroom . . . that is, until necessity forces him to borrow a pink rollerball pen from a classmate. The pen,

Cover of Richard Tulloch's middle-grade novel **Weird Stuff,** *featuring artwork by Shane Nagle.* (Walker & Company, 2004. Illustration copyright © 2004 by Shane Nagle. All rights reserved. Reproduced by permission.)

it turns out, is actually the purloined property of the classmate's romance-novelist mom, and when Brian uses it to complete a science test, his answers gain a certain literary flair. Soon, Brian finds himself in a special class for literary types, where the main attraction is the super-smart girl he has a crush on. His pink pen and newfound writing skill has more practical uses elsewhere, however: he turns it to penning convincing tardy notes for his fellow students. In her *School Library Journal* review of *Weird Stuff*, Emily Rodriguez called the book "an interesting premise couched in a contemporary, comical narrative," while a *Kirkus Reviews* cited the teen's "bemused" narration as well as his "triumphant" creative epiphany: Brian's writing ability turns out to be more talent than magic: he has it no matter what pen he uses.

Brian's adventures continue in *Awesome Stuff* as hopes of gaining a glance from his intellectual heartthrob make him the only boy enrolled in drama class. The teen's talent for writing excuse notes comes in especially handy here, allowing him to balance the gender scales by strong-arming some class-skipping friends into taking drama class with him. Things continue looking up for Brian when he is cast in the lead of *Cyberno*, a play written by his favorite author, Lancelot Cummins. Unfortunately, Brian's penchant for written confabulation seems to have a down side when combined with this new role: like the well-known and famously unattractive character Cyrano de Bergerac, on whom Cyberno is based, Brian's real-life nose seems to have enlarged. And like Pinocchio, the growth of Brian's nose seems to be related to his fibbing frequency. *Freaky Stuff* continues Brian's saga, his further adventures brought to life in quirky line drawings by Shane Nagle.

"I became a writer by accident," Tulloch once told *SATA*, admitting a similarity to the likeable Brian. "I grew up in the sports-mad city of Melbourne, and although I was a fair student, my main ambition was to play cricket for Australia. By the time I'd been dropped to the school's B cricket team, I'd changed my aim to something more reasonable—playing field hockey in the Olympic Games. I tried hard but never made it.

"During my last couple years at university, I discovered studying law was pretty boring and acting in plays was fantastic fun. Soon after graduating, I found myself working in a small professional theatre company, usually making up our own plays and performing them in theatres, schools, and out on the street. . . .

"A friend became director of the National Theatre in Perth, Western Australia, and offered me a job as an actor there. So I packed up again, this time with a Dutch wife and daughter, as well as the yellow fiddle. Although I loved acting, my writing and directing started to develop during our two-and-a-half years in Perth. I wrote six plays and became associate director of the company.

"In the early 1980s I wrote some short stories for very young children and submitted them to a radio program called *Kindergarten.* Most of my stories were rejected but enough were accepted to give me some encouragement. My son, Bram, was then about a year old. I tried in these early stories to see things from his point of view. Things which an adult may take little interest in—a line of ants on the kitchen floor, the garbage a dog has pulled from a bin in the street, a broken mug—could be fascinating for a little boy, and gave me ideas for stories.

"A lucky break got me into writing children's books," Tulloch continued. "My daughter told me that one of her friends at school had a mother who was an artist. That mum turned out to be Julie Vivas, who was already one of Australia's most successful illustrators. I was flattered when Julie asked to see the stories I'd written for *Kindergarten* and even more flattered when she said she'd like to illustrate them for what became my first children's book—*Stories from Our House.*

"Soon after *Stories from Our House* was published, I was asked to go and talk about my writing at a school. The children had lots of questions about how I write (and the usual one about how much money I earned) but the most fun we all had was when I read them some of my stories. I discovered the joys of being a story-teller, and now I spend a day or two most weeks doing this work. I learn all my stories by heart, devise simple ways to act them out, and inflict them on audiences in schools, theatres, and libraries. It's a way to combine my twin loves of performing and writing. Perhaps one day I'll find a way to work playing Olympic hockey into the act too!"

Biographical and Critical Sources

PERIODICALS

Bulletin of the Center for Children's Books, March, 1990, review of *Stories from Our Street,* p. 69; July-August, 2006, Loretta Gaffney, review of *Weird Stuff,* p. 520.

Horn Book, January, 1990, p. 238; July, 1990, pp. 42, 56; spring, 1992, p. 50.

Kirkus Reviews, April 15, 2006, review of *Weird Stuff,* p. 417.

Magpies, July, 1993, review of *Barry the Burglar's Last Job,* p. 28; September, 1993, review of *Could Do Better,* p. 34; March, 1997, review of *Mr. Fiffy's Battle,* p. 27; May, 1999, review of *Cocky Colin,* p. 23; November, 2004, Michael Janssen-Gibson, review of *Weird Stuff,* p. 417; May, 2005, review of *Freaky Stuff,* p. 39; November, 2006, review of *Beastly Tales,* p. 23.

Publishers Weekly, July 24, 1987, review of *Stories from Our House,* p. 186.

Quill & Quire, spring, 1989, review of *Stories from Our Street,* p. 25.

School Library Journal, February, 1988, Bonnie Wheatley, review of *Stories from Our House,* p. 66; February, 1992, Liza Bliss, review of *Danny in the Toybox,* p. 78; August, 2006, Emily Rodriguez, review of *Weird Stuff,* p. 131.

Times Educational Supplement, May 13, 1988, review of *The Fourth Year Are Animals,* p. B8; October 6, 1989, Ann Thwaite, review of *Stories from Our Street,* p. 32.

ONLINE

Random House Australia Web site, http://www.randomhouse.com.au/ (May 2, 2007), "Richard Tulloch."*

*   *   *

TULLOCH, Richard George
See TULLOCH, Richard

VALÉRIO, Geraldo 1970-

Personal

Born 1970, in Brazil. *Education:* New York University, M.A., 2000.

Addresses

Home—Vancouver, British Columbia, Canada.

Career

Illustrator.

Illustrator

Eileen Spinelli, *Do You Have a Hat?,* Simon & Schuster (New York, NY), 2004.

James Heneghan and Bruce McBay, *Nannycatch Chronicles,* Tradewinds Books, 2005.

Eileen Spinelli, *When You Are Happy,* Simon & Schuster (New York, NY), 2006.

Margaret Read MacDonald, *Conejito: A Folktale from Panama,* August House LittleFolk (Little Rock, AK), 2006.

Margaret Read MacDonald, *Go to Sleep, Gecko!: A Balinese Folktale,* August House LittleFolk (Little Rock, AK), 2007.

In his illustrations for Margaret Read MacDonald's Go to Sleep, Gecko!, *Geraldo Valério showcases his folk-art influences.* (August House Publishers, Inc., 2006. Illustration copyright © 2006 by Geraldo Valério. All rights reserved. Reproduced by permission.)

Illustrations also featured in books published in Brazil and Portugal.

Sidelights

The work of Brazilian-born illustrator Geraldo Valério has been praised for bringing to life picture-book texts by authors Eileen Spinelli and Margaret Read MacDonald. To complement Spinelli's rhyming text for *Do You Have a Hat?,* Valério uses stylized painted figures and bright colors in creating a visual history of headgear, prompting Roxanne Burg to deem the work a "great marriage of text and artwork" in her *School Library Journal* review. Appraising his illustrations for Spinelli's *When You Are Happy,* a *Kirkus Reviews* writer noted that the artist's "luminous" images, featuring "glowing, jeweled tones, . . . establish a dreamy quality" that enhances Spinelli's story about the joys and fears of childhood. Dubbing the picture book "an enchanting story of familial love," Wanda Meyers-Hines cited in particular Valério's acrylic paintings for *When You Are Happy,* maintaining that they "sparkle with . . . color, expression, and engaging design."

Valério's artwork has also been paired with several stories by well-known folklorist Margaret Read MacDonald. One of these works, *Go to Sleep, Gecko!: A Balinese Folktale,* retells a traditional story about a gecko who decides that some things in life serve no practical purpose whatsoever, at least certainly not to him. When he goes to a village elder with the request that the fireflies be relocated so he can sleep soundly at night, Gecko receives a reply that ultimately convinces him of the interrelatedness of all nature. Praising the "richly colored" art in *Go to Sleep, Gecko!,* Wendy Woodfill wrote in *School Library Journal* that Valério's "night scenes are luminescent with glowing fireflies and a midnight blue, starry sky." A *Kirkus Reviews* writer also noted the book's characters who, with their "goofy grins and exaggerated noses," enhance the strong dose of fun present in MacDonald's "bouncy ecological fable." Another story by MacDonald, the bilingual *Conejito: A Folktale from Panama,* receives what a *Kirkus Reviews* critic described as "a sense of exuberant motion" through Valério's warm-toned art. A story about a bunny who, with the help of his wise aunt, manages to outsmart several hungry predators, *Conejito* is given "movement and energy" from double-page images in which, as Lee Bock noted in *School Library Journal,* the artist's "folk-art motif . . . perfectly complements" Read's tale. Valério's use of "splashy tropical colors" and his "elongated, rubbery characters . . . capture the tale's bouncing energy," concluded *Booklist* contributor GraceAnne A. DeCandido.

Biographical and Critical Sources

PERIODICALS

Booklist, November 1, 2004, Diane Foote, review of *Do You Have a Hat?,* p. 494; March 1, 2006, GraceAnne A. DeCandido, review of *Conejito: A Folktale from Panama,* p. 51, and Julie Cummins, review of *When You Are Happy,* p. 101.

Bulletin of the Center for Children's Books, July-August, 2006, Maggie Hommel, review of *Conejito,* p. 508.

Kirkus Reviews, September 15, 2004, review of *Do You Have a Hat?,* p. 920; March 1, 2006, review of *Conejito,* p. 236; October 1, 2006, review of *Go to Sleep, Gecko!,* p. 1019.

Publishers Weekly, May 15, 2006, review of *Conejito,* p. 71.

School Library Journal, November, 2004, Roxanne Burg, review of *Do You Have a Hat?,* p. 118; March, 2006, Wanda Meyers-Hines, review of *When You Are Happy,* p. 202; April, 2006, Lee Bock, review of *Conejito,* p. 129; June, 2006, Elizabeth Bird, review of *Nannycatch Chronicles,* p. 158; October, 2006, Wendy Woodfill, review of *Go to Sleep, Gecko!,* p. 138.

ONLINE

August House Web site, http://www.augusthouse.com/ (May 10, 2007), "Geraldo Valério."

Geraldo Valério Home Page, http://www.geraldovalerio. com (May 10, 2007).*

*   *   *

VARELA, Barry 1963(?)

Personal

Born c. 1963; married Fiona Morgan (a professional writer and reporter); children: two daughters. *Education:* Grinnell College, B.A. (English).

Addresses

Home and office—Durham, NC.

Career

Author and editor. Former editor for Harper & Row, Random House, and Henry Holt publishers, New York, NY; Early Intervention Training Center for Infants and Toddlers with Visual Impairments, editor; freelance writer.

Writings

Palmers Gate, Roaring Brook Press (New Milford, CT), 2006.

Gizmo, Roaring Brook Press (New Milford, CT), 2007.

Coauthor and ghost writer for books, mainly in the field of children's literature.

Sidelights

Before penning his first young-adult novel, *Palmers Gate,* Barry Varela coauthored a variety of books within the genre of children's literature, sometimes as a ghost writer. Varela's debut novel deals with the difficult issue of sexual abuse, an issue depicted within the confines of a unique friendship between a young boy and his next-door neighbor. The novel's lead character is Robbie, a pretty typical ten-year-old boy who lives with his single mom. Things drastically change, however, when a new family moves next door and Robbie begins to notice strange things about these new neighbors. The boy is especially confounded by the family's daughter, Colleen, a classmate of Robbie's. In class, Colleen is unusually quiet. Because she wears outdated clothes, she quickly becomes the target of classroom taunting. Knowing that Colleen has family issues, Robbie begins to feel protective of her and the two preteens soon develop a secret friendship. When rumors about Colleen's bizarre behavior begin to circulate, Robbie ultimately sacrifices his own future in order to save the reputation of his friend.

A critic for *Kirkus Reviews* noted that, while Varela's ending is abrupt, in *Palmers Gate* he presents "a well-constructed portrait of a confused child." A *Publishers Weekly* reviewer described the book as a "strange and moving novella" that, in addition to being "gracefully written" "unfolds with excellent pacing."

Biographical and Critical Sources

PERIODICALS

Bulletin of the Center for Children's Books, July-August, 2006, Deborah Stevenson, review of *Palmers Gate,* p. 520.

Kirkus Reviews, May 1, 2006, review of *Palmers Gate,* p. 469.

Library Media Connection, November-December, 2006, Barbara J. McKee, review of *Palmers Gate,* p. 76.

Publishers Weekly, June 26, 2006, review of *Palmers Gate,* p. 52.

School Library Journal, July, 2006, Carolyn Lehman, review of *Palmers Gate,* p. 114.

ONLINE

Barry Varela Home Page, http://www.barryvarela.com (May 1, 2007)*.

* * *

VITALE, Stefano 1958-

Personal

Born August 27, 1958, in Padua, Italy; son of Guido Morassutti-Vitale (a landowner) and Carla Vitale (a homemaker); married Pamela Berry (an art director), May 28, 1988; children: Gianmarco, Anna. *Education:* Attended Bell School of Languages (Norwich, England), 1978, University of Venice, 1979, University of Verona, 1980-82, and University of California, Los Angeles, 1982-83; University of Southern California, B.S. (economics), 1984; Art Center College of Design (Pasadena, CA), B.F.A., 1987.

Addresses

Home and office—49 Sandy Hill Rd., Oyster Bay, NY 11771. *Office— Agent*—Lindgren & Smith, 250 W. 57th St., New York, NY 10107. *E-mail*—stefano@stefanovitale.com.

Career

Freelance illustrator. Advertising clients have included Absolut Vodka, Mercedes-Benz, Xerox, Marriott Hotels, and New York University. *Exhibitions:* Work has been exhibited at Ursitti, MacGuiness Gallery, Washington, DC, 1988; Art Director's Club, New York, NY, 1993; Chrysler Museum of Art, Norfolk, VA, 1996; New York Public Library, 1997; Delaware Museum of Art, Wilmington, 1997; Schloss Maretsch, Bolzano, Italy, 1998; Cedar Rapids Museum of Art, Cedar Rapids, IA, 1998; Galleria Civica, Padova, Italy, 1999; and other galleries and museums.

Awards, Honors

Three-dimensional Illustration Award, 1992; Society of Publication Designers Spot Competition awards, 1993, 1994, 1998; Children's Book of Distinction designation, *Hungry Mind Review,* 1993, for *The World in 1492;* certificate of merit, Society of Illustrators, 1993; Society of Newspaper Design award, 1994; Notable Book designation, American Library Association, 1995, 1997; Picture Book Silver Honor, Parents Choice, 1996; Aesop Prize, American Folklore Society/Library of Congress, 1996; Storytelling World Award honor book, 1998; gold award, National Parenting Publications, 1998; Reading Magic Award, *Parenting* magazine, 1999; seven American Illustration awards.

Illustrator

FOR CHILDREN

Jim Aylesworth, *The Folks in the Valley: A Pennsylvania Dutch ABC,* HarperCollins (New York, NY), 1992.

Jean Fritz, Patricia McKissack, and others, *The World in 1492,* Holt (New York, NY), 1992.

Nancy Jewell, *Christmas Lullaby,* Clarion (New York, NY), 1994.

Angela Shelf Medearis, *Too Much Talk,* Candlewick Press (New Yodk, NY), 1995.

Charlotte Zolotow, *When the Wind Stops* (originally published 1962), new edition, HarperCollins (New York, NY), 1995.

Judy Sierra, adaptor, *Nursery Tales around the World,* Clarion (New York, NY), 1996.

Valiska Gregory, *When Stories Fell like Shooting Stars,* Simon & Schuster (New York, NY), 1996.

Aileen Fisher, *The Story of Easter,* HarperCollins (New York, NY), 1997.

David Kherdian, *The Rose's Smile: Farizad of the Arabian Nights,* Holt (New York, NY), 1997.

Edward Field, *Magic Words* (poetry), Harcourt (New York, NY), 1998.

Nancy Jewell, *Sailor's Song,* Clarion (New York, NY), 1999.

Charlotte Zolotow, *Sleepy Book* (originally published 1958), new edition, HarperCollins (New York, NY), 2001.

Judy Sierra, adaptor, *Can You Guess My Name?: Traditional Tales around the World,* Clarion (New York, NY), 2002.

Charlotte Zolotow, *If You Listen,* Running Press (Philadelphia, PA), 2002.

Alice Walker, *There Is a Flower at the Tip of My Nose Smelling Me,* HarperCollins (New York, NY), 2006.

Alice Walker, *Why War Is Never a Good Idea,* HarperCollins (New York, NY), 2007.

OTHER

Illustrator of *The Creation Creation* (video), music by Bela Fleck, narrated by Amy Grant, Rabbit Ears. Contributor of illustrations to periodicals, including *Time, Newsweek, Business Week, Town and Country, Reader's Digest, Glamour,* and *Metropolitan Home.*

Sidelights

Stefano Vitale is known for creating folk-art-style paintings that, in addition to earned him numerous awards, have brought to life stories by a variety of children's book authors. Beginning his career as a fine-art painter of large canvases, Vitale moved to a smaller format when he refined his characteristic style: a primitive look that echoes the folk art of Mexico and the American Southwest and incorporates wood-grain texture and flat, saturated colors. Vitale's art has appeared in numerous picture books, among them Jim Aylesworth's *The Folks in the Valley: A Pennsylvania Dutch ABC,* Charlotte Zolotow's award-winning *When the Wind Stops,* Nancy Jewell's *Sailor's Song,* David Kherdian's *The Rose's Smile: Farizad of the Arabian Nights,* and Alice Walker's whimsically titled *There Is a Flower at the Tip of My Nose Smelling Me.*

Born in Italy in 1958, Vitale began his college education in the social sciences, graduating from the University of Southern California with a bachelor's degree in economics in 1984. Within the next three years he had refocused his interest, and in 1987 he received his B.F.A. from Pasadena, California's prestigious Art Center College of Design. Married the following year, Vitale marketed his artistic talents to advertisers, creating designs used in selling everything from hotels to motorcars. In his free time, he channeled his creative energy into the large-scale oil paintings that allowed him true artistic expression.

Stephano Vitale creates intricate folkstyle images to pair with Nancy Jewell's text for **Sailor's Song.** (Clarion Books, a Houghton Mifflin Company imprint, 1999.
Illustration copyright © 1999 by Stefano Vitale. All rights reserved. Reproduced by permission of Houghton Mifflin Company.)

"I began my illustrating career to finance my large-scale paintings," Vitale once told *SATA*. His first published illustration project, *Folks in the Valley*, appeared on bookstore shelves in 1992. Featuring a rhyming text, the book is "illustrated . . . with wit and naive charm," according to *Booklist* contributor Carolyn Phelan. Other book illustration assignments have followed, among them *Christmas Lullaby, When the Wind Stops,* and *Nursery Tales around the World,* the last a story collection edited by Judy Sierra. Focusing on the never-ending, cyclical characteristics of the natural world, *When the Wind Stops* is one of several stories by Zolotow that Vitale has re-envisioned for a new generation of young children. His update of the 1962 original features "exquisite" full-color illustrations that "gloriously depict heaven and earth and give concrete meaning to abstract concepts," according to *Booklist* contributor Lauren Peterson. Commenting on the visual references to Old Masters painters Vincent van Gogh and Marc Chagall that appear within the book, *School Library Journal* contributor Virginia Golodetz praised them as an "interesting detail." Using deep-hued oil paints to reprise Zolotow's 1958 picture book *Sleepy Book,* the illustrator creates a dusky, lullaby feel through the use of muted warm colors.

Noting that Vitale's use of color demonstrates "great sensitivity" to the medium of oil paint, *Booklist* reviewer Carolyn Phelan wrote of the artist's contribution to Nancy Jewell's *Christmas Lullaby* that he "uses line, color, and composition to achieve many different effects." Also admiring the illustrator's work, Cynthia Zarin commented in her appraisal of *Christmas Lullaby* for the *New York Times Book Review* that the book's "clear, enchanting illustrations are . . . [rendered] gracefully, without a trace of heavy-handedness." Another original story featuring the artist's work, Walker's *There Is a Flower at the Tip of My Nose Smelling Me* is transformed into what a *Publishers Weekly* described as "an illuminated prayer" by Vitale's inspirational images. A book that focuses on a young girl who is pondering the interrelationships that exist in the natural world, the work was hailed as "poeetic in its appeal" and "artistically stunning" by *School Library Journal* contributor Mary Elam.

Discussing Vitale's artistic contribution to Sierra's *Nursery Tales around the World* Mary M. Burns noted in *Horn Book* that his "folk-art style done in oil paint on wood panels, illuminates the collection's multicultural roots; intricately designed borders incorporate motifs" drawn from the cultures represented in Sierra's selections. Another anthology by Sierra, *Can You Guess My Name?: Traditional Tales from around the World,* also benefits from the Vitale touch. The fifteen tales included in the book are divided among the five traditional motifs embodied in "The Three Pigs," "The Bremen Town Musicians," "Hansel and Gretel," "The Frog Prince," and "Rumpelstiltskin." Discussing Vitale's contribution to the book, John Peters wrote in his *Booklist* review of *Can You Guess My Name?* that "Vitale paints

Cover of Edward Field's poetry collection **Magic Words**, *a work brought to life through Vitale's illustrations.* (Gulliver Books, Harcourt Brace & Company, 1998. Jacket illustration copyright © 1998 by Stefano Vitale. Reproduced by permission of Harcourt, Inc.)

on rough wood to add visual effect," enhancing each image with unique painted borders and "scenes of stylized but easily recognizable figures." Vitale's borders, described by a *Kirkus Reviews* writer as "vibrant and detailed," serve as "a strong component" of the book, and work to "create a mood and complement the [artist's] gloriously executed illustrations." "Beautiful to look at, [and] appealing in tone," *Can You Guess My Name?* "is an outstanding example of what folklore collections for children can and should be," concluded Burns.

Vitale's painted illustrations have found a welcome place in many other books, from Edward Field's poetry anthology *Magic Words* to several collections of folk tales and legends. In Angela Shelf Medearis's *Too Much Talk* his paintings bring to life a West African tale about a group of local neighbors who suddenly find that all manner of animals and vegetables around them have been given the gift of gab. Praising the book's illustrations, *Booklist* contributor Julie Corsaro noted that Vitale's "subtly colored spreads have stylized figures that evoke the region and flowing lines that echo the cadence of [Medearis's] text." A *Publishers Weekly* reviewer was even more enthusiastic, writing that, "even with lively, kid-pleasing narration, Vitale's . . . glowing, oil-on-wood paintings steal the show in this animated tale."

Deeming Vitale's illustrations "enchanting," *School Library Journal* critic Judith Constantinides also praised the artist's contribution to *The Rose's Smile,* Kherdian's reworking of the classic Arabian Nights saga for young people. Vitale's evocation of Persian miniatures and his use of "lush colors" elicited Constantinides' approval; as the reviewer noted, "each page is elaborately framed and, as with medieval and Eastern art, sometimes depicts more than one scene from the story—a nice touch." "The story moves quickly," agreed Karen Morgan in *Booklist,* the critic going on to write that "its appeal [is] magnified by Vitale's rich illustrations, which are lushly imbued with details of street and palace life and splendid gardens."

"Through the books I illustrate, I try to convey the images that the text suggests to me," Vitale once explained to *SATA.* "My working habits are like a nine-to-five job, interrupted by an occasional walk in the woods where I feel at peace." His advice to aspiring young illustrators? "Write your own stories and try to ignore this obsessive desire to be recognized."

Biographical and Critical Sources

PERIODICALS

Booklist, May 1, 1992, Carolyn Phelan, review of *The Folks in the Valley: A Pennsylvania Dutch ABC,* p. 1598; October 1, 1994, Carolyn Phelan, review of *Christmas Lullaby,* p. 333; July, 1995, Lauren Peterson, review of *When the Wind Stops,* p. 1879; January 1-15, 1996, Julie Corsaro, review of *Too Much Talk,* pp. 840-841; December 15, 1996, p. 729; January 1-15, 1997, p. 860; September 1, 1997, Karen Morgan, review of *The Rose's Smile: Farizad of the Arabian Nights,* p. 114; October 15, 1998, p. 414; November 1, 2001, Hazel Rochman, review of *Sleepy Book,* p. 480; November 15, 2002, John Peters, review of *Can You Guess My Name?: Traditional Tales around the World,* p. 599; April 1, 2006, Hazel Rochman, review of *There Is a Flower at the Tip of My Nose Smelling Me,* p. 47.

Bulletin of the Center for Children's Books, January, 2003, review of *Can You Guess My Name?,* p. 211.

Horn Book, March-April, 1993, p. 226; May-June, 1996, Mary M. Burns, review of *Nursery Tales around the World,* pp. 343-344; January, 2002, review of *Sleepy Book,* p. 49; October 15, 2002, review of *Can You Guess My Name?,* p. 1538; January-February, 2003, Mary M. Burns, review of *Can You Guess My Name?,* p. 87.

Kirkus Reviews, July 1, 2001, review of *Sleepy Book,* p. 950; October 15, 2002, review of *Can You Guess My Name?,* p. 1538; April 15, 2006, review of *There Is a Flower at the Tip of My Nose Smelling Me,* p. 418.

New York Times Book Review, December 18, 1994, Cynthia Zarin, review of *Christmas Lullaby.*

Publishers Weekly, October 23, 1995, review of *Too Much Talk,* p. 67; January 27, 1997, p. 97; September 7, 1998, p. 95; March 1, 1999, p. 67; September 3, 2001, review of *Sleepy Book,* p. 90; May 8, 2006, review of *There Is a Flower at the Tip of My Nose Smelling Me,* p. 64.

School Library Journal, May, 1992, p. 96; August, 1995, Virginia Golodetz, review of *When the Wind Stops,* p. 131; April, 1996, p. 130; October, 1996, p. 94; November, 1997, Judith Constantinides, review of *The Rose's Smile,* p. 109; December, 1998, p. 135; May, 1999, p. 91; August, 2001, Gay Lynn Van Vleck, review of *Sleepy Book,* p. 174; November, 2002, Lee Bock, review of *Can You Guess My Name?,* p. 148; May, 2006, Mary Elam, review of *There Is a Flower at the Tip of My Nose Smelling Me,* p. 118.

ONLINE

Lindgren & Smith Web site, http://www.lindgrensmith.com/ (May 15, 2007), "Stefano Vitale."*

*   *   *

VOAKE, Charlotte 1957-

Personal

Born 1957, in Wales; married; children: Chloe, William. *Education:* University of London, B.A. (art history).

Addresses

Home—Surrey, England.

Career

Children's book author and illustrator. Bluecoat Gallery, Liverpool, England, former gallery worker.

Awards, Honors

Reading Magic Awards Certificate of Excellence, *Parenting* magazine, 1988, for *First Things First: A Baby's Companion;* Best Books citation, *School Library Journal,* 1990, for *The Best of Aesop's Fables;* Nestlé Smarties Prize Gold Award, 1997, Reading Magic Awards Certificate of Excellence, *Parenting* magazine, and Sheffield Customers Book Award Commendation, both 1998, all for *Ginger;* Smarties Prize, 2002, for *Pizza Kittens.*

Writings

SELF-ILLUSTRATED

Tom's Cat, Lippincott (Philadelphia, PA), 1986.
First Things First: A Baby's Companion, Walker Books (London, England), 1988.

Mrs. Goose's Baby, Joy Street Books (Boston, MA), 1989.

Mr. Davies and the Baby, Candlewick Press (Cambridge, MA), 1996.

Ginger, Candlewick Press (Cambridge, MA), 1997.

Charlotte Voake's Alphabet Adventure, Jonathan Cape Children's Books (London, England), 1998.

Here Comes the Train, Candlewick Press (Cambridge, MA), 1998.

Pizza Kittens, Candlewick Press (Cambridge, MA), 2002.

Ginger Finds a Home, Candlewick Press (Cambridge, MA), 2003.

A Baby's Companion, Walker (London, England), 2004.

A Child's Guide to Wild Flowers, Transworld/Eden Project, 2004.

Hello, Twins, Candlewick Press (Cambridge, MA), 2006.

ILLUSTRATOR

Simon Watson, *The New Red Bike, and Other Stories for the Very Young,* Heinemann (London, England), 1978.

David Lloyd, *Top and Toby: A First Book of Letters,* Walker (London, England), 1980.

Simon Watson, *The Picture Prize and Other Stories for the Very Young,* Puffin (Harmondsworth, England), 1981.

Imogen Chichester, *Mr Teago and the Magic Slippers,* Viking Kestrel (London, England), 1983.

Philippa Pearce, *The Way to Sattin Shore,* Greenwillow Books (New York, NY), 1983.

Emma Tennant, *The Ghost Child,* Egmont Children's Books (London, England), 1984.

Emma Tennant, *The Witch Child,* Egmont Children's Books (London, England), 1984.

David Lloyd, *Duck,* Walker (London, England), 1984, Lippincott (Philadelphia, PA), 1988.

Over the Moon: A Book of Nursery Rhymes, introduction by David Lloyd, Clarkson N. Potter (New York, NY), 1985.

Jan Mark, *Fur,* Walker Books (London, England), 1986.

Sarah Hayes, *Bad Egg: The True Story of Humpty Dumpty,* Joy Street Books (Boston, MA), 1987, published as *The True Story of Humpty Dumpty,* Walker (London, England), 1998.

David Lloyd (adaptor), *The Ridiculous Story of Gammer Gurton's Needle,* Clarkson N. Potter (New York, NY), 1987.

Allan Ahlberg, *The Mighty Slide: Stories in Verse,* Viking Kestrel (Harmondsworth, Middlesex, England), 1988.

Martin Waddell, *Amy Said,* Little, Brown (Boston, MA), 1990.

Margaret Clark, adaptor, *The Best of Aesop's Fables,* Joy Street Books (Boston, MA), 1990.

The Three Little Pigs, and Other Favorite Nursery Stories, Candlewick Press (Cambridge, MA), 1992.

Vivian French, *Caterpillar, Caterpillar,* Candlewick Press (Cambridge, MA), 1995.

Eleanor Farjeon, *Elsie Piddock Skips in Her Sleep* (first published in *Martin Pippin in the Daisy Field,* 1937), Candlewick Press (Cambridge, MA), 1997.

Joy Richardson, *Looking at Pictures: An Introduction to Art for Young People,* Harry N. Abrams (New York, NY), 1997.

Geneviève de la Bretsche, *Grand Imagier* (picture dictionary), Scholastic (New York, NY), 2005.

ILLUSTRATOR; "FIRST DISCOVERY: MUSIC" SERIES

Marielle D. Khoury, *Henry Purcell découverte des musiciens* (includes audio CD), Gallimard (Paris, France), 2000, translated as *Henry Purcell,* Moonlight (London, England), 2001.

Yann Walcker, *Wolfgang Amadeus Mozart découverte des musiciens* (includes audio CD), Gallimard (Paris, France), 2000, translated as *Wolfgang Amadeus Mozart,* Moonlight (London, England), 2001.

Yann Walcker, *Ludwig van Beethoven découverte des musiciens* (includes audio CD), Gallimard (Paris, France), 2000, translated as *Ludwig van Beethoven,* Moonlight (London, England), 2001.

Catharine Weill, *Fryderyk Chopin, découverte des musiciens* (includes audio CD), Gallimard (Paris, France), 2000, translated as *Fryderyk Chopin,* Moonlight (London, England), 2001.

Pierre Babin, *Claude Debussy découverte des musiciens* (includes audio CD), Gallimard (Paris, France), 2000, translated as *Claude Debussy,* Moonlight (London, England), 2002.

Olivier Baumont, *Antonio Vivaldi découverte des musiciens* (includes audio CD), Gallimard (Paris, France), 2000, translated as *Antonio Vivaldi,* Moonlight (London, England), 2002.

Mildred Clary, *George Frideric Handel découverte des musiciens* (includes audio CD), Gallimard (Paris, France), 2000, translated as *George Frideric Handel,* Moonlight (London, England), 2002.

Paule du Bouchet, *Bach découverte des musiciens* (includes audio CD), Gallimard (Paris, France), 2000, translated as *Bach,* Moonlight (London, England), 2002.

Christian Wasselin, *Hector Berlioz découverte des musiciens* (includes audio CD), Gallimard (Paris, France), 2000, translated as *Hector Berloiz,* Moonlight (London, England), 2002.

Paule du Bouchet, *Franz Schubert découverte des musiciens* (includes audio CD), Gallimard (Paris, France), 2000, translated as *Franz Schubert,* Moonlight (London, England), 2002.

Sidelights

Opting for a degree in art history rather than art, Charlotte Voake has nonetheless followed her dream of becoming a picture-book illustrator. Beginning her career in the late 1970s—her first illustrations were published while Voake was still in college—she has become one of the most popular illustrators in her native Great Britain. In addition to the whimsical, humorous images she creates for stories by writers such as Jan Mark, Allan Ahlberg, and David Lloyd, she is also an author and illustrator of a number of original tales, among them the award-winning *Pizza Kittens* and *Ginger.* A testament to Voake's popularity came from the nephew of the late and highly awarded children's book author Eleanor Farjeon, who selected Voake as the perfect art-

Mrs. Goose's Baby *was one of Charlotte Voake's early self-illustrated picture books.* (Candlewick Press, 1989. Copyright © 1989 by Charlotte Voake. Reproduced by permission of Walker Books, Ltd. Published in the U.S. by Candlewick Press, Inc., Cambridge, MA.)

ist to create illustrations for *Elsie Piddock Skips in Her Sleep,* a story by Farjeon that was first published in 1973. Praising Voake's use of "deft, precise lines and delicate tints of color" in this work, *Booklist* contributor Carolyn Phelan added that the illustrator's "ink drawings with watercolor washes clearly establish the turn-of-the-century English setting" of Farjeon's tale.

One of Voake's early self-illustrated tales, *Tom's Cat* is a picture book aimed at children ranging from preschoolers to second graders. Its main character, Tom, listens to the strange, unidentified noises his cat is making, and imagines what the cat could be doing to create such odd sounds. When he finally investigates, Tom discovers that each noise actually accompanies a far more mundane activity than he had imagined. Another original story, *First Things First: A Baby's Companion,* collects a wealth of information—nursery rhymes, the alphabet, numbers, and information about the days of the week, plants, and animals—in a book that can be used by young children in various stages of development. A *Publishers Weekly* critic called *First Things First* "perfectly geared to babies and toddlers," and Denise M. Wilms dubbed it "a fresh, appealing choice to share" in her *Booklist* review. *School Library Journal* contributor Karen Litton applauded the book's structure, noting that Voake's "fresh and unconventional" book organization parallels the unique associations "made by small children discovering the world." A *Horn Book* contributor praised Voake's "tranquil and quiet" illustrations and called *First Things First* "an absolute winner for the very youngest child."

A tale of unconditional maternal love, *Mrs. Goose's Baby* describes a goose who finds an egg, cares for it,

and later raises the hatchling, even though the youngster is a chicken rather than a goose. A *Publishers Weekly* contributor wrote that, although Voake's story has an obvious ending, *Mrs. Goose's Baby* "is as reassuring as it is dear." In *Horn Book,* Ann A. Flowers praised the picture book as "a fine expression of mother-child affection." One of Voake's most popular characters is introduced in *Ginger Finds a Home* and *Ginger.* Ginger is a tiny grey kitten when readers first meet him in *Ginger Finds a Home.* A vagabond, he scrounges food from garbage cans and lives in a cluster of weeds. A little girl becomes the kitten's angel when she brings the scruffy feline food and eventually welcomes the cat into her home. Although Ginger is first afraid, he gradually warms up to his new home; as Carolyn Phelan noted in *Booklist,* Voake's "simple, good-hearted story will touch children as they identify with both Ginger's tentativeness and the little girl's longing."

In *Ginger* the kitten is now a full-grown cat; in fact, he is top cat in his new home. Ginger's positioned becomes threatened, however, when his owner unexpectedly brings home a kitten and the pampered pus finds that this young creature gets the lion's share of his owner's attention. A *Kirkus Reviews* critic observed that Ginger's story "parallels" a toddler's reaction to the arrival of a new baby in a household," a fact that give *Ginger* "a practical dimension." A *Publishers Weekly* contributor praised Voake's award-winning picture book for similar reasons, noting that *Ginger* is "a sound choice for children dealing with not-so-idiosyncratic reactions to the arrival of a newborn."

Kittens who behave like children also take center stage in *Pizza Kittens,* while *Here Comes the Train* and *Hello,*

Twins focus on sibling relationships. In *Here Comes the Train*, Chloe and her younger brother William enjoy spending Saturdays with their father, when they bike to a nearby bridge and anticipate the loud rush of the fast-moving trains they watch cross underneath. "Kids will recognize the excitement and also the magic" of Voake's family-centered tale, according to *Booklist* reviewer Hazel Rochman, while a *Publishers Weekly* contributor wrote that in *Here Comes the Train* "the sheer, giddy joy of the moment [is] . . . communicated . . . in phrases and art that even the youngest readers will respond to."

Another family-centered tale that is based on Voake's own experiences as a non-identical twin, *Hello, Twins* introduces Charlotte and Simon, who look different and have very different personalities, but have a unique relationship with each other. In simple, pen-and-ink and watercolor art, "Voake echoes the intensity of the twins' separate-but-together bond," wrote Gillian Engberg in her *Booklist* review, the critic adding that "all kids, not just twins, will find the messages about individuality and accepting differences reassuring" in *Hello, Twins*. The author/illustrator's "lithesome watercolor-and-ink illustrations are amusing and consistently expand" her "simple" story, maintained *School Library Journal* contributor Joy Fleishhaker, while in the *New York Times Book Review* Sara London viewed *Hello, Twins* as characteristic of Voake's ability to create "gesture-rich images" with "dynamic line [that] invests ordinary moments with energy and childlike pizzazz." "The importance of family bonds is at the heart of Voake's vision," London added, noting that the pictre book "reminds us that family harmony can happen even when the children sing separate songs."

Lucy, Bert, and Joe are three rambunctious kittens, and in *Pizza Kittens* the trio beg for pizza for dinner, but get only peas. The next night Mom and Dad cat try to encourage better table manners by serving the kittens their favorite food, but Lucy, Bert, and Joe still find ways to break a few rules of dinner-time etiquette. "Voake's signature style shines through in the sketchy watercolor-and-ink illustrations," wrote *School Library Journal* contributor Kathleen Kelly MacMillan, the critic adding that the author/illustrator's original "family story gets it right."

Biographical and Critical Sources

PERIODICALS

Booklist, January 15, 1986, p. 759; November 15, 1988, Denise M. Wilms, review of *First Things First: A Baby's Companion*, p. 588; May 1, 1989, p. 1555; October 15, 1993, p. 446; April, 1996, p. 1269; March 15, 1996, Carolyn Phelan, review of *Mr. Davies and the Baby*, p. 1269; February 1, 1997, p. 949; September 1, 1998, Hazel Rochman, review of *Here Comes the Train*, p. 129; November 1, 2000, Carolyn Phelan, review of *Charlotte Voake's Alphabet Adventures*, p. 99; May 1, 2002, Ilene Cooper, review of *Pizza Kittens*, p. 1537; June 1, 2003, review of *Ginger Finds a Home*, p. 812; July, 2003, Carolyn Phelan, review of *Ginger Finds a Home*, p. 1887; May 15, 2006, Gillian Engberg, review of *Hello, Twins*, p. 52.

Books for Keeps, November, 1990, p. 2.

Books for Your Children, summer, 1987, p. 21.

Bulletin of the Center for Children's Books, April, 1997, review of *Ginger*, p. 299; December, 1998, review of *Here Comes the Train*, p. 149; June, 2002, review of *Pizza Kittens*, p. 384; July, 2003, review of *Ginger Finds a Home*, p. 465; September, 2006, Loretta Gaffney, review of *Hello, Twins*, p. 39.

Horn Book, January-February, 1989, p. 62; May-June, 1989, Ann A. Flowers, review of *Mrs. Goose's Baby*, p. 366; May-June, 1990, pp. 330-331; November-December, 1990, pp. 757-758; January, 2001, review of *Elsie Piddock Skips in Her Sleep*, p. 68.

Kirkus Reviews, July 1, 1992, p. 855; January 1, 1996, review of *Mr. Davies and the Baby*, p. 74; January 1, 1997, review of *Ginger*, p. 66; May 1, 2002, review of *Pizza Kittens*, p. 668; May 1, 2006, review of *Hello, Twins*, p. 469.

New York Times Book Review, November 12, 2006, Sara London, "My Brother, Myself," p. 38.

Publishers Weekly, September 30, 1988, review of *First Things First*, p. 64; March 24, 1989, review of *Mrs. Goose's Baby*, p. 69; July 13, 1990, p. 54; March 2, 1992, p. 66; July 6, 1992, p. 54; January 13, 1997, review of *Ginger*, p. 74; March 17, 1997, p. 85; July 27, 1998, review of *Here Comes the Train*, p. 75.

School Library Journal, March, 1986, p. 151; May, 1987, Kathleen Odean, review of *Tom's Cat*, p. 94; December 1988, Karen Litton, review of *First Things First*, p. 95; July, 1990, p. 65; December, 1990, p. 20; August, 1992, p. 149; December, 1993, pp. 103-104; April, 1996, Marilyn Taniguchi, review of *Mr. Davies and the Baby*, pp. 119-120; October, 1998, Kathy M. Newby, review of *Here Comes the Train*, p. 116; October, 2000, Nina Lindsay, review of *Elsie Piddock Skips in Her Sleep*, p. 122; April 8, 2002, review of *Pizza Kittens*, p. 225; May, 2002, Kathleen Kelly MacMillan, review of *Pizza Kittens*, p. 129; June, 2003, review of *Ginger Finds a Home*, p. 122; July, 2006, Joy Fleishhacker, review of *Hello Twins*, p. 88.

Times Educational Supplement, November 27, 1998, review of *Here Comes the Train*, p. 12; December 1, 2000, review of *Elsie Piddock Skips in Her Sleep*, p. 25

ONLINE

British Council Arts Magic Pencil Web site, http://magicpencil.britishcouncil.org/ (May 15, 2007), "Charlotte Voake."

Walker Books Web site, http://www.walkerbooks.co.uk/ (May 15, 2007), "Charlotte Voake."*

W-Z

WANIEK, Marilyn Nelson
See NELSON, Marilyn

*   *   *

WILKINS, Rose

Personal
Daughter of an artist. *Education:* Bristol University, degree (classics); Oxford University, M.A. (classics).

Addresses
Home and office—London, England.

Career
Author and editor, working in London, England.

Writings

So Super Starry, Dial Books (New York, NY), 2004.
So Super Stylish, Macmillan Children's Books (London, England), 2005, Dial Books (New York, NY), 2006.
I Love Genie . . . Wishful Thinking, Macmillan Children's Books (London, England), 2007.

Sidelights
As the great-great niece of British author Charles Kingsley it was only natural for Rose Wilkins to enter a literary profession. Wilkins did not originally intend to pursue a novel-writing career, however; in fact, she wrote the initial draft of her first novel on a dare. As she explained in an online interview with *Word Mavericks:* "One night I was joking to my friends that I should start a romance novel. . . . I made a bet to write the opening chapter of a 'snogbuster' for teens within a week, but I found I was enjoying myself so much I

didn't stop there." A publishing house eventually bought the rights to Wilkins' draft and in 2004 *So Super Starry* was published.

Cover of Rose Wilkins' debut young-adult novel So Super Starry.
(Speak, 2004. Photo of girl © Reed/PictureQuest. Reproduced by permission of Speak, a division of Penguin Putnam Books for Young Readers.)

So Super Starry centers on Octavia, the daughter of a film producer and actress. Tired of being in the spotlight that shines on her parents, she prefers to remain low key and avoids the other celebrity offspring attending her elite private school. Citing Wilkins' humorous tone, a *Publishers Weekly* writer deemed *So Super Starry* an "entertaining debut." A sequel, *So Super Stylish,* continues the trials and tribulations of Octavia. In an attempt to live a more normal life, the teen transfers from her private school to a public school, hoping to fit in. Unfortunately, she soon finds herself in a predicament as a result of the media blitz that erupts when her actress mom is accused of having an affair with a well-known television executive. *Kliatt* reviewer Claire Rosser noted that Wilkins controls her sequel's eventful plotline "with finesse."

In her *Word Mavericks* interview, Wilkins advised aspiring writers to "read masses of everything." "Also," she suggested "keeping the diary—it will get you into the habit of writing in a disciplined manner and putting thoughts into words."

Biographical and Critical Sources

PERIODICALS

Booklist, October 15, 2004, Cindy Welch, review of *So Super Starry,* p. 399; February 15, 2006, Debbie Carton, review of *So Super Stylish,* p. 92.

Bulletin of the Center for Children's Books, November, 2004, Deborah Stevenson, review of *So Super Starry,* p. 151.

Kliatt, March, 2006, Claire Rosser, review of *So Super Starry,* p. 18.

Publishers Weekly, November 22, 2004, review of *So Super Starry,* p. 61.

School Library Journal, December, 2004, Tina Zuback, review of *So Super Starry,* p. 154; March, 2006, Heather E. Miller, review of *So Super Stylish,* p. 233.

Times Educational Supplement, May 21, 2004, Adèle Geras, "Pretty in Pink," p. C19; May 13, 2005, Adèle Geras, review of *So Super Stylish,* p. 25.

Voice of Youth Advocates, December, 2004, review of *So Super Starry,* p. 397; April, 2006, Angelica Delgado, review of *So Super Stylish,* p. 55.

ONLINE

Pan MacMillan Web site, http://www.panmacmillan.com/ (May 1, 2007), "Rose Wilkins."

Word Mavericks Web site, http://www.wordmavericks.com/ (May 1, 2007), interview with Wilkins.*

*　　　*　　　*

WILLEMS, Mo

Personal

Married; children: Trixie. *Education:* New York University, B.F.A.

Addresses

Home—Brooklyn, NY.

Career

Animator and illustrator. Children's Television Workshop, New York, NY, researcher, then script writer and animator for *Sesame Street* television series, 1994-2002; Nickelodeon, creator and director of animated series *The Off-Beats,* 1995-98; Cartoon Network, creator and director of animated series *Sheep in the Big City,* 2000-02, head writer of animated series *Codename: Kids Next Door,* 2002-03. Short films have appeared on MTV, HBO, IFC, Tournee of Animation, and Spike and Mike's Festival of Animation. Commentator for British Broadcasting Corporation's BBC Radio, 1994-97. Former member of Monkeysuit (comix collective), New York, NY.

Awards, Honors

ASIFA-East Awards for animation; six Emmy awards for work on *Sesame Street;* National Parenting Publications Award, 2003, for *Time to Pee!;* Caldecott Honor Book citation, American Library Association, 2004, for *Don't Let the Pigeon Drive the Bus!,* and 2005, for *Knuffle Bunny: A Cautionary Tale;* Book Sense Book of the Year Children's Illustrated Honor Book designation, American Booksellers Association, 2006, for *Leonardo, the Terrible Monster.*

Writings

SELF-ILLUSTRATED

Don't Let the Pigeon Drive the Bus!, Hyperion (New York, NY), 2003.

Time to Pee!, Hyperion (New York, NY), 2003.

The Pigeon Finds a Hot Dog!, Hyperion (New York, NY), 2004.

Knuffle Bunny: A Cautionary Tale, Hyperion (New York, NY), 2004.

The Pigeon Has Feelings, Too!, Hyperion (New York, NY), 2005.

The Pigeon Loves Things That Go!, Hyperion (New York, NY), 2005.

Time to Say "Please"!, Hyperion (New York, NY), 2005.

Leonardo, the Terrible Monster, Hyperion (New York, NY), 2005.

Don't Let the Pigeon Stay Up Late!, Hyperion (New York, NY), 2006.

You Can Never Find a Rickshaw When It Monsoons: The World on One Cartoon a Day, foreword by Dave Barry, Hyperion (New York, NY), 2006.

Edwina, the Dinosaur Who Didn't Know She Was Extinct, Hyperion (New York, NY), 2006.

Today I Will Fly!, Hyperion (New York, NY), 2007.

My Friend Is Sad, Hyperion (New York, NY), 2007.

Contributor to books, including *Monkeysuit,* Monkeysuit Press; *Cartoon Cartoons,* DC Comics; and *9-11: The World's Finest Comic Book Writers and Artists Tell Stories to Remember,* DC Comics, 2002.

Adaptations

Don't Let the Pigeon Drive the Bus! was adapted for the stage by Adam Bampton-Smith and produced by Big Wooden Horse Productions, 2005.

Sidelights

Mo Willems, an Emmy Award-winning television writer and animator, has also gained new fans through his work as an award-winning children's book author. A former writer and animator for the popular *Sesame Street* television program, Willems has also created more than one hundred short films, many of which have appeared on MTV, HBO, the Tournee of Animation, and Spike and Mike's Festival of Animation. The creator of the animated television series *Sheep in the Big City* and *The Off-Beats,* he also served as head writer for the Cartoon Network's *Codename: Kids Next Door* series. Since semi-retiring from television in 2003, Willems has channeled his creativity and quirky humor into picture books such as *Don't Let the Pigeon Drive the Bus!,*

Knuffle Bunny: A Cautionary Tale, and *Edwina, the Dinosaur Who Didn't Know She Was Extinct.* In Willems' books, while his characters sometimes make missteps, they ultimately join readers in a goodhearted laugh at their own foibles. As the author/illustrator told Susan Spencer Cramer in an interview for *Publishers Weekly,* "'Failure is pervasive in children's lives, but I don't know when it stopped being funny. It needs to be explored and enjoyed and laughed at and understood."

Willems' interest in cartooning began as a child. "I've been drawing funny cartoons my whole life," he noted on his home page. "I started out by drawing Snoopy and Charlie Brown and then started to make up my own characters. Luckily, no one has made me stop yet!" Willems decided on a career in animation during the 1980s, while a student at New York University. "My desire as a kid was to find a way to be funny and draw," he recalled to Martin Goodman in an interview for *Animation World.* "Animation turned out to be the best way for me to do that."

Willems made his first film, *The Man Who Yelled,* while still a student at New York University, and this was followed by the acclaimed short film *Iddy Biddy Beat Boy.* His job in the research department at the Children's

A cantankerous bird and a tiny duckling spar over a snack in Mo Willems' humorous **The Pigeon Finds a Hot Dog!** (Hyperion Books for Children, 2004. Illustration © 2004 by Mo Willems. Reprinted by permission of Hyperion Books for Children.)

Potty training can be fun, as Willems proves in his mouse-driven bathroom primer **Time to Pee!** (Copyright © 2003 Mo Willems. Reprinted by permission of Hyperion Books for Children. Publishing in the United Kingdom by Walker Books, Ltd. London.)

Television Workshop eventually found him working as an animator for *Sesame Street*. As Willems told Goodman, this opportunity was a "great fit because the kind of films I wanted to make were very close to the kind of films they wanted to air. I really felt that I was making personal work, even though I was teaching the 'letter of the day' or something like that." During Willems' time with *Sesame Street*, he garnered six Emmy Awards for his animation work.

In 1995 Willems began producing *The Off-Beats,* a series of animated shorts about Betty-Anne Bongo and her unusual friends, for Nickelodeon. The success of that series led to *Sheep in the Big City,* which debuted on the Cartoon Network in 2000. *Variety* reviewer Stuart Levine described *Sheep in the Big City* as "an amusing tale of a shy but determined woolly creature on the lam . . . after government bad guys try to kidnap and use him as a critical component of a high-powered weapon." After the series was canceled in 2002, Willems began writing for *Codename: Kids Next Door,*

which finds five ten year olds battling the forces of adulthood. In 2003 *Codename: Kids Next Door* became the highest-rated show on the Cartoon Network. That same year, Willems made the decision to leave television and become a stay-at-home father for his daughter, Trixie. He also embarked on his picture-book career.

Published in 2003, *Don't Let the Pigeon Drive the Bus!* jump-started Willems' authorial career and also began his series of picture books featuring a wily, cantankerous pigeon character. "The premise of this cheeky debut is charmingly absurd," wrote a contributor to *Publishers Weekly*. A bus driver steps out of his vehicle for a short break, asking that the reader keep an eye on things while he is gone. Before he leaves, the driver makes one special request: "Don't let the pigeon drive the bus." A big-eyed pigeon soon appears and tries to negotiate a spot behind the wheel, at various points telling the reader, "I'll be your best friend" and "I'll bet your mom would let me." Finally the pigeon throws a huge but futile tantrum as the driver returns, thanks the reader, and pulls away. The pigeon's disappointment is only temporary, though, as he spots a tractor-trailer coming up the road. "Willems hooks his audience quickly with the pigeon-to-reader approach and minimalist cartoons," noted the *Publishers Weekly* critic. Gillian Engberg, reviewing *Don't Let the Pigeon Drive the Bus!* for *School Library Journal*, remarked that "each page has the feel of a perfectly frozen frame of cartoon footage—action, remarkable expression, and wild humor captured with just a few lines."

Willems' wingéd hero makes a return appearance in *The Pigeon Finds a Hot Dog! The Pigeon Has Feelings, Too!, The Pigeon Loves Things That Go!,* and *Don't Let the Pigeon Stay Up Late!* In *The Pigeon Finds a Hot Dog!* Willems' plucky fowl spies a discarded hot dog and swoops in for a meal. Just as he is about to devour the treat, a tiny duckling scoots in and makes a number of seemingly innocent but calculated inquiries about the hot dog. According to Kitty Flynn in *Horn Book*, "the hot-headed pigeon humorously wrestles with a minor moral dilemma (to share or not to share) that will immediately resonate" with young readers. Though the pigeon is wise to the duckling's game, the incessant questions wear down his resistance, and the pair end up sharing the snack. Willems' "deceptively simple cartoon drawings convincingly portray his protagonist's emotional dilemma," Robin L. Gibson observed in *School Library Journal*. A *Publishers Weekly* reviewer found that Willems' design work adds much to the tale, stating that the cartoonist's use of "voice bubbles, body language, and expressive sizes and shapes of type . . . crafts a comical give-and-take between the characters."

In the board books *The Pigeon Has Feelings, Too!* and *The Pigeon Loves Things That Go!,* the cantankerous fowl's adventures are geared for younger readers. In the first title, the Bus Driver tries to get the pigeon to be happy, but that is a difficult task. In the second title, the pigeon explores all the various modes of transportation, finding that he likes all of them. Julie Roach, writing in the *School Library Journal*, found that "pigeon's fans will be excited to see this wacky bird and his friends again." In *Don't Let the Pigeon Stay up Late!* the reader is told to make sure that the pesky bird goes to bed early. However, in childlike fashion, the pigeon comes up with page after page of reasons why he does not need to go to bed. First he needs to watch a bird documentary on television, then he needs a drink of water. And, besides, he whines, "I'm not even tired." As a *Kirkus Reviews* critic noted, *Don't Let the Pigeon Stay up Late* showcases Willems' "wholehearted sense of fun."

In addition to his books about ducks, Willems has also written several standalone books for young readers, among them *Time to Pee!, Knuffle Bunny,* and *Edwina, the Dinosaur Who Didn't Know She Was Extinct.* "More pep rally than how-to," *Time to Pee!* "is perfectly attuned to preschoolers' sensibilities and funny bones," in the opinion of *Horn Book* contributor Kitty Flynn. Fea-

turing a band of cheerful mice who give advice and encouragement to youngsters undergoing potty training, the book showcases Willems' "genius for spare but expressive lines and an almost uncanny rapport with the preschool audience," according to *Booklist* reviewer Jennifer Matson. The mouse clan returns in *Time to Say "Please!",* a primer of basic manners that a *Kirkus Reviews* contributor praised as "an entirely kid-centered lesson" that will earn repeated readings at storytime. Calling the book "a painless introduction to good manners," Wendy Lukehart added that *Time to Say "Please!"* should be influential because Willems' "examples speak directly to a young child's experience."

A toddler loses her prized possession in *Knuffle Bunny,* a story Flynn predicted "will immediately register with even pre-verbal listeners." In Willems' quaint tale, little Trixie and her dad take a trip to the local Laundromat, but on the way home the girl realizes that her beloved stuffed bunny has been left behind. When the toddler's frantic attempts to communicate are misinterpreted by her clueless father, Trixie adopts a new strategy: she cries. Only after the pair arrive home and Trixie's mom noted the absence of the beloved toy does Dad realize his mistake. In a review of *Knuffle Bunny* a *Kirkus Reviews* contributor dubbed Willems "a master of body language," and Flynn praised the book's "playful illustrations," which feature cartoon characters "rendered in Willems's expressive retro style" and set against sepia-toned photographs of Brooklyn neighborhoods. The author/illustrator's "economical storytelling and deft skill with line lend the book its distinctive charm," wrote a contributor in *Publishers Weekly.*

Keying in to children's love of dinosaurs, *Edwina, the Dinosaur Who Didn't Know She Was Extinct* introduces a friendly neighborhood resident who just happens to be a dinosaur. Edwina is kind to everyone, even baking cookies for the local children, until know-it-all neighbor Reginald informs the oversized reptile that she is, in fact, extinct. Describing the sweet-tempered Edwina as "a masterful creation," a *Kirkus Reviews* writer praised *Edwina, the Dinosaur Who Didn't Know She Was Extinct* as "a tribute to the child's rock-solid faith in how the world should be." Monsters also have perennial child appeal, and in *Leonardo, the Terrible Monster* Willems casts a decidedly non-scary member of the Monster clan in what a *Kirkus Reviews* writer called "a sweetly original morality play" about friendship and differences. Calling the tale a "perfectly paced story," *School Library Journal* contributor Marianne Saccardi noted that it perfectly pairs with Willems' pastel-toned cartoon art, and in a *Booklist* review Ilene Cooper praised the book's "smart, striking design."

In Willems' picture-book career, he has reproduced many of the successes of his work in television. After only a few years, he earned some of the field's top awards, including two prestigious Caldecott Honor Book citations in recognition of his illustrations. In reviewing his books, critics often make note of the author/

A kindly throwback ignores a pesky realist in Willems' self-illustrated picture book **Edwina, the Dinosaur Who Didn't Know She Was Extinct.** (Hyperion Books for Children, 2006. Illustration copyright © 2006 by Mo Willems. All rights reserved. Reproduced by permission.)

illustrator's minimalist graphic style, a fact that pleases the former animator. As Willems told Goodman, "while I enjoy all forms of drawing, a single line, simply done, is more beautiful than a hundred little lines sort of approximating the same thing. I like my characters to be two-dimensional. Just because you can so something in 3-D doesn't make it better. I want my line to be focused, so the emotions of a character are clear."

Biographical and Critical Sources

BOOKS

Willems, Mo, *Don't Let the Pigeon Drive the Bus!,* Hyperion (New York, NY), 2003.

Willems, Mo, *Don't Let the Pigeon Stay Up Late!,* Hyperion (New York, NY), 2006.

PERIODICALS

Animation World, September, 1997, Arlene Sherman and Abby Terkuhle, interview with Willems; June 25, 2001, Martin Goodman, "Talking in His Sheep: A Conversation with Mo Willems."

Booklist, September 1, 2003, Gillian Engberg, review of *Don't Let the Pigeon Drive the Bus!,* p. 123; November 1, 2003, Jennifer Matson, review of *Time to Pee!,* p. 499; January 1, 2004, review of *Don't Let the Pigeon Drive the Bus!,* p 782; February 15, 2004, Gillian Engberg, review of *The Pigeon Finds a Hot Dog!,* p. 1064; September 15, 2004, Jennifer Matson, review of *Knuffle Bunny: A Cautionary Tale,* p. 241; June 1, 2005, Gillian Engberg, review of *Knuffle Bunny,* p. 1819; July, 2005, Ilene Cooper, review of *Leonardo, the Terrible Monster,* p. 1931; February 15, 2006, Ilene Cooper, review of *Don't Let the Pigeon Stay Up Late!,* p. 106; July 1, 2006, Jesse Karp, review of *You Can Never Find a Rickshaw When It Monsoons: The World on One Cartoon a Day,* p. 47; September 1, 2006, Randall Enos, review of *Edwina, the Dinosaur Who Didn't Know She Was Extinct,* p. 142.

Bookseller, April 16, 2004, Sonia Benster, review of *Don't Let the Pigeon Drive the Bus!,* p. 31; April 7, 2006, Katie Hawthorne, review of *The Pigeon Finds a Hot Dog!,* p. 13.

Bulletin of the Center for Children's Books, October, 2004, review of *Knuffle Bunny,* p. 103; November, 2005, Karen Coats, review of *Leonardo the Terrible Monster,* p. 127; May, 2006, Karen Coats, review of *Don't Let the Pigeon Stay up Late!,* p. 429; October, 2006,

Karen Coats, review of *Edwina, the Dinosaurs Who Didn't Know She Was Extinct*, p. 101.

CBC Magazine, May, 2005, Mo Willems, "How to Become Rich and Famous in One Easy Step (and Other Stuff That Has Nothing to Do with Making Kids' Books)."

Charlotte Observer, April 4, 2006, "Four Questions for Mo Willems."

Daily News (Los Angeles, CA), June 18, 2005, Sherry Joe Crosby, "Author Mo Willems Lets His Imagination Take Wing," p. U7.

Entertainment Weekly, October 3, 2003, review of *Time to Pee!,* p. 74.

Globe & Mail (Toronto, Ontario, Canada), June 14, 2003, Susan Perren, review of *Don't Let the Pigeon Drive the Bus!,* p. D15; July 17, 2004, Susan Perren, review of *The Pigeon Finds a Hot Dog!,* p. D11; October 23, 2004, Susan Perren, review of *Knuffle Bunny,* p. D22; June 18, 2005, Susan Perren, review of *Time to Say "Please"!,* p. D11; December 31, 2005, Susan Perren, review of *Leonardo, the Terrible Monster,* p. D13.

Horn Book, July-August, 2003, Kitty Flynn, review of *Don't Let the Pigeon Drive the Bus!,* p. 449; January-February, 2004, Kitty Flynn, review of *Time to Pee!,* p. 75; May-June, 2004, Kitty Flynn, review of *The Pigeon Finds a Hot Dog!,* p. 323; September-October, 2004, Kitty Flynn, review of *Knuffle Bunny,* pp. 576-577; January-February, 2005, review of *Knuffle Bunny,* p. 14; July-August, 2005, Kitty Flynn, review of *Time to Say "Please"!,* p. 462; September-October, 2005, Kitty Flynn, review of *Leonardo, the Terrible Monster,* p. 569; May-June, 2006, Susan Dove Lempke, review of *Don't Let the Pigeon Stay up Late!,* p. 308; September-October, 2006, Danielle J. Ford, review of *Edwina, the Dinosaur Who Didn't Know She Was Extinct,* p. 572.

Instructor, April, 2004, Judy Freeman, review of *Don't Let the Pigeon Drive the Bus!,* p. 65.

Kirkus Reviews, April 1, 2003, review of *Don't Let the Pigeon Drive the Bus!,* p. 542; October 1, 2003, review of *Time to Pee!,* p. 1233; April 1, 2004, review of *The Pigeon Finds a Hot Dog!,* p. 339; August 1, 2004, review of *Knuffle Bunny,* p. 750; May 15, 2005, review of *Time to Say "Please"!,* p. 597; June 1, 2005, review of *Leonardo, the Terrible Monster,* p. S22; July 15, 2005, review of *Leonardo, the Terrible Monster,* p. 797; March 1, 2006, review of *Don't Let the Pigeon Stay Up Late!,* p. 242; August 1, 2006, review of *Edwina, the Dinosaur Who Didn't Know She Was Extinct,* p. 799.

News-Leader (Springfield, MO), July 27, 2005, Samantha Critchell, "Author Quits Day Job to Write Kids' Books."

New York Times, April 16, 2000, Peter Marks, "Now Mom and Dad Are Going Cartoon-Crazy, Too."

New York Times Book Review, May 16, 2004, Claire Dederer, review of *The Pigeon Finds a Hot Dog!*

Publishers Weekly, February 10, 2003, review of *Don't Let the Pigeon Drive the Bus!,* p. 184; December 15, 2003, review of *Time to Pee!,* p. 71; April 5, 2004, review of *The Pigeon Finds a Hot Dog!,* p. 60; June 10, 2004, Nathalie op de Beeck, interview with Willems; August

16, 2004, review of *Knuffle Bunny,* p. 62; February 21, 2005, Susan Spencer Cramer, interview with Willems, p. 153; May 9, 2005, review of *Time to Say "Please"!,* p. 68; June 27, 2005, review of *Leonardo, the Terrible Monster,* p. 61; February 20, 2006, review of *Don't Let the Pigeon Stay up Late!,* p. 154; July 17, 2006, review of *Edwina, the Dinosaur Who Didn't Know She Was Extinct,* p. 156.

School Library Journal, May, 2003, Dona Ratterree, review of *Don't Let the Pigeon Drive the Bus!,* p. 132; December, 2003, Bina Williams, review of *Time to Pee!,* p. 140; May, 2004, Robin L. Gibson, review of *The Pigeon Finds a Hot Dog!,* pp. 126-127; October, 2004, Martha Topol, review of *Knuffle Bunny,* p. 136; August, 2005, Marianne Saccardi, review of *Leonardo, the Terrible Monster,* p. 108; Julie Roach, reviews of *The Pigeon Has Feelings, Too!* and *The Pigeon Loves Things That Go!,* p. 108, and Wendy Lukehart, review of *Time to Say "Please"!,* p. 108; September, 2005, Barbara Auerbach, review of *Knuffle Bunny,* p. 60; April, 2006, Joy Fleishhacker, review of *Don't Let the Pigeon Stay up Late!,* p. 122; September, 2006, Kate McClelland, review of *Edwina, the Dinosaur Who Didn't Know She Was Extinct,* p. 187.

Time, December 5, 2005, Christopher Porterfield, review of *Leonardo, the Terrible Monster,* p. W1.

Variety, November 13, 2000, Stuart Levine, review of *Sheep in the Big City,* p. 39.

ONLINE

CartoonNetwork.com, http://www.cartoonnetwork.com.au/ (April 7, 2006).

Cartoon Network's Friday's Fan site, http://fridays.toonzone.net/ (September 28, 2003), "Behind the Scenes Interviews: Tom Warburton and Mo Willems."

Mo Willems Home Page, http://www.mowillems.com (June 10, 2007).

Walker Books Web site, http://www.walkerbooks.co.uk/ (April 7, 2006), "Mo Willems."*

*   *   *

WILLIAMS, Laura E.
(L.E. Williams, Laura Ellen Williams)

Personal

Born in Korea. *Education:* College degree.

Addresses

Home—Hartford, CT.

Career

Children's book writer. Manchester High School, Manchester, CT, English teacher.

Writings

FOR CHILDREN

The Long Silk Thread: A Grandmother's Legacy to Her Granddaughter, illustrated by Grayce Bochak, Boyds Mills Press (Honesdale, PA), 1995.

Behind the Bedroom Wall, illustrated by A. Nancy Goldstein, Milkweed Editions (Minneapolis, MN), 1996.

Torch Fishing with the Sun, illustrated by Fabricio Vanden Broeck, Boyds Mills Press (Honesdale, PA), 1999.

The Spider's Web, illustrated by Erica Magnus, Milkweed Editions (Minneapolis, MN) 1999.

The Ghost Stallion, Holt (New York, NY), 1999.

Up a Creek, Holt (New York, NY), 2000.

The Executioner's Daughter, Holt (New York, NY), 2000.

(And photographer) *ABC Kids,* Philomel (New York, NY), 2000.

(Editor) *Unexpected: Eleven Mysterious Stories,* Scholastic (New York, NY), 2005.

The Best Winds, illustrated by Eujin Kim Neiland, Boyds Mills Press (Honesdale, PA), 2006.

Author of books in "Let's Have a Party" series.

"MAGIC ATTIC CLUB" SERIES; UNDER PSEUDONYM L.E. WILLIAMS

Rose Faces the Music, illustrated by Bill Dodge, Magic Attic Press (Portland, ME), 1997.

Cheyenne Rose, illustrated by Dan Burr, Magic Attic Press (Portland, ME), 1997.

Island Rose, illustrated by Tony Meers, Magic Attic Press (Portland, ME), 1998.

Champion Rose, illustrated by Bill Dodge, Magic Attic Press (Portland, ME), 1999.

"MYSTIC LIGHTHOUSE" MYSTERY SERIES

The Mystery of the Dark Lighthouse, Scholastic (New York, NY), 2000.

The Mystery of Dead Man's Curve, Scholastic (New York, NY), 2000.

The Mystery of the Bad Luck Curse, Scholastic (New York, NY), 2001.

The Mystery of the Haunted Playhouse, Scholastic (New York, NY), 2001.

The Mystery of the Phantom Ship, Scholastic (New York, NY), 2001.

The Mystery of the Missing Tiger, Scholastic (New York, NY), 2002.

Sidelights

Multicultural and multigenerational stories as well as mysteries and young-adult novels are among the books written by Laura E. Williams. Inspired by her own travels—born in Korea, she has also lived in Belgium and on the island of Hawaii—Williams began her writing career crafting original folk tales, as in her debut, *The Long Silk Thread: A Grandmother's Legacy to Her Granddaughter,* as well as *The Best Winds* and *Torch Fishing with the Sun.* Another picture book, *ABC Kids,* is self-illustrated and features what *School Library Journal* contributor Linda Ludke described as "stunning close-up photography" of young children at play. Williams' middle-grade novels *Behind the Wall* and *The Spider's Web* deal with the power of prejudice, both in

Laura E. Williams' picture book The Best Winds *is enhanced by the unusual perspective contained in Eujin Kim Neilan's detailed paintings.*

World War II Germany and among modern neo-Nazis, while the quandary of a modern teen and an environmentalist parent are the focus of *Up the Creek.*

A "graceful story" in the opinion of a *Publishers Weekly* contributor, *The Long Silk Thread* draws young readers back to ancient Japan and into a family tradition. As young Yasuyo listens, her beloved grandmother tells the stories of her long life while winding a ball from tied-together strands of silk. When the elderly woman dies, Yasuyo climbs the silk up to heaven, but learns that her true place is on earth with those who love her. In *Torch Fishing with the Sun* Williams crafts what a *Publishers Weekly* contributor described as "an affectionate original folktale" about a Hawaiian boy named Makoa who looks forward to being entrusted with an important task: like his grandfather, he will learn to capture the sun so that, unlike the other men of his village, he can fish without torchlight during the dark of night. In *Booklist* Lauren Peterson praised *Torch Fishing with the Sun* as "both appealing and timeless," while in *Booklist* Ilene Cooper noted of *The Long Silk Thread* that Williams' "telling is stately but is also full of warmth."

Another multigenerational picture book, *The Best Winds* focuses on Jinho, a boy who is frustrated by his immigrant grandfather's determination to retain his Korean ways. Ignoring the advice the man shares while the two are constructing a kite together, the boy decides to fly the new creation on his own, before the weather is appropriate. When the kite is damaged due to his inability to direct it, Jinho realizes that there is much he can learn from the elderly man; making a new kite, the two work together to make it take flight. In *School Library Journal* Amanda Conover Le praised *The Best Winds* as "a heartwarming tale," and *Booklist* contributor Kay Weisman deemed it a "great choice for spring story hours."

Moving to an older audience, Williams focuses on life in the Middle Ages in *The Executioner's Daughter*. Here readers meet Lily, a shy girl whose father is the village executioner. When other children shun her, Lily turns to the forest animals, and begins to care for those that are injured. After his wife dies, Lily's father asks that she take her mother's place as his assistant, which forces the girl to face the horrors of her father's job and the ironies of her age. Reviewing *The Executioner's Daughter* for *School Library Journal*, Bruce Ann Shook praised the book's "strong, insightful" heroine and called Williams' novel a "well-written story" that serves as "an excellent vehicle for demonstrating the harsh realities of life" in mid-fifteenth-century England.

In the middle-grade novel *Up a Creek* Williams introduces thirteen-year-old Starshine Bott and her single mother, Miracle. Involved in activist causes, mother and daughter live in a small Louisiana town with Starshine's grandmother. When Miracle's involvement in an effort to save a stand of old oak trees from destruction prevents her from caring for her mother when the elderly woman is hospitalized, Starshine must reexamine the values and choices she had formerly accepted without question. Praised by *School Library Journal* contributor Shawn Brommer as "a celebration of family and feminine strength," *Up a Creek* features "characters [that] are well realized and multidimensional." While noting that Williams "takes on momentous issues with mixed results," a *Publishers Weekly* contributor predicted that *Up a Creek* will inspire "budding environmentalists." In the view of *Booklist* critic Karen Hutt the novel will "appeal to girls struggling to define themselves and their relationships with their mothers."

In addition to standalone novels, Williams has also contributed to several novel series. In her "Mystic Lighthouse" mysteries, which include *The Mystery of Dead Man's Curve, The Mystery of the Bad Luck Curse,* and *The Mystery of the Haunted Playhouse,* Zeke and Jen are living with their aunt Bee in Maine, and their home is an old lighthouse. In the series, the siblings encounter ghostly visits, strange curses, phantom ships, and suspicious accidents, and ferret out each mystery with Aunt Bee's help. Each "Mystic Lighthouse" book includes a removable fill-in-the-blank page on which junior sleuths can record clues and other notes as the story unfolds.

Biographical and Critical Sources

PERIODICALS

Booklist, February 1, 1996, Ilene Cooper, review of *The Long Silk Thread: A Grandmother's Lecacy to Her Granddaughter,* p. 940; August, 1996, Hazel Rochman, review of *Behind the Bedroom Wall,* p. 1900; March 15, 1999, Lauren Peterson, review of *Torch Fishing with the Sun,* p. 1336; June 1, 1999, Hazel Rochman, review of *The Spider's Web,* p. 1832; July, 2000, review of *ABC Kids,* p. 2044; January 1, 2001, Karen Hutt, review of *Up a Creek,* p. 941; April 1, 2006, Kay Weisman, review of *The Best Winds,* p. 49.

Bulletin of the Center for Children's Books, May, 2000, review of *The Executioner's Daughter,* p. 340; October, 2000, review of *ABC Kids,* p. 87; February, 2001, review of *Up a Creek,* p. 240.

Five Owls (annual), 2003, review of *The Executioner's Daughter,* p. 30.

Horn Book, January-February, 1997, Hannah B. Zeiger, review of *Behind the Bedroom Wall,* p. 69.

Kirkus Reviews, January 1, 2006, review of *The Best Winds,* p. 47.

New York Times Book Review, June 18, 2000, review of *The Executioner's Song,* p. 25.

Publishers Weekly, July 10, 1995, review of *The Long Silk Thread,* p. 57; June 17, 1996, review of *Behind the Bedroom Wall,* p. 66; February 15, 1999, review of *Torch Fishing with the Sun,* p. 107; December 11, 2000, review of *Up a Creek,* p. 85.

School Library Journal, September, 1996, Amy Kellman, review of *Behind the Bedroom Wall,* p. 208; June, 1999, Steven Englefried, review of *Torch Fishing with the Sun,* p. 108; November, 1999, review of *The Ghost Stallion,* p. 166; December, 1999, review of *The Spider's Web,* p. 144; June, 2000, Linda Ludke, review of *ABC Kids,* p. 137, and Bruce Anne Shook, review of *The Executioner's Daughter,* p. 156; January, 2001, Shawn Brommer, review of *Up a Creek,* p. 135; January, 2006, Adrienne Furness, review of *Unexpected: Eleven Mysterious Stories,* p. 145; March, 2006, Amanda Conover Le, review of *The Best Winds,* p. 204.

Voice of Youth Advocates, February, 2000, review of *The Ghost Stallion,* p. 412; October, 2000, review of *The Executioner's Song,* p. 272; April, 2001, review of *Up a Creek,* p. 47.

*   *   *

WILLIAMS, Laura Ellen
See WILLIAMS, Laura E.

*   *   *

WILLIAMS, L.E.
See WILLIAMS, Laura E.

WINSTEAD, Rosie

Personal

Married; husband's name Patrick. *Hobbies and other interests:* Flea markets, rearranging her house, spending time with family.

Addresses

Home and office—Springfield, MO.

Career

Author and illustrator.

Writings

SELF-ILLUSTRATED

Ruby and Bubbles, Dial Books (New York, NY), 2006.

ILLUSTRATOR

Kathleen O'Dell, *Ophie out of Oz,* Dial Books (New York, NY), 2004.
Eileen Spinelli, *Someday,* Dial Books (New York, NY), 2006.

Ophie out of Oz, was adapted as an audiobook, read by Ann Marie Lee, Listening Library.

Sidelights

As a child Rosie Winstead would often draw family portraits depicting humorous renditions of her parents and eight siblings. In her work as a children's book illustrator she captures that same whimsical humor; as Winstead reported on the Adams Literary Web site, her aim in illustrating and writing children's stories is to create works that are "straightforward and simple, yet suggest subtle complexities through details, whether it be a certain gesture or something funny happening in the background." Winstead's illustrations are featured in Eileen Spinelli's picture book *Someday* as well as in Kathleen O'Dell's *Ophie out of Oz.* Winstead's artwork also appears alongside an original story in *Ruby and Bubbles.*

Winstead finds the innocence and unabashed confidence of younger children inspiring, and in her self-illustrated *Ruby and Bubbles* she creates characters who have these same virtues. *Ruby and Bubbles* is about a little girl named Ruby who buys a pet bird that cannot fly. Taunted by her friends about her strange pet, Ruby makes every effort to teach the bird—named Bubbles—to fly, but to no avail. Ultimately, the young girl realizes that she still appreciates Bubbles, even if

In **Ruby and Bubbles** *Rosie Winstead pairs her whimsical graphic illustrations with a story that features a likeable and spunky young heroine.*

the bird never takes to the sky. To bring to life her story, Winstead uses watercolor and pen-and-ink, creating "energetic illustrations [that] deliver the bulk of the book's humor," according to a *Publishers Weekly* reviewer. Carolyn Janssen, writing in *School Library Journal,* commented that Winstead's illustrations for *Ruby and Bubbles* "capture the girl's exuberant and independent style," in addition to "highlighting her dramatic fashion sense."

Biographical and Critical Sources

PERIODICALS

Bulletin of the Center for Children's Books, April, 2006, Karen Coats, review of *Ruby and Bubbles,* p. 377.
Horn Book, July-August, 2004, Robin Smith, review of *Ophie out of Oz,* p. 458.
Kirkus Reviews, April 15, 2004, review of *Ophie out of Oz,* p. 399; January 15, 2006, review of *Ruby and Bubbles,* p. 91.
Publishers Weekly, May 17, 2004, review of *Ophie out of Oz,* p. 51; March 6, 2006, review of *Ruby and Bubbles,* p. 74; August 21, 2006, review of *Ophie out of Oz,* p. 72.
School Library Journal, July, 2004, Linda L. Plevak, review of *Ophie out of Oz,* p. 83; February, 2006, Caro-

lyn Janssen, review of *Ruby and Bubbles*, p. 112; September, 2006, Cynthia Grabke, review of *Ophie out of Oz*, p. 72.

ONLINE

Adams Literary Web site, http://www.adamsliterary.com/ (May 1, 2007), "Rosie Winstead."*

* * *

WOOD, Douglas 1951-
(Douglas Eric Wood)

Personal

Born December 10, 1951, in New York, NY; son of James H. (a college professor) and Joyce (a college professor) Wood; married Kathryn Sokolowski (a teacher and singer), May 26, 1973; children: Eric, Bryan. *Education:* Morningside College (IA), B.Ed., 1973; attended St. Cloud State University, 1984. *Hobbies and other interests:* Canoeing and wilderness trips, tennis, fishing, reading.

Addresses

Home and office—3835 Pine Point Rd., Sartell, MN 56377. *E-mail*—doug@douglaswood.com.

Career

Writer and musician. Music teacher in Iowa and Minnesota, 1973-77; naturalist and wilderness guide in northern Minnesota, 1977—; host of weekly radio show, *Wood's Lore*, St. Cloud, MN, 1984-91; recording artist.

Awards, Honors

Named among Ten Outstanding Young Minnesotans by Minnesota Jaycees, 1991; Minnesota Book Award for younger children, 1992, and American Booksellers Book of the Year Award (children's division), American Booksellers Association, International Reading Association Children's Book Award, and Midwest Publishers Award, all 1993, all for *Old Turtle;* Minnesota Book Award nomination and North East Minnesota Book Award nomination, both 1995, both for *Minnesota: The Spirit of the Land*; Christopher Medal, 1999, for *Grandad's Prayers of the Earth.*

Writings

FOR CHILDREN

Old Turtle, illustrated by Cheng-Khee Chee, Pfeifer-Hamilton (Duluth, MN), 1992.
Northwoods Cradle Song: From a Menominee Lullaby, illustrated by Lisa Desimini, Simon & Schuster (New York, NY), 1996.

The Windigo's Return: A North Woods Story, illustrated by Greg Couch, Simon & Schuster (New York, NY), 1996.
Rabbit and the Moon, illustrated by Leslie Baker, Simon & Schuster (New York, NY), 1998.
Making the World, illustrated by Yoshi and Hibiki Miyazaki, Simon & Schuster (New York, NY), 1998.
Grandad's Prayers of the Earth, illustrated by P.J. Lynch, Candlewick Press (Cambridge, MA), 1999.
What Dads Can't Do, illustrated by Doug Cushman, Simon & Schuster (New York, NY), 2000.
What Moms Can't Do, illustrated by Doug Cushman, Simon & Schuster (New York, NY), 2001.
A Quiet Place, illustrated by Dan Andreasen, Simon & Schuster (New York, NY), 2001.
What Teachers Can't Do, illustrated by Doug Cushman, Simon & Schuster (New York, NY), 2002.
Old Turtle and the Broken Truth, illustrated by Jon J. Muth, Scholastic (New York, NY), 2003.
What Santa Can't Do, illustrated by Doug Cushman, Simon & Schuster (New York, NY), 2003.
The Secret of Saying Thanks, illustrated by Greg Shed, Simon & Schuster (New York, NY), 2005.
What Grandmas Can't Do, illustrated by Doug Cushman, Simon & Schuster (New York, NY), 2005.
Nothing to Do, illustrated by Wendy Anderson Halperin, Dutton (New York, NY), 2006.

OTHER

(And illustrator) *Paddle Whispers* (adult nonfiction), Pfeifer-Hamilton (Duluth, MN), 1993.
Minnesota, Naturally (adult nonfiction), Voyageur Press (Stillwater, MN), 1995.
Minnesota: The Spirit of the Land, Voyageur Press (Stillwater, MN), 1995.
(And illustrator) *Fawn Island,* University of Minnesota Press (Minneapolis, MN), 2001.

Lyricist on musical recordings, including *Solitary Shores,* EarthSong, 1980; *EarthSong,* NorthWord Press, 1985; *Northwoods Nights,* EarthSong, 1986; and *Wilderness Daydreams,* Pfeifer-Hamilton, 1988. Contributor of essays to *NorthWriters,* University of Minnesota Press, 1991; contributor of articles to magazines.

Adaptations

Several of Wood's books have been adapted as audiobooks.

Sidelights

Douglas Wood is best known for his book *Old Turtle,* called "a New Age fable" by *School Library Journal* contributor Shirley Wilton. This gently didactic book, which reminds readers of the unity of all living things, began with a modest first printing that sold out only a few weeks in Wood's native Minnesota. With continued demand, Wood—a folk singer, wilderness guide, and naturalist—embarked on a nationwide promotional tour, resulting in prestigious awards, a sequel, and Wood's new career as a children's book author.

"I never set out to write a children's book," Wood once told *SATA,* discussing *Old Turtle* in an interview. "And I sure never thought that it would touch so many people across the nation and the world. Clearly there is a resonance at work—it reaches both adults and children." Part of that resonance comes from the book's text, which is deceptively simple, like good song lyrics. Wood, who has been writing and performing music for years, is no amateur in this area. "My whole family is involved in music," he said. "My parents were both music instructors at the college level, and my two brothers are professional musicians. [In my family,] music was kind of like breathing." Trained in the piano and violin, Wood started playing guitar after he graduated from high school. While Wood continued to study the violin and majored in music at college, he was increasingly drawn to the simple yet eloquent themes of folk music. At the same time, he was plagued by a tension between his two loves. "I was always frustrated with music as a kid," Wood said, "because I didn't like to practice. I liked to be outdoors."

Music and nature continue to be the twin themes of Wood's life. While growing up in Sioux City, Iowa, the summers he spent in the north woods of Minnesota became synonymous with the outdoors. In 1975, fresh out of college and after a stint as a music teacher in Iowa, Wood and his wife moved north. Teaching in Minnesota, he was introduced to the naturalist writings of the Minnesotan Sigurd Olson. These books, plus an encouraging correspondence with Olson himself, was a turning point in Wood's life; he combined his twin loves by writing songs about nature. He also became involved in wilderness guiding, taking workshops at the Northwoods Audubon Center near his home in St. Cloud and eventually graduating to wilderness guide himself. "The first seven years were pretty awful," Wood recalled of his early years as a professional musician, "but my wife was very supportive, and we persevered together. I had this vision of making wilderness music, and here I was performing covers in smoky bars. I remember one night walking out of a bar after a gig, and I told myself that would be the last bar I ever played in."

Wood began playing more concerts, performing original folk music with his guitar and baritone vocals. He also began publishing cassettes and albums, on both his own EarthSong label and for others. He also began writing reflective nature essays for outdoor magazines, hosted a nature program, *Wood's Lore,* on a local radio station, and participated in artist-in-residence programs in the Minnesota public schools.

Douglas Wood mines Native American legend in **Old Turtle,** *a picture-book celebration of the natural world that features Cheng-Khee Chee's luminous paintings.* (Scholastic Press, 2001. Illustration © 1992 by Cheng-Khee Chee. Reproduced by permission of Scholastic Inc.)

Featuring Leslie Baker's luminous art, Wood's picture book Rabbit
and the Moon ***is based on a Cree trickster tale.*** (Aladdin Paperbacks, 1988.
Illustration copyright © by 1998 Leslie Baker. Reprinted with the permission of Simon &
Schuster Books for Young Readers, an imprint of Simon & Schuster Children's Publishing
Division.)

It was during one such public-school stint that Wood
was inspired to write *Old Turtle.* "I'd been working all
day with these kids, with their energy and love for creativity, and I was driving back to my parents' home,
where I was visiting. Suddenly the idea for *Old Turtle*
popped into my mind all of a piece. I knew exactly
what I wanted to say, exactly where the story would
take me. I got to my parents' house, said 'Hi,' and went
upstairs and set to work. In a half an hour I had the basic text of what became *Old Turtle.* It took another
couple of months to keep polishing and polishing, to
turn every word into glass so that meaning could shine
through clearly." Wood showed the manuscript to his
publishers at Pfeifer-Hamilton, who had been working
on inspirational tapes with Wood. "They saw that it was
a children's book," Wood said in his interview, "and
then they got hold of Cheng-Khee Chee to do the art
work. *Old Turtle* was born. The rest is history."

Essentially a teaching book in the manner of Sufi or
other religious texts, *Old Turtle* blends Wood's subtle
word play with Chee's lush watercolors to create a
message of love for one another and for the natural
world. Set in a time when all living and inanimate things
could communicate, *Old Turtle* tells of the discord
caused by an argument over the forms that God takes:
over knowing who or what God is. A cacophony en-
sues, which Old Turtle stops with sage words. To re-

mind the world of God's presence, humans are sent to
Earth, but they soon forget the message of love that
they themselves are meant to convey and begin to destroy the planet. Old Turtle once again has to remind all
creatures that God exists in all things.

Wood's "message of saving the Earth is told in lyrical
prose and pictures that delight the eye," Wilton wrote in
her *School Library Journal* review of *Old Turtle,* while
a *Publishers Weekly* critic cited the "lilting cadence of
the poetic text" in Wood's "enchanting book." Merry
Mattson, writing in the *Wilson Library Bulletin,* called
Old Turtle a "marvelous fable" that deals with the concept of God, the planet Earth, and the "interconnected-
ness" of all creatures.

Wood followed up his first book with *Paddle Whispers,*
an adult book of reflections on nature and humanity's
part in it. Written and illustrated by Wood, the book
records a metaphoric canoe voyage that mirrors one's
own journey through life. Although he has also written
several other volumes of adult nonfiction, Wood's focus
as an author has primarily remained in writing for
children. In addition to his adaptation of Native American folktales in *The Windigo Returns: A North Woods
Story* and *Northwoods Cradle Song: From a Menominee Lullaby,* Wood shares his belief in the potential of a
more humane world in books such as *A Quiet Place,
Nothing to Do, The Secret of Saying Thanks,* and
Grandad's Prayers of the Earth. His sequel to *Old
Turtle,* titled *The Old Turtle and the Broken Truth,* continues Wood's theme of tolerance; its story follows how
a core truth is broken in two upon its fall to earth, thus
causing undue suffering until a child reunites the truth's
two halves. As GraceAnne A. DeCandido noted in
Booklist, Old Turtle and the Broken Truth benefits from
John J. Muth's "gorgeous, shimmering" pen-and-ink
and watercolor art, while *School Library Journal* reviewer Marianne Saccardi predicted that Wood's "beautiful text" is "is sure to spark discussion among older
[elementary-grade] students."

In *The Windigo Returns* members of an Ojibwe tribe
notice that some of their people are missing, and the
terrifying Windigo is blamed. A pit is dug, and when
the Windigo is tricked into falling into it, the creature is
set on fire. His dying threat—that he will return to eat
the tribe and all succeeding generations—is considered
to come true the next summer in the stinging bite of the
mosquito. "The changing seasons flow through this
story like a slow river, linking the plot to nature's calendar," remarked a contributor to *Kirkus Reviews* of
Wood's porquois tale. Karen Morgan, writing in
Booklist, considered Wood's blend of horror and humor
utterly successful, citing the transformation of the monster's ashes into the ubiquitous and annoying mosquito.
In *The Windigo Returns* Wood offers readers "a blend-
ing of humor and spookiness that children will surely
love," Morgan concluded.

Northwoods Cradle Song is an adaptation of a Menominee lullaby that finds a Native-American woman rock-

ing her child and pointing out the ways in which other creatures in nature are also preparing to go to sleep. "The tender tone and quiet, respectful references to nature beautifully convey the timeless sense of night and lullaby," remarked Margaret A. Bush in *Horn Book,* while a *Publishers Weekly* contributor concluded that "Wood has crafted an image-rich, eminently musical lullaby."

In *Rabbit and the Moon* Wood crafts another Native-American folktale which, like *The Windigo Returns,* contains a pourquoi element. Rabbit wishes he could ride on the moon and convinces Crane to fly him up to the sky. Holding onto the bird's legs so tightly that they bleed, and patting the bird in thanks upon his arrival, Rabbit thus gives Crane its distinctive red legs and crown.

Like *Old Turtle,* the message of *Making the World* drives the story, as artists Yoshi and Hibiki Miyazaki join Wood to journey from continent to continent, observing how the world is continually altered by its interactions with wind and sun, animals and humans. "This ambitious, philosophical picture book, with its lyrical, simple prose, attempts to show how everything and everyone has a significant effect upon life and the landscape," Shelle Rosenfeld observed in *Booklist.* For Diane Nunn, writing in *School Library Journal,* the collaboration between illustration and text in *Making the World* "broadens a young child's awareness of our planet, its beauty, and everyone's ability to affect change."

In *Grandad's Prayers of the Earth* a young boy asks his father about prayer and receives an answer that encompasses all the creatures on earth. When the grandfather dies, the boy loses his ability to pray for a long time, until one day, when he returns to the forest where Grandad first explained it to him. "This is a depiction of the spiritual that is without reference to a particular faith or tradition, and that doesn't lapse into greeting-card platitudes," observed a contributor to *Kirkus Reviews.* By centering his story on the loving relationship between a grandson and grandfather, and through extensive use of tangible metaphors, Wood makes "a difficult religious concept somewhat more concrete for children," remarked a contributor to *Publishers Weekly.* Likewise, Shelley Townsend-Hudson concluded in *Booklist* that in *Grandad's Prayers of the Earth* "Wood presents the subjects of prayer and death in a way that stirs the imagination and offers hope."

In *A Quiet Place* Wood "hearkens back to a simpler time," according to a *Kirkus Reviews* writer. Enhanced by acrylic paintings by Dan Andreasen that evoke what *Booklist* reviewer Hazel Rochman dubbed an "old-fashioned *Saturday Evening Post*" nostalgia, the simple story follows a boy as he uses his imagination to expand his experiences beyond what he sees, ultimately finding the greatest serenity inside himself. Although several reviewers remarked that Wood's ode to solitude

Wood celebrates the reflection and creativity that solitude provides in A Quiet Place, *a picture book featuring Dan Andreasen's detailed and evocative paintings.* (Aladdin Paperbacks, 2002. Illustration copyright © 2002 by Dan Andreasen. All rights reserved. Reprinted with the permission of Simon & Schuster Books for Young Readers, an imprint of Simon & Schuster Children's Publishing Division.)

would appeal more to adults than children, Rochman maintained that "many children will welcome the change of pace," and that "the imaginary adventures" contained in Andreasen's paintings "are elemental." Citing a text "saturated with simile and metaphor," a *Publishers Weekly* reviewer called *A Quiet Place* "a vivid romp through a child's imagination," while a *Kirkus Reviews* contributor cited the picture book as "solid soul guidance for a media-saturated society."

Similar in theme to *A Quiet Place, Nothing to Do* is Wood's "picture-book celebration of the joys to be found in all-too-rare unscheduled time," according to a *Publishers Weekly* writer. Another reflective picture book, *The Secret of Saying Thanks,* focuses on acknowledging and appreciating the simple things in life. Employing a "gentle, assured tone and graceful phrasing," in the opinion of a *Publishers Weekly* contributor, Wood's message in this book is filtered through many faiths and reflected in Greg Shed's detailed paintings about a girl and her dog. *The Secret of Saying Thanks* serves as "a quiet, reflective piece on the importance of a grateful attitude," noted *School Library Journal* contributor Roxanne Burg, the book's focus extending to "the wonders of nature as well as the comforts of home and family," according to a *Kirkus Reviews* writer.

Wood is also the author of several humorous picture books featuring dinosaurs as main characters. In *What Dads Can't Do* and *What Moms Can't Do,* a young dinosaur narrator recounts the many things his parents cannot seem to get right without his help, from picking out clothes to sleeping in on Saturday morning. At the end of each book, however, the young dinosaur allows that one thing parents always know how to do is love their children. A similar format extends to books on the limitations of Grandmas, Grandpas, teachers, and even Santa. "This amusing picture book will tickle youngsters' funny bones and make every parent and child smile with recognition," predicted Wanda Meyers-Hines in a review of *What Dads Can't Do* for *School Library Journal.*

"I love writing for children," Wood once told *SATA.* "It is clearly different than writing for adults, which is not to say that one is less important. It's the focus I take that is different. I write for children in a pure way. It's idea-oriented, and my number-one priority is to find one good and meaningful idea. In that way, it's not so different than writing a good song. All my years spent song writing prepared me very well for writing children's books. That experience enabled me to hear and listen for the rhythm of a sentence. I'll spend two hours on a sentence getting the rhythm right. I'm always using my ear when I write."

As for the effect he hopes his work makes on his readers, Wood is very clear. "I came to a decision long ago that I was not going to be topical or political in my work. And I am not a scientist. What I am is a poet. I want to try to capture in my words and music the meanings of nature. And if by those words and that music I can help someone else fall in love with the Earth, then I've done my job, because they will find a way to become connected in it and to help re-establish a connectedness with others. To me, the natural world is inside us all as well as outside. We're all a part of one big thing called nature, and when we forget that, that's when bad things happen."

Biographical and Critical Sources

PERIODICALS

Audubon, November-December, 2001, Christopher Camuto, review of *Grandad's Prayers of the Earth,* p. 86.

Bloomsbury Review, December, 1991, p. 19.

Booklist, August, 1992, Julie Corsaro, review of *Old Turtle,* p. 2016; September 15, 1996, Karen Morgan, review of *The Windigo's Return: A North Woods Story,* p. 235; February 15, 1998, Elizabeth Drennan, review of *Rabbit and the Moon,* p. 1016; July, 1998, Shelle Rosenfeld, review of *Making the World,* p. 1892; December 1, 1999, Shelley Townsend-Hudson, review of *Grandad's Prayers of the Earth,* p. 715; April 15,

2001, Amy Brandt, review of *What Moms Can't Do,* p. 1567; February 15, 2002, Hazel Rochman, review of *A Quiet Place,* p. 1023; August, 2002, Connie Fletcher, review of *What Teachers Can't Do,* p. 1777; November 15, 2003, GraceAnne A. DeCandido, review of *The Old Turtle and the Broken Truth,* p. 604; May 1, 2006, Gillian Engberg, review of *Nothing to Do,* p. 94.

Bulletin of the Center for Children's Books, November, 1996, Betsy Hearne, review of *The Windigo's Return,* p. 112.

Horn Book, May-June, 1996, Margaret A. Bush, review of *Northwood's Cradle Song: From a Menominee Lullaby,* p. 331.

Kirkus Reviews, December 1, 1991, p. 1541; July 15, 1996, review of *The Windigo's Return,* pp. 1057-1058; January 15, 1998, review of *Rabbit and the Moon,* p. 120; November 1, 1999, review of *Grandad's Prayers of the Earth,* p. 1750; March 15, 2002, review of *A Quiet Place,* p. 429; June 1, 2002, review of *What Teachers Can't Do,* p. 814; October 1, 2005, review of *The Secret of Saying Thanks,* p. 1092; April 15, 2006, review of *Nothing to Do,* p. 419.

Los Angeles Times, August 29, 1992, Lynne Heffley, "Naturalist Sings, Writes of Love of Earth," pp. F5, F7.

Publishers Weekly, January 1, 1992, review of *Old Turtle,* p. 55; April 15, 1996, review of *Northwoods Cradle Song,* p. 67; September 16, 1996, review of *The Windigo's Return,* p. 82; February 23, 1998, review of *Rabbit and the Moon,* p. 75; August 10, 1998, review of *Making the World,* p. 386; September 27, 1999, review of *Grandad's Prayers of the Earth,* p. 97; May 15, 2000, review of *What Dads Can't Do,* p. 115; July 2, 2001, review of *Rabbit and the Moon,* p. 78; February 4, 2002, review of *A Quiet Place,* p. 75; September 22, 2003, review of *What Santa Can't Do,* p. 69; October 27, 2003, review of *Old Turtle and the Broken Truth,* p. 68; August 29, 2005, review of *The Secret of Saying Thanks,* p. 60; May 29, 2006, review of *Nothing to Do,* p. 57.

School Library Journal, June, 1992, Shirley Wilton, review of *Old Turtle,* p. 105; May, 1996, Ruth K. MacDonald, review of *Northwoods Cradle Song,* p. 109; November, 1996, Ellen Fader, review of *The Windigo's Return,* p. 102; July, 1998, Adele Greenlee, review of *Rabbit and the Moon,* p. 91; August, 1998, Diane Nunn, review of *Making the World,* pp. 147-148; January, 2000, Patricia Pearl Dole, review of *Grandad's Prayers of the Earth,* p. 114; May, 2000, Wanda Meyers-Hines, review of *What Dads Can't Do,* p. 159; March, 2001, Sally R. Dow, review of *What Moms Can't Do,* p. 224; July, 2002, Jody McCoy, review of *A Quiet Place,* p. 102; October, 2002, Louise L. Sherman, review of *What Teachers Can't Do,* p. 136; October, 2003, Linda Israelson, review of *What Santa Can't Do,* p. 69; December, 2003, Marianne Saccardi, review of *Old Turtle and the Broken Truth,* p. 162; July, 2005, Kathleen Whalin, review of *What Grandmas Can't Do,* p. 85: October, 2005, Roxanne Burg, review of *The Secret of Saying Thanks,* p. 134; May, 2006, Maryann H. Owen, review of *Nothing to Do,* p. 106.

Voice of Youth Advocates, April, 1992, p. 38.
Wilson Library Bulletin, December, 1993, Merry Mattson,
　　review of *Old Turtle,* p. 31.

ONLINE

Douglas Wood Home Page, http://www.douglaswood.com
　　(May 10, 2007).*

*　　　*　　　*

WOOD, Douglas Eric
See WOOD, Douglas

*　　　*　　　*

ZAPPA, Ahmet 1974-
(Ahmet Emuukha Rodan Zappa)

Personal

Born May 15, 1974, in Los Angeles, CA; son of Frank
Zappa (a musician) and Gail Sloatman (a business-
woman); married Selma Blair (an actress), June, 2004
(divorced June, 2006); children.

Addresses

Home and office—Los Angeles, CA.

Ahmet Zappa (AP Images.)

Career

Musician, actor, and writer. Member of band "Z"; per-
formed with father, Frank Zappa, and brother, Dweezil
Zappa, on recordings *Shampoo Horn* and *Music for
Pets,* and with Leather Dynamite. Host of television
programs, including *Based On, But Can They Sing?,
webRIOT,* and *Robotica.* Actor in film and on televi-
sion, including *Roseanne, Mad TV, Children of the Corn
V, Too Pure, Jack Frost, Grown Ups,* and *Ready to
Rumble;* voice actor on *Powder: Up Here* and *Gen 13.*
Executive producer of film *Fraggle Rock.*

Writings

(Self-illustrated) *The Monstrous Memoirs of a Mighty
McFearless,* Random House (New York, NY), 2006.

Adaptations

The Monstrous Memoirs of a Mighty McFearless was
adapted for film by Disney Studios.

Sidelights

Ahmet Zappa's childhood in the home of legendary
rocker Frank Zappa was unconventional in many ways,
and finding time to watch monster movies was a pas-
time shared by father and son. For the impressionable
young Zappa, such imaginative viewing made a strong
impression. "As a child, what Ahmet desperately needed
was an advice book on how to repel monsters, say,
when they emerged from under your bed and announced
they were about to eat you," reported Sharon Krum in
the London *Guardian.* Drawing on his childhood memories, the musician and actor wrote and illustrated *The
Monstrous Memoirs of a Mighty McFearless,* his first
novel for young readers. "I wanted to create a book that
would have been very useful to me as a child," Zappa
told Katherine Rushton of *Bookseller,* recalling his own
elaborate nighttime rituals to ward off monsters. "This
is me celebrating my life. I'm writing what I know."

The Monstrous Memoirs of a Mighty McFearless takes
readers into the lives of Max and Minerva, the children
of a "monsterminator." As they help their father fight
monsters, they are guided by an encyclopedia-with-
attitude named Ms. Monstranomicon. When their father
is captured, Max and Minerva set out to rescue him using a bag of tricks that includes concoctions made of
cat hair, coffee grounds, and toilet water. While noting
that Zappa incorporates some obvious gags, such as
naming a castle "Doominstinkinfart," a *Kirkus Reviews*
contributor concluded that "the lighthearted gross-out
humor, lavishly illustrated with photographs and childlike drawings, will provide plenty of silly entertainment." Diana Tixier Herald, writing in *Booklist,* wrote
that "Lemony Snicket fans who relish the strange and
yucky will find Zappa's barf-filled romp . . . mon-
strously entertaining."

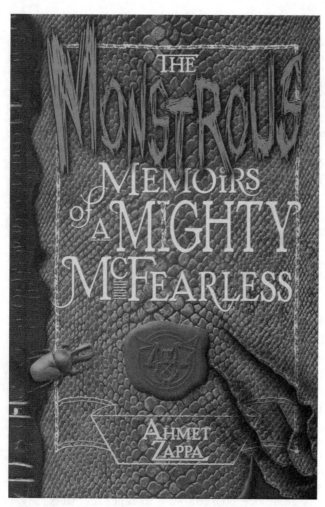

Cover of Zappa's The Monstrous Memoirs of a Might McFearless, *the author's first book for young readers.* (Random House, 2006. Used by permission of Random House, an imprint of Random House Children's Books, a division of Random House, Inc.)

Zappa struggled with learning disabilities as a child, and as an author he has made it one of his goals to create a text that is accessible to reluctant readers. To raise the interest level, he includes illustrations that depict monsters of all sorts, as well as brief bites of "factual" information about the monster world. In fact, Zappa originally conceived *The Monstrous Memoirs of a Mighty McFearless* as a series of illustrations rather than a novel; when his publisher told him they would only accept the illustrations if there was a story to go along with them, he pressed onward. The resulting text,

according to Rushton, is three times longer than that Zappa was required to write. According to a *Publishers Weekly* contributor, "Zappa's lively monster doodles and photo-illustrations of the main characters . . . add kooky, creepy graphic appeal" to the novel.

Of his lofty literary goals, Zappa stated on his home page: "My simplest wish was to be able write a book that everyone would enjoy, but more specifically, I wanted to write a book that would empower children to overcome their fears and inspire those who have suffered similar learning disabilities as mine to realize just how wonderful reading a book can be."

Biographical and Critical Sources

PERIODICALS

Booklist, May 15, 2006, Diana Tixier Herald, review of *The Monstrous Memoirs of a Mighty McFearless,* p. 59.

Bookseller, June 30, 2006, Katherine Rushton, "Monstrous Parenting," p. 23.

Guardian (London, England), July 29, 2006, Sharon Krum, interview with Zappa.

Kirkus Reviews, June 15, 2006, review of *The Monstrous Memoirs of a Mighty McFearless,* p. 639.

Library Media Connection, October, 2006, Betsy Ruffin, review of *The Monstrous Memoirs of a Mighty McFearless,* p. 73.

People, February 9, 2004, "Blair Hitch Project," p. 22.

Publishers Weekly, June 26, 2006, review of *The Monstrous Memoirs of a Mighty McFearless,* p. 52.

School Library Journal, July, 2006, Walter Minkel, review of *The Monstrous Memoirs of a Mighty McFearless,* p. 116.

Time, April 19, 1993, Sophfronia Scott Gregory, "Making Brotherly Music," p. 73.

ONLINE

Ahmet Zappa Home Page, http://www.ahmetzappa.com (April 28, 2007).*

* * *

ZAPPA, Ahmet Emuukha Rodan
See ZAPPA, Ahmet